Palaces of Revolution

PALACES *of*
Revolution

Life, Death and Art
at the Stuart Court

Simon Thurley

**WILLIAM
COLLINS**

William Collins

An imprint of HarperCollins*Publishers*

1 London Bridge Street

London SE1 9GF

WilliamCollinsBooks.com

HarperCollins*Publishers*
1st Floor, Watermarque Building, Ringsend Road
Dublin 4, Ireland

First published in Great Britain by William Collins in 2021

2024 2023 2022 2021

10 9 8 7 6 5 4 3 2 1

A catalogue record for this book is available from the British Library

ISBN 978-0-00-838996-3

Typeset in Adobe Garamond Pro by
Palimpsest Book Production Ltd, Falkirk, Stirlingshire
Printed and Bound in the UK using
100% Renewable Electricity at CPI Group (UK) Ltd

MIX
Paper from
responsible sources
FSC
www.fsc.org   FSC® C007454

This book is produced from independently certified FSC™ paper
to ensure responsible forest management.

For more information visit: www.harpercollins.co.uk/green

For Maud

Contents

Preface and Acknowledgements

When I laid down my pen after completing a history of Henry VIII's palaces in 1992 I decided that my next book would be about the houses of the Stuart kings. It was a slightly more ambitious task than I first imagined. Ten books and some thirty-five articles later I have finally completed it. The intervening twenty-eight years were spent writing the history of individual houses that formed the principal components of Stuart royal life. Books on Hampton Court, Whitehall, Somerset House, Windsor Castle, Oatlands, St James's and articles on Greenwich, Royston, Newmarket and Winchester were necessary steps in understanding the architecture of the Stuart court and its place in national, and international history.

Working first at Historic Royal Palaces, then the Museum of London and latterly at English Heritage for near three decades gave me privileged access to buildings, excavations, research, archives and the work of other scholars. Meanwhile colleagues in the Royal Collection, the British Museum, the V&A, the RIBA drawings collection and elsewhere have been generous enough to share and discuss their own research with me.

This book, in many senses, is a sequel to my work on Tudor royal architecture and court life, but it is also a stand-alone study of the Stuart world, a world far more cosmopolitan than that of the Tudors – a fact reflected in the geographical reach of what follows. The century or so I cover (1603–1714) was one of extraordinary political, economic and cultural change and the buildings that I describe were the stage upon which most of the important events of the period were enacted. Some of those buildings remain and can be visited today; many are gone, and my task has been to visualise these lost places both from documents and surviving plans and views. Archaeology has played its part, and some of the most important sites have been reconstructed from buried fragments of brick and stone. An important feature of this book is the many plans and maps that try and convey a lost world of remarkable places.

The decades since 1992 have also seen an explosion of interest in the Stuart monarchs, their courts, consorts, houses and cultural interests. Many of the scholars working in this sphere have become friends and I have hugely benefited from their research. An important source of debate has been the Society for Court Studies seminar series, a crucial forum for new thinking about courts.

Over the years many people have helped and advised me, most of whom are acknowledged in my previous publications; but some have been particularly generous with their help with this book and I would like to thank Warwick Rodwell, John Sutton, Andrew Barclay, Anna Keay, Anthony Geraghty, Judith Curthoys, Stephen Conlin, Olivia Fryman, Tom Campbell, Paul Pattison, Edward Impey, John Goodall and Mike Turner. Andrew Barclay and Anna Keay generously read the whole manuscript, diligently pointing out errors and making excellent suggestions. The editorial team at William Collins, Hazel Eriksson and Sally Partington, have also made many improvements for which I am grateful.

I would also like to thank my audiences at Gresham College who were the recipients of several chapters of this book in lecture form and asked penetrating questions and made useful comments. My lectures can be watched at https://www.gresham.ac.uk/series/theatres-of-revolution. Also accompanying this book is my website www.royalpalaces.com which contains much additional material.

Finally, I would like to thank my agent Andrew Gordon and my Commissioning Editor Myles Archibald for believing in this book, my assistant Kate Francis without whom nothing happens, least of all writing books, and my wife Anna Keay. Anna has worked on the Stuarts for as long as I have. Much of this book was written during the Covid 19 lockdown of 2020 and, as I worked on my text, Anna sat on the other side of our library in Norfolk writing her book *Interregnum* (also published by William Collins). Long evenings comparing notes and debating Stuart history with her has made this book immeasurably better. For that, and for everything else, I thank her.

King's Lynn
May 2021

Author's note

In quotations from contemporary sources, I have modernised spelling and punctuation to make it easier to read. The endnotes direct the reader to the original source.

Dates are shown as Old Style, but the year is calculated from 1 January. On occasion, where clarity requires it, dates are written 1687/8.

This book was completed during the global pandemic of 2020–21 and as a result it proved impossible to undertake some of the normal checking of primary sources in the National Archives and elsewhere. As a result, it is possible that mistakes remain in transcriptions and citations.

The sources upon which my plans are based are listed in the endnotes.

Prologue

Royal meltdown

Gold melts at 1,064 degrees centigrade. The know-how to reach this temperature had existed since ancient times, and the great brick furnaces in the Tower of London Mint were fired by oak charcoal, like that used by goldsmiths for a millennium or more. Clay crucibles, about nine inches high and six inches in diameter were packed into the burning charcoal whose heat was intensified by air directed from vast bellows aimed at their base. When the gold inside had liquefied, iron tongs extracted the brimming vessel and allowed the molten metal to be poured into an oiled mould.

The melting house in the Tower was in the outer ward, squeezed between two high medieval curtain walls. It was not in use every day, but the melters fired up their furnaces when there was enough material to fill their crucibles. They did not use gold ore, which was unavailable in England, but recycled plate, coin and jewellery brought into the Mint's plush Office of Receipt. The melters were actually subcontracted to the Master of the Mint and were managed, from the mid-1620s, by a goldsmith, Sir John Wollaston. His was a great contract to have as he charged sixpence a pound for melting gold and two pence for silver. He died an exceedingly rich man.

Despite having made his fortune by melting precious metal for the Crown he owed it little loyalty, declining to lend Charles I money for the assembling of his army in 1639 and refusing the king's orders to join him as he raised his standard against Parliament in 1642. He was, in fact, a Puritan deeply opposed to the king's religious policies. So was another official in the Tower of London, Sir Henry Mildmay, the Master of the Jewel House, the man in whose charge was the king's plate, personal jewels, and the state regalia.

It was probably therefore with mixed feelings on both sides that Wollaston received from Mildmay the Crown Jewels in the winter of 1649. With the king eight months dead, the monarchy abolished, and orders from parliament to destroy all symbols of sovereignty, Mildmay had commissioned a detailed list of the regalia. The chests in Westminster Abbey, where the coronation crown, sceptre, orb and spurs were kept, were broken open. The doors in the Tower of London Jewel House were also forced, yielding the state crown that had regularly been worn by James I and Charles I.

Gemstones, enamels and pearls were levered out of their mounts and metal shears cut the two crowns into small pieces. The sceptre was broken up, the orb beaten into a disk and then sliced into segments and the gilt spurs screwed into a ball. The fragments were pressed into crucibles and placed into the melters' furnaces. It was not long before the symbols of a monarchy 1,000 years old were being poured into the moulds of shallow ingots.

In happier times, the day before their entry into the City of London in 1603, King James I and Queen Anna of Denmark had paid their first visit to the Tower mint. Their tour of the melters' furnaces and coin mills over, they had themselves tried a hand at striking coins, afterwards distributing their efforts to a crowd of spectators. There was no way that they could have imagined that, just forty-six years later, regalia that James had proclaimed 'forever annexed to the kingdom of this realm' would, in those very rooms, be melted down and turned into coin.[1]

The Stuart century

The execution of King Charles I and the abolition of the monarchy is the central act in 100 years of Stuart history starting with James I's accession in 1603 and ending with the death of Queen Anne in 1714. It has become commonplace to regard the Tudor century that preceded it as one of high drama and momentous change. That it was, but the revolutions of the seventeenth century were as fast and more furious.

In a nutshell, James I was the bisexual king whose favourite son died and was succeeded instead by his second son, Charles, an out-of-touch aesthete. Charles I went to war against his own people on a matter of conscience and principle – lost and was executed. His son, also Charles, was crowned king in Scotland but exiled, held impecunious court in Europe. England under Oliver Cromwell, meanwhile, was still a monarchy in all but name. When Cromwell died nobody knew what to do. Short on options, Charles II was restored; but he had no legitimate children and, unlike Henry VIII, did not divorce his queen – the heir was his brother, a bigoted and narrow-minded Roman Catholic. When he came to the throne, he turned everyone against him and was driven out and replaced by his Protestant daughter, Mary, and her Dutch husband William of Orange. Mary tragically died and William left no heir, the throne going to James II's younger daughter, Anne. She also failed to have issue and the Stuarts were extinguished as a royal line.

Painted like this, the story of the Stuarts is a breathless soap opera – the reality, of course, is much more subtle and complex and must be understood in the context of the places where it happened. The physicality of the Stuart world determined the course of events, just as much as those events shaped the places in which they happened. This book places the story of the Stuarts in an array of spaces and places that cross Europe from Scotland, via Denmark, Holland, France and Spain to England. Its setting is not just palaces, it is churches, cathedrals, parks, gardens, town squares, tennis courts, shipyards, fortresses, stables, dog kennels and hunting lodges.

Because, during the seventeenth century, the sovereign's rule was personal all these places became centres of power while the monarch was there. The people that surrounded the monarch, the court, contained not only personal attendants and favourites, but those necessary to govern; everyone from secretaries of state and ambassadors to clerks and messengers. Their lives were regulated not only by the whim of their sovereign, but by carefully constructed protocols and ceremonial designed to lubricate the cogs of power.

But it is too easy to explain away the magnificence of courts, their architecture and ceremonies as merely projections of power. They were of course that, but they were also part and parcel of the being of the monarchs themselves. The Stuarts enjoyed luxury goods, admired art and architecture, felt comfortable in fine silks and brocades; they enjoyed hunting, laughed at comedies and tapped their feet to masques. Power by itself is not an adequate explanation for the architectural and material panoply of sovereignty – taste and pleasure in the art of commissioning, buying and owning are just as important, as this book will show.

ONE

Scotland

Baby James

Late sixteenth-century Scotland was a turbulent place. Riven by a jagged topography, divided in religion, fractured by inter-clan blood-feuds and threatened by foreign military intervention, leading barons were stabbed, poisoned, shot and blown up as factions jostled for power. As a result, baby James VI, born in June 1566, and crowned at the

Figure 1: View of Stirling Castle by John Slezer, *c.*1693. The twin towers of King James IV's gatehouse, now much reduced in height, lie to the right of the royal lodgings which just appear behind the high curtain wall.

delicate age of thirteen months, was placed under secure guardianship in Stirling Castle, impregnably sited on a volcanic crag, a safe distance from Edinburgh.

Stirling had been the focus of King James IV's cult of grandeur, an architectural programme to provide a monumental setting for his court and power. Between 1496 and 1508 he had laid out some £12,300 creating a fearsome show-front to the castle with great gatehouse, flanking towers and finely built ashlar curtain walls, all now much reduced. Within these rose a large great hall and beyond, a suite of lodgings for himself. Like his brother-in-law, Henry VIII, James IV favoured what I have called, in an English context, chivalric eclecticism – a blend of architectural influences from the Middle Ages and Renaissance Italy. Arthurian romances, biblical stories, classical allusions, and heraldic devices jostled happily to create a distinctive eclectic look.[1]

James IV's Stirling contained no lodgings for a queen and when, in 1537, his son James V married Madeleine of Valois, the eldest daughter of the King of France, and subsequently, after her death, one year later Marie of Guise, work began on the construction of a new self-contained royal residence within the castle called the *new work*. This was a quadrangular block of lodgings round a tight courtyard sometimes known as the Lion's Den. It was a simple, compact plan: from each end of a gallery the king's and queen's outer halls were reached and these led to great chambers for king and queen, a conjoined inner chamber and some small closets.[2]

This building was, for twelve years, the young king James VI's home. It must have often seemed like imprisonment as his guardians fended off attempts to seize him from rooms which, although magnificent, retain to this day their iron window bars. Here the king received a harsh, demanding and thorough education learning Latin, he claimed in later life, before he could speak Scots. He amassed in his schoolroom a substantial library which was not just a princely ornament; it was the foundation of the king's deep scholarship, of his love of debate and disputation.

In March 1578 the twelve-year-old king announced his intention to accept the responsibility of government in his own person and, in September

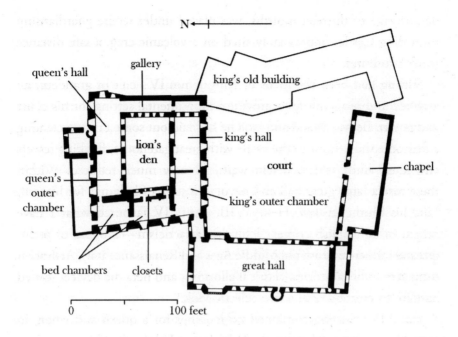

N ←—|———

queen's hall

gallery

king's old building

lion's den

king's hall

court

chapel

queen's outer chamber

king's outer chamber

bed chambers   closets

great hall

0   100 feet

Figure 2: Reconstructed plan of Stirling Castle showing
the royal lodgings at first-floor level.

1579, accompanied by many nobles and several thousand horse, he processed to Edinburgh, making a triumphal entry. During the reign of David II (1329–1370), Edinburgh Castle had become the principal residence of the Scots monarchy and seat of government. It contained the state archives, treasury and the royal administration. Rebuilt and enlarged in the fifteenth century, it retained its premier position in the royal itinerary until the completion of the new lodgings at Holyrood in 1505. Nevertheless it had been the place of James's birth in June 1566. His mother, Mary Queen of Scots, had been persuaded to retreat there for her confinement as a place of safety after the ghastly murder of her Italian secretary, David Rizzio, in her innermost room at Holyrood. The great rooms in the castle, fashioned by Mary's grandfather, King James IV, were richly furnished for the occasion. There was a great chamber, a large inner chamber and a small cabinet or closet, where the queen gave birth to James VI.[3]

Although many years later James was to return to the room of his birth, and redecorate it for posterity, he showed little interest in the castle in 1578. After a tour of his capital, he made straight for Holyrood on the eastern periphery of the city, sited in its own hunting park and dramatically overlooked by the Salisbury Crags and Arthur's Seat.

The Augustinian abbey at Holyrood, founded in the early twelfth century, had been a popular place for Scottish kings to stay but, in 1528, James V embarked on a reconstruction of the royal lodgings there, building a free-standing great tower of two storeys raised up on a vaulted basement. The king had an inner and outer chamber on the first floor and the queen an identical suite above. This sort of compact, fortified, tower lodging may have been appropriate for a teenage king fearful of kidnap but was not suitable for the 23-year-old monarch who was marrying a French princess. John Lesley, Bishop of Ross, who wrote *A History of Scotland* in 1570, describes what he calls the 'bigging of paleicis' in Scotland as having started because of King James V's marriage and experiences in France.[4] Certainly at both Stirling and Holyrood the royal lodgings became less defensive, more magnificent and 'bigger' in the 1530s.

At Holyrood a splendid new west range created a glittering entrance front with big glazed casements, three bay windows, turrets and a crenellated parapet. The facade owed a debt to the large brick palaces of the Tudors, such as Greenwich and Hampton Court, but unlike England the royal lodgings were entered by a broad external stair in the inner court. From this there was access to the large domestic chapel on the south and the king's outer or great chamber. There was then a second state room, which seems to have served as an audience chamber, and an ante room. The latter gave access to an inner chamber and to the great tower in which there was an ante room and the king's bedchamber.[5]

A flurry of work put these lodgings into good repair for the young king James VI and his household as he arrived in 1579. Amusements were prepared: a billiard table was re-covered, new tennis balls bought, the 'dancing house' repaired and sand laid for the king to run-at-the-ring, the mounted test of skill where a ring had to be lanced by a galloping rider. Holyrood became his usual winter residence and a regular stop-off on his tour round his realm. After all Edinburgh was the largest town, the seat of government and the meeting place of parliament.[6]

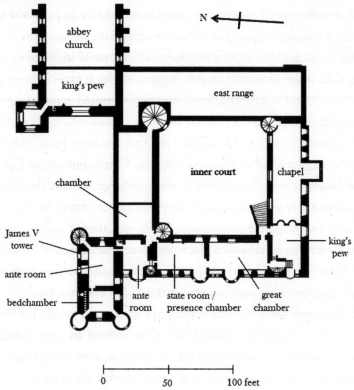

Figure 3a: The west front of Holyrood in *c.*1649 by J. Gordon. The royal lodgings were in the tower on the left and the outer chambers on the right, lit by giant windows.

Figure 3b: Reconstructed first-floor plan of Holyrood in the early seventeenth century, orientated to align with Gordon's view of the west front.

In 1580 the Scottish Privy Council decided to establish a formal court for James. The king's first great favourite, Esmé Stuart, sieur d'Aubigné, Earl of Lennox, became the king's lord great chamberlain and first gentleman of his bedchamber. Twenty-four gentlemen, all barons or sons of the nobility, served the king's chamber in shifts of eight, as instructed by Lennox. All the other necessary departments were established including kitchens and stables, a particular interest to James. But the court suffered from a fundamental problem: cash flow. James had the title of a king but not the means to support his status. His court was chronically underfunded and in continual financial crisis. In 1584 Mary Stuart's envoy Monsieur de Fontenay reported that 'the King is extremely penurious. To his domestic servants – of whom he has but a fraction of the number that served his mother – he owes more than 20,000 marks for wages and for the food and goods they have provided. He only lives by borrowing'. James frequently turned to Queen Elizabeth I for financial support who, between 1586 and 1603, sent some £58,000 north to sustain the king and his household.[7]

Denmark

Soon after James's court was established discussions began in earnest about his marriage. Royal marriages were international dynastic alliances in which countries established preferential trade links, military alliances and acquired diplomatic leverage. While James could expect a substantial dowry from an international match there was concern about whether the Scots court could sustain a queen financially. An English observer wrote that the king had 'neither plate nor stuff to furnish one of his little half-built houses, which are in great decay and ruin. His plate is not worth £100, he has only two or three rich jewels, his saddles are of plain cloth'. In fact he could not see 'how a queen can be here maintained, for there is not enough to maintain the king'.[8]

Although one of the options was a marriage to a French princess that would have helped cement the Auld Alliance with France and brought a huge dowry, the alternative was a match with Princess Anna, the younger daughter of King Frederick II of Denmark. Although this does not seem much of a contest, in the early seventeenth century Danish rule covered not only the territory that today bears its name but also Norway, much of Sweden, Schleswig and Holstein in what is now Germany and a constellation of islands in the Baltic and as far afield as Orkney, Iceland and Greenland. Through Holstein came membership of the College of Princes of the Imperial Diet of the Holy Roman Empire and so the King of Denmark was an Imperial Prince. Controlling access to the Baltic with a ring of mighty forts, and the finest navy in northern Europe, the Danes extracted tolls from merchant shipping making it an extremely powerful and wealthy monarchy.

In the expectation of relief from Danish tolls, it is no wonder that the merchant classes of Scotland wanted a marriage treaty with Denmark. It was ultimately also the match that James personally favoured. Anna, born in 1574, was fourteen, eight years younger than himself, tall, blonde, good-looking, and Protestant.

On 20 August 1589, in Copenhagen, James and Anna were married by proxy in a civil ceremony, and eight days later, James received the good news in Scotland. He immediately launched into preparations for the arrival of his bride and the church ceremonies that would see them man and wife in the eyes of God.

The 738 nautical miles from Copenhagen to Leith should have taken the sixteen Danish ships containing the princess and her trousseau some five days and so, believing them to have left on 1 September James anticipated seeing his wife within the week. On the 15th news arrived that, although the flotilla had sailed from Elsinore on the 5th, its where-abouts was now unknown. The fact was that the winds were gale force westerlies and the princess's ships had been battered back to harbour four times, Anna desperately seasick. James, in a frenzy of anxiety, imagining the worst, sent a ship of his own to try and find her. Colonel Stewart found the princess's ships sheltering off the southern tip of Norway. After fraught discussion it was agreed to abandon the attempt to reach Scotland and to make the crossing the following spring. The remaining seaworthy ships then took the princess north to Oslo.[9]

James, frustrated, impatient, and annoyed made a secret plan to go himself and rescue his queen. Secrecy was difficult because equipping five ships for such a voyage could not be done behind closed doors; nevertheless, he left Scotland and, three weeks later, arrived in Oslo, finally meeting his teenage bride. It was not long before Christian IV and his council of regency (he was only twelve) issued an invitation to the Scots party to spend the winter in Denmark; this James accepted, and he and his sparkling retinue of fifty or so attendants made their way overland to Elsinore.

The situation of Kronborg Castle at Elsinore is unforgettable. It sits on a sea-bound peninsular completely dominating the Straits of Øresund, the slender navigable artery between the Kattegat and the Baltic Sea from which the Danish kings harvested a toll from passing ships. The castle had been built in the 1420s to enforce the dues and was an unusually regular square of ten-metre-high masonry, inside which was accommodation for a garrison and the king. Kronborg remained a severe military installation until 1574 when King Frederick II, Queen Anna's father, resolved to transform it into a great palace.

Frederick was fascinated by architecture and recruited designers and craftsmen from Germany and Flanders to realise his ambition. Entered through a series of Renaissance-style gates, the palace was arranged

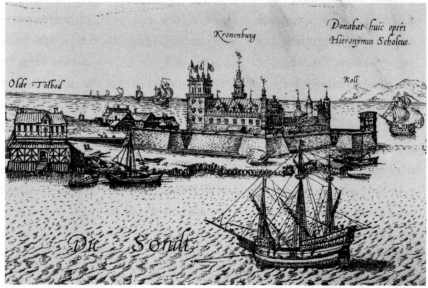

Figure 4: Kronborg Castle in 1582 from Braunius's *Theatrum Urbium*. On the left is the 'olde Tolbod' where the sound dues were collected.

round the inside of the medieval courtyard. To the south, on the first floor, was an enormous hall some 62 metres long beneath which, at its east end, was the palace chapel. On the opposite side of the court were the royal lodgings, the king in the west half, and the queen in the east. Each suite terminated in a tower, the king's of marble with a copper spire, containing his library, cabinet, workshop and a privy kitchen. On the floor above the royal suite were two guest suites with the best views over the sound. Linking north and south ranges was a service range on the west and a communication gallery to the east.[10]

All this had been built virtually without financial constraint after Frederick changed the shipping toll from a charge per vessel to a percentage of cargo value. The craftsmanship everywhere was superb, undertaken by the best Flemings and Germans and the design drew from Netherlandish and Italian sources. In the courtyard was a vast, complex bronze fountain cast in Nuremberg. Inside, the rooms were hung in gold-laced tapestries including a set in the great hall that depicted all 111 Danish kings from ancient times to the present. To ice the cake, Frederick had the whole of the outside of the castle covered in white sandstone and the roof tiles replaced with sheet copper.

Four months after she had sailed from Elsinore, Anna was returning home, no longer a virginal girl, and she and her husband were allocated the second-floor guest suites in the north wing. A catastrophic fire in 1629 destroyed most of the interiors that James would have seen but the vaulted chapel resisted the conflagration and is much as it was in 1590. Frederick's Lutheran chapel was embroidered with carvings and illuminated in colour. James, though baptised a Roman Catholic, was brought up by strict Presbyterians to whom any decoration was idolatry; it must have been the most magnificent church he had ever seen.

It was winter, short days and freezing temperatures, but no colder than Scotland, and James was determined to see as much of Denmark and its customs as he could. Heroic drinking bouts aside, he visited Copenhagen University, Roskilde Cathedral, Frederiksborg Castle and Uranienborg on the island of Ven, but architecturally the most up-to-date building he saw was Kronborg.

Figure 5: The chapel at Kronborg Castle escaped the devastating fire of 1629 and retains much woodwork from Frederick II's time, as well as the massive Tuscan columns supporting the vault.

Married bliss

In 1590, as the newlyweds arrived in Scotland, little was ready. Holyrood was still in disarray and a report sent to England claimed that Scotland was 'never in a worse state to receive a Queen than at this present, for there is nether house in repair but all most ruinous and want furniture'.[11] As usual the problems were eventually overcome and James and Anna made their entry into Edinburgh and established themselves at Holyrood.

For a royal match, the expectation was that the bride would be presented a jointure – lands to provide an independent income and residences for herself and her household. While still in Norway, James presented to Anna the Crown's portion of the Lordship of Dunfermline which included, as well as lands, three royal residences: Falkland, Linlithgow and Dunfermline. Soon after she arrived in Scotland Peder Munk, the Admiral of Denmark and one of the Council of Regency, led a delegation to inspect them. Although they were not much impressed, the young queen evidently took a liking to Dunfermline. It was here that she gave birth to Prince Charles and Princess Elizabeth; in 1601 James described it as 'the ordinary residence of the queen'.[12]

There is not enough evidence to create an accurate annual itinerary for James and Anna apart from a few isolated years. Occasionally James went on formal progress but more often hunted through the season, moving between his own houses and those of his courtiers with a small number of attendants. Hunting was his passion. A French visitor in 1584 remarked '[he] likes hunting above all the pleasures in the world, remaining there at least six hours together chasing all over the place with loosened rein'. On those hunting trips, like Elizabeth I, James preferred to stay at the residences of his nobility, but, in addition to the houses already described, there were two more of his own that he liked to visit.[13]

Linlithgow was the oldest of James's regular residences, having been started in the 1420s. It was a massive masonry quadrangle with an extremely large great hall on the east side. The king's lodgings were three rooms on the west, a hall, presence chamber and bedroom. The queen's lodgings were likely to have been on the north front.[14]

Falkland, built on a ridge at the foot of the east Lomond Hill, and situated in a fenced hunting forest stocked with deer and boar, was James VI's favoured hunting lodge where he regularly passed much of the summer. The palace which James VI knew was built by James IV between 1501 and 1513 and altered and embellished in the 1530s by James V. It comprised three ranges of buildings closed by a wall to form a quadrangle. On the north was the great hall and on the south next to a gatehouse was the chapel. The east range, joining the two, contained the royal lodgings: three rooms on the principal floor approached from the great hall in the north. It seems likely that, on the floor above, the king and queen had suites of two or three rooms which were for normal use, the rooms below being reserved for more public occasions.[15]

Between them Stirling, Linlithgow, Holyrood, Falkland and Dunfermline comprised the architectural setting of the Scottish court. Before James's marriage this was an all-male institution in which almost

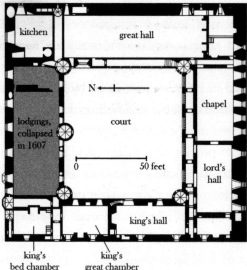

Figure 6a: Linlithgow palace from the west. From *Theatrum Scotiae* by John Slezer, 1693. Immediately to the right of the palace is St Michael's parish church. The west front, seen here, contained the king's principal lodgings.

Figure 6b: Reconstructed plan of Linlithgow palace at first-floor level in the early seventeenth century shown on the same alignment as Slezer's print.

anybody with an official position had access to the king. Because the architectural unit of his life was three rooms and a closet it made for an undisciplined and crowded environment. All twenty-four gentlemen had access to the king's bedchamber together with four valets and three pages. In the more private closet two gentlemen kept the door and one or two more were in attendance. The king's Lord Great Chamberlain, as also first gentleman of the chamber, had the right to sleep in his bedroom, and dress him.

In 1590–91 reforms were instituted to reduce the numbers of gentlemen and members of the Privy Council in an attempt at creating a more private and disciplined environment. But the regulations were flouted and access to the king was still fluid; part of the problem being that the wages of the king's guards were always in arrears and so they didn't police the rules of access. In 1601, there was again complaint of 'the confused number of persons of all ranks who have the entrée in his majesty's bedchamber'. Even after new restrictions were imposed, anyone of noble birth had access to the king's presence chamber.[16]

James and Anna's households grew as they had more children and, from the original complement of around 125 people in 1580, the combined households grew to 200 in 1591; only five years later the number had risen to 289.[17]

Like Elizabeth I James lived in houses constructed by his forebears. Unlike those of Elizabeth I, several of these buildings have survived. As a result, the physicality of James I's world in Scotland is much more real for us today than is possible for Elizabeth's, barely any of whose many hundreds of chambers survives in its original state. Elizabeth certainly struggled to maintain the vast number of houses left to her by her father, but her principal residences were kept in good repair. In contrast, the state of Scottish royal residences in 1600 was poor.

Both financial records and travellers' observations paint a picture of neglect and decay. In 1583 it was thought that if money was not spent on propping it up Linlithgow might fall down. The prediction was not proved wrong; by 1600 a quarter of it was ruinous and, in 1607, the north part completely collapsed.[18] A visitor in 1598 thought Falkland 'was of old building and almost ready to fall, having nothing in it remarkable'. Dunfermline was in such poor condition, before she rebuilt it in 1599, that Queen Anna was too ashamed to receive foreign ambassadors there. Stirling was also in bad order but, as the royal nursery house, the principal lodgings were kept in repair. Although Holyrood was the best kept of all the residences, an English visitor in 1600 observed that it was 'altogether ruinous'; an opinion that must have been accurate, given expenditure that year of some £1,300 on emergency repairs.[19]

The parlous state of the royal houses was partly due to a chronic lack of money but their repair was not one of James's priorities. His cultural leanings were essentially intellectual: he was a poet, a theologian and a political theorist and it was here that his interests lay rather than in the visual arts. There is no real evidence that while king of Scots he was specifically interested in building other than it being a necessarily magnificent setting to key moments in his rule. In Denmark, he spent time with theologians and philosophers rather than examining works of architecture.

Typical of his attitude are the events surrounding the baptism of his first son Prince Henry Frederick in August 1594. James wanted his first-born to enter the world at Stirling, where he had spent his childhood, and was crowned. On arriving for her confinement, Anna found the royal rooms in such a poor state that she had to stay in Lady Mar's lodgings. As the baby prince was the nephew of the King of Denmark and potential heir to the English throne, his christening was an international diplomatic occasion. Almost too late James realised that the chapel at Stirling was humiliatingly dilapidated and ordered it be rebuilt at great speed for the baptism.

The man in charge of the new building was almost certainly Sir William Schaw (*c.*1550–1602), a well-travelled polymath who had been to France and accompanied James to Denmark; he held a portfolio of important royal posts including Master of Works, Chamberlain to the queen and Master of Ceremonies at court. The king's interest in the new building was intense, principally because it had to be finished in time for the event rather than in the details of its architecture.[20]

What Schaw built, in just under seven months, was a stage set lined, on the day, with tapestry – even on the floor; canopies of state, rich textile screens and a pulpit draped with cloth of gold. But Schaw gave the building deeper meaning: like many architects before him, he based the dimensions of the chapel on those given in the Bible for the temple of Solomon. How many at the time recognised this is uncertain, but it is clear that Solomonic imagery was key to James's conception of his rule. Indeed, as he had entered Edinburgh as a thirteen-year-old the first tableau presented to him showed the judgement of Solomon.[21]

The external elevations of the chapel were also based on contemporary understandings of the biblical temple, but contained an important homage to Schaw's visit to Denmark and Queen Anna. The noble classical entrance portal is inspired by the great entrance portals at Kronborg which Schaw had seen a few years before; such portals are a defining feature of the Danish castle, leading into all its main parts and at Stirling represent the sole architectural expression of the king's Danish adventure.

Into England

Just before midnight on 26 March 1603 Sir Thomas Carey brought James the news that he was now King of England. Two days later, the official papers in his hand, he was proclaimed king of Great Britain and Ireland at the Cross in Edinburgh. There were few preparations that needed to be made for his departure and on 5 April, James I rode out of the gates of Holyrood to make his way to his new kingdom. On 1 June he was followed by the queen and three of her children in a cavalcade of coaches. The doors of Holyrood were closed and the shutters fastened. Just over a week later the Privy Council ordered an inventory of the contents of the house. There was a clock in the council chamber, some pieces of tapestry in the queen's closet, an old carpet and a broken bed in the master of works' rooms. By this time the furniture, the tapestries and all moveable valuables were in carts making their way south.[22]

At first James had no idea whether his arrival in England was going to be unopposed or whether he was to have to take the throne by force. His entry point was Berwick upon Tweed, the border town that had been sacked fourteen times before it finally became English in 1482. As the most vulnerable settlement in the country it had been heavily fortified, most recently by Elizabeth I who spent nearly £130,000 on an elaborate defensive system based on the latest Italian principles. From afar it was an impressive sight, although contemporary Scots opinion was dismissive of its strength.

An emissary sent by the king to ascertain whether he would be welcomed returned with the news that the keys of the city would be placed in James's hand when he arrived. When his cavalcade approached, the great guns fired round after round in salute to their new sovereign and as the smoke cleared, James entered his kingdom and began to familiarise himself with a new world.

James's youthful escapade to Denmark had been the only time he had left Scotland and his progress south was his introduction to the ways and the architecture of his new realm. Before James had left Edinburgh an itinerary had been agreed and his overnight stays scheduled.[23] Robert Cecil, Queen Elizabeth's secretary of state had wanted James to get to London quickly; indeed in the last months of Elizabeth's life, James had himself written that 'it shall be dangerous to leave the chair long empty, for the head being so distant from the body may yield cause of distemper to the whole government'. Yet the journey was not to be so quick.

From Berwick the king rode to Newcastle and then to Durham, where he stayed at the castle with the bishop. He must have been impressed by the gigantic cathedral and the lavishness of the Prince Bishop's palace. He also visited several private houses, Widdrington, Lumley Castle, Topcliffe and Walworth Castle. But it was in York that James first set foot in one of his own residences.

York was a great city, ancient, wealthy and beautiful, dominated by the great minster church and surrounded by high walls and stout gate-houses. James considered it to be the second city of England and instructed that, on his entry, formal royal etiquette should prevail for the first time. Up from London rushed trumpeters, heralds, mace-bearers and a baggage train containing jewels, regalia, robes and all that was needed to keep the monarch in state.[24]

The Council of the North, the administrative body that governed northern England, and York City Corporation had time to prepare for James's arrival on 16 April. Once the civic reception outside the walls was over, the king walked to the Minster and, after being greeted by the clergy and hearing a sermon, was to be escorted to his house. James rejected the royal coach that had been sent to York for his convenience and asked to walk so that he might be seen by the townspeople and so, beneath a canopy borne by four knights, and preceded by a sword-bearer, mace-carrier and the city sheriffs with their white rods he arrived at the King's Manor.

Henry VIII had fashioned himself a house out of the claustral buildings of St Mary's Abbey just outside the city walls. It was one of the former abbeys that he had converted into a residence in the late 1530s, and it was pressed into use when Henry made his one and only visit to York in 1541. By 1603 this building was ruinous, and the royal residence was in the nearby former prior's house which had been converted into a base for the Council of the North.

Here, nearly three weeks into his reign, James came face to face with English royal etiquette in one of his own houses. The King's Manor had a great hall and three chambers of state: a great chamber, a dining (or presence) chamber and a privy chamber. Above, on the first floor, was his bedroom, closets and a gallery leading to the council chamber. There

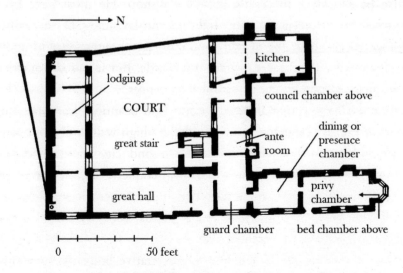

Figure 7: Reconstructed first-floor plan of the King's Manor, York, in 1603.

had been time to furnish the rooms richly, hanging them with tapestry, erecting a canopy of state and dais for the chair of state and installing a state bed. The king was met at the door by Thomas Cecil, Lord Burghley, president of the council, and was escorted by the sword- and mace-bearers to his chambers where the sword and mace were left while he was in residence. Burghley had stocked the extensive cellars and larders and, after feasting in the hall, James walked in the garden meeting local gentry. The next day he received the mayor, aldermen, sheriffs and others in his privy chamber where he received a gold cup.[25]

At the King's Manor, in rooms that still exist, James received his first lesson in the ways of the English court and its protocols. His tutor was Sir Robert Cecil, half-brother of the Lord President, Thomas, Lord Burghley. Cecil was secretary of state, the leading royal minister. He knew that there were pressing military and political problems, but the agenda was led by the delicate protocol surrounding the burial of the late queen, the king's southward progress, the makeup of his household, his entry into London and his coronation. Godfrey Goodman, Bishop of Gloucester, writing his memoirs some forty-five years later, recalled that the king first 'took state at York and put his court into an English fashion, for there was no such state in Scotland'. He went on to explain that no monarchy 'did observe such state and carried such a distance from the subjects as kings and queens of England'.[26]

Goodman was unquestionably right: Elizabeth's court had been stately and formal and both the queen's femininity and maintenance of Tudor regal dignity kept her at arm's length from her subjects. From the moment of James's accession he was surrounded by people hoping to secure titles, posts and offices, people hungry for pensions, grants and rewards, and those who simply came to catch a glimpse of their sovereign. Most people north of London had never seen their monarch and James's progress through the northern counties was the opportunity of a lifetime.

TWO

First Steps

James's peaceful accession is now so familiar as to seem inevitable; it was not so in 1603. Indeed, the peaceful accession to the English throne of the king of the country's oldest and closest enemy seemed to many people to be near miraculous. But there was no miracle about it. For two years the transfer of power to James had been secretly and expertly planned by Sir Robert Cecil with Henry Howard and his nephew Thomas, Lord Howard. Determined to destroy rivals at court and secure themselves in power they were eager for the king to speedily make his way to Westminster. At York Cecil and Howard realised that this would not be so simple. James was enjoying himself and was in no hurry to reach London – in the end his progress took thirty-seven days. What was agreed, however, was that the king would formally meet the late queen's council and household at Cecil's huge mansion Theobalds in Hertfordshire and there determine the composition of his new court. In this way, when he entered London, all important appointments would have been made.

The fortnight between leaving York and arriving at Theobalds (then pronounced, and often spelt, Tybalds) was spent hunting, enjoying the hospitality of his new subjects, and visiting royal castles within riding distance. He visited several modern aristocratic country houses, including Worksop Manor which had been rebuilt at much cost and in the best modern taste in the 1580s. But before arriving at Theobalds he also stayed at Burghley House, Thomas, Lord Burghley's magnificent mansion near Stamford. This had been built by his father, William Cecil, Queen Elizabeth's secretary of state in the 1570s and 80s. It was one of the largest and most magnificent houses in England which, in design, brilliantly melded traditional medieval forms with more modern classical influences. There was a full royal suite of rooms built by William Cecil in the hope that Elizabeth I might stay. She never came and so James I was their first royal guest.

Burghley House was the warm-up act for Theobalds, which James reached on 3 May and where he stayed four days. This vast house with four courtyards, begun in about 1567, also by William Cecil, was still being completed thirty years later when he died. Sited on the Great North Road only sixteen miles from Westminster, it became a favourite stopping place for Elizabeth I and Cecil had commissioned a new courtyard containing a suite of royal lodgings for the queen, and indeed, a future consort if she were to have one. Theobalds was thus an Elizabethan royal palace in all but name. Perhaps not as coherent a design as Burghley House, it was nevertheless a striking place furnished with several elegant loggias, towers, cupolas, roof walks and generously proportioned windows.

Division of the spoils

Although the architecture of Theobalds was the backdrop it was the hard-edged business of manufacturing the new regime that was the focus of the visit. Queen Elizabeth had eventually been buried on 28 April and her household, and many of the nobility who had held back in London for the ceremonies, were now free to join the king at Theobalds. It was a large mansion, but every room and every house and inn in the vicinity was needed to accommodate the huge numbers of official and unofficial visitors who made their way there. For the more junior members of the Elizabethan court, their reappointment was assured, but the king had to personally decide who would occupy the chief offices of state and senior positions at court. Cecil himself, the great

Svengali of Elizabethan England, was unsure how it would all turn out. 'I am pushed from the shore of comfort, and know not where the winds and waves of court will bear me', he told his son.[1]

The reason for Cecil's uncertainty was the complexity of melding together two courts which worked to different rules. The English court had been reshaped by two female sovereigns: the Tudor kings had welcomed large numbers of powerful men into their inner quarters, the Privy Chamber. This was never going to be possible with a woman on the throne. Under Queen Elizabeth, restricting access to her bedchamber and what were known as *secret places* was not only desirable to preserve her modesty and dignity but necessary. Elizabeth appointed four female attendants to be 'ladies of the bedchamber', a formal title used for the first time. These ladies were in daily intimate contact with the queen and controlled access to her person.

Under Elizabeth the men who were appointed to serve in the Privy Chamber undertook tasks in that room, and the other outer rooms of the royal houses, but not in close contact with the queen in her bedroom and secret places. Although ladies of the bedchamber might involve themselves in promoting various causes, they were not at the centre of national power politics in the way that members of Henry VIII's Privy Chamber had been. In Elizabeth's reign power moved out of the most private inner rooms of the royal houses and became concentrated in the hands of individuals, principally the royal secretary. The architectural locus of power was diffused – the council chamber, galleries, the hunting field all became places where power was brokered.

Although arrangements in Scotland were very different from England, James too had an inner group of body attendants who were collectively called his Chamber or *Chalmer* in Scots. These were long-standing close friends who would undertake his bidding. In theory there were only four gentlemen, but at various times their number was more; there were also cupbearers, carvers, grooms, pages, valets, ushers and musicians, in all perhaps twenty to twenty-five people. At a senior level, the Chalmer contained people whom James completely trusted and who were utterly loyal and, in theory, had sole access to his inner rooms. In reality things were less well ordered and there was a lack of discipline about access to the king's person.[2]

As James arrived at Theobalds in May 1603 the two systems stood opposing each other – the English system born out of the long rule of a female monarch, based on the centralised power of the queen's secretary and the subservience of court departments, and the Scottish model focused on the monarch himself but supported by a powerful inner department of close advisors and supporters. The English wanted to preserve the status quo, simply substituting king for queen. But it had already become clear by the time James arrived, that his view was that both the formal offices of state and the court departments should be divided equally amongst the Scots and the English. Cecil headed off an equal division of formal offices and equality on the Privy Council, although Scots were rewarded with some important roles; James's Scottish Chalmer, however, was simply renamed the King's Bedchamber and its Scottish staff retained in post.

Although it was perhaps not fully understood at the time, this was a Scottish takeover. The Jacobean bedchamber was not like the Elizabethan bedchamber filled with ladies of no real political conse-quence. James's bedchamber was much more like Henry VIII's Privy Chamber, containing the king's closest and most trusted friends at the centre of politics, patronage and faction. While the personnel of the Scottish Chamber were transposed into the English Bedchamber, it was a very different institution to what it had been in Scotland. While access to the king's bedchamber and closet in Scottish royal houses was often free and easy, it had never been so in Tudor England. The structures of the Privy and Bedchambers had been devised as mechanisms for restricting and controlling access to the monarch; James's new bedchamber took on this English characteristic. At Theobalds the new Bedchamber, filled with Scots, took formal and complete control of access to the monarch.[3]

Ludovic Stuart, 2nd Duke of Lennox, the king's cousin, oversaw the king's bedchamber, as he had in Scotland, where he had absolute control over access to the king's person. He was known as first nobleman of the bedchamber. The traditional English title for the king's closest body servant, groom of the stool, went to Sir Thomas Erskine of Gogar, the son of the king's childhood guardian, a close and loyal friend who was handy with a rapier in a crisis. Erskine was in constant attendance, carrying out the traditional role of attending the king as he relieved himself on his close stool, sleeping on a mattress at the end of his bed and helping him dress and undress. Four other Scots were appointed gentlemen of the bedchamber, all of whom had been in the king's Scottish Chalmer.[4]

Earthly inheritance

The deals brokered, the great men of both nations ordered, on 7 May the newly constituted court was ready to move from Theobalds. The roads and fields lining the way to London were packed with spectators many of whom had ridden or walked from London twelve miles away to catch a glimpse of their new king. At Stamford Hill, James was presented with the sword and keys of the city by the Lord Mayor. Five hundred citizens mounted, in their finery, now accompanied the vast procession through Islington and down towards the city.

Ever since King James was proclaimed both court and city had been in a frenzy of preparation to receive their sovereign. The Office of Works had to prepare the royal residence in the Tower of London which was the traditional place for a monarch to stay on their proclamation and then before their coronation. This was easier said than done. In 1588 the Elizabethan historian Holinshed had described the Tower as 'rather an armoury and house of munition . . . and place for the safekeeping of offenders than a palace royal for a king and queen to sojourn in'. Twenty years later a German traveller described the royal hall as 'almost falling to pieces with age'. In fact, the great hall was roofless and the royal lodgings had been used as storerooms for more than forty years. With no hope of building a new roof over the hall in time, a giant canvas tent was pitched over the hall resting on a new timber wall. Other emergency improvements included hiding a vast dung heap with a screen wall.[5]

The City meanwhile had to devise a civic pageant in its streets through which the king would process from the Tower to Westminster for his coronation. Such pageants were expensive and complex as they involved the construction of huge decorative arches under which the royal procession would pass.

The king moved to Charterhouse, the home of Thomas Lord Howard, sited immediately outside the city walls. Cecil and Howard had cooked up the king's route between them and used their residences to induct him into English ways. Howard's mansion was a former Carthusian monastery that had been converted into perhaps the largest courtier mansion near the City with a fine great hall, that still stands, and chambers of state including an elegant long gallery.[6]

It was from Charterhouse, impatient to see his principal residence, that the king made a private sortie to Whitehall. This could be done without entering the City by riding round the north of Westminster and entering St James's Park and then into Whitehall from the private steps on the north. We have no account of James's reaction to this visit, but Whitehall was unquestionably the largest royal palace he had ever seen. Unlike Theobalds or Burghley it was not a modern, ordered architectural composition but like a small town, an amalgam of dozens of structures of different dates knitted together by a matrix of long galleries. One of these crossed the main highway from Charing Cross to Westminster, carried over the busy road by a gatehouse later known as the Holbein Gate. On the east side of the road, adjacent to St James's Park, was the recreation centre, known as the park side, containing tennis courts, bowling alleys and a cockpit all constructed by Henry VIII in a festive chivalric style. The west side of the palace faced the Thames and, as well as the expected great hall, chapel and outer rooms, contained the privy gallery, the nerve centre of royal life. This long, three-storey building overlooked the palace gardens and was filled with tapestries, paintings, furniture and plate as well as Queen Elizabeth's wardrobe, jewels and personal effects. Even before James had arrived at Whitehall, he had said that he felt 'like a poor man wandering about forty years in a wilderness and barren soil and now arrived at the land of promise'.[7] His perception of a lavish inheritance can only have been strengthened by this visit.

The king stayed three nights at Charterhouse with the council in frequent attendance dealing with urgent issues of state. Foremost amongst these was plague. James's arrival in London had caused a surge in travellers entering the city. Some came to trade, some to win preferment, some to watch the coronation and others to beg, thieve and sponge in the crowded streets. These were ideal conditions for plague to thrive and by the time James arrived at Charterhouse the Privy Council had been informed that plague was in several parishes and had killed eleven that week. It was realised that the City was now too dangerous for the king to make his entry and, with the Tower now ready, on 11 May, James returned to Whitehall in private and boarded the royal barge and made his way under London Bridge to the Pool of London. Hundreds of cannons fired salutes as the king watched mid-stream before landing at Tower wharf and being presented the keys of the Tower from its Lieutenant.[8]

If the Whitehall privy gallery was the nerve centre of the monarchy the Tower was its engine room. During his brief stay there, as well as resolving the final details of his household and government, he inspected the armoury with its huge stores of military equipment; the ordinance house containing artillery; the royal wardrobe, a vast storehouse of tapestries, furniture and decorative objects; the jewel house where he could admire the royal regalia and plate; the national mint where coin was struck and the royal menagerie with its roaring lions.

The Tower was not a place of comfort or refinement. James was probably accommodated in the round towers of the early medieval royal lodgings overlooking the river, which would have been much more familiar to him as a residence than the expansive galleries of Whitehall.[9] At any rate his residence was a formality expected of a new sovereign and, after a couple of days, he was free to move on. But not to Whitehall. Plague deaths in Westminster were increasing daily and so James boarded his barge and made for Greenwich.

This extensive brick-built riverside residence that had been the birthplace of both Henry VIII and Elizabeth was a firm Tudor favourite. It was commodious, beautifully situated and luxuriously furnished and it was here, for a month, that the king based his court. It was certainly true that plague was still tearing its way through the city, but Greenwich was more than just a healthy bolt-hole. Sited on the river a steady two-hour row from Gravesend it was the gateway to the kingdom and here landed, in succession, emissaries from across Europe eager to present their congratulations to the new king. Ambassadors and junior members of princely houses came from the Emperor, the German states, the United Provinces, and a large embassy from France. These were not normal ambassadorial receptions; the court was heaving with spectators, the Venetian ambassador claimed that there were ten to twelve thousand people and that he couldn't get through the outer rooms let alone get near to the king.[10]

James was, from the first, deeply engaged in foreign policy. Amongst his first objectives were peace with Spain, ending the war which had, for nearly twenty years, blighted English relations with the continent, and finding wives for his sons and a husband for his daughter. James had no intention of delegating these crucial negotiations and, throughout his reign, kept tight control over them. The first great embassy was from France, a large and high-powered delegation led by Maximilien de Béthune, who later became 1st Duke of Sully, the French finance minister. In his memoirs Sully recalled being summoned to Greenwich by the king. He arrived at ten o'clock in the morning and after attending chapel (it was Sunday and he was a Protestant), the king sat with him and two others of his delegation at a great feast in the presence chamber. On the table was a glitzy centrepiece piled up with plate, some of which was set with diamonds. It was an unusually hot day and James talked about the weather and hunting, drank rather a lot of wine and 'at last quitted the company to go to bed, where he usually passed part of the afternoon, and sometimes even the whole of it'. Sully returned later in the week when the king took him into his privy gallery, and they were able to have a serious conversation.[11]

Almost immediately on arriving at Greenwich, and in anticipation of the onslaught of diplomatic activity, James created a new court post, the Master of Ceremonies. There had previously been no such role in

England but a similar post had existed in Scotland. The first holder was Sir Lewis Lewknor, a multi-lingual Roman Catholic former soldier whom Queen Elizabeth had used in her last years to help organise diplomatic missions. In his newly formalised role he was given three deputies, a salary and responsibility for the smooth running of what became a complex diplomatic programme with high political stakes. He rose to the challenge and was confirmed in post for life in November 1607. For the next twenty years he was royal diplomatic choreographer with a significant influence on court life and buildings.[12]

Family reunion

Queen Anna could not travel south with the king because all the ladies of the English court, essential to accompany her southern progress, were in deep mourning in London until Elizabeth's funeral. Before leaving Scotland, James had ordered that jewels from the late queen's collection should be sent north with horses, carriages and other rich goods for Queen Anna's eventual departure, which was set for 14 May. The English ladies made their way north to accompany her but a vicious row over custody of Prince Henry delayed her departure for nearly three weeks. When she eventually set off in a convoy of carriages and carts she was accompanied by Prince Henry and her daughter Princess Elizabeth; the journey, like the king's, was a magnificent progress punctuated by feasts, speeches and, at Althrop, in Northamptonshire, a masque.

As the queen's coaches rumbled along the pot-holed roads of the Midlands the king had been sightseeing, visiting courtier houses round London and viewing some of his own lesser residences. On 22 June he made it to Windsor. It was reported that he had inspected the castle and so liked it that it would be the place where he would first assemble his family in England. Five days later he rode north to Easton Neston where, surrounded by huge numbers of courtiers, he was reunited with the queen. That night they stayed in the village of Grafton Regis where one of Queen Elizabeth's former progress houses still stood.[13]

There now existed, for the first time since the time of Henry VIII, a permanent consort's household and this huge double conglomeration of courtiers made their way to Windsor. It had been long planned to hold a chapter of the Order of the Garter there on 2 July, and the royal family assembled in St George's Chapel in the lower ward where Prince Henry was installed as a member of the order; so was the Duke of Lennox and the Earl of Mar, Prince Henry's former guardian. The earls of Southampton and Pembroke, two English aristocrats to whom James had taken a shine were also installed.

Dudley Carleton described the arrival of the queen and the princess and their first days at Windsor to his correspondent John Chamberlain. 'We were much troubled here', he wrote, 'with certain wrangling Scots who, wheresoever they came, would have meat, drink, and lodging by strong hand.' It was not only the courtiers who were trying to prove themselves for James and Anna immediately set out to hunt in the park and 'In the afternoon she killed a buck out of a standing', James had no such luck and 'was so angry and discontented that she returned home without his company'.[14]

THREE

Royal Pleasures

A warm welcome

King James's first summer in England was framed by catastrophe. London was ravaged by plague, some 2,000 a week dying in August and September; the city had become virtually ungovernable, its population starving, the streets reeking of death and fear. On 25 July, St James's day, the king had made a dash into Westminster for his coronation which took place with skeletal ceremony and heavily reduced access. Even this subdued event attracted an influx of people and an upsurge in mortality. The sick fled the crowded streets, carrying disease into surrounding villages and, alarmingly, court followers spread the deadly bacteria in the king's wake. The court went on an enforced progress travelling further west, remaining for some weeks at the ancient residence of Woodstock. Access was denied without a certificate proving that the bearer had come from an uninfected district. But wherever it went, members of the royal households died and the court was forced to move on.[1]

The city was not deemed to be clear of infection until the following March, when the king finally made his long-delayed 'coronation' procession into London. There had not been an event such as this since 1559, and Queen Elizabeth's entry into the city had been a modest affair compared with the show laid on for James I, which cost the enormous sum of £36,000. Triumphal entries were an expression of loyalty from the capital and of the hopes that the governed had for their new governor – they were also pure spectacle, an opportunity for huge numbers of subjects to see and enjoy the splendour of their sovereign.

The procession started from the Tower, passed along Cheapside, past St Paul's, along the Strand, and ended at Whitehall where there was a firework display. The streets were packed with citizens, strewn with gravel, and the houses draped in tapestries. The procession passed beneath eight arches, ephemeral stage sets expressive of what was thought to be appropriately magnificent and regal for a new sovereign. The 'performances' given at each of the arches were composed by Ben Jonson and Thomas Dekker, rival poets and playwrights; the architecture was designed by Stephen Harrison, often described as a joiner, but no more a joiner than Inigo Jones – he was a designer of talent and creativity.[2]

The day was chaotic and noisy; few of the speeches were given as written and for everybody the most memorable part would have been the size and splendour of the procession. Every significant office-holder was included: archbishops, bishops, knights of the Bath, lawyers, heralds, lords and ladies in waiting, the lord mayor and aldermen and, in the midst, the king under a canopy held by sixteen knights, the queen in a litter of silver cloth and Prince Henry mounted. The arches were some 80 feet high with openings 18 feet wide and they stood for some weeks after and were a marvel of their age.[3]

The conceit was that the mayor, aldermen and city merchants had transformed the city into the king's own court and chamber for the day. The first arch was shrouded by huge silk curtains painted with clouds; these parted as the king approached, revealing a huge panorama of London labelled the 'king's chamber'. Singing voices welcomed him to his 'home' and beneath, a figure of the Thames spewed out water into which live fish had been cunningly introduced.

Figure 8: The first arch for King James I's entry into London on 15 March 1604 at Fenchurch Street in plan and elevation, designed by Stephen Harrison and engraved by William Kip, published in 1603. It shows London minutely and accurately portrayed as a coronet to the gateway. In the middle register are two balconies for choirs of boys to sing from. Below were figures representing the court of common council and the city's military might. Water flowed from a figure of the Thames, complete with live fish.

The eight arches were highly ornamental, each with a strong structure of columns and cornices, but decorated with the uninhibited and extrovert magnificence that is the essence of Jacobean design. The sources embraced the whole known world of iconography: there were real and mythological creatures of the earth and sea, plants, fruits and flowers.

There were carved figures from the Bible, mythology and British history and lavish use of chivalric and heraldic devices, emblems and mottoes. Architectural forms were exotic and, although loosely based on Roman architecture, defy conventional categorisation. Here, writ in gargantuan scale, was the concrete expression of the City's expectations of Jacobean royal magnificence. People admired the richness of ornamentation, the skill with which the many elements were fused together and the novelty of the creation.[4]

Once before, in September 1579, James had made a triumphal entry into a capital city as king. His reception into Edinburgh as a thirteen-year-old had involved a series of tableaux including a welcome to 'his town' by a man dressed as Bacchus sitting on a barrel of beer. The entry into London was on an entirely different scale. James was fascinated by the preparations and two days before had, in his coach, with the queen, made a secret visit to the Royal Exchange where work was in full swing. He was spotted and drew an immense crowd of noisy spectators who had to be shooed away.[5]

James's response to all this effort and expense was barely concealed impatience: an early biographer described how 'he endured this day's brunt with patience, being assured he should never have such another' and, reading the text of the orations today, one has some sympathy. Whether it was on this occasion that he 'in a sudden distemper would bid a pox or a plague on such as flocked to see him' is not known, but Sir John Oglander, a gentleman from the Isle of Wight, recalled him crying out as a crowd pressed round him, 'Gods Wounds! I will pull down my breeches and they shall also see my arse.'[6]

James had advised his son against seeking popularity with his subjects by being 'prodigal in joking or nodding at every step'. But this is precisely what Elizabeth I had done to such good effect, a contrast drawn out by the anonymous author of a petition to the king: 'It is said that your majesty of an ingenious and royal nature, not delighting in popular salutations, do pass by great troops of your commons with a kind of kingly negligence neither speaking nor looking upon them, the poor sort . . . prate of the manner of their late Queen, who when she was publicly abroad, would often stay and speak kindly to the multitude.'[7]

James was a profoundly different sort of monarch to his predecessor. The magisterial dignity of Elizabeth, built on an obsessively cultivated mystique and expressed in magnificent surroundings and pervasive panegyric, had no attraction for James. His style was homely, informal and private. His consort, Queen Anna, was more in the mould of Elizabeth, winning hearts on her journey south and responding graciously to their reception in the City. Sir Roger Wilbraham, an acute observer of the new royal family contrasted his first impressions of the king and queen in 1603: 'The Queen . . . though she bears a greater majesty, yet would she labour to entertain strangers, suitors and her people, with more courtly courtesy and favourable speeches than the king uses: who, although he be indeed of a more true benign and ingenious nature, yet the neglect of those ordinary ceremonies, which his variable and quick wit cannot attend, makes common people judge otherwise of him.'[8]

This, the English were to rapidly learn, was the way of their new sovereign and it had a huge impact on the king's houses, his itinerary and way of life. During the best part of his first year as king, when he was on-the-hoof, avoiding the plague, he took the chance to visit both royal houses at his disposal and houses of his subjects that he admired and, as a result, from 1605 James began to fundamentally redraw the royal geography of England, adding five new residences and bringing back into regular use a few more.

He had no interest in Kent, where he thought the hunting no good and the former Tudor houses at Dartford, Canterbury and Charing were given away. The large house at Woking was also granted away, presumably as he already had several big houses in Surrey. His most acquisitive period was the four years between 1605 and 1609 when he bought houses in Newmarket (Cambridgeshire) and Royston (Cambridgeshire/Hertfordshire border), the mansions of Theobalds (Hertfordshire) and Holdenby (Northamptonshire) and a house in Thetford (Norfolk).

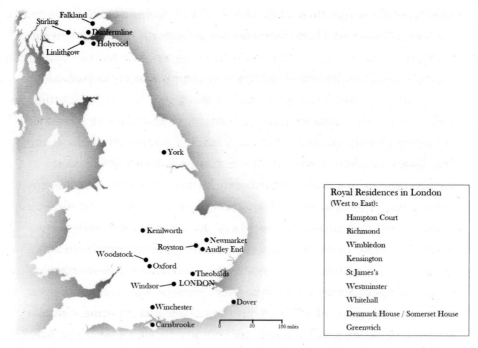

Figure 9: Map of Royal Houses in 1625.

To understand what these houses were, why James wanted them, and what he used them for, we are lucky to have a letter to the Privy Council written at the end of the Christmas holiday period in 1605. In it the king explained that for reasons of health he would not be residing in London for much of the year but living in the 'open air', far from places that were 'commodious for the ordinary residence' of the council. A few months later, in another letter, specifying the requirements for a new hunting lodge at Ampthill in Bedfordshire he described the sort of residence he was thinking of. The king wanted to be 'lodged, though not in state, yet sufficient to serve for the enjoying of his pleasures of hunting and hawking by the attendance of all such necessary officers and no more as are requisite for his royal person to have'. There was also to be space for the prince to stay and the queen, but the lodgings were not to be 'lodgings of state but lodgings of necessity'. Space was also required for the principal officers of the court such as the Lord Chamberlain, the king's secretary and Master of Horse but only attendants of 'necessity' not 'of pleasure'.[9]

This distinction between lodgings of state and necessity existed informally under Henry VIII, who would visit smaller houses for hunting and leisure with a tight-knit group of friends and attendants known as his riding household. Such an arrangement did not appeal to Elizabeth, but James I revived it both architecturally and institutionally. Already in Scotland people had observed that he liked to 'withdraw himself from places of most access and company to places of more solitude and repast with very small retinue'. In 1607 the Venetian ambassador, Nicholas Molin, noted that he 'more inclines to live retired with eight or ten of his favourites than openly, as is the custom of this country'. In the words of another Venetian, James favoured being 'in retirement in remote places of which he is very fond, free and enjoying himself, without pomp or gravity, which are contrary to his nature'. The new houses at Royston, Newmarket and Thetford were his houses of necessity, where he could be free, while Holdenby and Theobalds were houses of state for pomp and gravity.[10]

Houses of necessity

Royston was one of the places in which James had stayed on his way down the Great North Road. There he stayed in the old priory, the house of a local gentleman, Robert Chester. He only stopped a night, but the countryside round about, and its potential for hare coursing and hawking, pleased him. Chester, who followed the king to London, and was soon knighted, agreed to rent the king the priory for a year, and immediately a fourteen-mile-wide cordon was thrown around the town reserving all types of game for the king. A gamekeeper was appointed to kill 'noisome vermin and ravenous fowl' and a pack of hounds established in new kennels. Soon further regulations were issued requiring landowners to remove high hedges and not to plough their fields too deeply, to allow the king to ride with ease across the landscape.[11]

This sudden attention was unwanted by the people of Royston, who numbered about 1,000 in 1604. Accommodating even a reduced royal household put an enormous strain on local resources and in December 1604, the townsmen took desperate measures to persuade James to return to London. Kidnapping his favourite hound, a beast called Jowler, they attached a note to his collar which the king discovered when the dog was released the following day. It said 'Good Mr. Jowler, we pray you speak to the king . . . that it will please his majesty to go back to London, for else the country will be undone; all our provision is spent already, and we are not able to entertain him any longer'.[12]

The problem was that there were no proper facilities to support even a court of 'necessity', and so the king decided to purchase a number of town centre inns and houses 'for his highness and his train in the time of hunting there'. Royston was well provided with inns, as were all the towns on the Great North Road, and the Cock Inn, on the main road, was chosen to be the king's house; the nearby Greyhound was assigned to his guards, and the thatched house in between as the home of the king's privy kitchen.[13]

At first James was content to reside in a converted inn but, in 1607, he ordered the construction of a purpose-built block of privy lodgings containing a presence chamber and a privy chamber, the two principal rooms needed to conduct formal business. These were still linked to the old inn where the king apparently slept. The construction of the new lodging signalled the fact that the business of government would continue while the king was in residence and, indeed, a steady stream of ministers, officials and, occasionally, ambassadors made their way to Royston to conduct affairs of state.[14]

James's ongoing passion for Royston led, in 1609, to a decision to enlarge the privy lodgings. The locals grumbled again. Four hundred loads of timber had to be trundled into the town centre; it was harvest time, and they objected to their carts being requisitioned. Work went ahead nevertheless and a new brick frontage, one room deep, was built against the 1607 privy lodging in the middle of the street. Over the next few years this was embellished and decorated to become a fashionable brick town house with decorated gables, a clock tower crowned by obelisks, handsome cresting over the windows and a fine garden at the rear looking over an ornamental pond. The presence chamber, the king's throne room, which was moved into the 1609 block, had a large window looking straight up the Great North Road surmounted by the royal coat of arms; this enabled the king to watch traffic coming and going and every traveller to see that the obstruction in the road was a royal residence.[15]

The house was built by the king's Office of Works, whose head was Simon Basil, an appointee of Robert Cecil, now Earl of Salisbury, and still the king's principal minister. It is likely that Salisbury, obsessed by architecture, was behind the design of the new residence as it was similar, in many ways, to Cecil's brick-built Hatfield House, with its gables, cresting and clock tower, under construction at exactly the same time.

By 1617 most of the northern part of Royston had been bought up by the king. An inn called the Three Swans was purchased and fitted up for domestic offices; houses on the main road were bought and converted into lodgings for Prince Henry, extensive stables, kennels, and coach houses were constructed, some of which still survive although converted for modern uses. A circular cockpit was built to provide entertainment on days when the king didn't want to ride out. The parish church served as the royal chapel and was partly reconstructed for use by the court, though the king preferred to listen to sermons in the comfort of his presence chamber.[16]

During 2019 I made a careful survey of all the remaining sixteenth- and seventeenth-century buildings in Royston town centre and tried to equate them with the evidence provided by the royal building accounts and a survey of royal property taken in 1649.[17] Because one half of the king's privy lodging block still stands as a private residence, it is possible to have a good stab at the layout of Jacobean Royston. Working outwards from the king's building with the help of the brilliant illustrator, Stephen Conlin, we were able to do a reconstruction of this most unlikely of royal residences (plate 1).[18]

Twenty-five miles northeast of Royston, along the Icknield way, was the market town of Newmarket, sited at its junction with the arterial London to Norwich road. Half the size of prosperous Royston, its economy was based on its market and the inns that served travellers to and from England's second largest city. Newmarket is set in a highly distinctive landscape of grass heathland which, in due course, was to make excellent turf for racing but, in February 1605, when James first visited the town, the huge uninterrupted heath was deemed perfect for hawking and, in particular, hare coursing.[19]

The king leased the best inn in town, the Griffin on the high street and, in 1608, purchased it for £400. Work immediately started on building new privy lodgings containing a presence chamber, privy chamber and withdrawing chamber. The whole was a narrow range 80 feet by 20 feet linked to lodgings for the prince; the king's bedchamber seems to have remained in the Griffin. The building had a brick back wall which contained four big chimney flues but the street frontage was timber framed and the 'great cornice', windows (including a bay window) and doors painted to look like stone.[20]

In March 1613 the king entertained the Prince Palatine, who had just married the king's only daughter, Princess Elizabeth. In a break in the coursing and hawking Prince Charles took his new brother-in-law to Cambridge where they were subjected to a gruelling eight-hour oratorial performance. That night, while the king was in bed, his new lodgings started to collapse; he was only extracted in the nick of time as doors and windows began to break. Immediately orders were given for the construction of new lodgings which were completed for the autumn of 1615 at a cost of over £4,000.[21]

The king's new building was of brick with stone dressings, two storeys with an attic with dormer windows and a battlemented parapet. It contained a presence chamber, privy chamber, withdrawing room and dining room plus a room for his pages. Nearby, in separate buildings, were a privy kitchen, buttery and storehouse. Close too was an indoor tennis court with lodgings at either end, also battlemented.[22] The new lodgings inspired the king to institute a more comprehensive establishment in the town and, over the next six years, there was almost continuous building: new stables for the king and the prince, a new dog house with lodgings above; there was a brew house, a storehouse and an entirely new lodging block for Prince Charles.

By 1621 the king's Newmarket residence was essentially a courtyard house on the high street; nothing much survives now, although some stray walls embedded in the town centre shops may be part of the Jacobean works. The prince's lodging on the street was what you saw if you were passing by. It was built on the site of the old collapsed king's lodgings and the Griffin Inn and was a neat five-bay box of three storeys capped with a cornice and projecting timber eaves. The windows had key stones and friezes. Inside was a staircase that led up to the presence and withdrawing chambers on the street front and privy and bedchamber behind.[23]

This block was linked by a narrow two-storey gallery to the king's lodging that remained set back from the street: the gap between the two formed a courtyard closed by service buildings on the west. On the south side of the king's lodging was a garden and, across a lane, the parish church, which doubled, while the king was in residence, as the royal chapel.[24]

Newmarket and Royston were only ever used in the hawking and hare coursing season which ran from September to the end of February; the king was never there in summer which was the time for stag hunting. Stocks of hare were boosted by catching hares elsewhere and transporting them by cart. At Royston there was a hare warren where the keeper was paid the handsome allowance of two shillings a day. Hare coursing was done competitively against high wagers with pairs of greyhounds; it was a fast sport and could be watched from a static position or followed on horseback.

For hawking, as well as wild birds, partridges were imported and herons and ducks bred in a riverside enclosure. There was a hawk

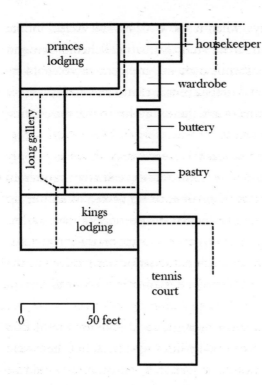

princes lodging

housekeeper

wardrobe

long gallery

buttery

pastry

kings lodging

tennis court

0   50 feet

Figure 10: Diagrammatic plan of the king's house at Newmarket from documentary evidence. The dotted lines are the current building boundaries.

mews at both Royston and Newmarket and, in 1611, the King of Denmark sent twelve falcons to Newmarket for the king; on another occasion a delegation from the King of France arrived bearing a gift of hawks. Shortly before his death, when James should not have been travelling, he insisted on going to Newmarket to 'see certain new hawks fly'.[25]

On the face of it, Royston and Newmarket were places designed to serve the king's obsession for hunting, but they were much more than that. In a typical week, in either house, he would hunt for only three days; the rest of the time he devoted to reading, writing, and business of state. The king was very bookish and was rarely happier indoors than when closeted away in his library with a group of scholars. While he ate, he would be read to, and then walk in the gardens arguing a point raised by what he heard. He loved the fact that Royston and Newmarket were close to Cambridge and books were sent from college libraries. As the houses were only used in winter, they were small and easy to keep warm; in the long winter days, when it was dark by four o'clock in the afternoon, the king could retire to his study and write. When the ground was frozen and the dogs could not pick up the scent there could be jousting, running at the ring and in the evening there were small masques and plays. Occasionally the king would go to Cambridge for the evening to watch a play in a college hall.[26]

Neither house had lodgings for the queen and there were only lodgings of necessity for his close companions, essential household and state officers. Ambassadors who came to visit were often put up in Cambridge where they could be lodged in appropriate state, or less often accommodated in the houses of aristocrats or the town inns. Receptions were informal: the Spanish ambassador was received in the king's bedchamber and the Swedish ambassador invited to dinner in the presence chamber.[27]

Royston and Newmarket were an entirely new kind of royal residence. Henry VIII had enjoyed the use of many hunting lodges, but these were used for short stays with his riding household and business would be put aside. At James's new houses he would stay for long periods transacting state affairs as necessary; but there was no state ceremonial, they revolved round the informality of royal life.

Both the king's new lodgings at Royston and Newmarket had been built under the supervision, and presumably to the design of, the king's surveyor Simon Basil. But he died in 1615 as the king's new lodging at Newmarket was completed and his successor, Inigo Jones, took over responsibility for the design of the new buildings. Two drawings have survived which probably are proposals for the prince's street-front lodgings. Both remained on the drawing board. Jones had designed a building larger and, crucially, statelier than was required in a house of necessity; what was built in the end was much more like a design for a town house in the City of London completed by Jones a few years earlier.

The colonisation of Royston and Newmarket required new infrastructure. To allow the king to continue to govern, an elaborate system of post horses was maintained for royal messengers to take a stream of

Figure 11: *Left*: Inigo Jones's design for the Prince's Lodging, Newmarket. Deemed perhaps to be too stately for a house of necessity, the surviving evidence from the building accounts show that what was built was much closer to Jones's drawing on the right, an elevation for Lord Maltravers at Lothbury in the City.

letters and papers to London, to Lord Salisbury's houses at Theobalds and Hatfield and to the queen and prince. The horses, like almost everything else, were purloined from the local populace; for one of Charles I's visits in 1636, 150 horses were requisitioned for the royal messengers.

Houses of state

The informality of royal life and architecture at Royston and Newmarket would have been completely baffling to the crowds who turned out to admire the triumphal arches of the king's entry into London in 1604. For Elizabethans, who had been used to the grandeur of Tudor royal houses, these new places were most undignified; Secretary Conway, in a dispatch from Newmarket, thought it too modest to lodge the Spanish ambassador as it 'bore nothing of grace'. The king appreciated that as well as houses of necessity he required residences in which he could appear in state as the majestic and magnificent. The problem was that, on the whole, he did not like the major Tudor residences he had inherited.[28]

In his first year in England James tried out all the great Tudor houses. Eltham, in East London, which had suffered a long neglect under

Elizabeth, was found not to be 'fit to be our abode'. It was surveyed, and proposals advanced to modernise it. More than £3,000 was spent in the first year of his reign bringing the queen's lodgings up to standard and creating a striking and symmetrical facade facing the park. Given that James subsequently barely visited the house, except for the occasional hunting trip, the initial concept may have been to provide a country residence for the queen.[29]

Hampton Court had been a backbone of the Tudor itinerary and, in 1603–4, with London still out of bounds because of plague, the court spent Christmas there. It was a lively time, with more than a dozen plays and masques performed, and the house crammed with guests. In January, with Whitehall still inaccessible, the king hosted the theological gathering known as the Hampton Court Conference, at which he listened to various opposing points of religion and commissioned the Authorised version of the Bible. After this long stay neither James, nor Charles I were ever to use the house so intensively again and, although it was regularly used for short visits, especially at the end of progress time, it was never a favoured seat.[30]

Windsor Castle, which had been one of Henry VIII's most visited residences, was also relegated. James normally took a short hunting break there in the early summer and would almost always end his progress at the castle for a final few days in the saddle, before rejoining the queen and receiving ambassadors at Hampton Court at the start of the autumn season. Windsor was thus more like a hunting lodge than a magnificent residence of state. Queen Elizabeth's favourite residence at Richmond upon Thames was completely abandoned by the king and assigned first to Prince Henry and later to Prince Charles as their summer retreat. Greenwich, where both Henry VIII and Elizabeth had been born, was enjoyed more than the other Tudor houses of state and was visited every year but one, for a few days hunting in May and June just before the court went on progress. James virtually never stayed at Greenwich outside these times and in 1614, he granted the house to the queen.[31]

All these Tudor favourites were big, chaotically planned, crammed with staff and courtiers and built in the glitzy, by then old-fashioned, taste of Henry VIII. It quickly became clear that James favoured Theobalds above any of the houses of state he had inherited. Theobalds was quite unlike any courtier house built since Cardinal Wolsey's Hampton Court, because it contained not only all the rooms and facilities needed for the monarch's chief minister to run the business of the state, but also a designated suite of lodgings for the monarch herself. In addition, as at Hampton Court in the 1520s, there were lodgings provided for many courtiers and aristocrats and their servants.

Elizabeth had liked the house a lot, visiting on each of eleven years after 1571; apparently, in 1583, she said that she 'was never in any place better pleased, and sure the house, garden and walks do compare with any delicate place in Italy'.[32] Her enthusiasm for the house led Cecil to start, in around 1572, the construction of a whole new court-yard to the west of the house to contain two sets of lodgings, one for the queen and a suite mirroring it for a future royal consort. The quadrangle was not completed before William Cecil died in 1598: the queen remained in her original lodgings on the south front and, of course, no consort was ever found. But what had been achieved by 1603, when Robert Cecil welcomed James to his father's great mansion, was a house of royal proportions – in reality far too large for even Cecil's purse. It is likely that, even before James acquired a taste for it, Cecil was hoping that he might pass the vast place on to the Crown.[33]

After James's momentous first stay at Theobalds in 1603, another nine visits followed in only four years, including a lavish entertainment for Christian IV of Denmark in 1606. These visits demonstrated to the king that Theobalds was ordered and regular, modern and elegant with a disciplined arrangement of royal rooms, quite unlike the Tudor houses of state. It was also set in newly laid-out pleasure gardens and integrated with a large hunting park which Cecil had formed, enclosing former adjacent common lands. Most attractive of all, perhaps, was its location, just fourteen miles from Westminster – a visiting German tourist in 1600 claimed that from the roof of the great hall he could see the Tower of London. Sometime in late 1606, James began negotiations for its acquisition and the following May, the house was transferred to the king in exchange for lands that included the manor of Hatfield, where Robert Cecil started a new house that remains to this day. In the deed of transfer to the king, Theobalds was described as being 'commodious for the residence of his highness' court and entertainment of foreign princes or their ambassadors' – in other words, a new house of state.[34]

The acquisition of a new royal house was a rare event and Ben Jonson devised an entertainment to accompany the handover. On 22 May the king and queen and the whole court had a celebratory dinner and then entered the great gallery; as they took their seats they saw a white curtain dividing the room. This was suddenly drawn aside and a 'gloomy obscure place' was revealed, covered in black silk where a single shaft of light illuminated a figure representing the genius of the household. He sat dejected, his cornucopia drooping, his wreath lying on the ground, his eyes downcast. Addressing the court, he complained that he must 'change the loved lord he had' for another. Suddenly the black silk was whisked away, and a scene of dazzling brightness was revealed, and the figure of Mercury announced that his new master was to be 'the greatest king, the fairest queen'. The genius's spirits were revived by this hearty news and the entertainment ended with a choir singing 'Oh blessed change, and no less glad than strange, where we that lose have won, and for a beam enjoy the sun!'[35]

As the king had decided that this would be a house of state, and would require adaptation to make it suitable, he appointed Cecil, together with the earls of Suffolk and Worcester and the Office of Works to devise the required improvements. They ordered that the service buildings that had flanked the forecourt should be converted into new lodgings for the household, and the former offices be removed to a new court to the north of the house. Meanwhile a large new stable yard was to be built with salvaged materials from the former royal house at Enfield. Internally there was not much to do. The king's painter lost no time inscribing royal ownership on the state rooms, painting the king's and queen's arms over each fireplace. The open loggia beneath the queen's privy gallery was walled in and divided into quarters for her ladies.[36]

Although only the merest fragments remain of this once vast mansion the survey made of it in 1650 by the parliamentary commissioners, together with a few surviving drawings, allows us to reconstruct what it would have looked like in the 1620s. The house was approached by a causeway from the main London to St Albans road; this opened into a walled forecourt with buildings (which were converted into household lodgings) to its north and south. Behind this were two brick-built courts divided by a central range containing the great hall and stair. The entrance front was deliberately low, allowing a view of the towering

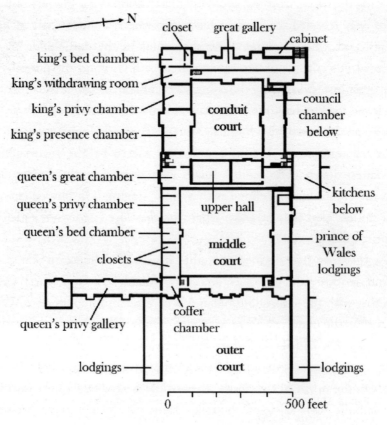

Figure 12: Diagrammatic reconstruction of the first floor of Theobalds, *c.*1625.

mass of the great hall crowned with a clock tower in the middle of the house. As was usual, the royal lodgings were on the sunny south front; they were approached through the great hall and up Cecil's grand stair that gave access, left and right, to the two royal suites. The queen's lodgings, on the east, were those that had been used by Queen Elizabeth; James chose the newer lodgings on the west which William Cecil had begun, and which Robert had completed after his father's death.[37]

The king had a vast presence chamber stripped of the whimsical decorations of William Cecil and richly panelled; this led to a privy chamber, withdrawing room and bedchamber and beyond the usual closets was a gallery, at the end of which a broad stair led down to the gardens where the king could walk, or take his horse. A large room on

Figure 13: Charles I, Henrietta Maria and the Lord Chamberlain, the Earl of Pembroke, in an interior which is almost certainly the great gallery at Theobalds. Engraving dated 1800 taken from the original in the Royal Collection. Charles I and his Queen, Henrietta Maria, are apparently being presented by Philip Herbert, 1st Earl of Montgomery (later 4th Earl of Pembroke), and received by his elder brother, William Herbert, 3rd Earl of Pembroke. Behind Pembroke, stands Jeffrey Hudson, a dwarf who lived in the queen's household.

the north of the house was allocated as the council chamber and next to it was a room for the king's clerks.

The queen's lodgings were similarly arranged and at the end of her privy gallery was a lodging that had been used by Queen Elizabeth's favourites, but now became her closet, an arrangement mirrored later at Denmark House.

Contemporary visitors almost run out of superlatives in attempting to describe the gardens. A particular feature was a series of canals or moats that were cut round the house, which allowed people to take a water tour of the gardens in a small boat.

Theobalds had a park well stocked with deer in 1607 and James enlarged it by purchase and enclosure to something approaching 2,500 acres. In 1620 he ordered that the whole be enclosed with a wall nine and a half miles long. Aware that this was quite a feat, at intervals of a mile, white painted stones were set into the wall, marking the distance with the date 1621 and the number of miles. Obsession is not too strong a word to describe the king's love of deer; there was nearly a major international rumpus when, in November 1611, the Spanish ambassador, visiting the king at Theobalds, brought him a leopard as a present. The beast, momentarily out of control, savaged a white red-deer calf that was being nursed for the king. In 1622 the king, then barely able to walk with severe gout-like symptoms, was carried round the park in a litter to inspect his herd and the following year he flew into a rage when he discovered that some of his deer had been poached.[38]

Theobalds became, by quite some way, King James's most visited country residence; but his stays were short, often only a night and on average over the reign only three days each. For such a big house this is surprising, especially as these short visits were generally brief hunting trips with only a small retinue in tow. Yet the house was used on occasion for big events and when it was first purchased, these may have been what he had in mind, as the principal extensions were made to the service quarters. In the 1610s he often stayed there for a fortnight or more, certainly hunting, but spending as much time reading and writing.

FOUR

The Royal Family

In 1603 England once again had a royal family: James I and Queen Anna had three children, nine-year-old Prince Henry, his three-year-old brother Charles, and Elizabeth, their sister, aged seven. It had

Figure 14: James I and his family, in an engraving dated 1623. James is seated at the centre, and to the left are Anna of Denmark and Henry Frederick, shown with skulls as they were both dead by the time the engraving was made. Two infants who had also died sit at the king's feet. Charles I as Prince of Wales rests his right hand on an open Bible, surrounded by the literary works of his father. To the right, James I's eldest daughter, Elizabeth of Bohemia, is accompanied by her husband, King Frederick, and by seven of their children.

been such a long time since this had been the case that Sir Robert Cecil was asked to investigate what arrangements should be made for accommodating and financing multiple households. Immediately three separate households were established, for the king, queen and for the royal children.

Queen Anna

Anna's immediate need was to have suitable lodgings at Whitehall. Queen Elizabeth had occupied Henry VIII's rooms and the consort's lodgings had been used for a variety of temporary uses. The Office of Works quickly brought these up to standard, constructing a new bedchamber and a cabinet.[1]

Anna had already received a jointure in Scotland; it was now up to Cecil to propose the scale and composition of one for England. He suggested that it be modelled on Katharine of Aragon's, the last royal princess to marry an English king. In all, he proposed Anna's settlement to be £6,376 a year from which the direct costs of her household were to be met. The cost of building and maintaining the queen's houses would be covered by the Crown. None of the estates held by Katharine was now available and the clutch of houses, castles and lands held by Anna were therefore a new assemblage.[2]

In terms of her private residences, the Tudor queens' traditional independent London home, Baynard's Castle, had fallen out of royal use before the end of Henry VIII's reign; Cecil had therefore to propose an alternative. Somerset Place was the obvious choice, even if it was incomplete and now rather old fashioned. James did not officially assign the queen a country residence until 1611 when she was granted Oatlands in Surrey, a large house with a big hunting park that had been used by the Tudor queens. In 1614 the king, who rarely used Greenwich, decided to add that to Anna's portfolio and then in 1616 he granted her Byfleet manor, another ancient royal residence in Surrey.[3]

Somerset Place was the great mansion on the Strand started by

Protector Somerset in the reign of Edward VI. After his fall from power, it became Crown property and had been used by Queen Elizabeth to lodge state visitors. In April 1604 the Venetian ambassador reported to the Doge, 'It is the most splendid house in London, after the royal palace [i.e. Whitehall].'[4] Before 1613 Anna had barely, if ever, stayed there and for it to become her home it needed significant expenditure. She had no fear of a large building project; indeed, in Scotland she had been a more dynamic patron of architecture than her husband, rebuilding her lodgings at Dunfermline Abbey.

Dunfermline Abbey was just that – an abbey. Until 1560, when it was sacked by Protestant zealots, the abbot had maintained, at his own expense, guest lodgings that were used by members of the royal family. In 1587 the abbey was appropriated by the Crown and, three years later, when it was granted to Anna, the buildings were in a poor state. William Schaw, the king's Master of Works, was commissioned to undertake urgent modernisation and repairs at a cost of £400, but the queen did not take up residence because of a complex legal wrangle over the abbey lands that took three years to resolve.[5]

The medieval royal lodgings comprised the usual three great rooms: a hall, a withdrawing chamber and a bedchamber. These lay on the south side of a courtyard at the east end of the abbey and were an old-fashioned state suite, rooms for receptions and business – not for daily life. In 1594, when the queen met ambassadors who had come to congratulate her on the birth of Prince Henry, she arranged to greet them at Falkland rather than Dunfermline 'lest they should see her at the Abbey where she lay not like a princess of such birth and virtues'.[6] She had to wait until 1599, when resources were available for her to commission what we could call a privy lodging to be connected to the principal lodgings on the south by a gallery, thus forming a more-or-less regular internal court.

The queen took some pride in the commission as, when it was completed, a plaque was attached to the outside commemorating her work. The privy lodging was located on the north side of the court, on the site of the medieval north gate and adjacent to the constable's lodgings to its east. As the plaque proclaimed, it was a *Propylaeum* – a monumental gatehouse.[7]

Its plan was a cross, three storeys and an attic, with a large oriel window over the entrance on the north side. A broad external stair led up to a first-floor entrance. At each of the principal levels there was a large room (or hall) and, in addition, there was a dining room and a dais chamber (a presence chamber) plus service rooms, including a wardrobe: eight rooms in all. The privy lodging was linked to the main lodgings by a gallery off which were various rooms. [8]

The disposition of parts at Dunfermline essentially recreated Anna's childhood home at Kronborg. Her mother's lodgings there, as at Dunfermline, were built in and around a gatehouse and linked to the rooms of state by a communication gallery (specifically provided by Anna's father); the gallery was balanced on the opposite side of the court by service rooms and lodgings. Anna was used to the very finest interiors and in 1600 she laid out some £1,300 on setting up her new rooms; the following year she moved all her possessions there.[9]

The architecture of the queen's lodging was tighter and more symmetrical in plan and elevation than the Scottish norm, but entirely devoid of the explicit language of classical architecture. Like Kronborg it was probably influenced by Netherlandish models and was almost certainly designed by William Schaw. James had taken Schaw with him to Norway and Denmark and, after seeing how splendid Kronborg was, sent him home to try and patch up Holyrood for the queen's arrival. In 1593 the queen appointed him Chamberlain of Dunfermline.[10]

Schaw had died in 1602 and had been succeeded as Master of Works by David Cunningham, whom James brought with him on his journey south. Before Cunningham had even reached the capital, he had been promised the English post of Surveyor of the King's Works and had been knighted. Fortunately for him the incumbent English surveyor was old and frail, and Cunningham was able to slip into his place immediately. Sir David himself may have not been a well man, as he gave up the surveyorship just over two years later. At this point Cecil

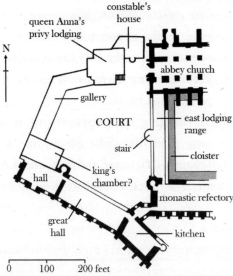

Figure 15: John Clerk of Eldin, *Dunfermline Abbey and Palace from the South West*. This is the only reliable image of Anna of Denmark's privy lodging at Dunfermline, which was demolished in 1797. From right to left can be seen: the west front of the abbey; the constable's house with a stair turret; the external staircase entrance to the queen's building; the three-storey central portion over the roadway, probably containing superimposed halls; a spiral stair tucked into the corner linking first and second floors; a blocked archway and demolished wall; and part of a gallery that linked the queen's building to the rooms of state. Two framed niches on the face of the building may have contained the queen's arms and a plaque commemorating the completion of the building in 1600.

Figure 16: Diagrammatic reconstruction to the first floor of Dunfermline Abbey/palace, *c.*1600.

put forward his own man, Simon Basil, the former comptroller of the royal works as the new surveyor, and it was to him that Queen Anna turned for the conversion of Somerset House.[11]

Somerset House had been in the architectural vanguard when first started in the 1550s, but by 1609 it looked old fashioned. By then Anna had been introduced to the architecture of Burghley and Theobalds as well as numerous other courtier mansions in the Elizabethan style; Somerset House, she decided, was to be made to look like them. So the Strand facade and the inner courtyard were modernised by the addition of fashionable features such as balustrades, a loggia, bay windows and lead flats rather than pitched tile-covered roofs.

These were economical improvements to its external facades; the main work was the rebuilding and extension of the queen's private rooms on a grand scale. The core Tudor rooms of parade on the south front remained, entered as was usual, by a great hall and a guard chamber. The presence and privy chambers looked out over the gardens towards the river. The presence chamber, with an added overmantle containing the arms of Denmark supported by wild men, was used for public dining and the reception of ambassadors. The privy chamber was used for more intimate and private receptions and the drawing room beyond was where the queen

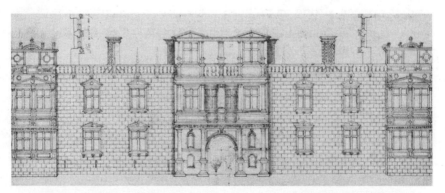

Figure 17: The Strand facade of Somerset House drawn by John Thorpe *c*.1610–11, possibly as a presentation drawing for the queen. The drawing shows the fashionable additions added to the earlier Tudor facade, including the balustrade, the cresting on the end bays and the central loggia.

could enjoy private discourse with her ladies and eat in private, served from the backstairs behind.

The great bedchamber was next and was closed to everyone except her ladies and members of her immediate family. It was the first room of a private suite in the inner courtyard that included a dining room and a second bedchamber. In creating these privy lodgings she imitated the layout of the larger and older royal houses. When, on his visit to England in 1606, her brother-in-law, the Duke of Holstein, presumed to enter her privy lodgings she was so furious that she refused to speak to him for two months.[12]

The original plan had been to add to these rooms a three-sided courtyard facing south, open to the Thames. Due to cost this was eventually reduced to an 'L' shape: the great gallery facing east and the cross gallery facing south. The great gallery, with four bay windows flanking an enormous central bow window, became one of the most magnificent rooms in London, with a throne canopy bearing the queen's arms with three 'high' chairs beneath it. The panelled walls were hung with paintings ranging from landscapes and portraits to devotional subjects and still lives. This vast room was the setting for private, but magnificent, audiences. The first time it was used was probably during a huge party thrown in February 1613, when a great banquet was held with a table running the entire length of the gallery and the queen sitting at its head. This was an exceptional occasion; more usually it would have been used for the most prestigious ambassadorial and diplomatic occasions.

At right angles to the great gallery was the cross galley, of two storeys supported on a loggia of six stone arches with a square bay window in the middle. This was divided into three, having ante rooms at either end and the gallery proper in the middle with a central fireplace and a great square projecting window. It was set up with a throne and throne canopy just like the great gallery, but its walls were hung with cloth of gold and gold curtains. There were cabinets, some tables and chairs, lots of mirrors and a selection of dynastic portraits. This was truly part of the queen's private domain but whom she saw in this room and how

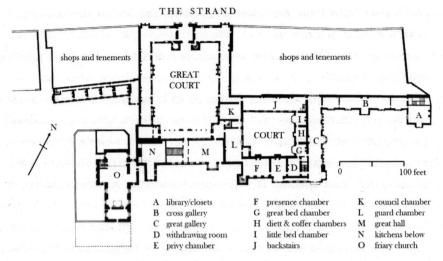

THE STRAND

shops and tenements

shops and tenements

GREAT
COURT

N

K

J

I

H

G

F E D

B

A

COURT

L

M

N

O

0   100 feet

A library/closets   F presence chamber   K council chamber
B cross gallery   G great bed chamber   L guard chamber
C great gallery   H diett & coffer chambers M great hall
D withdrawing room   I little bed chamber   N kitchens below
E privy chamber   J backstairs   O friary church

Figure 18: Reconstructed first-floor plan of Denmark House in 1640. The great court and rooms to the south and east of it were part of the original house, or added in the Elizabethan period. The cross gallery to the east, terminating in the queen's closet, was added by Queen Anna. The friary church was built for Henrietta Maria in 1630–35.

she used the throne and canopy can only be a matter for speculation. At the end of the cross gallery was the queen's closet and library, a three-storey tower containing the queen's most private and magnificent apartment. It was adorned with a monumental chimneypiece 14 feet high and 10 feet wide with nine Solomonic columns and two oval panels and a large stone vase.[13]

Although a gallery leading to a private closet was not the original intention, the arrangement had precedents; this was effectively the plan at both Kronborg and Dunfermline and, in fact, at Oatlands where, on the north front was a gallery leading to a closet set in the privy gardens.[14]

Gardens were central to the design of Somerset House and Anna employed the French hydraulic engineer and designer, Saloman de Caus to create for her gardens such as those found in the French royal houses with grottoes, automata, fountains and pools. The ground to the south of the house was levelled and raised walks built round it – in the centre was a pool with a pert rock grotto dubbed Mount Parnassus. This was made out of jagged rocks, minerals and shells planted with ferns and grasses; inside was a cave home to statues of the muses. Four river gods, one at each corner held cornucopia from which flowed streams named after the principal rivers of Britain, headed by the Thames. The confection was crowned with a gilded figure of Pegasus.

Anna of Denmark transformed Somerset House into one of the great buildings of Europe: great architecturally, but also important as a cultural centre. Ultimately the cost of completing and furnishing it was well over £45,000, making it the single most expensive royal domestic work of the early Stuart period. In comparison the cost of new buildings at Newmarket was £4,600, alterations at Theobalds £8,000 and Inigo Jones's Banqueting House at Whitehall £15,000. The importance of the queen's work should not be underestimated. Neither James I nor Charles I built for themselves on this scale and Anna's work at Somerset House was the first major reconstruction of an English royal palace since the death of Henry VIII.

Figure 19: Salomon de Caus, the rock grotto, Mount Parnassus, at Denmark House, from his book *Les raisons des forces mouuantes auec diuerses machines tant vtilles que plaisantes: aus quelles sont adioints plusieurs desseings de grotes et fontaines* (1615) Book 2, XIII.

Until his death in 1612 Robert Cecil, the queen's Lord High Steward, was the most powerful influence on royal building. In June 1608 he had been appointed keeper of Somerset House and furnished with lodgings in its gatehouse. At the start of work in September 1609 Sir Robert Aston, one of the king's boon hunting companions, wrote to Cecil telling him that the king was pleased that the queen was at Somerset House with her court, and that she had reminded him that he was paying for all the work there.[15] This reminder was probably timely given her extravagance in Scotland and the ambition and scale of works proposed at Somerset House. Godfrey Goodman, observer of James's court and later Bishop of Gloucester, noted that James used Cecil on at least one occasion to rein in his wife's expenditure on the project.[16]

Simon Basil was one of Cecil's protégés but, by 1609, Cecil was also turning to Inigo Jones for architectural advice. Jones was born in 1573. He seems to have started as a joiner, but by the time he was thirty he was valued by Roger Manners, 5th Earl of Rutland, for his skill as a landscape painter. Sometime in the late 1590s he had travelled abroad, probably in the household of the earl's brother Francis Manners, Lord Roos and had arrived in Venice where, amongst other souvenirs, he bought Andrea Palladio's recently published *Quattro Libri dell'architettura*. This was his guide to the ruins of Ancient Rome that he set out to study on this visit and on subsequent trips to France and Italy. Crucially it was in Italy where Jones first encountered the court of Denmark, probably through Danish musicians in Venice, who enticed him to go to Christian IV's court as a designer. There it is likely that he proved his considerable talents in devising for the Danish king a pageant to celebrate the swearing of an oath of allegiance by the city of Hamburg in 1603. Christian IV was portrayed as the sun king in a series of tableaux, the likes of which had never been seen north of the Alps.

Back in England the Earl of Rutland, Jones's first patron, had impressed James I by his hospitality and charm during the king's journey south from Scotland. As a result, he was chosen for the important diplomatic mission of attending the baptism of Christian IV's son (the queen's nephew) in Copenhagen and acting as proxy for James I, who was a godfather. It was natural that he should take Jones, who was familiar with the Danish court, in his entourage. It is not known whether Jones contributed to the festivities in Copenhagen, but he certainly cemented his position as an artistic link between the English and Danish courts.[17]

The following year Anna of Denmark's younger brother Ulrik arrived in London; he had previously visited James and Anna in Edinburgh, and now he stayed for six months in England, enjoying everything James had to offer. This included Ulrik staging a lavish masque at Candlemas for which the king reimbursed him some £10,000. It is tempting to suggest that this was designed by Jones, whose pageant in Hamburg he would have seen, but this cannot be proved. What is known is that on twelfth night that year, Jones, in collaboration with Ben Jonson, devised the *Masque of Blackness* for the queen at Whitehall, his first documented work for the English court.

A masque was neither a play nor an opera, nor a dance; it was a spectacle certainly, but most importantly it was the allegorical or symbolic setting of an idea, or ideas, in which the court participated – not as actors, but as themselves. It was inordinately expensive, and magnificent. Those who could not understand the symbolism (and that might have been many) would be left with a sense of wonder and amazement at the splendour of the monarch and their court.[18]

Masques had long been a feature of court life, but Jonson and Jones transformed them into a sophisticated and spectacular art form. The *Masque of Blackness,* for instance, began as a whim of the queen's; she wanted to appear, with her ladies, as Africans with blacked faces. The masque became an allegory on the power of kingship in which the twelve black nymphs of Niger were bleached by the bright light of the monarch in the white realm of Albion. The first part of the masque (the anti-masque) was performed by professional actors and presented a world of vice and disorder, this was swept away by the idyllic world of the court represented by the queen and her ladies. The spectacle ended with the courtly dancers inviting the aristocratic spectators to join the ball.[19]

Over the eight years following the *Masque of Blackness*, Jones continued to design masques, drawing inspiration from the spectacles of the Mantuan and Florentine courts and experimenting with architectural settings in deep perspective and flying mechanical novelties. By early 1608 he had acquired the patronage of Robert Cecil. Although Cecil was fascinated by painting, music and theatricals, building and gardening were his passions and he spotted Jones's capability, giving him some minor architectural tasks. At precisely the time Somerset House was designed for the queen, Jones was advising Cecil on his project for a shopping arcade, the New Exchange on the Strand, and on his own house at Hatfield.

The New Exchange was built in 1608–9, a hundred yards from Somerset House and the facades of the two buildings, completed within a very short time of each other, were symbiotic: the Exchange having elements of Somerset Place and Somerset Place having the skyline of the New Exchange. Given the existence of a drawing of the New Exchange in Jones's hand it seems unlikely that his advice would not have also been sought on Somerset House by Cecil, and probably also the queen.[20]

By mid-1613 Somerset House was more or less completed and Anna decided to throw a joint party; half housewarming and half celebration of the marriage of her favoured lady in waiting Jane Drummond to the Earl of Roxburghe. The centrepiece was the performance of a masque by Samuel Daniel, *Hymen's Triumph*.[21] A strong theme running through the text is the 'feminine commonwealth' in which 'no wild, no rude, no antique sport' is allowed. There is no doubt that the physical location of this commonwealth was the 'faire structure' of Somerset House whose 'roofs you reared of late', a domain 'sacred to integrity' where 'honour keeps the doore'.[22] The sense of Somerset House being a private world apart from the raucous climate of the king's household was further emphasised by a change in name. On Shrove Tuesday 1617 the queen entertained James to see the completed splendours of her house. The king, in her honour, declared that its nickname 'Denmark House' should henceforth become its official title.[23]

Anna's life had been transformed, not entirely for the better, by her move to England. Her influence in the small and incestuous Scottish court may have been significant, but in the tumult of Whitehall her voice was lost. The court which she created in Scotland now became a new type of English consort's household.[24] This was more restrained, private and dignified than the English expected. Her privy chamber was described as 'shut all day' and Jane Drummond, one of Anna's closest ladies of the bedchamber, wrote to Cecil in November 1611, 'I acquainted her Majesty with what your lordship wrote of her loving no body, but dead pictures in a paltry gallery: her majesty commanded me to return the answer, that she is more contented amongst those hermit's pictures in her "paltry gallery", then your lordship is with your great employments in fair rooms.'[25]

The queen's country houses

In the early part of James's reign he and Anna would cohabit at some of the larger royal houses but, after 1612, this happened less and less. Anna increasingly stayed with her household at Denmark House, Greenwich and Oatlands, and hardly ever went to Royston or Newmarket. In his turn James rarely visited Oatlands and never stayed at Denmark House; Greenwich he shared with the queen in the early summer. Occasionally Anna would accompany James on his summer progress and on a few occasions she made her own progress, but in most summers she used her own country seats.

The most favoured of these was Oatlands in Weybridge, Surrey where she spent much of each summer hunting. Nothing now survives of this once extensive mansion that was developed by Henry VIII as a retreat for his queens, but its site has been excavated and I was involved in writing up the results of this work after the death of the original excavator. What we learnt was that, despite Oatlands being favoured so highly by the Stuart queens, it remained little altered from its Tudor state. After 1611 (the year in which Anna formally took possession) the king's library, the queen's withdrawing room, bedchamber and the chapel were all modernised. In 1616 the queen had a new privy kitchen built and in 1616–18, the gardens to the south of the house were greatly improved. But otherwise the house was much as it had been left by Queen Elizabeth. What does not show up in the repair accounts is that Anna had the house completely redecorated inside. At her death not a single one of the tapestries that filled the house in Henry VIII's time remained, gone also were the great Tudor state beds and canopies; in fact Anna's house was entirely furnished with modern furniture and silk wall hangings in a rainbow of colours. The walls were adorned with easel paintings; for instance, in the gallery by the vineyard was her own portrait by Paul van Somer (plate 2) and portraits of her brother and her family in Denmark.[26]

Anna had always used Greenwich independently from the king and it was the place she chose for her many confinements. In 1613 James, who barely used the house, added Greenwich to her jointure and the following year, granted it to her for 100 years 'if she should live so long'. From this point she regularly held court at Greenwich herself, several foreign visitors subsequently noting that it was her 'usual residence'. The house was built on the riverside with the king's lodgings in a long north-facing range overlooking the Thames. The queen's lodgings were on the other side of the main court and looked south, opening, at ground level, onto the gardens with fine views towards the rising ground of the park. Anna's rooms were thus inherently more attractive than those of the king.

In 1582–3 Queen Elizabeth had re-faced the inner court to look like stone, adding a cornice, architraves and classical mouldings and a loggia with balusters. From 1607 this work of modernisation continued with the addition of a long gallery, cabinet and other rooms. One section, overlooking the garden, was supported by an Italianate loggia, echoing the Elizabethan loggia in the inner court and probably looking like that on the garden front at Denmark House.[27]

As well as these architectural attractions Greenwich was easy to get to by river from Denmark House or Whitehall and, with the tide going out, a barge would get the queen door-to-door in less than an hour. The house was beautifully situated: the royal gardens, which Anna embellished, were extensive, secure and peaceful and led to a large park of 188 acres. This was the real glory of the place; as the Thames valley rose steeply southwards, the sparsely wooded slopes were both ornamental and excellent for sport. The park was too small for the chase, but the king and queen could shoot coursed deer from a standing. When the Venetian ambassador arrived at Greenwich in June 1611, the king gave him a deer that he had just shot.[28]

The hunting park to the south, and the ornamental grounds to the north, were divided by the Deptford to Woolwich road and hunting parties had to cross this to get access to the park. Henry VIII had built a standing, or viewing platform, over the road which also acted as a pedestrian bridge to cross privately from one side to the other. In most royal houses, such as Hampton Court, the viewing point for the killing

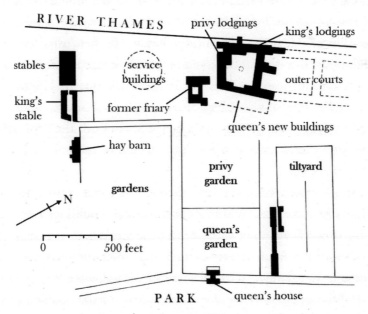

Figure 20: Diagrammatic layout of Greenwich Palace, *c.*1640.

ground of the hunt was from a balcony in the queen's drawing room. At Greenwich the drawing room was 1,000 feet from the park, and the standing contained a polite room for spectators in which, on two occasions in 1606, the queen entertained her brother to a banquet after a morning's hunting.[29]

This arrangement, while effective, was old fashioned and far from magisterial, and in 1616, Anna commissioned Inigo Jones to come up with a design for a new standing to watch the hunt from. In quick succession Jones produced two designs, one of which found favour and, in 1617, it was reported that the queen had commissioned a 'curious device' from him which would cost some £4,000. The building type was well established: an example of such a standing remains at Lodge Park, Sherborne in Gloucestershire built in *c*.1630 by Sir John Dutton, a socially ambitious Gloucestershire gentleman. This contained a gracious first-floor room for eating and a balcony for viewing. Like most standings it had a flat roof to provide more space for spectators. Jones's rendering of a standing for the queen was, however, both stylistically novel and architecturally ambitious.[30]

The building was to be of Portland stone with two parallel ranges either side of the road and a bridge linking them at first floor. Jones took the commission as an opportunity to draw on some of the models of late sixteenth-century residential villas by Andrea Palladio and Vincenzo Scamozzi he had seen in the Veneto. The new building was never intended to be a residence, least of all a copy of a Venetian villa, but he drew freely on the designs of these compact little residences for the queen's new building.[31]

As it rose from its foundations further improvements were made to the park. In 1619 work started on building an encircling wall and, as this was nearing completion, a great gateway was constructed giving access from the road. The gate aligned with the private royal thoroughfare which joined the stables to the park. Hunting parties now had a ceremonial route from stable to parkland and could assemble at the front of the magnificent new standing.[32]

Work on the new building stopped abruptly in April 1618 after most of the materials had been delivered and the lower courses laid out. The queen was economising, and her new building was one of the sacrifices she had to make. It was left a half-built carcass. Anna was not to know that within a year she would be dead, and that work would not start again for another fourteen years.

While King James's cultural interests were primarily intellectual and textual the queen's interests were much more visual. It was she who had first brought Inigo Jones into her employ and she who had given him his first major architectural commission in what we now call the Queen's House. Jones undertook this work, not as Surveyor of the King's Works, but privately paid for out of Anna's privy purse. She must have liked the Italianate design that he presented, and her acceptance of it must have made an impression at court and smoothed the way for his much more emphatically Italian designs for the Banqueting House a few years later.

In 1617–18 Anna commissioned Paul van Somer to paint another portrait of her. His previous portrait, in 1617 (plate 2), had been of

Figure 21: Wenceslaus Hollar, Greenwich Palace, seen from the south in 1637. Left, on the waterfront, are the Tudor stables with the riding way leading from them to Inigo Jones's gate to the park. The completed Queen's House occupies the centre, and behind it to the left is the long roof of the former Observant Friary. To the right in the background is the tower of the king's privy lodgings on the waterfront, and in front of that is Anna of Denmark's extension to the queen's lodgings. The tall building, centre right, is a Tudor recreation complex including viewing towers overlooking the tiltyard that can be seen with its low central barrier. Behind the tiltyard towers is the long low bulk of the chapel.

Anna as huntress and landowner; the new portrait was of Anna the connoisseur (plate 3). The gorgeously attired figure of the queen is minutely observed, but van Somer did not paint the elaborate architectural background; this was executed by another hand, someone extremely confident at handling deep architectural perspective correctly, conceivably Inigo Jones. The painting represents Anna the patron of *avant garde* architecture in the year before her early death, a fitting epitaph to early Stuart England's most important architectural patron.[33]

The royal princes

In 1603 it had been necessary to assemble an entirely new portfolio of lands to provide the queen with sufficient income. Providing for Prince Henry should have been more straightforward as, since the fourteenth century, revenues from the Duchy of Cornwall had been hypothecated to the use of the heir to the throne as they still are today. However, during the previous three reigns Duchy revenue had simply been mixed in with normal exchequer income and despite an attempt to disaggregate it, in 1603 the revenue continued to flow to the king.

Henry was still a minor and would not be in receipt of the Duchy revenues for some years, so the immediate task was to assign Prince Henry St James's and Nonsuch, the two houses built by Henry VIII to house his heir. Informally the prince and his brother and sister also used Richmond in the summer. St James's had been started by Henry VIII in the 1530s and was entirely within the walled compound of St James's Park; it could only be entered from the park or from the great gatehouse on St James's Street, which still stands. Early prints show that it had very few outward-looking windows and none on the ground floor: this was a secure nursery designed to keep the royal children safe from disease and ill-wishers.[34]

The house had two sides or suites, presumably originally designed for a prince and princess of Wales. Prince Henry was established on the prince's side and it can be assumed that the young Charles, Duke of York was given the consort's side. The boys had a 'school chamber' furnished with bookcases near Prince Henry's bedchamber.[35] Sir Thomas

Chaloner, Prince Henry's governor, and later his Lord Chamberlain, was given lodgings near the boys, as were Adam Newton, Henry's tutor and Sir Roger Aston, the king's eyes and ears in the princes' household. Three young noblemen were chosen as Prince Henry's special companions: Robert Devereux, 3rd Earl of Essex, William Cecil, Lord Cranborne and John Harrington, 2nd Baron Harrington of Exon. These boys were assigned rooms immediately adjacent to the prince; other young men were given more peripheral lodgings.[36]

The boys' education was typical for its age, split between the schoolroom and the saddle. James was determined that Henry should have a fine library as a basis for his studies and was lucky enough to be able to acquire, on his death, Lord Lumley's great library, one of the most important in England. His 2,000 volumes were transferred to St James's in 1609 and Patrick Young, the son of one of the prince's tutors was made librarian, a position he continued to hold throughout most of Charles I's reign.[37] A room was designated in the southeast corner of the inner court over the princes' privy kitchen. The interior was fitted out by Maximilian Colt, who had made his name carving Queen Elizabeth's monument in Westminster Abbey.[38]

The bookcases were decorated with eighty-one terms – tapering pedestals that melded into human busts or beasts at the top. There were four great arches with the prince's arms in the spandrels forming part of a vault over the room and smaller arches on the book cupboards which contained 620 shelves. On the east wall there was a massive fireplace with a vigorous chimney surround framed by two giant terms; such virtuoso chimneys were all the rage and Colt was, at that time, working on such a piece, in stone, for Robert Cecil's library at Hatfield. The library was furnished with desks and 'drawing boxes' before the books were delivered.[39]

Vigorous activity complemented hours studying leather-bound volumes in the schoolroom. Henry was mesmerised by warships, military hardware, riding and jousting. As well as butts for archery the prince ordered a stout platform from which he could fire small cannons at a 'strong large board of elm'. But above all he loved great horses upon which he could practise *haute école*, the art of schooling a horse to make supple and agile movements in a confined space. These equine dances were transferable to the tiltyard and enabled riders to perform remarkable feats for the watching crowds. James I's interest in horses was in hunters but Henry, Prince Charles and his friends Essex, Cranborne and William Cavendish, later Duke of Newcastle, devoted themselves to *haute école*.[40]

In 1607 Henry commissioned a new building at St James's at the cost of £150 in which to practise *haute école*. The building, the first purpose-built of its type in England, was of great interest at the time and was carefully surveyed by the architect Robert Smythson, whose drawing survives. The riding school was just that, a place for young aristocrats, led by Prince Henry, to learn the arts of horsemanship.[41]

When the princes tired of riding there were other amusements to hand. In St James's Fields to the north of the house was laid out a pell mell – a narrow alley half a mile long surfaced in crushed cockle shells rolled into loam. Either side were boards to prevent balls, whacked with a croquet-like mallet, going astray. The balls had to go through hoops positioned at points along the alley. Also popular with the boys was tennis. Henry was devoted

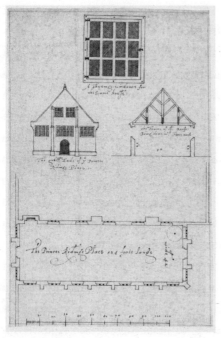

Figure 22: Robert Smythson, Prince Henry's Riding House at St James's Palace, as surveyed in 1609.

to the game and 'neither observed moderation, nor what appertained to his dignity and person' playing tennis for hours in just a shirt. He played at Whitehall, where a new changing room was built for him but, in 1619 for his brother Charles, a tennis court was built next to the pell mell in St James's Fields. Erected on the corner of St James's Street, near today's Berry Brothers wine shop, the court, and the house of its keeper, were set in a walled garden and were connected to the main house by a high-level bridge over the road. Charles, as prince and later king, played energetically, wagering large sums, which he lost when beaten.[42]

Prince Henry became the most popular member of the royal family; even taking into account the formulaic praise of his character by foreign ambassadors and others, he was clearly outgoing, charming and the very model of a future king. By 1607 his household at St James's had become a magnet for the young, fashionable and ambitious; it had swollen to many times its intended size and its cost was enormous. It was, in fact, in fashion if not in power, a rival centre to that of King James I.[43]

Coming of age

As Prince Henry entered his teens he became increasingly eager to estab-lish an independent income from his father and, in 1609, asked his auditor, the lawyer Richard Connock, to ascertain when he could come into his estates. In a detailed tract that listed all the income due to him, Connock explained that he should have gained the income at fourteen, an age which Henry had reached in February 1608. The passing of his fourteenth birthday had not been marked by any change of status and on his fifteenth birthday the prince petitioned his father for control of his revenues and formal creation as prince of Wales. His case was bolstered by a detailed analysis of the position of former Princes of Wales by Connock. Cecil, who was struggling with enormous financial deficits, was all for postponing the prince's independence for a couple of years but, in late 1609, saw a way that it could be turned to advantage.[44]

The only way out of the king's dire financial situation was for parlia-ment to grant money to pay off his debts and then agree some sort of ongoing financial subsidy. This parliament was reluctant to do despite being offered all sorts of concessions. The next parliamentary session was due to start on 9 February 1610, a week before the prince's sixteenth birthday: this coincidence, Cecil believed, gave him an opportunity. Connock's research showed that all but three former Princes of Wales were created in parliament, encouraging Cecil to devise a plan for a lavish parliamentary investiture for the popular and glamorous young prince that would win financial support for the Crown.[45]

In anticipation of this Prince Henry was already making improvements to St James's, including the completion of his new library; but the agreement to go ahead with his investiture, the forthcoming establishment of a full household and the promised release of income from the Duchy of Cornwall, injected a sense of urgency into the works.

St James's, like most royal residences, was arranged around several courtyards. Four, in fact: an outer, inner and a privy court with a kitchen court to the west. The inner court was surrounded on three sides by a gallery – three contiguous spaces 100 feet, 120 feet and 100 feet long respectively. Originally this immense 320-foot-long gallery was plastered and hung with tapestry but, in 1609 Prince Henry ordered it be panelled with square oak panels divided by fluted pilasters every ten feet and topped with a frieze and cornice. This was to be his picture gallery, hung with the best paintings he could acquire.

Work peaked at the end of the year, the prince desperate to complete his improvements in time for Christmas. On 6 January an indoor tournament, *The Barriers*, took place in the Banqueting House at Whitehall with the young men of the court fighting with swords and pikes. The public spectacle, with speeches composed by Ben Jonson and scenery by Inigo Jones, continued till three in the morning. The next day Henry rode to Whitehall from St James's and brought his parents and sister back to his house. There, in his new gallery, he gave them, his brother, and the cream of the court, supper on a table 120 feet long.[46]

This was the prelude to Henry's investiture. Funded by a loan of £100,000 from the City of London the ceremony, held on 4 June, was the first installation of a Prince of Wales for over a century. It

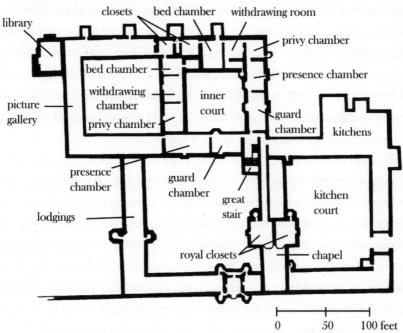

Figure 23a: Eighteenth-century engraving of the north facade of St James's Palace, showing the Tudor gatehouse and, to its right, the large window of the chapel.

Figure 23b: Diagrammatic reconstruction of the first floor at St James's Palace, *c*.1611.

would have been expected that the ceremony be held in the House of Lords, but the chamber was too small, either to admit all the Commons, or foreign guests who had been invited. The Office of Works and Great Wardrobe thus set up the Court of Requests, the largest of the state rooms in the old palace of Westminster (fig. 31). It was divided into two by a barrier; at the lower end sat the Commons on tiered benches with the speaker in a chair crowned with the royal arms. The upper end was dominated by a huge canopy of state elevated on five steps and flanked by tiered boxes for ambassadors and foreign dignitaries. The walls were hung with great tapestries and the boxes with rich textiles.[47]

The day before the investiture the prince had come by river from Richmond in a great flotilla and made a ceremonial entry to Whitehall. The following day the participants arrived in their barges and dressed in private: their robes had cost a staggering £7,000 and the prince's suit another £1,300. A lengthy procession entered the chamber full of peers in their parliament robes, the Commons in their finery and foreign guests and ambassadors outdoing each other with the magnificence of their outfits. Kneeling before his father on the steps of the dais Prince Henry heard his title read, and was invested with a ring, wand, sword and a golden coronet set with diamonds, sapphires and emeralds.[48]

A month or so earlier, on 9 May, while preparations for the investiture were underway, the composition of the prince's independent household had been agreed. It contained almost every office a prince would require from huntsmen to laundresses, chaplains to trumpeters, cooks to bottle-washers. Henry was eager to carry on building, telling Cecil that he was 'like enough to prove an unthrift', and his household was to have its own works department to be headed by Inigo Jones. It is likely that the prince, who had been an enthusiastic participant in many of Jones's masques, and had collaborated with him on the *Barriers* on twelfth night, made the decision himself to give Jones the senior role in his architectural establishment. But he would have encountered no resistance from Cecil or the queen, both of whom were Jones's patrons, or indeed from others in the prince's circle, such as the wily Richard Connock, who were Jones's close friends.[49]

The spectacular round of celebrations that launched Henry's independent life as Prince of Wales was a prelude to an ambitious programme of building. To St James's, in early 1610, the king formally added grants of the royal houses at Richmond and Woodstock. The Venetian ambassador reported that Henry was paying particular attention to his houses and had already ordered new fountains and buildings. 9 May had also been the date when Henry came into the income from his estates, which enabled him to draw some £50,000 a year; but cash did not start flowing immediately and, at first, improvements to the prince's residences continued to be funded by the Crown and Jones, although appointed, was not fully in charge of the work.[50]

The fifteenth-century royal residence at Richmond, which had been rebuilt by Henry VII, was a favourite of the Tudors. The royal lodgings were in a three-storey block with an elaborate ground plan, the upper parts encrusted with towers, turrets, bay windows and onion domes. The royal lodgings were surrounded by a moat crossed by a bridge that linked them to the great hall and chapel. Queen Elizabeth had died in the royal bedchamber there and, in an eight-month campaign of renovation starting in April 1610, the prince brushed away the fusty remains of the old lady's décor.

By the autumn of 1610 attention had switched to the gardens. Henry had been inspired by the *Mount of Parnassus* in his mother's garden at Denmark House, and asked Inigo Jones to embank the riverside at Richmond to create a regular platform for a new garden to be laid out by Robert Cecil's gardener, Mountain Jennings. Saloman de Caus was commissioned to design and construct a pair of large grottoes and the hydraulic systems to make them work.

Despite having the talents of Jones and de Caus at his disposal, Prince Henry craved the services of Italian designers and the Tuscan ambassador was asked whether two Florentines, the Francini brothers, could be released from the service of the French king and work, for higher wages, for him. The brothers had designed elaborate gardens and court spectacles for Henry IV, whom Prince Henry admired. The Francinis could not be released but the prince was offered the Florentine painter and

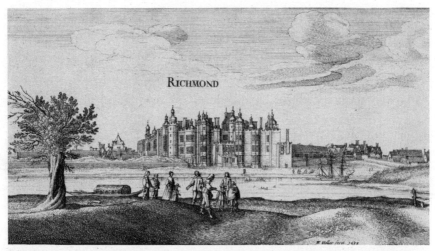

Figure 24: Richmond Palace, engraved by Wenceslaus Hollar, 1638. The Tudor privy lodging tower still stands; in front is the embanked riverside, designed by Inigo Jones for Prince Henry, and to the left are the remains of the conduit house, which would have powered the prince's grottoes.

garden designer, Costantino de' Servi who arrived in England in June 1611. He made straight for the queen's court where he was immediately employed as a portrait painter. But it was not long before Prince Henry had lured him to Richmond and commissioned a design for the gardens already underway.

The prince's enthusiasm for Richmond was spurred by discussions for his marriage. In the summer of 1612 serious negotiations for the hand of Maria, the daughter of the Duke of Savoy, were underway and the prince was facing the prospect of a Princess of Wales arriving before the end of the year. This is the context for de' Servi's magnificent design for Richmond which seems to have been accepted by Henry and shown to the king. It was not only an ambitious remodelling of the gardens, creating a scalloped oval jousting arena in front of the palace, but proposed two new wings to the royal lodgings overlooking the arena and facing the river for the prince and a princess. In July 1612 Henry was urging work on so that when his wife arrived, she would find it built.[51]

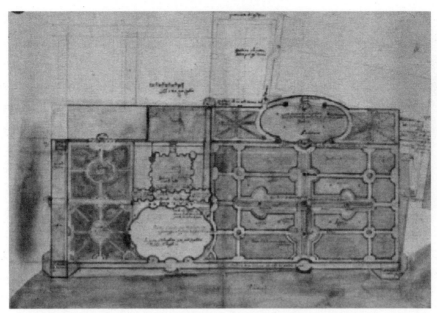

Figure 25: Costantino de' Servi's presentation plan of Richmond Palace. The Lancastrian and Tudor palace was kept and reset in a matrix of new gardens; on the riverfront were added two new pavilions in a style to match the original. De' Servi was not being employed to bring Italian Renaissance architecture to Richmond but to embellish the fifteenth- and sixteenth-century palace.

Even with the receipts of the Duchy of Cornwall, to which had been added those from the Principality of Wales and the earldom of Chester, Prince Henry was finding it hard to make ends meet. His diets (food for his table and household) cost some £10,000 a year, his wardrobe, £3,000 and his privy purse £4,000. Preliminary works at Richmond, paid for by the king in 1610–11 cost very nearly £4,000 and the following year, paid on the prince's account, the bill was £2,422. No wonder Richard Connock told the prince 'in a time so necessitous, and in years so young, you may well forebear the heat and haste of building; building much better fits old men, whom age and infirmity confine to their houses, than in young men, whose youth and heroic and valiant actions princes are to lay a foundation to their fame, before they enter into costly fabrications, serving only for ornament'. Amongst his many gripes de' Servi complained not only of not being paid, but that he doubted that the money was available to carry through his ambitious plans.[52]

Despite the fine library provided for him by his father and the diligent labours of his tutors the young prince fashioned himself not as a scholar, like his peace-loving father, but as a prince in the saddle of a warhorse. He was reported to have said 'it is not necessary for me to be a professor, but a soldier and a man of the world'. The theme of the *Barriers*, the spectacle which marked the culmination of his coming out on twelfth night 1610, was proposed by the prince himself as the revival of the chivalric glories of the past under a new Prince of Wales. In a carefully selective review of English history, narrated by the Arthurian wizard Merlin, Ben Jonson, the author of the spectacle, placed the prince in a lineage of English chivalric heroes from King Arthur, culminating with the Elizabethan knights who 'defeated' the Spanish Armada. Henry was presented as the heir of Tudor chivalry.[53]

The front curtain of Jones's design for the *Barriers* depicts the crumbling ruins of 'the fallen House of Chivalry'; in front of this the Lady of the Lake is in mourning. The cloud above opened to reveal King Arthur himself who handed a shield to Prince Henry; the curtain was then raised, and the audience perceived that chivalry had been restored by the young prince who made his entrance in front of St George's Portico. This building encapsulates the dreams of Prince Henry – it is no classical pavilion, but a gothic concoction set amongst various Roman buildings, many ruined.

The portico expressed the prince's tastes: he admired Richmond for its chivalric associations with the early Tudor kings, for its romantic skyline that would provide a backdrop to future tournaments fought in its shade. His Italian designer de' Servi respectfully planned two new wings in a Tudor style to match the old building. The gardens were full of Tudor and Stuart heraldic badges and devices designed to be seen from raised walks and the windows of the palace. On the east side there was to be a copy of Trajan's column, the carved triumphal pillar that celebrated the Roman Emperor Trajan's victories in the Dacian wars. Nearby was to be a statue of Neptune so large as to have several rooms inside and a dovecote in his head. These represented hopes that Henry would lead a nation to great victories on land and sea.

As if none of this was enough, almost immediately upon coming into his lands Henry also started negotiations to buy what was certainly the most magnificent and romantic castle in England. Kenilworth had been a royal property, but Elizabeth had made it over to Robert Dudley, the Earl of Leicester, her great favourite. Leicester had constructed spectacular new royal lodgings which James I's surveyors thought as modern as anything being built then. In the autumn of 1611 Prince Henry

Figure 26: St George's Portico, backdrop designed for Prince Henry's barriers by Inigo Jones, 6 January 1610. The extraordinary confection in the middle of the scene is Jones's architectural representation of a chivalric pavilion. Through it the prince and his companions entered the middle of the hall divided by a barrier marked with gilded obelisks. The scene is also the earliest known perspective stage set in England.

snapped the castle up for a mere £15,000 and immediately issued instructions for the improvement for what he called 'my first purchase'.[54]

Prince Henry's masques, his plans for Richmond and purchase of Kenilworth show his architectural interests as being quite different from those of his mother; his obsession with chivalry, castles and military prowess resulted in his admiration not of refined Italian Renaissance architecture, but of the chivalric eclecticism of the Tudors and Elizabethans. These tastes, together with his outgoing character and youthful good looks contributed to his popularity and eventually to the outpouring of grief for his death. For nobody could have predicted when he contracted a slight fever at the start of October 1612 that it was typhoid and that on 6 November, he would be dead. His workmen were immediately dismissed, his household dissolved, and his revenues reabsorbed into the exchequer.

Financial crisis

The royal Office of Works, the court department responsible for building and maintaining the royal residential estate, was a well-established organ of state. During the early Stuart period it enjoyed a considerable stability in personnel; only three men served as head of department, the surveyor: Sir David Cunningham, Simon Basil and Inigo Jones. Beneath them was a well-ordered and professionally staffed office which also enjoyed considerable continuity. In the late Elizabethan period, the office had been little more than a maintenance department disbursing some £4,000 a year. On the accession of James expenditure had leapt to £7,000, the following year £11,000; the bills for the eighteen months 1606–7 were £23,000 and for the same period of time in 1609–10 a vast £51,800. These were levels of expenditure not seen since the reign of Henry VIII.

Underlying this soaring expenditure was a loss of financial control. Under Elizabeth estimates were obtained and budgets agreed: James ignored these 'unnecessary' administrative niceties and ordered works to start without consideration of the cost. When, in 1608 Robert Cecil took over as Lord Treasurer he issued strict new orders to ensure that work was undertaken as efficiently as possible and that the officers were not illegally enriching themselves (which they had been). The reforms, however, did not deal with the real issue, which was that the king believed that money was not his problem.[55]

Travelling south from Scotland, receiving lavish entertainment at every halt, then arriving in London and taking possession of a score of large, richly furnished palaces set in huge hunting parks, James described himself as being in a 'paradise of pleasure'. The ecstasy did not last long. With a growing financial crisis, in October 1605 he complained that 'the glorious sunshine of my entry here should be so soon overcast with the dark clouds of irreparable misery'. Two years later he wrote likening himself to a patient and the Privy Council the physicians: 'the only disease and consumption which I can ever apprehend as likeliest to endanger me is this eating canker of want'.[56]

There was no reason why James should have understood how shaky English Crown finances were: a more-or-less static income since the 1550s had been whittled away by inflation and the pound in the Stuart royal pocket was buying only 60 per cent of what Henry VIII's had done. This situation could have perhaps been managed in peacetime by careful husbandry and retrenchment, but James was determined to enjoy his new kingdom and had no intention of holding back. Bishop Goodman, recalling a conversation with the king, reflected upon the profligate spirit of the age, it 'being a time of peace we fell to luxury and riot; no kingdom in the world spent so much in building as we did in his time . . . for excess in apparel and expense besides, the number of law suits, and many other ways which might exhaust a kingdom, under his happy and peaceable government we did exceed'. When Salisbury became treasurer, he ordered a comparison between expenditure in the last five years of Elizabeth's reign and the first five of King James's. It showed that the privy purse had increased from £5,100 to £25,800, the wardrobe from £21,300 to £77,900, the cost of the household from £30,000 to £164,900 and so on for another ten categories.

With a larger royal family and the expenses of marrying the royal children some increase in expenditure was inevitable, but a great deal of it was the king's personal whim. He could not bear to seem mean and granted away some £68,153 to favourites in his first four years. A fortune was spent on personal adornment – while Elizabeth I had spent around £10,000 a year on her wardrobe towards the end of the reign, James was spending £36,000 annually at the start of his. In his first year alone he spent £47,000 on jewels and the marriage of his daughter Elizabeth in 1613 cost a staggering £100,000.[57]

When, in 1615, Inigo Jones became surveyor the financial crisis was in full flood. The surveyor's work was onerous with heavy financial responsibilities and it was necessary first to be a capable administrator. Basil had certainly been this, but Jones had been employed, not primarily for his administrative skills, but because he was recognised as the most talented designer at court. But his artistic genius was allied with a brilliant grasp of administration and under him the Office of Works had barely ever been better run: looking back from the vantage point of 1667 one informed observer was to claim of his tenure that there was 'scarcely any one office in his majesty's court of greater reputation both for able officers, good conduct, frugality of expense and sure payment than the Office of Works'.[58]

Jones, as this book will show, was pulled every way by his many duties. As well as the surveyorship he was responsible for co-producing court masques and supporting the royal players at court; he acquired the leading role in royal ambitions to improve the capital and its principal buildings, served Charles I as an artistic advisor and was a hard-working Justice of the Peace and Member of Parliament. His office was thus much like a large architectural practice today where the principal led on the big ideas and client interface, and the details of design and supervision were left to his team.

The men in the Office of Works at Jones's side were much more experienced in building than he; many could draw plans and elevations, and all had overseen major building projects. The mason and carver William Cure had his own successful family workshop in Southwark; Nicholas Stone also had an extensive private practice as an architect and mason. Francis Carter was chief clerk of works; he was another experienced architect who had the crucial role of supervising the eight junior clerks each responsible for a group of royal houses. Several of these were architects too, including Robert Stickells who designed a banqueting house for James I in 1609. The master craftsmen: the locksmith, plumber, bricklayer, plasterer, glazier etc. were also part of the office, bringing specialised technical knowledge to the works.

By far the majority of the office's work was the repair of existing medieval and Tudor structures and the erection of relatively minor ancillary buildings. In fact, Jones's tenure as surveyor was a low point in the output of the Office of Works. The only significant new building was the Whitehall banqueting house completed by 1622. For the whole of King Charles's reign there was not a single new commission of note that got off the drawing board. Early Stuart financial resources were not put into architecture but into clothes, jewellery, plate, works of art and hospitality. Some new work did come the way of the office; the largest royal commissions of King Charles's reign, remodelling St Paul's Cathedral, and designing Covent Garden Piazza, both of which are described in the next chapter, were not royal palaces and were undertaken outside the Office of Works. In these projects, from 1628, Jones had his own personal assistant, a relative by marriage, John Webb.

Webb was to later claim that Charles I had encouraged Jones to take on a pupil as a plan for the succession of the surveyorship; this may have been true, but more importantly Jones urgently needed a talented assistant who could produce the technical drawings necessary for both the theatre and St Paul's Cathedral. Some of this work was redrawing sketches by Jones at scale for the craftsmen, but most of the designs for theatre and masques show that Webb had mastered the technicalities of stage mechanics and designed under his own initiative.[59]

It was Webb who described Jones as the 'supreme officer' of the king's works, an epithet that hints at control-freakery. Ben Jonson the poet and playwright, Jones's early collaborator in masques, with whom he catastrophically fell out, called him a 'joiner who will join with no man', and the Papal Agent at Henrietta Maria's court thought him 'very conceited and boastful'. Jones cannot always have been an easy man to work with, but he knew how to handle his royal masters, and they came to rely on him to achieve their aims.[60]

FIVE

Jacobus Rex Magnae Britanniae

Capital city

From the moment of Elizabeth's death James knew in his heart that he was now no ordinary monarch. He was the first king of Britain and his overwhelming ambition was to unite his two kingdoms under a single crown which he was to wear. In a sense he had prepared for this all his life, contemplating its implications during his 33-year reign in Scotland.

Although he continued two separate administrations in 1603, his aim, as soon as parliament met, was to pass the legislation to unite them. The English Parliament was not to be so compliant. James's suggestion that he should be styled King of Great Britain was eventually quashed by arguments put forward by the judiciary and he was forced to adopt it, not by Act of Parliament, but by proclamation. The king's efforts to create a flag and common currency for Britain met with similar hostility.[1]

Despite James's failure to achieve a political union the idea and ambition behind it never died; nor, more importantly, did James's own image of himself as King of Britain. The weight of dignity conferred upon him by his new title remained central to his thinking about the setting of his rule. In this, London, his new capital, was now the capital

Figure 27: James I on horseback with the City of London and Southwark
in the background. This is one of a set of three engravings of James I,
Queen Anna and Charles I on horseback, published by Compton Holland
in *c.*1616. The print proclaims James as King of Great Britain and remarks on
the millions who depend on him, including the inhabitants of his capital city.

of Great Britain and a city vastly elevated in status by the marriage of
two nations that he had achieved.

In 1500, London had had around 50,000 inhabitants; in less than a
century it had grown to over half a million. In 1580, in order to control
its growth, Queen Elizabeth issued the first of a series of proclamations
forbidding the building of houses on new sites within three miles of
the gates of the City. An Act of Parliament, and a further proclamation
followed, but failed to make any real difference. In 1603, when King
James arrived, he found a city gripped by pestilence, and amongst his
first acts was a proclamation regulating the construction of poorly built

and crowded housing. It was the first of twelve such proclamations between 1603 and his death in 1625.

Frustrated at his inability to control the spread of shanty development, in October 1614 the king asked for a detailed survey listing all the new buildings erected in the City of London since he came to the throne. This doomsday survey of illegal property does not survive but its contents must have been alarming because, in April 1614, the king created a muscular new Commission to enforce his proclamations comprising the entire Privy Council and twenty-two others. Up until this time the Lord Mayor, aldermen and justices of the peace were responsible for policing new development, but the new commission, armed with powers to investigate, interrogate and prosecute now took the lead.

It may have been as a result of the initial meeting of this large commission that James felt impelled to clarify what it was he was trying to achieve. On 16 July another proclamation was issued in which James stated that 'Our City of London is become the greatest or next the greatest city of the Christian world' but that it was in need of improvement and that he wanted to oversee a transformation for the better: 'As it was said by the first emperor of Rome, that he had found the city of Rome of brick, and left it of marble, so We, whom God hath honoured to be the first King of Great Britain, might be able to say in some proportion, that we found our city and suburbs of London of sticks, and left them of bricks.'[2]

James, as always precise in his instructions, appended to the proclamation a list of the buildings he liked, and which be regarded as models for new development to follow. Not surprisingly he had licensed all of them and most had been designed by architects in the orbit of the Crown: Sutton's Hospital (now the Charterhouse) was erected under royal patent and designed by Francis Carter, clerk of works to the Prince of Wales and later Master Carpenter to the king; the New Exchange in the Strand was built by the king's secretary the Earl of Salisbury, designed by Simon Basil the surveyor of the king's works and advised upon by Inigo Jones; Hicks Hall, the court room for the Middlesex sessions in

Clerkenwell was erected by Sir Baptist Hicks whose brother was the Earl of Salisbury's secretary and who was the lead supplier of cloth to the king. The new city gate at Aldersgate was designed by Gerard Christmas, carver to the Royal Navy who sculpted a large equestrian statue of James I in bas relief on its north face. None was particularly architecturally novel, distinguished or ambitious, but all were well-built in brick and stone and represented the standard the king felt appropriate to this new capital of Great Britain.[3]

Up until 1618 the efforts of the Crown to control the number and quality of new buildings in the city had been essentially legal and administrative but that year King James called in Inigo Jones to help protect an area of undeveloped land between Westminster and the City. After the death of Prince Henry, Jones had been offered the reversion of the Surveyor of Works, which meant that all he had to do to gain the post was to wait until Simon Basil died. Safe in the knowledge of his prospects, and riding high in the opinion of the greatest English artistic connoisseurs, Jones accompanied the Earl of Arundel and his countess on a European tour. Crucially Jones was now able to spend a year in Italy where he explored in depth the architecture of Palladio and Scamozzi as well as examining ancient Roman buildings and some contemporary ones. Simon Basil died in October 1615 and over the following years Jones's talents drew him into more and more royal projects.

Lincoln's Inn Fields had been targeted by a speculative developer and the lawyers of Lincoln's Inn petitioned the Privy Council to preserve the land as an open recreational space. James asked Jones to come up with a scheme to do this which, the king believed, would be 'of great ornament to the City, pleasure and freshness for the health and recreation of the Inhabitants thereabout, and for the sight and delight of Ambassadors and Strangers coming to our Court and City, and a memorable work of our time to all posterity'. For a second time a proclamation expressed royal motivations: and in 1618, to a general desire to give London the status it now deserved, was the imperative for it to be a magnificent place for the reception of ambassadors engaged in marriage negotiations for the hands of the king's children.[4]

London was no stranger to royal marriage discussions and, during the first half of Elizabeth's reign, had played host to a series of delegations hopeful of concluding a marriage treaty with the queen. Whitehall, as the principal seat of the Crown, was one site of these but, in 1581, faced with the prospect of the arrival of a favoured suitor, Francis, the French king's brother, the queen ordered that the palace be prepared for a possible future husband. In particular a new Banqueting House was to be built in which to feast and entertain the French. It was raised up on a basement with walls framed in timber and covered in canvas painted in imitation of stone. This Banqueting House, intended as a temporary structure, had its life extended by a series of repairs for a remarkable twenty-five years, entering the Jacobean era as an embarrassing monument to Elizabeth's unconsummated nuptials.[5]

Banqueting houses

The 1581 Banqueting House fitted neither with James's ambitions for his new capital, nor with those for the reception of ambassadors, and amongst his first orders to the Office of Works was one for repainting the great canvas ceiling with clouds and his coat of arms. George Weale, the clerk of works at Whitehall was commissioned to survey the Banqueting House and adjacent buildings in preparation for their replacement. The Elizabethan architect and naval engineer Robert Stickells provided a design for the new building, and so possibly did Sir David Cunningham, but Cunningham died, and the architect's job seems to have rested with Stickells.[6]

Stickells was interested in architectural theory and wrote several pompous theoretical tracts on the subject. His design, a large central space surrounded by aisles with galleries above in two classical orders, was based on his understanding of the 'Egyptian hall' described by the ancient Roman writer Vitruvius. But as Vitruvius's text was not illustrated, he turned to the Netherlandish engraver Hans Vredeman de Vries who had published a perspective view of a large hall, with colonnades very similar to those described in the Banqueting House.

Figure 28: Hans Vredeman de Vries, engraving entitled 'Ionica super Dorica', 1606.
The building accounts for the Banqueting House at Whitehall describe a building
very similar to de Vries's engraving including the columnation, double orders and
balcony. Robert Stickells used de Vries as a source for other buildings and
may have drawn inspiration from his engravings for Whitehall.

King James was excited by this, his first major English commission,
and in September 1607, when work on the building was well advanced,
diverted his progress to the west, travelling from Windsor to Whitehall
specially to see it. What he saw horrified him. Stickells's design may
have looked good on paper, but inside the forest of columns made it
difficult to see anything. It even made it hard to see out of the windows
as the columns lined up with each window opening instead of, more
sensibly, being between them. James was not only displeased, but was
furious with his architect. Perhaps not surprisingly Stickells never worked
for the Crown again. But the Banqueting House was finished, nevertheless, and was launched in January 1608 with the *Masque of Beauty*,
written by Ben Jonson. For this the hall was decked out with raked
seating on the floor and in its gallery. The unfortunate Office of Works
clerk who had the task of describing the vast rotating throne encrusted

with greenery and set in a maze which was the centrepiece of the entertainment struggled to find the appropriate words.[7]

The Banqueting House became the ceremonial hub of the kingdom. In 1614, for instance, the royal works first dismantled the seating and stages for the New Year masques, then set up tables for the Maundy ceremonies; soon after which seating was again erected for the king to receive parliamentarians at the opening of the session. This came down for the St George's day feast. Then the hall was prepared for entertaining Christian IV of Denmark including converting one of the windows into a box to watch bear-baiting outside. Amidst all this they were making alterations to the windows so that a Dutchman could demonstrate a scientific discovery to the king.[8]

There is only one detailed description of this Banqueting House in use: following his attendance at a masque in 1618 Orazio Busino, the almoner to the Venetian Embassy, described the experience: 'A large hall arranged like a theatre, with well secured boxes all round. The stage is at one end and his Majesty's chair in front under an ample canopy. Near him are stools for the foreign ambassadors . . . Whilst waiting for the King we amused ourselves by admiring the decorations and beauty of the hall, with its two orders of columns, one above the other, their distance from the wall the full width of the passage, the upper gallery supported by Doric columns, above these rise Ionic columns supporting the roof. The whole is of wood, including even the shafts, which are carved and gilt with much skill. From the roof of these hang garlands and angels in relief, with two rows of lights.'[9]

On 12 January 1619, this Banqueting House, crammed full of painted oilcloth, went spectacularly up in flames. The chief officers of the household were, at that moment, in the City Guildhall at a meeting of the king's commission for London. Rushing back to Whitehall they saw that the Banqueting House was beyond rescue and concentrated on saving the rest of the palace.[10]

The king's reaction is nowhere recorded but, he wanted it to 'expeditiously be new built'. Just as he had done on acquiring Theobalds, James assembled a commission of courtiers to take responsibility for determining the next steps. The men who served on it were chosen with characteristic care: foremost had to be the two most important court officers, the Lord Chamberlain, William Herbert, Earl of Pembroke and the Lord Steward, Ludovic Stuart, Duke of Lennox. They were responsible for the daily functioning of ceremonial and would have strong views about the functionality of a new building. Given the Crown's financial situation the chancellor of the exchequer, Sir Fulke Greville was to sit with the chamberlain and steward. Two other courtiers were chosen for their expertise: Sir John Digby was vice chamberlain of the household, but more importantly, James's leading diplomat who had been responsible for conducting marriage negotiations in Spain for the king's sons. Digby knew more about foreign courts and diplomacy than anyone else. Then there was Thomas Howard, Earl of Arundel who did not hold a major court post, though he desperately wanted one; his qualification for being on the commission must have been as a connoisseur and leading member of the king's commission for building in London.[11]

As the committee sat, Queen Anna became gravely ill and died on 2 March, plunging the court into mourning and the Office of Works into frantic preparations for her funeral. The royal coffers empty, the funeral had to be put off until the money could be raised to bury her with due solemnity, which didn't happen until 13 May. In this interval Inigo Jones, preoccupied by funeral arrangements, began to produce designs for the commission. Their deliberations are lost but two elevations survive as well as some associated plans. These show that various options were considered before a final design was chosen. This had been achieved by 19 April when an estimate, signed by the officers of works, was submitted to the Privy Council, and approved. The budget was £9,850.[12]

Jones's designs show that commissioners were debating the eventual width of the building on Whitehall and how it would join with the existing structures. The south end was straightforward as the new building would join the king's privy gallery just as the old one had done. But access from here was for the king only and access at the north end, for ambassadors and others, had to be up a public staircase, and there was no room to build this without demolishing and redesigning the fifteenth-century court gate – the principal entrance to Whitehall. There was certainly no money available for this and so the Banqueting House was eventually built with a temporary stair at its north end which could be taken down and replaced later when the court gate was more comprehensively redesigned.

The design of the new building was something quite out of the ordinary. Jones, who had been brought up amongst the exoticism of flamboyant Elizabethan design, instead derived inspiration from the ancient language of architecture where a limited suite of components could be assembled according to a set of principles to achieve a proportional harmony of the parts. The completed facades of the Banqueting House sprang from a deep understanding of the rules of Renaissance architects and even more remarkably of the ancient architecture from which they derived.

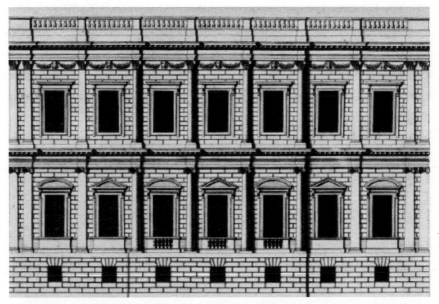

Figure 29: Inigo Jones, the Banqueting House at Whitehall, as depicted by Colen Campbell in *Vitruvius Britannicus*, 1715. The lower order of columns is Ionic, and the upper is a composite order. There is no conventional frieze, but a line of swags is hung, as it were, between the capitals. The building was re-faced in the nineteenth century and none of the original external stonework now remains.

The new building was constructed of three types of subtly contrasting stone: brownish Oxfordshire stone for the basement; a warm Northamptonshire stone for the upper walls, and bright white Portland for the columns and balustrade. The whole was rusticated, that is to say the wall surface was channelled to give the impression of being composed of massive individual blocks of stone. Seven bays wide, the central three slightly project with round columns, the flanking bays framed by flat pilasters. The completed building was like nothing seen before in Britain; it was the first use of the classical orders in a manner that conformed to rules set out in Renaissance treatises of architecture, no wonder the letter writer, John Chamberlain, thought the Banqueting House 'too fair' for the rest of Whitehall.[13]

Nothing that King James had commissioned before 1619 had prepared people for this, and nothing built by the Crown for another forty-five years came even close to it in the correct use of the classical orders of architecture. This is because the Banqueting House was no ordinary royal domestic building, it was the expression in stone of James's ambitions as King of Great Britain. Inside on a tablet was inscribed 'I[acobus] R[ex] M[agna] B[ritannia], a shortened version of the originally intended plaque that was to explain the purpose of the building as being for 'festive occasions, for formal spectacles, and for the ceremonials of the British court'.[14]

The king's royal dignity as King of Great Britain was emphasised by an entirely novel architectural device at the south end of the new main hall. Here was a shallow apse based on Andrea Palladio's reconstruction of ancient Roman basilica; Jones had intended the royal throne to sit in this niche so that James could rule from the place the Romans associated with judicial authority. But the idea was too theoretical. For centuries English kings had sat beneath square-headed textile canopies on a carpet-covered dais. This ill-suited an ancient Roman apse and so only a few years after its completion the apse was demolished, and the traditional arrangement adopted. Yet the idea must have been accepted, not only by the Banqueting House commission but the king himself.

The Banqueting House was not only a glorification of the new British king, it was designed to be a model for the public architecture of the new capital city. James himself wrote in his book 'the peace-maker' of 1619, 'O London blessed Mrs of this happy Britanniae build thy new gates there's peace entering at them . . . Let Whitehall (fit emblem for her purity) be her chief palace and let it say *Ades Alma salus.*' The role that the Banqueting House could play in the revival of the capital was recognised by the City members of the Commission for Building who offered, on the destruction of the 1581 Banqueting House, to pay for its reconstruction. The financial trail goes cold in the surviving exchequer papers, so it is unclear how much of the £15,000 that the building eventually cost was raised from the City. But, in 1621, a scene in the Lord Mayor's pageant suggests that the Corporation felt able to take some credit for both the completion of the Banqueting House and the work that James had encouraged to improve the dilapidated state of St Paul's Cathedral. Thomas Middleton, who composed the tableau, devised a gloomy and tattered figure lying collapsed over the ruined battlements of the 'tower of fame'. When the Lord Mayor and aldermen arrived, hot from an audience at Whitehall, the figure looked up, threw off his rags, and standing erect proclaimed 'virtue's fair edifice raised up like me, why, here's the city's goodness, shown in either, to raise two worthy buildings both together'.[15]

The building of the Banqueting House in London was important enough to be news in foreign courts and the ambition of the project came to the ears of Peter Paul Rubens, then the most successful and famous painter in northern Europe who was just completing a huge commission to paint canvases for the ceiling of the Jesuit Church in Antwerp (now St Carlo Borromeo). On the very day the church was consecrated he wrote to William Trumbull, the English resident agent to the court in Brussels, offering to paint the ceiling of the new Banqueting House. It was an audacious request as the building was not even complete, but while King James was distracted by financial and political events, the queen mother of France asked Rubens to decorate her palace at the Luxembourg in Paris. Marie de' Medici wanted to commission paintings for the two long galleries that ran the whole length of her house on each wing. The paintings on one side were completed by the end of 1624 in time for the celebrations for the marriage of her daughter Henrietta Maria with Charles Prince of Wales.[16]

James was extremely proud of his new hall, visiting it in construction, and the intended inscription, which dates from around 1621, proclaims that the building 'strikes the eye by its majesty and speaks most magnificently of the soul of its Lord, razed when scarcely made of brick, but now the equal of any marble buildings throughout Europe'. Before it was completed, the king had already commissioned the Flemish artist Paul van Somer to paint him standing in front of it (plate 5). James is shown before a window in the guard chamber with the east elevation of the Banqueting House seen across the court through an open casement. Van Somer must have been furnished with a drawing of the building as intended by Jones as it is not shown as finally completed.

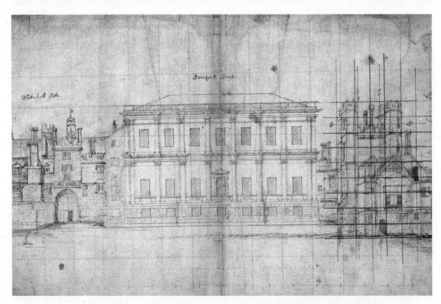

Figure 30: Inigo Jones, drawing for a scene in the masque, *Time Vindicated to Himself and to His Honours*, performed in the Banqueting House on 19 January 1623. To to the left of the Banqueting House is the fifteenth-century court gate and, squeezed between that and the north wall of the Banqueting House, a structure containing a staircase. To the right is the so-called Holbein Gate with the end of the tiltyard gallery in front of it. The elevation of the Banqueting House is unfinished.

The king, however, is portrayed in all his majesty, in his coronation robes with orb and sceptre: his intention is clear, the Banqueting House was intended to be the principal theatre of his majesty.[17]

For twelfth night 1623, the Banqueting House was used for the first time for a masque; *Time Vindicated to Himself and to his Honours* opened with a cloth that depicted the Banqueting House with the buildings of the old palace to either side. England now had a building which could compare, in style, to the modern palaces of Europe, a building in which the king would feel proud to entertain foreign princes, ratify treaties, receive the houses of parliament, create new peers and celebrate the feast of St George. It was a building created to magnify the greatness of the first king of Great Britain and his capital city and James comprehensively used it as such.[18]

The first glittering international occasion in the hall was, as the king had envisaged, the reception of Spanish ambassadors engaged in the detailed negotiations for the marriage of his son. On 29 July 1623, leaving the palace chapel, the king led the two ambassadors into the Banqueting House, hung with the great sixteenth-century set of Abraham tapestries and dressed with two enormous buffets laden with eight cartloads of plate brought from the Tower. The silver-gilt buffet stretched across the full width of the lower end of the hall, pierced in the centre by an arch so that the door was in the middle of it. The second was to the right hand of the king sitting in his niche, very tall and all the plate of gold. In front of the king was a table, the width of the hall, behind which the king sat and, at a small distance, either side were the two Spaniards.[19]

The Palace of Westminster

James lost little time in calling his first parliament. He knew, of course, how to manage one, and had many years of experience in Edinburgh where, so he said, he was heard 'not only as King but as councillor', but his experience of the English Parliament alarmed him. He was unused to a body that defied his will, was bored by his rhetoric, rejected his suggestions, questioned his motives and was hostile to his fellow countrymen. He also had to contend with a parliament that had two chambers, not one as in Scotland. At first, he looked on parliamentary proceedings with incomprehension; later this turned to frustration and eventually to anger.

Parliament met in the Palace of Westminster, the ancient seat of the English monarchy, the only one of its residences normally referred to as a palace. During the Middle Ages, one by one, the administrative, financial and judicial offices of state made their homes there and, by the reign of Henry VII, the palace was more like a small town than a building. The largest, and oldest, structure was Westminster Hall, built by William Rufus from 1097 and given a spectacular timber roof 200 years later in the reign of Richard II. Leading off this colossal hall were the great medieval rooms of state and further south, a maze of smaller chambers for more intimate functions – the so-called privy palace. This part of the palace was destroyed in a fierce fire in 1512. Henry VIII moved out and, by 1530, had re-established himself at Whitehall a few hundred yards north. The Palace of Westminster was never again to be used as a royal residence, although to this day, it remains the property of the sovereign.

From the mid-1530s more and more administrative functions were established in the abandoned old palace and new structures were built to house them. Westminster Hall remained the home of the most important law courts, the Common Pleas, King's Bench and Chancery, set up in partitioned sections of the vast draughty space. Up a few steps was the Court of Wards and Liveries and beyond that, in the White Hall of the old palace, was established the Court of Requests. The House of Lords met in the former queen's chamber, one of the larger medieval state rooms. Access for the peers was through the courts or up some steps from Old Palace Yard; the bishops and the king had their own, separate, entrances. The Commons had historically assembled in the refectory of Westminster Abbey. After the suppression of the abbey and the college of St Stephen in the Palace of Westminster, Edward VI granted the Commons permission to meet in St Stephen's Chapel, bringing together the two houses in a single building for the first time.

The chapel required very little alteration to make it suitable, the speaker sitting on the raised altar step and the MPs occupying the position of the former choir stalls.

The law courts sat regularly and predictably during the four legal terms of the year but parliament met irregularly and relatively unpredictably and for most of the year the majority of the palace was occupied, on a variety of tenures, by officers of state, members of the royal household, and some private individuals. There were taverns and alehouses; three named Hell, Heaven and Purgatory were particularly successful. There were many shops and booths, some selling necessaries for the legal profession like books and stationery, others selling food, drink and luxury goods. People had the right to alter and adapt their residences to add rooms, pentices, attics and cellars. This created a maze of small courts and passages.[20]

Because the old palace was home to the law courts, hordes of plaintiffs, defendants, witnesses, lawyers, students, clerks and judges filled the lobbies and galleries around. When parliament was in session it became a scrum; peers were accompanied by their servants and MPs brought with them the recorders and aldermen of their boroughs, as well as their wives eager to shop in Westminster's fashion district. Officials such as the parliamentary clerks, doormen, serjeants at arms and scriveners worked side by side with servants who stoked the fires, brought in refreshments and swept the floors. To ferry members to and fro there were coachmen, footmen and watermen who clogged the entries and staircases waiting for a fare. The lobbies to each of the Houses were filled with people presenting petitions, sending messages to members in their chambers or simply wanting to be first with news of the latest deliberations.[21]

It was this jumbled architectural incoherence and teeming human chaos that confronted King James when his first parliament assembled in March 1604. Some small alterations were made to the Lords' chamber, so as to provide a place for the queen, and more seats and a gallery were built in the Commons chamber to accommodate the growing number of members, but over and above dressing the rooms with tapestries and new mats, little was needed for the new monarch. In line with the tradition established by his predecessors, on the first day James processed from Whitehall to Westminster Abbey where, after a service and a sermon, he made another procession to the House of Lords where he opened his first parliamentary session.[22]

In July 1603, amongst the vexations of dealing with a parliament that had no interest in the unification of his two realms, two Roman Catholic plots against his person were uncovered. James had been deeply scarred by the various plots he had endured in Scotland, and annually celebrated the defeat of the Gowrie conspiracy in 1600, in which he had nearly been stabbed to death. The English plots served to increase both his anxiety and his vigilance. In fact they probably saved his life for, in 1605, on his orders, the most dastardly plot of all was uncovered.

The fanatical Catholic terrorists who plotted to obliterate the king on his chair of estate in the House of Lords exploited the inadequacies of the Palace of Westminster to brilliant effect. In June 1604, one of the plotters, Thomas Percy, was appointed a gentleman pensioner, one of the ceremonial guards who stood in the outer rooms of royal houses on special occasions. He used his appointment as cover to rent a house in the Palace of Westminster from a Yeoman of the King's Wardrobe of the Beds, John Whynniard. This house, a perk of office, itself sublet, was on the Thames waterfront next to the House of Lords. On the first floor it connected to a long narrow room over a passage which led directly to the Lords' chamber.

All the principal rooms in the palace were on a raised ground floor, and beneath them were a series of undercrofts used for storage and service. The plan was to tunnel into the space beneath the House of Lords from Percy's house and plant an enormous bomb there; this would be ignited as the king opened parliament, vaporising the king, queen, Prince of Wales and most of the peers. One of the co-conspirators, Guy Fawkes, a tall red-headed Yorkshire gentleman, who had made a career as a mercenary in the Spanish Netherlands, donned the disguise of Percy's servant, moved into the little house, and started mining.

The fourteenth-century stonework, set in iron-like mortar, did not yield to his increasingly violent blows and it says a great deal about the noisy and chaotic nature of the palace that the sound of his hammering did not cause suspicion. What Fawkes then realised, was that the space directly under the Lords' chamber was rented by Whynniard to a Mrs Skinner, and so Thomas Percy turned his charm, and purse, towards getting her to sublet it to him. His pretext was that his wife was to join him during the forthcoming parliamentary session and that he needed space for coal and firewood. Thanks to a large number of nocturnal ferry trips across the Thames, Fawkes and his aides brought some thirty-six barrels of gunpowder, approximately half a ton, across a garden and into the undercroft and hid it under 3,000 bundles of kindling. There was enough gunpowder in the room to reduce most of the southern part of the old palace to rubble.

Due to a tip-off, the undercroft was searched, but not thoroughly, and afterwards King James liked to tell the story of how, on his personal instructions, the keeper of the palace, one of his Privy Chamber, Sir Thomas Knyvett, undertook a more thorough search, arrested Fawkes and discovered the bomb.[23]

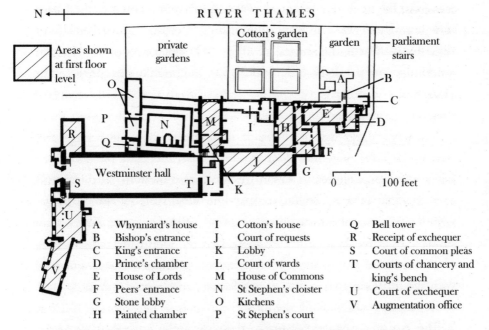

Figure 31: Diagrammatic reconstruction of Westminster Palace at ground and first-floor levels in the early seventeenth century.

Whitehall

The Gunpowder Plot contributed to James's dislike of London and reluctance to stay at Whitehall because it shared many of the characteristics of uncontrollable Westminster Palace. Like Westminster, Whitehall was also a vast dispersed complex covering some twenty-three acres including courts and gardens.

The sovereign's lodgings were extensive and richly furnished, so much so that during James's long reign very few changes were made. He ordered a painted and gilded weathervane be added to his private drawing room in the privy gallery which was connected, by means of an iron rod, to a dial in the room showing the king which way the wind blew. This gave it a new name: the vane room. The king also renovated and enlarged his library, always a personal concern. The queen's lodgings had not been regularly used since Henry VIII's reign and were remodelled and decorated for Anna of Denmark. Likewise, the Prince of Wales's riverside lodging, last used by a member of the royal family in Mary I's reign, were modernised and brought back into use. There was no accommodation for either Prince Charles or his sister Elizabeth and the palace keeper was ejected from his comfortable lodge on the Park Side which was assigned to the prince. The smaller of Henry VIII's two indoor tennis courts nearby was converted into a neat residence for Elizabeth.[24]

James, who regarded Whitehall as a necessary evil, came and went, staying just long enough to discharge his duties. His main period of residence was the so-called court season: this was the period from mid-December to mid-January, the coldest and darkest time of the year, but also the period with the greatest concentration of festivals: Christmas, St Stephen's day, St John's day, Holy Innocents, New Year's Day, Epiphany, Michaelmas, Hallowmas and Candlemas. These religious festivals, although not kept with the liturgical elaboration of the Tudor period, were excuses to stage court entertainments filling the long evenings.[25]

The court normally reassembled at Whitehall three more times before the summer. Although Candlemas formally marked the end of winter, Shrovetide, which normally fell in February, was the last festival of the cold season. It was a chance for overindulgence before the start of Lent when eating meat was forbidden. It was also a time for popular sport and, while the city apprentices played football, at court there was cockfighting, the occasional tournament, plays and a masque (on Shrove Tuesday). The king's accession day, 24 March, was almost always celebrated at Whitehall and accompanied by a tournament in the tiltyard. The bells of the city churches rang out and the populace would flood into Whitehall hoping for a chance to glimpse the action. The last big Whitehall event of spring was normally Easter although this was not as reliably held at Whitehall as the previous festivals. Although the intense ceremonies of the Roman Catholic church had been stripped back and sublimated into a festival of preaching, at court, Holy Week and Easter were celebrated with some formality and it was one of the times that the king wore his robes and received communion publicly in the chapel royal.

For most of the period from Easter to November James was not at Whitehall. He would come for a day or two to receive ambassadors, meet the Privy Council, attend to family matters, but the next regular fixture in the Whitehall calendar was the anniversary of the Gunpowder Plot, 5 November, which had been turned by the king into a national religious festival with prayers for the royal family and a reminder of how wicked Roman Catholics were.

Jacobean Whitehall was thus the ceremonial hub of the kingdom, not its principal royal residence. This had major implications for the king's Office of Works. This venerable court department had long been quartered in Scotland Yard; it was here that the surveyor had his residence and drawing office and the financial officers exercised their oversight of the works. Nearby, master craftsmen stockpiled materials and had their workshops. Under James the focus of their work profoundly altered. While architecturally little new was done at Whitehall, in the twenty-two years of his reign, the winter months were marked by intense activity preparing the palace for masques, plays, tournaments, dances, feasts and other ephemeral events. Jones used the muscle of the Office of Works to make the elaborate machinery and scenery required. The Serjeant Painter John de Critz and one of the royal contract painters Edward Pierce both painted large-scale scenery for Jones. The joiners were particularly busy: for one masque it took eighteen carts to transport the infrastructure for its staging to Denmark House and back to Scotland Yard.[26]

There were essentially three types of court performance: plays, masques and feats of arms. Of the latter, the most remarkable were tournaments. Tournaments had been a central part of court festivities for more than two centuries before James came to the throne. Henry VIII had built facilities for tilting at most of his larger houses and, at Whitehall, on the Park Side, between the road and the park, was a tiltyard – a walled enclosure with a central timber barrier designed for tournaments. It had been heavily used by Elizabeth, under whom tournaments had become an elaborate chivalric display complete with scenery and outlandish costumes at which young men strove to outdo each other to win the approval of their queen.

It is perhaps strange that James I, who loved nothing more than to be in the saddle, was uninterested in jousting. On a couple of occasions he ran at the ring in public, a test of skill with a lance that required the rider to spear a hanging ring. He much preferred to be a spectator at the annual accession day tournaments, and on special occasions such as weddings and ambassadorial receptions. Prince Henry and Prince Charles, on the other hand, were enamoured with both the skills and the chivalry of the tilt. At St James's there was a roofed course to practise running at the ring and before his death Prince Henry had excelled at the sport. As Prince of Wales, Charles twice led spectacular processions into the tiltyard and jousted in front of the king.[27]

On these occasions the Office of Works erected tiered seating along the sides of the tiltyard for spectators. A 'judging house', an elaborate roofed grandstand, was put up overlooking the anticipated point where the participants would clash. The king would watch from the tiltyard gallery, an extension of the privy gallery carried over King Street by the Holbein Gate, where there was a balcony beneath which staging for the most important spectators was erected.[28]

Although these Jacobean tournaments were regular events which seem to have been enjoyed by the king, spectators thought them less good than those under Elizabeth. The apparent enthusiasm for the tiltyard shown by Prince Charles somehow never made up for the death of Prince Henry and the king's perceived indifference; courtiers were less willing to spend a fortune on their costumes and the gradual exclusion of the less well-off spectators robbed the events of their popular frisson. James much preferred masques and plays which, in a sense, continued the spectacle of the Elizabethan tournament, but indoors. Under Charles I, after a single tournament welcoming Henrietta Maria, the tiltyard was never again used for its original purpose.[29]

By the time King James arrived at Whitehall court drama was well established. Companies of players had long entertained Elizabethans and the Lord Chamberlain's Men, the theatrical company of which Shakespeare was part owner and resident playwright, had staged thirty-three of the sixty-eight plays recorded at court between 1584 and 1603. The company's title derived from the patronage of Henry Carey, Lord Hunsdon who became Lord Chamberlain in 1597. In 1603, the company, despite having lost its first patron, achieved the remarkable coup of winning a patent from James I to become his personal company of players. Two other companies soon achieved similar official status: the former Admiral's Company, run by Edward Alleyn and Philip Henslowe, became Prince Henry's Men and the former Worcester's Company became Queen Anna's Company.

Senior members of the company, now renamed the King's Men, became court officials and, like the royal barbers, musicians, keepers of hounds or silkworms, assumed the honorific title of grooms of the chamber and were issued court livery to wear on official occasions: a doublet and hose and a scarlet cloak with the royal arms and badges embroidered in gold. It is known that Shakespeare and his fellows turned out in their liveries for the signing of the peace treaty with the Spanish ambassadors at Denmark House in 1604 where they stood to attention in the outer rooms as the ambassadors passed through.[30]

During Elizabeth's reign there had been on average half a dozen plays a year at court; under James this rose to nineteen – in all, 421 performances in his twenty-two years on the throne. The King's Men were most intensively employed during the court season, the pinnacle of which was twelfth night, or Epiphany, the feast of the coming of the three kings. James himself told a visiting ambassador that it was 'the greatest of all festivals'. On twelfth night there was a masque, not a play, although this often involved one or more of the companies taking the speaking parts.[31]

The production of such a large number of plays, let alone the masque, which was hugely complex to stage, required a considerable underpinning infrastructure. Henry VIII had established a household department called the Revels and from 1572 it had a headquarters in the former priory of St John in Clerkenwell. Here scenery was painted, costumes made, and rehearsals undertaken. In 1607 King James dissolved the Tudor arrangements; both masques and plays were now directly commissioned from individuals or companies by the Lord Chamberlain. For masques the Office of Works and the Wardrobe provided the equipment and royal musicians and composers the music. Anything else that was needed was funded direct from the exchequer. The role of the Revels was restricted to setting up the complex system of lights on stage and in the hall. The Blackfriars headquarters of the Revels was sold in 1607 and the remaining staff had to rent accommodation.[32]

Father and son

For Elizabethan courtiers, daily life in England's royal houses underwent a revolution in 1603. Not only was there a new monarch who had been bred and brought up in an entirely different tradition, but the arrival of the king's Scottish companions brought both new blood into the inner sanctum of sovereignty, and new attitudes, expectations and assumptions. Unlike the Elizabethans at court, comfortable in their imagined cultural and economic superiority, the Scots courtiers were men who knew their king, understood his foibles, appreciated his strengths and managed his weaknesses.

The deal forged at Theobalds and the Tower of London in May 1603 created a situation in which the levers of state largely remained with the Elizabethan old guard but the personal attendants round the king were entirely Scottish. In institutional terms this meant that the Bedchamber, the part of the household that provided personal service to the king in the inner rooms of the royal houses, was staffed by Scots and the Privy Chamber, the more honorific body that manned the outer rooms, together with the Privy Council, were a mixture of Scots and English.

The architectural framework of this division was fundamental. Scottish royal houses, as has been explained, were public and compact with three rooms and a cabinet; there was no barrier other than rank or familiarity that excluded courtiers from the presence of the king. In England, since the time of Henry VIII, a rigid architectural matrix had been developed in a series of six or more chambers that progressively restricted access to the monarch. By the time of Queen Elizabeth the matrix was three-fold: the outer chambers, great hall, guard chamber and presence chamber were open to almost anyone respectable; the territory of the Privy Chamber which occupied two rooms – the privy chamber itself and the withdrawing room, to which access was restricted by membership and invitation; and then the bedchamber and so-called secret places, which was highly restricted to Elizabeth's ladies and those who were personally invited.[33]

These were two entirely different systems, the one, in Scotland, designed to facilitate access to the monarch, the other, in England, to frustrate it. In 1603 the Scottish system of access was grafted onto the architecture of restriction with all sorts of unexpected consequences. The most important of these was that the Bedchamber immediately became politicised. No longer staffed by ladies of the court, who had been largely politically inert, it was now the preserve of the king's politically active Scottish companions who had control over access to him in his private rooms. The head of the Bedchamber, in theory, was the king's cousin Ludovic Stuart, Duke of Lennox, but in practice the head man was Sir Thomas Erskine, groom of the stool.[34]

Erskine was also captain of the guard; this unique combination (from an English perspective) reflected James's paranoia about his personal security. Erskine had helped save the king's life at the time of the Gowrie conspiracy and was his most trusted friend, the ideal person to command a personal bodyguard. Elizabeth had 142 Yeomen of the Guard and Erskine increased the number to 200 and, at the same time, increased their pay by four pence a day, in all nearly doubling their annual cost. Dressed in their embroidered liveries, bearing the initials JR, 120 guarded the king, 60 the queen, and 20 the Prince of Wales.[35]

Erskine was no more familiar with English court etiquette and architecture than the king, but immediately helped James bring suitable majesty to the new King of Great Britain's court. The Venetian ambassador thought that James, 'of his own accord, would probably hardly have changed his modest habit of life which he pursued in Scotland, where he lived like a private gentleman, let alone a sovereign, making many people sit down with him at table, waited on by rough servants, who did not even remove their hats, treating all with a French familiarity'. But now, in England 'the Government are re-introducing the ancient splendours of the English Court, and almost adoring his Majesty, who day by day adopts the practices suitable to his greatness. On Sunday last he dined in state, as it is called, waited upon by the greatest lords of the realm; it was a splendid and unwonted sight'.[36]

The cumbersome formality of the English court and its restrictive regulations were quickly found to meet royal purposes. Erskine was able to use the English system to exclude all but James's Scots companions from his presence. At Whitehall, and the other larger residences, privy councillors and officers of state were now required to wait for the king to emerge from his bedchamber for an audience. In the smaller houses of necessity attendance on the king was reduced solely to his bedchamber and a selected group of court officials. The Archbishop of Canterbury was of the opinion that 'there are now two councils in England of which that of Newmarket is higher'. This was true up to a point. James was a diligent monarch who required the attention, and often the presence, of his ministers. Before his death in 1612 Cecil always had access to the king and, although he could not curb the excesses of the Bedchamber, it could not exclude him from the royal presence.[37]

In 1610 a former Gentleman of the Privy Chamber pointed out that 'the Scottish monopolise his princely person, standing like mountains betwixt the beams of his grace and us'. The mountain was not only ethnic, it was emotional. James famously could not resist the company of entertaining comely young men, and the intimacy of the bedchamber was the perfect hothouse for raising favourites. Both Robert Carr, later Earl of Somerset, and then George Villiers, later Duke of Buckingham rose to favour in the Bedchamber and were able to monopolise the king, not only through personal affection, but by the institutions and geography of the court.[38]

Behind the closed doors of the bedchamber the king was extremely free-and-easy with his companions. Sir John Finet, who was to become the sober and dignified Master of Ceremonies in the court of Charles I, was christened by James as chief fool. Adept at larking about, singing ribald songs and devising practical jokes, he would entertain the king after dinner when he was in drink. James himself had a quick wit and a dry humour and liked practical jokes. On one of his many stays at Wilton House with the Earl of Pembroke, knowing that Pembroke hated frogs, James put one down his favourite's neck. Pembroke later took his revenge by sneaking a live pig into the king's close stool room.[39]

The subtle, but important, changes James made to the privy lodgings at Whitehall facilitated this free-and-easy private life. In 1614–15 he ordered the construction of a back staircase that led, via some private closets, directly to the vane room. This allowed members of his Bedchamber direct access to him, circumnavigating the outer rooms and the privy gallery. On the north side of the privy gallery was the council chamber, a block of building that contained the council room itself, a waiting room known as the stone table chamber, a lobby and a back stair. After Queen Anna's death in 1619 the council was relocated out of the privy gallery to the now vacant queen's privy chamber. The old council chamber was given to the Duke of Lennox who had been squeezed into the upper floors of the Holbein Gate. Thus the Privy Council was removed from the king's privy lodgings and replaced with the lodgings of a Scottish favourite.[40]

Yet James insisted on dignity when the occasion required it, in particular on religious and diplomatic occasions. The creation of a Master of Ceremonies brought order and dignity to diplomatic protocol, and he was most interested in dignity and ceremonial in court religion.

SIX

The Connoisseur King

Peace in our time

The Treaty of London, signed in August 1604, ended a state of war with Spain that had dominated English politics for almost twenty years. Protestant England had been isolated from the Catholic powers ever since Elizabeth I's excommunication by the Pope in 1570. Spanish territories spread across more or less the whole of Europe including most of Italy and, although France was not formally at war with England, travel abroad by the English was dangerous and ill advised. Many luxury goods that were common in Paris and Madrid struggled to make their way into the Port of London and, in many ways, England was cut off from the cultural currents of contemporary Europe.

The treaty was ratified by King Philip III of Spain in the presence of Charles Howard, Earl of Nottingham and around 500 English courtiers. It was the most splendid and extravagant appearance of the English court abroad for nearly a century. Their trip to Spain was a visit to the centre of the European world, the capital of Europe's largest and most powerful empire and, as the English wagon train of 800 mules made their way across the sun-scorched landscape, the cream of the Jacobean court were exposed to a novel set of cultural influences.[1]

They assembled at Valladolid, the Castilian city to which King Philip III had moved his court in 1601. As the capital of Castile, it was a fine place with an ambitious but unfinished sixteenth-century cathedral and many large houses, churches and colleges. The royal palace was originally a private mansion built between 1526 and 1534; in 1600 it was acquired by the Duke of Lerma, who sold it to Philip III the following year.

Philip III's palace remains, but much altered from its early seventeenth-century state. What the English visitors saw was a double-courtyarded residence in an early Renaissance style similar to many of Henry VIII's houses. It was far smaller than Hampton Court or Greenwich, but familiar in the arrangement of rooms graduating from the public to the private quarters of the king. On the street front was a great festival hall overlooking a square in which the principal events of the reception were held. It must have been an exotic and exciting time because the Spanish laid on magnificent entertainments: a triumph, bull fights, a tournament, a parade, masques and feasts. It was noted that the royal palace was 'furnished with many excellent pictures, all the good ones made by Italians or come out of Italy'.[2]

The ratification of the Treaty of London opened the way for a huge

Figure 32: Elevation of the principal facade of the royal palace at Valladolid by Ventura Pérez, from his 'History of the very noble and very loyal city of Valladolid. Compiled from various authors in this year of 1759'.

exodus of the English aristocracy seeking adventure, novelty and education on the continent. They did not make for the sweltering, arid plains of Spain, except on business, but for Paris and the cities of Italy. So much so that James I, alarmed, registered his disapproval at the Privy Council, but instructions to English ambassadors to keep tabs on travellers were meaningless as Italy was now teeming with them.

Noble travellers needed chaperones who could speak French and Italian and who were experienced in travelling on the continent. There was a small pool of such men who had through trade, academia or diplomacy travelled in Europe under Elizabeth. One of the best-travelled, and most important, of this first generation of Jacobean travellers was Henry Wotton who, through his extensive knowledge of Germany, Italy and Switzerland, and his command of several European languages was, in 1604, appointed first resident ambassador in Venice since 1550. Almost immediately Venice became the centre of English interest in Italy: Jacobeans were overwhelmed by its lustre. They admired its unique constitution which had guaranteed a millennium of political stability, they marvelled at its wealth built on east–west trade, respected its naval prowess, and enjoyed the resistance of the Venetian republic to claims of Papacy supremacy. They, like us, were also entranced by the liquid topography of the city, its architecture, textiles, glass and painting.

Wotton, who served three terms as English ambassador in Venice, was one of the first Englishmen to develop a sophisticated eye for Italian paintings. It was this skill, rather than his diplomatic achievements (which were few) that recommended him to leading Jacobean courtiers. From 1608 Wotton began to send a steady stream of items to England from Venice, including a large number of easel paintings. That year he sent Lord Salisbury a consignment of paintings including Palma Giovane's canvas, *Prometheus Chained to the Caucasus*. This Salisbury offered to Henry Prince of Wales, who hung it in his gallery at St James's. Thus came to court the richness and vibrancy of Venetian painting, a complete contrast to anything hanging in any royal house at the time.[3]

Giovane was a pupil of Tiziano Vecellio, known to the English simply as Titian. Titian had broken away from the prevailing technique of overpainting a drawing on a gessoed wooden panel and had perfected the use of paint richly, and thickly, applied to canvas to achieve a startlingly fluid effect. So radical was this departure from what the English were used to that Wotton wrote to warn Salisbury that *Prometheus Chained to the Caucasus* and the other Venetian paintings he had sent were done 'naturally but roughly *alla Venetiana*' and should therefore 'be set at some good distance from the sight'.[4]

Wotton was a gentleman, not a great aristocrat, and it was England's senior peer, Thomas Howard, Earl of Arundel, who became the expert in Venetian painting and arbiter of court taste. Arundel, whose grandfather and father had both been convicted of treason, enjoyed a family rehabilitation in the early years of James's reign and entered Prince Henry of Wales's court circle, where he rubbed shoulders with other young aristocrats fascinated by European culture. In the summer of 1612 Arundel gained permission to go abroad and it was then that he met Peter Paul Rubens, who painted his portrait (now lost). After returning to England briefly following the death of Prince Henry, Arundel set off again on his travels, this time taking the multi-lingual and multi-talented Inigo Jones as his translator and guide.

They travelled Italy, where Arundel became enamoured not only of Venetian painting but with the whole breadth of Italian art, architecture and decorative arts from the ancients to the modern. He was a wealthy man and he bought voraciously. We don't fully know what Arundel returned with when he eventually unpacked his crates at Arundel House, on the Strand. But we do know that he started to rebuild his house as a setting for the collections he had acquired.

Wonder boys

Arundel shared his passion for Venetian painting with Henry Prince of Wales. At St James's, in the huge three-sided gallery in the privy lodgings, Henry established a picture gallery in conjunction with his library. The late sixteenth century had seen an explosion of collecting across the princely courts of Europe; galleries and cabinets were filled with old master paintings, sculptures, coins and medals, manuscripts and books. Through his mother Anna of Denmark, and people like Arundel and Wotton Henry knew of the great collections of the Medici and of the emperor Rudolph II in Prague and the prince and his advisors set out to imitate them.

Prince Henry started buying paintings in January 1611, and soon afterwards it was public knowledge that he had set out to create a great gallery of painting. A request to Vincenzo Salviati, the Florentine ambassador, led to the receipt that June of a large shipment of paintings delivered by Costantino de' Servi at Richmond. As the paintings were unpacked Henry asked the Italian 'about the decoration of their Highnesses galleries and if there were subject pictures and what kind of statues, and he confirmed his intention of using the foresaid pictures for his new gallery'. Soon a major shipment of paintings from Venice arrived for which the prince paid the vast sum of £400. Thus, in a very short time, Henry Prince of Wales had created the largest picture gallery in England, over 325 feet long and hung with perhaps as many as fifty paintings, most of which were Italian and many Venetian.

In 1611 work was underway on the prince's cabinet, a small room set aside for collections of antique coins, medals and bronzes, which he started collecting in 1610. The cabinet was unfinished at the time of his death and its precise location cannot now be pinpointed. The combined cost of building a library, painting gallery and cabinet at St James's was some £2,800 and represented a unique undertaking. Henry VIII had combined galleries with cabinets of treasures before, but what the prince was doing was deliberately creating an encyclopaedic collection of the world's knowledge in imitation of the cabinets of other European princes. Neither Elizabeth I, nor James I were interested in such an enterprise, but his brother, Charles, was to continue his endeavours with vigour later in the century.

Charles's first interests were not in painting or sculpture but tapestry. Tapestry was unquestionably the primary art form at the Stuart court. The cavernous outer rooms of royal houses had huge expanses of wall; tapestries, hung floor to ceiling, edge to edge, provided richness, colour and interest as well as improving the acoustic properties and warmth in the hard plastered interiors. After the first quarter of the sixteenth century, tapestries depicted large, lifelike figures in deep perspective and suites of tapestries telling well-known biblical or classical stories provided coherent expanses of rich narrative. As there was little furniture in the outer rooms they could be appreciated at the sweep of an eye and at a distance.[5]

The best sets were only hung on important occasions and were transported from palace to palace. On progress the royal Wardrobe would load tapestries of an appropriate size onto carts and take them to remote residences; even during the Civil War and into exile, Charles I, Henrietta Maria and Prince Charles carried sets of tapestries with them to adorn their ad hoc royal palaces.

Rich textiles, more generally, were at the heart of courtiers' aspirations and men and women wore suits of clothes that were considerably more expensive than a painting, for instance. A suit bought by Charles I in 1629, richly laced with gold and silver embroidery, cost £266, whereas the painting of him wearing it by Daniel Mytens, now in the National Portrait Gallery, cost only £66. Suits such as this, sparkling with gold and silver thread, and sometimes with precious stones and pearls, were the foreground of tapestries that themselves were woven with gold and silver thread. This came into its own at night; candles creating a rippling surface of gleaming light on people and walls alike.[6]

During the sixteenth century the centre for tapestry manufacture was the Netherlands; but the industry was decimated by war in the last quarter of the century and it was only with the gradual ending of conflict after 1600 that it began to recover. It was vulnerable, though, to the head-hunting of its weavers by royal courts ambitious to establish their own manufactories. The French were first, in 1609, with the establishment of a works in Paris powered by Flemish expertise; and James I, who was seized with a mission to stimulate native crafts, decided in 1618 to investigate the possibility of a similar project in England. A commission assembled, with the French articles of association to hand, and established that the best way to proceed was to award a monopoly to an imaginative and capable entrepreneur. That man was Sir Francis Crane, a courtier and administrator, who had been patronised by the Duke of Lennox, the king's cousin and groom of the stool. Through him Crane had served in the households of Prince Henry and Prince Charles and had been knighted in 1617.[7]

Through the services of William Trumbull, James I's resident diplomat in the Spanish Netherlands, whole families of weavers were recruited to come and work for Crane in his new workshops in Mortlake, just west of London. As in France, the workshops were to be launched by royal commissions, and the first, in 1620 was for Prince Charles, a copy of a set of nine tapestries of the story of *Vulcan and Venus* already in the royal collection but with the addition of new borders and the Prince of Wales's feathers. In its early years the new workshop lacked original cartoons to work from, and Crane pressed Trumbull to procure high-quality Italian tapestry designs for him, a task which he found extremely difficult. The Prince of Wales himself set out to buy designs and, in 1620, laid out £40 for a cartoon for the month of December, for a suite of tapestries depicting the months of the year. Soon after, Charles was told that a set of cartoons by Raphael Sanzio of Urbino might be available. These were designs for tapestries woven for Pope Leo X in 1515 for the Sistine Chapel, the most famous and admired tapestry commission of its age. Crane was instructed to purchase them for £300 and bring them from Genoa to London.[8]

At the same time as this stunning acquisition, Prince Charles managed to secure, from the court of Christian IV of Denmark, the services of the painter Francis Cleyn. Cleyn was brought to his attention by Sir Henry Wotton who had met him in Venice. Cleyn entered the service of Charles I in 1625 and was immediately taken on by Inigo Jones to help with the triumphal arches being prepared for the reception of Henrietta Maria. Indeed, Jones and Cleyn may have already met each other in Venice. In Cleyn, Charles acquired a second creative genius to match that of Inigo Jones. Not only did Cleyn produce dazzling designs for the Mortlake works, but he began to supply designs for the interiors of royal houses, particularly for the queen.[9]

Buckingham and the Spanish match

Despite embodying the future hopes of king and country, in his teens, Prince Charles was a lost figure at court. He had been robbed of his brother in 1612 and, the following year, his beloved sister Elizabeth had married Frederick V, Elector of the German Palatinate, one of the seven princes who chose the Holy Roman Emperor. When they left England Charles was left to his own devices at St James's, where he continued to receive a princely education devised for him by the king. James made little effort to involve him in the governance of the land and Charles had no political influence.

Worse still was the fact that in 1614 the king's eye fell upon a new favourite, George Villiers, who accelerated himself into James's affections, capturing them completely by early 1616. Charles was now, more than ever, a bystander at court, his father's attention completely captured by his new love. Soon the king had adopted Villiers as his 'son' and the king became his 'dear Dad'; the only way forward for Charles was to join this new extended family as a junior member, which is what he did in 1618 as 'baby Charles'. For the last six years of James's reign England was effectively governed by this triumvirate.

Buckingham rose from virtually nothing to become, in 1623, the only duke in England and his rise to wealth and power was accompanied by all its trappings, including those of art and architecture. It is likely that Villiers' interests in this sphere helped stimulate those of Prince Charles, who began to take a greater interest in the collections amassed by his brother, still on show at St James's. Villiers brought into his service a Huguenot refugee, Balthasar Gerbier, a multi-lingual painter, art dealer, architect and connoisseur who became his personal shopper, travelling all over Europe hunting out art and antiques, especially Venetian paintings.[10]

After the death of his brother, Prince Charles became the focus of intense discussions about his marriage. These centred on the possibility of him marrying the Infanta Maria Ana, the Roman Catholic daughter of Philip III of Spain, a project which had strategic benefits to both nations, but which was beset with problems. The marriage was promoted by the Spanish ambassador in London, Don Diego Sarmiento de Acuña, Count Gondomar and by George Digby, Earl of Bristol, the English ambassador in Madrid who painted such a picture of the Infanta that Charles fell for the idea of her completely.

In early 1623, with marriage negotiations bogged down in matters of religion, Charles and Buckingham conceived a plan to appear, unannounced, at the Spanish court in Madrid and to win the hand of his princess, blasting away contractual niceties. Like his dead brother, Charles was seized by visions of chivalry and romance and saw himself embarking on a princely quest to win his bride.[11]

It was a highly risky scheme. It was winter, and Lent, and Charles and Villiers planned to ride incognito across France with only three servants arriving, unannounced, at Europe's most splendid and formal court with nothing but their riding habits. In March 1621 King Philip III had died and his heir, Philip IV, was a youth of just sixteen dominated by his tutor Gaspar de Guzmán, Count of Olivares. Philip's was an enormous, but fragmented, monarchy that stretched across the world. In Iberia alone he held three crowns and to these had to be added sovereignty over the Spanish Netherlands, the Duchy of Milan, the kingdoms of Naples and Sicily and the territories in the New World. Philip was *el rey planeta*, the planet king, an epithet that not only referred to his vast territories but to his personal glory. For Olivares ensured that Philip was a model of princely magnificence, reserved, dignified, pious and excelling in all princely virtues from hunting to connoisseurship. The reception the Prince of Wales would receive at this mighty court, breaching every known diplomatic protocol, was completely unknown.

The importance of the eight months Charles was away from England cannot be overestimated. The prince's trip was no weekend mini break: he lived at the Spanish court for five and a half months completely immersed in its etiquette, entertainments and architecture, and observing, first hand, its religious practices. To get there, he had travelled across France; his first stop was Paris where he spent a day seeing the sights. In fear of being unmasked he and Villiers (travelling as Jack and Thomas

Smith) bought new periwigs and, in disguise, obtained access to the court at the Louvre where they saw the queen mother dining in public, the king in his gallery and the queen and her ladies practising for a masque. Leaving Paris, they embarked on a ten-day, 500-mile dash for the Spanish border which they crossed at Irún and, three days later, on 7 March, they reached Madrid. Having ridden on ahead, Charles and Villiers arrived at the house of the Earl of Bristol with only one servant: his surprise was complete and his consternation absolute.[12]

Madrid had become the principal seat of the Spanish court in 1561 and had only begun to acquire the appearance of what we would call a capital city after 1610. It was not a particularly promising location – at the centre of the land mass, with a meagre river, it was boiling in summer and freezing in winter – but nevertheless, by 1623, there were some 10,000 private houses, including many mansions belonging to the nobility. King Philip III had commissioned his court architect, Juan Gómez de Mora, to build a huge civic square symmetrically lined with houses built above arcades. This, the Plaza Mayor, according to Sir Richard Wynn, one of the English sent by sea to attend Prince Charles on his arrival, was 'the only thing in that town which a man would stand and look at'. A broad street, the Calle Mayor, led up to the Alcazar, the royal residence sited in a large medieval fortress on rising ground to the west of the city.[13]

Bristol, in conference with Gondomar, who was in Madrid at the time, decided that Villiers should pave the way with King Philip and he was taken by Olivares to the Alcazar where, by the backstairs, he was ushered into the king's private apartments for an audience with the eighteen-year-old monarch. The Spanish court was gripped by a crisis of etiquette. Charles could not meet the king's sister, Maria Ana, without considerable preparation and so it was arranged that he should at first spy her from his shuttered carriage, the princess wearing a blue ribbon to mark her out. She was beautiful, and the glimpse of his future wife further inflamed Charles's desire. The protocolists convened a council to determine the proper steps for a reception of the prince at court. The cost of doing this properly would be enormous and it was joked that Charles had managed to sack Madrid without an army.[14]

Before he had left England, James had furnished the prince with letters of presentation for King Philip which explained that his son was 'a prince, the sworn king of Scotland'. This ingenious piece of mumbo-jumbo was to guarantee that Charles would be treated as sovereign and not just a prince of the blood. It worked. Preparations were advanced on the basis that Prince Charles had equality with the king and members of the Spanish royal family. Key to this was his introduction by way of a public entry, the mechanism by which Spanish royalty took the public stage. On 16 March Charles was accorded this honour.[15]

Charles and Philip rode through the carefully swept and richly decorated city streets beneath a canopy carried high by twelve gentlemen, accompanied by drummers and trumpeters and surrounded by foot guards. Behind them rode Olivares and Villiers and an assortment of

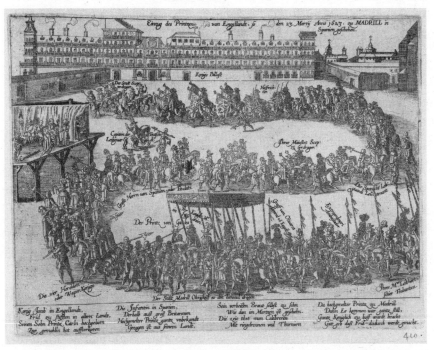

Figure 33: The Entry of Charles, Prince of Wales into Madrid, 23 March 1623, published in Franz Christoph Khevenhüller's *Annales Ferdinandei*. Drawn from an eyewitness account, the details of this rare depiction of a Spanish court event are accurate. In front of the new facade of the Alcazar, completed in 1621, lay the Plaza de Palacio, a vast public square.

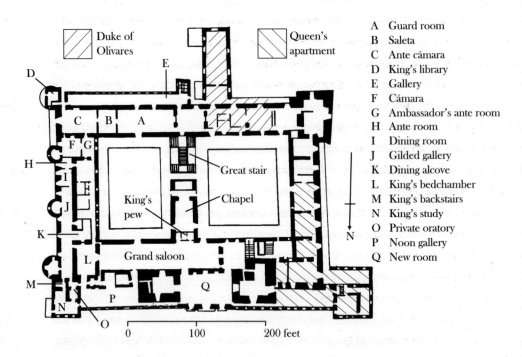

A	Guard room
B	Saleta
C	Ante cámara
D	King's library
E	Gallery
F	Cámara
G	Ambassador's ante room
H	Ante room
I	Dining room
J	Gilded gallery
K	Dining alcove
L	King's bedchamber
M	King's backstairs
N	King's study
O	Private oratory
P	Noon gallery
Q	New room

Figure 34: First-floor plan of the Alcazar of Madrid in the 1620s.

ambassadors and nobles; a contemporary print shows the procession arriving at the Alcazar where they were met by the queen in her audience chamber. Charles was then escorted to the prince's quarter where he was delivered into his very bedroom where, within an hour, the queen's lord chamberlain arrived laden with valuable gifts.

Although the Alcazar of Madrid was an ancient Moorish fortress in origin it had been adapted and extended by the Hapsburgs to form a large double-courtyarded palace with a principal facade only completed two years before the arrival of Prince Charles. Sir Richard Wynn thought the front 'very fair', though the rest of the palace was not 'worth much observation', Lord Roos who had seen it a few years before thought it not very large 'but beautiful commodious and stately'. In truth the facade was more impressive by its size and apparent regularity than by any sophistication of its architecture.[16]

In plan the Alcazar would have been of a familiar type to the English visitors. It comprised two courts, one for the king and the other for the queen; the royal family occupied the principal floor, below were not only the offices of state but also various commercial enterprises. Access to the royal apartments was via a grand stair that occupied the block between the two courts, this gave onto an upper cloister that ran round the interior of each court. The first chamber on the king's side was for the royal guards and led to a small hall which was where the king would dine in public. Beyond this was the king's principal reception room, known as the ante-chamber. In here there was a canopy and chair of state, beneath which Philip received councillors and washed the feet of poor men on Maundy Thursday, a ceremony observed by Charles during his stay.[17] Then came the principal audience chamber, the *cámara* containing a ceremonial bed in its corner. As ambassadors were received in here, and royal councillors attended to kiss the royal hand, it was part of the outer part of the palace, not the inner apartments. These started at the *cámara* door and access to them was highly restricted to gentlemen of the bedchamber and other named court officials. This was not unlike the Elizabethan court, where a tiny proportion of courtiers had access to the queen's privy lodgings. The access that Prince Charles was given to Philip's private apartments on the west and southwest of the Alcazar was exceptional. Here there were three small rooms for the private reception of ambassadors, but beyond these, at the end of a long gallery, was the king's study, where few courtiers ever penetrated. A back staircase gave access to rooms below, where the Prince of Wales was lodged. Philip generally ate alone, served by his groom of the stool, in an alcove off the gallery and his bedchamber was only accessed by the groom and a small number of menial servants. Spanish kings lived a much less public life than had become the norm across the rest of Europe, principally venturing from their private apartments on religious and court feasts, and then with great splendour.[18]

On the south side of the Alcazar was originally the great hall of the ancient fortress but in the years immediately before Charles's visit a new range of rooms was built against it, giving Philip IV two great new chambers in which to hang his paintings and conduct affairs with his family. The room that would be later called the hall of mirrors had been painted and gilded and was hung with easel paintings while Charles was living there, including several canvases by Titian. In due course this room was to contain the cream of Philip's collection of paintings.

The largest hall was the *salón de las comedias*, the hall of plays; in 1626 this was described as 'the great hall in which celebrations with plays and balls are held and in which the king and queen dine in public on the wedding day of ladies who marry in the place'. Sir Richard Wynn described the staging of a play in the hall of comedies which he called 'an indifferent fair room'. It contained a canopy of state under which there were five chairs for the king, queen, Prince of Wales and the two royal brothers.[19]

Philip had decreed that the prince be served exactly as he was, and he sent him half his personal bodyguard and assigned him a chamberlain or mayor-domo to be in charge of his household. Not giving the prince gentlemen for his bedchamber, he presented him, instead, with two gold keys, which were the master keys to the apartments; these he passed on to Buckingham and the Earl of Bristol. Various aristocrats were also assigned to the prince's household to wait upon him.[20]

The king saw to it that there were few days when there was no entertainment for Prince Charles. In quieter times the prince would hunt and hawk in the parks near to Madrid, but every week there were plays, bull fights, displays of martial skill, music, pageants, feasts, firework displays, torchlight processions, picnics, visits to places of interest, in short an itinerary that gave a fun-packed facade to the hard-nosed marriage negotiations behind the scenes.[21]

On his third day in the Alcazar the Prince of Wales was taken by the king on a tour of paintings in the royal apartments. Philip was already a connoisseur of painting, literature, poetry, music and theatre and had inherited perhaps 2,000 paintings from his father hanging at the Alcazar and the other royal houses. To these he was already adding acquisitions of his own, especially Venetian paintings. Charles had the opportunity to examine much of this collection at leisure. Two of the servants who had ridden across France with him were Francis Cottington and Endymion Porter; both extremely knowledgeable about Spain and about painting, they were soon joined in Madrid by Buckingham's artistic advisor Balthasar Gerbier.[22]

Covetousness filled the prince's eyes, especially for the king's Titians, of which there were many. Charles dropped hints and hoped for a big gift and was rewarded by two large and important canvases: Titian's portrait of the *Emperor Charles VI with a hound* (now in the Prado) and his *Venus du Pado* (now in the Louvre). Gerbier, Cottington and Porter scouted Madrid for other paintings, both those that were commercially available, and also those in private collections. According to the contemporary art critic, Vincente Carducho, who observed the prince, every painting he saw was at risk from the acquisitive Englishmen. A score or more paintings were bought and crated ready for shipping to London, mainly, but not exclusively Italian sixteenth-century pieces, including Titian's erotically charged *Woman with a fur coat* (now in the Kunsthistorisches Museum in Vienna) and the enigmatic *Conjugal allegory* (now in the Louvre).[23]

Charles was also a guest at El Escorial, the colossal palace-cum-monastery twenty-eight miles north of the capital. The Escorial had been started by Philip's grandfather and was something of a mystery to many of the English who went there. Lord Roos described it as 'so great, so rich, so imperial a building that in all Italy itself there is nothing that deserves to be compared with it'. Sir Richard Wynn praised it as 'the only thing talked of in those parts to be worth seeing' and was impressed by its size and beauty but, 'when they had showed us most of the house . . . we desired to see the king's lodgings, which we found poorly furnished and nothing proportionate to the rest of the house' confirming his opinion that 'it was never intended for the king's palace but for the goodliest monastery in the world (which it is)'.[24]

There Charles must have met Giovanni Battista Crescenzi, the Italian aristocratic painter, art dealer and architect who had come to Spain and won the commission to design and decorate the royal pantheon at the Escorial. He seems to have taken a shine to the character and talents of Crescenzi as, in 1631, with Charles king and Crescenzi a royal architect,

Charles invited him to come to England, an offer he politely declined, instead sending Charles a painting.[25]

The English royal party, and their swollen baggage train, began to make their way to the coast in September after extracting themselves from the Spanish with treaties, promises and oaths, all soon to be broken. The prince travelled via Segovia where he visited the cathedral and the palace, where he was put up and feasted. They then went on to the former royal capital at Valladolid where he went shopping and perused the royal picture collections in the palace, where he was given a fine sculpture by Giambologna and a luscious *Mars and Venus* by Paolo Veronese (now in the National Gallery of Scotland).[26]

The Spanish chapel

Negotiations for a marriage between a Protestant prince and a Catholic princess were never going to be straightforward; nor were the European power-politics that lay behind the proposed dynastic alliance. Discussions were detailed, vexed and lengthy and, as negotiations dragged on in Spain, and while Charles and Buckingham consumed the £30,000 that they had brought with them, preparations were afoot in England to receive the Infanta. The day after Charles and Buckingham arrived in Madrid the secretary of state, Edward, Viscount Conway consulted the Lord Chamberlain and Inigo Jones on which houses would be most suitable for receiving the Infanta and her entourage. They thought Denmark House would be the cheapest and easiest to prepare; but St James's was the seat of the Prince of Wales and it was decided that this would be the Infanta's 'constant seat', although Denmark House would be assigned to her as her London residence in due course.[27]

In preparing St James's the most complicated issue was provision for the princess to exercise her religion. In April 1623 the Pope granted a dispensation for the marriage on the condition that her religion could be freely practised in her own establishment, not only by her but by Londoners who wished to attend, and that her children should be brought up Roman Catholics.

This necessitated new chapels at both Denmark House and St James's and the refitting of the old Savoy Chapel for the princess's household. The two residences were inspected by the Spanish ambassador, Don Carlos Coloma, who was insistent on the importance of both chapels. These were required, by an advisory panel of Spanish theologians, to be 'public churches' which were 'sufficiently large in which all the divine offices may be celebrated . . . [and] where Catholics may be buried with the ceremonies that are customary'.[28]

On 3 May Inigo Jones was ordered to prepare designs for a church, or more properly a chapel, for St James's 'with great state and costliness'. He must have worked fast, for eleven days later designs were sent to Spain for approval. Not waiting for a reply, Jones submitted the following day an estimate for £5,475 11s 11d, covering the construction of two chapels, and the day after that the Spanish ambassador laid the foundation stone. Things were moving incredibly fast.[29]

The new chapel was to be built on the east side of the palace, connected by a gallery to what would be the princess's rooms. For its design there were no English models; it had been nearly 100 years since a church had been built for Roman Catholic worship in England. The design had to adhere to the (lost) specification from the Spanish royal household, but, more significantly, drew on the most up-to-date ecclesiastical architecture Jones had seen in his two trips to Italy; in fact, he had probably studied more contemporary Roman Catholic churches than any living Englishman.

Of these, perhaps, the most relevant was the small church of Santa Maria Nova attached to the Augustan convent in Borgo Porta Nova in Vicenza. The convent was patronised by the wealthy of the city and in 1578 the Vicentine noble Lodovico Trento commissioned a church that was almost certainly designed by Andrea Palladio and completed by 1590. It was a simple rectangle of similar dimensions to the St James's chapel with a hipped roof and a heavy modillion cornice. The design owed much to the Roman temple at Nîmes that Palladio had illustrated in his *Quattro Libri*. As a chapel attached to a convent for aristocratic patrons, this church may have been in Jones's mind as he considered his response to the commission in London.[30]

Figure 35: Plan and elevation of the church of Santa Maria Nova in Vicenza, probably designed by Andrea Palladio in 1578–90 and published by Ottavio Bertotti Scamozzi.

His response to the brief was, however, very much in an English vein. The austere and astylar west front of the St James's chapel was a variation on an unexecuted design prepared for the prince's new lodgings at Newmarket. (Fig 12) The tripartite division of the west front articulated, at Santa Maria Nova, by Corinthian columns was achieved at St James's by plain, but boldly moulded, fenestration constrained by corner quoins and a string course.[31]

Inside the chapel was a double cube, a proportion used nearby at the Banqueting House. The west end contained the royal closet, elevated and separated from the body of the chapel by a screen with Corinthian pilasters and festoons. The ceiling was barrel vaulted with square coffers based on Palladio's reconstruction of the Roman Temple of the Sun and the Moon and the east window is the first use in England of what became known as a Serlian or Venetian window. Although there was

Figure 36: Henry Flitcroft, long section (west to east) of the Queen's Chapel at St James's Palace, *c.*1720. Although drawn (at the command of Lord Burlington) after the chapel had been modified many times, Flitcroft's section shows the simplicity and elegance of Jones's design, with the queen's elevated pew to the left containing Jones's chimney piece.

Figure 37: The west facade of the Queen's Chapel today.

no structural chancel the presbytery was marked by the gilding of the twenty-eight coffers above.[32]

Despite the rush to construct the new chapel for the Spanish bride, in early October 1623, Charles and Buckingham returned to England empty handed and to great rejoicing; the heir to the throne had safely returned, and without an unpopular Spanish wife. The bells in the City rang out and the streets surged with rejoicing citizens. In the king's privy chamber at Royston, father, son and favourite reunited, hugged and kissed while at St James's there was the carcass of a large chapel.

In the afterglow of the collapse of the Spanish match, a parliament was called which Prince Charles and the Duke of Buckingham hoped would help reset foreign policy away from a treaty with Spain towards war. Buckingham's performance in persuading both houses was masterful and, during the session, the prince attended the Lords regularly and impressed everyone, even the French ambassador, who thought that he 'gains daily reputation, glory and good will from parliament'. As parliament dispersed in the summer of 1624 the duke emerged effectively as chief minister and Charles as a skilful independent politician. Buoyed with success, orders were given to Inigo Jones to come up with designs to redecorate the House of Lords, known at the time as 'The Parliament Chamber'.[33]

The chamber, as previously described, was part of the medieval palace and had a timber wagon roof and gothic-shaped windows; at its upper end, raised up on four steps, stood the chair and canopy of state for the sovereign. This was the most important architectural set piece of the English monarchy where, crowned, in parliament robes, the sovereign addressed the peers – no wonder Guy Fawkes had identified this as his target.

Jones blocked the gothic windows, moved and redesigned the fireplace and, under the barrel roof, inserted a new moulded plaster ceiling adorned with ribs in a pattern of intersecting crosses and octagons. This Roman ceiling was painted to resemble stone. Light was now provided from a series of dormers and the lower walls freed to take tapestry hung beneath a new deep cornice. Jones had recreated the Parliament Chamber in the guise of a Roman basilica.[34]

Nobody knew at the time that within half a year King James would

Figure 38: Wenceslaus Hollar, The Trial of Archbishop Laud, 1644. This is the
earliest depiction of Inigo Jones's redesigned Parliament House (House of Lords).
The monarch's setting in the house was enormously enhanced and improved by
the scheme. Given the background to the parliament, it is likely that the initiative
for the work came from the Prince of Wales and Duke of Buckingham.

be dead, but it must have been a good guess that Prince Charles was likely to be the next monarch to address the Lords in the chamber. The new chamber was a much more dignified, modern and impressive setting for the monarchy and set the scene for the accession of the second Stuart king.

SEVEN

Dignity and Order

In 1625 Charles I's reign started with a revolt against the behaviour of his father's court. A proclamation of May 1625 stated: 'in the late reign of our most dear and royal father, we saw much disorder in and about his household by reason of the many idle persons and other unnecessary attendants following the same; which evil, we, finding to bring much dishonour to our house, have resolved the reformation thereof'. Charles was a small, neat and private man whose world picture was ordered, moral and hierarchical. He had been repulsed by the Jacobean court's disorder, coarseness and sexual ambiguities and was uncomfortable with his father's lack of dignity and majesty. Within days of his accession he reasserted court regulations that dated from Tudor times. He was also structuring his own life, establishing regular times and days for all his activities, a habit he kept until the end of his life.

At first he was forced to retain some of his father's servants and court officials, a factor that must have inhibited his reforms, but four years into his reign, with more of his own men in place, he asked a commission to propose the best means of effecting a court of what he called 'civility and honour'. As a result, in 1630–31, a series of regulations were published governing conduct in the king's and queen's courts. As well as ensuring that people entering court precincts were vetted for respectability, the new rules forbade drunkenness, swearing and public immorality. These were not empty threats, as the gentlemen of the privy chamber who were sacked for swearing found out.

The emphasis on dignity and order was reinforced by the king's marriage to the moralistic and prudish French Princess Henrietta Maria, and by his experiences in the Spanish court in 1623. Here, just two years before he ascended the throne, he had been exposed to the extreme privacy and asceticism of the Spanish monarchy. Restraint, ceremony and deference reigned in a way that he had probably never thought possible in the chaos of James I's Bedchamber. Returning to England he even briefly adopted the extremely sober Spanish fashions of court dress. No wonder John Chamberlain, a close and acute observer of the court, thought that it was 'more straight and private than in former time', and in the 1670s Sir Philip Warwick could call it 'the most regular and splendid court in christendom'. A more sceptical observer was Lucy Hutchinson, daughter of the Lieutenant of the Tower of London and wife to a Parliamentarian colonel, who could recall that 'king Charles was temperate, chaste and serious, so that the fools and bawds, mimics and catamites of the former court grew out of fashion'. But she also noticed that 'the nobility and courtiers, who did not quite abandon their old debaucheries, had yet that reverence to the king to retire into corners to practise them'.[1]

It was a fact that attempting to regulate the behaviour of so many people, particularly during the court season when hundreds of courtiers were cooped up in London for three or four months, was never going to be simple. By the mid-1630s, several court observers thought that Whitehall was chaotic, 'filled with the families of every mean courtier . . . the king's servants wait pell-mell without any order'. In fact 'all things in court, both above stairs, beneath, and in the stables; all of which are out of order, and need great reformation'. In 1637–8 a new committee was established, meeting weekly, consulting the lord chamberlain's archives back into the reigns of Henry VII and VIII, to introduce new rigorously enforced orders.[2]

What would have been most noticeable early in Charles's reign were not the new rules and regulations but their enforcement. In his memoirs

Sir John Finet, Master of Ceremonies, a man used to easy access round the court of King James, describes his first duties at the Caroline court and how he was barred from old routes of access and forbidden to enter certain rooms. Gentlemen ushers at the door of the privy chamber, gentlemen pensioners in the presence chamber, the yeomen of the guard and even the porters at the gate, now enforced rules of access to the letter.[3]

Controlling access and enforcing good behaviour was the foundation upon which a new emphasis on ceremony was built. While James I did, on occasion, dine in public in the presence chamber, this ritual was revived by Charles I together with the full ceremonies of Henry VIII's reign. Sometime soon after 1635 Charles commissioned Jan van Belcamp, a painter retained at court for the alteration and copying of paintings, to record the king dining in public. He took an imaginary architectural interior, painted by the Dutch painter, Gerrit Houckgeest, and added a scene of Charles, Henrietta Maria and the five-year-old Prince Charles dining.

The scene is extremely accurate and depicts exactly what took place according to Charles I's household regulations. The yeomen of the guard in their red liveries bring food into the hall. Dressed in black, and waiting on the king, are the cupbearer, the carver and the sewer: the carver at the table (with the regulatory towel on his shoulder), the sewer standing by the buffet displaying plate and the cupbearer with a wine jug making for an enormous wine cooler on the floor. The three of them are allowed to stand on the king's carpet, as are privy councillors, bishops, peers, the dean of the royal chapel and the clerk of the closet; the latter can be seen in his skull cap at the end of the table presumably having said grace.

Also permitted to stand on the carpet were the gentlemen ushers; these were the men responsible for the security, order and smooth running of the outer chambers. One can be seen leading the yeomen of the guard into the hall; another stands at the king's left hand giving him something. Behind the king is the man to whom the gentlemen ushers answer, the Lord Chamberlain, the Earl of Pembroke with his blue Garter sash and wand of office. Spectators are held back behind a balustrade by two of the Gentlemen Pensioners, men of good breeding who made up the inner guard bearing great halbards. The painting is a remarkable document bearing testimony to the ordered dignity of Charles's court.[4]

In the 1630s another court painter, Sir Anthony van Dyck, more famously captured the atmosphere of the Caroline court. In a series of portraits he encapsulated both the dignity and formality of the court and the intense domesticity of the royal family. Van Dyck's paintings make the Caroline court seem brilliant, but the genius of his painting conceals the fact that James's court had been a far more open-minded and intellectually vibrant place than that of his son. After all, it was headed by a bookish intellectual who thrived on debate and disputation. It was at James's court that Shakespeare played, where Ben Jonson and Beaumont and Fletcher worked. Francis Bacon, the Lord Chancellor, was an exceptional philosopher and historian; there were brilliant theologians including John Donne and Lancelot Andrewes and of course there was Inigo Jones the all-round designer and connoisseur of the visual arts. James's court was a centre of new thought and innovation.

James's approach to architecture also had an intellectual underpinning: he had a political interest in his capital city and principal residence reflecting the glory of New Britain; he had an historical interest in framing London in the guise of Rome, and himself as its emperor. Buildings of state had to express the dignity and majesty of the King of Great Britain, but houses of necessity, that is all his favourite residences, were what today we would call Jacobean – exuberant, vibrant, eclectic buildings drawing inspiration more from Dutch artists like Vredeman de Vries than from Italian sources such as Palladio. When Jones proposed a design for Newmarket that was too stately, he was ordered to simplify it. Buildings had to be appropriate to their use.

He also liked to take advice and started to appoint commissions to advise on cultural matters. There was a commission for his new tapestry workshop, for the restoration of St Paul's Cathedral and for the rebuilding of the Banqueting House. James liked to debate and to listen to the conclusions of his councillors on these matters. But he was ultimately his own master in matters of taste; once, when told by his English courtiers that it was not the fashion to have a masque on Christmas night, he replied, 'what do you tell me of the fashion? I will make it a fashion'.[5]

Charles I was not his father, nor did he share his open-minded intellectual curiosity. Under Charles debate stultified, and court culture narrowed and became more inward-looking. Taste was led by a king who was an acknowledged connoisseur of art and architecture, a man who knew his own mind.

Whitehall and St James's

On 28 March 1625, the day after King James's death, the Privy Council assembled at St James's and kissed the hand of King Charles. As a mark of respect Charles, at first, kept to his bedchamber but presently, dressed in black, dined in his privy chamber and, after dinner, went to chapel. The body of James was laid in state at Denmark House and so, on 5 April, King Charles slipped through St James's Park and took up residence at Whitehall.[6]

Historians are very rude about Whitehall Palace. It is generally considered to be incoherent, confusing and old fashioned. It is sometimes said that the Banqueting House was the first step in rebuilding it on a more classically based plan but there is no evidence for this – James's commission was for a new chamber of state, not for a new palace. King James had little time for Whitehall, or indeed for London, over and above the requirement to have a ceremonial seat. It was in fact a well-ordered, carefully maintained, and smoothly functioning royal residence. Throughout the Elizabethan and Jacobean years great care had been taken to ensure that new additions elegantly blended in with older work. It was also a treasure house, a point comprehensively made by surviving sixteenth-century inventories and dozens of foreign visitors.[7]

Yet in 1625, Charles had only recently returned from his visit to Spain where the Escorial, in particular, had made a big impression on him and his companions. Within a month of his accession it was common knowledge that the king wanted to rebuild Whitehall, but there are no official documents to show what was in his mind. A drawing now at Chatsworth House shows a design, probably dating from this period, and possibly in the hand of Isaac de Caus to rebuild the privy gallery and create a new wing in the privy garden, but it is not known whether it was even seen by the king.[8]

Whitehall was by far and away Charles I's most favoured and frequently visited residence. In contrast to his father, Charles would move to Whitehall whenever he had the opportunity and the winter court season was extended at both ends to become a four- or (in the 1630s) a five-month, continuous residence. Like his father, during the summer months he was only there on occasion for business but then, most of the aristocracy and the whole of fashionable society were in the country.

The bride who was eventually welcomed to Whitehall was not the Spanish Infanta but a French princess, Henrietta Maria. As was common in international matches their union was not about personal preference but international diplomacy and wedded bliss was an exception rather than a rule. Yet, after a shaky start to their marriage Charles and Henrietta Maria gradually reached an accommodation, and then fell in love. The queen gave birth to a stillborn child in 1629 but, in early 1630, she was pregnant again and Charles, fastidious as ever, and eager to maintain the utmost decorum and tradition, ordered a search of the records to ascertain the etiquette used by Henry VII and VIII for the lying-in of a queen. It was decided that St James's would be the place where she should give birth, being close to Whitehall but far enough away to be free from the infections that made unsafe the more crowded royal residences. Between 1630 and 1637 Henrietta Maria eventually gave birth to five children there.[9]

To great national rejoicing the queen had a healthy son, Charles, who was christened at St James's on 27 June 1630. At the moment of baptism, by the richly coped Bishop of London, trumpets and drums were the signal to hoist a flag on the roof of the gatehouse. This being spied by a lookout on the Banqueting House, a flame was lit that was visible from the Tower of London. The signal spotted, an order was given to fire the castle's cannons and to let off ordinance from the naval vessels in the Pool of London.[10] St James's now became the royal nursery house, the role originally envisaged for it by its builder, Henry VIII. From here King Charles could make the short journey across the park and enter Whitehall through its back door.

The king's privy gallery, the backbone of his private quarters at Whitehall, ran east–west and was carried across King Street, the road between Charing Cross and Westminster, by the Holbein Gate. The portion of the gallery to the west of the gatehouse was known as the tiltyard gallery, there had always been a spiral stair here that allowed monarchs to descend to the park (fig. 43), the back door to Whitehall, as it were; but Charles rebuilt this to be a broad and impressive staircase supported by Corinthian and composite columns with a sweeping roof. This was now part of what became a well-trodden route between Whitehall and St James's; indeed in Charles's reign Whitehall and St James's were integrated, with the king seamlessly moving between the two.[11]

From 1630 Prince Charles was the principal resident of St James's. It was here during the winter and autumn that he spent most of his time; in summer he was based at Richmond in the old Tudor manor. He was joined at St James's by his eldest sister Mary in 1631 and by his brother James who was born there in November 1633. In due course there were three more children: princesses Elizabeth (b.1635) and Anne (b.1637) and Henry, Duke of Gloucester (b.1640). The children were given their own kitchen to the west of the house and Prince Charles was given a flower garden next to the Queen's Chapel.[12] The prince was also given a Chapel establishment which was supplied with fine vestments, linen and plate and used the Tudor Chapel Royal.[13]

In 1645 the thresholds of the doors in the privy lodgings at St James's were cut down 'to avoid tumbling' by the toddlers and a swing was erected. In 1638 when he was eight, Prince Charles's household was formalised and the Duke of Newcastle made his governor; under him was a household in miniature with grooms, ushers, gentlemen and servers – fifty people in all. A set of regulations, an 'establishment book' was issued setting out the duties and entitlements of household members and how they should conduct themselves appropriately in the presence of the boy-prince.[14]

The king and queen were far more attentive to their children than was often the case with seventeenth-century monarchs and were regular visitors to St James's. Soon after the birth of Prince Charles they began to design a new garden there together, as a private retreat for their family. Henrietta

Figure 39: An engraving by Wenceslaus Hollar
after a painting by van Dyck. It shows
Prince Charles when he was about eleven.
Hollar, who published the print in 1649, added
the Banqueting House in the background
as if the viewpoint was from St James's.

Maria had been interested in gardens before her arrival in England, and sent to France for one of the most fashionable designers of the day, André Mollet, who was appointed chief gardener and asked to redesign the gardens at St James's. Mollet laid out the privy garden as an elaborate parterre in box, quite a novelty in England at the time. The orchard next door was in a different style with 'fruit trees, planted in a checker pattern, with a big wooden post in the middle, which spouts water'.[15]

The Banqueting House

The birth of Prince Charles secured the Stuart dynasty and, before he was three years old, his image was a central part of a huge painted ceiling in the hand of Peter Paul Rubens. Rubens was an astonishing talent. Born into a modest family in 1577, his genius propelled him to the pinnacle of social, economic and artistic success by his death in 1640.

While Rubens was working on the Luxembourg Palace the peace between the Hapsburg territories and the rest of Europe, which had been held together by a truce, dissolved into hostility. Across Europe there erupted a period of intense diplomatic activity as states attempted

Figure 40: Whitehall Palace from the north. The wide open area of King Street lies in front of the Banqueting House. To the right is the outline of the tiltyard gallery with the great tennis court behind. To the left of the Holbein Gate are four bays of the privy gallery, and to the left of the Banqueting House is the court gate – the palace's main entrance.

to realign themselves. In this Archduchess Isabella asked Rubens to become her envoy. Painters and connoisseurs had easy access to the courts of Europe and were used to moving in princely circles. They were also unobtrusive and reliable diplomats without complex personal agendas. For three years, between 1627 and 1630, Rubens's life was taken up with attempting to smooth the way for international alliances on behalf of the archduchess. Key to this was the effort to bring about an alliance between England and Spain. In this Rubens was not an ambassador, he was a diplomatic envoy preparing the way for the arrival of a full embassy to achieve her ends. So Rubens's arrival in London and reception by Charles I on 5 June 1629 was not a formal ambassadorial reception, but it was an immensely important moment and, for many in England who hated Catholic Spain, an immensely unpopular one.

Rubens knew about the English court. He had not only met Buckingham, but also English envoys, connoisseurs and merchants. He believed Charles I to be 'the greatest amateur of paintings amongst the princes of the world', and he had met Queen Henrietta Maria at her mother's palace of the Luxembourg before she had been queen. Yet Rubens must have had his reservations about a Protestant country and when he arrived in London and saw the royal houses his reservations may have been greater. Although Charles I's residences contained some remarkable paintings, tapestry and a little sculpture the buildings themselves were essentially all of Henry VIII's time.

It took Rubens three months to set up an agreement for a full exchange of ambassadors, but he was ordered to remain in London until the arrival of the Spanish ambassador which wasn't, in the end, to be until January 1630. He would have liked to return home and to see his young sons, but he suffered an enforced exile which he made the most of. Luckily in his extensive baggage train Rubens brought to London his paints and he accepted a number of English commissions, including the king's invitation to paint a ceiling for the Banqueting House at Whitehall.

Rubens had pitched to paint the canvases in 1621 and it is likely, (though there is no firm evidence) that his offer was accepted, but no progress was made until he was in London. Here he met Inigo Jones and the two men discussed the commission in detail. Architecturally the model for the hall was a basilica from Ancient Rome, but for both Rubens and Jones the idea for the ceiling painting came from the Sala del Collegio (the Hall of the Council) in the Doge's Palace in Venice which both men knew. This great room was where foreign delegations were received and granted an audience by the Council. The hall had been completely redecorated by Andrea Palladio after a fire in 1574 and the gilded ceiling frames a series of works by Paolo Veronese. The function of this room was essentially the same as that intended for the Banqueting House.

From the early Middle Ages, the audience rooms of English kings had been painted with murals setting out their dynastic history and their God-given right to rule. The Painted Chamber built by Henry III lay at the centre of the medieval Palace of Westminster. When in the 1530s Henry VIII replaced Westminster Palace with Whitehall he recreated a dynastic audience chamber which Hans Holbein the Younger painted for him. The Whitehall mural showed Henry VIII receiving the throne from his father and passing it on to his son: the same subject that Rubens painted for the Banqueting House.

The new ceiling presented huge challenges to Rubens. Never had he worked on such a scale; the painted area was in total nearly 2,500 square feet. In fact, these were the biggest ceiling canvases in northern Europe; larger could only be found at the Doge's Palace in Venice. The canvasses would eventually be viewed from 50 feet below and, generally, at an angle. A series of sketches helped him to master the perspectival problems and, when he had done so, he painted a complete sketch of the whole ceiling that was sent to Charles I. The king suspended this from the ceiling of his cabinet at Whitehall and must have lain on the floor to appreciate the full effect.

The canvases were completed by May 1633, but lay, folded up in Rubens's studio in Antwerp for nearly a year before they were sent the 100-mile distance to Dunkirk on a wagon. From there they crossed the Channel and arrived in London. They were unfolded on the floor of the Banqueting House, presumably in the presence of an excited king. There was, however, a problem. It was realised that the canvases did not fit the recesses in the ceiling. This was despite extensive correspondence and careful supervision by both Rubens and Jones. The problem was that the length of a foot differed from country to country. Rubens misunderstood which version Jones had specified and so in at least four cases fairly drastic alterations had to be made to Rubens's paintings on site.

The work of extending and repainting the canvases and tacking them to their timber stretchers was finished quickly and they were finally lifted up into place by early 1636. Before they had arrived Jones had supervised the redecoration of the interior. The original plain white scheme was replaced by walls painted in imitation of marble and a ceiling grained to resemble timber and encrusted in gold leaf.

In this way the building begun for James I as a celebration of his reign was completed by his son as his memorial. This is how the Banqueting House should be read today: as a cenotaph to King James. The two rectangular canvases on the ceiling celebrated the king's greatest achievements and the central oval God's judgement of his success.

The compartments were carefully designed to be seen from specific viewing points. The canvas over the door is invisible as people enter (it is directly above the viewer's head) and can best be seen either from the throne itself or as visitors turned to leave after addressing the monarch. It depicts James's greatest achievement: his unification of the crowns of England and Scotland as first king of Britain.

The central canvas is set so that people entering the hall would see it first; this is important because it was intended to convey the central message of the whole scheme. The central oval encapsulates the early Stuart concept of monarchy: the sovereign's authority derived directly from God, and it was to God that he was answerable for his actions when he died. The central painting depicts James I being escorted to heaven to give an account of his rule before God. As he is lifted heavenwards his earthly crown and orb, the accoutrements of a Christian king, are being removed and he rises bareheaded to meet his maker. He is dressed in his parliament robes to stress his constitutional role as king in parliament.

The oval would have not been clearly seen by the monarch sitting on his throne, and the southernmost canvas, the one above his head, would have been invisible. There James is shown seated in a niche, symbolising the ruler's role as judge of his people and upholder of the law in parliament – the keeper of the peace. The theme of peace ran deeper still as the painting also celebrated James's achievements as a political peacemaker. The king's imperial crown is being lifted and a triumphal crown is about to be placed on his head by two winged victories. With a sweep of his hand, and with the help of Minerva, James is expelling Mars, the god of war and his ghoulish monsters in the fiery depth beneath him.

So familiar are we with the work of Rubens that it is now impossible to adequately convey the impact and novelty of the ceiling in 1636. The vast majority of visitors to the Banqueting House would have never seen painting like this before. It was so far divorced from the stiff, representational mode of portraiture familiar to the English as to be a completely different way of representing the world. The taste was the king's and the complete silence in historical record about their reception perhaps reflects the bemusement that many people felt.

Drama at court

Masques took place in mid-winter, in the middle of the night, in a cold hall. There is no record of the number of lights used in the various Whitehall banqueting houses but, for a masque performed before the king at the Merchant Taylors' Hall in 1634, 54 pounds of wax was bought for burning as well as 456 candles, 348 'torches' and three flambeaux weighing 12 pounds each. These lit 52 chandeliers (20 of these were described as 'great') and 116 wall lights. The Whitehall banqueting houses were much larger and the numbers of burning lights, hung from wires stretched across the hall, must have neared 1,000.

Beeswax candles have a high melting point (68°C) and the lights not only provided brilliant illumination but were the sole source of heating in a vast chamber without a fireplace; 1,000 candles made a considerable difference when the temperature outside was below zero and courtiers shivered in their silks and satins. Expensive wax candles, well made, burnt quite cleanly, but when there was a draught, or if the candle had a large wick (which the 'torches' did), they produced soot and moisture. Smoking candles and condensation were everyday facts for the Stuart court and with the installation of Rubens's paint-ings it was realised that the Banqueting House would no longer be suitable for the staging of masques.

The Banqueting House had other drawbacks as a theatre. The acous-tics were poor and it was unsuitable for increasingly innovative stage machinery, especially as the stone vault meant that it was not possible to use machinery under the stage. And the biggest problem of all was the expense and effort of setting up and then dismantling the staging when the hall was in use as a theatre. For the very first masque in the new Banqueting House temporary staging seven rows high was installed along each side and a vertiginous four rows high in the galleries. This had to be erected and dismounted, putting the room out of use typically for five weeks.[16]

As a result, in 1635, the Tudor great hall was set up with a stage and seating for a pastoral called *Florimène*. Three plans and an elevation exist for this in the hand of John Webb showing in detail the installation of the stage and amphitheatre. These illustrate the precise nature of the tiered staging, royal seat and stage which were constructed throughout the early Stuart period in the great hall, showing the locations of the boxes of favoured courtiers and the scale of the stage.[17]

The great hall was, however, little better than the Banqueting House and so, in September 1637, Inigo Jones was instructed to construct a new 'temporary room' to provide a setting for masques. It was of clap-board, partly built in the preaching place and partly in the outer court. This was the first purpose-built theatre at court, but it got little use. After the staging of *Salmacida Spolia* in February 1640, it was never

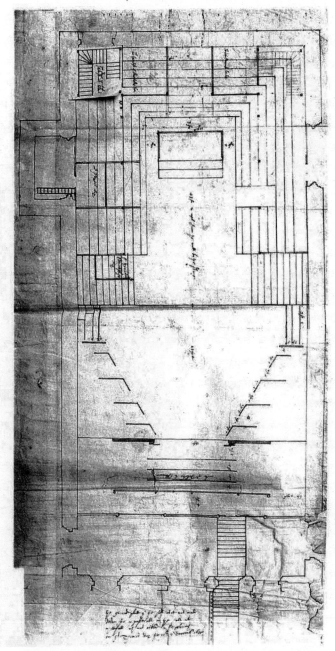

Figure 41: John Webb, survey and plan of the Great Hall at
Whitehall showing the tiers of seating and royal box installed for
the performance of *Florimène* in December 1635. Inigo Jones's
own reserved seat is marked. The stage is in the lower half of the
image showing the receding scenic flats and backdrop.

used again and two years later the Parliamentarians demolished what they called 'the queen's dancing barn'. This extremely large timber building, the same size as the Banqueting House, but with a pitched roof, must have always been intended to be temporary. Indeed, it is likely that as well as serving as a hastily erected venue for *Britannia Triumphans* in 1638 it was intended to be a test bed for Jones to build a permanent court theatre. He could achieve the perfect technical specification in timber and then translate this into a new structure. As will become apparent, this was exactly the period when the king was contemplating a complete rebuilding of Whitehall.[18]

The investment in a masque was enormous, not only in terms of the construction of the theatre, but in costumes and the time and energy put into rehearsals. The king, queen and royal family would be completely absorbed for weeks in practice for their parts and dances. The closest we can now get to this is a gigantic canvas, *Apollo and Diana*, by Gerrit van Honthorst that now hangs in the queen's staircase at Hampton Court. It shows a masque scene in which the Duke of Buckingham, as Mercury, the messenger of the gods, leads the seven liberal arts into the light, presenting them to Charles I as Apollo, the god of art and learning. By the king's side is Henrietta Maria as Diana (Apollo's sister). The costume, allegory, and favoured Jonesian device of a god descending from the clouds, all point to this being the representation of a masque.

At the recommendation of Charles I's sister, Elizabeth of Bohemia, Honthorst was in London in the summer and autumn of 1628 during the preparations for the winter masque, the subject of which is now lost. It is possible that this colossal canvas (which in its current size is cut down) was painted by him as part of the masque itself. Honthorst's assistant tells us that it was painted for the Banqueting House which, at this stage, was without Rubens's ceiling. It may have subsequently been used as a sort of shutter or curtain – it was certainly stored in a service room next to the Banqueting House in 1639 where it had presumably been placed after the abandonment of masques in the hall.[19]

While the principal point of masques and plays was the entertainment of the royal family and their close friends, a much wider audience also enjoyed them. The masques, in particular, were staged in an arena that could seat perhaps 1,000 people who flocked to see both the theatrical spectacle and the royal family dancing in all their finery. Aristocrats and court officials automatically gained access, but others were required to have an invitation. The Gentlemen Ushers had an unenviable task as doormen as people used every excuse to gain entry; in due course entry was only by turnstile to control the crowds. Masques tended to start at around ten in the evening and were normally over by one o'clock in the morning, at which point the king led the masquers to a banquet in the presence chamber. He would not stay to eat himself and withdrew to the privy lodgings while the guests fell on the feast.[20]

Masques needed a great deal of space as there had to be a clear dance floor between the royal seat and the stage; plays, on the other hand could be accommodated in smaller buildings and the first permanent court theatre was set up for these in 1629. Charles I enjoyed plays as much as his father and acquired patronage of the King's Men company in 1625. During his first court season they performed ten plays and the king granted them £100 for buying new costumes. His decision to create a permanent theatre must have been, at least in part, an attempt to reduce the chaos and expense caused by the construction and dismantling of stages each year.

On the west side of Whitehall stood Henry VIII's cockpit, an octagonal building 60 feet in diameter with tiered seating and a central area for fighting cocks. It was a substantial structure with a flamboyant roofline and, when not in use for cockfights, James I had watched plays there. Judging by records kept for fitting up the space this was a regular occurrence: at least thirty-nine were staged before the building fell out of use in 1622. Internally the cockpit was a riot of colour and carving. In 1629 Inigo jones constructed a permanent stage with a scenic front adorned with two tiers of columns, niches, swags, busts and a great central portal with a segmental pediment. Directly inspired by the Teatro Olimpico at Vicenza which had been visited by Jones, it became the second most classically correct structure in England, although only ever seen by a few courtiers.

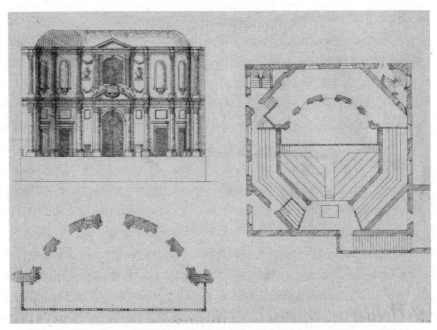

Figure 42: John Webb, plan of the Cockpit Theatre and elevation of the scenic front, designed and erected by Inigo Jones in 1629. The drawing dates from the early Restoration, and the plan shows the octagonal cockpit squared-off by John Webb for Charles II.

The court season at Whitehall that year, which lasted four months, saw a bonanza of plays, sixteen in all in a run that ended on Candlemas. Whether this extraordinarily large number was in celebration of the new theatre or to blot out the appalling memory of the assassination of the Duke of Buckingham, is not clear. What is known is that plays were a vital component of the court season, and in a year like 1633, when the queen was unwell and there were few plays, courtiers complained bitterly that there had never 'been a duller Christmas than we had at court this year'.[21]

King Charles at Whitehall

The king's private life, that is to say life outside ceremonial pleasures and duties of state, was conducted in the Bedchamber. This was not a private area in a sense that we would recognise today; monarchs were never alone, not even on the close stool; but they could choose who they wanted to be near and exclude those whom they did not. James I and Charles I had different ways of managing personal attendance, but both relied on the architecture of their houses to facilitate any rules they put in place.

Whitehall had the most extensive privy accommodation of any residence. Confusingly the whole range of buildings was called the privy gallery, but it also contained a long gallery called the privy gallery. The range connected to the queen's privy lodgings and the matted gallery. The latter was a 380-foot-long gallery fronting the privy garden and leading to Prince Charles's lodgings. Whitehall can be characterised as 'home' for Charles I and the static court season was his time for pursuing his cultural interests: music, drama, masques and collecting works of art.

Charles was a serious collector: collecting was a structured, almost empirical, activity which combined connoisseurship, scholarship and classification. Soon after his return from Spain he ordered his first inventory of paintings including the Titian he had bought in Madrid. Two years later, when he became king, he began to commission and purchase large numbers of pictures. In 1627, most famously, he bought a spectacular collection of paintings and sculpture from the Duke of Mantua for nearly £16,000. In fact, in the first five years of his reign, Charles spent some £30,000 on buying paintings and tapestries.[22]

Most of these objects came to Westminster and almost all were placed in the privy gallery at Whitehall and at St James's. Although the privy gallery had been built by Henry VIII it had not been altered in structure by either Elizabeth I or James I. Such decorative changes as there had been retained the essential structure of a series of rooms backing onto a long gallery with bay windows overlooking the privy garden. The gallery was the spine of the building and ran from the river to St James's Park and, although it had different sections, was essentially a 600-foot-long passage. The part called the privy gallery was a relatively short section from the door of the vane room to the Holbein Gate.

On the north side was the council chamber which was restored to its former use by Charles at his accession. This was not only the meeting place of the Privy Council but where ambassadors would be brought discreetly up the council stairs to wait for private audiences with the king. Charles I banned the use of the privy gallery by anyone other than members of the Bedchamber, Privy Chamber and Privy Council.[23]

Charles hung the privy gallery with seventy-three Tudor and Jacobean portraits with a very small number of more recent portraits. The older portraits were paintings inherited by him and already hanging at Whitehall. Courtiers using the gallery would thus see the array of traditional dynastic royal painting. Those who wanted to see some of the king's personal collection would need to get access to the matted gallery or the privy lodgings. The colossally long matted gallery was one of the wonders of Whitehall. It faced west, overlooking the privy garden and in 1639, on its east wall, was an almost continuous display of 103 paintings, the majority Italian pictures acquired as part of the Mantua purchase. Dotted along the gallery's length were antique marble sculptures on timber pedestals.

There were a few contemporary pieces, the most significant of which was van Dyck's 'Great Piece', a monumental family portrait of the king and his family set at Whitehall itself. It is not specified where in the gallery the painting hung; however it was 9 feet 8 inches high and 8

Key to Figure 43

King's Lodgings
1 – Guard chamber
2 – Presence chamber
3 – Private chamber
4 – Privy chamber
5 – Withdrawing room
6 – Vane room
7 – Wardrobe (below)
8 – Backstair
9 – Matted gallery
10 – Bedchamber
11 – Breakfast chamber
12 – Closets
13 – Cabinet or green room
14 – Council chamber, store chamber, clerks rooms and council stairs
15 – Third privy lodging room
16 – Second privy lodging room
17 – First privy lodging room
18 – Adam and Eve stairs
19 – Privy gallery
20 – Rooms and stairs
21 – 'Holbein' gate
22 – Tiltyard gallery
23 – Stairs to park

Queen's lodgings
a – Presence chamber
b – Privy chamber
c – Withdrawing chamber
d – Bedchamber, closets, stairs etc
e – Queen's gallery

Other parts
A – Chapel closets
B – Privy kitchen
C – River gallery
D – Privy bridge (landing stage)
E – Princes' lodgings
F – Great indoor tennis court
G – Great outdoor tennis court
H – Lodging range and Gallery
I – King Street gate
J – Bowling alley
K – Small outdoor tennis court
L – Princess Elizabeth's lodgings
M – Gallery/Lodgings
N – Cockpit theatre
O – Gallery
P – Pulpit

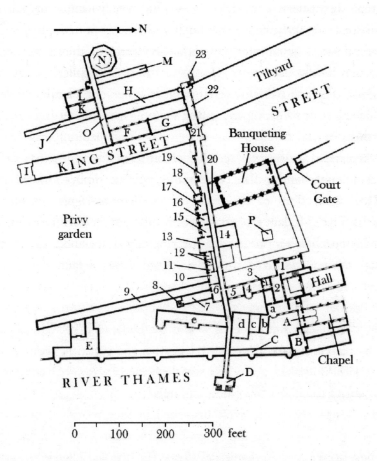

Figure 43: Reconstructed first-floor plan of Whitehall Palace, *c.*1630. The plan omits the large area of service buildings and courts to the north.

feet wide and the only place where it could have been properly seen in a gallery only 15 feet wide would have been on the end wall; this must have been the wall at the south as the north end had two doors in it. The view in the background of the painting is the very view of Westminster that would have been seen out of a window in the south end of the gallery, had there been one. The painting depicted the domesticity of Whitehall, the fidelity of the royal couple and their affection for their children. Symbolically a crown, sceptre and orb on the table lie directly under the silhouette of St Stephen's Chapel, the meeting place of parliament. This great gallery of painting was thus presided over by the king and queen in an illusionistic setting composed for them by van Dyck.

The matted gallery was accessed either from the vane room or from the king's bedchamber. The bedchamber, and the seven rooms beyond it on the south front of the palace, were restricted only to the king's Bedchamber staff. James I had sometimes allowed ambassadors and others into his bedchamber but in 1626 the king had all locks changed to treble locks and keys restricted to just the Lord Chamberlain, the king and queen. This was an inner sanctum, hung with a series of new Mortlake tapestries of the *Months of the Year* and containing paintings of his wife, siblings, nephews and nieces as well as the Duke of Buckingham and his family placed over the chimney. Next door the breakfast room was also hung with Mortlake tapestry and over the fireplace was van Dyck's gorgeous painting of the king's five eldest children.

The king's collections were displayed in four rooms in the western half of this range entered, by everyone but the king and his closest friends, from a door in the privy gallery. The first was filled with canvases by Titian and the following two rooms overflowed with paintings by Raphael, Correggio and others. The largest room in the privy lodgings was the king's cabinet. Most of the contents of this had, until 1638, been kept at St James's and was, in origin, the collector's cabinet of his brother, Henry Prince of Wales. When Prince Charles (the future Charles II) acquired his own household in 1638 the king had to relocate the cabinet to Whitehall. The new Whitehall cabinet contained some eighty paintings including works by Raphael and Leonardo da Vinci but also bronzes, books, medals, drawings and other works of art. Into the ceiling was set Rubens's sketch for the ceiling of the Banqueting House.[24]

Before 1638 St James's was, in effect, an extension of the Whitehall privy lodgings. The king had not stripped the paintings from the great U-shaped gallery, nor denuded the library of books or even extracted the bronzes, medals and coins in the cabinet. In fact he reinforced St James's as a centre of royal connoisseurship by appointing Prince Henry's former collections' curator, the Dutch artist and expert in coins and medals, Abraham van der Doort, as keeper of both the cabinet room and, soon after, surveyor of his pictures – the latter an entirely new post. For thirteen years the king added royally to the existing collections at St James's.[25]

In 1630 as the sculptures, part of the king's Gonzaga purchase, were being unpacked, a new gallery was being built for them in the orchard at St James's. On top of the raised bank, on its south side, was erected a 70-foot-long Tuscan arcade with columns 10 feet high. This was filled with full-length antique sculptures on plinths. The picture gallery also received artworks from Mantua including heads of Caesars painted by Titian and smaller portraits of mounted emperors by Giulio Romano.[26]

It was perhaps the success of the *great piece*, painted in 1632 for the matted gallery, which inspired, the following year, a second huge canvas by van Dyck to perform the same function at the east end of the privy gallery at St James's. The equestrian portrait of King Charles I and M. de St Antoine was 12 feet high and more than 8 feet wide and hung more-or-less floor to ceiling, dominating the view down the 18-foot-wide privy gallery. The architectural setting for the mounted king could have been part of the panelled gallery itself and the illusionistic effect of the archway must have given the impression that the king was riding in from the park.[27]

The king's collecting was almost exclusively concentrated at Whitehall and St James's. At Hampton Court, by contrast, a house richly furnished with hundreds of tapestries and paintings, there were no contemporary Mortlake tapestries, contemporary paintings or fine sixteenth-century continental works; instead the house was hung with portraits, religious painting, and subjects of classical mythology. Mantegna's *Triumphs of Caesar*, which were hung there in 1630, were placed in the privy gallery away from public gaze. This is probably the reason why, when Abraham van der Doort made his inventory of the royal collection in 1638–9, he did not list a single painting at Hampton Court, although there were around 350. Nor was there any contemporary furniture; Charles slept in Tudor state beds and received ambassadors each autumn under canopies of state made for Henry VIII. This was a self-conscious decision. Hampton Court was framed by the early Stuarts as a great ancestral seat and treasure house of antiques.[28]

It has been a trope of historians to link royal art collecting and the display of power, but what is abundantly clear is that none of Charles I's collections were accessible to anyone outside his Bedchamber and a few invited guests, and those almost exclusively at Whitehall and St James's. In fact, nobody outside this charmed circle had any access to either his high Renaissance paintings or the contemporary works of art. Indeed, the only contemporary painting publicly on show anywhere in the royal houses was the Banqueting House ceiling. This is the fundamental truth about Charles's court. The king's art collection was private, inward looking and sustained for the pleasure and enjoyment of the royal family and their closest friends, it was never about the external representation of power.

Whitehall underwent no transformation under Charles I. In fact he was a careful custodian of the Tudor fabric, carefully repairing carvings, conserving Holbein's great mural of Henry VII and VIII in the privy chamber, touching up the painting of Adam and Eve that gave his backstairs their name and piecing in linenfold panelling in the privy gallery as a backdrop for the paintings.

For those who had access into the great outer rooms, and that was most people of good fashion and behaviour, the principal change was in the arrangement of tapestries. In 1637 the king had bought the Mortlake tapestry manufactory from Richard Crane and it had continued to produce spectacular sets of high-quality tapestry designed by Cleyn and others. Tapestry was always on the move between rooms and between residences and sets were taken down and erected for special occasions; but Whitehall was in receipt of several Mortlake sets that were hung in the outer chambers. Their lively, fresh colours with rich borders and big figures gave the outer rooms a brighter and more contemporary feel than the grand antique sets.[29]

On the move

In the early seventeenth century monarchs were public property. Because government was personal to the sovereign, his subjects had a stake, not only in his opinions, beliefs and competence, but in his health and well-being. Seeing the king in person was not only a novelty, it was a reassurance in the proper order of things. King James faced criticism that he hid himself away at Royston and Newmarket; that he was uncivil to his subjects when he came face to face with them. King Charles's way was different. Although spending a third of the year in Westminster the rest of the time he was either itinerant, shuttling between his houses in the Thames valley, or on progress.

Charles made a summer progress every year of his reign up to 1640. His itinerary was more restricted and conservative than that of his father, visiting a relatively small number of places on multiple occasions, and these mostly close to London. Although he enjoyed hunting and was a brilliant horseman and capable shot, his enjoyment did not amount to obsession, as had his father's; yet hunting drove his summers' activities and took him to both his own parks and those of his courtiers.

The logistics of the Caroline progress were formidable: The king travelled with some 400 carts, guarded by 100 yeomen of the guard and accompanied by more than 1,000 household officers from kitchen scullions to the noblest aristocrats. On an average two-month progress there would be ten to fifteen moves, and on the two extended progresses to Scotland in 1633 and 1639, there were three times that many. The household was a finely tuned machine and meticulous preparations went into determining the route, identifying and preparing places to stay. Very occasionally things went awry. In March 1631 the court left Newmarket for Theobalds, but found that their bedding had not arrived and had to divert to Whitehall; finding that unready also, they had to go to St James's.[30]

A surviving set of the king's 'gests' as they were called – the list of his progress stops – shows his two-month route in 1633 when he travelled out to Woodstock and back again, staying mostly in royal houses in between. Woodstock, although one of the oldest royal houses, was extremely large and sited in a hunting park that had been enlarged by successive monarchs. King Charles enlarged the park further, building a stone standing from which to shoot driven deer.[31]

The progress of 1634 was into the Midlands and took in royal and private houses and a visit to Leicester. The king's gentlemen ushers delivered details of the visit to the Mayor of Leicester on 9 May five weeks before the progress was scheduled to begin. First of all the mayor was obliged to provide a certificate showing the town free from disease; this accepted, preparations for the arrival of the court were intense. The town gates were repainted, householders were required to paint the outside of their houses 'decent and convenient colours' and pave the streets in front. Forty citizens were designated as the guard to keep watch at night and provided with 156 torches sent up from London to light the streets. Just before the royal arrival the roads outside were laid with sand and gravel and the streets were strewn with rushes. New liveries were made for the mayor and aldermen and golden bowls with pictures of the king and queen were fashioned as gifts. The Earl of Huntingdon, the Lord Lieutenant, was sent ahead to ensure that St Martin's Church was properly arranged for the Sunday when the king would attend divine service. Such preparations gripped the towns and houses in the royal route.

EIGHT

Queen Consort

Affairs of state

Henrietta Maria had married Charles I in Notre Dame Cathedral in Paris on 1 May 1625. The king, who was 215 miles away in London at the time, was represented by his distant relative the Duke of Chevreuse. His bride was not yet quite sixteen and prepared to leave Paris knowing that the Pope himself had commanded her to be a missionary to a heretical nation.

The Duke of Buckingham had control of preparations. Guided by precedent, it was decided to replicate the reception of Anne of Cleves, the last queen consort to arrive on English soil from overseas. An emergency programme of works was ordered at Dover Castle. It was a massive operation as the queen's eighty attendants, twenty-eight priests and the Duke and Duchess of Chevreuse and their households all had to be accommodated. In addition, suitable lodgings had to be found for senior English courtiers. Buckingham, who had been appointed Constable of Dover Castle the previous year, had his own extensive lodgings.

In the centre of the castle Henry II had constructed a great tower, visible from the coast of France, as his lodging. In the 1630s this contained two principal floors, the upper one for the monarch and the one below for his consort; each had gigantic presence and privy chambers, a bedchamber and closets. After a century of neglect Charles I's plasterers inserted coved plastered ceilings, replaced doorcases and painted panelling in preparation for a huge delivery of tapestries, hangings and furniture from the Great Wardrobe in London. The king ordered the enlargement of a window in his presence chamber and construction of a balcony, perhaps so he could stand and take the sea views with his bride. The basement, normally used for storage, was given a raised floor and divided up for additional accommodation. The Lord Chamberlain, the Earl of Pembroke, who would take charge of ceremonies once the queen had landed, was given a huge lodging opposite the entrance to the tower.[1]

The queen disembarked on a pontoon and was carried by litter into Dover town where she received a civic welcome before boarding her coach, ascending the steep hill to the castle and entering through the mighty constable's tower. As well as the luxuries of her mother's up-to-the-minute palace of Luxembourg in Paris, Henrietta Maria was perfectly used to medieval fortresses and the sight then, as today, must have been impressive. The cortege wound their way through the outer ward and into the inner bailey to be confronted with the largest keep in England sporting a new porch, designed by Inigo Jones, crowned with the royal arms.

By now it was evening and Henrietta Maria requested a night's grace before meeting the king. Soon she was seated at a magnificent banquet laid on in her privy chamber after which her first night in England was spent, alone, in a bedchamber built when France was ruled from England. The king arrived the next morning, finding Henrietta Maria at her breakfast table. A visitor to the castle ten years later noted that a small plaque marked the place where they first met: 'all places of this castle, only this / where Charles and Marie, shared a royal kiss'.[2]

From Dover the royal couple made their way, in stages, overland to Gravesend where the royal barge was waiting. In this they were rowed up river, past the royal palace at Greenwich and into the Pool of London, crammed with spectators on land and in river craft. The guns of the Tower let loose salvo after salvo, while to these echoes, the barge made

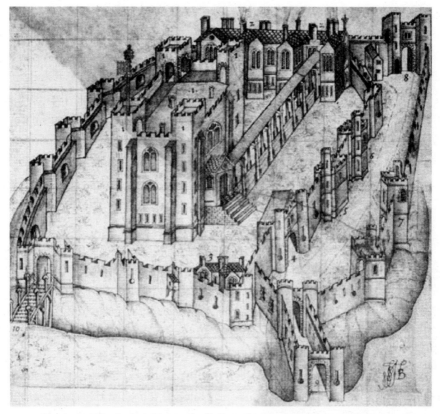

Figure 44: Elizabethan Dover Castle from the west, showing, in the centre,
the great tower containing the royal lodgings. Drawing by John Bereblock, *c.*1570.

its way to the privy stairs at Whitehall where Henrietta Maria entered
her new home.[3]

Although only fifteen when she arrived in England, Henrietta Maria
was no ingenue; she was, like Anna before her, the daughter of a monarch,
and brought up in the most fashionable court in Europe. Though what
education she had concentrated on religion and etiquette, these instilled
in her a clear perception of her rank and the deference due to it. In
1625 there had not been a queen of England for more than five years
and the queen's lodgings in all the royal houses had either been put to
other uses or shut up. The Office of Works and the Wardrobe undertook
a massive renovation and refurbishing project to bring the queen's sides

up to standard. And the moment she arrived she began to address their interior décor with gusto.

Over the following fifteen years her taste infused all the major royal houses, not so much in bricks and mortar but painting, tapestry, furniture, textiles, upholstery, plate and domestic utensils. To this has to be added the influence of Catholic France on ceremonies and festivals at her residences: the masques, the pastorals, the dancing, music, food at her table and above all liturgy in her chapel. Most daily discourse was in French, at least until the mid-1630s. Thus in every area of her existence, the influence of France and of Catholic Europe prevailed.[4]

In her first years in England the queen received money directly from the exchequer while a permanent jointure was worked out. It took some time to assemble and in fact was never formally granted; however, between 1626 and 1639 she was in receipt of lands and houses which yielded an annual income of some £28,000 a year. During the 1630s this sum was regularly topped up by the exchequer. The king granted his wife seven houses. The first and most important, on St Valentine's Day 1626, was her official London residence, Denmark House with all its contents. Then came her first country houses: Richmond in February 1627 and the following month Oatlands and Nonsuch. Exactly a year later the queen was formally granted the manor of Greenwich. In August 1629 the parks at Greenwich and Oatlands and another large country house, Holdenby in Northamptonshire; finally, in 1639, Charles I purchased Wimbledon Manor for her. In addition, of course, she had extensive lodgings in all the major royal houses such as Whitehall, Hampton Court and Theobalds.[5]

By the late 1630s Henrietta Maria had established a pattern of residence in these houses only interrupted by her regular pregnancies and outbreaks of plague. Pregnancy normally meant a confinement at Greenwich and removal to St James's to give birth and plague heralded an exit from London and its surrounds often to Hampton Court but, in extremis, further afield. The queen was in London for the court season, often at Whitehall and St James's, but frequently holding her own court at Denmark House; Christmas observance she kept in her own chapel. She would sometimes accompany the king on his spring hunting trips but in May normally went to Greenwich for the early summer. There she was joined by the king just before they both left for their summer progress.

The king and queen had their own progress itinerary but, at larger royal or courtier houses, they would sometimes join up. Henrietta Maria would often include Oatlands in her progress and the king would join her there. Short trips to Richmond, where the royal children spent their summers, or Nonsuch were also common before king and queen were reunited at Hampton Court for the start of the autumn season.

Hers was a very different sort of court to that of Anna of Denmark; Anna's court was essentially a private one, independent of the king's, moving in its own orbit. Her successor's was almost indistinguishable from the king's. After 1628, the king and queen were closely entwined in all they did. Under Anna Denmark House had been a female refuge rarely visited by James, and then only briefly, but Charles, his children and courtiers were regular visitors, the king often staying the night despite the proximity of Whitehall.[6]

The refurbishment of Denmark House and the building of the queen's Roman Catholic chapel there was her first architectural project and financed by the king, partly because it was an obligation of their marriage treaty. Thereafter Henrietta Maria's building projects were paid for out of her own resources, even if she commissioned the king's Office of Works to undertake the work. Either way her chief designer was Inigo Jones serving as royal surveyor or her own master of works for which he received a pension of £20 a year from 1630.[7]

Exploring her lodgings at Whitehall Henrietta Maria discovered that the Office of Works had set up a small oratory for her private use but this was clearly not the publicly accessible church she had been promised. She also discovered that the St James's chapel that might have fulfilled that role, was unfinished, and nobody was in a hurry to complete it. Begging the king to restart works he unsympathetically remarked that if her closet was proving too tight she should use her great chamber, that if that were too small she should use the garden, and if that was not large enough she should move into the park.[8]

The French must have been given details of the St James's chapel as designed by Inigo Jones because Henrietta Maria's extensive trousseau contained everything that was needed to furnish two chapels and equip their staff. Jones's drawings would have indicated, for instance, the number, position and size of the altars and the queen's trousseau contained several altarpieces to fit them: three large ones for the chapel and a smaller one for the sacristy. These ornaments and many others were installed at St James's by Easter 1626 when the queen and her ladies walked to it from Denmark House to visit an Easter Sepulchre.[9]

When Henrietta Maria arrived at Dover she was accompanied by twelve Oratorian priests who established themselves at St James's, publicly celebrating Mass for the first time in England since the reign of Queen Mary I. As this began to inflame popular outrage, tensions increased at court. While the king and queen dined together in public their Catholic and Protestant chaplains vied to have their own grace heard loudest. As it turned into a shouting match, the king grabbed the queen and left the table in a fury. At the end of July 1626, the Oratorians, and the majority of the queen's French household, were expelled.[10]

In November 1627 it was finally agreed that the queen should have a new chapel establishment: a bishop, Capuchin friars, a confessor and musicians. The Catholic chapel at St James's would be completed and a new one built at Denmark House. The Capuchins were an order of Observant friars noted for their repudiation of worldly things and their proselytising zeal. Before the Reformation the Observants had friaries at Greenwich and Richmond and were the favoured order for the early Tudor kings. So, the start of work on a friary and chapel at Denmark House was a return to an arrangement very familiar in England 100 years previously. But unlike its Tudor precursors, the Denmark House friary was not a private chapel; it was a public Roman Catholic church entered completely separately from the main palace. Unlike her other chapels it remained open when she was not in residence and welcomed Catholics from all over London.[11]

By 1630 Inigo Jones had experience at designing for Roman Catholic worship but the design of the new friary must have been discussed with the superior of the Capuchins and the queen herself. It is known that Jones used prints of French Jesuit churches for specific elements of his design and these were most likely given to him by his patrons. The Denmark House chapel was architecturally more ambitious than St James's, it was raised up on a vaulted brick undercroft approached by a staircase and had shallow transepts. At the south (liturgical east) end there was a vestry and at the north end, at second-floor level, was the royal pew; further north were the residential buildings of the friary. Inside there was a beamed ceiling like that in the Banqueting House comprising a central rectangle and flanking circles and ovals for canvases; over the presbytery was a coffered Roman ceiling. The front of the queen's pew, which was supported by Doric columns, was highly carved and decorated with cherubs' heads and scallop shells, the latter presumably symbolising pilgrimage.

The first Mass was a spectacle not seen in England for a century. Its setting was a fashionable type of Roman liturgical theatre designed and executed by the Roman-trained Flemish sculptor François Dieussart. He created a 40-foot-high monstrance over the high altar in which a Host was held in a large oval flanked by prophets and supported by two pillars that soared through seven layers of 'clouds' amongst which nestled 200 angels. This concealed a real human choir whose singing appeared to come from the massed heavenly host on the clouds. The whole contraption, lit by 400 lights, was hidden behind curtains when the congregation entered and at the crucial moment Dieussart drew them aside. The queen wept with joy and Charles was so fascinated that he spent an hour and a half examining it after Mass was over. In January 1637 the king was observed entering the friary again, visiting the church, the friars' cells and then dining with them in the refectory.[12]

Figure 45: Isaac Ware, survey drawing of the front of the queen's pew in the
Denmark House friary church, designed by Inigo Jones, engraving published in 1735.

There were no significant architectural changes to the residential parts
of Denmark House but the queen ordered a thoroughgoing redecoration
of her privy lodgings, in particular of her bedchambers. When Anna of
Denmark extended Denmark House she had specified two bedchambers:
a great bedchamber placed, as normal, next to the withdrawing room
and a little bedchamber sited beyond a private dining room and a
wardrobe (fig. 18).

The great bedchamber was the more formal of the two where she
was attended by her Bedchamber staff; the little bedchamber, perhaps,
was where she slept. As the Earl of Worcester explained to the Earl of
Shrewsbury in 1603, 'we have ladies of divers degrees of favour; some
for the private [ie privy] chamber, some for the drawing chamber, some
for the bedchamber'. He noted that those who were of the private or
privy chamber were often 'shut out' of the inner rooms. Household
regulations drawn up for Henrietta Maria in 1627 set out these access
rules in detail and justified them as being those which were used in
Anna of Denmark's time.[13]

Yet there was a fundamental difference between Anna's and Henrietta Maria's bedchambers. At the French court the bedchamber occupied a central position in the ceremonial life of the monarch; it was the room in which the most important audiences would be held, treaties signed and proclamations made; the monarch standing by the bed, frequently behind a gilded or silvered balustrade (fig. 46a). In expectation of such a bedchamber in England Henrietta Maria's trousseau contained a complete set of French royal bedchamber furnishings of red velvet with gold and silver trimmings. These were delivered to Whitehall where the bed was set up on a red-covered dais and crowned with four great plumes of white ostrich feathers. Three chairs and six coffers of matching velvet and three large Turkish carpets were also provided.[14]

Financial crisis and poor relations with the king had hindered any significant remodelling of her bedchambers at Denmark House in her first years in England. The queen appointed a new upholsterer, Ralph Grynder, probably a Frenchman, and he made do and mend with the royal beds he found, transforming them, as well as he could, into the French style.[15]

Ever since his accession, plans had been in the making for Charles to undertake a journey north to be crowned in Edinburgh and in November 1631 the Privy Council there was informed that the king would be arriving in April 1632. Henrietta Maria was to remain in London and, while not granted any formal powers of regency, was to be nominally in charge and responsible for state ceremonial. She was also to hold a formal weekly audience with the Privy Council. In preparation for this new role the queen's Denmark House great bedchamber was finally redecorated.

Inigo Jones designed a new white marble chimneypiece, and a 10-foot-square platform 6 inches high was built and a richly embroidered green and white satin bed delivered. This was accompanied by 'A Rail and Ballaster to encompass round ye bed silvered and varnished over'. The ensemble also included a second bed, a *lit d'ange* known in the later seventeenth century as an angel bed as the canopy was suspended from above by chains rather than supported by posts at the feet. This too was of green without and white within. The great bedchamber was thus transformed into a French room of state ready for her new duties. In 1641, when the king went to Scotland again, and the queen was left at Hampton Court nominally in charge, in the same way her bedchamber there was remodelled and redecorated for the purpose.[16]

While Henrietta Maria's little bedchamber was certainly a female preserve the point of a great bedchamber, decorated with her arms, and with a bed raised on a lavishly covered dais behind a rail, was that it should be a room into which honoured guests would be invited. Indeed, a contemporary engraving of her mother Marie de' Medici in her bedchamber at St James's Palace during her visit to England in 1638 shows a French bed with its rail and the queen mother receiving the Lord Mayor of London and the aldermen in a formalised setting. It seems a fair assumption that if Marie was using her great bedchamber in the French fashion, her daughter, less than a mile away, was doing likewise.

Figure 46a: Marie de' Medici receiving the Lord Mayor and Aldermen in her bedchamber at St James's Palace with a French bed and bed rail. Illustration to Jean Puget de la Serre, *Histoire de l'entrée de la Reyne Mère dans la Grande Brétaigne* 1639.

This was not the only form of French court etiquette practised at Denmark House. The principal court occasion in the queen's weekly calendar was the circle. This was an event instituted by the 1630s whereby the queen's presence chamber was thrown open to select ladies and gentlemen of the court who would gather round the queen, seated under her throne canopy, for conversation and gossip. The queen brought the circle to England from Paris where the event was later formally known as a Salon. Once again an engraving of Marie de' Medici shows the queen mother hosting her circle at St James's. Henrietta Maria's circle was not only held in the queen's lodgings at Whitehall, but also frequently at Denmark House.[17]

For some, the circle made it easier to see the queen than the king; it certainly institutionalised informal social interaction in the queen's court in a way that did not exist in the king's. The queen's lodgings were thus open to the politically aware classes, and perhaps, for the privileged, her great bedchamber was open too. This was important in the late 1630s, in an atmosphere where contact with the queen's Catholic court with its foreign ways was a matter of concern and even fear amongst sections of the population.

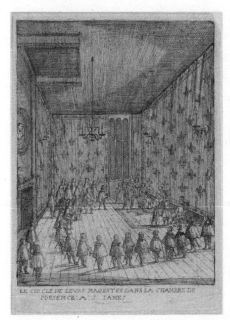

LE CIRCLE DE LEURS MAGESTES DANS LA CHAMBRE DE PRESENCE A S. IAMES

Figure 46b: Marie de' Medici holding a circle in the presence chamber at St James's Palace with the king, queen and their children in attendance. Such circles were pioneered by Henrietta Maria and became the most important events at the court. Illustration to Jean Puget de la Serre, *Histoire de l'entrée de la Reyne Mère dans la Grande Brétaigne*, 1639.

Denmark House also provided a secure location in which the king and courtiers of varied religious orientations could consort with Catholic envoys. Since the time of Henry VIII, an important function of the queen's side of a royal house had been to allow the monarch to mingle with courtiers and visitors outside the restrictive regulations that governed behaviour in his own rooms. Sir John Finet, Charles's Master of Ceremonies, observed that private ambassadorial ceremonies at Denmark House were undesirable as they took place outside the established conventions. More worrying to many was the access that the king had to the papal envoy George Con who had arrived in England in 1636 and was presented at Henrietta Maria's court at Denmark House. The king enjoyed Con's company and saw him frequently at Whitehall and at Denmark House where he had the official status denied him at the king's court. None of this was good for the king's image as little distinction was made between the court of the queen and that of the king himself.[18]

The queen at leisure

With the disability of hindsight, the 1630s seems a period of snowballing problems, a prelude to a shattering Civil War. Yet, for the Stuart court, at least, it was its gilded age. The decade began badly, with the assassination of the Duke of Buckingham in August 1628, but the death of the great favourite seems to have cleared the way for a deep and passionate love affair between the king and queen. Their sexual chemistry infused the court: for more than half the 1630s the fecund Henrietta Maria was pregnant, giving birth to a succession of healthy children. Like Victoria and Albert the royal couple became a model of idealised love and family life. By the end of 1630 short but expensive wars against both France and Spain had come to an end and ushered in a decade without war: the Earl of Clarendon was able to write in the late 1640s that such 'peace and plenty and universal tranquillity for ten years was never enjoyed by any nation'.[19]

In the 1630s Henrietta Maria was in her twenties. It was her decade: she was energetic and vivacious, financially independent and possessed of taste refined in Europe's most fashionable court. She was adored by

Figure 47: Henrietta Maria on horseback, with a view of
Greenwich Palace and the newly completed Queen's
House in the background. There are several versions
of this image with differing backgrounds; this
one was reissued after the completion of the Queen's
House illustrating its significance to the queen.

her husband, a man little concerned with the details of rule; unlike his
father he was lazy and work-shy preferring hunting, plays, masques and
art to the minutiae of state affairs. He thrived in the company of his
wife and together they were devoted to pleasure and the arts.

In 1629 Henrietta Maria had been granted Greenwich Palace and
decided to recommence work on the park side pavilion begun by her
predecessor. Soon after work restarted, she seems to have commissioned
Jan van Belcamp to paint the royal family and their friends enjoying a
summer's walk in Greenwich Park. He added the figures onto a fine

landscape done by another Dutchman, Adriaen van Stalbemt, in the background of which is the stumpy single-storey hulk of the incomplete Queen's House (plate 12).[20]

It is not known what was in Henrietta Maria's mind when she ordered Inigo Jones to take up where he had left off eleven years before, but it seems that the structure designed in 1616 was that which he brought to completion in 1638–9. Its decoration and use, however, were reinvented by its new owner.

The queen was no less enthusiastic a huntress than Anna of Denmark, retaining her own pack of hounds, huntsmen and a personal crossbow maker. She and the king regularly shot deer in Greenwich Park but, as work restarted on what we now know as the Queen's House, it was not on the park side of the building. Anna of Denmark's house had addressed the park in function and form, but Henrietta Maria turned its aspect northwards to face the palace and river by building a terrace approached by sweeping semi-circular staircases. While the building rose as a single unit, only the northern interiors were advanced and, by 1636, the queen was laying out an extensive garden in front of them. When work stopped in 1640 the northern half of the house overlooking new pleasure gardens was largely complete and inhabitable: the project had cost at least £7,000.[21]

Visiting the Queen's House today gives no sense of what it was like on the eve of the Civil War. Set austerely in manicured lawns it appears as an architectural jewel, a shrine to its architect and to the style that much later became known as Palladianism. If a drawing of the house from the 1630s is to be believed, the upper portions of the garden front were originally painted with colourful grotesques and the windows of the queen's bedchamber and withdrawing room had iron balconies; roof terraces above provided more views over the gardens, palace, river, and distantly, the City of London. It was, in fact, a garden pavilion described by one contemporary as a 'house of delight'. Such buildings had a long pedigree and since the fifteenth century, Greenwich had been conceived in two parts, incorporating a secluded garden retreat known as a pleasaunce. Henrietta Maria was thus reinstating a traditional form of private royal residence. Decorating this house came to be the queen's principal interest in the mid-1630s and she was frequently to be found inspecting the progress of work. In close collaboration with Inigo Jones, who was handsomely rewarded for his efforts, the king's and queen's international network of connoisseurs were mobilised to create a series of bejewelled interiors.[22]

Figure 48: Henrietta Maria, to the left, is depicted holding a prayer book and standing beside the figures of her three eldest children, Charles II, Mary, Princess of Orange, and James II, within an open courtyard, with a putto flying above, holding a depiction of Prince Charles – the first son of Henrietta Maria and Charles I – who died in infancy. With a view of an ornamental garden in the background and with English verses below: 1633. While this is a celebration of the queen's fertility, it shows her standing on a balustraded terrace overlooking a pleasure garden. It was a view such as this that one would have seen from the north side of the Queen's House Greenwich (or the terrace at Wimbledon Manor) in 1640.

In 1626 the Tuscan painter Orazio Gentileschi entered the service of Charles I. He had previously been working for Henrietta Maria's mother, Marie de' Medici, in Paris and had come to England with her blessing. He was quickly assimilated into the group of connoisseurs and collectors round the king as both painter and advisor but he was superseded in royal favour in the early 1630s by van Dyck and was, instead, absorbed into the queen's circle. Gentileschi painted two large canvases for the great hall at the Queen's House and was commissioned to paint its ceiling. Like the Banqueting House, the ceiling was divided up into compartments by great beams and, in these, Gentileschi painted his *Allegory of Peace reigning over the arts.*

While the ceiling survives, it is not in situ, and has been badly mutilated. This is a shame because while Rubens's Whitehall ceiling publicly trumpeted the triumph of the Stuart dynasty the iconography in the Queen's House was more intimate, representing the national cultural rebirth over which the king and queen saw themselves presiding. All twenty-six figures in the complex allegory are female, acknowledging the role their sex played in the arts. Indeed, the subjects in the wall canvases were female too; the single male presence in the hall was the exquisite bust of the king commissioned by Henrietta Maria from Gianlorenzo Bernini.[23]

No less attention was applied to the two first-floor rooms. Sir Balthasar Gerbier was enlisted to secure the services of the leading Flemish painter Jacob Jordaens to paint twenty-two canvases for the withdrawing room. Elaborate instructions were prepared by Jones; still smarting from the debacle of the Rubens canvases not fitting his ceiling, a piece of string, the length of an English foot, was enclosed to prevent another mix-up. The subject was to be Cupid and Psyche (thinly disguised as the king and queen); the gods surrounding them were to be easily recognisable and required 'ye faces of ye women as beautiful as may be'.

Unlike Jordaens' paintings, none of which survive, the queen's bedchamber remains largely intact and is the only early Stuart royal interior where today one can get a sense of the king and queen's private existence. Through the papal agent at her court the queen secured the

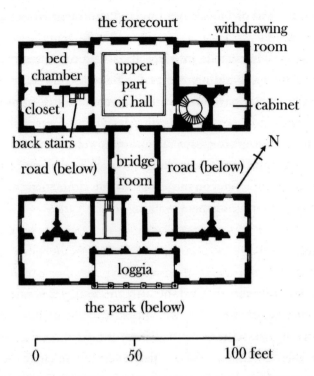

Figure 49: The Queen's House, Greenwich, reconstructed first-floor plan
showing the building as used by Henrietta Maria.

services of Guido Reni to paint the central canvas in a ceiling decorated
by the English Office of Works. Guido's painting never reached England,
but the coving is a unique survival of decorative painting in an early
Stuart royal interior (plate 13). Royal taste was strongly for Italian
Renaissance grotesque work, a form of decoration popular in England
for a century or more but brought to a state of high sophistication by
designers such as Francis Cleyn.[24]

Cleyn and the Office of Works painters John de Critz and Matthew
Goodrich specialised in the intense colours and writhing forms of animals
and men in fantastic architectural compartments that were the essence
of grotesques. Books of prints (including one by Cleyn) circulated to
provide inspiration for these schemes, but their essence was the free rein

of the imagination. The queen's bedchamber also incorporated the arms, badges and crowns of France and England and carefully placed symbols of the Virgin Mary.

The Queen's House tells us more about the early Stuart court than any other surviving building, except the Banqueting House. Conceived as a private pleasure pavilion and dedicated to their love of each other and the love of the arts, Henrietta Maria and Charles I used their contacts across Europe to create a luxurious jewel casket set in a gorgeous landscape. Like the king's privy lodgings at Whitehall and St James's it was only open to a tiny privileged group of close friends, epitomised by Belcamp's painting of them walking in the park.

Wimbledon

The sequence of events that led, in 1639, to Henrietta Maria purchasing Wimbledon Manor is not known. Situated south of the river, an easy six miles from Westminster, it had been built by Thomas Cecil, Lord Burghley in 1588. Thomas had married an heiress in 1564, adding to the family's great wealth. Building seems to have been Thomas's chief interest and it is likely that he took the major hand in designing their spectacularly located and elegantly planned suburban home. Cut into the hillside the house was approached by a series of terraces behind which, on gently rising ground were extensive pleasure gardens.

James I had been a regular visitor to Thomas Cecil in Wimbledon but after Cecil's death the house passed to his son, General Sir Edward Cecil, who spent much of his career abroad. A foreign tourist who visited in 1629 raved about its beauty and especially the gardens the likes of which, he thought, were 'rarely found in England'. When Edward died without a male heir the estate was put up for sale.[25]

There is no evidence that Charles and Henrietta Maria were visitors to the house during the 1630s, or that they were looking for another residence and, with Greenwich, Oatlands, Richmond and Nonsuch it must be wondered why the queen wanted another house. The answer lies in the house itself and the queen's subsequent changes to it.

Though not one brick remains there is surprisingly good information about Wimbledon, enough in fact, to accurately reconstruct it in Henrietta Maria's time. The original manor was not large; only one room deep, its plan was U shaped with the east arm containing galleries, the central section a hall, great chamber and dining room and the western arm containing Cecil's apartments. The beauty and novelty of the place was the way it was cut into the hillside and looked out onto one of the largest and most ambitious gardens of the time in England.[26]

The house was bought for the colossal sum of £16,789 'at the desire of the queen' and was paid for out of revenues of the Court of Wards rather than the queen's own income which could not have supported such a bill.[27]

Although the gardens were already the fame of the place, the queen commissioned André Mollet to restructure them in contemporary fashion. The Tudor garden had been an asymmetrical assemblage of walled compartments containing ponds, a banqueting house and monuments. Mollet imposed a new regularity and symmetry with a strong central axis aligned on the main door on the south front. The sunken garden on the east side became the orange garden laid out with four squares of parterre and an orangery for storing the sixty potted trees over winter.

The principal gardens were approached by a bridge vaulting a sunken area containing lawns, a fountain and an aviary. Either side of the central walk were symmetrically placed square parterres that led to a great avenue that crossed the site, a feature from the Jacobean garden. At either end of this, circular banqueting houses were erected. Beyond was a maze and a more loosely planted area – a wilderness, and in the far south a terrace with two more banqueting houses.[28]

As Mollet and his assistants were at work in the gardens Inigo Jones oversaw remodelling the house, receiving both a fee of over £580 and a special 'bounty' from the queen for his efforts. The east wing had been designed in tandem with a sunken garden and, in the undercroft, Cecil had built a shell grotto. Jones remodelled the principal floor with a new chapel and a large marble parlour giving out onto the terrace overlooking the orange garden. The great first-floor rooms remained much as they were but on the west side Cecil's rooms were remodelled. Here the king and queen had new bedchambers and a shared withdrawing room. Each bedchamber had its own bathroom with tiled floors, lead baths and hot and cold running water. Nearby was a linen room. Adjacent was also a highly ornamented study that had previously been Cecil's with a Dutch stove and various secure cupboards.

The most remarkable addition was Inigo Jones's cruciform stone gallery. The southern arm, ten feet wide with 'many compendious sentences' painted on the walls, led to a bridge into the garden. The north arm opened out into an alcove in which there was a crimson velvet bed with cloth of silver and gold with three chairs, six stools and a carpet to match. The east–west arm ended in a balcony and at the crossing was a stove. How the crossing was handled is not known, but a seventeenth-century plan shows engaged columns and so it was most likely a quadripartite vault. It is a unique layout, and a unique conception: a royal bedchamber that opened directly onto a garden. At the garden door was 'the lord's chamber' presumably a room where someone could be stationed to control access.[29]

The cross gallery contained what was almost certainly the first bed alcove in England. The alcove was a fashionable new feature from French aristocratic houses. At the start of the seventeenth century French bedchambers were large rooms containing a bed, often doubling up as a reception room, but in the late 1620s bedchambers began to be used for more private intercourse and an intimate space was created in the chamber called the ruelle. This was simply the area between the side of the bed and the wall, a place where the owner could receive specially favoured friends. The ruelle gradually became architecturally defined by a niche or alcove in which the bed could be set. The first recorded bed alcove in Paris was at the demolished Hôtel de Rambouillet in the 1630s and, by the 1640s, they were fairly common. For Henrietta Maria to build an alcove at Wimbledon in 1639–40 showed her in tune with the ultimate in contemporary Parisian fashion, an architectural feature associated with privacy and intimacy.[30]

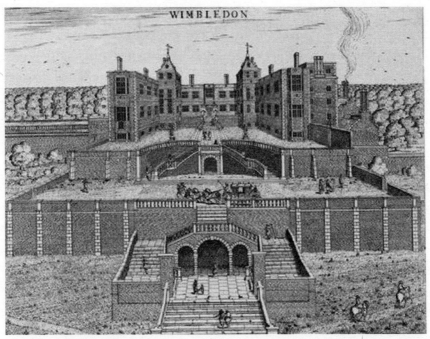

Figure 50: Henry Winstanley, Wimbledon Manor in 1678. The brilliant use of the topography to create a series of spectacular terraces is emphasised by Winstanley's perspective view taken while the house was in the ownership of Lord Danby.

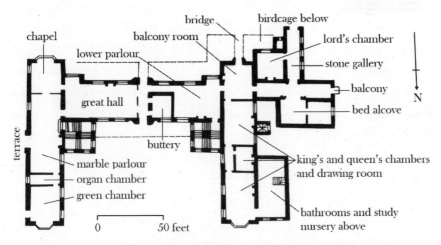

Figure 51: Reconstructed ground-floor plan of Wimbledon Manor in 1649, orientated to align with Winstanley's perspective.

The house contained an extremely limited number of household lodgings – there was a room for a maid, and a pallet chamber for ladies on duty but otherwise there were rooms for only the queen's two closest friends, her childhood nurse Françoise de Monbodiac and Susan Feilding, the Countess of Denbigh, the queen's first lady of the bedchamber, mistress of the robes and holder of her personal purse-strings. On the first floor there was also a nursery suggesting that the queen intended to bring her children to the house.

All this adds up to a unique royal residence without a single traditionally named room of state or any division between outer and inner lodgings. This was a private hideaway, indeed, a royal love nest; a house where the king and queen could reside in complete privacy and enjoy uninterrupted intimacy. The bathrooms, shared withdrawing room, an alcove bedroom, direct access to the gardens are all things impossible even at the newly constructed Queen's House. Wimbledon Manor was the ultimate expression of the king's and queen's love for each other.

NINE

Capital Improvements

Despite all the energy that James I had put into proclaiming new standards for building in London there had hardly been any prosecutions for unregulated building. This was because a royal proclamation expressed the will of the monarch and was not law; for a proclamation to lead to prosecution there had to be a breach of law in the common law courts. The solution to the problem was for James I to get an Act of Parliament putting his ambitions for London's buildings into law.

When parliament met in 1621 and the member for New Shoreham was ejected for procedural irregularities he was replaced, after a by-election, by Inigo Jones. It is likely that Jones was shoe-horned into the seat by the Duke of Buckingham, who controlled it. Jones took his seat on 26 March and two months later a bill for 'the ordering and settling the manner of buildings, and for restraint of inmates and dividing of tenements in and near the Cities of London and Westminster' was given a first reading in the Commons. Its provisions were transparently drawn from the previous series of royal proclamations which had been masterminded by Jones.

The plan to insert Jones into the House of Commons to get a bill through was brilliant, but spectacularly failed. The parliament, which started harmoniously enough, descended into acrimony and the impeachment of the Lord Chancellor. The Commons, scenting blood, wanted to move on to impeach the Duke of Buckingham at which point the king at first suspended and then dissolved the house without a single piece of legislation being passed.[1]

Just over a month after Charles I came to the throne in 1625 he issued his first proclamation regulating building in London. It was the most comprehensive one yet and the detailed architectural specifications were again drafted by Jones. It was clear that the new king was determined to continue his father's ambitions for London. Charles's proclamations had as little chance of success as those of his father but, unlike James, Charles had seen in person how royal intervention could shape a capital city. He had been profoundly impressed by the Plaza Mayor in Madrid. In this huge civic square, commissioned by Philip II and built in 1583–5, Charles had been treated to the most spectacular festival of his stay. The tournament in his honour, according to a Spanish witness, was attended by some 50,000 people and was memorialised in a series of paintings (plate 6). The Plaza Mayor was the centrepiece of Philip's remodelling of Madrid, achieved through private owners building to specifications set out and policed by court architects. The completed square became the principal marketplace of the city, surrounded by uniform brick-built houses raised up on a stone colonnade. Shops under these porticoes sold luxury goods to the court and, from the balconies above, residents watched spectacular royal festivals. In 1623 Charles had also spent two days in Paris and must have seen the Place Royal, Paris's first formal square built by Henry IV and completed by 1612.

In 1629 an opportunity arose for the king to emulate the Spanish and French monarchs. One part of the vast Westminster estate that was not held by the Crown was a forty-acre area on the east side of Westminster known as the Covent Garden. This had been acquired by John, Baron Russell, 1st Earl of Bedford. In 1629 the entrepreneurial 4th earl decided to try and develop this land despite royal prohibition. Charles I instantly took an interest in his plans and viewed the site with his building commission with Inigo Jones at his side. The earl's plans, he decided, were not ambitious enough and the king ordered Jones to draw up a scheme that would create a square like the Plaza Mayor. As building commenced, the king and Jones intervened several more times to ensure that the development accorded with his vision, even to the degree of approving building materials during construction. According to the earl interference by the king and by Jones cost him an additional £6,000 on the development.[2]

In the hands of Inigo Jones, the new square became something far more sophisticated and elegant than the Plaza Mayor. It was never a full square, or Piazza, as it was christened, as only the north and east sides were intended to be built up; the west was occupied by the new church of St Paul and the south opened onto the gardens of Bedford House. But the sides that were erected were raised on an elegant rusticated arcade that became known to Londoners as the 'piazzas'. The design drew on town squares Jones had seen on his continental travels, particularly the Place Royal in Paris and, if John Evelyn is to be believed, on the Piazza d'Arme in Livorno which both he and Jones had seen.[3]

The Earl of Bedford was typical of Caroline courtiers who wanted to live close to Whitehall. During Charles I's reign they started to build and buy houses in the parish of St Martins. While official policy was

Figure 52: Covent Garden, the Piazza looking southeast, 1768.

to discourage this, if new building could enhance the capital city special exceptions were made. It cannot be proved that the king attempted to control the design of all of them but, in the case of Robert Sidney, 2nd Earl of Leicester, he certainly did. Sidney was a leading Caroline diplomat who bought four acres of St Martin's Fields from the Crown. Prohibited from developing it by royal decree, in August 1631, he acquired a licence from Charles I to build a house 'with necessary outhouses buildings and gardens', on the condition that 'the forefronts and all the utter walls and windows of the premises bee wholly made of brick and stone or one of them, the forefronts to be made in that uniform sort and order as may best beautify the place'.[4]

A clutch of half a dozen aristocratic town houses, and the Covent Garden Piazza, show the king working closely with Jones to dignify Westminster with fine regular architecture. But their ambitions were for the whole of London and not just for the court quarter. It may be that Jones alluded to this in *Britannia Triumphans,* a court masque performed in 1638. Five months before its performance the Commission for Buildings had ordered a survey of the London suburb of Southwark to determine which buildings were acceptable and which not. One of the backdrops for *Britannia Triumphans* was a scene 'London far off' which showed the city as seen from Southwark and the view was framed by buildings that were evidently acceptable to Jones and similar in style to those built in Westminster.[5]

The view also contained a building that was unacceptable: St Paul's Cathedral. The cathedral had always been both the public arena of the monarchy and the symbol of the commercial virility of London. In the 1630s it was neither. Battered by a lightning strike that had destroyed the spire and triggered a blaze, it was in a sorry state. James I had wanted to restore this 'famous monument' and had established a commission to oversee the work in 1620. King Charles was even more determined that St Paul's would once again be 'a princely ornament of that royal city, the imperial seat and chamber of this our kingdom' and established a second commission in 1631.

It was not until February 1633 that it was announced that the king's architect, Inigo Jones, would be in charge of the restoration and not

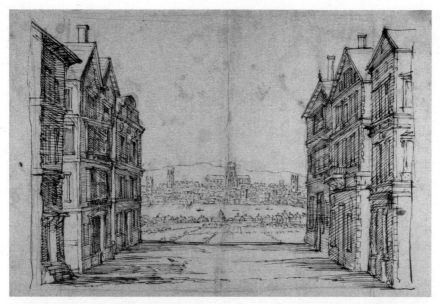

Figure 53: Inigo Jones, 'London far off', a backcloth design for scene I of *Britannia Triumphans*, the masque by William Davenant performed at Whitehall in January 1638.

until the following year that the king would personally finance the most prominent part of Jones's design, a vast Corinthian portico on the west front. This remarkable structure drew on Jones's deep study of Roman architecture and was perfected by means of a series of drawings and a scale model. On the parapet stood statues of Charles and James I, and the entablature bore an inscription naming the king as its builder. Unlike the Banqueting House, which happily blended sixteenth-century Italian sources, this was fiercely, and deliberately, Roman and was intended to be a monument to Stuart sovereignty and Godly rule. In his copy of Vasari's *Lives of the Painters* Jones scribbled 'Rich Princes should leave behind them a fame by building richly': Roman architecture was seen to be the most appropriate way to achieve this.[6]

In early 1632 Jones had produced a masque, written by Aurelian Townshend, called *Albion's Triumph*. It was set in London in the guise of an imperial capital, Albiopolis. King Charles played the part of the emperor Albanactus who wooed Albion's goddess, Henrietta Maria, dressed as Alba. It opened with a proscenium with painted figures of the theory and

Figure 54: Thomas Wyck, the west front of St Paul's Cathedral, *c.*1672, after
the neglect of the Civil War and republic and the Great Fire. The statues of Charles I
and James I have gone, but King Charles's inscription remains. The massiveness of the
balustrade was an important part of the design, giving the portico weight
when seen from Ludgate Hill.

practice of architecture and the first scene was a Roman atrium beyond
which was a glimpse of a royal palace. After the main dance the emperor
and goddess sat together and the scene changed to 'a landscape in which
was a prospect of the king's palace of Whitehall and part of the city of
London seen afar off'. Over this vision innocence, justice, religion, concord
and 'affection to the country' reigned. Charles was fashioned as the emperor
of his imperial capital and Jones was making it all possible.[7]

Three years later, in April 1636, at the request of the City Corporation,
the Privy Council considered the repair of Temple Bar. This was the
gatehouse that spanned Fleet Street at its junction with the Strand defining
the administrative boundary between Westminster and the City. There
were many such gatehouses in London, including the two at Whitehall

Palace, but Temple Bar, a timber-framed structure, was by far the least impressive, and arguably the most prominent. The City Recorder and aldermen were instructed by the Privy Council not to just repair the gate but to work with Inigo Jones on a completely new structure. Jones turned to the arches of Septimius Severus and Constantine in Rome, adapting them to the width of the street, creating a spectacular triumphal arch. The arch was both the entrance to the City and to Westminster, so while on the Strand face there were roundels based on Roman medals depicting shipping and commerce, on the City side, medallions proclaimed the joyfulness and good humour of the body politic. Jones copied the medals from a book in the king's cabinet at Whitehall, suggesting that the images were jointly selected by the king and Jones.[8]

Figure 55: Inigo Jones, sketch elevation for a triumphal arch at Temple Bar, 1636. Jones shows the face towards the City that would have marked the entrance to Westminster. Pasted onto the back of one of the roundels is the note 'medal from ye King's Prints', referring to a book of medals in the king's cabinet at Whitehall. The sculptural panels are copied from prints of the Roman originals.

Grand projects

King Charles's vision for a more majestic London came to a culmination with two immensely ambitious projects that would have transformed the status of the capital and the monarchy within it. Both were brought forward in 1638 at a turning point in the king's life and reign.

In July 1637 the king had told his nephew, the Elector Palatine, that he was 'the happiest king or prince in all Christendom'. He would have been ungrateful to think otherwise. He was in his prime, happily married, with healthy sons, the country was peaceful and prosperous and the legality of his non-parliamentary taxation, Ship Money, had been upheld in court. Just eleven months later this self-satisfaction had been shattered, and he was involved in military preparations to go to war against his Scottish subjects.

Charles was a Scottish king, but he was not a Scot. Although he retained Anglicised Scots in his household, he had little affinity with his country of birth. The king, obsessed with correct form and ceremony, occupied with his collections, tucked away with his family, and with an unshakable belief in his monarchical authority, was fundamentally out of harmony with his northern subjects. It took him eight years to make the journey to Scotland to be crowned and, when he arrived in 1633, it was the first time Scots had seen their monarch for more than fifteen years. The king's sojourn in his northern capital convinced him to ignore the strongly held Presbyterianism of the Scots Kirk and impose uniformity of religious practice across his dominions. In 1637 he ordered the compilation of a Scottish prayer book to be used in all churches north of the border.

It was the imposition of this new form of worship by Scottish bishops under royal authority that triggered a revolt. In February 1638, the protestors drew up a covenant in defence of religion asserting parliamentary supremacy and questioning Charles's authority. By the early summer a furious king, unwilling to concede either his power, or that of the bishops, was already considering military action against the covenanters. In the short space of a year a happy, quietly confident monarch had been transformed into a prince determined to assert his might, majesty and right against his subjects.

Over the next three years Charles was a more visible presence in his capital than he had been during the previous decade. In October 1638 he welcomed his mother-in-law Marie de' Medici with a magnificent formal entry watched by tens of thousands of citizens; in April 1640 the opening of parliament, the first in eleven years, was accompanied by the king riding in state in his parliament robes surrounded by the nobility and, in the autumn of 1641, he made a full state entry into the City on his return from Scotland.[9]

This is the context in which, in 1638, Inigo Jones was instructed to consider the Strand elevation of Denmark House. Like most medieval town mansions the street frontage of Denmark House was a narrow gatehouse set between rows of shops let commercially to city traders; this brought in a handsome income to the queen, but inevitably reduced the architectural presence of the house on the street. In fact, on an occasion such as the entry of Marie de' Medici, the facade of Denmark House was an architectural nonentity compared to the boastful facades of courtier houses such as Northumberland House at Charing Cross.

Jones produced a scheme, approved by the king and queen, to boost the impact of Denmark House with a new 35-bay facade of two storeys and an attic. The central eleven bays were closely based on a grandiose scheme by Andrea Palladio for re-fronting the Ducal palace in Venice. The range was two rooms deep and contained a central gateway giving access into the main courtyard and a second entrance to Denmark House Yard and the Catholic chapel. It added no new state rooms to the queen's palace which remained behind the facade, and the ground-floor frontage, at least, was intended to retain shops let on a commercial basis. The scheme was not a functional necessity, it was a magnificent re-rendering of the status quo to aggrandise the queen's majesty. The Office of Works began to assemble materials for the start of work, but nothing more is heard of the project after 1638.[10]

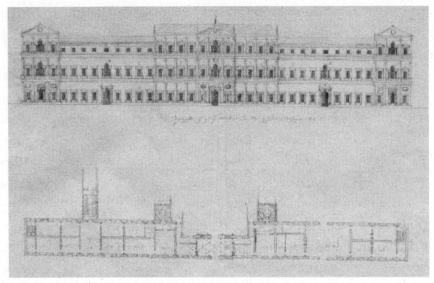

Figure 56: John Webb, street facade and plan for Denmark House
marked 'taken' 1638. The plan shows shops on the Strand front
and the earlier courtyard behind.

The second project under consideration that year was a complete
rebuilding of Whitehall Palace. The ideas that seem to have been briefly
contemplated in 1625 were for a reconstruction of the privy gallery, but
in 1638 the scheme was for a hugely ambitious recasting of the whole
of Westminster. The problem with Whitehall had always been that it
was bisected by a main road; half of the palace was in St James's Park
and the other half on the riverside. This had a purpose when the principal form of transport was barge, but Charles I mostly travelled by
coach and direct river access was no longer essential. Equally important
was the fact that Whitehall, with Scotland Yard and the palace gardens,
occupied the entire waterfront from Charing Cross to modern day
Richmond House Terrace, denying Westminster any meaningful
commercial wharfage.[11]

Jones devised a plan that rerouted King Street further east to run
alongside the river joining Charing Cross with Cannon Row and terminating on axis with the north door of Westminster Hall. This was a
new commercial thoroughfare, but it was also a ceremonial way. The
new road was the culmination of a parade that would have begun at

the massive portico of St Paul's Cathedral, passed under the triumphal arch at Temple Bar, passed the new facade of Denmark House, with its street-fronting balconies, and then, turning north at Charing Cross, passed Whitehall to the east and ended aligned on the twin towers of Westminster Hall, the most ancient symbol of English monarchy.[12]

The new Whitehall, itself with a spectacular street frontage, would be, like St James's, within the secure walled compound of the royal parkland. Jones, and his draughtsman, John Webb, must have been intensively concentrating on the project because forty drawings for it survive, perhaps only half of the number originally produced. The idea was for a single rectangular building perforated by eleven court-yards, the central one a great colonnaded square. Unconstrained by pre-existing structures a square is an obvious form to adopt, but it is possible that Jones was asked to base his plan on the Escorial, seen by King Charles in 1623, to which the Whitehall design bears a strong resemblance. It is also possible that Jones was influenced by a conjec-tural reconstruction of the Temple of Solomon published in 1596 by a Spanish Jesuit, Juan Bautista Villalpando, which is also a square containing multiple courts.[13]

What is certain is that as the plans developed the king was closely engaged. Sketches were shown to him and options discussed; the favoured solutions were marked 'taken' and the rejected options crossed out. Indeed the drawings that remain are an extraordinary chronicle of the evolving ideas about what a new royal palace should comprise. Amongst them there are some that are highly finished and obviously designed for presentation but because many drawings have been lost, it is now impossible to discern the chosen plan if, indeed, there was one.

In most, if not all schemes, the Banqueting House was to be demol-ished and presumably its treasured ceiling relocated. The royal lodgings were to face the park and the principal public facade would face the new street that ran alongside the river. Ranged on the first floor, and approached by a magnificent stair, the layout of the state rooms, and the privy lodgings that adjoined them, replicated existing arrangements at Whitehall: the challenge was how to arrange the public spaces.

One of the earliest plans proposes a truly remarkable double-height colonnaded council chamber with an apse and coffered barrel vault. Jones had built an apse in the Banqueting House alluding to the seat of judgment in a Roman basilica and an unbuilt scheme for the Court of Star Chamber at Westminster from 1617 prefigured the Whitehall design in many of its elements. Yet such an emphatic setting for the meeting of the Privy Council conceived at the end of the period of the king's personal rule speaks to Charles's conception of royal government revolving round his own council. In a variant scheme there is another astonishing architectural statement: a vast domed chapel built on a Greek cross plan; detailed sketches show an altar in a niche with a life-size crucifix in a pedimented aedicule. Such a Roman Catholic composition would have made the Denmark House chapel seem like a Puritan preaching box.[14]

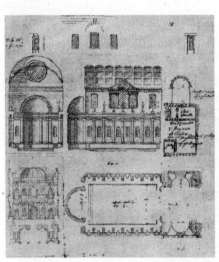
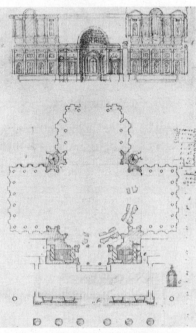

Figure 57: Drawings by John Webb c.1638. *Left*: sketches for the new Whitehall council chamber, a room of unparalled Roman grandeur in England at the time, the apse perhaps the symbolic seat of the king in council. *Right*: sketches for the proposed new chapel, at the east end a raised royal pew, and at the west a chancel focused on the high altar. Deep transepts contain side altars.

In the most complete scheme that survives, the excessive expressions of monarchical rule and religious ceremonialism have been watered down and the most striking feature is a circular colonnaded courtyard on the park front linking the state rooms at first-floor level and providing a covered way below. Neither Jones nor the king had seen the circular courtyard in the early sixteenth-century palace of Charles V at Granada but Jones would have known Scamozzi's reconstruction of Pliny's villa at Laurentium that included such a feature. The circular court would have been spectacular, but had no obvious function; it created an arena in the middle of the royal lodgings and perhaps could have been used for performance.

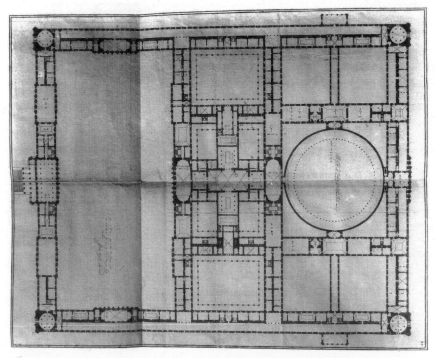

Figure 58: Henry Flitcroft's redrawing of John Webb's rendering of Inigo Jones's scheme for Whitehall, published in William Kent's *Designs of Inigo Jones*. In this scheme the Banqueting House was probably intended to be retained and is shown at the bottom left of the great court. Round the circular court to the east are the state rooms, with the privy lodgings overlooking St James's Park on the far right.

The same scheme incorporates the Banqueting House, either in situ, or dismantled and re-erected further west. If it is shown in its original position the Thames would have had to be embanked and the east facade of the new palace would have been on the waterfront. The road would have continued much on its existing alignment and great gate-houses either side of the central court would have defined the public highway which would have run through the middle of the palace.

The facades, some of which were drawn to a fine presentation standard, are impressive in their unforgiving horizontality broken by occasional gables and pediments. They are made of a series of small blocks themselves composed of the whole canon of ancient and Renaissance architecture lavishly applied from plinth to entablature. It is a rich plate and perhaps a bit indigestible; while the Banqueting House is satisfying in its balance and harmony Jones struggles in these elevations to create something greater than the sum of its parts. But the public rooms, if they had ever been built, would have conveyed an appropriately senatorial atmosphere for a monarch modelling himself on a Roman emperor.

While none of these schemes ever left the drawing board there was one symbolic intervention that was achieved. The Tower of London had long been a symbol of the might and majesty of monarchy. It was the place where ambassadors disembarked and transferred to their coaches before being driven through the city of London. In 1629 Charles I had ordered that on all 'solemnities or triumphs' the new British flag should be flown from the White Tower, the massy Norman keep at the centre of the castle, and a new flag 33 feet long was delivered and flown from a flagpole 60 feet high.

In 1636 the king had resolved to do something about the dilapidated state of the Tower but nothing meaningful was done until 1638. That year, as ordnance was being amassed for war in Scotland, the king personally inspected the stores, and a massive repair programme began on the White Tower, by far the most visible part of the fortress. Work started on the west side, the elevation facing the city. Decayed stone was cut out and new Portland stone windows were inserted to the design of Inigo Jones. These were in a gentle sub-Norman style in harmony with the ancient fabric. As works drew to a close the whole White Tower was whitewashed, leaving it a gleaming symbol of royal authority.[15]

Charles the builder

On 31 October 1634 Phineas Pett, England's leading shipbuilder, presented a large model of a warship to Charles I in the privy gallery at Hampton Court. Just under four months previously, on one of his periodic trips to Pett's shipyard in Woolwich, the king had expressed the ambition to build a truly giant warship, the largest ever constructed. It was to weigh 1,637 tons and have 100 guns, something that the port authorities thought impossible; the largest ship that fought against the Spanish Armada had weighed only 760 tons. The model at Hampton Court was the result of this commission. After scrutinising it, and cross-examining Pett, it was taken from Hampton Court to Whitehall and work on detailed design began.

Charles was fascinated by the navy, by ships and sailing and from early in his reign stressed to his admirals that England should gain sovereignty over its waters. As war with France and Spain had ended in 1630 he had begun a shipbuilding programme, the culmination of which was the *Sovereign of the Seas*, easily the most powerful warship in the world. The ship was immediately celebrated in paint, engravings and elegiac books; it was a legend, known to terrified Dutch mariners as the 'golden devil'.[16]

Charles loved the technicalities of marine engineering, but he was also obsessed with aesthetics. The *Sovereign* was a floating work of art covered with a programme of carvings devised by the dramatist and poet Thomas Heywood and approved by the king. His scheme enlisted classical, heraldic, mythological and historical themes to emphasise Charles's rule over what he called the English seas. The figurehead depicted King Edgar on horseback, the supposed founder of the Royal Navy trampling seven kings underfoot. The ship was painted black and the carving was gilded – there were no other colours. The ship was the most expensive to be built for a century to come: the final bill was £65,586 16s 9d, of which the carving and gilding alone accounted for £6,691, only £600 less than what it cost Henrietta Maria to complete the Queen's House, Greenwich.[17]

King Charles loved nothing more than to be with designers, architects, painters and craftsmen; he liked to discuss his own projects and those of his courtiers, opining on matters of style and taste. His sister, Elizabeth of Bohemia, when commissioning a new house in Rhenen in Gelderland, sent designs to Sir Dudley Carleton, the former English ambassador at The Hague; Charles I asked to see them, sending back his detailed views on the design to his brother-in-law. This was typical of the close interest he took in artistic matters.[18]

One of the king's earliest biographers, Sir Edward Walker, Garter King of Arms, Charles's secretary of war and close confidant, described

Figure 59: John Payne, 'The true portraiture of his Majesty's royal ship *The Sovereign of the Seas* built in the year 1637'. This massive print, three feet long, was commissioned by Phineas Pett, the ship's designer, in 1638. It was intended for public display and was a popular celebration of the national flagship.

his master in 1651 as 'magnificent and a lover of order', a point emphasised, he thought, by 'the reception of ambassadors, regularity of his court and attendance, solemnity of his service, state of solemn feasts, riches of his household-stuff, and by his pious care and great expense in the rebuilding of the west end of St Paul's Church, with his design to have new built his palace at Whitehall'.[19]

Like his father, Charles I held a distinction between architecture of state and architecture of necessity. Walker's 'magnificence and order' well summarise Charles's attitude to the architecture of state – these buildings represented his sovereignty. The Banqueting House, the portico at St Paul's, and the designs for Whitehall were monuments of state, and the classical orders of architecture which they used articulated his vision of an ordered hierarchy in which his own divinely ordained authority was supreme. Inigo Jones understood how to express this, using components of public buildings from classical antiquity. It should be no surprise that the Banqueting House and St Paul's had negligible impact on contemporary architectural design: they were buildings specifically fashioned in the style of majesty, an architectural language appropriate only to the king.[20]

Charles's personal architectural taste was quite different. Under James I architecture had been underpinned by heraldic and chivalric display and an eclecticism inspired by the international market in architectural prints. Starting in and around London in the early 1620s taste for a plainer and more simple type of building developed. These buildings were not inspired by Roman public architecture with columns and heavy entablatures, they were astylar, that is to say without columns or pilasters on their facades. In fact Jacobean architects used columnar architecture more than Caroline ones; the new style of buildings were plain, reserved and relied on the proportions of wall to window to achieve an elegant austerity. Inside they were suffused with the richness of the Italian Renaissance, especially the influence of Venice. The Earl of Pembroke's house at Wilton, which Charles I admired more than any other new country house, and which can still be visited, encapsulated this taste.

The coming of Charles's court had seen a changing aesthetic spirit. Although Prince Henry had been seized with chivalric ideals, Charles's boyish enthusiasm for the chivalric exploits of the tiltyard had died by the time he became king. Elizabethan and Jacobean chivalric display in court festivities ends after 1625. King Charles wanted a new Whitehall to express his sovereignty through the architectural apparatus of Ancient Rome, not as the heroics of the high Middle Ages. His private residences likewise were shorn of Jacobean exuberance and re-fashioned as Italianate villas with gorgeously rich interiors. The king's architectural tastes were, like his life, split between his persona as anointed sovereign, and that of a devoted husband and family man. Underlying both was an unshakable conviction in his God-given responsibility to rule.

TEN

God and My Right

The religion of James I

Religion was the pivot on which the court turned. Before the Reformation it was hard to disentangle secular and religious royal ceremonial: both glorified God and the sovereign in a mutually reinforcing pact. Royal houses had their household chapels, private oratories, and the larger ones, attached friaries and colleges of priests; the royal itinerary and the monarch's calendar was fixed by religious observance in these theatres of devotion.

Henry VIII took the first steps to change this. To sweep away opposition to his divorce he abolished court monasteries and centred royal religion on the Chapel Royal, his independent, personal, ecclesiastical establishment. But ceremonial and liturgy at court remained much as it had done before. In 1558 the sweeping changes in religious practice that had taken place under Protestant Edward VI and Catholic Mary I presented a complicated inheritance to Queen Elizabeth. The problem she faced in her own palaces was that Protestant reforms had extracted from court religion its ceremonial and hierarchical content. Whereas the old creed had provided a vehicle for display and magnificence emphasising the special relationship between God and his chosen ruler, the Church of England did none of this. In fact, Elizabeth would have probably agreed with King Charles II who remarked to the French ambassador that 'no other creed matches so well with the absolute dignity of kings' than Catholicism.[1]

The Chapel Royal under Elizabeth therefore developed a unique type of ceremonious Protestantism only found at court. It retained and adapted elements of traditional religion to uphold the dignity of queenship: the queen's chapel retained images, crucifixes and candles banned in the parishes, maintained an elaborate musical tradition, and was architecturally more splendid than parish worship. Elizabeth's weekly procession to chapel and back again became a quasi-liturgical event with people falling to their knees as if being blessed by a bishop, cardinal, or the Pope himself.

Elizabeth inaugurated a new type of religious observance for a new sort of Protestant court. The hybrid she created was not only a public expression of her personal beliefs, it advertised the religious preferences of the supreme head of the Church of England. This is why what took place in the Chapel Royal was not a private matter, it was of enormous concern to the nation as a whole. While the Elizabethan chapel was grudgingly accepted by most, for others, the so-called Godly, who wanted the Protestant Reformation to go further, it was symbolic of crypto-Catholicism at the heart of the state.[2]

James I was no stranger to this sort of religious controversy. The Scots Reformation had not been triggered by an act of state, as in England, but by a rebellion against authority. In 1560, in defiance of their monarch, the Scots parliament had dismantled the Catholic Church. The reformed church, or Kirk, emphasised its independence from the state: the Godly argued that there was a spiritual Kingdom and a temporal one, in the former the king was merely a parishioner and only in the latter he ruled. Many of them also argued for a Presbyterian church, a self-governing federation of parishes without a hierarchical structure under bishops.

In 1584, on assuming his majority, James launched his kingship with a series of Acts of Parliament asserting his supremacy over both church and state. Although these were christened the *Black Acts,* and although he crossed swords with the Godly in the Kirk, James was, as he said of himself in 1607, 'ever for the Medium in every thing'. While his court contained several prominent Roman Catholics, a minister of the Kirk was invited to write the preface to his first book on theology.[3]

The headquarters of James's personal chapel in Scotland was at Holyrood. Here, the large fifteenth-century chapel on the south side of the court had been purged of what were regarded as popish ornaments during James's minority. In 1583, in preparation for his independent rule, it had been refitted to his 'honour' with a royal seat and new panelling and pulpit. It does not seem to have been a particularly impressive room, unlike the splendid new chapel that James built at Stirling, described previously. In 1586 James appointed a master of his chapel in charge of music and six choirboys; there was also a lutenist, three chaplains and ministers who were responsible for preaching.[4]

If the king's new chapel at Stirling represented his preferences in ecclesiastical architecture James would have found the richly decorated Elizabethan royal chapels much to his liking. Perhaps an early indication of his tastes in England was the cleaning in 1603–4 of a painting of the Virgin in the Whitehall chapel and the alteration of another to depict Joseph. James maintained Sunday as the principal court day, processing to and from the chapel royal ceremoniously attended by leading courtiers; his household staff attended their own service earlier in the morning. James also always attended on Tuesday mornings in thanksgiving for his deliverance from the Gowrie conspiracy in 1600. He was also, no doubt, pleased to be able to celebrate Christmas in style, something impossible in Scotland where it was regarded as a papistical festival.[5]

More than anything James liked to listen to sermons; his progress south in 1603 has been characterised as an orgy of hunting and feasting; it was equally an orgy of sermonising which reached its culmination at the king's arrival in Greenwich when he appointed eleven chaplains in ordinary to his Chapel. They preached in a rota in which the king took great interest. In addition to Tuesdays and Sundays, the series of Lent sermons, which were a feature of Tudor court life, continued and these were normally delivered in the preaching place, the large courtyard at Whitehall adjacent to the council chamber. In a pulpit in the middle of this court sermons were delivered to hundreds of listeners, and to the king and his guests, listening from the window of the council chamber.[6]

Court preachers would follow the king out of London: at Royston and Newmarket sermons would be delivered in the presence chamber or, on occasion, the king would hear them in the parish church; the church at Royston seems to have been partially rebuilt for the Jacobean court. On a Tuesday, when the king was hunting, the sermon would be at eight o'clock in the morning, before he took out his hounds. One sermon at Royston was so good that after he returned from the hunt he put it beneath his pillow at bedtime, but as he also ordered an hourglass for the chapel – his lust for sermons had limits.[7]

After many promises, and a few false starts, 'with salmon-like instinct', as he described it, James finally decided to return to his homeland in the spring of 1617. The previous May orders had been given for the repair of Edinburgh Castle, Holyrood, Stirling and Falkland, none of which had been in royal use for fourteen years. Large sums were expended: £40,000 at Holyrood, £20,000 at Falkland and a colossal £53,000 at Edinburgh Castle where the royal lodgings were virtually rebuilt.

Bracing itself for the influx of some 5,000 people, Edinburgh was surveyed to ensure there was enough suitable accommodation. The streets were to be swept, beggars removed, the city tennis courts cleaned, and hay and oats procured for 5,000 horses. Special care was taken to ensure that there would be lodgings close to Holyrood for the king's personal servants.

James had many reasons for his pilgrimage north, but perhaps the most important was to further the cause of religious uniformity in his kingdoms. The Kirk had refused to accept the ceremonies of the Church of England and James's participation in the English rite in Edinburgh was intended to set an example. Inigo Jones was instructed to redesign the chapel royal in Holyrood which was to be brought into line with the royal chapels in England. He engaged Nicholas Stone, England's leading sculptor, and Matthew Goodrich, a painter much employed by the king, to execute the designs. The joinery was made in London and shipped to Edinburgh and Stone and Goodrich followed in person. The chapel was to be refitted in English style with a west screen and royal pew with windows into the body of the chapel; there was to be an elaborately carved organ and choir stalls, statues of the Evangelists and Apostles and an interior richly painted and gilded. The statues of the apostles were scrapped after James received a letter of complaint from the Scottish bishops; not, the king assured them, to ease their consciences but because there was not enough time to make them.

The king arrived in Edinburgh on 16 May 1617 accompanied by his chaplains, including the then Dean of Gloucester, William Laud, and twenty-four choristers of the Chapel Royal who had arrived by sea. For the Scots, even more contentious than the 'graven images' carved by Nicholas Stone, was kneeling to take communion, as this 'Romish Practice', they believed, was a veneration of the bread and wine. On James's second day in Scotland a choral service was celebrated in the new chapel and on Whit-Sunday he took communion; some Scottish noblemen and a few bishops knelt, but many were unhappy with this, the use of vestments and the prayer book.[8]

In the aftermath of the royal homecoming (as it was billed), in the so-called Five Articles of Perth, James forced through orders to kneel at communion as well as the full celebration of Christmas and Easter. For good measure he also ordered that, after his departure, sung services should be continued daily at Holyrood. Without the king's presence the order was not obeyed. Sir Anthony's Weldon's witty and barbed account of the Scots during the royal visit speculated on the fate of the Holyrood chapel: 'but for those graven images in his new beautified chapel, they threaten to pull them down soon after his departure, and to make of them a burnt offering to appease . . . the almighty for suffering such idolatry to enter the kingdom. The organs I think will find mercy, because, as they say, there is some affinity between them and bagpipes'.[9]

In the English court, from about 1618, there was an increasing emphasis on the decoration and embellishment of royal chapels, the so-called 'beauty of holiness'. This was accompanied by changes in the liturgy and its musical setting to make it more ceremonious – indeed a comprehensive integration of 'beauty' into worship. After William Laud became Archbishop of Canterbury in 1633 this became a national programme

often known as *Laudianism*. In most churches it merely meant an attempt
to impose a sense of order and decorum on the perceived chaos of Jacobean
parochial worship, principally through the introduction of altar rails and
the use of vestments. But elsewhere, particularly under private patronage
at the universities of Oxford and Cambridge, there was a re-emergence
of forms of decoration and images absent since the Reformation – angels,
cherubs, saints and even the occasional Madonna and child.[10]

These concerns were brought to the royal chapels by a series of royal
deans with what can be described as a Laudian outlook. Lancelot
Andrewes was the first of these and he was succeeded by William Laud
himself, William Juxon, and then Matthew Wren. These four men were
closely associated and shared a reasonably common and coherent vision
that saw royal chapels primarily as sacramental space rather than being
merely preaching houses.[11]

Changes in liturgy and decoration in the royal chapels began around
1620. In 1621–2 the ceiling of the Whitehall chapel was gilded, two statues
were repainted and their garments gilded, the stained glass was carefully
repaired. Then at Greenwich a much more thoroughgoing refitting was
undertaken. While the chapels at Whitehall and Hampton Court had
had first-floor royal pews separated from the body of the chapel by a
glazed screen, Greenwich had not. In 1622–3 a great new window lavishly
carved with pendants, putti bearing the king's arms, and winged victories
was installed, the walls were painted with an elaborate mural scheme by
John de Critz and the ceiling was repainted and gilded.

In 1623 James issued a set of regulations for behaviour in the royal
chapels enforcing dignity, order and reverence. Courtiers were instructed
to approach and enter the chapel in an orderly fashion not wearing boots
or spurs. Once inside strict rules were laid down, setting out where the
various ranks were entitled to sit and how headwear was to be worn –
excepting privy councillors, courtiers beneath the rank of a baron were
forbidden to enter the royal pew.[12]

These changes, while undoubtedly in tune with the views of Dean
Andrewes, had a far more practical aspect to them. On 20 July 1623 the
marriage treaty between Prince Charles and the Spanish Infanta was

ratified. This act was a prelude to what James hoped to be the magnificent celebration of the royal marriage in his own palaces at Whitehall and Greenwich.

The religion of Charles I

Charles's Spanish trip gave the Catholic world hope that the next King of England would not be a heretic. In fact, it was assumed in Madrid in 1623 that his arrival heralded the prince's imminent conversion, and the Pope himself wrote encouraging him to take the great step. The Spanish court set out to demonstrate not only the truth but the splendour of Catholicism and, as it was Easter, they redoubled the scale and elaboration of ceremonial. Corpus Christi, which followed in June, was even more magnificent with the greatest procession that had been seen up until that time in Madrid. At its heart was a consecrated host in a magnificent monstrance; as it passed, everyone, including Prince Charles knelt in adoration.

This was, in fact, exactly what James had ordered his son to do faced

Figure 60: William Marshall, frontispiece to *Eikon Basilike*, 1649. Charles I in his parliament robes looks towards a heavenly crown. On the floor is a heavy earthly crown, put to one side as he grasps the crown of thorns (symbolising suffering). Outside is the rock of his faith in stormy seas, and a palm tree still standing though weighed down with cares.

with such a situation. The king had issued detailed instructions for the prince's chapel in Spain: his chaplains were instructed to act in a way 'as near the Roman form as can be lawfully done for it hath been my way to goe with the church of Rome *usque ad aras* (as far as the altar)'. The prince's chaplains were laden with plate, vestments, altar frontals, carpets, curtains and even prayer books in Spanish. Ironically what seemed to James and Charles like a chapel on the verge of Rome was assumed, by the Spaniards, to be deeply Calvinist and an insult to their religion.[13]

Charles's experience of court religion in Madrid did not push him nearer to Rome, but unquestionably impressed him with its ceremony and splendour. Matthew Wren, one of the chaplains who had accompanied the prince, and later became Dean of the Chapel Royal, was quizzed on Charles's religious beliefs on his return from Spain; he assured Lancelot Andrewes that, when king, Charles would uphold the doctrine and discipline of the Church of England better than his father. Unlike his father's faith, founded on theological disputation, Charles I's was founded on his private devotions and on the proper ordering of his places of worship, the 'beauty of holiness'. This extended to his bedchamber and his closet which were filled with devotional books and paintings as much as the royal chapels. Charles himself, unlike his father, joined in prayers at chapel rather than arriving in time to hear the sermon and insisted on order and decorum amongst the congregation. He reissued his father's regulations and, in the 1630s, issued a new series of orders for the governance of the chapel.[14]

When William Laud became Archbishop of Canterbury in 1633 he found that his chapel at Lambeth Palace, his London residence was, in his words, 'nasty' and he could not use it without 'distain'. The works he commissioned to beautify it were later recorded by William Prynne who obtained entry to the chapel after Laud's arrest. Prynne was a lawyer who wanted to record the archbishop's 'Popish' and 'superstitious' innovations to aid his prosecution. The plan he produced of the Lambeth chapel is as close as can be got to understanding the layout of royal chapels in Charles I's reign.

For the Godly reformers like Prynne, who disliked the increasingly rich decoration of the royal chapels, the real abomination was the positioning of the communion table against the east wall like an altar. This meant that communion was celebrated with the celebrant's back to the congregation in the Catholic manner, rather than everyone equally participating round a table. The Lambeth plan shows this precise arrangement; on the altar were candlesticks and a large basin. It was raised up on steps that are themselves part of a raised and railed platform. There was also a music desk, a lectern raised up on three steps, and a table at which 'they kneel to read the litanie'.[15]

In the 1630s all the chapels royal were embellished and reordered to conform to the Lambeth plan. Charles I believed that this was merely reinstating the forms of worship adopted by his Tudor predecessors. Defending the arrangements at Whitehall in 1641 Matthew Wren pointed out that 'in the King's Royal Chapels . . . the Holy Table hath ever since the Reformation stood at the upper End of the Choir'.[16]

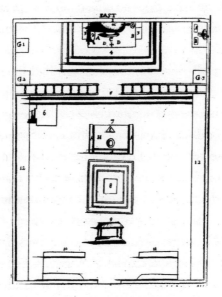

Figure 61: William Prynne, plan of Archbishop William Laud's Lambeth Palace chapel in 1646. Laud was the guiding hand behind the reordering of the royal chapels, and this plan shows how the Chapels Royal must have been set up in Charles I's reign. The altar is at the top, sited against the east wall and raised on five steps. A reading desk is in front of the ensemble.

Charles I in Scotland

Charles I ruled over three kingdoms, each with a different religious settlement and each split within itself as to the nature of the national church. James I had hoped for some sort of uniformity in his dominions and had used his 1617 visit to Scotland to try and encourage this. On his accession, in 1625, Charles returned to the issue, requiring Scots to kneel at communion and insisting that the Scottish Privy Council take communion in the Holyrood chapel at the sound of a trumpet. These were, at first, remote requests but, in the early 1630s, they became urgent and personal as Charles began to plan a visit to Scotland.[17]

Ever since his accession Charles had promised a 'homecoming' to the land of his birth which he had left aged three and had no memory of. He returned as a 33-year-old monarch knowing he was God's anointed lieutenant on earth. This powerful conviction was not scaffolded by a deep schooling in practical politics for, although James had larded his son with advice, he gave him no practical experience of rule. Charles was thus principally guided only by the most powerful force in his life – his conscience.

In considering his homecoming Charles had no real understanding of Scotland or the Scots and had to rely on reports from others as to the state of his northern kingdom. Nevertheless, he had two strongly held ambitions, both of which had architectural consequences. First, he wanted to impose episcopal discipline on the Scottish church, to establish a bishopric in Edinburgh and a cathedral in its principal church, St Giles'. Secondly, he was determined to preside over the Scots parliament in a magisterial setting that dignified both his office and the Scottish nation. As a consequence, in the spring of 1632, the town council of Edinburgh, under royal instruction, began to lay plans for rearranging St Giles' Church and building a new Parliament House. The first was for the proper setting of divine service and the second for the 'convenience' of parliament and as a 'credit to the kingdom'.[18]

In 1561 St Giles' Kirk had met the full force of the Scottish Reformation. The chancel had been walled up to create, in the nave, a more visible and audible preaching place surrounded by galleries. The former chancel became part of the Tolbooth, Edinburgh's principal municipal building, courthouse, prison, and sometime meeting place of parliament. The king's orders were to eject the secular activities from the church and reinstate the chancel. The new dean was sent to Durham Cathedral to examine the chancel there as a model.[19]

Meanwhile work started on a new building for parliament, the Privy Council and the Lords of Session, the highest Scottish law court. It was designed by the King's Master of Works in Scotland, James Murray,

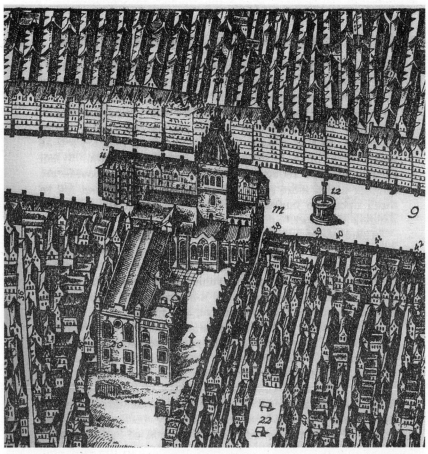

Figure 62: James Gordon of Rothiemay, Map of Edinburgh, 1647. This detail shows St Giles' Cathedral (as it was known in 1633–8 and 1661–89). South of it is the Parliament House, lying on a north-south axis, and the civic square to its east.

whom the king knighted (in absentia) during the design process. Just as Charles II later remotely controlled royal building works in Edinburgh from London, his father did the same, and must have approved of Murray's plans which created not only the new building but a civic square expressing architecturally the symbiosis of church and state.

The new parliament building contained three rooms on the ground floor: entered through a massive triumphal doorcase towards its north end, a great hall served as the meeting place for parliament. At the south end, raised up on six steps, was the royal chair and canopy of state; the representatives of the shires and burghs sat in the middle and the bishops and nobility on benches round the edges. Although the hall had an openwork timber ceiling that emphasised tradition and continuity, externally the flat parapets proclaimed a more modern aspect. The two other chambers were used by the Privy Council and the Lords of Session.[20]

In anticipation of the king's visit debate had been intense as to where in Edinburgh his coronation should take place. St Giles' was not going to be ready and so it was decided that it would be staged in the Abbey Church of Holyrood, where Charles's mother had been crowned and many of his ancestors buried. In fact, the Abbey Church had also lost its chancel and, since 1570, had been just the nave which was used as a parish church. In January 1633 orders were given to urgently make this truncated church suitable and some £17,000 was laid out on rebuilding the east and west gables, installing a fine new east window and reordering the interior to create a royal pew at the west end. The west steeples were rebuilt and, in one, a new peal of bells hung, sent up by sea from London.[21]

There was a large communion table set like an altar at the east end covered with tapestry. On the table stood a richly bound bible and prayer book, two candlesticks, and a large alms dish; behind was a tapestry depicting the crucifixion. Charles had shipped from London five paintings, presumably of sacred subjects, which were also hung in the abbey. The new windows were punched into the formerly gloomy church, filling it with light and illuminating the new furnishings and vestments and robes of the participants. On 18 June the king's coronation procession came from the royal lodgings at Edinburgh Castle to

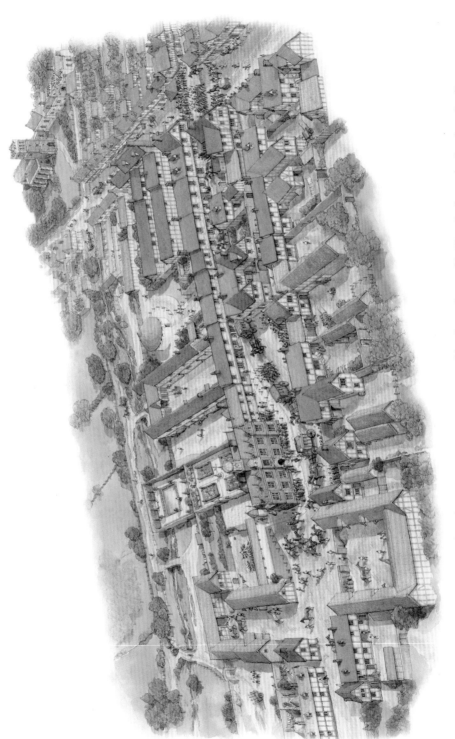

Royston town centre as it may have been in c.1620 as reconstructed by the author and brilliantly drawn by Stephen Conlin.

Paul van Somer, Anne of Denmark, 1617. This painting shows the queen at her favourite house, Oatlands, with her hunting dogs and her gardens in the background. It is the image of a country woman, devoted to sport, but the scroll over her head reminds the viewer of her regality, with the motto 'My greatness is from on high'. The Queen commissioned this painting which hung in her gallery at Oatlands.

Paul van Somer, Queen Anna of Denmark 1617–18. In this sumptuous portrait van Somer employed another hand to create the architectural fantasy in the background. Possibly executed by Inigo Jones, it shows Anna as a patron of avant garde architectural styles.

Robert Peake, Prince Henry of Wales, c.1610. This painting was probably commissioned to send to the Duke of Savoy as part of marriage negotiations. The Prince chose to be depicted in front of a castle, possibly Kenilworth with its hunting park behind.

Paul van Somer, King James I in his coronation robes at Whitehall, with the Banqueting House as the background, *c.*1620. This painting is not only valuable for what it tells of the importance James accorded to the Banqueting House, but also for the details it gives of the interior of a Jacobean state room. The wall and windowsill are covered in tapestry and the floor laid with a gorgeous carpet. The windows have the king's motto in stained glass.

Juan de le Corte, Fiesta in the Plaza Mayor in honour of the Prince of Wales, 1623.
The painting records the tournament held in Prince Charles's honour on 21 August 1623.
He sits on the balcony in the centre of the painting next to the Infanta (it was the first time
he was allowed to sit next to her). The horsemen engaged in combat include King Philip.

Gerrit Houckgeest, Charles I, Queen Henrietta Maria, and Charles II when Prince of Wales
Dining in Public, 1635.

The Banqueting House Ceiling by Inigo Jones with canvases by Peter Paul Rubens.
The paintings were commissioned by Charles I in 1629 and installed in 1636.
The central oval is James I being carried to heaven, the rectangle above, the vision
of the cross, and below the peaceful reign of James I.

Gerrit van Honthorst, Apollo and Diana, 1628. The liberal arts are ushered into the presence of Charles I dressed as Apollo. They are: Grammar holding a key and book; Logic with scales; Rhetoric with a scroll; Astronomy with an astrolabe and dividers; Geometry with a globe and dividers; Arithmetic with a tablet; and Music with a lute. It is likely that the painting was made as scenery for a masque.

Sir Anthony van Dyck, Charles I, Henrietta Maria, Prince Charles and Princess Mary, 1632. Known as The Great Piece, this was commissioned for the end of the matted gallery at Whitehall where the view behind the royal family was the actual view towards Westminster. The painting dominated the hugely long gallery hung with the cream of Charles I's collection.

Sir Anthony Van Dyck, King Charles I and M. de St Antoine, 1633. This painting was commissioned for the privy gallery at St James's where it hung between 1633 and *c*.1650. Its position at the end of the gallery made it seem as if the king was riding in from the park. St James's was a centre of royal equestrian activity where Prince Charles and Prince James learned to ride. A painting showing the king with a riding master was very appropriate.

Figure 63a: Frederick de Wit, engraving of Gordon of Rothiemay's view of the Parliament House from the east, 1646.

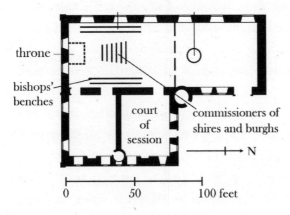

throne

bishops' benches

court of session

commissioners of shires and burghs

→ N

0   50   100 feet

Figure 63b: Reconstructed ground-floor plan of the Parliament House in the seventeenth century.

the west door of the abbey; as the king entered he genuflected to the altar before ascending the throne platform facing east. The service was conducted by bishops in vestments who bended their knee at the crucifix. Nothing in the service would have been out of place in London, but in Edinburgh the setting and liturgy were seen as scandalously popish.[22]

Only a privileged few saw the coronation in the abbey; the citizenry had to wait to see the king at worship until the Sunday after the opening of parliament, when he attended St Giles' Church. Here, in full view, the preacher, in rich vestments and flanked by a phalanx of clergy in surplices, delivered his sermon. The Scots were disgusted by the perceived popery, and the king by the building which, with its packed galleries, Archbishop Laud described as more like a theatre than a church.[23]

Charles left Edinburgh to tour the principal royal houses of his northern kingdom, each of which had been given a brush-up for his arrival. At Falkland there still remains the painted decorative scheme in the chapel ceiling and north wall bearing the date of the king's visit. More interesting, though, is the chapel at Stirling. This had been built for James I using the biblical description of the temple of Solomon in Jerusalem. Solomon's temple was a benchmark for the Laudian vision of a church – a house sanctified through beauty for the worship of God. In preparation for Charles's arrival at Stirling the painter Valentine Jenkin executed an extensive decorative scheme on the roof, walls and panelling, some of which still remains. An eighteenth-century print shows that there was also an elaborate wooden screen with a segmental pediment supported by Corinthian pillars. Stylistically this emphatic construction seems to date from around 1630 and is similar to Counter-Reformation models in Paris that were published in books of design during the 1620s and 30s. There is no information as to where in the church this screen was positioned but it was surely a reredos. If it was, it was the king's most emphatic and provocative innovation in Presbyterian Scotland.[24]

Work on the Parliament House and on the restoration of St Giles' was largely complete in late 1637, but by then the king's project for Scottish uniformity had collapsed in chaos.

The Scottish church managed to combine Calvinist theology with an episcopal structure. It worked because the bishops did not exert themselves and, dressed like ordinary ministers, were happy to work with synods. Charles went one step further, and one step too far. After returning to England his determination to enforce uniformity was strengthened and, in 1637, he gave orders that a prayer book, drafted by the Scottish bishops, and approved by himself, should be introduced. It did not go well. On its first outing, in newly created St Giles' Cathedral, the Dean and Bishop of Edinburgh were attacked by a furious mob. Charles's subsequent efforts

Figure 64: Woodcut showing what was probably the reredos in the Stirling chapel royal, erected for Charles I in 1632–3. From William Fowler, 'True reportarie of the most triumphant, and royal accomplishment of the baptisme of the most excellent, right high, and mightie prince, Frederick Henry A True Reportarie . . .' (1764).

to impose the prayer book led to hundreds of thousands signing a solemn covenant not to accept the hated liturgy.

Thus started the stand-off with the Scots that Charles regarded as a direct assault on his kingship and on the principle of monarchy. By the start of 1639 both the Covenanters and the king were preparing to resolve the dispute by military action. To pay for this the king called the English Parliament for the first time in eleven years, unleashing, in due course, a torrent of grievances that were eventually to be collated in the Grand Remonstrance. Charles was defeated in Scotland and had to agree to the abolition of episcopacy and the establishment of Presbyterianism. Meanwhile his third kingdom, Ireland, exploded in rebellion, the Catholic majority rising up, emboldened by royal capitulation in Scotland. The king's failed attempt to arrest five MPs on the charge of treason and his subsequent abandonment of London was the prelude to his assembling an army to fight against his own parliament. On 22 August 1642 he symbolically raised the royal standard at Nottingham, launching civil war.

The attack on the royal chapels

When parliament met in London in April 1640 one of its first acts was to set up a committee to investigate issues of religion including the position of the communion table and setting up crosses and statues in churches. But parliamentary processes were slow and were overtaken by Londoners spontaneously tearing altar rails and steps out of parish churches. In this febrile atmosphere it was inevitable that attention would turn to Denmark House where the queen maintained her Capuchin friary. In November that year, as parliament reconvened, the first riots took place outside the chapel.[25]

Disorder, rioting and violent behaviour were hallmarks of life in early Stuart London but in 1640–42, stoked by plague, trade depression, political crisis and religious radicalism London was nearly out of control. Thousands of citizens took to the streets to take the law into their own hands. At the heart of this disorder was a view, passionately held by some, that there was a Roman Catholic conspiracy at court involving the queen, her priests, and a few of the king's closest councillors. Tracts circulating in London spread the belief that the Denmark House friary was contaminating the king with popery. In Amsterdam, in December 1642, safe from the censor's pen, a satirical broadsheet entitled *Magna Britannia Divisa* showed the capture of the king by the *Processio Romana*, a procession of subversive foreign papal influence. At the heart of the procession was Henrietta Maria who had fled London for the continent eleven months before the broadsheet was published. She is portrayed holding her crown with her confessor and an ugly group of menacing Capuchins, armed beneath their habits.[26]

By this stage everyone, except the king, could see that the Capuchin friary was a huge liability for the royal family and that, without its dissolution, Charles would have no chance of convincing parliament that he did not favour Catholics. Despite repeated strident requests from the Commons that the friars be expelled, nothing was done and, in January 1642, several 'rude boys and other lewed persons' succeeded in breaking into the queen's chapel causing quite a lot of damage; the following month a hungry crowd

Figure 65: '*Processio Romana sive Rex sine parlamento*' (The Roman procession
or the King without parliament), 1642. Published under an assumed name in Holland,
this incendiary satire shows Henrietta Maria as number 28 behind three European
Catholic queens. Charles I is number 60 being dragged into the popish procession
in chains. Almost every figure is identified in an accompanying text and
they include most English Catholic peers.

gathered outside the house in anticipation of the arrest of the friars.[27]

Denmark House was not, of course, the only building to be singled
out. The Palaces of Westminster and Whitehall were also mobbed and
put under guard, especially in the days after the Long Parliament assembled.[28] Denmark House was different. Whitehall was far out west,
separated from the main population of the city. It was heavily guarded
and its approaches could be controlled if necessary. Denmark House
was in the heart of the most populous part of the Strand and at the

hub of the metropolitan news network. Rumours of what went on there circulated within the capital in a score of minutes.[29]

This is why, in March 1643, without the formal consent of the House of Lords, Sir John Clotworthy an MP and religious fanatic, with two others, broke ranks and forced entry into Denmark House friary with a trained band from the city.[30] Two French aristocratic members of the queen's household tried to stop them, claiming that the friary was protected under the terms of the queen's marriage treaty. They were ignored and seven friars taken into custody. Clotworthy then climbed onto the high altar and hacked to pieces Rubens's altarpiece with a halberd and had it thrown into the Thames. He then moved on to the side chapels where he did the same to paintings of St Francis and the Virgin, smashed a large statue of the Virgin and Child in the vestry before finding two more statues of St Francis and the Crucifixion in the garden. He destroyed these, according to the French, by banging their heads together. The mob then moved to the presbytery, reredos and altars all of which were demolished. The vestry was ransacked and a bonfire outside was fed with books, furniture and confessionals.[31]

The following month a more formal step was taken with the establishment of a committee of ten MPs under the chairmanship of Sir Robert Harley to receive information on 'monuments of superstition and idolatry' and demolish them. The committee's work led to an ordinance, passed in August, for the removal and demolition of all altars, altar rails, altar steps, candlesticks, crucifixes and painted images by 1 November.[32]

In September 1643, a case of delinquency was opened against the Surveyor of the King's Works, Inigo Jones. He was deprived of his post in favour of Edward Carter, Jones's executive officer at St Paul's Cathedral. An ordinance for the seizure of the king's property was passed the same month and Denmark House was almost immediately broken into by a mob. The state apartments were ransacked; furniture and paintings were stolen and smashed. At this point the House of Lords realised that while it might be acceptable to condone officially sanctioned iconoclasm, wanton vandalism by the London mob was a different prospect. A resolution was passed securing the royal palaces and banning entry by anyone unless accompanied by two MPs and a peer. The ordinance gave parliament power to appoint its own officers to administer the king's estate and allowed Edward Carter officially to assume the duties of Surveyor.[33]

Throughout this period, other than at Windsor, the royal chapels had remained much as they had been. But on 9 March 1644 the committee opened discussions with the Lords for the demolishing of all superstitious pictures and monuments in Whitehall and the other royal houses, particularly in the chapels. If any further sanction were needed a further ordinance passed in May added vestments, holy water fonts and organs to the list of superstitious elements to be demolished or defaced.[34] These acts finally heralded the assault on the Caroline royal chapels.

The first to be cleared was the queen's chapel at St James's where the reredos, altar and steps were taken out. Less symbolic, but closer to the seat of power, was the Whitehall chapel. In May Harley's men smashed the stained glass which had only been inserted twenty years previously, and new clear glass was set up. The same month the rood cross was dismantled, panel paintings planed and the boards painted plain colours. The following month Harley ordered that the stem of the cross should be converted into a support for a heraldic lion holding the king's arms. In July a communion table was supplied to replace the altar and the walls were stripped of their murals and plastered over. The work of 1644 transformed the Whitehall chapel into a white preaching auditorium, but still a Chapel Royal bearing the royal insignia.[35]

Greenwich was next. In late 1644 the stained glass was destroyed and replaced with plain, the organ removed, and the organ loft bricked over.[36] Hampton Court was last. Far from London, with an uncertain future and a royalist housekeeper the house was out of the limelight. In late 1645 the altar was taken down and the step on which it stood levelled, the stained glass was broken up and a large painted crucifixion over the altar was destroyed. Thus in three short years the beauty of holiness created by James I and Charles I, and a good deal of Tudor work too, was destroyed and reduced to monochrome austerity.[37]

ELEVEN

Civil War

In Oxford

When in August 1642 the king raised the royal standard in Nottingham, he had been on the road since 10 January, when he had abandoned London after his botched attempt to arrest five members of parliament. Hastily exiting from Whitehall, he arrived late at Hampton Court which was quite unprepared to receive the royal family; it was cold and only partially furnished when Charles entered his privy lodgings, and the whole family had to sleep in one bed. But the king's main concern was security, not comfort, and preparations were undertaken at lightning speed for the king and queen to move to the safety of Windsor Castle. It was noted that 'things are done in such post-haste that I have never heard of the like for the voyage of persons of so great dignity'.[1]

These were the first rushed, unplanned, moves of hundreds that the king was to make over the next six years before he eventually returned to London as a prisoner at the end of 1648. The royal itinerary was normally planned months in advance to allow houses to be furnished and repaired and larders and cellars stocked. But, at war, Charles and his family often stayed in makeshift accommodation, the king sleeping under a hedge at Lostwithiel in Cornwall and in his coach in Wolvercote in Oxfordshire, while the queen, under heavy Parliamentarian shelling, hid in a ditch in Bridlington. It is remarkable that, despite makeshift accommodation, the Caroline court managed to maintain order, dignity and a degree of splendour.

The first great battle of the Civil War was at Edgehill ten miles or so northwest of Banbury and, in its aftermath, it was natural that the court and army should move to Oxford. The university was fervently loyal to the Crown and the city, in the crook of three rivers, easily defensible. Greeted outside the city by the vice-chancellor, the king explained that he would only stay until 'we can with safety to our honour and person in peace return to the Jerusalem of our nation, our City of London'. He could not have envisaged that for three and a half years Oxford would become the seat of the court, headquarters of the army and, in effect, the Royalist capital city. It was also a garrison town, a fact demonstrated by Charles's appointment of a board of civilian Lords Commissioners and Jacob, Lord Astley, as military governor. These officials had to liaise with the mayor and aldermen on the one hand and the vice-chancellor and the heads of the colleges on the other. Governing royalist Oxford was complex and sometimes fraught.[2]

The king made his headquarters at Christ Church college, founded by Cardinal Wolsey and begun in 1525. It was intended to be the largest college in Oxford or Cambridge, with a great cloister flanked to north and south by the hall and chapel. The scheme was interrupted by Wolsey's death in 1530 and although the hall, the most magnificent in Oxford, was completed, the great cloistered quad (measuring 264 by 261 feet) was only half built and the chapel barely begun. Instead, the partly dismantled priory church became the chapel. But not for long. The episcopal reorganisation that took place after the Reformation saw a new diocese of Oxford formed and the chapel become Christ Church Cathedral with its own dean and chapter.

This combined arrangement of college and cathedral was unique, but what made it even more unusual were the provisions in the founding statutes of the college which specified that it was to be used by the monarch, his eldest son and their households when they were in Oxford.[3]

Where Wolsey intended the royal lodgings to be is uncertain but when, in 1566, Queen Elizabeth exercised her right to reside there, she stayed in the deanery which occupied the north end of the east range of the great quad. It was here also that Charles I stayed in 1636 when he was the guest of William Laud who had risen, by 1633, to be not only Archbishop of Canterbury but dean of the Chapel Royal, privy councillor and Chancellor of Oxford University.

At Oxford Laud had built a magnificent new quadrangle at his former college, St John's, that was the object of King Charles's visit in 1636. The Canterbury Quadrangle is a remarkable blend of traditional and *avant garde* design; while the north and south elevations of the court were utterly conventional, the east and west sides incorporated round-headed loggias and flamboyant frontispieces encrusted in writhing carvings inspired by French and Flemish pattern books. Beautiful though the effect is, the punch is packed by the iconography – the two frontispieces contain the royal arms and those of Laud and niches with full-size bronze statues of the king and queen by Hubert le Sueur. Even the rainwater heads contain lead mitres and crowns. Charles's reaction to the courtyard is unknown, but as it represented, in stone, lead and bronze, the union of Church and Crown for which he and Laud were to fight it is unlikely to have been unfavourable.[4]

Royal visits, and the expectation of more, drew attention to the fact that half-built Christ Church had all the prestige of a royal foundation but none of the expected architectural magnificence, a want highlighted by Laud's spectacular new courtyard at St John's. At Christ Church Dean Brian Duppa, and his successor Samuel Fell, both fervent royalists, set out to complete Wolsey's unfinished works, but the only new building to be completed before the outbreak of war was a stair leading up to the hall, which was covered with a fan vault of great size and beauty.[5]

In October 1642 the arrival of the court in Oxford was, in one sense, an unexceptional event. On progress the court was frequently established in towns and cities and, because of the status of Christ Church, the

Figure 66: The Canterbury Quadrangle, St John's College, Oxford, commissioned
by Archbishop Laud in 1630 and completed in 1636. Several designers were
involved under Laud's close supervision.

king's arrival there was much like entering one of the many royal progress
houses maintained by the Crown. Yet there was a difference. The royal
family rarely moved together and when the queen joined the king in
1643 there were, unusually, four households in total including those of
the princes. There was then the army and its officers and increasing
numbers of officers of state; because of the war, some brought their
wives and children with them. The court always had followers, but in
Oxford it became a magnet for dispossessed, penurious or simply fright-
ened royalists of all classes. To make matters worse, for every man of
any status there was at least one horse and the requirement for stabling
and fodder was immense.

There were three authorities charged with finding lodgings in Oxford
for this swelling entourage: the quartermaster of the army requisitioned
lodgings for soldiers; the royal harbingers billeted members of the royal
households and the governor of the city housed the Oxford garrison.

Everyone else had to scramble for a bed. In order to ease the pressure, the king issued a series of proclamations ordering people who were not part of one of the royal households to leave.[6]

Householders were paid an allowance of 3s 6d a week for feeding a soldier and colleges charged their guests for board and lodging, rather as they did students. Private owners could exchange billets (accommodation notices) issued by the royal harbingers for cash. The pressure on accommodation was acute. In 1643 Ann, Lady Fanshawe, was summoned by her father, Sir John Harrison, to join the court at Oxford. Sir John, a diehard royalist, had his estates sequestered by parliament and, by the time he reached Oxford was, in Ann's words, 'as poor as Job'; she remarked that 'from as good house as any gentleman of England we had come to a baker's house in an obscure street, and from rooms well-furnished to lie in a very bad bed in a garret'. She describes the plague and sickness 'by reason of so many people being packed together, as I believe there never was before of that quality' but most, she claimed, 'bore it with a martyr-like cheerfulness'.[7]

The king moved directly into the dean's lodgings at Christ Church. These rooms are still occupied by the dean and before the mid-nineteenth century alterations of Dean Liddell (who was enriched by the profits of a Greek dictionary he compiled) had been little changed since the seventeenth century. Yet enough original work survives to work out the plan of the rooms in King Charles's time. On the ground floor was a great hall and what were described as two parlours in 1612. It is hard to discern these now, but what remains, in all its glory, is the original kitchen and parts of the larders and entry to them. The stairs to the first floor, where the king's lodgings were, were replaced in 1855 but an eighteenth-century plan shows that they rose at the north end to a gallery off which was, in 1642, a room described as the presence and privy chamber – a single room serving both functions. Further south were three more rooms; one was the withdrawing chamber and the southernmost was the royal bedchamber, a room that survives much as it was in the seventeenth century. The backstairs linking the private rooms with the kitchens and service rooms below also remain in a modified form.[8]

The rooms, though smaller in number than was usual in a royal house, were large, well-lit and overlooked the dean's private garden onto which the ground-floor parlours opened. In January 1642 the Council of War discussed and agreed regulations to govern the operation of the royal lodgings. Guards were to stand at the foot of the stairs up to the privy and presence chamber, gentlemen ushers manned the doors to the withdrawing room and pages of the bedchamber guarded the backstairs to the bedchamber. Unusually these regulations were published in the royalist newspaper *Mercurius Aulicus*, to emphasise that this was no temporary billet, but a formal royal residence.[9]

The Privy Council seems to have met in the cathedral chapter house and the Council of War met in the Audit House, the old infirmary of the priory hung with portraits of former deans. The royal lodgings were furnished with tapestries, textiles, plate and other furniture from the royal wardrobe. Some items were sent from London including clothes, drugs, drink and saddlery but most furnishings were in the king's vast baggage train that had accompanied him as if on progress. When the baggage train was captured after the battle of Naseby it contained some 200 wagons.[10]

Although Archbishop Laud had characterised Christ Church as having 'many fair lodgings for great men' there was not enough space to accommodate all the offices or officers of state let alone the wider royal household. To the east of Christ Church were two colleges that were contiguous, Corpus Christi and Merton; across a narrow lane was a third, Oriel. All three were effectively absorbed into the royal residence.

After Henrietta Maria joined the king in Oxford in July 1643 she was given lodgings at Merton. In 1629 the king and queen had been feasted here by the warden, Sir Nathaniel Brent, but Brent had elected to side with parliament and had been ejected from his lodgings in the fifteenth-century Fitzjames gateway. This gatehouse now became the queen's lodgings; it was directly adjacent to Fellows Quadrangle, one of

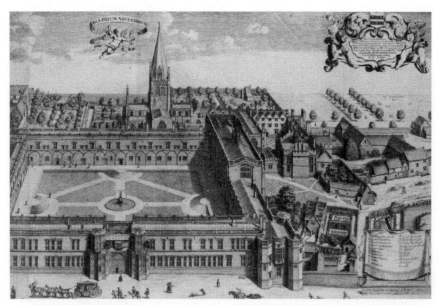

Figure 67: David Loggan, view of Christ Church college, 1673. Much as Charles I would have known it, this fine print shows the dean's lodgings, used as a royal residence in the 1640s, at the back left-hand corner of the main quad. The cathedral is in the top right-hand corner.

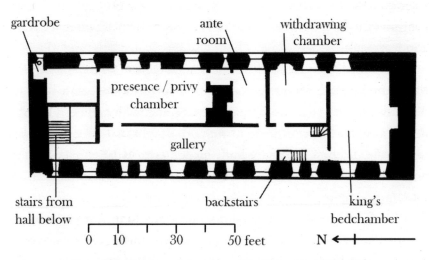

gardrobe

ante room

withdrawing chamber

presence / privy chamber

gallery

stairs from hall below

backstairs

king's bedchamber

0   10   30   50 feet   N ←

Figure 68: Reconstructed first-floor plan of the dean's lodgings at Christ Church college, as occupied by Charles I in 1642.

the most modern in Oxford, completed in 1610, and adorned with James I's arms – in here were placed the queen's household. In order to link Merton and Christ Church, doorways were cut in the garden walls either side of Corpus Christi and a gravel path laid between them. At Corpus lodged John Ashburnham, Treasurer-at-War, who was visited there by both the king and his sons, the bursar tipping the royal trumpeters and footmen who accompanied them.[11]

Oriel College had been entirely rebuilt in the early part of Charles I's reign and adorned with a large statue of the king over the hall door. Its provost, John Tolson, a fervent royalist who became vice-chancellor in 1642, played a major role in the fortification of the city. Oriel was home to the Lord Treasurer, Francis Cottington and the dean of the chapel royal, Richard Steward, as well as thirty-five other royal servants and army officers. Cottington chaired meetings of the executive committee of the Privy Council there.[12] Perhaps the college's most important role was as editorial office for *Mercurius Aulicus* or the *Court Mercury*, the newspaper published in Oxford which became the mouthpiece of the Royalist cause.[13]

Although the ordered cloisters, quads and gardens of Christ Church, Corpus and Merton might seem to have been the perfect royal enclave they were also a war zone. Oxford was a walled city and the king supplemented the medieval defences by a series of modern bastions and gun emplacements. A plan of the fortifications drawn by the Flemish military engineer Bernard de Gomme, who had been brought to England by Prince Rupert to support Royalist military operations, shows the defences hurriedly built by conscripted labour. Two buildings are identified by name – Oxford Castle and Christ Church, the two most important strategic locations in the city. A tower on the town wall at Merton was cut down for a gun platform covering the Christ Church water meadow which had been deliberately flooded. A magazine was set up at New College, an artillery park at Magdalen College Grove and a cannon foundry at Christ Church. In the Schools building small arms were repaired, drawbridges manufactured, and armour and uniforms stored. Powder, meanwhile, was prudently milled

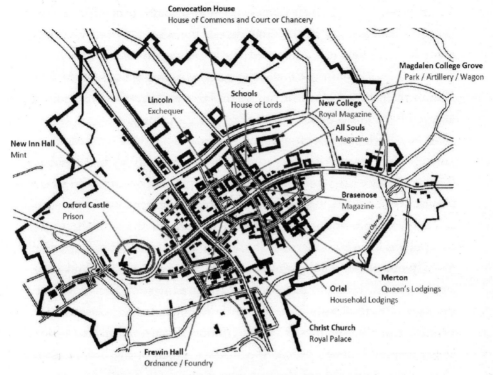

Figure 69: Map of Civil War Oxford, *c.*1643 showing the
principal places mentioned in the text.

on the outskirts of the city. Oxford was full of soldiers often short on
pay and temper; the city was over-full, prone to disease, squalor, fire
and disorder.[14]

At the gates of Christ Church is St Aldate's, the parish church that
gives its name to the long street that leads from Folly Bridge to the city
centre. This was where the bulk of the royal household was accommodated.
In private houses on the street lodged the king's surgeon, his tailor, his
barber, his apothecary and the royal seamstress, all of whom held posts
that brought them into close contact with the king. Others, in lesser
accommodation, included a royal poulterer, two royal bakers, the
coal-carrier and various other humble servants. Eighty of the king's
red-coated lifeguard of foot were also billeted in St Aldate's, including
their colonel, Montagu Bertie, Lord Willoughby de Eresby, who was
also, from 1642, the king's Lord Great Chamberlain.[15]

These people made their homes in Oxford, many remaining in residence when the army left to campaign in the summer. Some married, many had children, and a few died: the burial records of Christ Church Cathedral include entries for an officer of the counting house, the Clerk Comptroller, two yeomen of the wardrobe, two garter heralds and the keeper of the Great Seal.[16]

As royal etiquette, reinforced by the new household regulations of January 1642, restricted access to the king's person in his bedchamber, Charles decided to promote key figures in the army and city giving them direct access to his person. The most prominent was the almost simultaneous promotion of William Seymour, Marquess of Hertford, to be a Lord Commissioner of Oxford, Vice-Chancellor of the University and Groom of the Stool, combining three key posts in the hands of a single courtier. Hertford had lodgings at Christ Church from where he exercised his responsibilities. Colonel William Legge, Governor of Oxford, and Royalist master of the armoury (who lived in St Aldate's at the gates of Christ Church) was made a groom of the bedchamber, as was John Ashburnham the treasurer-at-war, both acquiring right of access to the king.[17]

On 14 July 1643 the queen made her ceremonial entry into Oxford, the streets lined with soldiers. First came a carriage containing her ladies followed by her servants and gentlemen pensioners. Next came the heralds and serjeants at arms in their uniforms, the sergeant carrying a mace; preceding the royal coach was the queen's chamberlain, the Earl of Dorset. After a speech of welcome at Carfax she proceeded to Christ Church where she was welcomed by the vice-chancellor and then escorted by the king to her lodgings at Merton where the orator of the university gave another speech. Henrietta Maria was accompanied by her Catholic confessor, priests and attendants. There was anxiety about holding Church of England services in the Merton chapel while she was in residence, but the queen insisted they continue, and she heard Mass with her household elsewhere in the college.[18]

Ceremonies in Oxford

Summer was the campaigning season and king and army were in the field, but as the court retired to Oxford in the winters of 1642–3, 43–4 and 44–5 court life became almost normal. The Royalist army officer Sir Henry Slingsby described the king's daily routine in 1644: 'He kept his hours most exactly, both for his exercises and for his dispatches, as also his hours for admitting all sorts to come to speak with him. You might know where he would be from any hour from his rising, which was very early, to his walk he took in the garden, and so to chapel and dinner; so after dinner, if he went not abroad, he had his hours for writing or discoursing, or chess playing, or tennis.' As before the Civil War the king spent much of his leisure time in the queen's lodgings where he could be free of the restrictive etiquette of his own apartments. As their youngest child was conceived in Oxford he probably also spent the night there. Their request to the Westminster Parliament to have their two youngest children, Elizabeth and Henry, sent to Oxford to join them was rejected and they remained, in Parliamentarian care, at St James's.[19]

The annual round of court ceremonial continued uninterrupted. A chapter of the Order of the Garter was held in March 1645 in the presence and privy chamber, where two new knights were created, and the St George's day service was held in the cathedral. A book recording payments to household members at the creation of new peers lists twelve occasions when the king ennobled close supporters. The young John Aubrey recalled often watching the king dining in public in the great hall and, in April 1643, two humble artillery soldiers knelt and kissed the king's hand on his way to dinner. There was no shortage of food, for the royal table at least, and Christ Church hall set up for public dining made a regal impact.[20]

A parade of foreign ambassadors was received, given formal receptions in the great hall, and private conference in the deanery. In 1643 the French ambassador was welcomed by a salute of cannon fire as he entered the city. After dining at St John's where he was staying, he was visited by the king and queen who conversed with him for two hours. The next day at four o'clock he processed in state to Christ Church where he had an audience and was feasted in the great hall.[21]

Parliamentarian representatives also came to Oxford to negotiate with the king. Early in 1643 Bulstrode Whitelocke was one of a twelve-man deputation who came to present parliament's proposals. They had their first meeting with the king in the gardens of Christ Church where they kissed his hand and read their scripts; later negotiations were more hospitably conducted in the king's rooms, including his withdrawing chamber. The king called parliament to Oxford in January 1644 and 83 peers and 175 MPs attended him in the Hall of Christ Church for its opening. Later they took their seats – the Commons in the Convocation House and the Lords in the upper Schools.[22]

What was perhaps most important to the king was the strict observance of the court's religious calendar. In the early 1620s Dean Richard Corbett had commissioned a splendid new organ for Christ Church Cathedral and his successor Brian Duppa reordered its interior, dividing the chancel from the chapels by screens, building box pews, repaving the floor and elevating the communion table on marble steps. Most controversially he commissioned a glorious scheme of painted glass which included scenes from the nativity, crucifixion and the burial of Christ. Duppa had been the king's host at Christ Church in 1636 and, two years later, had been appointed as tutor to the Prince of Wales and Duke of York. He had been elevated to the see of Chichester in 1638 and after only three years on to Salisbury. The arrangements for royal worship at Christ Church Cathedral were thus very much to King Charles's ceremonious tastes.[23]

As parliament stripped away the ceremonies of the Church of England, abolishing the prayer book and banning Christmas, the king made Christ Church an exemplar of ceremonious Protestantism. Each Christmas season carols were commissioned that embodied Charles's world picture emphasising his divine role in society; Easter was also celebrated with traditional rites. Lenten sermons were preached: on the first Sunday in Lent 1643 the preacher's title was *The sovereign's power and the subject's duty* – it was later published and distributed. On Maundy Thursday 1643 Charles washed the feet of twelve poor men in the great hall.[24]

The ordered maintenance of court and state etiquette was as important to the king as the military effort. For Charles to be visibly king and to be afforded due deference was crucial, not only to his own dignity, but to the dignity of his office. The fiercely loyal Lady Mary Stafford got Parliamentarian passes to make three journeys from Oxford to St James's Palace, and on one of them, succeeded in bringing to Oxford a mass of jewels and the king's crown; the latter he was able to wear on collar days including the Epiphany services in the cathedral. The Oxford court was no ramshackle compromise; it was conducted with deliberate regality and magnificence.[25]

While the ceremonial side of the king's life was upheld there was no neglect of pleasure. Charles hunted with his own pack of hounds in the royal park at Woodstock and elsewhere and, in poor weather, he played tennis with the Prince of Wales, Duke of York and Prince Rupert. There was a tennis court at the back of Christ Church near Oriel and, in November 1643, the king asked his Master of the Robes to send a servant from London to Oxford to bring a bolt of taffeta and 'two pairs of garters and roses with silk buttons' to make him a tennis suit.[26]

Although most court musicians stayed in London a few came to Oxford and accompanied services at Christ Church and the queen's chapel as well as performing chamber music for the king and queen and accompanying ceremonies with trumpets and drums. Likewise, a small number of actors came to perform plays and masques at court, although without the complex scenery that had become commonplace at Whitehall. In February 1646, when it was clear that Oxford would be lost, a play was acted before the king 'to keep up his spirit in stead of good success from his soldiery'.[27]

In 1643 the king issued orders for all royal servants to join him at Oxford. This was the prelude to an attempt to relocate the central organs of the state to his new temporary capital. The Chancery, Exchequer and the courts of law were all ordered from Westminster to Oxford where they were set up in colleges and university buildings. Parliament had taken control of the Mint at the Tower of London and the king had initially established a mint in Shrewsbury using his own plate and Welsh silver to mint coin. In January 1643 the Shrewsbury mint was ordered to Oxford and set up at New Inn Hall (the site of St Peter's College). It was remarkably successful in producing coin for the war effort. One coin struck there deserves special mention. The Oxford Crown minted in 1644 has a detailed representation of Oxford from the north on one side. The legend advertises the king's intention to uphold the Protestant religion, the laws of England and the freedom of parliament.

This remarkable coin must have been struck on the king's orders for while the slogan proclaiming his aims was common to most Civil War coinage, the depiction of Oxford was unique on an English coin. The

Figure 70: Charles I silver crown, 1644. The Oxford mint was overseen by Thomas Bushell and Sir William Pankhurst, former wardens of the Shrewsbury and Tower Mints. Supplied with silver from Oxford and Cambridge colleges, together with foreign coin, the mint covered the king's needs for coinage during the war. It closed in May or June 1646 when the city was taken by Parliament.

king was extremely proud of Oxford, its buildings, beauty and history and was determined that it should not be damaged by the war. In 1645, when there was still the opportunity to move the court to the West of England, he resolved to stay as Oxford was the only city that could have accommodated the court in comfort and the only place suitable to his and its magnificence.[28]

Henrietta Maria was pregnant and found overcrowded Oxford increasingly intolerable. Eventually the 34-year-old consort informed her husband that she was going to leave. In April 1644 she slipped out of the city and made for the South West where, in Exeter, she would eventually give birth to her last child, Princess Henrietta. Only a month later, she boarded ship and sailed for the Low Countries; Charles never saw her again. After losing the battle of Naseby in June 1645 and surrendering Bristol it became clear that the war was lost and, on 27 April 1646, the king rode out of Oxford disguised as a servant and accompanied by three attendants, abandoning his temporary capital, his cousin Prince Rupert and his young son, the Duke of York.

On 25 June the keys of the surrendered city were handed to General Fairfax who, with the other senior Parliamentarian officers, entered and made for Christ Church. Prince James, Duke of York, remained in the dean's lodgings. One by one they kissed the twelve-year-old's hand: only one of their number knelt at his feet as they did so. That man was Oliver Cromwell. Even in the humiliation of defeat the magic of monarchy was alive.[29]

In July the royal lodgings at Christ Church were dismantled. The king's crown and seals of office were handed over to the Parliamentarian generals but most of his other possessions were sent to Hampton Court, the remainder travelling with the Duke of York to St James's where he joined his brother, the Duke of Gloucester and Princess Elizabeth. The Prince of Wales had escaped and was on his way, via the Isles of Scilly and Jersey, to France where he eventually joined his mother.[30]

In prison

The king had surrendered to the Scots who took him north to Newcastle before handing him over to the English parliament. A deal struck in January 1647 allowed him to be moved south again, under close guard; first to Holdenby House in Northamptonshire, then on to Royston and Hatfield, and finally to Hampton Court. Hampton Court was to be his resting-place from 24 August for about eleven weeks. What is usually described as Charles's imprisonment was barely house arrest. Not only did he have free movement about the palace and parks, he retained his own attendants, enabling him to hold a court in miniature maintained by parliament's official sanction.

The house was specially refurnished for his arrival and plate was issued from the jewel house at the Tower for his table. It also seems that Charles requested paintings of his family to be sent from Whitehall. He success-fully petitioned parliament for his children to visit him and, between June and November 1647, they came several times a week, talking, hunting and playing tennis with their father. In October Charles requested that they should be allowed to stay overnight – a request that was granted. Princess Elizabeth slept in a bedroom off the privy gallery; she asked for the king's guards to be moved further off as she claimed that their noise kept her awake.

Charles's stay at Hampton Court was happier than it might have been in such circumstances. Royalist supporters came from London to see him and pay their respects. Also came senior Parliamentarian officers including Oliver Cromwell and Henry Ireton, with whom the king discussed the so-called 'Heads of Proposals', the draft agreement which was being touted by them as the best constitutional settlement on offer. On 9 or 10 November Cromwell wrote to Colonel Edward Whalley, Charles's supervisor, warning him that the army might try to assassinate the king. Whalley showed the letter to Charles, and the following night, under cover of darkness, the king escaped.

He slipped down the backstairs from the privy lodgings and out through the south front gardens. Accompanied by John Ashburton, groom of the bedchamber, he reached the waterside where a boat ferried him across the Thames to a waiting horse. There was no agreed plan, and it was not until the party had passed Farnham that the king finally decided that he would make for the Isle of Wight where there were no army units and, it was believed, the new Parliamentarian Governor, Colonel Robert Hammond might be sympathetic. Twenty-six-year-old Hammond had been one of the army officers who came to Hampton Court to pay respects to the king in his confinement but, asked to shelter the king at Carisbrooke Castle he was horrified. The king, too, was lukewarm about the idea of placing himself in the hands of a Parliamentarian officer with conflicted loyalties, but had little choice and so, made the short sea crossing to the Isle of Wight and on to Carisbrooke.[31]

Carisbrooke had long been strategically important and had most recently been remodelled as an artillery fort to guard against the threat of Spanish invasion in the 1590s. The massive new stone-faced outworks had been erected under the authority of the island's captain, Sir George Carey. Carey was the son of Lord Hunsdon, the queen's cousin, and inherited his titles in 1596. In 1583 he had been appointed to the Isle of Wight as captain and over the next three years created a large residence in the castle on the site of the twelfth-century great hall. It was in this thirteen-room mansion, with 'a fayre pair of large stairs' that Charles, as Prince of Wales, had been feasted in 1618.[32]

In November 1647 things were rather different. The king received a number of island dignitaries in the constable's lodgings and explained that 'my resolution in coming here being but to be secured till there may be some happy accommodation made'. How long this was going to take nobody knew and so Charles successfully requested that some of his household left behind so suddenly at Hampton Court could join him. A large posse arrived at the end of November with several cartloads of furnishings which transformed the large and elegant Elizabethan constable's lodging into a handsomely furnished palace in miniature. A month later the royal coach, with liveried coachmen and footmen were shipped across by sea and delivered to the castle. At first the king was remarkably free to travel round the island, sightseeing and hunting, but

Figure 71: Carisbrooke Castle from the northwest in the early nineteenth century before Victorian restoration. The house marked '2' was the location of the king's lodgings.

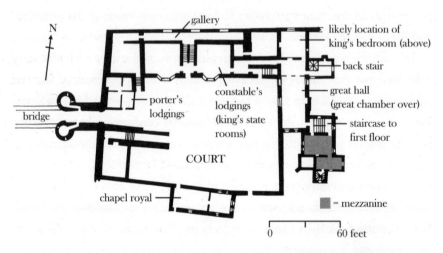

Figure 72: Reconstructed plan of Carisbrooke Castle lodgings at ground level.

by the end of the year security was tightened and the king went out much less; after a feeble attempt by some local people to rescue him, the excursions ceased and he was effectively imprisoned.[33]

What is striking about the king's initial establishment is that he was accommodated in great style: he slept in a magnificent green velvet bed laced with silver and gold fringes; matching it there were twelve stools, two armchairs with cushions and a footstool. The walls of the bedroom, and the presence chamber, were hung with tapestry; that in the presence chamber depicted the Roman emperors. It seems as if the chairs and stools of state in the presence chamber were upholstered in yellow satin. There were carpets, six silver candlesticks, two large silver sconces and a velvet-covered close stool with a silver chamber pot. There were enough books in the castle for the king to keep a list of them, and he begged and borrowed more during his stay.[34]

Even after parliament purged his household of suspect servants there were some thirty royal attendants. They managed to continue royal life with a considerable degree of formality: the king ceremoniously dined in public, went to daily prayers, received visitors, read, wrote, listened to music, touched for the king's evil and, after the construction of a bowling green in the castle's east bailey, regularly played bowls. Towards the end of the summer a pavilion was built at one end of the green for the king's shelter; it was clearly a building of some pretension.[35]

In July 1648 parliament voted to reopen negotiations with the king and, because they didn't want to negotiate with a prisoner, they allowed him to leave the castle and set up at the house of his friend, William Hopkins, in Newport. The royal Wardrobe immediately refurnished the house in some style and set up a canopy of state and a long table in the local grammar school where negotiations with the Parliamentary Commissioners would take place. Charles was allowed to reassemble his advisors and servants and was permitted to ride freely round the island. He was overcome by a surge of optimism – his coachmen were granted new liveries, he encouraged a scheme to mine silver in Cornwall and wrote to the Royal Librarian, Patrick Young, asking him to arrange the royal coin collection at St James's Palace, placing specimens in date order and removing duplicates. Orders were given to his tailor in London to prepare new suits of clothes for a return to his capital and he also sent for Inigo Jones's assistant John Webb.

The treaty discussions, which lasted eleven weeks, were intense and, for the first time, reached a conclusion, the king conceding thirty-eight of parliament's demands in return for only four of his own. Even before the negotiations began it was clear that there were three sides to any settlement and that while the King and Parliament might come to some agreement, the Army would be much harder to satisfy. The stakes were high as it was increasingly apparent that if the army seized the initiative the king's future would be bleak. Charles was closely engaged in every turn of the negotiations but in the evenings became increasingly philosophical, reflecting on his rule and on the constitution. He received a draft of *Eikon Basilike,* a compilation of thoughts and explanations he had been working on since 1642. He also composed a series of letters to Prince Charles rationalising the concessions he was making and laying out his views on kingship.[36]

With these papers on the king's desk were also plans by John Webb for a new Whitehall. Webb had been an active royalist supporter maintaining contact with the court and supplying the king with a survey of Parliamentarian fortifications round London, indicating points of weakness. In the absence of Jones, old and confined to his quarters, he was the closest person the king had to a Surveyor of Works.

The new Whitehall designs were a development of those that Webb had worked on with Jones in 1638–9, but these were not only in Webb's own hand but in his style. The busyness of Jones's facades had given way to a more monumental approach achieved using a giant order in the central section and end pavilions. The surviving elevation is a skeleton, perhaps hastily drawn, without details inked in and, marked 'taken', probably represents the king's liking of an idea to be worked up by Webb on his return to London.[37]

Figure 73: John Webb, design for the east elevation for a new palace at Whitehall, 1638, inscribed by Webb as the one chosen by Charles I in 1648. This scheme retained the Banqueting House and replicated it as a balancing block on the other side of a great hall faced with a monumental portico.

The accompanying plan, which is also marked 'taken', is the most remarkable design for a royal palace devised between Henry VIII's Whitehall in the 1530s and Sir Charles Barry's scheme for a new Palace of Westminster in the mid-nineteenth century. Every element has been deliberately and minutely planned and, although some of the original intentions cannot now be divined, the bones of the scheme are quite clear.

Like previous plans it allows for a new road to be built along the riverfront and incorporates the Banqueting House in a long elevation facing the street. A vast portico led to a central entrance hall that would have been flanked by the Banqueting House and a hall of matching design. It is not clear how these two public reception rooms would have been used; their connections with the rest of the palace are not monumental and so they may have been intended as stand-alone halls for court festivities.

Behind the street range was the vast rectangular great court. The royal lodgings faced not onto this, but looked west over the park, ranged round a circular court like that conceived ten years before. The state rooms are very conventionally planned: indeed, precisely as Henry VIII would have built them a century earlier, even down to the finesse of a private oratory lying between the presence and privy chambers. The privy lodgings are on the park front and throughout the plan the bedchambers are signified by alcoves which, in places, have the beds dotted in. Just as at Wimbledon Manor these alcoves were in private rooms, for intimate delectation.[38]

The astonishingly long galleries that run, between circular closets, the whole length of the north and south sides must have been for the royal painting collection; they would have measured 1,000 feet, much longer than the matted gallery in Old Whitehall that performed the same function. The circular closets may have been intended as tribunes for the display of sculpture. A cross gallery linked the privy chamber with these galleries, allowing the king and queen to invite guests to view the collection without approaching through the privy lodgings.

To understand the complex of rooms that occupy the centre of the palace it is necessary to look forward precisely fifty years to the destruction

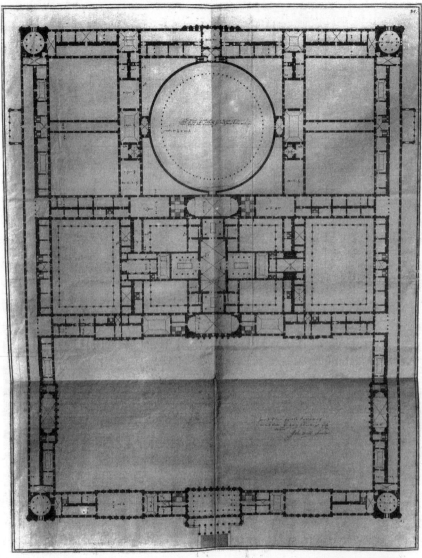

Figure 74: John Webb, scheme for a new palace of Whitehall, 1648.
The plan was marked 'taken' by Webb after the king's death, but there is no
reason to doubt that this was the plan chosen by the king during the
negotiations for the Treaty of Newport. North is to the right. At the top are the
privy lodgings overlooking the park. Either side of the circular court are the state
rooms, and in the centre are the two houses of parliament with their lobbies.
At the bottom, either side of a central hall, are two more halls,
one of which was the Banqueting House.

of Whitehall by fire in 1698. After the cataclysm of the fire, Sir Christopher Wren was ordered to design a new palace and both he and Nicholas Hawksmoor referred to the mass of Whitehall drawings done for Charles I, and still in the Office of Works in Scotland Yard. William III had asked Wren to include in the design provision for a new Parliament House (fig. 134). This design contained a cruciform arrangement of two chambers entered from a shared double-height hall. The plans for William's new parliament were, in fact, copied directly from Webb's plan agreed by Charles I in Newport, for the complex of rooms at the heart of his new palace were nothing less than a new home for the houses of parliament.

Webb's planning here is sublime. MPs and peers would have crossed the great court and ascended stairs into a great ante room with apses at either end. Passing through a square chamber they would have entered a central vaulted hall; this was the lobby, a crucially important space thronged with people during parliamentary sessions. Off this, left and right, were the two double-height chambers. Slightly shorter than St Stephen's Chapel (the Commons chamber), the new chambers were wider and, like St Stephen's, may have had balconies on either side, judging by the columns. They were top lit through skylights and clerestory windows. Either side were small rooms for committees.

In the central north–south spine, back to back with the two chambers, were two other large rooms: to the south was the chapel, again double height, with a shallow structural chancel and an elevated pew to the north. On the north side, in the position occupied by the council chamber in earlier schemes, were what seem to have been the kitchens. Webb shows two massive blocks of chimney stacks either side of a ground-floor room with a vault. The final refinement were four small suites of lodgings, presumably for the royal children. The two larger ones were entered from the king and queen's guard chambers, the smaller ones from the east vestibule.

During the Middle Ages monarch and parliament had met in the same building, the old Palace of Westminster, an arrangement terminated by the burning of the residential parts of the palace. From the reign of

Edward VI, Commons and Lords had met in the old palace while the monarch had resided at Whitehall. Webb's plan of 1648 recreated the medieval arrangements of sovereign and parliament co-located in a single building. The plan must have been conceived in September or October 1648, before Charles became disillusioned with negotiations. Then, still believing that he could return to London and be 'settled in a condition of honour, freedom and safety', Webb's blueprint reflected the king's aspiration to turn back the clock and recreate the constitutional balance of the early Tudors. In a letter to Prince Charles, part of a manifesto for the future published in *Eikon Basilike*, he advised: 'nor would I have you to entertain any aversion or dislike to parliaments which in their right constitution with freedom and honour will never injure or diminish your greatness but will rather be as interchangings of love, loyalty and confidence between a prince and his people'.

Webb's plan was not only about functionality and representation, it was about magnificence and order. Charles had already shown interest in the setting of the House of Lords in 1624 and in 1633 had commissioned a new parliament house in Scotland. The plan for new chambers was a logical extension of the king's quest for dignity, regality and order in the state. But by November 1648 it was too late. Speaking of the unreason-ableness of the two houses' propositions for future government, that month the king remarked 'they will ask so much and use it so ill, that the people of England will be one day glad to relodge the power they had taken from the crown where it is due'. Webb's plan captured the thoughts of the king as he contemplated a future that was never to be.[39]

TWELVE

Republican Residences

The army coup

While most MPs willed the Newport treaty to succeed, and wanted the king, and normality, to return, the army had lost patience. They thought parliament had betrayed what they had fought for and, in December 1648, staged a military coup occupying London and ejecting from the Commons MPs who opposed them. The partisan Parliamentary Rump that remained soon voted the Newport negotiations 'destructive to the peace of the kingdom' and resolved to bring the king 'speedily to justice'.

Early in the morning of 1 December the army captured Charles I, hastily removing him from Newport and taking him across the water to Hurst Castle. This was not a residence, but a military installation on a spit of gravel surrounded by water. Secured by the army, preparations were now made to move the king to London. His passage from Hampshire to Windsor was almost like a progress of old. Although lodged in private houses, people flocked to see him dine and pay their respects. Arriving at Windsor Castle on 22 December he was welcomed by loud crowds in the streets, but visitors were prohibited within the castle walls and so, as he retired to his old bedchamber, he was attended only by six servants and the army's guards.

Windsor had been appropriated by parliament in October 1642 to prevent it becoming a Royalist stronghold. For much of the following six years it had been heavily garrisoned and, on occasion, served as headquarters of the army. In the state rooms the royal furniture and fittings remained, although the castle's first governor had purged St George's Chapel of superstitious images. In this purged chapel, on Sundays, the king listened to the governor's chaplain preach.

Just before Christmas the king's tailor arrived bearing the new suits he had ordered in Newport. Although nobody was there to see him in them, laced and velveted, he dined in state on Christmas day. On the 27th the army forbade any further ceremonies and cut the number of personal attendants. The king now dined alone in his bedchamber.[1]

His journey from Windsor to Westminster was shorn of all ceremonial. As the king's coach and six bumped its way through Hammersmith, accompanied by a troop of guards, the king entered Westminster, anonymously, alone and without ritual. One of the royal bedchambers at St James's had been prepared for him, and he found his gentlemen had prepared dinner in the presence chamber under a canopy of state. He was served there with all the usual dignity by his cupbearer, carver and sewer on bended knee. These were the last ceremonies performed in a reign defined by the maintenance of royal dignity. For after the king's trial had been announced the army had passed a resolution that he should not dine in state but be served privately. Now he was confined to his bedchamber and was not allowed to leave to eat, pray or even relieve himself. Soldiers were posted on rota in the room and drank and smoked in his presence.[2]

The king's trial

Westminster Hall was the national seat of justice, the place where not only the great like Sir Thomas More and the Earl of Strafford had been tried but where thousands of lesser legal disputes were settled by the royal courts. It was a place that legitimised and normalised the trial of the king, an act that had no precedent in law or constitution. Although the hall is now a vast open space, in the 1640s it was divided up by partitions in which the courts sat. Orders had been given to clear these and create, on the raised platform at its south end, a court. On the large, matted area the judges sat behind a long table, the President, John Bradshaw, with a crimson velvet cushion before him, the light from the high gothic windows behind him. Before them was a table covered in a Turkey rug on which a sword and mace were placed, symbols of the court's authority. The king sat on his own chair facing them.

In the hall itself were grandstands from which the wealthy and well-connected got a good view, while behind double rails at ground level humbler spectators squeezed in to hear the proceedings. In their midst was a line of troops, armed, ready to quash trouble. The arrangements were designed to minimise the likelihood of anyone hearing what Charles, 40 feet away from the closest spectator, had to say, but to allow everyone to witness an ordered and dignified process. The king was brought to his chair through the well-guarded backways of the palace and not through the main entrance in the north, past spectators.[3]

In the event the king said little, refusing to enter a plea, or even recognise the authority of the court. On Saturday 27 January, after going through the motions for a week, the judges pronounced the King of England a tyrant, traitor, murderer and public enemy. He was sentenced to death.

The proceedings over, Charles was conveyed in a closed sedan chair from Westminster back to St James's. The Duke of Gloucester and Princess Elizabeth were brought from Syon House to say goodbye; the emotional scene recorded by his valet Sir Thomas Herbert. Two musketeers had been ordered to stand in the king's bedchamber but Herbert and Bishop Juxon won him his last night in peace and contemplation. On the day of his execution the army was determined to prevent disruption and the way across the park to Whitehall was lined by foot soldiers. On the morning of 30 January King Charles walked to Whitehall between two companies of Halbadiers, their great drums beating; there he was taken to his bedchamber for his last prayers. From here he made his way across the privy gallery, through the Banqueting House, and out onto a timber platform encased in black cloth built in front of it.

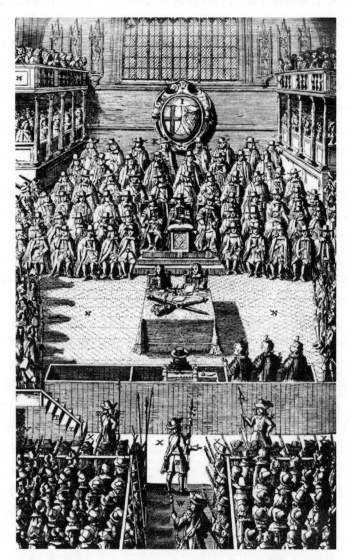

Figure 75: Westminster Hall during the trial of Charles I. The king
sits wearing his hat in a chair facing his judges, with a table bearing
a sword and mace between them. The central aisle of the hall is full
of troops, but the sides are packed with spectators. Balconies inserted
into the hall contain well-off observers. This print from Nalson's
Record of the Trial of Charles I, published in 1688, presents a more
orderly picture than written accounts suggest.

Aristocrats and members of the royal family had historically been decapitated privately inside the Tower of London; traitors were executed on Tower Hill where a large audience could witness it – this had been the fate of the Earl of Strafford in 1641. Parliament elected for neither but uniquely an execution on a public highway in Westminster. King Street widened north of the Holbein Gate, creating an open space in front of the Banqueting House. The area was not large, far smaller than Tower Hill, and would limit the risk of a large crowd that could get out of hand. The space had already been strengthened and fortified by the army and guns could be trained from the Holbein Gate in case of trouble.

Security was vitally important, but so was symbolism. The Banqueting House was the visible expression of early Stuart sovereignty, its pale-faced stone facade discordantly overbearing the red brick and stucco of the Tudor buildings. Inside, Rubens's canvases silently advertised the God-given right of the Stuarts to rule. At around two o'clock on 30

Figure 76: The execution of King Charles I outside the Banqueting House, from a Dutch broadsheet published in 1649, which was widely copied in Germany but of which there are no known English versions.

January 1649 Charles I must have looked up at the ceiling as he walked through the Banqueting House for the last time. A glazed casement had been cut out of a window for the king to access the scaffold where he faced companies of foot soldiers and cavalry on all sides. Beyond was a crowd, but too far away for them to hear the words he spoke. Soon after, the king's decapitated body was placed in a pre-prepared coffin in the king's lodgings and taken back to St James's before being moved to Windsor for burial.[4]

The Council of State at Whitehall

In August 1643, when the king's absence from the capital was expected to be only short-lived, orders had been given that the palaces and their contents should be safeguarded and a keeper was appointed to take control of Whitehall. But, by the start of 1648, after five years of absence and conflict, the palace began to assume the role of a military base. The Holbein Gate was the ideal place to control access to Westminster from the City, its windows were blocked and gun loops inserted while the adjacent walls were strengthened. Ordnance was set up in the street and in Scotland Yard. Soon the Charing Cross Mews became a cavalry barracks and in December Sir Thomas Fairfax, Lord General of the Parliamentarian forces established himself in Whitehall with four regiments of soldiers in attendance. For the following eight months Whitehall was effectively the army headquarters. Yet, though Fairfax slept in a grand bed in a fine lodging, the rank and file used peripheral areas and not the royal apartments which remained furnished and carefully guarded.[5]

In February 1649, with the king dead, the monarchy abolished and the establishment of a new executive body, the Council of State, parliament ordered that Whitehall would be its home. On the one hand this was a practical solution for housing the new executive body, on the other it was a symbolic appropriation of the palace by the new regime. But it was easier said than done: the palace was full of soldiers, and the buildings had seen virtually no maintenance for seven years – peeling paint, flaking plaster, leaking roofs were everywhere.

In 1643 Inigo Jones had fled London, and left John Webb in charge of the Office of Works. Both men were hopelessly tainted as royalists, and Jones was identified as a 'delinquent' and fined in absentia. Webb was thrust out of the Office of Works and replaced by Edward Carter, Jones's Presbyterian deputy at St Paul's Cathedral. It was to Carter that the task fell of repairing Whitehall for the Council of State. He was assisted by Clement Kynnersley, one of Charles I's officials from the Great Wardrobe. In the first few years of the Commonwealth nearly £10,000 was spent on remedial works on royal houses, most of it on Whitehall and its gardens.[6]

The queen's former presence chamber became the council chamber and her guard chamber next door its ante room. A new way was made through to the council rooms, giving the councillors direct access to the landing stage on the Thames. Most other large rooms were allotted to parliamentary committees: the old royal council chamber was allocated to the Committee of Trade, the Committee of Examinations met in the rooms outside the chapel and the queen's withdrawing room, while the Holbein Gate was the meeting room for the Committee for Scottish and Irish Affairs and the Committee for Jamaica sat in the stone gallery.[7]

Life at Whitehall had always revolved round an individual but executive power was now vested in the forty-one members of the Council of State who had elected John Bradshaw, president of the court that had tried the king, as their chairman – or Lord President as he became known. Bradshaw was as close as the Commonwealth came to having a head of state and took up lodgings at Whitehall together with other members of the council and several parliamentary committees. Quickly the palace filled up with councillors, their clerks, serjeants, messengers, porters and less legitimate residents who wormed their way in. Soon dinners were being provided from the various kitchens and ushers, doorkeepers and grooms employed for controlling access, keeping the galleries clean and directing visitors. Security was tight and pass keys were issued to councillors to allow them to move about the galleries and lodgings freely.

The chapels at Whitehall and Denmark House quickly found a new use as public places of worship. In fact, the decision to convert the Denmark House chapel had been taken in January 1647. Workmen had dismantled Inigo Jones's altar and concealed the scar on the floor with black and white marble paving. They created a plain auditorium for preaching with galleries and wooden benches. Soon after the king's execution, permission was given for public services to be held there and a preacher from St Clement Danes was licensed to use it on Thursday afternoons for sermons.[8]

At Whitehall the former preaching place with its terraces was demolished to avoid unregulated preaching and in November 1649 orders were given to enlarge the Whitehall chapel for the delivery of public sermons. While this work was underway the Banqueting House was designated as a chapel.[9] In December 1651 the Dutchman Lodewijck Huygens attended a sermon in the enlarged chapel: 'It is', he remarked, 'panelled round almost up to the roof. The people are mostly seated in a gallery, which runs round the upper part of the church. The pulpit is oblong but divided into two parts, and behind the minister stood two or three men who wrote down his sermon. More than 20 others, both men and women . . . were doing the same thing.'

This chapel, scrubbed clean of the Laudian beauty of holiness, became the official place of worship for the Council of State. Their use of it was no less susceptible to precedence than the Chapel Royal had been. In October 1651 a committee of eight was established to 'appoint a fit place in the chapel where the members of Council may sit'. But unlike Charles's chapel it was open to a wider congregation. The fact that, in 1652, during a sermon a woman stripped naked and ran through the chapel shouting 'welcome the resurrection!' shows that it was easy of access.[10]

Reusing the royal estate

Of the many problems the Council of State faced was the pressing one of royal debts. The cost of the army had virtually bankrupted the state and the war had left many former royal servants and suppliers with substantial unpaid bills. The latter became the excuse for a fire sale of royal property, at least that part of it that the council would not require itself. Acts were passed in 1649, and 1651, for the sale of both the buildings and their contents. Parliament limited to £20,000 the value of royal goods that the Council of State could reserve for its own use. But only months later, goods totalling some £54,000 had been set aside.

There were reasons for this. First, all the outer rooms at Whitehall were designed to be hung with tapestry – without it there was bare white plaster on the cold walls. Large-scale tapestries were the most expensive items valued and so merely to clothe the palace walls the council was forced to appropriate some of the most valuable items in the royal collection. Then there was the need to furnish former courtier lodgings for members of the new administration. In the king's time people brought their own furnishings, but these new men requisitioned former royal beds, carpets, wall hangings, curtains and other items to adorn their new apartments.

Parliament itself was not exempt from the cherry-picking. Before the Civil War the great chambers at Westminster Palace were dressed with rich tapestry only when parliament met; but from 1640 it sat continuously for over twelve years. In 1649 the Commons reserved the tapestries in their chamber for themselves and requisitioned the magnificent set depicting the defeat of the Spanish Armada to hang in the House of Lords, which had been dispensed with in January 1649.

Only in the instance of the king's library was there a plan to use the former royal collection for greater public benefit. A small number of the Council of State recognised that the library was one of the finest in Europe, the loss of which Bulstrode Whitelocke claimed 'would be a dishonour and damage to our nation, and to all scholars'. The council appointed Whitelocke as Library Keeper, giving him lodgings at St James's. He was one of a small group who planned to convert the Queen's Chapel into a public library filled with the king's books. Despite orders being given to start work, the project faltered and St James's became the barracks providing guards on a 24-hour rotation to Whitehall.[11]

For more than a century Whitehall had combined the lodgings and workplaces of the officers of state with the ceremonial functions of the monarch. With the monarch gone, parliament was now sovereign, and the ceremonial of state was a matter for MPs and their council. Some felt that all ceremonies were superfluous and only matters of fact and substance should be recognised. Another, more pragmatic approach, that recognised the complete diplomatic isolation of the fledgling republic, was to develop a new set of protocols for the regime. It was this latter course that was elected, the Council of State appointing a former royal diplomat, Sir Oliver Fleming, to oversee diplomatic cere-monial. Fleming not only had the advantage of experience but was Oliver Cromwell's first cousin and therefore had reason to be trusted as an insider.

Whitehall was now a complex of government offices and Westminster the ceremonial hub of the republic. Fleming relocated diplomatic recep-tions to the House of Commons where ambassadors were received with great pomp and show, while lesser envoys were received in the former House of Lords where they were subjected to the jingoistic Armada tapestries. Westminster's appropriation of state ceremonial was reinforced by the demise of St Paul's Cathedral. Before the abolition of the Dean and Chapter in 1649 the cathedral had already been used as quarters for Parliament's cavalry, but afterwards it became home to a variety of separatist congregations, to vagabonds, souvenir-hunters and pilferers. After scaffolding supporting the vaults was purloined part of the roof collapsed and permission was given to use the lead from it to mend City water pipes.[12]

Westminster Abbey was not a cathedral, but a royal church, and was seized by Parliament in early 1644 and handed to a parliamentary committee to manage; prominent members settled in the abbey precincts and John Bradshaw was given the dean's house by a grateful parliament. The abbey's income was appropriated, and its services controlled by parliamentary decree. The state began to use the abbey as the place to bury its heroes, the first being the Parliamentarian John Pym who died in December 1643 and who was given a state funeral. It was also now the venue for national thanksgiving for military victories, for the ceremonials, prayers and sermons before the meeting of parliament and for public preaching authorised by the state.[13]

While it was perhaps obvious to incorporate Westminster Abbey into the state's orbit, it was less obvious what was to be made of the twenty or so private royal residences. Most of these were eventually sold but in May 1649 parliament decided that as well as Whitehall and St James's they would reserve for state use Greenwich, Hampton Court, Theobalds, Windsor and Denmark House – which now reverted to its previous name, Somerset House. Ultimately Greenwich and Theobalds would be sold, but the others were kept.

Somerset House was cleared to create an art repository and saleroom for the former royal goods. Cartloads of furniture, paintings, tapestry and domestic utensils were brought there and laid out in the state apartments. The rooms were thrown open for people to come and see the trappings of monarchy for sale – the symbols of ceremonialism now available for a few pounds. But the sales were slow, chaotic and expensive. The market was flooded, buyers reluctant to come forward and there was confusion over what the Council of State wished to reserve for its use. In all the sale failed to yield anything like what had been predicted.[14]

St James's was integrally linked to Whitehall and was retained for use by the army. In December 1651 a young gentleman from the States General found the palace completely inaccessible, heavily garrisoned and full of prisoners. In fact, at no point from the execution of the king to the Restoration did Westminster return to a purely civilian state. In 1656 the Venetian ambassador wrote that 'the exquisite court, once

the most sumptuous and joyous in the world . . . is now changed for
the perpetual marching and countermarching of troops, the ceaseless
noise of drums and trumpets, and numerous companies of officers and
soldiers at their various posts'.[15]

Self-images

In April 1653 three entrepreneurial painters, Balthasar Gerbier, George
Geldorp and Peter Lely, suggested painting a series of pictures for the
Banqueting House at Whitehall of 'the most remarkablest Battails' of
the Civil War together with a vast group portrait of members of the
House of Commons. The Parliamentarians were to be painted on the
south wall, the canvases presumably hung on new walls to be built on
the long flanks. This was to be a celebration of the achievements of
parliament to hang in the company of Rubens's Banqueting House
ceiling, Holbein's privy chamber mural and the other triumphant history
paintings in the galleries of Whitehall.

The suggestion found no favour. Presumably, there was reluctance
to pay for it, but more important was perhaps the fact that
Commonwealth politicians did not care for such personal glorification.
Instead it was decided that the royal tapestry manufactory at Mortlake
would be reserved from sale and commissioned to produce a series of
tapestries for state use. Andrea Mantegna's ten panels of the *Triumph
of Caesar* had already been reserved and, in 1653, were sent from
Hampton Court to Mortlake to be used as cartoons for the new set.
The tapestries, over 11 feet high, would have been too small for the
Banqueting House, but were perhaps intended for either the Commons
chamber or the former queen's presence chamber where the Council
of State met.

The triumph of Caesar was a theme that the classically educated
gentlemen of the Rump and Council of State well understood. Indeed
their political self-image may well have been influenced by a reminder
of republican virtue and imperial vice. Very few purely decorative
items were reserved from the royal collection, but those that were sent

to Whitehall were almost exclusively antique Roman pieces. These full-length statues were placed in the privy garden while busts were deployed in the galleries. Although for some these pagan figures, some nude and therefore lascivious, were abominations, for the councillors at Whitehall they represented a link with the past in which some of them saw themselves represented.[16]

The Protectorate

By the time of the king's execution England's most powerful and famous commoner was General Oliver Cromwell, a position he consolidated in a series of military triumphs in Ireland and Scotland and crowned in his victory over Charles II at the battle of Worcester in 1651. Returning from campaign to Westminster he became increasingly frustrated at parliament's inability to achieve the reforms he believed that the army had fought for and, in April 1653, he forced its dissolution. Out of the power vacuum he had created came the proposal to make Cromwell Protector.

On 16 December 1653, in Westminster Hall Oliver Cromwell took the oath of office that inaugurated the Protectorate. He was now 'his Highness, the Lord Protector of the Commonwealth' and St James's, Whitehall, Somerset House, Greenwich, Windsor Castle and Hampton Court were put at his disposal for 'the maintenance of his state and dignity'. As a country seat Cromwell chose Hampton Court. The reasons for his choice were never made explicit. He could have chosen Greenwich, or Windsor, but Hampton Court was still the most lavishly furnished and most beautiful country residence. Cromwell spent most weekends there, uprooting his family, court and officials each Friday and moving as discreetly as possible in a heavily guarded barge or coach to the country. Each Monday he would return to Whitehall in the same manner.[17]

Whitehall was his principal residence, and over Christmas 1653–4 the Council of State, and its many hangers-on, were hurriedly relocated. The Cromwells, as prominent members of the new regime, had lodgings in the cockpit since 1650 and the palace was familiar to them. Now they were to move into the royal apartments. Although at first apparently reluctant, Cromwell's wife Elizabeth took an active role in decorating their rooms, working closely with Clement Kynnersley of the Wardrobe. It took until 14 April to get everything ready for them to move in.[18]

The Protectoral private quarters were in Henrietta Maria's former lodgings on the riverfront, rather than the king's rooms overlooking the privy garden. The rooms were light, east facing, with a large balcony; they were furnished with a mixture of former royal items and nearly £12,500 of new furniture bought by Kynnersley. Some recently sold royal goods had to be re-purchased, especially hangings to furnish the larger former state rooms. When John Evelyn visited in 1656 he thought the palace 'very glorious and well furnished'.[19]

Cromwell was, at first, uncomfortable with ceremonial but within a short time he was using former king's rooms for business in much the same way as Charles I. The old royal council chamber was brought back into use. The council was now of between thirteen and twenty-one members, half the size of the previous Council of State and would fit comfortably into the well-arranged royal council chamber with its ante room, rooms for the clerks and backstair. As his principal reception room he used the privy chamber, renamed the Henry VIII chamber after its vast mural of Henry VII and Henry VIII painted by Hans Holbein the Younger. Although an image of monarchical supremacy, it had been Henry VIII who had broken with Rome and Edward VI, painted at his side, who had secured England as a Protestant nation. The room thus celebrated those who had laid the foundations for the Godly Commonwealth of which Cromwell was now Protector.[20]

In 1655, a large delegation had arrived at Whitehall from Lambeth landing at the watergate directly entering the privy gallery. They had come to present a petition to Cromwell personally. Discovered by the ushers they were hastily bundled into the courtyard and ordered to enter formally through the outer chambers. Here they were poked and prodded by the halberds of Cromwell's guards before a small number were allowed to progress through the outer chambers and wait in the privy chamber for the Protector's arrival. Here Cromwell received them by the fireside 'in great majesty'. Security aside, Cromwellian Whitehall was a place governed by protocol and dignity.[21]

Cromwell saw to it that the ceremonial hub of the nation returned from Westminster to Whitehall and the Banqueting House re-established as the arena for ambassadorial receptions, richly hung with tapestries and the tables and buffets laden with gold and silver plate. Rooms at Somerset House were set aside for the accommodation of foreign embassies in suitable splendour. He also used the Banqueting House for his own ceremonies. In February 1657, celebrating the defeat of an assassination attempt, a service of thanksgiving was held at St Margaret's, Westminster. Afterwards some 200 MPs dined with Cromwell in great splendour in the Banqueting House. To the strains of the Protector's strings, courses were brought from the palace kitchens to long tables arranged beneath Rubens's canvases some 50 feet above. Just as the Holbein mural could be read as a celebration of Protestantism, so Rubens's image of King James could have been perceived as of the monarch who sponsored the authorised version of the Bible. [22]

The banquet of February 1657 apparently ended in a bun fight between Cromwell, Colonel Thomas Pride and their friends on the top table before the high-spirited party crossed the Holbein Gate to the cockpit. Here, in Inigo Jones's theatre the party enjoyed a choral concert into the small hours. The Cockpit Theatre was retained by Cromwell as a place for entertaining both his close friends and larger assemblies. In December 1656 it had been the location for the private premiere of a piece for six voices and instruments by the composer John Hingston. In 1658, after Cromwell had taken everyone by surprise by dissolving parliament, he assembled 200 army officers in the Cockpit in order to bolster their loyalty. Cromwell took the stage and spoke to the throng who had, like him, drunk more than was good for them.[23]

The rhythm of life at the Stuart court was regulated by attendance at chapel. So was life at the Protectoral court. Only a couple of weeks into the Protectorate Cromwell and his generals attended the Whitehall chapel for several hours 'of fast and humiliation' and in 1655, after a disastrously wet summer, Cromwell and the whole council 'attended at devout prayers and triple sermons' from the best preachers 'to invoke divine assistance' to save the harvest. Such events were open to a much wider congregation, indeed so wide that conspirators attempting to incinerate Cromwell in the Whitehall chapel got as far as lighting a basket full of gunpowder and brimstone before they were apprehended.[24]

Soon it was ordered that the chapel be rearranged for the Protector and his family. The glazed windows in the royal pew were removed, creating a balcony for the Cromwells' personal devotion. Here each day at ten in the morning and six in the evening the family said their prayers and listened to the words of their chaplain.[25] Sundays were almost always spent at Hampton Court, where Cromwell enjoyed prayers and preaching. In September 1655, the son of the governor of Hampton Court told Cromwell from the pulpit that he was ruling with tyranny and would fall with infamy. The plucky preacher was promptly imprisoned.[26]

Parliament paid for a substantial household containing all the above-stairs officials and downstairs servants necessary to run Whitehall as the residence of the head of state. Court tables were established for communal dining, as in royal times. Cromwell and the lady protectoress had their own tables, although Elizabeth, by her own declaration, played little part in politics or public ceremonies. There were also tables for the chaplains, visitors to court, the stewards and gentlemen, for coachmen and other domestic servants.[27]

As Cromwell assumed his new role, so responsibility for state buildings was transferred from Edward Carter as Surveyor of Works to the former royal sergeant plumber John Embree. Embree was more in tune with the new regime, purchasing a large quantity of former royal artworks at the Somerset House sales. He speculated in church lands and even bought former royal buildings in Scotland Yard. He was an active surveyor whose focus was the buildings occupied by Cromwell as Protector: Whitehall, the Charing Cross Mews and Hampton Court. Yet he also had to take care of St James's, Somerset House and the remaining buildings at Greenwich.[28]

In all some £55,000 was dispersed by Embree during the Protectorate: of this more than half was spent in its first three years. This was because the royal estate was in terrible condition. Whitehall had been kept watertight but little had been done decoratively other than to the principal rooms; Hampton Court had been used as army accommodation and the expectation was that it would be sold and demolished for its building materials. St James's and Somerset House had been barely maintained and Greenwich had been a prisoner-of-war camp and stables. It took until 1656 to get the buildings in order, a process that Cromwell actively supervised.

Oliver Cromwell was, after all, a country gentleman and, in former times, had known well his uncle's house at Hinchingbrooke outside Huntingdon and the responsibilities that maintaining it involved. But there was no new building, no adaptation and no modification over and above the decorative necessity to expunge the royal arms in prominent locations. It was the only eighteen-year period in the history of the English state when nothing new was built.[29]

King Cromwell

On 26 June 1657 Cromwell had his second installation. Many had hoped that it would be a coronation but, despite pleading, Cromwell refused to accept the title of king, although he was willing to accept its powers. As before, the installation took place in Westminster Hall, but this time he sat in Edward I's coronation chair brought from the abbey; he wore a robe and was invested with a Bible, sword and sceptre. He could now nominate his successor and his council was called the Privy Council, not the Council of State.

Cromwell had just over a year to live, and his health was rapidly declining. In 1659 a detailed inventory was taken of Hampton Court and this is the only surviving document that throws any light on Cromwell's tastes. The compilers made a distinction between goods belonging to the state and goods belonging personally to Cromwell and this shows that Cromwell, in five short years, had amassed a considerable wardrobe of fine furnishings and works of art at Hampton Court.[30]

As at Whitehall he had decided not to use Charles I's rooms himself, and they were left as offices and lodgings. The king's former bedchamber was left empty and its closet became the bedroom of a menial servant. Several of the protectorial officers occupied the same rooms as their royal predecessors. Cromwell's daughter and son-in-law John Claypole were assigned the same lodgings as Charles I's master of the horse. Cromwell's granddaughters had, as their nursery, part of the Archbishop of Canterbury's former lodging below. The comptroller of Cromwell's household, Colonel Philip Jones, was assigned the former lord chamberlain's lodgings and the cofferer, John Maidstone, was granted the lodgings of the royal captain of the guard. The chapel vestry was converted into a servants' dining room; the king's oratory was set aside as a lodging for one of Cromwell's court preachers.

Cromwell himself moved into the queen's lodgings, rooms he shared with his wife, a break with royal tradition. The queen's guard chamber on the north side of cloister green court became Cromwell's 'great presence chamber'; the next room, the queen's former presence chamber, was his privy chamber, and the queen's old privy chamber became Cromwell's supping or withdrawing chamber. Then came the queen's former withdrawing room which had a balcony looking out into the courtyard and contained a couch and elbow chairs. Beyond this came a closet, and then the queen's former great bedchamber overlooking the park. This room was Cromwell's 'rich bedchamber', it led into the former queen's dressing room, Cromwell's study, which contained a single elbow chair and a 'fine Counterfeit Ebony Table'. In here the privileged were taken for intimate business. Next door was Cromwell's little bedchamber hung with the story of *Vulcan and Venus*, with his dressing room beyond.

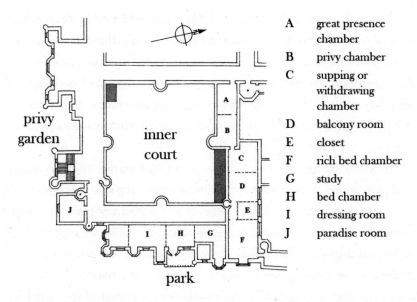

A   great presence chamber
B   privy chamber
C   supping or withdrawing chamber
D   balcony room
E   closet
F   rich bed chamber
G   study
H   bed chamber
I   dressing room
J   paradise room

Figure 77: Diagrammatic reconstruction of the first floor of the inner court at Hampton Court during the Cromwellian Protectorate.

Cromwell had moved into a suite of rooms that had been remodelled by Henrietta Maria to provide a great and little bedchamber. In the 'rich bedchamber', Cromwell's state bedchamber, the trappings of the Stuart monarchy were still in place and supplemented with fashionable new furniture. On the walls hung a sixteenth-century set of tapestries, *The Triumph of the Gods*, while a pier table and pier glass flanked by torchères stood between the windows. It must be likely that Mr and Mrs Cromwell slept together in the little bedchamber in the more private part of the east front. This begs the question of the use of the state bedchamber. In France such a room was used as a reception room for honoured guests, as it was in England after 1660. Could Cromwell have used it in the same fashion?

Cromwell tended not to use Hampton Court for state business. The Swedish ambassador, Christer Bonde was invited to visit Cromwell at Hampton Court and considered it a great honour. When he got there he found a very relaxed atmosphere: he 'heard music; walked in the park, killed a stag; then to bowling green and played bowls; then kissed the hand of Cromwell's wife, and his daughter's cheek; then drank a glass of Spanish wine, and returned to London'. These privileges were rarely granted and a royalist observer reported that Cromwell was 'exceedingly intimate' with Bonde. The visit was thus atypical, but the description of one of Bonde's entourage suggests that the presentation to Mrs Cromwell and her daughter may have been intimate and private, conceivably in the state bedchamber.[31]

From the execution of the king to 1660, successive regimes struggled to find a model of rule that would balance the powers of the executive, the army and parliament. The royal estate played an important role in this, first legitimising rule, and then defining it. Because the Council of State did not use Whitehall for ceremonial it was genuinely able to create a new model of government. But the Protectorate regimes occupying the former royal palaces and dominated by an individual were forced by their very layout to adopt monarchical patterns and procedures. Whitehall and Hampton Court, barely altered in form or decoration from the 1630s, were the setting for the reign of King Cromwell.

Cromwell's death and the succession of his ill-equipped and ineffectual son, Richard, left an executive vacuum at the heart of government. After Richard's deposition by the military there was a struggle between parliament and the army for power; St James's became the headquarters of the army, with Richard Cromwell living at Whitehall. Eventually General George Monck, whom Cromwell had made commander-in-chief in Scotland, marched south to defend parliament against the military radicals. Parliament offered him £1,000 and St James's as his base if he would consent to come to London to safeguard the Commons. Thus from March 1660 it was from St James's that Monck choreographed the Restoration and, as he made his way to Dover to welcome King Charles II, the last of the troops were ejected from St James's and Whitehall and preparations began to restore it to the Crown.[32]

THIRTEEN

The Court in Exile

Island kingdom

For three years of civil war Prince Charles was kept closely at his father's side but, in early 1645, the king became worried that they might both be taken and decided that his increasingly independent fifteen-year-old heir should take his own command. The prince was placed in nominal control of Bristol and the Royalist forces in the West. But, before he had a chance to influence events, the king's army was all but wiped out at the battle of Naseby and, now virtually unstoppable, the New Model Army took the West of England. In March 1646, realising that he was in imminent danger of capture, Charles sailed for the Scilly Isles from where he fled to the safety of Jersey.

Due to the loyalty and determination of Sir George Carteret, its bailiff, Jersey had been recaptured from the Parliamentarians and still held out for the king. In 1594, to defend the island against possible Spanish invasion, a new fort had been built on a tidal spit guarding St Helier. Elizabeth Castle, as it had become known, contained the house of the governor of Jersey built in around 1600 for Sir Walter Raleigh, who then occupied the post. This was as close as Jersey got to having a royal residence. For three months Prince Charles, and his swelling household, were based in this Elizabethan fort.

Elizabeth Castle has a spectacular location, made even more impressive as, for fourteen hours a day, the rising tide transforms it into an island. On the highest point is the upper ward crowned by a circular keep – a great gun platform protecting the bay. Just below this is the governor's house. In the much larger lower ward, in addition to the garrison barracks, storerooms, stables and houses for the officers, were the remains of the twelfth-century priory of St Helier.

Prince Charles's 300 or so household officers, council and guards, plus a train of suppliers and tradesmen were squashed into the lower ward and into private houses in St Helier, while the governor's house became a makeshift royal residence. The house still stands, although it has had a chequered history.

It was a substantial building with a cellar, two floors and an attic. On the ground floor was a hall and a parlour, presumably used for the royal guards and for receptions, and a large kitchen. Stairs led up to the first floor where the king's bedroom at the west end had its own gardrobe and views over the bay. The two other chambers at this level must have been used as ante or withdrawing rooms. Charles had arrived with three ships, one of which contained the paraphernalia of majesty and he was able to hang the rooms with tapestry and set them with fine furniture. When he was not enjoying yachting in the bay, he dined in public in his parlour on gold plate, watched by spectators, and held receptions for the island gentry.

The nave of the priory church, which had been converted for military purposes, was now transformed into a chapel royal. It was lined with whitewashed planks which were presumably covered in tapestry; there was a pulpit and a raised choir containing the royal pew. The exiles used this chapel but on several occasions Charles preferred to ride in procession to the parish church in St Helier where he could be observed at prayer in all the majesty he could muster.[1]

In the middle of June a high-powered delegation arrived from Henrietta Maria insisting that Charles join her in France; it had become clear that the Scots were not declaring for the king, but holding him under guard and, after some heated debate, it was agreed that it was

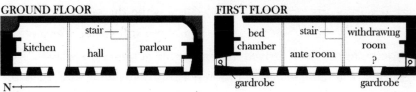

Figure 78a: Wenceslaus Hollar, Elizabeth Castle from the north, 1651. The governor's house is at the intermediate level below the circular keep. The large building in the lower bailey is the priory church, converted into a chapel by the royalists.

Figure 78b: Ground- and first-floor plan of the governor's house as used during the occupation by Charles Prince of Wales and later Charles II.

best for the prince and his mother to be reunited. Although Charles sailed from Jersey in July 1646 imagining, perhaps, that he was bidding the island farewell, he was to return in September 1649 after the execution of his father.

His second visit, accompanied by the Duke of York and 300 followers, was to be longer and, this time, he was king. He was welcomed by the islanders and held court, once again, at Elizabeth Castle. Arriving with three coaches and wagons full of furnishings once again, the house was now transformed into a monarchical residence. Here in the castle chapel, for the first time, he exercised his regal powers of touching for the king's evil, the laying on of sovereign hands that supposedly cured the glandular disease scrofula. Though Charles hunted and hawked, found time to draw a map of the island, was entertained by many of the gentry and held a great party at the castle for the Duke of York's birthday, this second visit was not as happy. Money was incredibly short, supplies from overseas were throttled by bad weather and the Parliamentarian navy, and the household became shabby and fractious as the winter drew in.

On 30 January 1650 the court commemorated the execution of Charles I in the parish church at St Helier, draped in black cloth. A fortnight later Charles departed for the last time; the following year, in the face of a determined siege Carteret surrendered the island and the final toehold on sovereign soil fell to parliament.[2]

At the French court

Henrietta Maria had arrived in France in summer 1644 with four boatloads of attendants. Her brother, King Louis XIII, had died the previous year and her nephew, the four-year-old King Louis XIV had succeeded him. Too young to rule, his Spanish mother, Anne of Austria, took the Regency assisted by her first minister, and lover, Cardinal Mazarin.

Central Paris, in the 1640s, was a product of the visionary ambition of Louis XIV's grandfather, Henry IV, who ruled from 1589 until his assassination in 1610. He had been responsible for bringing the French wars of religion to an end and had entered Paris in 1594 with a determination to make the city the locus of the monarchy and visibly capital of the nation. For two centuries previously, French monarchs had paid lip service to Paris as their capital, actually preferring to live outside the city but Henry initiated a programme to transform its appearance. The Place Royal (now called the Place des Vosges), the Place Dauphine, the rue Dauphine and the Hospital of St Louis were his most important public works, but these were public expressions of a much more radical programme to bring the streets and promenades of the city under royal control and to regulate private building.

Henry IV's first Parisian project was to improve the Louvre, the ancient seat of the French Crown. In the sixteenth century a programme of rebuilding had begun to transform the forbidding medieval fortress into an elegant modern palace; but the project was incomplete and the Louvre had never become the principal residence of the Crown in the way Whitehall had in England. In 1594 it was a shabby and incoherent compromise. Only a quarter of the main building, round the central Cour Carrée had been rebuilt; the rest was still the medieval stone fortress. Some distance to the west, just outside the mighty city wall, was the queen's residence, the Tuileries. Henry IV's idea was to link the two buildings with an enormously long gallery (le Grande Gallerie) which was largely completed by his death. His successor, Louis XIII, built another quarter of the Cour Carrée, but when he died in 1643, the palace was still an unfinished building site.[3]

In October 1643, five months after her husband Louis XIII died, Anne of Austria, and her two young sons, moved out of the Louvre. Nearby was the great town house constructed by Louis XIII's chief minister Cardinal Richelieu. This elegant modern residence had been given to the king and renamed Le Palais Royal; it now became the home of the queen regent and the toddler king Louis XIV. This meant that, when Henrietta Maria was welcomed into Paris by Queen Anne in November 1644, the Louvre was empty and, as a reigning queen consort, Anne presented her with the queen's apartments to be her Parisian home.[4]

Henrietta Maria was no stranger to the Louvre. She had been born there. So when Anne of Austria ceremonially escorted her to the cabinet of her apartment she was, in a sense, coming home. The queen's rooms were on the first floor of the south side of the Cour Carrée overlooking the river. This wing had been completed by 1578 and had been occupied by Louis XIII and Anne of Austria, but any decorative improvements they had made were swept away in the mid-1650s and by later redecorations. Consequently, although the layout of the rooms can now be discerned, their precise appearance cannot.

The queen's apartment was approached by its own staircase and an antechamber. The principal reception room in a French royal palace was the *chambre de parade* which contained a *lit de parade* – a ceremonial bed, in front of which the queen held audiences. The cabinet beyond was where the queen ate and beyond this was a small bedchamber and a great bedchamber where also she sometimes received favoured guests. The rooms were furnished with a mixture of items provided by Anne of Austria and the queen's own brought from England. Amongst these was one of the most spectacular sets of Mortlake tapestry, the *Hero and Leander* series, and paintings by Guido Reni and van Dyck. The French supplied tapestries of the story of the conversion of Saul and a magnificent red satin bed with gold embroidery for her bedchamber. In addition to the queen's own apartment there were, according to one report, '30 furnished rooms for her ladies-in-waiting, her daughter, her chambermaids, and the principal of her officers'.[5]

A generous settlement was agreed upon; as the daughter, sister, and now aunt, of a King of France Henrietta Maria was to have an allowance of 360,000 livres a year and, as well the queen's apartment in the Louvre, the use of her childhood home at St Germain en Laye, a large royal summer residence twelve miles west of Paris. The head of her household was Henry Jermyn who had been an attendant of the queen's since the 1620s, had become her master of horse in 1638 and, in Oxford, had been appointed her chamberlain. Jermyn also acted as her treasurer, chief diplomat and advisor.[6]

Prince Charles arrived in Paris and joined his mother with a small retinue and his personal baggage in July 1646. Although the prince was half French his grasp of the language was weak, and he had never been to France before. Just as his father's arrival in Spain in 1623 had thrown the Spanish protocologists, Charles's arrival set a conundrum for the French. Charles was the grandson of a French king and thus was technically a member of the French royal family. The English argued that he should be accorded equality with King Louis just as his father had been with Philip IV in Madrid. As in Madrid, the initial introductions were managed behind the scenes: it was agreed that the royal families should meet by 'chance', in carriages, in the forest of Fontainebleau. After this successful meeting Charles stayed incognito at Fontainebleau for three days and was placed at the right hand of the boy king by

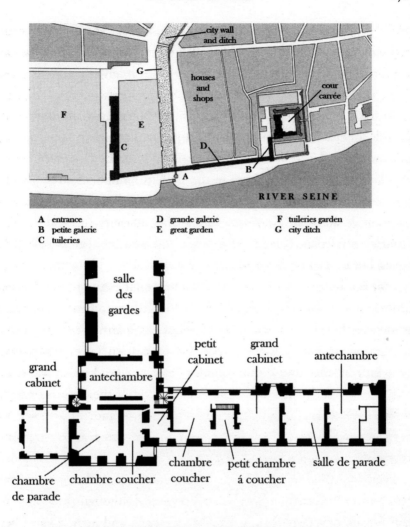

A entrance
B petite galerie
C tuileries
D grande galerie
E great garden
F tuileries garden
G city ditch

Figure 79a: Paris: The Louvre and the Tuileries in the 1650s.

Figure 79b: First-floor plan of the king's and queen's apartments at the Louvre in the 1650s. The detail is from the left-hand corner of the Cour Carrée shown on the map above.

'coincidence'. Ultimately Charles's status was never formalised, a situation to the advantage of both sides.[7]

Paris and its environs were Charles's home for nearly two years. His mother's allowance had been increased by the queen regent and Charles was now tied to both his mother's purse and apron strings. He was assigned lodgings near Henrietta Maria's in the Louvre, it is not known precisely where. Although on a short leash, under the protection of the French Crown Charles was able to properly devote himself to the most fashionable city in Europe, the place to learn manners, how to dance, dress, ride and how to seduce.[8]

At first Charles maintained a company of English players employed to provide entertainment for the exiled royalists. Even after they had been disbanded at the end of 1646 it was possible for the English court to stage an elaborate New Year masque in the Louvre. Charles enjoyed going to the theatre and promenading in the summer months in the royal gardens; he hunted, attended court assemblies and, towards the end of 1647, attended an Italian comedy and music followed by a great ball at the Palais Royal. The problem of precedent was solved by neither Charles, nor the boy king taking the throne and it being left empty as they watched. On another occasion he was invited to Fontainebleau and was entertained with excursions by day, comedies by night and a ball in his honour.[9]

The Louvre has been characterised here as a shabby compromise in 1594 but, by the time Prince Charles came to live there in the 1640s,

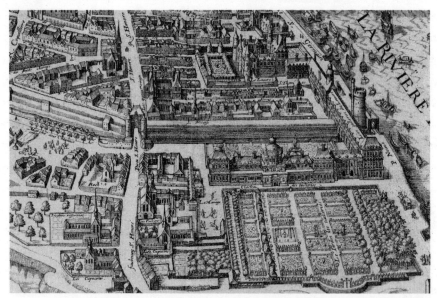

Figure 80: Matthäus Merian, *Map of Paris*, 1615, detail of the Louvre and Tuileries.
This view shows that the Tuileries were outside the city walls, but
connected to the Louvre by the Grande Galerie.

and then again in the 1650s, it had been much improved and beautified by first Henry IV and then Louis XIII.

The king's pavilion, like the queen's, comprised an ante room, *chambre de parade*, bedchamber and cabinet. A small bridge carried a narrow passage linking the *chambre de parade* to the *petite galerie* built in the 1560s. To the English exiles its exterior must have looked much like a Jacobean building, richly decorated, rusticated and adorned with sculpture. Inside it contained a genealogy of portraits of French kings beginning with St Louis IX and ending with Henry IV, twenty-eight in all. This led into the 442-metre-long *grande galerie* that linked the Louvre and the Tuileries. From the river this presented a broadly symmetrical facade with balancing pavilions at either end. The eastern half, which was built first, had a busy and crowded front, but the western half was confidently monumental with giant composite pilasters supporting alternating trian-gular and segmental pediments. The first-floor windows cut into the entablature giving the facade a baroque swagger. This was unquestionably impressive and quite unlike anything in London either in scale or style.[10]

Prince Charles left France for the United Provinces in mid-July 1648. James Duke of York had escaped from house arrest at St James's and made his way across the Channel to The Hague. The two brothers were now reunited and joined their sister Mary, the Princess Royal, who had married William II, Prince of Orange. Charles was royally received at the Binnenhof by the States General who awarded him a time-limited pension and assigned him a house reserved for foreign ambassadors. A few days later he moved to join his sister and brother-in-law in a fine suite of rooms in the Binnenhof itself.[11]

Figure 81: Elevation of the south facade of the Grande Galerie facing the river as it appeared *c.*1665. From Jean Marot's *L'Architecture Française*. The east pavilion (right), which is the short end of the Petite Galerie was rebuilt and heightened after a fire in 1661. Before the fire, the elevation would have appeared more symmetrical. The eastern section of the gallery was completed by 1604, and the more monumental western section was completed by 1610.

The Binnenhof did not belong to the Prince of Orange, it was the seat of government, but contained the stadtholder's quarters: a long range containing two suites of apartments one above the other for the stadtholder and his consort. The apartments had been extended and redecorated in 1632–4 by Prince Frederick Henry and so were modern and comfortable (fig. 121). Lodged in dignity three of Charles I's children now held a war conference. It seemed likely the Scots would form an army under Prince Charles's leadership to invade England and, best of all, the English fleet had declared for the king and was anchored off Helvoetsluys. The rest of the summer and the autumn were spent in negotiation and indecisive naval engagements, but all was interrupted by the devastating news that reached The Hague on 4 February. The king had been beheaded and Prince Charles was now king.[12]

William and Mary immediately recognised him as sovereign, a gesture which was also a recognition that Charles now outranked his hosts. He was soon assigned new apartments suitable to his sovereignty. None of the crowned heads of Europe willingly followed suit, indeed not even the Estates General in the Netherlands were willing to imitate the stadtholder's lead in case they upset the English Parliament. Nevertheless, in his travels over the following months in the Spanish Netherlands, Charles engineered a monarchical welcome, being lodged in the royal palace of the Coudenberg in Brussels and dining on equal terms with his French cousin Louis XIV as he passed through Compiegne.[13]

Charles I had been king of Scotland as well as of England and the Scots were outraged by his unilateral execution by English parliamentarians, immediately proclaiming Prince Charles king in Edinburgh. This turned out to be cold comfort to Charles II because a gulf lay between the Scots and himself in matters of religion and parliamentary authority. But in desperate straits, with no other options, he was forced to come to an agreement with his opponents, and landed in his northern kingdom in June 1650.

It is a fact that, during the fifteen months Charles spent in Scotland and his reckless dash into England, that ended in the rout of his ramshackle army by Oliver Cromwell at Worcester, he spent most of his time in military encampments. In Scotland he did visit some of the houses of his grandparents for the first time: he stayed at Dunfermline, Falkland and Stirling, but the unhappy state of his relations with the Scots lords, and especially the Scottish Presbyterians, soured the few moments spent in his ancestral halls. Back in Paris, where he arrived exhausted, humiliated and penniless in October 1651, he said of Scotland that 'there was not a woman to talk to and the barbarism of the men was such that they thought it a sin to play the violin'.[14]

The Paris to which Charles returned in 1651 was very different from that which he had left only three years before. In 1648, as a struggle between Crown and Parliament was reaching its climax, Paris was primed to explode in violent demonstrations against the arbitrary powers of the Crown. The series of conflicts that ensued between court and country between 1648 and 1653, and known as the Fronde, had two effects on the exiled Stuart royal family. First it gnawed away at Henrietta Maria's pension; payments became irregular and then almost dried up. It was reported in November 1651 that Charles and Henrietta Maria were 'keeping a very spare house, and having but one table for themselves: and for the Duke of York and the young princess, and that very indifferently furnished'. Second, it caused the French court to flee Paris, leaving Henrietta Maria the sole representative of the royal family in the Louvre. At one point a furious mob besieged her complaining she was ruining France (as she had already ruined England!).[15]

When Anne of Austria and Louis XIV returned to Paris in October 1652 they moved back into the Louvre. It was a more secure location than the Palais Royal and reoccupying the ancient seat of the monarchy was a deliberate assertion of the authority of the Crown. The English exiles were hurriedly assigned the Palais Royal instead. The Palais Royal was destroyed by fire in 1763, a tragedy as its builder, Cardinal Richelieu, was the greatest architectural patron of his age, and his mansion the most spectacular residence in Paris. His architect was Jacques Lemercier, who was forced to design the building piecemeal as Richelieu gradually bought up plots of neighbouring land in the densely packed streets close to the Louvre. In the end the building sprawled over eight courtyards, overlooked a huge garden and contained a 3,000-seat theatre. It was perhaps always destined to be a royal residence as, when the bachelor Richelieu presented it to Louis XIII in 1636, it contained two suites of lodgings as if for a monarch and consort.[16]

Eighteenth-century plans, drawn after later alterations, allow us to envisage the rooms that Henrietta Maria occupied. She took the magnificent suite, known as the summer apartment, that had been occupied by Anne of Austria. It had a parade of state rooms built by Cardinal Richelieu and a series of more intimate chambers on the garden front set up by Anne. Nowhere is it made explicit which part of the Palais Royal Charles II occupied, but there can be little doubt that he used the king's apartments – rooms that had been used by the young Louis XIV and before him by Cardinal Richelieu.[17]

The monarch's lodgings were T-shaped; a long wing to the north containing the private rooms including a bedchamber, closet and large chapel, and to the south was the *chambre de parade*. The Gallery of Illustrious Men, which stood at the junction between the two wings, was decorated with paintings depicting the great supporters of the French Crown, including Richelieu himself. Both the *chambre de parade* and the king's bedchamber contained elaborate bed alcoves and magnificent upholstered French beds. There is no image of either, but the engravings of Jean Lepautre capture the appearance of bedchambers of similar status.[18]

The Palais Royal was in the vanguard of French fashion. The apartments displayed the latest in planning, even in advance of the Louvre where an alcove bedchamber was not built until 1654. The rooms of state were set in enfilade, the doors aligned on the window wall creating an impressive perspective through the principal chambers. Chimneys were built with flues in the depth of the walls allowing chimneypieces to be placed flat on the wall plane and not on chimney breast projections. Ceilings were increasingly coved rather than being composed of flat decorative beams. Interior decoration was harmonised and doors, window shutters, even floors, were part of a single

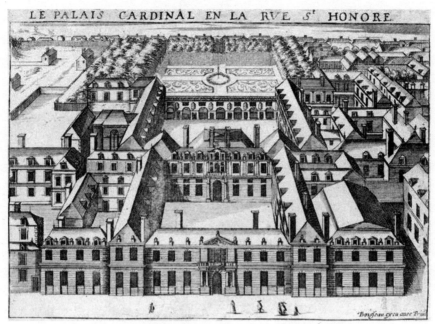

LE PALAIS CARDINAL EN LA RVE St HONORE.

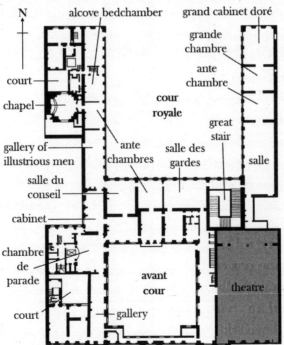

N

alcove bedchamber   grand cabinet doré

grande
chambre

ante
chambre

court

chapel

cour
royale

gallery of
illustrious men

ante
chambres

salle des
gardes

great
stair

salle

salle du
conseil

cabinet

chambre
de
parade

avant
cour

theatre

court   gallery

Figure 82a: The Palais Royal, *c.*1641, looking toward the north
from the south side of the rue Saint-Honoré.

Figure 82b: First-floor plan of the Palais Royal in the same orientation as the
perspective view. Charles II occupied the principal apartment in the left-hand wing.

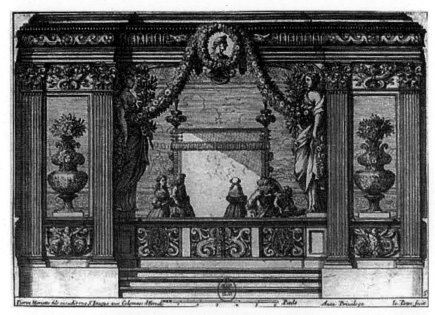

Figure 83: Jean Lepautre, an alcove with five people and giant urns, from
Alcoves a L'Italienne, published in 1656–7. At the height of their fashion in the
1650s aristocrats, churchmen and members of the royal family installed bed alcoves
in their houses. There were two in Charles II's apartment in the Palais Royal.

composition. All these fashions became familiar to King Charles in his new surroundings.[19]

The Stuart royal family relocated to their elegant new home, but elegance was, apparently, in short supply. In his play *Thomaso or the Wanderer,* Thomas Killigrew, the English playwright and impresario, called the Palais Royal a 'Coney-warren fill'd with Cavaliers of all Trades' and noted 'they eat so seldom, and dung so small, you may as soon step in a Custard as a Turd in the Court'. Two Dutch brothers, clearly hostile to the Royalist cause, claimed that the rag bag of impoverished royalist exiles camping in the Palais Royal, had almost destroyed it, shaving gilding off the gallery walls to make coins and picking lead out of the windows to sell. Surviving financial accounts for Charles's court show that he was periodically able to pay for his bedchamber servants and stable, but plentiful correspondence shows that he was unable to fulfil the expectations of the large numbers of cavaliers who wanted

Figure 84: Double-height chimneypiece from the salles de gardes in the
Palais Royal, with two life-size chained captives and the figures of
peace and justice. Engraving by Lemercier, 1633.

pensions, offices and honours. Indeed, there were occasions when the
king himself had to eat in taverns rather than at his own table.[20]

Nevertheless, for the next three years Charles lived at the Palais Royal,
not as an English prince but as the crowned king of Scotland. Despite
the acute lack of cash the young English monarch made the most of
his time in Paris: he hawked in the winter, swam in the summer, played
tennis and billiards the year round, danced, drank, gambled at cards
and had a small number of love affairs. In December 1653, after a season
of masques and plays at court, Charles was able to throw a dinner for
Louis XIV, a compliment returned by the king.[21]

There was also a serious side to his existence; determined to win back
his English throne he was enmeshed in complex discussions, negotiations,
plots and plans. For any of these to be successful he needed to behave

as a sovereign and, at the Palais Royal, strict court protocol prevailed. As in England the court was divided into three – the bedchamber (for the king's personal attendants), the kitchens and the stables. Bedchamber servants orchestrated courtly etiquette which was a blend of French and English practice. The rooms in his apartment were named in the English style, presence, privy chamber etc., but the king received people in the *chambre de parade* or bedchamber in the French fashion. Sustaining the necessary magnificence strained the teetering royal finances and while some thought the English court fine and splendid Edward Hyde, later Earl of Clarendon, thought that 'until, the king be more a king in his own house, all will not be well'.[22]

William II of Orange's death of smallpox aged only twenty-six, in November 1650, robbed Charles of his ally in the Netherlands and, in 1654, Mazarin began negotiating a treaty with Oliver Cromwell, who had just been made Lord Protector. These events would effectively close France and the United Provinces to him, but Charles had hopes that the German princes might support him financially. It was time to move. Mazarin, keen to get the exiled Stuarts off French soil even provided a cash grant to allow Charles and his baggage train to leave in suitable splendour.

End of exile

Via Aachen where, in the cathedral, he admired the bones of Charlemagne, Charles arrived in Cologne in August 1654. To his surprise he received a warm civic welcome and rented a large mansion; Cologne was to be his home for eighteen months. During the Second World War three-quarters of the city was destroyed by bombing and there is now no trace of where King Charles lived. But his residence in the city was not important for its architecture because, while Charles's stay at the court of France was to exercise a huge influence on his tastes, his experiences in Cologne were of a different kind. Not required to maintain rank at a competitive court he was able, more or less, to live within his means. Although money was chronically short, his outgoings were reduced, and cash that arrived in fits and spurts enabled him to live the reduced and dignified life of an exiled monarch.[23]

Charles spent time mastering both French and Italian and perfecting various courtly dances; he hunted, played tennis, went on brisk walks, swam in the Rhine and kept spaniels and a pet monkey. In late September 1655, with a group of companions, he went from Cologne to Frankfurt for the winter fair. They travelled most of the way on the River Main in a large barge with two subsidiary barges attached for their luggage; it was huge fun but ruinously expensive. All this time he was forced to live a life far more informal than he had ever done before. Yet surviving financial accounts show that he named rooms in his house presence chamber, withdrawing chamber, bedchamber and closet with a prayer room, rather than a chapel. But though he lived ceremoniously his life was, of necessity, unostentatious.[24]

In 1655 the diplomatic tables of Europe were reset. England and Spain were now at war and Mazarin concluded his treaty with the English, including a clause that barred Charles from France. The Spanish empire still comprised territory in Iberia, the Netherlands and Italy and, with both the United Provinces and France closed to Charles II, the Spanish Netherlands were the only feasible place from which to launch a seaborne attempt to regain his kingdom. To secure this, in May 1656, he entered into treaty negotiations with the Governor of the Spanish Netherlands. The Spanish, as always, obsessed with regularity of behaviour and correct form, would not acknowledge Charles publicly, nor even accommodate him in their headquarters in Brussels: he therefore set up in Bruges.

Bruges, much admired today for its beauty and quirky charm, was then a remote backwater of the Spanish Empire and not where Charles wanted to live. Arriving in April 1656 the Marquess of Ormond complained that 'the king is in no sort provided of a house' and he lodged temporarily in the home of a fellow exile, the Irish peer Anthony Preston, Lord Tara, 'with trouble to the Lord and some great inconveniency to himself'; other members of the royal household were scattered throughout the town. The king complained that 'houses, lodgings and furniture are had with more difficulty than in Cologne'; nevertheless a large house was found in the centre of the town.[25]

The House of the Seven Towers was a medieval merchant's mansion which was rapidly set up for the king with rented furniture. Here Charles was required to live incognito, but accompanied by the Duke of York, his sixteen-year-old brother the Duke of Gloucester, and a household of 156, he was a prominent new resident. Although the Seven Towers remains, it was rebuilt in 1717, and it is the king's kitchen accounts that reveal there was space for a full suite of royal rooms, presence, withdrawing, bedchamber, closet, backstairs and prayer room. In January 1659 with a fleeting influx of cash from the Spanish he moved to a new house rented from Count Basseny for 2,000 florins a year. Tapestries were hired for the presence and privy chambers and the eating room for 346 florins. For the king's own chamber new hangings were made and a bed alcove constructed for his own damask-covered bed. Here the king was able to hold court in greater style than at any time since he left the Palais Royal.[26]

In cahoots with the Spanish Charles, with a royalist 'army' of several thousand men, engaged in fighting against the French and the English. He personally moved to Brussels nearer the centre of things, but money problems remained acute and a planned assault on England was stillborn when it became apparent that there was no appetite for it amongst the cowed royalists in London. Worse still, Cromwell's troops fighting with the French routed both Charles's royalist army and the Spanish in a series of military encounters. Just as all looked lost, and Charles was considering a new arrangement with the United Provinces, Cromwell died.[27]

FOURTEEN

Restoration

Figure 85: Richard Gaywood's 1660 portrait of King Charles II
standing in St James's Palace with the Banqueting House in the
background. The image is a self-conscious sequel to Hollar's image
of Charles as a boy in the same location, published in 1649.

In his years of exile Charles II acquired many debts, both personal
and financial and, the moment it became apparent that the
Restoration would become a reality, his ragged and impecunious court
was flooded with royalists looking for jobs. A few of Charles I's household, like Nicholas Lanier, his Master of Music, had survived through
the 1650s to reclaim their posts in 1660. Others held the reversion of
offices (that is to say the promise of a post when the holder died);

many more had been granted an office by Charles while in exile. But there were still hundreds of posts to be filled and many times that number of hopeful supplicants. In the first eight months after the Restoration the king granted 478 patents, rapidly filling offices of state and the household.[1]

The Office of Works was one of the departments that was to be restored exactly as it had been before the Civil War and was typical, in that the appointments made in 1660 were a mixture of men resuming positions they had held before 1649, those who could prove they had a reversion, and people who succeeded in claiming a reward for loyalty during the interregnum. John Embree, who had served as the Protector's surveyor, had bought parts of Whitehall Palace as a property speculation and was persona non grata. The man who won the coveted post was the poet, playwright and royalist conspirator, Sir John Denham.

Figure 86: Richard Gaywood, *Charles II riding from Whitehall to his first Parliament at Westminster.*

In 1642 Denham had published *Coopers Hill,* a 22-page poem whose theme upheld the notion of monarchy. That November, as Charles I's forces entered Surrey, Denham was appointed sheriff of the county and governor of Farnham Castle, a role that ended in his humiliating surrender to the Parliamentarians. Joining the king in Oxford, *Coopers Hill* was republished as a work of royalist propaganda; Charles himself complimented Denham on his verses but wanted him to perform more serious services. This Denham did at the king's side at Hampton Court, on the Isle of Wight, in London and at the court of Henrietta Maria in France. With most of his lands sequestered by 1648, he was with Prince Charles at The Hague where he acted as messenger between Charles and his mother. At St Germain, with no money to reward Denham's services, the king promised him that, when he was king, he would succeed Inigo Jones as Surveyor of Works. It might have seemed a hollow reward at the time but, in 1660, the king kept his word.[2]

Back in England, on 2 May, only a week after parliament had voted to restore the monarchy, John Webb lodged a petition with the Council of State requesting that he be made Surveyor of Works. Appointing someone to oversee physical preparations for Charles's return was pressing. On 5 May parliament had agreed some £30,000 to be spent on the preparation of the royal houses and on the 8th, the day of the king's proclamation, a Commons committee was established to supervise it. This committee, and a similar one established by the House of Lords, also required the return of former royal property sold during the Commonwealth. Webb was instructed to prepare Whitehall, Somerset House and St James's and the hefty inventories of Charles I's possessions were handed to him to help with reassembling the royal interiors. Webb was assisted by a stalwart former royal servant Clement Kynnersley, the Master of the Wardrobe who knew the royal collection better than anyone else.[3]

The Lords committee, ignorant of the appointment of Denham in Breda started to refer to Webb as 'His Majesty's surveyor'. Webb, highly experienced, was the obvious candidate for the job. Much in favour with Charles I, and active in the Royalist cause during the Civil War, in 1656 he had obtained permission to travel to France from where he joined Charles's court in exile in Bruges. By 1660 he was back in London, denying himself the opportunity to press his case for the surveyorship in person. Instead, when Charles II arrived in London, he found Webb's petition setting out his credentials. It was too late; Denham had moved into the Scotland Yard offices and had formally relieved Embree of his duties.[4]

Meanwhile the king appointed another loyal royalist as Paymaster to the Works. This was Hugh May, an extremely capable architect from a court family who had been in the service of the Duke of Buckingham and had been at Charles II's side at the battle of Worcester, fleeing with him to the continent afterwards. Long in exile, he had served the king and studied continental architecture at leisure. He had also hoped for the surveyorship, and, although his duties as paymaster were officially financial and administrative, Denham asked him to undertake most of the design work of the early Restoration.[5]

Charles II returned to Whitehall on 29 May 1660, his thirtieth birthday. His procession to the City was more like a military triumph than a traditional royal entrance. At Blackheath Charles reviewed the army and watched as the flags, banners and arms of the Republic were tossed on a huge bonfire. These had been replaced in a rushed programme to emblazon the royal arms on everything from warships to carriages, flags to drums and hundreds of buildings. The City was draped in tapestry, the roads lined by the trained bands in their uniforms, and huge bonfires were lit on street corners; passing through the City, packed with cheering citizens and escorted by a huge train of attendants, officials and dignitaries, the king reached Charing Cross at which point the mass of spectators parted allowing the king to enter through the Whitehall court gate.

The day had started at five in the morning and by the time Charles entered the withdrawing chamber in the evening, it was past seven and the lights were lit. After receiving a short speech and the Lords kissing his hand, he entered the Banqueting House, chandeliers blazing, to receive the House of Commons.

Since 1649 there had been few architectural changes at Whitehall and, on returning, Charles would have been familiar with everything he saw. What had changed were his expectations of what a principal metropolitan residence should look like. Whitehall may have been large with many splendid interiors, but the Palais Royal, it was not. It was not only the residence that disappointed him, but its setting and, indeed, London as a whole.

There was little the king could do about this immediately and so, while he contemplated rebuilding Whitehall and remodelling its environs, his own living quarters claimed his attention. The first task was his bedchamber. In the Palais Royal he had slept in a fashionable alcove bedchamber and he probably knew of the French royal architect, Jacques Lemercier's, plans to build an alcove for Louis XIV at the Louvre. Though the contracts for this were not signed until June 1654, a couple of months before he left Paris, the design had been settled several years before.

The new Whitehall bedchamber bore a strong resemblance to Louis XIV's new Louvre bedroom. Its front was decorated with carved wooden curtains hauled up by flying putti and a shield flanked by eagles. The front of the alcove was closed by a gilded rail with opening gates. The floor was laid with parquet, one of the first instances of this being used in England. On the ceiling was a painting by John Michael Wright celebrating the Restoration. New furniture soon arrived including a state bed and a matching suite of furniture. Charles used the new bedchamber in the French fashion as a room in which to receive honoured guests. This was quite unlike either Charles I or even Henrietta Maria, who had built an alcove at Wimbledon; both of them had used bedrooms as private rather than public spaces.

The king's dressing room and cabinet nearby were also redecorated. Initially the old bathroom on the floor below was refurbished but, in 1663, Charles ordered it be rebuilt. The room, which contained a deep sunken bathing pool, was panelled and garnished with carvings and a painting over the chimney. The walls were hung with silk, a feather bed was installed in an alcove and, to preserve the king's privacy, a palisade was erected in front of the windows.[6]

Sir John Denham's Office of Works was quite different to that of Inigo Jones who preceded him, or Sir Christopher Wren who followed. Denham had won the post of surveyor through his loyalty and services to the Stuarts, through his artistic sophistication, but also through his bonhomie. Charles liked Denham, giving him subjects upon which to versify to while away the boredom of exile; he became part of an inner circle of men who gambled, whored and drank with the king and were given diplomatic tasks to fulfil. The high favour he enjoyed was reflected in his creation as a knight of the Bath at the coronation. In 1660 Denham was forty-five and past his hell-raising days; he became a surveyor of smooth administrative ability and sophisticated architectural tastes and drew on a pool of architects and designers who were assigned projects either by royal preference or for their technical expertise. It is likely that, in 1660, John Webb was asked by Denham to remodel the Cockpit Theatre at Whitehall for both these reasons.[7]

The king had enjoyed theatre during his long exile and, as the Cockpit had been regularly used by Cromwell, it was in good condition, but for musical concerts not plays. In 1660 two courtiers, William Davenant and Thomas Killigrew, succeeded in winning royal patents to form two companies of actors, the King's and the Duke's, who had the exclusive rights to act on the London and the court stage. But, in 1660, before anyone could tread the boards the Cockpit Theatre needed reconstruction.

The modifications to the Cockpit, that included squaring off the previously octagonal building with triangular staircase towers, and improving the sight-lines and lighting, were good enough for a few years, but new plays were increasingly demanding of scenery, and the semi-circular format of the auditorium was limiting for both audience and actors. In 1665 the king gave orders to convert the great hall into a permanent theatre and Denham again asked John Webb, the only man in England with the necessary experience, to design it. A proscenium arch with a curtain faced a deep stage to take scenery; there was a pit, an auditorium with a balcony, raked seating and a royal box. At first the Tudor hammerbeam ceiling was concealed by stretched canvas; later a boarded and plaster ceiling was inserted. By the end of the reign there were side balconies for the public to watch plays, but initially the theatre was to entertain the court.

From the outside the great hall was still the Tudor flint and stone hulk built by Cardinal Wolsey, but inside it rivalled the two principal commercial theatres for beauty and convenience. In the winter there were plays every week, many by the English patent companies, but some by French or Italian travelling companies; a highlight was the arrival of Scaramouche and his fellows from the Palais Royal for the summer of 1673. Plays took place in the evening and the stage and auditorium was lit with hundreds of candles: all the departments of the royal household were involved – the king's violins played the music, the Office of Works built the scenery, the Wardrobe made the costumes and the kitchens provided the refreshments.[8]

Sir John Denham was a highly cultured man. *Coopers Hill*, his famous poem, was a reflection on landscapes and buildings seen from the top of the eponymous rise near his home in Egham, Surrey. Windsor Castle, St Paul's Cathedral and the ruins of Chertsey Abbey became emblems illuminating his view of monarchical rule. This sensibility to place and its meanings must have been developed and honed in the company of Charles II in exile and after 1660 may have influenced Denham's thinking about London.[9]

The thoroughness with which the royal estate in Westminster was recast in the years 1661–5 suggests that in the early part of 1661 the king must have agreed what would now be called a masterplan for it; but who, apart from the king himself, devised this remains unclear. St James's Park was completely redesigned: the waterways were reorganised to create a vast central canal 2,800 feet long and 120 feet wide flanked by double avenues of trees and a great semi-circle at its east end. Other pools and streams were regularised, including the construction of a decoy for duck trapping. A new pell mell alley was built in front of St James's to replace the earlier one outside the park wall and bordered by another double avenue.[10]

Along the north wall of the park the former royal gardens were replanted by the French gardener André Mollet and his nephew Gabriel to be a private retreat from Whitehall. At its east end, by Charing Cross, was another garden in which Prince Rupert built himself a splendid house. The old tiltyard, and the sheds and houses in it, were demolished and a fine new headquarters for the king's horseguards built. Its centre-piece was a pedimented pavilion with a viewing platform and a clock turret; either side were taller blocks capped with pediments on the street side. In front was a parade ground, the first such thing in England.

Meanwhile the Office of Works staked out the path of a new road, Pall Mall, to run from Charing Cross to St James's Palace, creating a

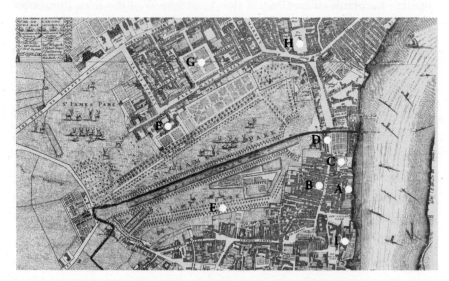

Figure 87: William Morgan, *A prospect of London and Westminster*, 1682.
By this date Charles II had extended St James's Park into the area
we now know as Green Park.

A – Whitehall palace	E – St James's Park
B – The parkside or cockpit	F – St James's Palace
C – Scotland Yard	G – St James's Square
D – Horseguards	H – The Royal Mews
	I – Westminster Palace

more rectilinear layout. To the north of this was land on which Henry Jermyn, the Earl of St Albans was given permission to develop a new aristocratic quarter, a square or 'Place Royal', for the accommodation of leading courtiers. As in Covent Garden the design of the houses was reserved for the king's approval. Work had begun on what became St James's Square by 1663.

Denham was deeply involved in all these projects, acting in the same capacity as his predecessor Inigo Jones, formally approving designs and engaging the Office of Works in technical issues. In 1661 he was returned as MP for Old Sarum and was prominent in achieving legislation necessary for metropolitan improvements. Hugh May was also engaged in the Westminster works as paymaster and one of May's elder brothers, Adrian, who was a groom of the bedchamber and seems to have had an aptitude for gardening, was given charge of the gardeners.

The centrepiece of this great scheme, and the building for which the setting was being created, was a new palace of Whitehall. In 1660 John Webb must have believed that his chance had finally come to build the palace that he had designed for Charles I, and it is likely that with his petition for the surveyorship he included a proposal for a new palace. The king was enthusiastic and ordered a survey to be made of the existing buildings of Whitehall in December 1660.

Several drawings survive by Webb, all of which include the Banqueting House and are of a much more realistic scale than the plans of 1648. One of these found enough royal favour for Denham to commission a wooden model of it. Two of Webb's drawings show the proposed siting of the palace: one puts it on the riverfront, like the scheme approved by Charles I. Another, dated October 1661, is more ambitious and shows the complete remodelling of Charing Cross, Pall Mall and the Strand to create a vast forecourt in front of the palace. By autumn 1661 it had become clear that Charles II wanted not a mere rebuilding, but a completely new palace in a magnificent landscape setting much more like the Louvre.[11]

While work continued on the park, Pall Mall and St James's Square, design work on the palace stalled. This was partly because Restoration

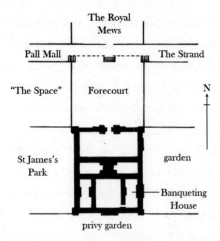

Figure 88: John Webb's proposal for a new Whitehall Palace, dated October 1661. It shows King Charles's aspirations at their most ambitious. The River Thames is to the right.

Whitehall was a whirlwind of activity: The king was crowned and married, there was a deluge of diplomatic missions, the so-called Cavalier Parliament sat four times, a deal on religion was struck and England descended into war with the Dutch. Charles was in near continual residence for four years, the longest time an English monarch, up to that date, had ever resided in one place.

The king was not the only resident: after 1660 Whitehall quickly filled up; the Duke and Duchess of York had the largest lodgings, followed by Prince Rupert and the Duke of Monmouth, Charles's eldest illegitimate son. A series of mistresses would be given large apartments: Barbara Palmer, Countess of Castlemaine (who bore the king five children); Nell Gwynn (who had two sons), and Louise Renée de Kéroualle (with a son). In addition to Monmouth's lodging in the cockpit, there was also an extremely large apartment for George Monck, now the Duke of Albemarle, and the Duke of Ormond, Lord Lieutenant of Ireland. The Duke of Lauderdale, Secretary of State for Scotland, had rooms in and around the King Street Gate. All these people had household servants and those with political office or court responsibilities had assistants, clerks and deputies. Restoration Whitehall was a residence but also a governing machine clogged by diplomats, petitioners, messengers, clerks and MPs.[12]

In October 1660 the king had instructed that his household should be established on the model of Charles I's in 1631. This meant recruiting more than 300 servants who would provide communal meals (diets) for around 225 members of the royal household in the outer rooms of the palace twice a day. Provision was made by parliament for financing this, but the costs proved higher than anticipated and the income less than expected. At the end of 1662, to stave off a financial crisis, all but the most senior courtiers lost their diets and the others were put on boardwages – a payment in lieu of dining rights. It was not enough. In August 1663 Charles was forced to stop all diets, boardwages and pensions save for the queen and Prince Rupert. At a stroke expenditure on the household was halved and the number of staff reduced to fewer than 150.[13]

These financial problems contributed to the lack of progress for a new Whitehall, but they also began to determine the nature of any new building. For, although any new palace would need to accommodate the king's large extended family and functions of state, it no longer had to provide for hundreds of menial servants engaged in the provision of daily diets. From 1663 no royal house would ever again need to be so large.

Wife and mother

Unlike the triumphant return of the king, Henrietta Maria's arrival in London was low key and met with tepid enthusiasm. She was only fifty and, though chastened by a decade of exile, was still the same forceful and entitled princess that had gone into exile. After an immediate payment of £20,000, her jointure was restored to her by parliament plus a pension of £30,000 a year and she moved back into the queen's lodgings at Whitehall on 2 November 1660.

Charles was unmarried, and Henrietta Maria was still a queen. Established in the queen's lodgings at Whitehall she held court and gave orders for Somerset House to be rebuilt and the Queen's House, Greenwich to be repaired. Wimbledon Manor she sold for £10,000. Her second queenly reign only lasted a few months and, in January 1661, she left England to see her daughter Henrietta Anne marry the duc d'Orléans in Paris. Four months later the king announced that he would marry the Portuguese Princess Catherine of Braganza and so it was clear that, when his mother returned, it would be in a different role.[14]

Work on Somerset House was put in the hands of Sir John Denham, a trusted friend who was appointed her Surveyor General with a pension of £20 a year. Work was entirely funded by the queen and Denham was responsible for signing the wage books. Her executant architect was Hugh May who took wages as her architect, an £80 annual pension and, in 1664, a £500 reward 'for his paines'. It makes complete sense that he would have won this, the first important architectural commission of the Restoration, having been well known to the queen mother in exile. Work at Somerset House was extensive, and it was agreed that, while underway, the queen mother would reside at Greenwich in the Queen's House. This put considerable pressure on to get the work completed for her return.[15]

It is clear, however that plans for Greenwich, as they coalesced, were for Charles II and his bride and not just for the queen mother. Greenwich had been a favoured royal residence for some two centuries and, though it was in appalling condition in 1660, Charles II wanted it to resume its prominent place in the royal itinerary. Concurrently with plans for a new Whitehall, the king was devising a scheme for a replacement palace at Greenwich. The diarist and architectural connoisseur John Evelyn records a conversation with Denham about ideas for a new palace at Greenwich in October 1661 and two months later, a wooden model was made of it.[16]

But initially the focus was not a grandiose scheme for a comprehensive rebuilding, but the necessity to bring the Queen's House up to standard. One of the designers with whom Sir John Denham worked during his nine-year surveyorship was the Dutch sculptor and architect

Willem de Keyser. In July 1661 de Keyser, who had worked in England before the Civil War, and had returned from Amsterdam where he had been during the Republic, was asked to draw plans and elevations of Greenwich for Denham. The next month work began on converting the Queen's House into a miniature royal residence.

The Queen's House was two blocks of building linked by a bridge straddling the road; the 1661 scheme added two more bridges creating a king's side and a queen's side approached from the central hall on the north front. Each side had presence and privy chambers and a bedroom overlooking the park. It was small: the presence chamber only 32 feet by 18 feet, a fraction of what was needed for any state occasion but, perhaps, perfect as a private retreat. It was finished by August 1662 when Henrietta Maria returned to England and moved in pending the completion of works on Somerset House. It was there that she met her Portuguese daughter-in-law, Catherine of Braganza.

Catherine had landed at Portsmouth on 15 May and had taken to bed recovering from a fever while the king dealt with the end of a parliamentary session, joining her only on the 20th. They were married in a makeshift presence chamber according to the Anglican rite, a secret Roman marriage ceremony having already taken place.

Hampton Court was the only country residence in a condition to receive the king and queen and the Office of Works embarked on a frantic programme of repairs and improvement in anticipation of their arrival. A cordon had been placed around the house to prevent unauthorised persons having access before the king and queen arrived on the 29th. An encampment of tents and wagons sprang up, some full of undelivered luggage, others belonging to stallholders and costermongers selling souvenirs, snacks and other goods for the crowds that were assembling. An air of chaos reigned – in one tent lay the body of one of the king's choristers who had been run over and killed by a cart, in another was one of the king's cooks who had drowned while swimming in the Thames. John Evelyn was one of those who managed to get a ringside view of the royal arrival. He had travelled down to Hampton Court on 25 May where he saw the queen's newly decorated bedchamber and examined her bed, a

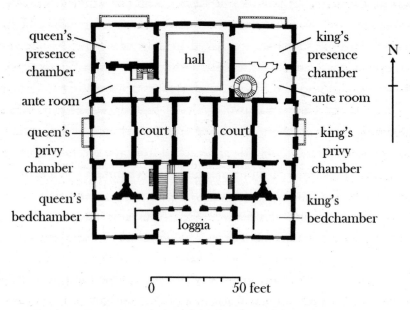

Figure 89: Reconstructed plan of the first floor of the Queen's House,
as completed for Henrietta Maria and Charles II in 1662.

gift from the States of Holland. It was hung with crimson velvet hangings embroidered with silver. Some of the furniture in the queen's apartments was the queen's own and Evelyn especially noted the 'Indian cabinets' and lacquer trunks, novelties in England.[17]

The king and queen did not arrive until about nine o'clock at night, and so the assembled crowds saw little; the royal carriage drove through the outer court in a cloud of dust between massed ranks of guards. They alighted in the inner court with the Duke of York at their side. From here Catherine processed to her bedchamber, passing through her lodgings, where in each chamber were stationed, according to rank, the nobility of England.

Hampton Court was a stepping stone to her arrival in London, but while Whitehall was being prepared Charles and Catherine made a trip by carriage to Greenwich, where Henrietta Maria met the new queen on the terrace of the Queen's House at the front door. The new rooms must have smelt of drying paint as the queen mother showed them round.

Figure 90: Dirk Stoop's illustration of the arrival of Queen Catherine at
Whitehall, 1662. Entitled *Aqua Triumphalis*, it shows the king's barge containing
Catherine and Charles being welcomed by the lord mayor and the citizens of
London. The lord mayor's barge is labelled, as are the smaller boats containing
pageants by the various city guilds. Whitehall is depicted to the right.

Their eventual entry into London was by river. The royal barge with
twenty-four oarsmen was fitted with a crimson and gold canopy under
which the newlyweds were seated; their vessel was surrounded by hundreds
of others; Samuel Pepys, the naval administrator and diarist, who had a
rooftop vantage point, could see no water for the number of craft. They
landed at the privy stairs and entered Whitehall to the booming of guns
on the south bank. Once more, the queen's apartments were filled with
the cream of society in the best dress money could buy.[18]

Between Catherine's arrival in May 1662 and Henrietta Maria's final
departure from England in 1665 there were two queenly courts in
London. Henrietta Maria's rebuilding of Somerset House, that was
largely complete by October 1664, had created a dazzling setting for
hers. The brief must have been settled with Hugh May before her
departure to France and involved both enlarging the house and bringing
it up to date stylistically.

May's solution was simple but ingenious. He constructed a new block
of rooms on the south side of the great hall in the garden neatly set between
the chapel on the west and the old presence chamber on the east. A giant
five-bay rusticated arcade supported the new facade with pilasters and
pedimented windows. The design was a variation on Italian Renaissance
palazzo designs such as the Palazzo Magnani in Bologna finished in the

1580s. It was an extremely sophisticated composition, especially as it was May's first documented architectural work in England.[19]

The facade was important for another reason: May, perhaps using French craftsmen summoned by the queen mother, installed what were almost certainly the first sash windows in England. Sliding frames of glass counterbalanced by weights worked by leather straps and pulleys were an absolute novelty in 1661, but were rapidly adopted at Whitehall from where they set a fashion that was to take England by storm.

Inside the new range a spectacular staircase created a new circulation hub. Pepys describes descending it and trying the 'brave echo on the stairs – which continues a voice so long as the singing three notes concords, one after another, they all three shall sound in consort together a good while most pleasantly'. Little wonder it echoed, for it rose through almost four storeys. At first-floor level there was a new presence chamber and privy chamber.[20]

From the Tudor great hall a door in the centre of the south wall took visitors to the dowager's presence chamber. This was a much larger room than that which it replaced and was intended for staging the queen's weekly Circle which she re-introduced as the court's principal weekly social event after a gap of some twenty years. After the king's marriage to Catherine of Braganza, Henrietta Maria's circle remained the leading court social event, the young queen joining her mother-in-law beneath the throne canopy.

Courtiers arrived in the outer court and assembled in the old great hall, now used by the queen's guards, before moving into the queen's presence. The great staircase allowed the king, queen, Duke and Duchess of York to disembark from their barges and cross the garden ascending to enter the circle directly. In August 1662 Pepys attended a Somerset House circle, being ushered into the presence chamber by the queen's attendant and surgeon James Pearse. Under the canopy sat the queen mother and the queen attended by the Countess of Castlemaine and the Duke of Monmouth amongst others. Soon they were joined by the king and the Duke and Duchess of York.[21]

Henrietta Maria's rejuvenated Somerset House was furnished with paintings, furniture and tapestry recovered from the Commonwealth

THE STRAND

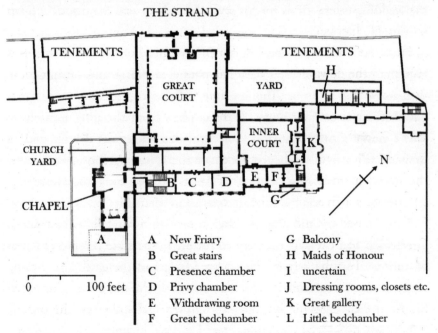

A	New Friary	G	Balcony
B	Great stairs	H	Maids of Honour
C	Presence chamber	I	uncertain
D	Privy chamber	J	Dressing rooms, closets etc.
E	Withdrawing room	K	Great gallery
F	Great bedchamber	L	Little bedchamber

Figure 91a: Leonard Knyff and Jan Kip, Somerset House from the south published in *Britannia Illustrata*, 1707. Knyff's view is extremely accurate and depicts the river facade and the new rooms as built for Henrietta Maria by Hugh May. On the left-hand side is the large stable building designed for Catherine of Braganza by Robert Hooke.

Figure 91b: Reconstructed palace of Somerset House at first-floor level as rearranged for Henrietta Maria in 1662, in same orientation as the perspective.

sales, with items sent from France and newly commissioned pieces. Some craftsmen and materials were also brought from France, in particular craftsmen to lay newly fashionable parquet floors. The appearance of the painter John Michael Wright in her accounts might suggest that painted ceilings were commissioned in some of the rooms.[22]

Although the king appointed Henry Jermyn, Earl of St Albans, Henrietta Maria's closest friend and treasurer as keeper of Greenwich house and park, some agreement, now lost, must have existed between the king and his mother assigning the use of Greenwich to the Crown. For while works to Somerset House were underway the king's plans for Greenwich were developing.

As at Whitehall, the king was thinking ahead and wanted to lay out the landscape and, in particular, plant trees as soon as possible. During the wedding celebrations for his sister, Henrietta and the duc d'Orléans in 1661, Henrietta Maria had been feted at Vaux-le-Vicomte, the gorgeous house of Nicholas Fouquet, Louis XIV's finance minister. There she had met the French landscape designer André le Nôtre and admired the gardens he had laid out. This meeting led to a commission to design a new landscape at Greenwich. Despite pleas from the king himself, le Nôtre never visited England, but provided Henrietta Maria with a drawing for a new landscape south of the Queen's House. Pepys saw the trees for this being planted in April 1662, although le Nôtre was still being chased for his final designs more than two years later.[23]

From its foundation as a royal house in 1439 the attraction of Greenwich had been its capacity to couple major state ceremonial with an intimate private retreat. Henrietta Maria had perfected this by the construction of the Queen's House, although the Civil War prevented her from fully enjoying it. Greenwich's principal state function was its role in ambassadorial receptions. Sited on the Thames, four miles east of the capital, it was the first royal house encountered by visiting dignitaries who normally landed at Gravesend. At Greenwich an initial formal welcome took place by senior members of the royal household after which ambassadors transferred to the royal barge for their ceremonial cruise to the City of London. Greenwich needed to be magnificent enough to impress foreign diplomats and intimate enough as a weekend retreat. This was never more so than in the early 1660s when a flood of diplomats made their way to Charles II's restored court. By July 1662 no fewer than twelve full-scale embassies had been received by the king. In December 1662 the Russian ambassador, who was sick from his journey, was forced to camp at Greenwich while he recovered. Plans for a new Greenwich therefore needed to recognise its dual role.[24]

In 1663 John Webb was asked to join the Office of Works team working on designs for Greenwich and was given the title of 'surveyor assistant to Sir John Denham' for the job. He was, of course, familiar with the site and had been involved in discussions about it with Denham a few years before. Now however, a comprehensive scheme for an entirely new palace was being formulated. The first drawings for this are not in Webb's hand and incorporate the ideas of several people, including the king, for a new type of royal house.[25]

The new palace was to be divided between public reception rooms and self-contained private apartments. What is probably the first of two proposed schemes shows an H-shaped palace with a great fore-court facing the river. On the west were the king's state lodgings and facing it across the court was not a side for the queen but a massive range of reception rooms in the centre of which was an extremely large domed chapel. Chapels were key to diplomatic cere-monial as the places where thanks were given for safe transit, farewells were said, and where treaties were solemnly signed in the presence of the Almighty. James I had enhanced the Tudor chapel at Greenwich for exactly this reason and, although Charles's own marriage had already taken place, the new chapel would have been a crucial tool in diplomatic negotiations for the marriages of Charles and Catherine's anticipated children.

On the south side of the house, facing the gardens and looking up the hill, were the privy lodgings, the king's and queen's apartments facing each other with bedchambers and south-facing closets. This scheme did not find favour, perhaps because the Queen's House, now a comfortable refurbished retreat, would have had no obvious use. So

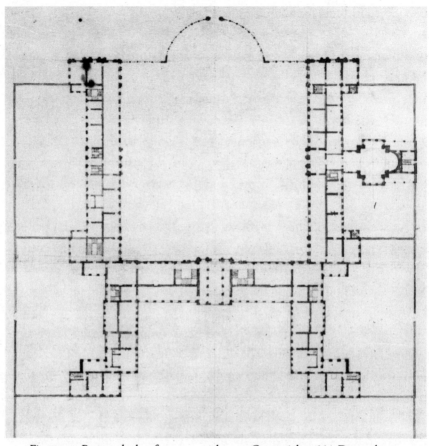

Figure 92: Proposed plan for a new palace at Greenwich, 1663. Drawn by an unknown draughtsman employed by the Office of Works, it shows a unique arrangement with only one suite of state rooms for the king and symmetrical privy lodgings for the king and queen overlooking the park. The massive range facing the state apartments contains no recognisable rooms other than a gallery and chapel: it was probably designed for diplomatic receptions.

a second scheme was prepared, much like the first, but siting the private lodgings in the Queen's House rather than as part of the main palace.

For this, in May 1663, work started on enlarging the Queen's House by adding pavilions to the corners. This would have increased its architectural impact seen from the river as well as provided expanded royal accommodation. Pepys saw the foundations laid for the king's state block by the river the same month.

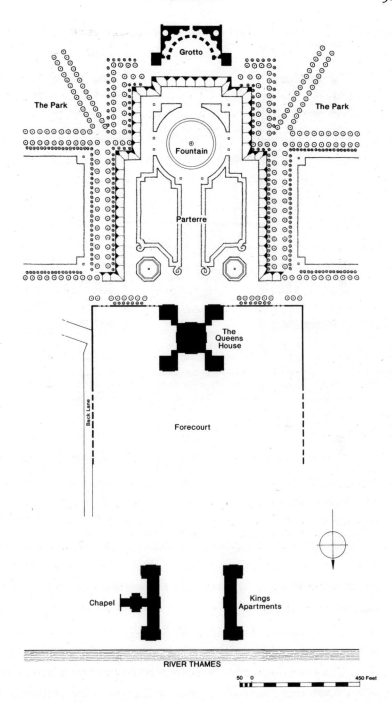

Figure 93a: Reconstructed plan of Greenwich palace as envisaged by Charles II in 1663. Work to realise this ambitious scheme was started but abandoned by 1670.

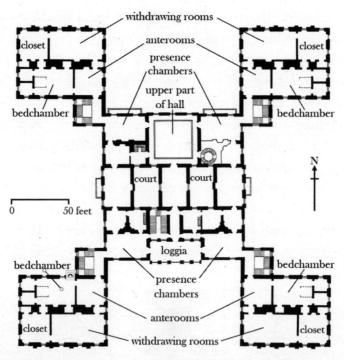

Figure 93b: Reconstructed plan at first-floor level of the Queen's House, Greenwich, as intended in 1663. The scheme was begun but soon abandoned.

The conception was bold. Landing diplomats would have seen two enormous stone-built blocks flanking a vista terminating in a much-enlarged Queen's House. Behind this were rising terraces of garden culminating in a large hilltop grotto. Le Nôtre's designs for this were sketchy and were worked up by Webb into a remarkable classical belvedere. It was perhaps at this juncture that the king asked for the Queen's House to be built higher to provide a more imposing structure in the vista from the river.[26]

Given the financial crisis that engulfed the court in 1663, and the far greater one that crippled London in 1665–6, it is remarkable that anything was done, but with ingenuity money was found from various sources to keep this extremely expensive scheme going. Webb's king's block, his masterpiece, and a masterpiece of English architecture, was of stone and heavily modelled with rustication, pilasters, and a giant order in the centre. The design was a development of Webb's elevations for Charles I's Whitehall and drew its inspiration from designs by Andrea Palladio, as had the Banqueting House, but this was bigger, bolder, more coherent and more majestic than anything yet built in England. It was neither a cheap nor an easy building to construct. Although things moved very slowly work began on designing the interiors in early 1665; a huge trunk of drawings, books and prints was brought to Scotland Yard from Webb's house in Somerset, presumably to provide inspiration for the designs.[27]

Many of Webb's drawings survive, including a beautiful design for the king's bedchamber with a spectacular bed alcove. These reveal that as well as the first-floor state chambers, on the ground floor was

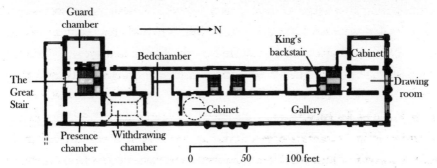

Figure 94a: The east facade of John Webb's state suite for Charles II, with state apartments on the first floor and a public dining room on the ground floor.

Figure 94b: Reconstructed plan of the first floor of the king's lodgings as intended in the early 1660s.

a suite of rooms specifically designed for public dining. Charles II revived the practice of dining in public in 1660 with greater splendour and formality than under his two predecessors. The king always had breakfast and supper in his own apartments, but dinner, taken mid-afternoon, was frequently a public event in the presence chamber; when he dined with the queen it would be in her presence chamber. Such occasions were very popular, and rails were erected to keep people at a distance.

Public dining usually accompanied diplomatic events and it would have been expected that this took place in the presence chamber. But Greenwich provided the first purpose-built dining room in any royal palace. A separate vaulted entrance from the forecourt (which still survives) led to a waiting room and ante room where spectators were vetted by the guards and the gentlemen ushers before being admitted into the dining room next door – a room larger than the presence chamber above. Unfortunately, no drawings exist of the proposed interior, but judging by drawings that survive for the first-floor rooms it would have been a magnificent space.[28]

Given the generosity of the facilities designed at Greenwich, and their undoubted splendour, it appears that the king was intending to make Greenwich the focus of diplomatic ceremonial and that the Queen's House was intended to operate as an entirely separate and self-contained residence for the royal family.

FIFTEEN

The First Decade

All the king's men

A t the Restoration many of those who had endured a decade or more of privation in exile were rewarded with a place at court. This meant that most of those closest to the king had an intimate experience of the continent, and in particular of Paris and the French court. French fashions were not just the prerogative of the half-French king, but infused everyone's taste.

From 1660 almost all the king's designers and decorators had been to Paris or, indeed, were brought from Paris. The old royal upholsterer John Baker junior, for instance, who had held the post for forty years was asked, in 1660, to work alongside John Casbert, a French upholsterer who came over with the king and learnt his trade under Louis XIII. In the Office of Works John Denham and Hugh May were both *au fait* with the latest French fashions. Other travellers who gained royal commissions included John Webb, but also William Samwell and Sir William Bruce who will be mentioned below.

Before the Restoration it was already accepted that the best person to design a building was one who had toured Europe. Architectural education was increasingly a process of reading and foreign observation – and books and travel cost money. Designers now had to be well heeled; the master craftsman of old could not afford a long period of foreign travel and study. The designers at Charles II's court were therefore different from those before the Civil War: almost all were gentlemen of means rather than craftsmen tutored on building sites.[1]

John Denham typified this new breed of designer. It is not known whether he could draw plans and elevations, but he certainly directed not only architectural administration but also design. It is impossible now to quantify his lasting influence, but another figure has a claim to be perhaps the most influential of his generation. John Evelyn is best known for his diary, but he was also a connoisseur of wide scientific and artistic interests. A committed royalist, but no soldier, he had conducted an extended Grand Tour of Europe during the 1640s and had married the daughter of the English Resident in Paris. There he had been a figure on the fringes of the exiled court. At the Restoration he published books and pamphlets drawing comparisons between France and England. His translation of Roland Fréart's *Parallèle de l'architecture antique avec la moderne*, dedicated to the king and to Sir John Denham (whom he had known in Paris), and published in 1664 with the encouragement and help of Hugh May, was the first and most important architectural book of the Restoration.

Fréart's *Parallèle*, illustrated by high-quality plates, brought to English architects, craftsmen and connoisseurs a detailed exposition on the ancient orders of architecture, showing that they were not just 'pillars' but were a whole system of design based on geometry. Fréart made it clear that designing a building was not about garnishing it with columns but using the basic geometric principles that lay behind the orders. Inigo Jones had understood this point, but few, if any other English architects had done so before the Civil War. Evelyn's translation was in the library of every architectural connoisseur and designer for more than fifty years.[2]

In Rome, Evelyn had become good friends with another important figure in Restoration architecture, Roger Pratt. Like Evelyn he had an extensive Grand Tour during the Republic and wrote keenly about architecture, but his works were never published. He did however scoop several of the most important architectural commissions of the

Restoration, including building Clarendon House on Piccadilly. He does not seem to have been commissioned by Denham but, as will appear, Charles II chose him to be one of the three commissioners for rebuilding the City after the Great Fire of London and knighted him in 1668, Pratt becoming the first to be knighted as an architect.

While these men all played a role in the architecture of the Restoration court, their favour was to be eclipsed by a young astronomy don from Oxford, Christopher Wren. Wren's royalist credentials were impeccable. His father, a clergyman also called Christopher, started in the household of Lancelot Andrewes, Dean of the Chapel Royal, and was appointed Dean of Windsor after his brother Matthew vacated the post. The dean was ex officio registrar of the Order of the Garter, a job he took very seriously, and which brought him into close contact with Charles I. The young Christopher spent much of his youth in the dean's capacious lodgings at Windsor and was well known to the royal family.

The Wrens were ejected from Windsor in May 1643 and the whole family, perhaps, was in Oxford with the court before retreating to their country parish in Wiltshire; Dean Wren was imprisoned for short periods and, after losing his living, retired to Oxfordshire with his books, dying in 1658. Meanwhile his son, whose talents were recognised by all who met him, went up to Oxford University where he lived with the warden of Wadham College and quickly became admired for his mathematical ability. A fellowship at All Souls College was followed by the Gresham professorship of astronomy in London and finally the Savilian chair of astronomy at Oxford.

Wren was a royalist and a courtier to his bones. In August 1660, on bended knee, he returned to the king, in person, his father's registers of the Order of the Garter. Unless Wren had managed to make a trip to the continent to visit the king in exile, which is unproven, the two had not met since they were teenagers. The 28-year-old Wren, two years the king's junior, was now widely recognised as a genius and, a couple of months later, he was found at Gresham College with Charles II gazing at the stars through his telescope; soon he was entertaining the king with his meticulous drawings of fleas and lice and received a commission to make a globe of the moon for the king's cabinet.

At the Restoration, Wren took his place amongst the coterie of courtiers with scientific and technical ability round the king. The mind of Charles himself was of that bent. Although a well-informed lover of beautiful things he was not a committed connoisseur like his father, nor a book-worm like his grandfather. Science, engineering and architecture fascinated him and, like many a gentleman, he had his own laboratory at Whitehall where experiments could be undertaken. The founding of the Royal Society, the world's first scientific institution, promoted by great men of learning, was approved and encouraged by the king.[3]

In the mid-seventeenth century the modern distinctions between disciplines did not exist, and architecture, engineering and surveying were seen as mathematical sciences, like geometry and astronomy. Christopher senior had been very interested in architecture and, amongst the remarkably wide interests of Christopher junior, which spanned acoustics, medicine, print-making and fishing, architecture and engin-eering took a prominent place.[4]

Although Wren was probably involved in engineering projects in Oxford before 1660, at the Restoration Charles II asked him to go to Tangier, recently acquired by the English as part of Catherine of Braganza's dowry, as chief engineer. There he was to design fortifications and would be rewarded not only with a handsome salary, but with the reversion of Sir John Denham's post of Surveyor of the Works. Wren passed the opportunity of relocating to North Africa to a much more experienced engineer, Jonas Moore, and instead answered the royal command to assist with the repair of Old St Paul's Cathedral, whose south transept had collapsed during the Interregnum. These were regarded as tasks of geometry, mathematics and engineering, not archi-tectural design and, as far as is known, Wren's first original architectural compositions were produced in 1663 for Pembroke College Chapel, Cambridge and the Sheldonian Theatre, Oxford. Wren's wooden model for the latter was sent to London to be shown to the Royal Society and the king, who much admired it in April 1663.

That month the king formed a Commission for the repair of St Paul's Cathedral. As a symbol of the national church, of the monarch as its head, and of the magnificence of the capital, its repair was a priority. The commission included Sir John Denham, but otherwise comprised those who would have to find ways of financing the project from the City and the Church. They were empowered to take advice from appropriate technicians. Denham initially asked John Webb and the master mason Edward Marshall for advice, but the circle was soon widened to include Pratt and May. Wren, it seems, was engaged on another royal project.[5]

Amidst the deluge of work, and the orgy of pleasure, that consumed Charles II in the first years of the Restoration his project to rebuild Whitehall faltered. But in October 1664, in a conversation with John Evelyn in the privy gallery at Whitehall, the king sketched out on a sheet of paper his new ideas for the palace. These are unlikely to have been the same as Webb's. Although a designer of great talent, Webb was chippy and socially awkward and this held him back from high office. The king's new darling, Christopher Wren, had none of this. While the voluminous documentation on his life gives few clues about his character, no one frequently in the company of Charles II prospered unless they were socially at ease. Wren was not only a royalist and a genius, he had social *savoir faire*.

The new designs for Whitehall devised in 1664 were by Wren and, with royal approval, were translated into a large-scale timber model. The design, Wren's first royal commission, included a three-storey building connecting the Banqueting House with a two-storey portico. It is a beautiful piece of work and shows Wren's brilliant draughtsmanship meeting the geometrician's rule. The elevation is made of carefully proportioned rectilinear compartments filled with subtly balanced decorative details: Wren saw architecture as a 'mathematical science'. Already, in this early essay, the bones of his future style were to be seen, yet there was something missing. Wren was the only one of the king's favoured designers who had not been to Paris. In early 1665 it was decided that Wren should go on a study tour to France. The queen mother was planning to leave England and Wren was to be attached to her household. John Denham and John Evelyn furnished him with advice and contacts and, at the end of June, Henrietta Maria and her entourage left England, with Wren in attendance.

There was nothing particularly unusual about sending Wren to Paris. Other royal servants had been sent to learn French fashions: the composer Pelham Humfrey was sent to learn composition, Thomas Betterton travelled to Paris on a number of occasions to consult experts on the construction of theatres and writing plays and John Banister was sent to learn how to compose musicals. For Wren, who had up to this point known French buildings only through books and prints, a tour of Paris would put him on a level with May and Pratt, who had studied European architecture at leisure, and it would equip him for the great task of redesigning Whitehall.[6]

As Wren arrived in Paris the cognoscenti were in a frenzy. Gianlorenzo Bernini, the most brilliant and famous architect and sculptor in Europe, was in town pondering the best way to transform the Louvre, while carving a portrait bust of Louis XIV. Wren was amongst the hundreds who crowded into his studio hoping for an audience with the old Italian; like most of his hopeful audience Wren caught only a few moments of bad-tempered attention and snatched a glance at some of his drawings for the Louvre.

While his meeting with Bernini might have been a let-down, Wren's tour of the buildings in and around Paris was inspirational. Closed doors swung open at the name of the queen mother, and Evelyn's contacts provided Wren with like-minded companions. Wren observed craftsmen and engineers, took notes, bought books and prints and discussed architecture and science with his French counterparts. After a full eight months he packed his trunks and made his way back to London, bringing with him 'all Paris on paper'. Although this was to be his only foreign trip, Wren maintained his interest in architectural developments abroad, hungrily devouring new books on continental architecture as they were published.[7]

Court religion

Charles II owed his crown to his Anglicanism, yet within months of his return to Whitehall he was negotiating a marriage with the Catholic daughter of the King of Portugal. From the king's point of view there was much in favour of this; it helped balance the great powers of Europe to English advantage and brought with it a dowry that would handsomely boost royal finances. His subjects were less enthusiastic, and Charles parried parliament's hostility by pointing out that if he waited for their approval, he would die a bachelor.[8]

Charles was diligent preparing for the arrival of Catherine of Braganza. He recalled Father John Huddleston who had hidden him after the battle of Worcester and had taken Benedictine orders in exile. As the most prominent Catholic at court, Huddleston was asked to establish a house of Benedictines for the queen made up from English Catholics in exile.[9]

Catherine arrived with four priests, a choir master, several musicians and some choirboys. She found her house of hand-picked Benedictines at St James's where, in the east window of the chapel, a huge stained-glass crucifix flanked by the arms of Braganza and Stuart had been installed. An organ had been brought from Whitehall and the royal pew luxuriously furnished. For her private devotions, which she meticulously observed, Catherine used the oratory that had been prepared for her at Whitehall, but on feast days she crossed the park to St James's. On these occasions she could be seen by anyone who attended the chapel and, according to Pepys, the congregation was a complete cross-section of society from duchesses to beggars.

Although a Catholic chapel was now re-established at St James's it was not the leading congregation in London. On her return Henrietta Maria had made it a priority to restore her Capuchin friary at Somerset House and, by 1664, it was the most magnificent Roman Catholic chapel in England. Stripped of all its fittings in the 1640s, Inigo Jones's chapel was a blank canvas for Hugh May in 1660. He was commissioned to redesign the interior, providing a huge new altarpiece as a focus for the queen's worship. In his extensive travels across Europe, May would have seen many of the leading churches in Italy and France and may have also owned some of the books or loose sheet prints of altarpieces published in France from the 1630s.

The new altarpiece was based on French Counter-Reformation models with pairs of fluted Ionic pillars supporting an attic with a segmental pediment. Niches either side contained statues of saints and a rectangle over the high altar was designed to take a painting. Pepys, who enjoyed gate-crashing services in the Catholic chapels, attended on Ash Wednesday 1664 and thought the chapel very fine and ten times fuller than the queen's chapel at St James's.[10]

Figure 95: Isaac Ware, survey drawing of the altarpiece in the Roman Catholic chapel at Somerset House, c.1735. Now known to have been designed by Hugh May and built in 1662–4, this impressive composition ironically went on to be the inspiration for hundreds of Anglican altarpieces from the 1670s.

In 1665 Henrietta Maria left England and her band of Capuchin friars. Their community continued at Somerset House but, with the queen mother gone, Catherine became England's leading Roman Catholic. She appointed a new Grand Almoner, Philip Howard, who decided to build a friary at St James's to accommodate a band of Franciscan friars of the Spanish order of St Peter of Alcantara. The Benedictines were provided with lodgings in the old tennis court at St James's and twelve Alcantarine friars and a father guardian were invited to London; unlike the suave aristocratic English Benedictines they were simple, severe and ill-educated.[11]

A fully functioning friary with two cloisters, refectory, dormitory, cells and a choir for the brothers had not been seen in England since the Reformation. Both Denham and May could have known continental friaries but they must have been following the lead of Philip Howard and the queen who was reported, in 1669, by the visiting Belgian abbot, Claudius Agretti, to have a special interest in 'al decoro della Chiesa'. A notable feature of the friary was the friars' choir, a first-floor chapel behind the high altar. Such chapels were to be found in Spain, but the inspiration was most likely the Paris Oratory founded in 1611 and designated the royal chapel of the Louvre by Louis XIII in 1623. François Mansart had added an oval eastern choir as the Oratorians' private chapel. He also designed such a chapel behind the high altar at the abbey of Val-de-Grâce. Both these churches were well known to Henrietta Maria and to English Catholics and may well have been visited by Hugh May.[12]

In January 1667 Pepys was proudly shown round the new friary by Philip Howard himself and wrote that he 'saw the Dortorie and the cells of the priests, and we went into one – very pretty little room, very clean, hung with pictures – set with books . . . A pretty library they have, and I was in the Refectory, where every man has his napkin – knife – cup of earth – and basin of the same – and a place for one to sit and read while the rest are at meals. And into the kitchen I went . . . Their windows looking all into a fine garden and the park'. Cosimo III de' Medici, Grand Duke of Tuscany, who saw the friary a few years later reported that the friars observed the monastic hours in their upper choir and participated in monthly processions round both cloisters carrying relics or a consecrated host. In these the queen herself participated.[13]

In September 1669 Henrietta Maria died and Somerset House and all its contents were finally transferred to Queen Catherine. She decided not to use it as her principal residence, much preferring to live at Whitehall. She did however relocate her chapel from St James's to the larger and more splendid Somerset House. Here, immediately, she began to build new conventual buildings around the chapel: a dormitory, refectory and cloister for the friars and, in the chapel, extensions and modifications for a larger congregation. It was in this way that, within

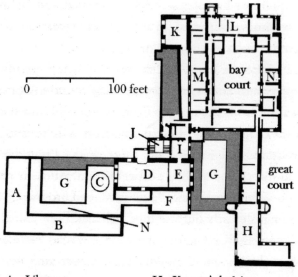

A	Library	H	Keeper's lodging
B	Friars' cells	I	Queen's withdrawing room
C	Friars' choir	J	Chapel stairs
D	Chapel	K	Royal library
E	Queen's Pew	L	Duke's lodgings
F	? Private oratory	M	Princess Anne's lodgings
G	Cloister garth (below)	N	Princess Mary's lodgings

Figure 96: Reconstructed first-floor plan of the Alcantarine Friary at St James's Palace as built for Catherine of Braganza in 1665–9. The plan only shows the eastern section of the palace, which was occupied by the Duke and Duchess of York during Charles II's reign.

a decade of the Restoration, Somerset House once again hosted a large and energetic Roman Catholic congregation in the centre of the highly populated Strand.[14]

Country houses

By fortune the Restoration of 1660 had not been accompanied by outbreaks of plague such as the catastrophic episodes of 1603 and 1626 but 1661 saw a severe outbreak in Turkey and from there the plague spread across Europe, reaching London in the spring of 1665. By mid-June the deadly bacteria was killing more than 100 a week in the City.

On 29 June cases close to Whitehall caused a general remove of the court in 148 carriages to Hampton Court. But Hampton-on-Thames and the surrounding villages soon became infected and, at the end of July, one of the king's guard died. It was decided to remove to Salisbury where the court arrived in early August.[15]

The plague reached its peak in October with 4,327 recorded deaths, but unlike previous outbreaks it did not disappear after Christmas and the spring of 1666 saw a resurgence. It was impossible for the court to go back to London and, after spending Christmas at Oxford, the king returned to Hampton Court on 27 January. By this time his presence in London was imperative and, with the plague abating, he returned to Whitehall in early February, where he received the Lord Mayor to express his gratitude for his efforts on behalf of the City.[16]

The seven months that Charles spent on the road in 1665–6 high-lighted the fact that, other than Hampton Court and Windsor, the Crown no longer had any habitable domestic residences outside London. In March 1666, determined to rectify this, Charles made a trip eastward to Saffron Walden in Essex, where lay Audley End, one of the greatest Jacobean houses in the land. It had been begun in 1603 by Thomas Howard, 1st Earl of Suffolk, who subsequently became James I's Lord Treasurer. It was a house designed from the first to host royalty with matching king's and queen's sides round an inner court. About a third of the house remains today, and it is still vast. The cost of the house was crippling and Howard died passing heavy debts to his son and grandson.

James Howard, the 3rd earl, was Earl Marshal at the 1661 coronation and his wife became groom of the stool to Catherine of Braganza. Husband and wife were in a good position to sell the delights of their overblown Essex home to the king. A deal was struck that was mutually advantageous: the king would purchase the house and its contents for £50,000, £30,000 in cash and £20,000 as a loan from Howard. Howard would retain the interest, most of the estate, less the hunting park, and become the keeper of the house with a large private apartment there.

Like many a spur-of-the-moment purchase, Audley End did not live up to reality. Although it was large and able to accommodate the whole court, and though the long gallery was a much-admired feature, it was in Wren's words 'gay but old-fashioned'. The court visited a handful of times, and not at all towards the end of the reign.[17]

Charles II was a great sportsman; he loved to walk, ride, swim, fish, play tennis, pell mell and bowls, race greyhounds, fly hawks, hunt stags, hares, foxes and otters, fight cocks, and sail yachts. He was a man full

Figure 97: Henry Winstanley, engraved view of Audley End House, with figures and horses and carriage in the foreground, 1688.

of energy and enthusiasm for life. Ranking his pleasures would be impossible, but racing was one of his favourites, and one of the reasons why, in March 1666, he stayed at Audley End House. It was only twenty miles from the pre-war royal sporting centre of Newmarket and had fine paddocks and stabling.

During the Republic the Jacobean palace there had been all but demolished. Charles had either forgotten what Newmarket was like, or it had substantially changed since the 1640s, as he tipped a guide ten shillings to take him round town. It was perhaps his original intention to use Audley End as a base to visit Newmarket, but he quickly decided that he wanted to stay in the town itself. The Earl of Arlington, spotting that Newmarket was being restored as a royal centre, bought an estate at Euston, twenty miles north and commissioned a magnificent remodelling of the house there.

Two years later, after unsatisfactorily using Audley End, the king bought a plot of land on which to build a new house at Newmarket and Denham appointed William Samwell as architect. The Samwells were a well-connected gentry family from Northamptonshire with a penchant for radical political thought. William's first cousin was James Harrington, an unlikely favourite of Charles I, whose book of political philosophy, *Oceana*, was briefly an influence on Republican thinking. The Samwells declared for Parliament and, as well as occupying important positions in the county, bought former property of Westminster Abbey in Dean's Yard, Samwell, his father, and James Harrington all living there from the late 1640s.

Harrington acted the elder brother to his relations, promoting his brother William Harrington's career as an architect and as a fellow of the Royal Society, and it was probably he who, in 1648, secured for the twenty-year-old William Samwell a position in the bedchamber of the dukes of York and Gloucester at St James's at a salary of £100 a year. He may have also encouraged young William to follow his example and travel on the continent as, by the time he took up architecture in the early 1660s, he was clearly well-versed in continental architectural developments.[18]

It is not clear how Samwell met his first patron, Edward Proger, but Proger had been in the royal household as a page to Charles II as Prince of Wales and subsequently in exile before returning to London in the 1650s. At the Restoration he was appointed to the Bedchamber, becoming close friends with the king, and was ordered to build 'for our service' a new lodge at Hampton Court where Proger had been granted the keepership of the north park. Samwell designed a near-square building with a striking roofscape of stacked dormers with a distinctly Dutch feel.[19]

Samwell also seems to have been involved in dealings with the Earl of Arlington and may have had a hand in the design of his house at Euston Hall in Suffolk not far from Newmarket. But it is perhaps most likely that his commission for Newmarket came via the Duke of York

Figure 98: Pen-and-ink drawing by Bernard Lens of Bushy House, as completed by William Samwell for Edward Proger in 1664–5. The windows have stone casements and the roofline is decorated with two storeys of dormers.

in whose household he had been placed in 1648, and for whom he was later to work at the Royal Mews at Charing Cross.[20]

What Samwell designed at Newmarket was an elegant essay in Caroline Dutch classicism. It was brick, of two storeys with attics, similar to his surviving range at Felbrigg Hall in Norfolk. In plan it was very interesting. Samwell adopted the French pavilion plan, in other words the creation of small square linked pavilions in which the king's and queen's lodgings were more or less self-contained. This arrangement had been proposed at Greenwich by John Webb but never built before in a royal palace.

It is not known precisely how the rooms were laid out, yet it is certain that the room in the south pavilion was the king's bedchamber in which his bed was positioned in an alcove behind a gilded rail. The other pavilion was probably the queen's, approached by its own staircase. The room on the front overlooking the road was the king's presence chamber, used for dining in state.

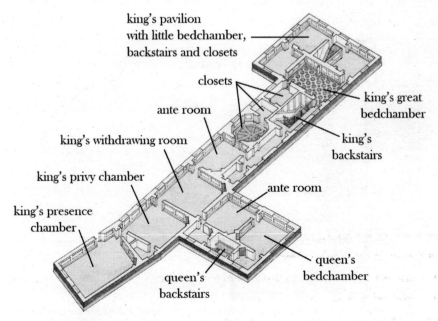

king's pavilion with little bedchamber, backstairs and closets

closets

king's great bedchamber

ante room

king's withdrawing room

king's backstairs

king's privy chamber

ante room

king's presence chamber

queen's bedchamber

queen's backstairs

Figure 99: Reconstructed cut-away plan of the first floor of the king's lodgings at Newmarket, as designed by William Samwell.

Samwell's design was right up to date, incorporating both corner fireplaces and sash windows. One of the latter survived bricked up only to be rediscovered in the 1990s; it is the earliest sash to survive in England. Although Samwell's building was technologically and architecturally advanced its overall effect was less than impressive to contemporaries. Cosimo de' Medici, who visited soon after it was completed, thought that it 'did not deserve to be called a king's residence' and John Evelyn thought the buildings the 'most improper imaginable for an house of Sport and Pleasure'. Despite these remarks Charles II liked the house and spent much time there in the 1670s.

Evelyn spent the night at Newmarket in October 1671 and found 'the jolly blades racing, dancing, feasting and revelling, more resembling a luxurious and abandoned rout than a Christian Court'. Racing was not the only entertainment at Newmarket; there was a tennis court and a bowling green and most important of all a cockpit. Sometimes while the court was in residence there were cockfights twice a day. At night there were plays. One by the poet Thomas Shadwell is set at Newmarket and one of its main characters, Prig, is described in the *dramatis personae* as 'A

Figure 100: Francis Barlow, 'The last horse race run before Charles the Second of blessed memory by Dorsett Ferry near Windsor Castle, August 24 1684'. Races at Newmarket were very similar.

coxcomb that never talks or thinks of anything but dogs, horses, hunting, hawking, bowls, tennis and gaming; a rook [cheat] and a most noisy jockey'. The description could have applied to many at Charles's Newmarket.

Yet not all was pleasure. The king received ambassadors at Newmarket and undertook other ceremonial duties. This is important because it demonstrates that Newmarket was more than a pleasure palace, it was a place of serious royal business and ceremony and Samwell's buildings were designed to be a backdrop to the theatre of state.

As the new residences at Audley End and Newmarket were being discussed, the country was not only ravaged by plague, it was at war. The conflict with the Dutch that had begun in March 1665 was joined by Louis XIV in January 1666. Known to history as the Second Dutch War, it was a disagreement about trade and navigation fought at sea by the navy. Its costs were enormous, some £5 million in all and, in its midst, the most famous event in London's history took place.

Fire

The Great Fire of London, which began on Sunday 2 September 1666, obliterated the commercial heart of the nation. For a government that had relied on borrowing from the City and taxing its trade this was a disaster. For a king who set store by the appearance of his capital it was an opportunity. A royal proclamation a week after the fire expressed the king's hope that the city would be quickly rebuilt for both 'use and beauty', and that the world would regard it 'purged by fire . . . to a wonderful beauty and comliness'. 'Rules and directions' for rebuilding would take time to prepare and 'hasty and unskilful building' in the meantime was not to be allowed, but Charles promised that the 'whole design' of the city would be quickly agreed. To this end he ordered a survey to ascertain property ownership and form the basis of a master plan for reconstruction.

By the time these instructions were issued Christopher Wren had already presented the king with his plan for a new layout for the city and, on the very day of the proclamation, John Evelyn presented another. A third scheme, devised by Robert Hooke, Gresham Professor of

Geometry, and approved by the Royal Society and the Corporation of London, followed a few days later. With hindsight such ambitions were already doomed. England was at war and parliament preoccupied with raising money for the navy rather than rebuilding the city. Pressure from residents and traders to rebuild immediately was intense, and the negotiations necessary to value and purchase thousands of parcels of land to enable a new layout would take years, even if it could be afforded – which it couldn't.[21]

In the end the practical details of how to rebuild was delegated to a commission of six: for the king, Wren, May and Roger Pratt, and for the City Robert Hooke, the city's bricklayer turned architect, Peter Mills and its mason, also an architect, Edward Jerman. These were the six best-qualified and most talented architects in England. By the spring of 1667 it was clear that they were to proceed, not to a new plan, but more or less to the old layout of streets and buildings. Care must be taken not to underestimate their achievement because the new city was more elegant, more spacious, ordered and built in brick and stone. In fact, the City had now caught up with the West End, its finest mansions reflecting the architecture of St James's Square.

The king himself took great interest in the progress of work, intervening in both town planning and architecture. In this he showed himself to be a well-informed and discerning patron. Evelyn's book *Fréart's Parallèlle de l'architecture* was not just a translation of another man's work, it contained an essay on 'Architects and Architecture'. In this he identified three participants in the process of design: an *Architectus Ingenio* or superintendent, an *Architectus Sumptuarius*, or patron and the *Manuarius*, or workmen. All the Stuart kings acted as *Architectus Sumptuarius*, but Charles II was also *Architectus Ingenio*. In 1664 Sir Balthasar Gerbier published a book on architecture dedicating it to the king, pointing out that Charles had seen more stately palaces and buildings than any of his predecessors: this was the key qualification for any designer in Restoration England.

On a visit to Languard Fort in Suffolk, accompanied by his chief military engineer, Sir Bernard de Gomme, Charles II examined plans

Adriaen van Stalbemt, A View of Greenwich with Charles I and Henrietta Maria among a group of courtiers, c.1632. On the far left with his garter ribbon is probably the king's groom of the stool, James Hay, first earl of Carlisle, called camel-face by the king's daughter. Wearing an indoor cap, he is talking to the immediately recognisable Endymion Porter, a fellow connoisseur and close friend of the king's. The man in blue labouring up the hill also with a garter ribbon may be the 4th Earl of Pembroke. The darker of the ladies behind the queen could be Lucy Percy, Countess of Carlisle and the man in black, also wearing his ribbon is Richard Weston, 1st Earl of Portland, Lord High Treasurer. In the background is Greenwich Palace and the Queen's House as it was left by Anna of Denmark.

The queen's bedchamber at Greenwich, photographed in the 1980s as arranged in the time of Catherine of Braganza. In Henrietta Maria's time the room contained a magnificent bed behind a rail. The central ceiling panel is later but the cove and frieze are those painted in the late 1630s. The fireplace is a copy of the original.

Peter Lely, Peter Pett and the *Sovereign of the Seas*, *c*.1645.
Shown in minute detail is the lavish decoration of the stern of
Charles I's flagship, ordered by the king himself.

Isaac Fuller, the arrival of Charles II at Whitehall in 1660,
c.1660. The Banqueting House is on the right and next to it,
the Court Gate, the main entrance to the palace.

Hendrick Danckerts 1676–80. From left to right this painting shows the new horseguards headquarters with the Banqueting House behind; the Holbein Gate and tiltyard with Inigo Jones's stairs; the cockpit lodgings with the turret, or the old Tudor Tennis Courts.

Sir Christopher Wren, presentation drawing for a new palace at Whitehall, 1698. On the left is the Banqueting House.

Sir Peter Lely, self-portrait with Hugh May. This painting showing the two friends in front of May's masterpiece, Windsor Castle, was painted in the late 1670s. Hugh May holds one of his plans and others are on the table.

The inner court of Holyrood Palace, designed by Sir William Bruce with Robert Mylne, constructed for Charles II and completed by 1678.

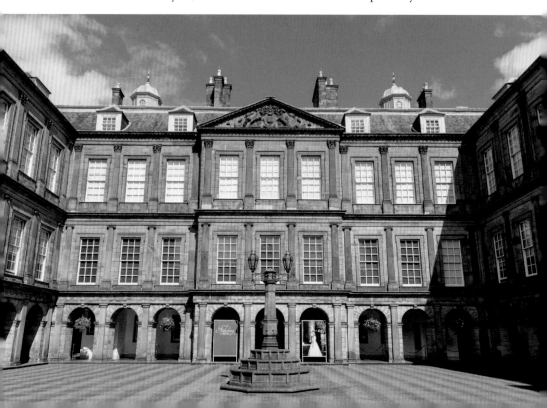

Henri Gascars, Charles II and the Yeomen of the Guard, with the Duchess of Portsmouth *c*.1682. This painting was probably commissioned by George Villiers, 4th Viscount Grandison the captain of the Yeomen of the Guard as a present for Louise de Keroualle, Duchess of Portsmouth. Grandison was uncle to Barbara Castlemaine, the king's discarded mistress, and needed to curry favour with Louise. It shows the king in a fictional setting, but one closest to St George's Hall at Windsor, a residence where Louise had extensive apartments. The Guard in the middle is Grandison and in the background is Louise with her ladies.

Anonymous, view of St James's Palace from the south, *c*.1690. The privy garden is in the foreground, and the nursery built by the Duke of York in 1677; next to this is the balcony of the drawing room. The Banquet House can be glimpsed across the park.

Hieronymus Janssens, Charles II dancing at a ball on 22 May 1660 at the Mauritshuis on the eve of his departure for Britain, c.1660. Charles II and his sister Mary are dancing the *courante*.

Leonard Knyff, Hampton Court from the east, c.1712-13. Knyff shows the palace at the height of its glory, with William III's gardens laid out and the juxtaposition of the new state rooms and the Tudor palace.

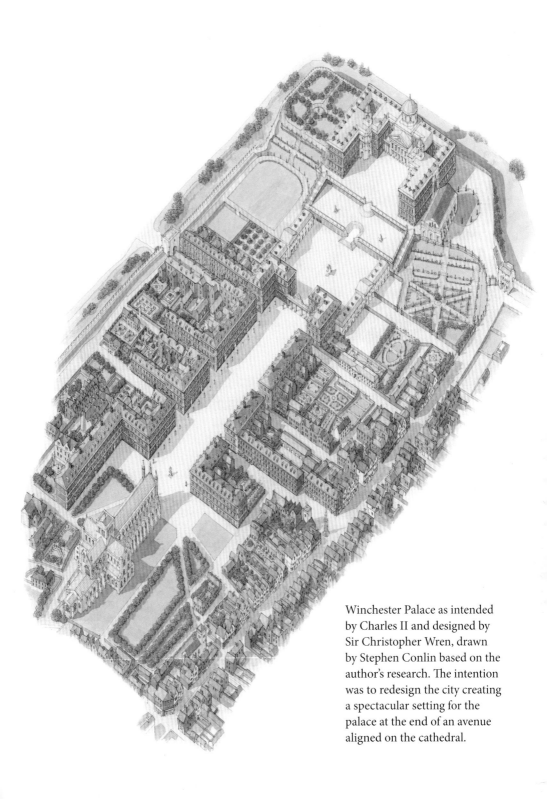

Winchester Palace as intended by Charles II and designed by Sir Christopher Wren, drawn by Stephen Conlin based on the author's research. The intention was to redesign the city creating a spectacular setting for the palace at the end of an avenue aligned on the cathedral.

The King's House at Newmarket as designed by William Samwell for King Charles II. The earlier Jacobean range can be seen on the street front. The three bay square queen's pavilion is at the bottom left. The long king's range overlooks the garden terminating in another square pavilion. Drawing by Stephen Conlin based on the author's research.

made by de Gomme, a brilliant designer and draughtsman. He then sat down and made alterations 'with his own hand by black lead pen and ruler'. The king had also taken up pencil and paper with Evelyn in a window seat at Whitehall to sketch his ideas for a new palace. At Holyrood in 1671 Charles asked that the entrance be large enough for his carriage and for corner fireplaces as at Newmarket. He first said that he didn't much care for columns on the outside if they could not be afforded, but later agreed to the 'pillar work' round the interior of the courtyard. Even greater concern was taken for the commissioning of statues of himself. For the equestrian statue erected in the courtyard at Windsor alternative designs were presented to the king while he was at his levee; after examining them he chose the version with himself as a Roman emperor, a choice he made again for his statue at the Royal Exchange. He was always eager to keep up with architectural developments in Paris: the Earl of Arlington sent to Paris for plans of the Louvre and the king's son, the Duke of Monmouth wrote to Louvois asking for a plan and elevations of Les Invalides because 'the king would be very glad to see it'. In fact, not since Henry VIII had there been a monarch more actively engaged in architectural design.[22]

In February 1667 Charles had the map of the city brought to him and he pointed out which streets he thought must be widened or straightened; he pronounced on the architecture to line the Thames, the closing of vistas and the appearance of the principal thoroughfares. His influence was particularly felt in the design of public buildings. His first concern was for the only royal building to be destroyed – the customs house. The Office of Works was ordered to immediately start work on designing a new one as without it the receipt of customs dues would be hindered. It is not known whom Denham asked to take control, although he and possibly the king had some hand in its design, but Charles was clear that he wanted an impressive stand-alone building on the riverfront. Yet the site was a leasehold and by the time the legal issues were resolved Denham was dead and Wren was in charge. To the protests of his own officers Wren rejected the existing designs outright and persuaded the Treasury to agree to his own, pricier, scheme.

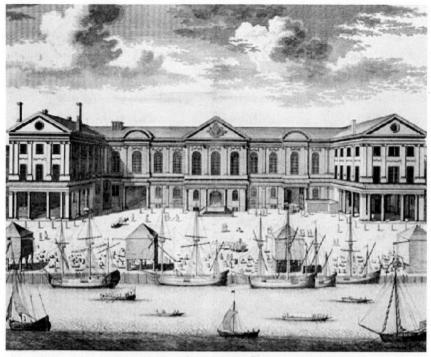

Figure 101: Sir Christopher Wren, the Custom House, London: his first
building as Surveyor of Works and Charles II's first foray into
influencing the rebuilding of the City after the Great Fire.

This was Wren's first building as Surveyor and demonstrated how
he was able to take a complex functional specification and give it
architectural presence. The ground floor and basement contained ware-
housing but the whole of the central block running between two
terminating pavilions was a grandiloquent first-floor room where the
customs officials sat. The pavilions contained elegant offices and below,
colonnades allowed for the delivery of merchandise. Sited on the waterfront the two temple ends of the pavilions and the central portico gave
an impressive facade to the river. This was the image of the new London
the king was anxious to craft.[23]

The other great commercial building in the city was the Royal
Exchange, part shopping emporium, part trading centre. The
Elizabethan building had been reduced to rubble and Edward Jerman,
the architect chosen by the City Corporation to design the new one,

presented his design to the king at Whitehall with the Lord Mayor at his side. The king liked it, in particular the south portico, and asked that the building be set by itself, free of adjoining buildings as it was 'of so public and eminent a concern for the honour of the city'. On 23 October 1667 Charles laid the first stone; Pepys failed to get in on the ceremony but afterwards got a look at the large tapestry-lined timber shed in which the king had dined on bacon, anchovies and caviar under a great throne canopy. With work underway Sir John Denham was royal representative, regularly reporting back on progress. After Denham's death and Wren's appointment, it was he who asked the king's permission for the design to be altered and two of the admired porticoes to be omitted.[24]

Of all the buildings in London, other than his own palaces, the building that most interested the king (and, indeed, his father and grandfather) was St Paul's Cathedral. The cathedral had been Wren's introduction to the City and just four months before the fire he had presented a report suggesting continuing Inigo Jones's refacing of the exterior and replacing the central tower with a dome. In 1666 a much greater problem was faced when the dean and bishop, with the king, had to decide whether to rebuild or repair. At first it was thought it might be possible to repair but, by 1668, with further collapses in the shattered ruins, it was clear that an entirely new cathedral had to be built.[25]

The story of how Wren, the dean, bishop, archbishop and the king navigated the process of design through seven alternative schemes has been told many times, but the crucial fact is that Charles himself was closely engaged throughout. Plans presented to him were circulated amongst the architectural cognoscenti at court before he uttered his opinion. The first model was taken to Whitehall in 1670 and remained there on show for near two years. Then a series of options were presented – one of which the king approved. Filled with enthusiasm, Charles ordered the construction of a huge model of this which would be 18 feet long and a special building was erected for it, arranged in such a way that spectators could stand inside. When the finished model was unveiled there was a storm of protest from the king's own commission set up to oversee the rebuilding. They thought the cathedral too popish and not English enough and the king pragmatically overrode Wren who only submitted, in tears, after a fight.

The replacement design, one much more in line with the plan of the old cathedral, was admired by the commission but received a lukewarm reception from the king. Yet a warrant was signed for this to be built, the king privately telling his architect that he was free to alter the details as he saw fit. The design, in fact, continued to evolve for duration of construction but on 21 June 1675 the first stone was laid.

Whitehall

The Great Fire injected a streak of realism into Charles II's thinking about Whitehall. With royal finances shot, a scarcity of building materials, and the country at war a more modest project than a total rebuilding was inevitable. In early 1667 Denham, or the king himself, assigned the job of designing a new wing of privy lodgings to Hugh May; these became known, in due course, as the volary lodgings, named after the volary, or aviary on the site of which they were built.

The addition was extremely skilful, integrating a handsome modern building into the complex matrix of existing galleries and courts. From the river it appeared as a 'U' plan of brick, two storeys with attics and a steeply pitched roof. There were big new sash windows and corner fireplaces, much admired by Pepys as a novelty. The king had a new great bedchamber linked to the state rooms and, in the north wing at right angles to the river, a private bedchamber and closet that could be accessed by a private backstair. There was also a library and a new laboratory with its own water cistern. The king moved in during the early summer of 1668. The project had cost just over £6,000 at a time when Pepys estimated that the navy was costing £24,000 a week. The king probably considered his new lodgings as small-change.[26]

Figure 102: Vignette of Whitehall from the river, from John Ogilby and
William Morgan's map of London, 1682. On the far left are the volary lodgings
connected to the privy bridge (the royal landing stage). To the right of these
are the queen's lodgings, with their broad river terrace. Behind them is the
Banqueting House. The large building on the riverfront in front of
the great hall (by this date used as the court theatre) houses the kitchens.

In his heyday in Paris Denham had probably contracted syphilis and,
in April 1666, he experienced symptoms consistent with the tertiary
stages of the disease. His 'madness' incapacitated him and, after apparently telling the king that he was the Holy Ghost, Hugh May was
appointed Surveyor until he was better. By the late summer, he seems
to have been in remission and returned to duty, serving on various
committees for the rebuilding of the City. But this 52-year-old, although
mentally recovered, was a physical wreck. At the start of 1669, now
really ill, he requested that Christopher Wren be formally appointed his
deputy and, when he died a fortnight later, the king appointed Wren
Surveyor.

It appears that Denham had been specifically asked by the king to
make Wren deputy and had also insisted on Wren as his successor. There
is no record of Hugh May baulking at the appointment, but perhaps
he was too sophisticated to try and reverse a royal *fait accompli*. At any
rate the king liked May and awarded him a compensatory additional
pension of £300 a year. Webb, characteristically, railed against the

appointment, pointing out that Wren knew nothing of the Office of Works. Furious, ignored and rejected he left London to live in Somerset, where he died in 1672.[27]

It was the Great Fire that both determined the direction of Wren's career and sealed his appointment as Surveyor. The length of his tenure exceeded all before and after; his longevity, with superb skills as a courtier and Stuart loyalist, secured his position under four monarchs. His grip on administration enabled him to ride the tectonics of Treasury finances under successive treasurers. His skill at spotting talent and drawing it into his office guaranteed its capacity to undertake a scope of work larger and more diverse than any of his predecessors. The fertility of his imagination and ability to create solutions to structural and architectural problems was second to none. And his reputation as an architect has stood the test of time.

The Surveyor of Works was instructed by the Lord Chamberlain, who at the start of the reign was Edward Montagu, 2nd Earl of Manchester. Soon after Wren came into office, Manchester was briefly succeeded by Henry Jermyn, Earl of St Albans, a friend of Wren's with whom he had travelled to France, but three years later, Charles replaced the seventy-year-old earl with Henry Bennet, Earl of Arlington. Bennet was one of the king's closest friends, a right-hand man in exile, the longest serving secretary of state, ambassador to France and father-in-law to one of his sons. Arlington was also unquestionably the leader of taste at court. His country house, Euston Hall, was a centre of fashion and a regular haunt of the king's; his London residence at the west end of St James's Park was described by John Evelyn as having 'the best and most princely furniture that any subject had in England'. The king never left architectural decisions entirely in the hands of Arlington, or anyone else, always taking a personal interest, but building required hundreds of small decisions, many of which were taken by Arlington and Wren.[28]

In 1669 it was widely known that Wren's first commission was for a new Whitehall. Just as in 1660–61 the inspiration was the Louvre and Sir Joseph Williamson, Arlington's workaholic deputy, and information-gatherer for foreign affairs, was trying to obtain plans of it from Paris in June 1669. His agent told him that the best plans were still in the hands of ministers, and what printed materials there were, were not yet publicly available. A handful of drawings for a new palace, in Wren's hand, probably date from this period and seem to be influenced by Bernini's Louvre schemes.[29]

The most important document to survive from Wren's first year as Surveyor is, however, a comprehensive large-scale survey of Whitehall. It was no ordinary measured drawing such as might be commissioned before a rebuilding, it was, in fact, an occupation survey identifying how many people lived in the palace, the extent of their lodgings, and the nature of their tenure. Whitehall was not just a royal residence and seat of the executive; it was like a vast overpopulated, and slightly shabby, hotel with some 1,500 rooms occupied by officials and household servants.

Many held rooms as part of their remuneration: some, like the porters, only when they were on duty and others, like the secretary of state, as a permanent perk. There were others who retained a toehold in the palace as pensioners or widows without official employment. Both categories of occupant normally held their lodgings for life and so, when there was a need to alter or extend (as a result of a growing family, for instance) swaps, leases, subletting and renting were common. New building had to be paid for by the occupant and thus lodgings were an investment to be traded and an asset to be jealously guarded. John Denham was not untypical in constructing a range of buildings for the Office of Works at his own cost as an investment. He and his heirs held them on a long lease independent from Crown interference. The Lord Chamberlain and the gentlemen ushers were the policemen of this chaotic system, one so complex that the king himself had to rent from his own courtiers if he needed more space.

Wren's survey of 1670 set out to make sense of the mind-boggling complexity of tenures at Whitehall, colouring walls to indicate which ones were private property and which were royal responsibility. For a man who had spent four years frustrated by entrenched property rights in the City of London, what the Whitehall plan told him must have been deeply depressing. It showed that nothing could be done at

Whitehall without identifying and then buying out a myriad of private interests. Indeed, the Treasury noted that private property interests at Whitehall made it 'more difficult to have his majesties palaces . . . reformed, beautified, or new built'. It is likely that the 1670 survey finally killed Charles II's vision of a new Whitehall – at any rate, little is heard of any new scheme for the palace after 1670 and a new series of projects began to emerge outside the capital.[30]

SIXTEEN

Grand Finale

Windsor Castle

Restoration England was staunchly anti-Catholic and the religious settlement agreed by parliament, contrary to Charles's hopes for greater toleration, was fiercely Anglican. The king was careful to publicly demonstrate his commitment to the established church against a foreign policy that saw England fighting Protestant powers and the queen and queen mother maintaining friaries next to their houses.

In December 1670 England signed a treaty with France. Unbeknown to all but a tiny minority this was the public face of a secret treaty negotiated at Dover earlier in the year. Its terms were explosive: not only would the king receive £230,000 a year from Louis XIV to fight the Dutch, but he would receive £150,000 for declaring himself a Roman Catholic. As England began to prepare for what is now known as the Third Dutch War, the king issued a Declaration of Indulgence that lifted the penal laws against dissenters and Catholics.

Parliament, called by Charles to grant revenues to prosecute the war, was furious. It saw the Declaration as a measure to favour English Catholics and demanded a new law to require anyone holding public office to be Anglican. The Test Act, that required office-holders to denounce Catholicism and take Anglican communion, was passed in March 1673. Its most high-profile victim was a Catholic convert, the king's brother and heir to the throne, the Duke of York, who resigned all his public offices that June.[1]

The conversion of the heir to the throne and his subsequent resignations put the court under intense scrutiny and Charles responded by tightening up court regulations. Controlling access became increasingly important, especially during religious feasts, as taking communion was now a badge of political allegiance, not just an act of devotion. At Easter 1674, Charles moved the whole court to Windsor. The king knew that as the first Easter since the Duke of York resigned his offices, it would attract huge attention and that at Windsor, with its high walls and guarded gatehouses, access could be controlled.

The king enjoyed his stay at the old, unmodernised, castle and returned in July for 109 days. It was a summer of high jinks that included hunting in the restocked parks, plays in St George's Hall and the re-enactment of the Duke of Monmouth's stunning military exploits at the siege of Maastricht. At the end of the visit Charles announced his intention to rebuild the castle and make it the normal summer residence of the court.[2]

Rebuilding a royal palace, especially one as large and ancient as Windsor, was a complex undertaking. Windsor had long retained its own surveyor who often operated independently from the Surveyor of the King's Works. In 1673 Hugh May had been appointed to this and so it was he who was responsible for realising the king's vision for a new Windsor. It is likely that the appointment of Lord Arlington as Lord Chamberlain in 1674 was specifically to oversee the project.

Charles II, like most monarchs who build, was in a hurry. He did not want the castle out of use for five years; aged forty-four, he wanted to get on and enjoy the completed building and so it was decided to undertake the work in two phases: first, the royal lodgings which were to be completed in time for the court's summer visit of 1678. Then a second phase that would transform the hall and chapel which, in the end, was completed in 1684. It was an ambitious programme and would prove to be hugely expensive, in all costing some £200,000.[3]

The first Dutch war combined with the economic catastrophe of plague and fire was a toxic cocktail that poisoned Crown finances. In 1672 the crisis reached its peak when the Treasury defaulted on its interest payments to ease revenue cash flow. But the measures introduced after this doomsday laid foundations for a more sustainable position. The first instalments of money from the secret Treaty of Dover began to flow directly into the king's privy coffers and could be discreetly directed towards building. The Third Dutch War had inconclusively ended in early 1674 and the new Treasurer, the Earl of Danby, steered national revenues back into the black. For the first time since 1660 the king felt confident enough to bring a major building project to a conclusion.[4]

May's scheme, worked out with Arlington and the king, was ingenious. Much of the earlier building was to be retained, including the volumes of both the king's and queen's principal state rooms, but a large section of the medieval north front was demolished to make way for a new block of royal lodgings to contain the king's privy chambers. As at Somerset House, May designed a magnificent staircase by which the royal lodgings were approached. The king's stair was entered through a giant triumphal arch pierced by windows that lit a spectacular double staircase joining at a landing at the door to the king's guard chamber. The queen's stair, of more traditional form, was no less magnificent.

The king's and queen's suites contained the usual set of rooms but uniquely their drawing rooms were linked by an eating room. This was a similar idea to that planned, but never completed, at Greenwich: a separate room for public dining. At Windsor it was not in the public domain but approached from the drawing rooms and contained two alcoves for the king's violins to play during dinner.

In 1672 Arlington had seen the work of the painter Antonio Verrio at the French court and subsequently invited him to England to paint

Figure 103: Unknown eighteenth-century Office of Works
draughtsman, a survey of the east elevation of Horn Court,
Windsor. This is the great triumphal front designed by Hugh
May as an entrance to the king's apartments. Steps lead up to
a vast arched opening within which rose a double staircase.
The arched headed openings were probably niches, while the
openings at capital level were windows throwing light onto
Verrio's painted ceiling inside. Tragically the staircase was
demolished without record in 1800.

murals at both his London house and Euston, and it was at Arlington's
houses that king and court first saw the genius of Verrio's work. Arlington
brought Verrio and his assistants to Windsor at just the same time that
John Evelyn introduced the brilliant Dutch limewood carver Grinling
Gibbons to the king.[5]

Verrio and Gibbons elevated the interiors at Windsor above what
Charles had already achieved at Whitehall. The royal lodgings were first
wainscoted with oak dados, doorcases, window reveals and chimney
breasts, all unified with a moulded cornice. This oak carcass was then
enriched by a team of carvers led by Henry Philips and Grinling Gibbons
who carved elements of the wainscoting and added frames for pictures
above the doors and chimneypieces. The deeply coved plaster ceilings
were painted by Verrio and the gilding added by René Cousin; in all

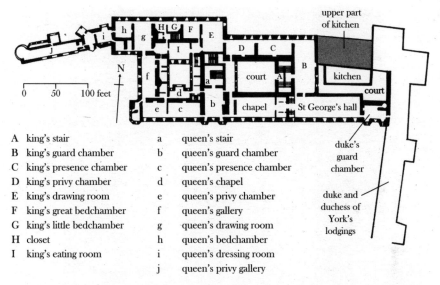

A king's stair
B king's guard chamber
C king's presence chamber
D king's privy chamber
E king's drawing room
F king's great bedchamber
G king's little bedchamber
H closet
I king's eating room

a queen's stair
b queen's guard chamber
c queen's presence chamber
d queen's chapel
e queen's privy chamber
f queen's gallery
g queen's drawing room
h queen's bedchamber
i queen's dressing room
j queen's privy gallery

Figure 104: Reconstructed plan of the first floor of the royal lodgings in the upper ward at Windsor Castle, as remodelled for Charles II, *c.*1683. The regular ten-bay building on the north front was Hugh May's star building, named after a huge tin garter star affixed to its exterior.

Verrio completed twenty ceilings at Windsor as well as three staircases and the enormous chapel and hall. New suites of furniture were commissioned and installed and paintings were brought from other residences and raised up for the king to see their effect before being hung. The state rooms were ready for Charles to bring the court to stay the summer of 1678.[6]

Windsor was designed to be a summer pleasure retreat. Charles only transacted essential business there and preferred to enjoy the park and the sports it had to offer. There was no council chamber, for instance, and when the Privy Council was convened it met at Hampton Court, the king sometimes walking the twenty miles between the two.

While work was underway at Windsor Charles turned to the immediate issues raised by passing of the Test Act. Like his predecessors, he attended chapel every Sunday and on all the principal feast days of the year, ceremonially processed to his pew, took his chair of state, and patiently listened to sermons. He encouraged church music, asking that his own violinists should accompany the anthems. The royal tradition

Figure 105: Pieter van der Banck, etching of the ceiling of the king's
withdrawing room at Windsor Castle, *c*.1684. The ceiling, painted by Verrio,
depicts the Restoration of Charles II. Van der Banck was a French engraver
who recorded several of Verrio's ceilings and helped popularise illusionistic
ceiling painting across Europe.

was only to take communion three times a year: at Christmas, Easter
and Whitsun; on these occasions the chapel was especially full as people
crowded in to see their sovereign communicate.

The royal chapels were designed on an identical model with a lower
chapel for the court and a raised pew at the west end divided into two
sections, one for the sovereign and his attendants, and the other for his
consort and her ladies. Since the death of Henry VIII the consort's pew
had rarely been used and, with the absolute necessity to show that senior
members of the royal household were Anglicans, the king decided to
abolish it and create a single large royal gallery in which specified courtiers would transparently join him at service. The Whitehall pew was
rearranged in the summer of 1675 and soon after Wren was ordered to
design a new reredos, similar, in fact, to that constructed for Henrietta

Maria at Somerset House, but stripped down and translated into a plain Anglican form.[7]

The same year the queen decided to spend Easter at Somerset House so she could perform all the ceremonies of Holy Week publicly. English Catholic priests had been expelled the previous month and the queen relied on her Portuguese friars who ministered to a congregation that was mainly English, though it contained some foreigners. The state apartments at Somerset House were redecorated: new furniture was delivered, including a great cloth of state bearing Catherine's arms. Huge crowds of Catholics were expected and it was decided to add galleries to the chapel to make space.

The queen's intensive use of her chapel did nothing to improve her image; in fact it contributed to her being a focus of the Popish Plot of 1678. The fabricated plot, revealed to the king while he was at Windsor, centred on his assassination to clear the way for Catholic James to ascend the throne. The queen was allegedly complicit and, to cover up the evidence, it was claimed that Catherine's Catholic servants had murdered the investigating magistrate, Sir Edmund Godfrey at Somerset House with the queen's knowledge and approval. Somerset House was even searched for evidence.[8]

Scotland

The popular hysteria generated by the Popish Plot was intensified by the fact that, in 1673, after the death of his first wife, James married the teenage Roman Catholic, Mary Beatrice of Modena, who it was felt would certainly bear him a Catholic son. The prospect of generations of Catholic rule motivated parliament to propose a bill for the exclusion of the Duke of the York from the throne. Charles was adamant that parliament should not tamper with the succession and, to defuse the crisis, banished James and Mary Beatrice first to Brussels and then to Edinburgh. Between November 1679 and March 1682 James and Mary Beatrice lived at Holyrood with a short break in England in 1680.

Cromwell had built a barrack block over the entrance front of Holyrood, signalling its new use as the Edinburgh headquarters of the army. In 1661 the Scottish Privy Council smartened the palace up and in 1663 there was some thought that it might be remodelled, but nothing happened until, in 1670, it was decided to almost completely rebuild it.

What was built between 1671 and 1679 was no normal palace. At the time it seemed very unlikely that Charles II would ever visit Edinburgh let alone live there but Holyrood was a visible symbol of the restored Stuart dynasty and an expression of the status of Edinburgh as a national capital. Its rebuilding was therefore symbolically important as well as being necessary to serve the practical needs of the King's Commissioner to Parliament, various government officials and the Scottish Privy Council.

The prime mover was John Maitland, Earl, and later Duke of Lauderdale, the brutal, boisterous, red-haired Scot whom Charles appointed Secretary of State for Scotland in 1660. By deftly neutralising and discrediting his rivals, by 1669 Lauderdale, in Pepys's words, had 'got the whole power of Scotland into his hand' becoming the king's representative, or commissioner. Between October 1669 and January 1670 he held magnificent state in the king's lodgings at Holyrood while parliament met to consider a union with England.[9]

The attempt at unification failed and, by the end of 1670, it was clear that Scotland, as a separate kingdom, would continue to maintain a parliament, Privy Council and a monarchy which would require a viable seat. Lauderdale, and the Privy Council, now felt that, in its depressed state, Holyrood did not do justice to Scotland, Edinburgh, their monarch, or themselves. As the Scots were prepared to fully fund it, Charles gave orders that Holyrood be rebuilt.

Lauderdale must have been responsible for suggesting to the king that Sir William Bruce be the architect. Bruce was another royalist who had spent some of the 1650s touring Europe studying architecture. In 1659–60 he had been given a knighthood and lucrative posts in Scotland. His architectural debut was at his own house, Balcaskie in Fife, which was so admired by Lauderdale that he commissioned Bruce to work on his own houses in Scotland, retaining William Samwell for his Thames-side villa, Ham House.[10]

Bruce, as a fierce Stuart loyalist, had been chosen as one of the commissioners to discuss the unification of the two nations. On 3 September 1670, with fifteen other Scottish commissioners, Bruce kissed Charles II's hand in the vane room at Whitehall and received instructions for the sitting of the committee. Over the following nine weeks the commissions met at Whitehall, the exchequer in Westminster and at Somerset House and, between sessions, Lauderdale hosted them in his lavishly decorated lodgings at Whitehall. During his long stay in London Bruce had the opportunity to visit all the newest buildings and Lauderdale's house at Ham. He must have also met Wren, May, Samwell and other English architects.[11]

Lauderdale presumably sang the praises of Bruce and it is likely that before he left London he was already in possession of a commission to redesign Holyrood for the king. Bruce's collaborator was the king's Scots master mason, Robert Mylne, in whose hand the surviving designs are probably drawn. These were with Lauderdale in London on 2 June and he presented them to the king at Windsor the following day.

The correspondence that survives for this scheme is the most detailed record of the genesis of any British royal building project of the seventeenth century. Charles evidently carefully examined the plans and elevations and, while he found much to like, replied with several pages of detailed comments, to which, on rereading, he added further points.

Presumably at the suggestion of Lauderdale, Bruce had designed three sets of state rooms; the third was probably intended for the Duke of York or perhaps even for Lauderdale himself. In terms of an English royal house the plan was messy and confused and the king sent clear instructions for the rooms to be rearranged along English lines with two suites of apartments joined by a privy gallery. The king didn't want a household chapel and the space allocated for it would be set aside as a council chamber. Meanwhile instructions were given to remove the parochial congregation from the former abbey church and to convert it into the chapel royal.[12]

Notwithstanding these criticisms the king liked the design of the house 'in general' and formally appointed Bruce as Surveyor General of royal castles and palaces in Scotland. New plans were drawn, and work commenced. The new palace, like the old, was arranged round a courtyard. Its entrance front was a brilliantly conceived blend of old and new. The north tower had contained the lodgings of Mary Queen of Scots and weighed heavy with national and dynastic symbolism: Bruce retained this and built a matching wing to the south. Between the two was a lower screen wall containing a swaggering entrance portal framed by coupled Doric columns and crowned by a cupola and vast coat of arms. This front, that still greets visitors at the bottom of the Royal Mile, is both venerable and modern, militaristic and gracious, fashionable and romantic – designed to present the modern face of an ancient dynasty.

A remarkably magnificent state stair in the southwest corner is the fulcrum of the state rooms. Straight on, at the stair top, the visitor enters the king's apartments, to the left the queen's and to the right an ante room that led to a magnificent new council chamber. The king's and queen's rooms were linked on the north side by a privy gallery that ran the whole length of the inner courtyard. The courtyard itself, on which the state rooms look, was a refined exercise in classicism with superimposed orders. The first- and second-floor rooms were of equal height; the second-floor rooms being for officers of state. Originally the windows were casements giving the facade an old-fashioned look to English contemporaries. The Duke of York ordered the replacement of those in his closet with more fashionable and convenient sashes. Nevertheless, the careful symmetry of the court was much admired by Scottish aristocrats who went on to regularise and classicise their baronial seats in imitation.

To decorate the interiors Lauderdale and Bruce assembled an international team of craftsmen: from London, plasterers to produce high-relief decorated ceilings, from the Netherlands wood carvers and

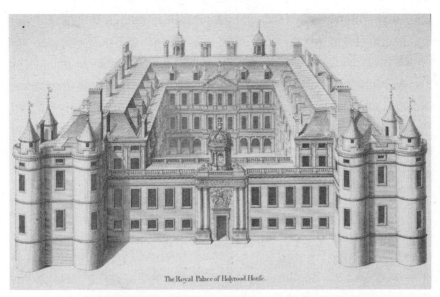

Figure 106: Holyrood from the west, engraved in *c.*1750.

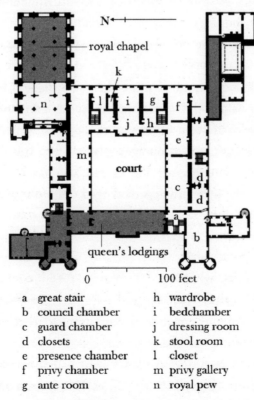

a	great stair	h	wardrobe
b	council chamber	i	bedchamber
c	guard chamber	j	dressing room
d	closets	k	stool room
e	presence chamber	l	closet
f	privy chamber	m	privy gallery
g	ante room	n	royal pew

Figure 107: Reconstructed first-floor plan of Holyrood, as designed for King Charles II, on the same orientation as the perspective above.

a painter; timber came from Norway and ready-cut fireplaces from London. Much of this survives, making the king's suite the best preserved of all Caroline state interiors. Work was still not complete in 1678 when Lauderdale fell out with Bruce and sacked him. Some of the decoration was completed during the occupation of the Duke of York; in fact, on his arrival, the palace had to be hurriedly furnished; Lauderdale lending tapestries to cover the walls while the duke's own made their way by sea to Scotland.[13]

The duke's arrival coincided with the fall of Lauderdale and, for three years after 1679 Holyrood became a fully working royal palace where power and display, architecture and etiquette melded together in perhaps the way the Privy Council had originally intended. In terms of its plan Holyrood was an English import, with the full suite of state rooms arranged in the standard English manner. No Scottish royal house had ever had enfilades of state chambers or a rigid distinction between the state and privy lodgings. Charles had made it clear that he wanted arrangements existing at Whitehall and Newmarket incorporated into the design.

James and his household of more than 100 made a big impact on Edinburgh and James did everything to seem calm, reasonable and gracious. He held drawing rooms at the palace, attended the Privy Council, played golf and encouraged plays. Mary Beatrice found the northern capital less engaging; she missed London and her daughter Isabella. In fact, the little princess died aged only four with her mother in Scotland.[14]

Windsor again

With James in Scotland, three successive English parliaments attempted to exclude him from the throne. In an attempt to cool the political temperature in the capital, the third was called in Oxford. Once again, a King of England in dispute with his own parliament had set up his residence at Christ Church. But Charles II was in a much stronger position than his father. In the second parliament the House of Lords had defeated the exclusion bill and the king felt he had the initiative. In a dramatic moment on 27 March 1681 Charles took a sedan chair to the Geometry Schools where the Lords were sitting. After attending for a few minutes he slipped out as if to relieve himself. On his return he was crowned, in full state robes – he summoned the Commons and announced to clamorous disbelief that parliament was dissolved. Retiring to the great hall of Christ Church he dined in public and then, summoning his coach, left for Windsor. As he drove off he remarked that England now had one king, not 500. Parliament was not to meet again in his reign.[15]

A year later James, Duke of York returned to London filled with the conviction that 'the monarchie must be either more absolute or quite abolished'.[16] His brother might not have put it quite like this, but during the exclusion crisis the court underwent a distinct change. Charles had always known how to use ceremony and etiquette to emphasise his regality. Indeed, in exile it was often all he had to distinguish himself from any other man. But in the last six years of his reign he insisted on following court protocol to the letter in the most formal and majestic form. Previously the king had chosen to receive individuals and delegations in his more private rooms, in the vane room – like the Scottish commissioners, or even in his bedchamber. Now delegations were received in the presence chamber with stiff disdain, petitioners being left on their knees as they spoke and the king only communicating through an intermediary. Meanwhile in his state bedchamber he instituted a formal ceremony of rising each morning – a *lever*, and each night an equivalent bedtime ceremony, a *coucher*. The rising and retiring were undertaken with studied formality, distancing the monarch from spectators and attendants alike.[17]

In April 1680 Charles II went to Windsor to view the completed carcass of the last two great new rooms, the household chapel and St George's Hall. It must have been then that he and Arlington discussed with Verrio a scheme for painting them. Sketches were made, agreed by Arlington and presented to the king for approval. There is no doubt that the king liked what he was getting from the painter; he was lavishly

Figure 108: The cartographer John Ogilby presenting Charles II with the book of subscribers to his map of London in 1682. The room depicted is unlikely to be a representation of a specific room at Whitehall, but the general impression is accurate. The presentation appears to be taking place in a state bedchamber.

rewarded and, on the completion of St George's Hall in July 1684, he was given £400 by the king in gratitude.[18]

St George's Hall was decorated, not as a banqueting hall, but as a colossal throne room, or presence chamber; it was, in fact, the successor to the Banqueting House at Whitehall, the most magnificent space available for royal audiences and receptions in the kingdom. Just as Inigo Jones had originally constructed an apse at the north end of the Banqueting House as a setting for King James I's throne, Verrio painted an illusionistic apse for Charles at the upper end of St George's Hall.[19] Both alluded to Roman basilicas where magistrates sat in judgment. The niche was draped with a trompe l'oeil crimson backcloth with an image of St George and the Dragon, in front of which was a substantial marble dais five steps high. On this stood a remarkable new throne firmly railed off by a decorative balustrade.

Throne was not a word used lightly or often in the seventeenth century. Presence and privy chambers in the royal palaces had chairs of state. But in St George's hall was a throne, more like a coronation chair – a concoction made by Lewis Vanupstall and Jan Vanderstaine, that included large figures of prudence, fame and justice as well as two great urns and three trophies – no wonder a visitor to the completed room described the ensemble as 'Outshining the Chariot of the blazing Sun'.[20]

At the west end of the hall, on an axis with the throne, was a great portal that led through to the chapel, smaller than the hall but no less rich. The window wall was defined by giant trompe l'oeil columns, painted by Verrio, but the focus was the west wall; here was an ensemble worthy of a great church in Rome. Framed by Solomonic columns was a vast painted niche containing a huge painting of the Last Supper. Below was an altar raised up on several steps and enclosed by a magnificent rail. On the north wall illusionistic Solomonic columns framed a scene of Christ healing the sick, a scene closely based on one of Raphael's cartoons, part of Charles I's collection. The ceiling was the apotheosis of Christ.

Royal chapels had, of course, always been richly painted and hung with tapestry, but this was on a much larger scale. It was a chapel painted by a Roman Catholic who had a legal dispensation to work in England. It was commissioned by a king, and his Lord Chamberlain, both of whom were alleged to have made deathbed conversions to Catholicism. The imagery and the disposition of the west end drew on Parisian Counter-Reformation models. Yet the purpose of the chapel was secular and monarchical. Like the hall this was part of Charles's elevation of his majesty in response to the challenges of the late 1670s.[21]

In the same period the king began to rapidly increase the scale of his healing ceremonies – touching for the king's evil, the magical curing of scrofula. In the middle years of his reign he had been touching perhaps 3,500 people a year, but in 1682 he touched nearly 9,000. The new chapel became the setting for these weekly ceremonies and the image of Christ healing the sick was the backdrop. The impact of Christ and Charles

juxtaposed in these big court ceremonies cannot have been lost on either
the sufferers or spectators. Charles was not so much making a religious
statement, but one about the nature of his monarchy. Nobody could be
in any doubt that this king was put on his throne by the Almighty.[22]

Redrawing the map

In March 1682 there was a huge blaze at the queen's friary at St James's.
One witness, with glee, reported 'The fire yesterday fell amongst the
priests and fires at St James's burned down all the priory and the queen's
chapel. People condole not much seeing that it fell amongst them and
say that the [rosary] beads cracked and rattled like anything'.[23]

Catherine immediately summoned Wren and ordered him to rebuild
the friary and restore the damaged chapel. The queen, presumably
emboldened by her brother-in-law's conversion, wanted to enhance the
performance of liturgy both for the friars and for the congregation and
Wren's visit to Paris stood him in good stead to do this. There was to
be a new chapel for the friars up behind the high altar. Again the circular
and oval chapels at the Louvre and Val-de-Grâce must have been the
inspiration for Wren's new chapel fitted with fourteen 6-foot-high stalls
raised up on five steps and laid out in a semi-circle beneath a dome.
Wren had already designed two domes – one at St Stephen's Walbrook
in the City and the other at the Theatre Royal in Drury Lane. This one
was painted inside by Jacob Huysmans, a Roman Catholic painter from
Antwerp and self-styled painter to the queen.[24]

The remarkable friars' choir was a private space, not so the queen's
chapel. Here the instructions were to provide a much larger space for
the liturgy and a full-scale Counter-Reformation-style reredos. Wren
again looked to the Jesuit churches of Paris for inspiration. In the centre
of his reredos was a painting of the Holy Family by Jacob Huysmans
in an elaborate frame by Grinling Gibbons; either side were quadrants
containing niches and, against the outer walls, portals leading to a
passage behind the altarpiece. On top of each of the portals was a large
carved angel and above the blocked east window were carved putti

carrying the queen's arms. Two large niches were cut out of the walls to take statues. These were filled with effigies of St Peter and St Paul by John Bushnell moved from the Somerset House chapel.[25]

Figure 109: The Queen's Chapel, St James's, *c*.1685. Set up for Catherine of Braganza, Wren designed an elaborate reredos containing a painting by Jacob Huysmans. Statues by John Bushnell are in raised niches; the presbytery is a vast area enclosed by a rail.

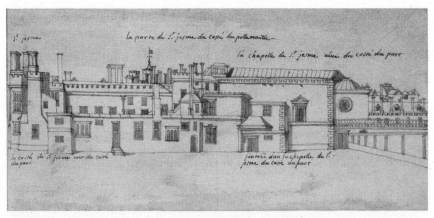

Figure 110: St James's from the south by François Gasselin *c.*1693. On the far right the dome of the friars' first-floor chapel can be seen, with its circular window. The Queen's Chapel has an entrance porch to allow people to approach from the park. To the left are the buildings of the royal library and at the far left the end of the Duke of York's lodgings.

The queen's friary exceeded Henrietta Maria's chapels in richness and beauty. Nothing like it had ever been seen in London and as, apart from the embassy chapels, it was the only Catholic church in London it received a large congregation. It also became a target for those who regarded the queen's religion with horror. A guard room was built to keep out troublemakers and pass keys were distributed to the friars so they could gain access to the private parts of the friary. The prominence of Catholic worship at court, the duke's conversion, the exclusion campaign, and the Popish Plot provoked a political and constitutional crisis that led to violence, disorder and rioting in the streets of the capital. The London crowds were manipulated by opposing political factions and the authorities several times nearly lost control, especially in the crisis years of 1681–2.[26]

This meant that there was a strong imperative to spend more time outside London. The project at Windsor had established a magnificent summer hunting retreat, but the court was only there a few months a year. Hampton Court had never much appealed and by 1670 it had been made over to Barbara Palmer, Countess of Castlemaine, a former lover of the king's by whom he had five children. Hampton Court became their family home. Work at Greenwich had gradually tailed off and it was abandoned by 1670, the carcass of the king's riverside block being boarded up. The king had never taken to Audley End and in the atmosphere of the 1680s, Newmarket was becoming less and less agreeable. There had never been enough accommodation at Newmarket and now Charles's increasingly formal court did not well accord with a house built for informality. Newmarket town was small and dirty and the hunting round about was increasingly disappointing. In 1683 much of the town was destroyed by a fire, making it even less attractive.[27]

In 1682 the king accepted an invitation from the city of Winchester to attend their races. The whole court moved there in August for a visit which was a huge success. Within days it was common knowledge that the king wanted to build a new residence there. As the ancient capital of England, the town had a long royalist pedigree and one reinforced by its loyalty during the exclusion crisis. In easy reach of Portsmouth, which the king was then refortifying, it had excellent connections to London, a splendid cathedral and plentiful inns, taverns and stables.

In early 1683 the lawyer and architectural connoisseur Roger North was at a meeting of the Treasury in the royal presence. Wren had been summoned, and the subject was the financing of the new palace. The king asked how long it would take to build; Wren answered two years, but Charles thought this too long and enquired whether it could be built in one. Yes, Wren replied, but with 'great confusion, charge, and inconvenience'. Notwithstanding this warning the decision was made to proceed and, on 9 February the Treasury authorised expenditure of £36,000. The site of the old royal castle was chosen, preserving the early medieval great hall in which a vast round table hung, believed at the time to have been King Arthur's. The site was on the top of a rise, the land falling to the west front of the cathedral; the main palace buildings would be at the highest point and the outer court on the falling land below; a park of 352 acres was planned to the south.[28]

Designing a new palace was the opportunity for which Wren had long waited. In Paris he had seen Louis Le Vau's Collège des Quatre Nations (now the Institut de France) under construction. On the banks of the Seine, opposite the Louvre, it was founded by Cardinal Mazarin in 1661. Wren had drawn on the *collège* for his designs for Trinity College Cambridge and it also became the prototype for Winchester. Unlike Versailles, with which Winchester shared its receding courts, the *collège* was crowned by a central dome above a portico. It was also brilliantly integrated into the Parisian cityscape on an axis with the king's apartments in the Louvre. This idea Wren took up at Winchester, which was set in a new urban landscape with a great avenue aligned on the west front of the cathedral.

A coloured perspective drawing and a large-scale model were made which were approved by the king. These were for no hunting lodge, but a full-scale, fully equipped, palace designed to house the whole court and royal family for long periods of time. Unlike Windsor it was to have a large council chamber and rooms for the council clerks, showing that the king intended to use it for state business. As in the queen's side at Windsor, the state rooms were divided from the privy lodgings by a privy gallery, making the king's wing into a self-contained

Figure 111a: Engraved perspective of Winchester Palace from John Milner's *History of Winchester* (1798–1801), based, so the text says, on 'a coloured drawing made by the architect himself'.

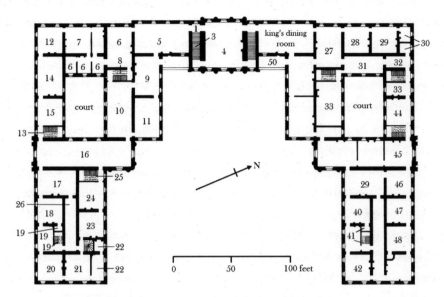

1 – Entrance for the King's Coach
2 – Guard chamber below stairs
3 – Principal stairs
4 – Lobby

King's Side
5 – Presence chamber
6 – Passage and ante chapel and closet above the screen
7 – Chapel
8 – Stairs to the closet
9 – Privy chamber
10 – Drawing room
11 – Lobby, or dining room on the King's side
12 – Ante room to council chamber and clerks' seats
13 – Stairs to council chamber
14 – Council chamber
15 – Closet to council chamber
16 – Privy gallery

17 – Ante room
18 – Bed chamber
19 – Lobby, stool room and private stairs
20 – Cabinet
21 – Inner bed chamber
22 – Dressing room, closet and stairs to the inner bed chamber
23 – Inner room of backstairs
24 – Waiting room of backstairs
25 – Backstairs
26 – Passage

Queen's Side
27 – Presence chamber
28 – Drawing room
29 – Bed chamber
30 – Closet and stool room
31 – Dressing room, robes and private stairs
32 – Waiting rooms and backstairs
33 – Chapel

Figure 111b: Plan of the first floor of the palace as intended, showing probable planned usage of the rooms in the same orientation as the print.

residence if required. There was a household chapel and fine lodgings for the Duke and Duchess of York; a third large apartment was presumably for Louise Renée de Kéroualle, Duchess of Portsmouth, who had entirely captured the king's affections and held court as almost an alternative queen – Evelyn thought her 24-room lodging at Whitehall ten times finer than Catherine's.[29]

This was the first entirely new royal palace since the time of Henry VIII and in its plan it encapsulated all the developments in royal etiquette and planning that had taken place over 150 years. Unencumbered by pre-existing buildings Winchester was the perfect machine for governing smoothly, integrating royal domestic and administrative requirements. The roof was leaded the very week Charles II died.

The king's death and James's disinclination to finish the palace robbed history of the opportunity to understand how it would have changed the royal itinerary, and possibly re-mapped the political geography of England. Winchester was potentially an alternative capital, with the new palace invested with the history and infrastructure necessary for rule. Whitehall would always have been important, but Winchester may have been intended as the new normal seat of the monarch.

The death of the king

In the early 1680s Charles II spent more and more time out of London. After the completion of the state rooms at Windsor he had a bang up-to-date country residence and rapid progress at Winchester promised to deliver a brand-new urban seat. He had resolved not to call parliament and that removed an important reason for being in Westminster. Yet Windsor did not replace the ceremonial functions of Whitehall, and Winchester was not ready to take them. Charles thus continued to use Whitehall as his ceremonial hub, touching for the king's evil, holding Chapters of the Garter, full council meetings, ambassadorial receptions and keeping house there at Christmas.

With all idea of comprehensively rebuilding Whitehall abandoned the king decided to rebuild his state bedchamber to replace the now

150-year-old bedroom he had revamped in 1660. In March 1682 the Duke of York moved out of his riverside apartment and it was temporally set up for the king; the court made its way to Newmarket and then on to spend the summer at Windsor.

Wren was left to undertake some rapid and ingenious architectural keyhole surgery. His brief was to demolish the old buildings between the privy gallery and the volary lodgings and insert a new drawing room, state bedchamber, ante room and eating room. The rooms had no external architectural expression being squeezed into a densely packed section of the palace. Although the work was meant to only take a couple of months, the king did not move back into his lodgings until October and his opulent new furniture only arrived the following May. The distinct improvement in the sovereign's accommodation at Whitehall did not lure Charles back to London for long periods: other than over Christmas, the new rooms were sparely used during the remainder of his reign. But it was at Whitehall where, on 2 February 1685, Charles had the massive stroke that was to kill him four days later.[30]

SEVENTEEN

Nasty, Brutish and Short:
The Reign of James II and VII

When James II came to the throne, he had abstained from publicly taking the Anglican sacrament for thirteen years and had, for nine of them, been a papist recusant. Now, as king, nothing was to hold him back and he was able to embark on his life's crusade: returning his dominions to the Roman Catholic fold. On the second Sunday after his accession, he attended Mass in his wife's chapel at St James's, leaving the doors wide open. People were scandalised for, although it was widely known that he was a Catholic, Charles II had been extremely careful to keep all Catholic devotions at court behind closed doors. Now, all fears were confirmed, England once again had a Roman Catholic monarch.[1]

Although the brothers James and Charles shared many characteristics, not least a belief in their God-given right to rule, the two men were entirely different. While Charles was not a man of principle, happy to change his mind, to dissemble and tell people what they wanted to hear, James was more like his father. For him his personal conscience was everything and he was prepared to die for it. As Duke of York, Charles described his brother as being 'as stiff as a mule'; as king, James refused to take advice, except from the flattering coterie of Roman Catholic advisors who came to surround him.

On the positive side, James was a reformer who diligently attended to state paperwork, was active in the administration of his realm and was a responsible steward of resources. On his accession he brought new rules into his household and initiated a cull of posts and privileges that reduced the household's size by a third, from some 1,200 to around 800. The reforms hit the staff below stairs hardest, merging the household kitchen with the privy kitchen and amalgamating other service departments. While economy was a strong motivation it is also likely that James wanted his court to look and feel different from his brother's. Perhaps he wanted a more sober, regulated court as a moral symbol of his religious intentions.[2]

Whitehall

Those intentions were made concrete within months of his accession. By May 1685 James had, in his hands, plans and an estimate from Sir Christopher Wren for the rebuilding of the queen's lodgings at Whitehall and for constructing a large new Roman Catholic church there. It quickly became apparent that he had little interest in Winchester and wanted to establish himself at Whitehall as the most effective place to enact his religious crusade. The reconstruction of Whitehall that began in 1685, was only completed by Queen Mary II in 1689, and finally gave London the metropolitan palace it deserved.

The new king's bedchamber of 1682 had left the 150-year-old privy gallery as a vestige of former times, inhabited by officials and courtiers; it could now be emptied and demolished for a new construction. What James built completely reorganised the geography of the palace. From Pebble Court there was a magnificent top-lit marble stair that provided access to the privy gallery, a new council chamber with attendant offices, and the Banqueting House. The latter was reordered and the throne canopy moved to the north end; this necessitated the repositioning of the ceiling canvases that had been designed to be seen from the other direction. The same stair and gallery led to two novel state rooms. These were neither part of the king's nor the queen's lodgings, but a withdrawing room and eating room where the king and queen could hold court together.

The final component of the new range was a suite of state rooms for the queen replacing the Tudor riverside lodgings. These overlooked the privy garden and contained the normal sequence of chambers. The king's and queen's state apartments were now laid out in a long line, separated in the middle by the old vane room. This became the 'great waiting room', or guard chamber to the two suites and in here the yeomen of the guard were ordered to stand. The former Tudor outer chambers were redecorated and preserved but seem to have played no part in the modernisation plans.

Wren's handling of the architecture was very skilful. For the first time the Banqueting House was stylistically integrated into the royal apartments, in elevation the new council chamber was raised up on a rusticated plinth matching Jones's basement, cornice heights and entablatures. The queen's range, which had a facade to the garden, was very austere, much like the wings of the Royal Hospital Chelsea, but without a portico in the middle. This perhaps reflected the speed at which the

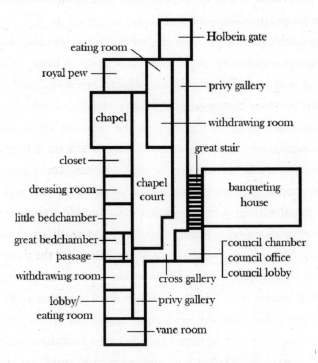

Figure 112: Diagrammatic plan of the first floor of
the royal lodgings at Whitehall in 1688.

building had to be erected, the acute shortage of Portland stone, and the fact that it was a private facade. The elevations in the public court were much grander.[3]

While work was underway at Whitehall, James and Mary Beatrice remained at St James's. This had been James's home since 1660 and, in a reign that lasted less than four years, two and a half were spent at St James's. The Roman Catholic chapel there was now the centre of royal religion and two chairs of state were ordered for the elevated royal pew, allowing James and his consort to sit side by side and, in anticipation of a royal baptism, a large niche was cut out of the brickwork for a font. Benedetto Gennari was commissioned to paint a huge Holy Family for the high altar; this was designed to be replaced over Holy Week by two other paintings of the same size: a crucifixion on Good Friday and a resurrection for Easter Day. James re-established the St James's friary as a Benedictine monastery. Thirteen monks and two lay brothers were drawn from three English Benedictine houses and placed under Augustine Howard as Superior.[4]

The accession of a Roman Catholic to the throne presented an apparently insuperable problem of protocol. Not only was the sovereign the head of the Anglican church, his attendance at the Chapel Royal was a central act of court ceremonial and kingly display. Weekly processions to the chapel took place on Sundays and far larger processions on collar days (the feasts when the king wore his Garter collar). On these occasions, the king made an offering at the altar and took communion. James announced that he wanted to be escorted in procession to his Catholic chapel with full ritual and that non-Catholics could either wait outside during the service or leave as the priest raised the consecrated host during Mass. Senior courtiers fell into line with the request and the royal pew in the Queen's Chapel at St James's was altered so that the king and queen could descend and make their offering at the altar and take communion according to royal tradition.[5]

The new arrangements put the Catholic chapels at the centre of court ceremonial but, even if James had wanted to, he could not abolish the Anglican Chapel Royal as his daughter, Anne, was Protestant, as were the overwhelming number of courtiers. In December James appointed a new Dean of the Chapel Royal, Nathaniel Crewe, Bishop of Durham, his closest Anglican associate and supporter, and the clergyman who had conducted his marriage to Mary Beatrice. Seeing that the king was attending Mass at St James's, and had no intention of using the Chapel Royal at Whitehall, Crewe gave orders to close the royal pew. His instructions were countermanded by James and new orders were issued governing the pew which had the effect of requiring attendees at chapel to give the king's empty chair the respect that was due to the king if he had been sitting on it. Henceforth there would be two chapels at court with equal status, but the king would only attend one of them.[6]

Improvements to the St James Chapel were a stop-gap until a new Roman Catholic church could be built at the far western end of the new privy gallery at Whitehall. By the time Wren received the commission to design this the Office of Works had sixty years of experience in Catholic architecture and many of its architects, including Wren himself, had studied churches abroad. Yet, for this most prestigious of commissions, Wren turned again to the chapel of St James, in plan a simple rectangle. Both chapels were around 40 feet wide but the new building at Whitehall, at 107 feet, was 22 feet longer. Unlike the Anglican chapel at Whitehall the new building was correctly orientated, facing east with the royal pew on the west lit by a large venetian window onto the public highway.

As in previous English Catholic royal chapels the decorative emphasis was on the reredos. Grinling Gibbons and Arnold Quellin, the greatest carvers of their day, were given the £1,800 contract to build a piece 39 feet 6 inches high and 33 feet wide, the entire width of the chapel's east end. Their contract specified that the altar should be finished by 25 September 1686, else they forfeit £100 of their fee. It was an incredible task and Gibbons and Quellin employed almost fifty carvers, joiners, painters, stonemasons and polishers to assist them. The altarpiece was of white marble, three storeys high, topped with two life-size kneeling marble angels. Benedetto Gennari supplied his masterpiece, an annunciation measuring 7 feet by 8 feet, for the space over the main altar.

Verrio painted the chapel ceiling which depicted the Assumption of the Blessed Virgin. Gibbons was also contracted to provide a pulpit carved with figures of the four evangelists, a picture frame for Gennari's altarpiece and a holy water pot. Opposite the altar was the royal pew, or tribune, containing a canopy of nine carved and gilded cherubs and a gilded crown and sceptre suspended over the king and queen's thrones.

The first time the new chapel was used was on Christmas Eve 1686. The procession, led by the sword-bearer, made its way along the as yet incomplete privy gallery and the king entered his pew from the shell of the new eating room, many courtiers remaining outside.

Figure 113: The reredos from the Whitehall Chapel installed in Westminster Abbey in 1706 after being removed before the catastrophic Whitehall fire of 1698. The configuration was modified to fit the abbey, but in its essentials this image represents what James II ordered.

Others crowded in to view the spectacle. Seated on their thrones James and Mary Beatrice listened to an Italian choir singing Mass while a Roman Catholic bishop presided in his mitre and rich cope. Ten Jesuit priests with rich vestments swung censers filling the chapel with incense. John Evelyn was shocked at what he saw. 'I could not have believed that I should ever have seen such things in the King of England's palace.'[7]

The opening of the Whitehall chapel was the cue for setting up a parallel Roman Catholic chapel establishment to the existing Anglican one. Twenty-eight staff were appointed and an annual budget of some £2,000 allocated. A cosmopolitan mix of French, Italian, German and English musicians who were familiar with Catholic liturgy were recruited and their wages pushed the chapel budget up to nearly £4,000 a year compared to just £2,500 for the Anglican establishment. Sir Edward Petre, a Jesuit who had been implicated in the Popish Plot, was appointed Clerk of the Closet and *de facto* head of the Roman establishment; he was granted extensive lodgings at Whitehall where he held court.[8]

At Christmas and Easter it was traditional for the king to receive communion at the high altar but Wren's chapel had made no provision for a stair to allow the royal couple to descend from the pew to do this. A few days after Easter 1687 Wren received instructions to alter and enlarge the chapel. He was asked to build a processional staircase, a side chapel for a subsidiary altar above which should be an organ loft, and next to this was to be a vestry. The wording of the royal warrant to Wren suggests that he was given drawings and a specification, probably devised by Father Petre. Wren had originally designed a chapel for private devotions along the lines of St James's, but the king wanted a fully operational chapel royal where the full force of royal majesty and piety could be displayed. The rebuilt Whitehall chapel shared a plan with that at Somerset House which was never a private chapel but a conventual church open to Catholics from all over London. It was in this way that the English court now had two chapels royal, one Catholic and one Anglican existing with equal architectural and institutional status, an arrangement unique in all Europe.[9]

King James continued to use Windsor as the summer residence of the court; here there was a small private Catholic chapel on the queen's side which he initially used. During the court visit of 1686 James announced that he would be taking over the recently completed Chapel Royal for Catholic worship. New vestments, linen, plate and candlesticks were purchased, and a new organ ordered. Meanwhile the works department replaced a communion table with an altar on a marble step and made a new 'confession chaire'. The following summer the king received the Papal Nuncio at Windsor in a ceremony unparalleled since the days of Mary I. He arrived in a cavalcade of thirty-six coaches each pulled by six horses. The nuncio rode in the king's coach with the Master of Ceremonies and the Duke of Grafton; his own coach followed, empty. They got out in the inner court, the nuncio accompanied by ten of his own priests, after which he was received in St George's Hall, where 'were the King and Queen seated on two chairs under a canopy'.[10]

Scotland

James's promotion of Catholicism was never confined to England but extended to Ireland and, in particular, Scotland. The dominant Scots at court were the Drummond brothers, Lords Perth and Melfort who converted to Catholicism early in James's reign and gained effective control of Scotland. Because, as Duke of York, James had lived at Holyrood, he regarded it as part of the core royal estate in a way that Charles II never had. Orders were given at the start of his reign to convert the new council chamber into a Roman Catholic chapel for 'exercising with the more decency and security' Catholic worship. After the dismissal of the talented William Bruce in 1678, Lauderdale's brother briefly held the post of Surveyor. He was soon eclipsed by the Catholic architect James Smith who had travelled through Europe and lived in Rome where he had begun to train as a priest. Returning to Scotland he married Robert Mylne's daughter and was engaged to work on Holyrood under Bruce. Smith made the necessary alterations to the council chamber and received, at Leith Docks, an altar, vestments, paintings and other equipment sent from London to furnish it.

In December 1687 Smith was called to Whitehall where he was able to see the new chapel and other new buildings and receive detailed instructions for the conversion of the abbey church at Holyrood for Roman Catholic worship. Given the recent experience with the Whitehall chapel the king must have approved the designs personally and Smith received £120 as a reward for 'the performance of his duty'. Although Smith's work was demolished by a 'giddy multitude and enthusiastical mob' in 1688, its appearance is known from a drawing by a Dutch artist later published as a print.[11]

James envisaged the chapel being the home of a revived Order of the Thistle along the lines of Garter knights at St George's Chapel at Windsor. The twelve knights were to sit in stalls facing each other, six a side, each

Figure 114: The Chapel Royal at Holyrood set up in the abbey church for King James II and VII. Engraving by Peter Mazell, based on a lost drawing by Jan van Wyck of 1687/8.

set within canopies supported by Corinthian columns. At the west end, raised up on seven steps was an elaborate throne framed by a giant order and crowned by military trophies. The throne setting was reminiscent of St George's Hall at Windsor, but the whole conception was more daring, evoking Christ presiding over the twelve disciples. No image of the reredos survives but, given the magnificence of the rest of the church, it must have been large and impressive.[12]

James decreed that much of the woodwork be manufactured in London and sent north to be fitted in place. Ostensibly this was because it was cheaper, but in reality James must have wanted to keep an eye on the fittings as they were made. Concurrently with the Whitehall chapel work was underway on the capacious and restrained chapel at Chelsea Royal Hospital. Here one of the leading carvers working on the altarpiece was William Morgan and he, together with Grinling Gibbons, was instructed to liaise with London merchant James Fowlis to make and transport the fittings to Scotland.[13]

As at Whitehall, the abbey church was no private chapel: it was a fully-fledged Roman Catholic church and the king's intention, with the help of his Catholic team of Smith, Melfort and Perth was to turn it into a conventual church, establishing a monastery there. By 1688 there was already a Jesuit College at Holyrood funded from the Treasury. The establishment of the Catholic chapel at Holyrood had caused rioting in the city but news of James's unseating by William of Orange in December 1688 fired the mob to destroy the chapel; Perth was lucky to escape with his life, and Scotland lost one of the finest interiors of the age.[14]

Son and heir

When James and Mary Beatrice re-established themselves at Whitehall in 1688 the atmosphere was increasingly tense, as the queen was four months pregnant and the king had required churches across England to give a general thanksgiving 'upon the occasion of the queen being with child'. Catholic priests at court were happy to tell anyone who listened that it would be a boy. A male heir would remove the king's

Protestant daughter Mary as heir presumptive and guarantee Roman Catholic rule into the foreseeable future. Scrutiny around the child's birth was therefore intense. It was assumed that the queen would give birth in her new bedchamber at Whitehall, but she unexpectedly announced that she would have the child at St James's. The queen's lying-in there, and the birth of a healthy son in June 1688, was destined to be a turning point in English history, and the source of the greatest conspiracy theory of the age.

The conspiracy theorists believed that the queen's pregnancy was a fabrication aided by blood and milk-filled sponges applied to her underwear. The baby was allegedly smuggled in a warming pan and St James's chosen for the birth as it was where there was 'a convent adjoining where a woman might be kept at the time of her bigness, or come into it any evening and none perceive . . . it being a large place within walls and cloisters, out of all hearing'. A plan was published showing any not convinced by twenty-one pages of detailed argument the route by which a child born in the friary was smuggled into the queen's bedchamber.[15]

There is no doubt that James Francis Edward Stuart, the Old Pretender, was the king's son. When James heard that Mary Beatrice was in labour, he came from Whitehall with almost the whole Privy Council who heard the queen's shrieks as she gave birth, and soon after, saw the child itself. A nursery was set up for the young prince at St James's with his own kitchen and room for a governess. On 15 October, in a ceremony of great splendour the Prince of Wales was christened in the Queen's Chapel at St James's with Catherine of Braganza and the Pope (represented by Count d'Adda, his nuncio) as godparents.[16]

The birth of Prince James Edward dashed the hope of succession long nursed by William of Orange, the husband of the king's daughter Mary. On 28 September William declared that he would invade England to rescue its people from popery and arbitrary rule, triggering the events which would lead to the revolution of 1688. Rioting in London led to violent attacks on Catholic chapels and in December, as London erupted in an explosion of anti-Catholicism, the government was alerted to a mob who wanted to demolish the chapel at St James's. A troop of eighty

De Koningin van Engelant, vlught met d' Prins van walles uijt London.

Figure 115: The departure of James II from Whitehall in 1698 from a
Dutch news sheet. The configuration of Whitehall is confused,
but individual elements are broadly correct.

horse guards were sent to secure it; they arrived just as rioters had broken
in and had started to destroy the organ. The plate had been removed
from the Whitehall chapel to protect it and, as the rioters became bolder,
eighty cavalry, 300 foot soldiers and three cannon were set up to protect
Whitehall and the palace precincts.[17]

It was from Whitehall, in a barge, that James II made his escape from
London in the face of William III's troops. He left behind him a palace
half-finished and his project to convert the nation half-begun. His legacy
at Whitehall and Holyrood was quickly erased and the reign of his
daughter and son-in-law that followed ensured that his vision of a court
where Anglicans and Roman Catholics co-existed was forgotten.

EIGHTEEN

Domesticity and Splendour: William and Mary

Figure 116: Romeyn de Hooghe, an allegory of William and Mary, c.1689. The king and queen are seen with the riverfront of Whitehall in the background. Henry Compton, the Bishop of London, is shown bowing before them. The royal arms are flanked by medallions showing Orange and Stuart rulers.

As Charles II sailed for England to take his crown in 1660 one of those who saw him off at the quayside in Scheveningen in the Dutch Republic was the nine-year-old William of Orange, who would, unbeknown to everyone, one day be crowned King of England. In

1660 William was a ward of the Dutch state and the role of Stadtholder, which his father had held till his sudden death in 1650, was in abeyance. The stadtholder was not a sovereign head of state, he was the first and supreme servant of the States of Holland and head of the Dutch army.

William was to grow up in the Netherlands as the head of the house of Orange Nassau. This was a European dynasty closely related to the royal families of England, France and several German princely states. They had substantial private revenues of perhaps a million guilders a year from their estates in the Dutch Republic, France and Germany, maintained a series of magnificent residences and hosted a populous court. This was Prince William's world until, at the age of thirty-eight, he inherited the residences and estates of the kingdoms of England and Scotland.

William was middle-aged in 1688, and like Charles II arrived at Whitehall with tastes shaped by long experience of life abroad. The ancient seat of the Nassau dynasty was at Breda, where a massive square moated castle was begun in the 1530s and furnished by William's grandfather with a great series of tapestries celebrating members of the house of Nassau. By the time William's father became stadtholder in 1647 this was no longer a principal residence and their favoured family home was Honselaersdijk, seven miles from The Hague towards Delft.

Honselaersdijk had been built between 1621 and 1646 as the principal summer residence for the Orange court. Set in fine hunting country, it was also furnished with extensive stables. Its layout was heavily influenced by the Palais de Luxembourg in Paris. The main block was connected to two pavilions by galleries that made up three sides of a courtyard; a colonnade and gallery closed the fourth side. On the first floor were symmetrical apartments sharing a hall and leading to antechambers. In square pavilions at each corner were the presence chambers, bedchambers and closets, each connected to a long gallery. The famous gardens, like the house, underwent several stages of development, and were set within a matrix of canals and waterways. In the 1630s, the French horticulturalist André Mollet, who also designed gardens in England for Charles I, laid out the parterres. The arrangement was captured by the brilliant cartographer Balthasar Florisz van Berckenrode in around 1638; his view emphasises that although the house was extremely beautiful, framed by waterways and intensely cultivated gardens, it was an exquisite rather than magisterial place.[1]

While Honselaersdijk was the closest thing William's father had to a modern residence of state, he also owned two hunting lodges. Huis ter Nieuburgh was begun, five miles east of The Hague, at Ryijswijk in 1630, as a private lodge, without accommodation for court officials. It was also designed after the French pavilion system but not in a courtyard – rather as a single range. Here two remote pavilions were linked by galleries to a central block that contained the principal rooms. Like Honselaersdijk it was set in extensive gardens. His other lodge was at Dieren in Gelderland

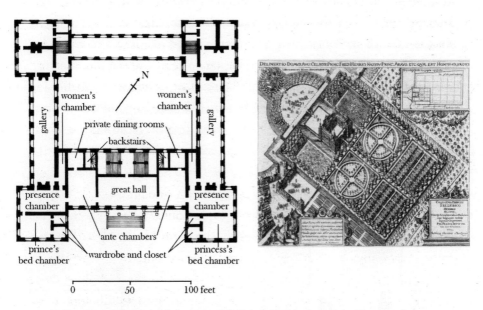

Figure 117: *Left:* Plan of the principal floor of Honselaersdijk. The plan became the model for most of William and Mary's palaces in that there was a shared state room and individual apartments linked to it. *Right:* Bird's eye view of the house and gardens at Honselaersdijk by Balthasar Florisz van Berckenrode, *c.*1638.

on the southeastern border of the excellent hunting grounds of the Veluwe. This was also inherited by William from his father who had purchased it in 1647. In the first part of his reign as stadtholder William spent as much as ten weeks a year here hunting far and wide.[2]

In 1645 William's grandmother had begun Huis ten Bosch (literally House in the Wood) as her dower house. Right beside The Hague, this was designed by Pieter Post, the stadtholder's official architect, with the assistance of Jacob van Campen, the chief exponent of Dutch classical architecture. The house was a square villa with a central domed hall that became a celebration of the Orange family in the way that the Banqueting House at Whitehall was a celebration of the Stuarts. Around the central hall were two sets of apartments each comprising an anteroom, used as a presence chamber with a canopy of state; this led to a bedchamber with a bed of state behind a balustrade, and a large private closet, a smaller closet and a dressing room.[3]

In 1668 William turned eighteen and his minority came to an end. He inherited his estates, their income, and all these residences, apart from Huis ten Bosch in which his grandmother still lived, and which finally came to him in 1686. At the same time, he entered political life, starting to attend meetings of the Council of State as an ordinary member.

While William was a rich man, he was also owed considerable sums by the Stuarts whom his family had loyally supported during the Civil War and Interregnum. It was to reclaim these funds that William accepted,

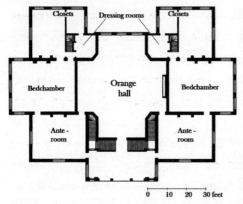

Figure 118: *Left:* Plan of the principal floor of Huis ten Bosch; and *right:* cross-section by Jan Mattysz, after a design by Pieter Jansz, 1655.

in 1670, an invitation from his uncle, Charles II, to visit England. The twenty-year-old prince arrived at Whitehall in November that year and was given specially fitted up lodgings in the cockpit. He remained at the English court until the end of February 1671, being entertained in lavish style. He visited Windsor Castle, Oxford and Cambridge, he went to the races at Newmarket, was dined by the Lord Mayor of London and spent many nights at the king's table. He made a good impression, though he was thought to be a bit dour and reserved. The king encouraged him to get drunk one evening; apparently William could not hold his drink and ended up smashing windows in the maids of honour's lodgings.[4]

William had no idea that his duplicitous uncle had concluded a secret treaty with France and that he would declare war on the United Provinces the following year. In 1672 as the English led an attack by sea, Louis XIV's armies invaded the Spanish Netherlands and pressed on towards the United Provinces. The Dutch were hopelessly unprepared, their army collapsed like a deflating balloon and in July 1672 Louis XIV made a triumphal entry into Utrecht. The situation was catastrophic; described by the English poet, Andrew Marvell, as 'an earthquake, an hurricane and the deluge'. William was now the only hope and, by popular acclaim, was made Captain General of the army and Stadholder. It was not only his family name that made him first the leader, and then the hero of the Dutch fightback: he quickly proved himself to be a talent on campaign and in the council chamber. Nevertheless, his struggle against France would continue for the rest of his life – becoming almost the reason for it.[5]

Peace was concluded with England in early 1674 and a few months later William bought a farmhouse, Huis Soestdijk in the province of Utrecht. While this was certainly to provide new hunting grounds, it was also to establish a seat in the west of the country where the Oranges had little presence. In 1670 William had appointed as his personal architect Maurits Post, the 25-year-old son of the former stadtholder's architect Pieter Post. He extended the original farmhouse, adding two wings for William and a future consort; unusually the main rooms were on the ground floor approached, not by a grand staircase, but by a common entrance hall. The consort's side had only an antechamber,

AMSTERDAM
Huis ten Bosch
Het Loo
DEN HAAG
Honselaardijk
Soestdijk
De Voorst

Figure 119: Map of the United Provinces
showing William III's principal residences.

a bedchamber and a gallery; William's side had an additional room – a dining room. The exterior was extremely plain and restrained but inside the house was densely decorated with contemporary paintings including a ceiling adorned with hunting dogs.[6]

William had inherited fine gardens laid out by his grandfather, but at Soestdijk he was to create his own. Gardening became, with hunting, his greatest passion, and Soestdijk was his first experiment undertaken with a new gardener and the collaboration of Hans Willem Bentinck, his closest friend and fellow gardening fanatic. The house was flanked by two gardens containing a pair of parterres each with a great statue in the middle. The parterres were bounded by orchards of dwarf fruit trees planted in rows. Great avenues thrust their way out from this inner core, penetrating the parkland where deer roamed free.[7]

As well as architecture and gardening, a more peaceful life caused William to think about matrimony. Despite Charles II's double-dealing

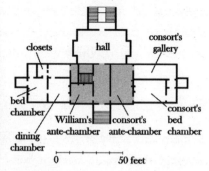

Figure 120: Diagrammatic plan of the principal floor of Huis Soestdijk as first constructed by William as stadtholder. The original farmhouse remained at the core of the new hunting lodge and is shaded in grey tone. On the left is a view of Soestdijk the early eighteenth century.

it was clear to him that a marriage with Mary Stuart, the Duke of York's eldest daughter, would potentially secure him the British throne. Meanwhile Charles II saw the benefits of marrying her to William, cementing his rickety Protestant credentials at home without, he believed, destroying his relationship with France. Before William made his move, he made detailed enquiries into what Mary was like: he had enough trouble in his life, he told the English ambassador at The Hague, without a wife who might add to it. Fully satisfied with what he heard, William made his way to England in October 1677 to discuss a possible marriage.

William was now head of state and his arrival demanded considerable expense and meticulous planning. He was received by Charles II at Newmarket where he was accommodated in the Duke of Ormond's house and furnished with a retinue of fifty English attendants who joined forty of his own. At Whitehall the Duke of York vacated his lodgings on the waterside at the end of the matted gallery in preparation for William's arrival. The Wardrobe refurnished the apartments and hired in new furniture including four large tables set up to feed William's entourage twice a day. Mary's lodgings were at St James's and it was there that her father told her that she was to marry William in just a few days' time. They married on William's twenty-seventh birthday at nine in the evening in Mary's bedroom at St James's and, after the blessing, she was undressed and taken to her bed. When William was safely tucked in beside her, the king drew the curtains crying 'Now nephew to your work! Hey! St George for England!' and the couple were left to get to know each other.[8]

William and Mary in the Dutch Republic

William and Mary arrived in Holland in terrible weather after a ghastly crossing; they made straight for Honselaersdijk where Mary and her ladies were escorted to her apartment. What expectations the tall, dark and vivacious fifteen-year-old had is not known. But she was probably pleasantly surprised by the elegant and symmetrical house with its beautiful gardens and well-ordered and compact lodgings. Only the year before, writing to her friend and confidante Frances Apsley, she reflected on what happiness was, and mused 'I could live and be content with a cottage in the country and a cow, a stiff petticoat and waistcoat in the summer, and cloth in winter; a little garden to live upon the fruit & herbs it yields'. Honselaersdijk and her husband's hunting lodges may have fulfilled that fantasy. They were everything her homes at St James's and Richmond were not: they were small-scaled, comfortable, modern and spotlessly clean.[9]

Mary had five days to explore her new home and prepare for her formal entry to The Hague. This was conducted with great splendour by the Estates General and included the obligatory triumphal arches, under which Mary's carriage passed, crushing beneath its wheels the sweet herbs strewn by twenty-four young virgins. She arrived at the Binnenhof, the official residence of the stadtholder and seat of government; in English terms, the equivalent to Whitehall and Westminster.[10]

The stadholder's quarters were on two floors linked by a large stair that gave access to both. The first room was for the guards and, after an anteroom there was the so-called great room, that led to a drawing room. Beyond this came William's new rooms, the most important of which was a state bedchamber containing an alcove for a state bed. Beyond a small cabinet was a long gallery, at the end of which was a large room called, in the eighteenth century, the music room. The ceiling

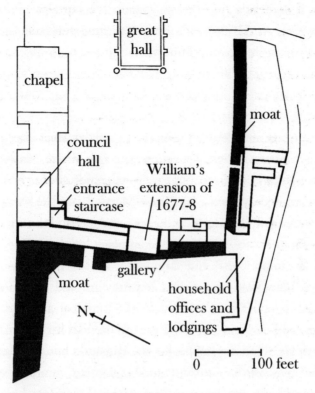

Figure 121: General plan showing the layout of the Stadtholder quarter in the Binnenhof and the new building erected by William in 1677–8.

of Mary's bedroom, beautifully painted with representations of morning and evening, is all that survives (now in the Rijksmuseum). Although he was brought up in the Binnenhof, William did not like living there, he hated the crowds of suitors; only the theatre which he had built in the old riding school would hold him there longer than a few days.[11]

Mary's marriage treaty allowed her a residence in The Hague, another in the country and freedom to practise as an Anglican. It was this last provision that, from an English point of view, was vital as Mary, who was second in line to the throne, had to be protected from becoming contaminated by Dutch Calvinism. To safeguard her, the Bishop of London appointed George Hooper, one of the archbishop's chaplains, to be her almoner. He arrived in the Dutch Republic soon after Mary, and found that none of William's houses had private chapels and that, because his residences were so small, there was no space to put one near Mary's lodgings. At the Binnenhof Mary vacated her dining room and it was fitted up with a communion table raised up on two steps and a chair for her near it. William, who had been brought up to be a strict Calvinist, was disparaging about the little closet, but Mary diligently said her prayers there every day.[12]

William's household had 13 noblemen in attendance, 24 household officials, 26 footmen in green liveries, 22 pages dressed in blue satin, crimson and gold, 32 manservants, 27 Swiss guards in blue cloaks, three chambermaids and 15 in the kitchens. Mary's household was another forty people mainly comprising her English attendants: in all, the combined number was 200, small compared with the English royal household of around 900, but large even for a great nobleman. The stadtholder's household were well cared for and used the prince's own physicians and were fed at his tables. At Honselaersdijk and Rijswijk there were extensive kitchen gardens and ice houses producing and storing fresh fruit and vegetables for the court.[13]

Like all sevententh-century princes, William was an obsessive huntsman and kept a large stable and packs of hounds. Although his hunting lodge at Dieren was sufficient for a bachelor, it was no place for the married stadtholder and, in 1678, William ordered that it be extended. In the early 1680s William and Mary spent much time here, and at Soestdijk, closeted with a very small company. While William hunted, the queen arranged her Chinese porcelain, did needlework with her ladies, and tended the gardens. Mary seems to have been seized by the beauty of the Dutch countryside and soon after arriving in Holland acquired an interest in botany and garden design. At Honselaersdijk an orangery was built, and she received, each week, flowers in season for her apartments. At Dieren, where there had been no garden, new walks, fountains, grottoes and arbours were laid out for Mary to enjoy while William was hunting.[14]

Mary had an intense sense of her royalty that was reinforced by the terms of her marriage, which insisted that she be treated with all the honour that she was used to in England. One consequence of this was that William was the only one of sufficient rank to dine with her. As William had previously held an open table with eight or ten companions, the newlyweds at first ate separately, Mary in stiff formality and William with his friends. Then a compromise was reached: William kept a table in the middle of the day and, in the evening, he retired to dine with Mary, banning political or military conversation and joking and laughing with his wife. Their relationship was unusually intimate for people of their rank, they even slept in the same bed.[15]

Mary's sense of status inhibited intimate friendships with the ladies of the Dutch Republic and so she passed time playing cards, doing needle-work, enjoying music, reading, collecting botanic specimens and at her prayers. Like many a bored millionaire she was a shopaholic and spent recklessly on luxury goods, often leading, and sometimes making, the fashion. Her jointure was £4,000 a year, but William frequently had to top this up. In the Royal Library at Windsor Castle one of her account books details what she spent on everything from jewellery, through gloves and fans to Chinese porcelain. In a marginal note in 1688 she wrote that she hoped William would 'forgive the debts I have made, if God gives me life I shall pay them, as fast as I can, if not I hope the prince will let none be wronged by my follies'. Despite her profligacy anxiety Mary had an extremely happy life, noting on her return to England that she 'had no small reason to doubt if ever I should be so happy in my own country'.[16]

Heir presumptive

The death of Charles II, and the accession of James in February 1685, was completely unexpected, placing William and Mary next in line to the British throne. Soon a stream of visitors came from England, both those opposing the rule of James II and those sent by James hoping to win support. Now, acutely conscious of their new status, William embarked on an aggrandisement of both his court and residences. Mary had always retained a sense of her regality but this markedly increased after Charles II's death; it was noted that now she was served at table by kneeling pages.[17]

William and Mary's elevation almost exactly coincided with an influx of architectural talent to their court. Maurits Post, the stadtholder's architect, had died in 1677 and was succeeded by a man of lesser capability, Johan van Swieten. Other than the construction of an orangery at Honselaersdijk no major commissions came his way, and his annual salary of just 600 guilders suggests that he was responsible mainly for minor works and maintenance. The important work of new design was passed to the former sculptor turned architect, Jacob Roman, who was first paid for design work in the stadtholder's accounts in 1684. Five years later, when William was king, Roman was to inherit the post of stadtholder's architect, at an increased salary of 1,000 florins a year, but before that he had already won William and Mary's confidence and become their principal architectural designer.[18]

In 1685 Louis XIV revoked the Edict of Nantes which had given protection to French Protestants (Huguenots). In the resulting exodus of refugees was the astonishingly talented and versatile 24-year-old designer Daniel Marot who quickly came to the notice of William and Mary. By 1686 he was so integrated into their architectural projects that he was calling himself 'architect to his highness', although he never occupied the position. Before Marot, the work of Dutch architects, like those in England, was confined to the architectural shell of a building and patrons, with their upholsterers and suppliers, decorated interiors to their taste. Marot took control of the whole appearance of William and Mary's houses, gardens and court festivities, integrating architecture, furnishing and planting.[19]

The third new talent to enter William's circle was a gardener, Daniel Desmarets, a Dutch expert in exotic plants who had first been employed at Honselaersdijk and who was to take over the botanical side of William's gardening as his 'intendant of gardens and plantations'. He answered directly to Bentinck who had been officially appointed gardening mastermind in 1681. It was also in this period that William appointed a curator of his collections, Robbert du Val, a painter who was in charge of keeping an inventory up to date. [20]

From the mid-1680s, this new team began to transform the setting of the stadtholder's court. This can be seen vividly in an engraving Marot made of a party at Huis ten Bosch in 1686. William's grandmother had left Huis ten Bosch to her daughters in 1675 and, for a decade, they had struggled to maintain the house and gardens. In 1686 William was finally able to persuade them to sell it to him for 10,000 guilders. Mary immediately commissioned Marot to redecorate their apartments and, in December that year, threw a tremendous ball in honour of William, although he was unable to attend. Marot took control of the event and his engraving shows the Oranjezaal with a ceiling newly painted by him and the princess's royal crowns prominently displayed above each door. He also redecorated William and Mary's apartments re-hanging the walls with silk, painting two ceilings and re-displaying Mary's porcelain collection.[21]

By this stage Roman, Marot and Desmarets were collaborating on a new venture, a hunting box or *lusthof* (literally pleasure house) in the Veluwe not far from Dieren called Huis Het Loo. The medieval castle there was purchased in 1684 and William seems to have approached Louis XIV's Académie Royale de l'Architecture for preliminary designs, probably in late 1684, but if plans were sent, it is unlikely that they had much influence, as Het Loo is entirely within the pre-existing traditions of stately architecture in the Dutch Republic. The house, which was built on a new site, and complete by 1687, was essentially a Palladian villa like the Villa Thiene at Cicogna or the Villa Badoer at Fratta Polesine. The main block was square and quadrant colonnades linked it to flanking service blocks. It was built around a central hall and stair leading up to a first-floor hall either side of which were two identical three-room apartments – neat, symmetrical and compact. Similar in plan to any number of contemporary small French country houses, it was, in many ways, rather old fashioned.

Either side of the house were his and hers gardens. Mary's was devoted to her passion for exotic flowers; plants in tubs in the summer were relocated to an orangery in the cold months. On William's side, as well as the parterres, there was a bowling green. Behind the house were the more public gardens laid out with parterres of cut grass

Figure 122: Daniel Marot, 'The Oranjezaal at Huis ten Bosch on the occasion
of the great ball of 1696'. Marot inserted a new painted ceiling beneath the existing
one, his first exercise in design in the Dutch Republic. Note the crowned M
over the door illuminated in fairy lights. Vignettes show the guests arriving
and Mary receiving her ladies in waiting.

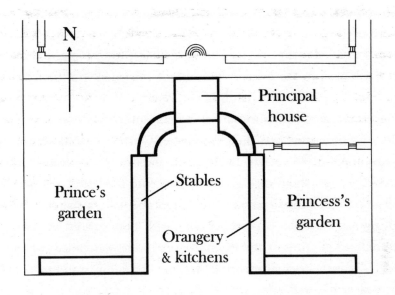

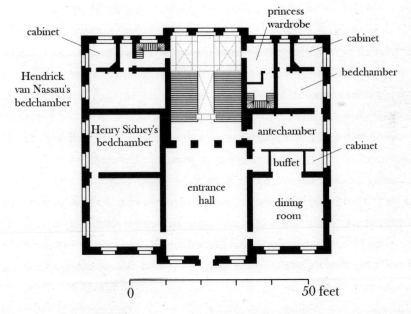

Figure 123a: Diagram of Het Loo in 1687, showing the original layout of house and grounds.

Figure 123b: Reconstructed plan of the ground floor of the building in 1685. The room labels are those in use in *c*.1692 and show that to the left of the hall were the rooms of William's Master of Horse, Hendrick van Nassau, and his First Gentleman of the Bedchamber, Henry Sidney. On the right is another large courtier lodging and the prince's dining room. The princess's wardrobe is connected to her dressing room above by a staircase.

bordered with beds, garnished with statues and managed by an English expert in turf.[22]

The great pediments of Het Loo were filled with carvings of hunting and hawking, proclaiming the purpose of this small but perfect oasis set in the heaths and moorlands of the Veluwe. Though today Het Loo is the most prominent survival of William and Mary's houses, in the 1680s Honselaersdijk was their showpiece. Only seven miles from The Hague, fashionable society could drive out for the evening and be received. Some joined card games, others just walked in the gardens. William would sometimes join the ladies and take a hand of basset. William had an audience chamber hung with cloth of gold and crimson embroidered in crimson and green; Mary's rooms were filled with gold-flecked lacquer, oriental embroideries and her Chinese cabinet had a mirrored ceiling reflecting shelves of porcelain. Her gallery was hung with portraits of the Stuart dynasty, emphasising her royal lineage.[23]

The biggest changes after 1685 took place at the ancient Nassau seat of Breda. Here William fashioned the only residence that the contemporary English might call a palace. An English visitor went so far as to say that it was equal to Windsor, though smaller. It, with Honselaersdijk, was the only residence to possess a throne room and, after 1685, a complete suite of royal apartments in the English style. Off a great hall there were three ante rooms before a presence chamber with a throne. Beyond this were the state bedchamber, a cabinet and a dressing room. Beyond the backstairs there were more private lodgings. William furnished the castle with dynastic portraits and antique tapestries. He added three new tapestries to his grandfather's set representing members of the house of Nassau, showing himself and Mary, emphasising his lineage and reinforcing the effect of an ancient family home.[24]

In the 1680s William and Mary created for themselves a string of perfect architectural jewels, set in beautiful gardens. Sparsely but richly furnished, their neat, compact apartments were clean and well ordered. There was no bustling bureaucracy, no rigid rule of etiquette, no clawing court, no hungry heir, few obligations for hospitality and even fewer of state: in short William and Mary enjoyed considerable domestic freedom

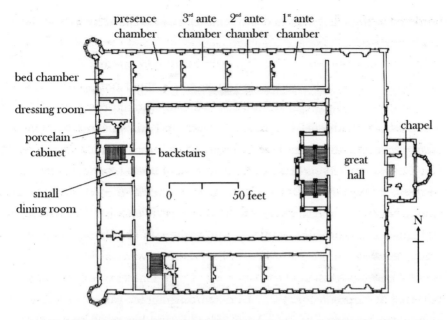

Figure 124a: Reconstructed plan of the first floor of the palace of Breda, showing the English-style state apartments.

Figure 124b: A contemporary engraving showing the 1667 signing of the peace treaty of Breda with the English by Romeyn de Hooghe. The depiction of the interior of the castle conveys the impression of ancient magnificence that William was to enhance after 1685.

and, while William was not on campaign, they made the most of a happy domestic existence together.

The Glorious Revolution

By September 1688 it was public knowledge that William of Orange was preparing an army ready for invasion. The corridors of Whitehall were filled with rumour and a palpable sense of unease. James was beside himself with anxiety and sent orders to mobilise the army. A royal proclamation was issued stating that it was a pretence that he had threatened the 'liberties, property and religion' of the English and that these lies were being used as a cover to facilitate the conquest of England by the Dutch. In a state of panic James began to systematically overturn all the pro-Catholic actions that he had introduced since his accession. It was not enough. Everyone knew that the moment the threat of invasion subsided, James would simply reinstate the unpopular measures. On 28 September the king and queen retreated to the new Whitehall chapel where they began a forty-hour service of continuous prayer for divine assistance.

Even James knew that prayer was not going to be enough and by mid-October his army was positioned along the south and east coast and his navy was ready to sail. All they awaited was a favourable wind for William to leave Holland. On top of the Banqueting House, in the heart of Whitehall, the king's blacksmiths laboured to erect a huge wind-vane. It is still there on the north side, easily visible from the street. When this showed an easterly wind James knew that his hour of destiny had arrived. On 1 November 1688 the gilded vane flipped eastwards signalling that William's fleet was on the way. It landed four days later, on 5 November, at Brixham.

James moved to Salisbury where a large part of his army was waiting for William. It was not a happy visit. Parts of the English army were deserting to his son-in-law and the stress caused James to have a two-day-long nosebleed that prevented him from travelling. He decided to retreat to the Thames valley and stage a strong defensive line around London.

But by the time James returned to Whitehall he found that the drizzle of defections had turned into a deluge. Worse, amongst the defectors were some of James's closest and oldest friends, and some of the most important men of the court. The most crushing news was that his daughter Anne (later Queen Anne) had left Whitehall with the Bishop of London and was on her way to join William of Orange's camp. Already there was her husband George of Denmark.

Even James now realised that his reign was untenable. Both his daughters, both his sons-in-law and his closest and oldest friends were now all against him. The court had shrunk to a tiny group of Catholic advisors and a few minor Italian diplomats. He heard that Dover Castle, his obvious escape route to the continent, had gone over to William. It would be surprising if James, sitting in Whitehall on the night of 9 December was not thinking of the execution of his father, not thirty yards from where he slept. Over a tense and unhappy supper James and his wife Mary of Modena agreed to flee.

At two o'clock in the morning on 10 December the queen, disguised as an Italian laundress, left Whitehall with the Prince of Wales, two nurses and a single attendant. She was smuggled to Gravesend in a coach from where she embarked for France. The king, meanwhile, was struggling with his own conscience: should he stay or should he abandon his duty and go? In the early hours of 11 December, less than twenty-four hours after the queen, James boarded a carriage in the inner court at Whitehall. It took him to the horse ferry at Lambeth where he crossed the river. In his luggage he had the Great Seal of England, the instrument by which parliament was called. In the wintry darkness the heavy metal mould, the symbol of royal authority, was slipped into the river. Although few knew that he had thrown the Seal away, the very action of his abandoning the throne at a time of national crisis was to count against him. Kings were expected to rule and if they could not a council of regency should have been established. James had simply dropped the reins of power.

Etiquette restricted access into the king's bedchamber and so it was not until the middle of the next morning that it became clear that he had fled. His attempt to escape was a disaster. The whole of the Thames estuary and most of Kent was full of parties of armed peasants and townsmen looking for papists. It was not long before a rough band apprehended the king's party and James found himself in captivity. His rough cloak, short wig and a patch on the side of his face concealed his identity from his captors. He was stripped, searched and his crucifix confiscated. When he arrived at Faversham he was recognised as the king and eventually, treated as such.

William of Orange was now at Windsor Castle, and James believed that, even at this late stage, he could strike a deal with his son-in-law that would heal the wounds and secure his throne. To start negotiations, he returned to Whitehall. In London James was welcomed by cheering crowds and celebratory bonfires. In his absence there had been terrifying riots, the houses of known Catholics had been ransacked and Catholic chapels burnt. Londoners, seeing their king, hoped that he had done a deal with William and that peace would return. Everyone, William and James included, wanted to avoid bloodshed and chaos. That night, 17 December, was surreal. With William at Syon House on the outskirts of London, and James buoyed by his reception, Whitehall almost returned to normal. The king regally summoned his Privy Council to the new council chamber and welcomed his Catholic advisors back to his apartments. At midnight he ostentatiously heard Mass in the chapel.

In the middle of the following night the king was woken in his bedchamber by the secretary of state, the Earl of Middleton. William had stationed Dutch guards round Whitehall and the king's own grenadiers had defected to the prince. James, crushed by the news, agreed to leave Whitehall. At eleven the next morning a small flotilla of barges pulled up at the steps of Whitehall and rowed away England's rightful king to Rochester from where, on Christmas Eve, he left for France. Only five hours later Prince William of Orange rode into London and established himself at St James's. The glorious, and bloodless, revolution had been effected.

At first coming to England at the head of his army, the provisional government held back from offering William the use of any of the royal houses. William, acutely aware of the symbolism accorded to residence in a royal palace, trod very carefully. At Windsor Castle where, with his Whig supporters, plans were laid to oust James and enter the capital, he occupied the ground-floor rooms, only going upstairs to dine in the state eating room. Similarly, on his arrival in London William moved to St James's, the seat of the heir, not Whitehall, the sovereign's palace. Mary arrived in Greenwich on 11 February and, after composing herself, and being briefed by William, made for Whitehall the following day. Whatever her real feelings, entering her father's new apartments in the privy gallery, the 26-year-old queen went from room to room enthusiastically inspecting the furniture, opening the cupboards and examining everything in great detail. Radiating positivity, either genuine, or to convince the English ladies that she was comfortable with deposing her father, she then made for St James's where she spent the night for the first time since 1677.[25]

The following day William and Mary were declared joint sovereigns and, the day after, the Privy Council met in the Whitehall council chamber. Their positions officially acknowledged by parliament, William and Mary could now take up residence in Whitehall. It was now William's turn to gloat over the royal collection, moving from room to room noting the paintings and making plans to relocate them. The general expectation was that the king and queen would reside at Whitehall but William did not like the vast, rambling, overpopulated urban residence lying low beside a polluted river and surrounded by hundreds of belching chimneys. It was not the place for a man who loved small houses in the countryside and was plagued by respiratory ailments. Nine days into their reign the royal couple had moved from Westminster to Hampton Court.[26]

The melding of courts

Unlike King James I, who came to London ignorant of the workings of the English court, Mary had been brought up there, and William had several times been an honoured guest; yet neither was much enamoured by it. The queen privately expressed her dismay at what she regarded as the vanities of court ceremonial, particularly as it concerned her coronation and ritual in the Chapel Royal. But more generally they had designed their lives in Holland to be free from restrictions: Mary regarded their move to England as a 'loss of liberty'.[27]

Although William's personal inclinations were towards informality, he embraced the ceremonious formality of the English court life, first because he had to demonstrate his legitimacy, and royal power in England was inextricably bound up with the ability to play the part of sovereign. But he also needed to persuade his new subjects to back his war with France, and the best way to do that was to be the magnificent monarch they expected. It is the case that William's English court was different from that of his predecessors. He was not a gregarious socialite like Charles II, nor was he an anti-social recluse; he was a prince who enjoyed small company and held himself with dignity in a large gathering. His court also had a unique dual dynamic while Mary was alive; she played a more important role than either of the preceding queen consorts. Crucially it was also a court from which William was regularly absent abroad. As a result, ceremonial was episodic, marked by his regular departure in early summer and return in the autumn. As William left London political and fashionable society left for the country while Mary held court at Whitehall sustaining a degree of formal activity through the summer until parliament returned in September.

Despite the king's opponents complaining that England was now overrun with Dutchmen, the reality was that William kept his two administrations entirely separate and a tiny number of Dutch gained political posts in England. Six went to the House of Lords, one onto the Privy Council but otherwise the entire political establishment was English. At court, the key posts went to men who had served William in the Netherlands. Most important was the groom of the stool, head of the king's Bedchamber, Hans Willem Bentinck, who had served William since being taken on as a page in 1664 aged fourteen. Bentinck not only shared the king's great interest in gardening and hunting, but was his closest friend and most trusted advisor. He went on to become Earl of Portland and the only Dutchman to sit on the Privy Council.

His brother-in-law, Edward Villiers, Mary's master of the horse, became the Earl of Jersey and Lord Chamberlain in 1700 and William's second cousin, Hendrick van Nassau-Ouwerkerk, became Master of Horse. These appointments ensured that William was surrounded by close friends while the complexities of English politics remained with the English Privy Council. This was not so very different to what James I had established in 1603. The rest of the court, some 1,000 posts, went to Englishmen. In 1688–9 William oversaw the reassemblage of a court on the scale of Charles II, undoing the reforms of James II that had slashed numbers. William also ruled that he would adopt the court regulations established by Charles II, populating his palaces with staff geared to the smooth functioning of public ceremonial.[28]

When in February 1688 William and Mary left the capital for Hampton Court Mary was returning to a place she knew from her childhood. But her memories, if they had been fond, were deceptive: she wrote to a Dutch friend, 'At the moment I am in the country in a place which has been badly neglected, it is about four miles from London but lacks many of the commodities of Dieren (although the house has four or five hundred rooms).' William 'found the air of Hampton Court agreed so well with him, that he resolved to live the greatest part of the year there; but that palace was so very old built and so irregular, that a design was formed of raising new buildings there for the king's and queen's apartments'. The bed of state which had been at Windsor, the official summer residence of Charles and James, was moved to Hampton Court, and Wren was commissioned to come up with a design.[29]

The king, melancholic, homesick, and unwell was eager to move in as quickly as possible and orders were given for the court to remove from Whitehall to Hampton Court. The decision was met with horror. Keeping the court out of London was bad for the city's economy and dreadful for the sanity of his ministers, all of whom lived in or near Westminster. So the king was persuaded to look for somewhere closer to Whitehall and quickly settled on the 2nd Earl of Nottingham's house in Kensington. Just a month after their coronation William bought it, and its surrounding grounds for £20,000. The Jacobean mansion was no more suitable than Tudor Hampton Court and Wren received a second commission from his new masters to modernise and extend Kensington House. Meanwhile the king and queen rented Holland House in Kensington from where Mary urged on both projects.[30]

It was in this way that King William, in a matter of months of his accession, redrew a centuries-old pattern of royal habitation. Whitehall was now to be principally the centre of the national bureaucracy while Kensington was to be William and Mary's normal town residence and Hampton Court the palace of state. This arrangement replicated their pattern of existence in Dutch Republic: Whitehall was equivalent to the Binnenhof, a little-liked official urban residence; Huis ten Bosch

Figure 125: Nottingham House as it must have looked when purchased by William and Mary in 1689, as reconstructed by Dr Edward Impey.

was like Kensington, a suburban residence close to the capital and Hampton Court the treasure house of state, more like Honselaersdijk or Breda Castle.

Whitehall, the theatre of state

Although William disliked Whitehall it was inescapably the administrative and ceremonial hub of the kingdom. The Banqueting House was the theatre of diplomatic ceremonial and William played a full part in the formal reception and leave-taking of embassies there. It was also the headquarters of the Chapel Royal and, on all the major church feasts, William attended chapel in the royal pew taking communion in public and washing the feet of poor men on Maundy Thursday. Amongst other state offices it contained the Treasury and William regularly attended meetings of the Treasury Board in their chamber there. In short, the wheels of the British state could not turn without the sovereign's presence at Whitehall.[31]

This quickly gave William a problem. In June 1690 he departed at the head of an army to Ireland where he was to meet his father-in-law in battle and, almost every year thereafter, he spent considerable time abroad on campaign. To cover his absences parliament passed an Act of Regency giving Mary authority to 'exercise and administer regal power and government of the kingdom'. In undertaking this task, one at first she did not relish, she was fortunate in having the Whitehall privy lodgings that her stepmother had started and left incomplete. For Mary of Modena, Wren had designed one of his most attractive buildings: a square six-bay block in rubbed brick and stone on the waterfront, intended to replace the accretion of rooms that made up the Tudor and early Stuart queen's lodgings. On the riverfront it contained a double-height drawing room of four bays with a balcony overlooking the river; next door was an eating room and, in the range behind, a bedroom and dressing room. The west side overlooked an extraordinary hemi-circular court around which ran a gallery, lit by sixteen circular windows, joining the new building with parts of the old.[32]

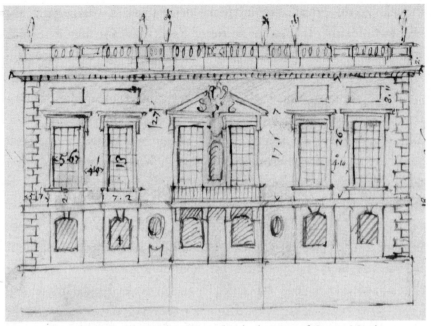

Figure 126: Sir Christopher Wren, sketch elevation of Queen Mary's
riverside privy lodging at Whitehall, much as it was built.

The new riverside lodgings became a self-contained private residence for
Mary each summer as the king was on campaign. She was able to attend
Privy Council meetings in the council chamber and receive ministers on
state business. In her state rooms she conducted receptions, gave audiences,
held drawing rooms and danced with her ladies. At the end of the day she
could withdraw to part of the palace similar to that which she had enjoyed
in Holland. Mary loved to build and to decorate and, in 1689, she had the
privy lodgings refurnished and a library built for her voracious reading
habit. Yet Whitehall was a poor substitute for Kensington, and she wrote
to William in August 1690 as a 'poor body' who had been 'so long condemned
to this place, and see nothing but water or walls'. She was in residence in
April 1691 when a major fire broke out in the stone gallery, obliterating
most of the southern part of the palace but being extinguished before it
reached the royal lodgings. After the fire, determined to escape the envel-
oping 'walls' she ordered a complete rearrangement of her lodgings.[33]

Lacking any private garden, Mary commissioned a large terrace to be built into the Thames using rubble from the 1691 fire. A stair led from her lodgings to a delicate parterre and sweeping quadrant steps to landing stages enabling her to take to the water. The former eating room was converted into a new great bedchamber overlooking the river and connected to the king's bedchamber in the volary lodgings next door. Richly upholstered beds were ordered and a suite of wall hangings in velvet for winter and damask for summer. A new white-tiled bathroom with a furnace for hot water was built next to her bedroom.[34]

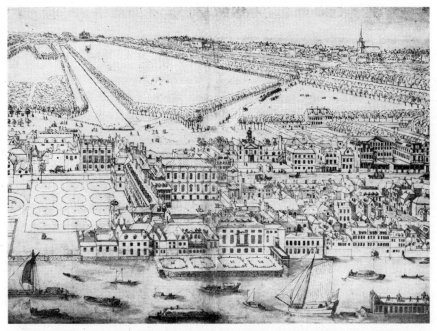

Figure 127: Leonard Knyff, a bird's-eye view of Whitehall from the east, *c.*1695–7. This remarkable panorama shows Whitehall after the fire of 1691 that destroyed its southern part. The queen's new lodgings and terrace are very prominent on the waterfront. The two windows on the left are to Queen Mary's bedchamber. All the rooms were double height. To their left is the volary lodging, built by Charles II and containing the king's privy apartments. Behind them to the left of the Banqueting House is James II's new range of state rooms with the Catholic chapel at the far end. The right of the drawing is dominated by the packed workhouses and offices of Scotland Yard. In the distance across St James's Park is St James's Palace, and to its right stands the newly built church of St James Piccadilly.

Religion at court

The Revolution of 1688 was in some senses a religious one and, within days of its achievement, steps were taken to expunge all traces of Catholicism at court. Foremost was the decision to convert James II's Roman Catholic chapel at Whitehall into a library and the dismantling of its interior began immediately. Although, under the terms of her grant from Charles II, the St James's catholic chapel was still Catherine of Braganza's, she had no use for it and, in 1688, it was granted to a congregation of French Protestants. The St James's Chapel Royal, which remained in service, was redecorated in a simplified fashion.[35]

William, who was a Dutch Calvinist, reappointed Charles II's dean, Henry Compton, Bishop of London, as Dean of the Chapel Royal and he immediately issued orders forbidding music, other than organ music, and singing other than anthems and the Gloria, in the Chapel Royal. As expected, William appointed his fiercely loyal friend and religious and political advisor Gilbert Burnet as clerk of the closet and, after his elevation to the bishopric of Salisbury, John Tillotson took his place. Tillotson, who became Archbishop of Canterbury in 1691 was, like Burnet, known for his attacks on popery. Therefore within the royal household, both private royal devotions and public displays of piety were rapidly reformed and a rhetoric of Godly reformation adopted from the royal pulpits.[36]

During her first stay at Hampton Court, in February 1689, Mary ordered that the altar in her private chapel be removed and a communion table provided. That Easter William and Mary were at Hampton Court and experienced the full ceremonialism of the Caroline court in the Tudor chapel royal. The queen recorded in her journal that they received the sacrament together alone, a 'foolish formality'. By Christmas etiquette had been reformed and, when they next received communion publicly at Whitehall, members of the court accompanied them. Ever since Henry VIII's time a closet, sited between the presence and privy chambers, had been the king's private oratory. The oratories at Hampton Court and Whitehall were abolished, signifying the king's abandonment of the old ways; when plans were drawn up in 1689 for the new king's lodgings at Hampton Court and Kensington there was no obvious provision for private devotion.[37]

There was, however, a small household chapel built at Kensington. It was a double-height space with a traditional elevated royal pew. There was a communion table with a rail and the royal crowns over the door; marked on a plan of 1695 it appears as an extremely domestic space with no concession to traditional ecclesiastical features. Their principal place of worship, and headquarters of the Chapel Royal, remained at Whitehall. Mary instituted regular weekday sung prayers and a series of sermons on Wednesday afternoons. For these the pulpit was embellished to include much carving and a canopy relocated to it from above the king's seat – a symbolic reassignment of significance. The queen had a new private chapel for herself constructed close to her privy lodgings where she said her daily prayers.[38]

Mary's regular presence at Whitehall in the years immediately after 1688 provided an important strand of continuity with her father's reign, especially for those uncertain about William and his right to the throne. Mary was unassailably in the line of succession; she was an Anglican of unquestioned virtue, and she held court, as was traditional, at Whitehall. All these strengthened confidence in the infant regime even if it didn't satisfy the Jacobites.

Kensington and Het Loo

In 1689 Kensington House was a compact rectangular Jacobean villa with a central hall and rooms to either side. The plan was to enlarge it by the addition of four corner pavilions and a long gallery connected to an entrance on the west. The southeast pavilion was the king's, the northwest for the queen, while the northeast pavilion contained the council chamber and the southwest the main stairs. Kensington was, in fact, closely based on William and Mary's houses in the Netherlands: the shared entrance chamber and compact residential pavilions were the essence of their residences at home: Wren had, in fact, designed a palace planned in the Dutch style.[39]

Figure 128: Noel Gasselin, view of Kensington Palace from the southeast, seen over the boundary wall with Hyde Park. Three of the new pavilions can be seen, and, in their midst, the gable and central turret of the Jacobean house.

In 1689 Wren had been Surveyor of the King's Works for twenty-one years. He had faithfully served both Charles II and James II as a courtier and a Tory and was deeply implicated in the old regime. William and Mary's arrival caused a radical redistribution of government and court offices and, on the face of it, his hold on the surveyorship must have been, at best, uncertain. In all this change Mary was a strand of continuity. The new queen knew how the court worked socially and politically. Her resuscitation of normal Stuart court life was vital in establishing the legitimacy and efficacy of William's reign. So too was the normal and efficient functioning of the Office of Works, including the immediate construction of two palaces and the completion of the queen's privy lodgings at Whitehall. Ultimately only two of the personnel of the Office of Works were replaced in 1688 and their head, Sir Christopher, survived. This was probably due to Mary's favour towards a diehard Stuart courtier and her admiration for the now famous architect of St Paul's. For Mary the completion of the cathedral was a vital part of the spiritual reformation that she believed England badly needed.[40]

Design work for Hampton Court and Kensington therefore took place against the background of uncertainty at the Office of Works and Wren's attempt to secure a fruitful and effective *modus operandi* with his new patrons. Into this mix we know that William and Mary introduced their own architectural advisors. By December 1689 Jacob Roman was in London and, soon afterwards, so too was Daniel Marot who stayed until 1696. These two had led the translation of the stadtholder's architectural image into a kingly one in the Netherlands. There is no evidence that Roman's views were sought on either the design of Kensington or Hampton Court, but he understood William and Mary's liking for modest brick-built houses designed on the pavilion principle. It is entirely possible that the final appearance of Kensington owed something to three-way conversations between Queen Mary, Roman and Wren. If its layout was influenced by Roman to reflect the king and queen's domestic preferences, its interiors also reflected their Dutch tastes. The queen's rooms were decorated with 787 pieces of porcelain arranged in the manner of Daniel Marot; although, again, there is no evidence to prove it, during his three-year stay in England, Marot was probably acting as an interior decorator and (as will be suggested) garden designer to Mary.[41]

Despite the Dutch influence on Kensington, it was necessary to shoehorn the traditional sequence of royal rooms into the first floor.[42] Here, after the obligatory guard chamber, there were two formal reception rooms (presence and privy chambers) containing two chairs of state and a table for dining in public. If formal receptions were necessary, it was in the privy chamber that they took place; William's most frequent duty was giving audiences to ambassadors, but he also received delegations in here. The king had two bedchambers, one formally presented with a state bed and hung with fine tapestry, which he occasionally used for receiving people. Beyond was his closet, essentially his room of business where he conducted private audiences. The council chamber was a separate pavilion with its own stair, waiting room and room for the clerks. In here at six o'clock on a Sunday evening, at a great table covered with a carpet, William sat on his chair of state, his lords on blue velvet chairs, and attended to state business. If the council were to meet without the king, it would be at Whitehall.[43]

Design work for William's houses in Holland and England was

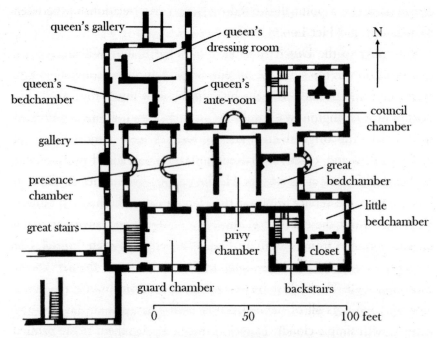

Figure 129: Plan of the first floor of Kensington Palace in 1694. This reconstruction of the original arrangement is based on surviving plans and building accounts as no complete contemporary plan of the house at this date exists. It shows that the state rooms were in old Nottingham House, while the king's and queen's own rooms were in opposing pavilions. There was a floor below of privy lodgings, and attics above for staff and servants.

undertaken concurrently. Designs and models were prepared wherever William was and were sent back and forth. At Huis de Voorst, in Gelderland, built between 1695 and 1700 by William III for Arnold Joost van Keppel (created Lord Albemarle in 1697), a wooden model seems to have been made in England under Jacob Roman's supervision for the approval of William and Lord Albemarle. In December 1700, while William was at Hampton Court, Charles Hopson, his English master joiner, arrived bearing a model he had made of the staircases at Het Loo which the King's English sergeant painter was sent to decorate. But Kensington, as the private residence of William and Mary, may have been singled out for special attention by William and Mary's Dutch design advisors; a point illustrated by the stylistic relationship between Kensington and Het Loo.⁴⁴

Returning to the Dutch Republic as a king in 1691 William realised that Het Loo was too small for the entourage that now accompanied him everywhere and decided to make his 'princely seat into a royal seat'. The design of Kensington was fresh in his mind and, in fact, provided the model. The original quadrant colonnades were removed and set in the gardens and, exactly as at Kensington, Roman added two pavilions to the central block at its corners. He then added two further pavilions to link these to the service wings at the front. In plan he had reproduced Kensington, but the effect of gradually receding compartments focusing on the entrance front was more like Winchester or even Versailles in giving it a sense of scale. At the same time the interiors of the new rooms were upgraded. In the first phase Loo had been very much a hunting lodge, its interiors all of painted timber: the ceilings were boarded and painted with simple clouds. Daniel Marot now gave them richly painted and gilded plaster ceilings with deep mouldings of fruit and flowers.⁴⁵

Het Loo also had rooms necessary for a stadtholder and his wife who were now king and queen of Great Britain. For Mary there was a large Anglican chapel with a royal seat facing a pulpit and an altar behind a rail; for William there was a new public dining room. Marot gave special attention to this with rich, deep painted and gilded plaster mouldings and tapestries integrated into wall compartments. On the first floor the original three-room apartment was supplemented by a second apartment of state with an audience chamber, bedchamber and closet. William continued to use the original bedchamber (or *slaepcamer*) which, after all, overlooked the gardens. The new bedchamber (*bedcamer*) was a state bedchamber and it contained a monumental angel bed (*lit d'ange*), an extremely tall and grand structure without foot posts and supported invisibly by chains (notionally by angels).⁴⁶

The relocation of the original quadrants to the garden, framing a pool with a great jet, created a new area which was laid out to a design by Marot. There was now a strong central axis at the back of the house aligned on pools and fountains. Keeping such an elaborate garden in order required at least twenty-five staff and came with a sizeable bill; but William was passionate about the house, gardens and the hunting landscape around it.

Mary died before she ever saw the second phase of work at Het Loo and William did not use it much before 1698, and so their intended long-term pattern of use cannot be known. But it was seventy miles, a good twenty-four hours' ride, from The Hague, and it is clear that, although William needed a small suite of state rooms, the house was, as explained at the time, a place for the king to withdraw to be 'free from wars or weary of government' and English travellers certainly thought it 'rather neat than magnificent'. William himself was anxious about this perception for he wanted it to be splendid as well as comfortable. Nevertheless Loo was never a palace in the English sense, it remained principally a hunting seat for the king's pleasure.[47]

Hampton Court, the architecture of magnificence

There is a danger in exaggerating the novelty of Kensington. Every Stuart monarch had built smaller residences to escape the formality of the full court, James I at Royston, Charles I at Greenwich and Wimbledon and Charles II at Newmarket. The unique aspect of Kensington was that it was in London and the king decided that it was from there he should rule. What is not known is how the use of Kensington would have changed if William had lived longer to enjoy the completion of his other great architectural project, Hampton Court.

Hampton Court was designed to be magnificent. What is most surprising is that the exterior of the palace and its layout was designed over an incredibly intense period between the first week of March and the second week of April 1689. By then William had approved the final design and foundations were being dug in June. It was a moment of triumph for Wren; for his entire career he had been waiting for the order to rebuild one of the major royal residences. Despite work at Whitehall and Winchester he had never completed a royal palace, and

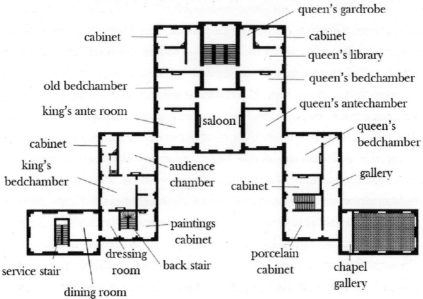

Figure 130a: Perspective of Het Loo as completed in *c*.1700.

Figure 130b: Reconstructed plan of the first floor of the palace on same alignment as the perspective above. The shaded area is the chapel on the ground floor.

William and Mary's enthusiasm for a new Hampton Court must have seemed like his best chance yet.[48]

The first plans were over-ambitious and involved sweeping away the whole Tudor palace except Henry VIII's great hall; but time was against William and he agreed to a piecemeal approach, first completing the royal lodgings and then moving on to the rest of the palace. Compromises had to be made in plan and elevation to accommodate the join with the Tudor buildings, and account had to be taken of pre-existing garden features, particularly Charles II's long canal on the east front. So, although the plan of the rooms has a smooth functionality, the external elevations wrapped round them bear little relationship to the rooms behind – with one exception. The two most important rooms, the king's privy chamber and the queen's drawing chamber, respectively the key rooms in each apartment, were in the centre of the south and east fronts, signified by elaborate stone frontispieces.

In the English tradition, since the early Stuart period, the privy chamber had become the principal reception room. But, due to the innovations of Charles II, by 1688 the great bedchamber had taken on many of the most formal functions of the privy chamber. This French custom was not reflected by Wren in any of the Hampton Court schemes, and was barely recognised in the household regulations, which clung to the etiquette of the early Stuart court. Indeed, in 1689, while thought was being given to the arrangement of the new royal apartments it was ordered that their plan should be the same as the old ones, dating from Tudor times.

The fact was that the alcove bedchambers of Charles II's time were no longer fashionable. A state bedchamber with an alcove was, after all, the appropriation of an arrangement originally designed for intimacy for a public function. William's III's great bedchamber had a rail across the room in front of the bed, but the room was large and spacious and, although William did have a *lever*, it was not of the formality and grandeur of those late in Charles II's reign.[49]

The year 1689, which had started so well, ended disastrously for Wren. First, in early November, a section of roof at Kensington fell, bringing down walls and floors with it. One workman was killed and several more injured. To make matters worse the queen had been there only a little while before. A much greater calamity was to follow. On 11 December a much larger part of the south range of Hampton Court also collapsed, killing two carpenters and injuring eleven others. Understandably Wren was upset and very 'troubled'. The resulting inquiry was to undermine Wren's credibility with William and led, eventually, to him losing the commission to complete Hampton Court.

Mary threw herself into the court that she had left eleven years before as a teenager. She reflected that in Holland she had 'led the life of a nun' but now she was in a 'noisy world full of vanity'. While she craved her quiet and elegant Dutch life, being Queen of England had its compensations: her greatest love was in building, decoration and furnishing, and while work continued on the main building at Hampton Court her attention focused on the creation of a pleasure house for herself at the riverside. She chose the large and well-built Tudor water gate, built in 1529–36, and used by successive monarchs as a riverside hideaway. Its last occupant had been Charles II's mistress, Barbara Palmer, by then Duchess of Cleveland, who had created, in the 1670s, a dairy and bathing room there. Here Mary created a luxurious retreat filled with lacquer work and blue and white Chinese export china modelled on her rooms at Honselaersdijk and Huis ten Bosch.

Between 1689 and 1694 William and Mary established a new rhythm to court life, melding long-held traditions with new ceremonial. The leave-taking and welcoming audiences that framed William's annual travels were an innovation. In either June or July, the king would receive delegations from the City, the church and the judiciary as well as the aristocracy and gentry to bid him *bon voyage*. On his return, normally in early October, he would receive a ceremonial welcome lasting several days; large numbers attended, as they signalled the start of the winter parliamentary and court season. Soon after his return was the annual City of London Mayor Making that included a great water pageant; William and Mary watched from the Whitehall balcony surrounded by courtiers after receiving the civic party in their apartments.[50]

The traditional 5 November celebration acquired extra meaning as it was also the day that William landed in 1688. The king's birthday was on the 14th and so the festivities were doubled: there was normally a concert and a ball and occasionally a play in the hall theatre; these were sometimes followed by dining in public and fireworks. Before 1698 these were held at Whitehall but at the end of the reign, at Kensington. On this day London was *en fête*, the shops were closed, church bells rang, and ordnance at the Tower was discharged. The queen's birthday, in April, was also celebrated with balls, music and sometimes a play; this continued, after her death in 1694, celebrating Princess Anne's birthday. Balls were also held on the anniversary of the coronation, in fact, between 1689 and 1696 at least seventeen balls were held at Whitehall, mostly in the great hall. Chapters of the Order of the Garter were regularly held at Whitehall and Kensington and some Garter feasts took place at Windsor. For the installation of the Earl of Portland one such feast involved the consumption of three oxen, eighteen calves, twenty-five sheep and vast quantities of poultry.

In the summer William would sometimes give concerts on a specially erected stage at Kensington. Mary would occasionally go to the theatre in Covent Garden, but William enjoyed plays at court; these were performed at Whitehall but, after 1698, he commissioned a theatre at Kensington and another for the great hall at Hampton Court; he maintained a fully operational theatre at the Binnenhof even while in England. William and Mary, in fact, presided over the most expensive court of any of the Stuart monarchs, costing some £300,000 a year and, in 1702, William left Queen Anne £307,000 of debts – more than twice those left by Charles II.[51]

NINETEEN

The Magnificence of Sovereignty

Just before Christmas 1694 Mary contracted smallpox, the infection that had killed both of William's parents. To his intense grief she died at Kensington a week later. William shut himself away, refusing to eat, sleep, or see anyone. Every wall at Kensington was hung with black fabric and orders were given for the household to drape their coaches in black and dress their servants in black livery. The queen's funeral was one of the most spectacular and costly ceremonial events of the entire century. Her coffin was taken from the Banqueting House, where it had lain in state, to Westminster Abbey along an avenue defined by rails covered in black cloth. For the first time in history it was accompanied by the members of both houses of parliament. There was genuine nation-wide sorrow, but the funeral was also a powerful expression of William's right to reign alone.[1]

Work at Hampton Court, then in full swing, stopped. In truth, that Hampton Court and Kensington should have been built at all is remarkable given the financial climate of the early 1690s. In 1689 the king and queen had been granted approximately £940,000 a year for four years. This was at least half a million short of what was required to run the household, and did not make provision for the £200,000 required annually to service the war debt. On this inadequate sum William restored a huge household, purchased Kensington House and launched the rebuilding of Hampton Court. By the queen's death £131,000 had been spent there and £92,000 at Kensington, not including a further £83,000 on gardens. William and Mary were spending twice what Charles II had done at his most extravagant. By 1695 the salaries of servants below stairs were sixteen months in arrears, so stopping work at Hampton Court was as much a financial necessity as an emotional response to the queen's death.[2]

Despite one early pregnancy, Mary never bore a child and her death left the succession in the hands of her sister Anne. In 1683 she had married Prince George of Denmark, whom Charles II thought boring, but to whom Anne was devoted. They were assigned lodgings in the Whitehall Cockpit where they held court and where Anne concentrated on producing an heir. Before 1700 she had seventeen pregnancies and produced eighteen children, only five of whom were born alive and all of whom died before reaching adulthood. She and Prince George had supported the revolution of 1688 and the settlement in 1689 had made her children next in line to the throne after William and Mary's. Months later Anne gave birth to a healthy boy at Hampton Court; he was named William after his uncle and immediately created Duke of Gloucester. An undignified public argument over Anne's financial settlement caused a rift with the king and queen, one that was deepened by Mary's dislike of Sarah Churchill, Anne's closest friend. In 1692 Anne exiled herself from court, establishing herself at Berkeley House in Piccadilly. The estrangement had not healed at the time of Mary's death.

In January 1695 William was reconciled with Princess Anne, now heir apparent, and began to pay special attention to the young Duke of Gloucester. William and his sister-in-law now had to manage the court between them and, with Hampton Court incomplete, they needed to enlarge Kensington. Even before the queen's funeral on 5 March orders had been given for its extension and remodelling. There were two aspects to this: the rearrangement of the old core of Nottingham House to create much larger and better proportioned presence and privy chambers and a new larger drawing room; and the creation of a new suite of king's lodgings incorporating a new long gallery. Work went ahead at a blinding rate and in early September William was supervising the hanging of pictures in his new gallery.[3]

The construction of the king's new gallery across the face of the two southernmost pavilions gave the palace, for the first time, an impressive facade. Its finely tooled brick elevation was very austere and rather Dutch, with tall flat brick pilasters and protruding attic topped with urns. The elevation comes from a different stable from that which was concurrently being designed by the Office of Works. The pilasters and attic are strikingly similar to the Het Loo pavilions and to Huis de Voorst and the Office of Works may have been given drawings of Het Loo or perhaps Jacob Roman was asked to provide advice.

The state rooms were now significantly larger, especially the drawing room, where William and Anne now hosted assemblies. But the king's first-floor apartment, identical in plan to that proposed at Hampton Court, was also intended for receptions. Through the great bedchamber and two closets the privy gallery was reached. This was hung with over seventy choice paintings from the royal collection and furnished with card tables for court assemblies. At one such regular Monday evening 'appearance' Princess Anne and Prince George, with sixty ladies of fashion, took card tables in the gallery with the king circulating amongst them. A French visitor was 'ravished with astonishment at the sight of so many great beauties'; some may have been sitting on the sofas provided, a novelty at the time. There was a little bedchamber on the state floor, but William's private lodgings were on the floor below and here there was a library, several closets, a private bedchamber, a billiard room and, on the south front, a vestibule that led directly out into the gardens.[4]

Bentinck had been appointed superintendent of the royal gardens in 1689 and he quickly brought leading Dutch horticulturalists to England to work at both Kensington and Hampton Court. England's most successful garden designer, George London, was appointed deputy and William Talman, already comptroller in the Office of Works, added garden comptroller to his duties. Kensington was laid out between 1689 and 1693 and its parterres bear a resemblance to those designed by Marot

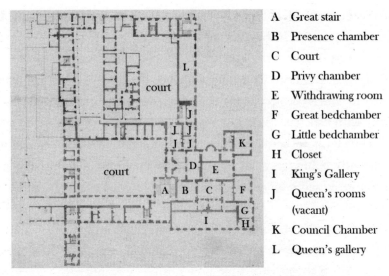

A   Great stair
B   Presence chamber
C   Court
D   Privy chamber
E   Withdrawing room
F   Great bedchamber
G   Little bedchamber
H   Closet
I   King's Gallery
J   Queen's rooms
    (vacant)
K   Council Chamber
L   Queen's gallery

Figure 131: Detail of a first-floor survey of Kensington undertaken in 1717.

for William and Mary in Holland; indeed he may have been the designer creating a garden that was an undoubted novelty in England. But few would have been able to marvel at the intricate designs and carefully judged planting as it was bounded by a high wall to keep it private. This is probably why the entrance to the mansion house was from the west, down a long corridor that didn't overlook the garden. Unlike the later Hampton Court gardens which were for court use, this compact garden of only fifteen acres was for private delectation.[5]

In October, while furnishings were still being delivered to his new rooms, William decided to make a progress. It was his first and only tour, and one that, though partly motivated by the upcoming general election, was largely driven by his curiosity to see the country which he ruled, and the great houses of his nobility. He had travelled little in England and in 1689 had ordered a large map of the country for the council chamber as a reference point. Although late in the year, he was blessed with fine weather and enjoyed great hunting, generous welcomes and lavish hospitality for twenty-six days. He visited some of the most important houses in the Midlands including Boughton, Burghley, Belton and Warwick Castle. He was impressed by architecture, interior decoration and the

Figure 132: Bird's-eye view of Kensington Palace *c*.1715,
showing the formal gardens and surrounding fields.

paintings he saw, even making two visits to Burghley to study the interiors painted by Verrio. That winter William found himself at leisure at Kensington, devoting himself to rearranging his gallery and reading up about the latest ideas on architectural design.[6]

In October 1695 William offered Anne St James's as a residence and William of Gloucester the Garter, a household and a residence of his own. At St James's Anne was expected to keep court 'as if she were a crowned head' and work began to make the house suitable. William had made it clear that this was to be at her own expense and in 1696–7, she outlaid some £2,200 in the construction of new buildings including a ball room, the first instance of a room with this name being added to an English royal residence. Balls had been new to England in 1660, Charles II having acquired a taste for them in France. Charles II loved French dances, especially the *courante*, an apparently simple dance, which few mastered.[7]

Therefore, when in 1696 a ball room was built at St James's, balls had been an integral part of court life for nearly forty years. Anne's dancing days were over – she had to be carried upstairs in a sedan chair, her legs were so bad. The ball room was not for her pleasure, it was built because she now assumed the role of consort and had to perform the social functions previously undertaken by Mary. Hosting balls was one of the most important, particularly the annual ball held for the queen's birthday – a highlight of the court almanack.[8]

The new ball room was designed by Wren on the west side of St James's, raised upon a rusticated Portland stone arcade and lit by nine large sash windows on the north front. A large external staircase provided access separately from the state apartments which made it much more like the Banqueting House at Whitehall than a reception room integrated with the rest of the house. The first time the room was used was for Princess Anne's birthday in February 1697, and for the next three years the room played host to February court balls.[9]

Out of the ashes

In 1697 the treaties of Rijswijk were signed, ending the Nine Years War that had dominated northern Europe since 1688, put tens of thousands of Englishmen under arms, and relentlessly sucked cash from English taxpayers. William returned to London in November to wildly cheering crowds and the hope of a calmer existence. Just over eight weeks later the mood was changed with a huge blow to national pride. Whitehall, which had been the principal residence of the Crown for 168 years, caught light again. On 4 January fire tore into the tightly-packed buildings with their tinder-dry roof structures, panelling and floors. Firefighting was complete chaos, impeded both by residents attempting to save their possessions and by looters. The gates were locked as parts of the building were detonated to create firebreaks, but the explosions only hurled more timbers into the flames. At one point it was believed that the fire was out, but the red-hot cinders reignited and parts of the palace that had been secured were now completely consumed. William gave orders that the Banqueting House be saved at all costs and, amidst the heat and smoke, a daring workman bricked up its great north window, stopping the fire from incinerating Jones's masterpiece.

News spread fast across Europe and, in his Journal at Versailles, the duc de Saint Simon recorded 'a fire destroyed Whitehall, the largest and ugliest palace in Europe'. William thought the loss 'considerable', but 'less to me than it would be to another person, for I cannot live there'. Yet, he did as his country expected and vowed, 'if God will give me leave, I will rebuild it much finer than before'.[10]

Whitehall housed many offices of state which required relocating if the work of government was to continue smoothly and Wren was ordered to set up rooms in the old west side cockpit for the Treasury, Council of Trade and as a council chamber. Rooms were also set aside for the king including a privy chamber, drawing room, bedchamber and two closets. The Secretary to the Treasury was provided with an office and a new meeting room for the Lords of the Treasury was constructed. The Whitehall fire also robbed the Crown of the principal chapel royal. It was decided to use the Banqueting House as a chapel so that the major Anglican royal liturgies such as Maundy Thursday could be celebrated in public. But this was not an everyday solution and it was decided that William should normally use the Chapel Royal at St James's.[11]

William soon gave orders to rebuild Whitehall. The designs which survive, drawn by Hawksmoor, in great haste, under the eye of Wren, have no commentary to illuminate the thought process behind them, but William, so intensely in control of everything, and so experienced a patron, would have briefed Wren on his precise requirements. Like Charles I and Charles II, William wanted to recast the whole of Westminster. Inigo Jones had envisaged a triumphal way from Whitehall to Westminster Hall, but this plan involved the demolition of the Banqueting House. Since Jones's time the Banqueting House had acquired layers of meaning that made it central to the iconography of the Stuart state and, in any case, in 1698 it had just been saved from the flames. Wren's scheme retained the Banqueting House and memorialised it as an ancestral hall at the centre of the palace. Much more ambitiously William's idea was also to replace the crumbling Palace of Westminster where parliament met and create a purpose-built House of Commons and Lords linked to the new palace by a long corridor.

The two houses faced each other in chambers of equal size and between them was a vast two-storey hall lit by Diocletian windows. In the archives of the Office of Works were the Whitehall plans drawn for Charles I that incorporated new chambers for the two houses, and it is clear that Hawksmoor's designs owed a debt to these.

A 700-foot-long gallery linked the new parliament to the royal palace aligned on the banqueting hall. The front of the new parliament faced north and was on a direct alignment with the north front of Westminster Hall, seemingly the only part of the old palace to be retained in the scheme. An apron of land in front of the palace was presumably the public highway, relocated from its position running through the middle of the old palace.[12]

Since the Restoration the Crown's relationship with parliament had evolved rapidly and the events of 1688 instituted changes which recast the relationship for good. After 1689 parliament met every winter and the triennial act meant elections every three years. The monarch now had to rule through ministers who were acceptable to a majority in parliament and the king had to sway parliamentarians to achieve his ends. William was thus the first monarch for whom the essence of rule was the management of the legislature.

This was easier for him than it would have been for his uncles and grandfather. In the Dutch Republic, the stadtholder was technically only a minister of the sovereign States assemblies and from birth, William was schooled in a polity that exercised power through them. In 1651–5

Figure 133: Nicholas Hawksmoor, riverfront of William III's new Whitehall, designed January–March 1689. In the centre is the Banqueting House, adorned with a giant Corinthian portico. It is flanked by two domed stair towers. In the foreground are the ends of two wings facing the river.

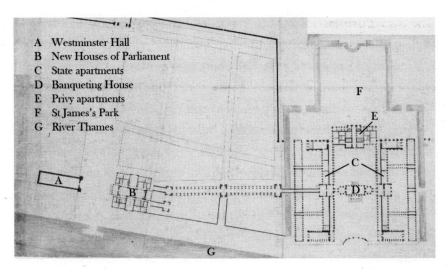

A Westminster Hall
B New Houses of Parliament
C State apartments
D Banqueting House
E Privy apartments
F St James's Park
G River Thames

Figure 134: Nicholas Hawksmoor, William III scheme for a new Whitehall linked to the new houses of parliament by a long corridor, 1698. The houses of parliament were based on Inigo Jones's design of 1649 (fig. 74).

the States had built themselves a new assembly hall at the Binnenhof to the design of Pieter Post. Constructed on the abolition of the post of stadtholder, it reflected their new-found power; it also reflected well on the Republic and William may have felt that crumbling Westminster Palace, where the English parliament met, was not a fair reflection of national status.[13]

Yet despite his republican education, William had a strong sense of his royal ancestry and acquired sovereign status and the 1698 plans for Whitehall and parliament were an embodiment in stone of his conception of rule. At the heart was the Banqueting House, the architectural symbol of the Stuart dynasty: this was to be a shared entrance to two suites of state rooms on the north and south that led to a block containing the privy lodgings, aligned on a new garden incorporating the existing St James's Canal. These seem to have been arranged much like Het Loo with a central shared hall and compact suites either side.

From an ante room in the king's state rooms a gallery, similar to that at the Louvre leading to the Tuileries, led to the Parliament House. The

king could process in state to parliament and parliamentarians could
easily gain access to the palace. This latter point was perhaps the key
to the design. Engagement with parliament was essential to further royal
policy and attracting parliamentarians to court, and keeping them there,
had been increasingly difficult as William spent more time away from
Westminster. The new palace would fuse king and legislature together
in a single building.

William's popularity with the English ebbed and flowed and 1698
was a personal high water mark boosted by the peace at Rijswijk and
bruised national pride after the Whitehall fire. Yet even standing in the
sunlight of popular admiration, it was clear that the scheme was too
grandiose and too expensive to survive and, as an alternative, Wren
recycled ideas that he had in the late 1660s, when he had been contemplating rebuilding the palace for Charles II. The Parliament House may
not have been part of this, but the same basic building blocks were
assembled on a reduced scale, to create a forecourt facing the river and
the privy lodgings overlooking gardens in St James's Park.

Even if the finances for this were agreed, building at Whitehall would
not be complete for many years; in the meantime William needed a
palace where he could conduct state business. Hampton Court was
half-built and so he temporarily switched major court ceremonial to
Windsor. For the next two years the castle played host to the most
important court events.

In April 1698 the Swedish ambassador had his public audience at
Windsor and William entertained him to a great feast; the following
month it was the turn of the French ambassador to be similarly treated.
The following year the king was in residence again and, in May, held a
'great court' there. With the ceremonial came hunting. Over Christmas
1699 he was in the saddle in the great park with 'a great concourse of the
nobility and gentry'. In the absence of financing for the Whitehall project
orders were given to Wren to devise a scheme that would effectively finish
May's remodelling of the castle. He intended to rebuild the south side of
the upper ward and replace Henry VII's tower and Elizabeth's gallery on
the north. Meanwhile the French royal gardener André le Nôtre was asked

for a plan for the gardens; these were eventually made by le Nôtre's nephew, Claude Desgots, who came to England in 1700.[14]

The last phase: Hampton Court

William, and the English, had to have a magnificent palace as a matter of national prestige, as much as to serve the practical requirements of traditional monarchy, and Hampton Court was to fulfil that role. Construction at Hampton Court had been possible because Mary had been supervising it. William was away for the entire building season each year and without the queen to keep an eye on work it was impossible to continue with such a massive project. For three years after Mary's death, work at Hampton Court had been frozen, but the peace of Rijswijk eased William's financial situation, and parliament finally granted him a permanent, unencumbered civil-list revenue of £700,000 per annum. William now pruned his household, removing at least fifty posts, and focused on art and architecture.[15]

The first room to be restarted at Hampton Court was the great gallery, now the cartoon gallery, that was prepared to take Raphael's *Acts of the Apostles* cartoons. Ever since Charles I acquired them, they had been in dozens of narrow strips but now they were glued together in vast sheets and hung on the bare brick walls. Thrilled with the effect, William gave orders for customised panelling to be installed to fit them. The east front gallery, originally intended for the queen, but now part of the king's domain, was to be hung with Andrea Mantegna's *Triumphs of Caesar* – William thus incorporated the two largest and most important suites of Renaissance painting outside Italy in his own apartments.

Wren must have imagined, when the king asked him to submit an estimate for completing the interiors, that it would be a matter of course that he should be commissioned. But this was not to be. His deputy William Talman slipped in a cheaper estimate for undertaking the work: Wren was sacked, his designs scrapped, and Talman won the job of fitting out the brick shell. Talman's friendship with Portland almost certainly swung him the job; but it was a tricky one. Most of the fundamental decisions had already been taken, Talman had tied himself to a budget of a mere £5,500 and the king was breathing down his neck. The day after his appointment William met Talman at Hampton Court to discuss the designs. After one more brief visit the king left for the Netherlands on 4 July 1699, not intending to return until October. During his absence Talman drove works forward as fast as he could, as William had expressed a desire to move in immediately on his return.[16]

When he got back William spent his first night at Hampton Court in over a decade and, as a result, decided to abandon his plan to stay at Windsor until the work was completed and instead remain and supervise it in person. Between October 1699 and April 1700 William visited the palace at least thirty times, issuing a stream of instructions for the completion of the rooms on the south front and the gardens.[17]

Figure 135: Simon Gribelin, the cartoon gallery at Hampton Court, 1720. The earliest depiction of any of the interiors, this engraving celebrated the Raphael cartoons, Hampton Court's most famous artworks. It also shows the restrained austerity of the interiors, which were panelled with oak garnished with carvings. The bolection chimneypieces were marble.

The architecture of the new interiors was plain, with coved ceilings and oak joinery only enlivened by Grinling Gibbons's virtuoso limewood carvings which, in almost white limewood, contrasted with their oak back boards. The principal decoration was tapestry from the royal collection, which gave the rooms richness and colour and helped deaden their echoing qualities. Ralph Montagu, Earl and later 1st Duke of Montagu, Charles II's Master of the Great Wardrobe, had been out of favour under James II but resumed his former post under William. A great patron of architecture, painting and the decorative arts, William had visited Montagu's Francophile country house, Boughton, on his 1695 progress. Montagu oversaw the furnishing of Hampton Court and was faced with transforming the architectural shell created by Talman on a very tight budget.

As Montagu was organising new furniture William Bentinck, the Earl of Portland, the man who knew William's personal tastes better than anyone else, was in Paris as Ambassador. Between punishing sessions of contorted diplomatic chicanery Portland was shown the gardens of Versailles, sampled the hunting, examined the furnishings of royal houses and went luxury shopping. He was of the firm opinion that William would not like French furniture because it was made in an old-fashioned way to match existing antique pieces. He disliked the over-use of gold and silver braid and the shape of the beds. When William toyed with ordering a Parisian bed for Dieren, Portland put him off. He emphasised that everything he had seen was better made in England. He was right and, in the end, almost all the furnishings for Hampton Court were made in London. Much of the damask was made in Spitalfields and bought through London merchants; the glass plates for the mirrors came from Vauxhall, and the giltwood furniture was made in the parish of St Martin-in-the-Fields. Indeed, by 1715 Elizabeth Charlotte of Orlèans wrote that 'one can no longer send fashions' from France to England 'because the English have their own, which are followed here now'.[18]

The state rooms were ponderously hung with dynastic portraits and the king's private rooms with a dense hang of small-scale Dutch and Italian old masters. The greatest paintings were all reserved for the king's gallery and closet at Kensington to where, early in the reign, he had moved them. William had always envisaged that the ceilings of the state rooms at Hampton Court be painted. All his houses in the Dutch Republic had richly painted interiors and the Oranjezaal at Huis ten Bosch, conceived by Jacob Jordaens to glorify Fredrick Henry, William's grandfather, was one of the greatest painted rooms in northern Europe. William's interiors at Het Loo had been less ambitious and more architectural, but the audience chamber, painted by Marot was a masterpiece of illusionistic art. Antonio Verrio, the greatest muralist working in England, had left London to work at Chatsworth and Burghley House in 1688 refusing, as a Catholic, to work for William and Mary. William admired his work at Windsor and even pardoned Verrio's son, who had fought with the Jacobites at the battle of the Boyne, because of it. William finally met Verrio at Burghley in 1695. Five years later, the 61-year-old painter was persuaded to come to Hampton Court and start work on the new interiors.

By William's death, only three ceilings had been painted, but he had also started the great staircase with an elaborate allegory whose theme was the triumph of William, and Protestantism, over James II and the Catholics. Though it has suffered from repeated restoration the stair still conveys a sense of regal magnificence, and its symbolism would have been obvious in 1702. More triumphal in a personal sense than the stair, was Godfrey Kneller's vast equestrian portrait of the king in the presence chamber. This was not William the conqueror, but William the peacemaker of Rijswijk.[19]

In June 1699 William announced that in future all foreign ambassadors were to have their audiences at Hampton Court, marking a decisive shift away from London, and in April 1700, there was a remove of the entire court to the palace for the first time since 1689. It remained in residence for ten weeks, the Privy Council meeting at a great table in the cartoon gallery. The new apartment was supplied with both a presence chamber and a room for dining in public. This room, called the eating room, was never used by William but in it, the royal household was ordered to keep open tables 'with abundance of persons of

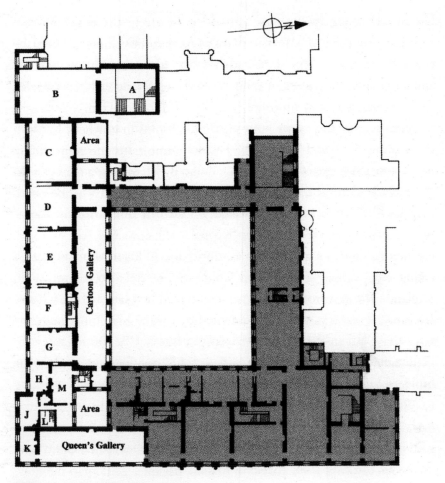

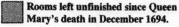

Rooms left unfinished since Queen
Mary's death in December 1694.

Feet

A – King's Great Stair
B – King's Guard Chamber
C – King's Presence Chamber
D – King's Eating Room
E – King's Privy Chamber
F – King's Withdrawing Room
G – King's Great Bedchamber

H – King's Little Bedchamber
J – closet
K – closet ('Queen Mary's')
L – King's Back Stair
M – King's Gentleman of the
    Bedchamber

Figure 136: Hampton Court, first-floor plan, 1702, showing the
state apartments, and in grey shade the parts of the palace that were
still a bare shell on William's death in 1702.

honour'. Drawing rooms were hosted by the king each week, William sitting in the privy chamber under a canopy, his hand being kissed by those he received. The state bedchamber was occasionally used for audiences and the closet beyond for private and detailed discussions with ambassadors and ministers.

William used the upper floor purely for his state duties; he lived on the ground floor and here were several closets, a bedchamber, dining room and study together with an orangery that led directly out into the privy garden. The rooms were small-scaled, panelled with oak with marble chimneypieces and connected, on the east front with the rooms of his favourite Arnold Joost van Keppel.

Direct access to a garden was a priority for William who had started laying out gardens at Hampton Court immediately on his arrival in England. The east front garden was completed first, aligned on Charles II's canal; it was a vast parterre designed by Daniel Marot, probably the largest laid out in the whole seventeenth century. The south garden, to be designated the king's private garden, could only be started when the builders' huts had been removed; In 1700 the parterres began to be dug to William's specifications. He was much involved in discussions over every element and in the summer of 1701 he ordered the whole southern section be dug up and the ground lowered by five feet so he could have a view of the river from the state rooms.

Legacy

In July 1700 the eleven-year-old William, Duke of Gloucester, died. William had just made over to him Mary's former apartment at Kensington; the king was distraught, and the boy's mother, Princess Anne, utterly devastated. This was a personal, dynastic and political disaster and when William, now ill and frail, returned to England it was to a court without youth or hope: William struggled to remain on stage at the centre of court life. For a dying man he was extraordinarily resilient, undertaking a punishing diary of deputations, conferences and council meetings, opening parliament in state on New Year's Eve 1701 and sealing two Acts

Figure 137: Hampton Court, the south front of the king's apartments and the privy garden from the south as completed in 1695. Depicted by Sutton Nichols. The garden was later extended further south to the present extent.

of Parliament on his deathbed. It was pneumonia, brought on by a fall from his horse in Hampton Court Park in February 1702, which eventually killed him. William received the last rites in the little bedchamber at Kensington, the door open so that the court, in the state bedchamber next door, could watch.

The accession of his sister-in-law was uncontested, and she inherited Hampton Court and Kensington with their exquisite gardens furnished and operational. That William should have achieved so much in a reign that lasted thirteen years was remarkable when ruling two countries, fighting the French, resisting the Jacobites, juggling English politics, riding huge budget deficits and confronting cumulative personal and dynastic disaster. Amidst a complex and testing life William was fascinated by houses, gardens and their decoration and even, on his long march to London in 1688, took time to stop at Wilton House to admire the paintings by van Dyck. There were always two or three building projects on the go and he was intensely interested in them all, personally giving instructions to his architects: in 1700 he gave Jacob Roman's son, Fabrice, money to study architecture in Italy for two years. William's personal involvement in garden design and planting was perhaps even more intense and his plantsmanship considered impressive. He was a connoisseur of fine paintings incessantly moving them between houses, carefully rearranging the works at Kensington.[20]

On his death, William's architectural legacy was assured but not universally admired. Contemporaries gave Hampton Court mixed reviews. Edmund Gibson thought 'the Additions made to it by *King William and Queen Mary* do so far excel what it was before, that they evidently show what vast Advancements, Architecture has Received since that time'. But a more discerning critic, Roger North, found the whole new building lacking: 'It is towards the garden and park, of a square form, pink't full of holes, some round, and some oblong, others square . . . . But that which is worst of all, there is nothing rising at the angles, as pavilions . . ., nor no large rising front with a grand order in the Middle, but a small one, having short columns, like the middle door in an old fashioned cabinet.'[21]

Fashions in architecture change and yesterday's masterpiece is tomorrow's eyesore and so William's reign has to be judged on a broader canvas than mere taste. The enduring legacy was the disentangling of the private life of the monarch from the administration of the state. This had been a theme of the entire Stuart period and William and Mary had already taken steps to separate their lives from the government by building Kensington, but the burning of Whitehall provided a decisive turning point. It was a moment in history when a fundamental change in the infrastructure of rule coincided with shifts in the balance of power and influence to create an entirely new topographical and political model. A model inherited by William's sister-in-law, Queen Anne.

Epilogue

I t is perhaps unfair to consign the reign of Queen Anne to an epilogue, but in the history of royal building in England the burning of Whitehall in 1698, and death of King William III four years later, marked a crucial watershed. During the century before Anne's accession royal residences had been the stage on which the drama of the Stuart century had been enacted. They were the theatres of successive revolutions. This was because royal buildings contained all the people and powers necessary to determine the course of the nation. But by the end of the Stuart century, where once the court had been a major instrument of power and influence, and the royal palaces an expression of the monarch's personal preference, the court was increasingly peripheral.

The root of this change lay in the exclusion crisis that led to the emergence of two distinct groups in parliament between 1679 and 1681. Originally the Whigs and Tories had been divided by their views on the monarch's right to rule, the Tories believing in divine and hereditary right and the Whigs in the right of parliament to choose. Yet as time moved on the divisions were defined by religion and the relative merits of religious toleration (the Whigs) and support for the conservative element of the Anglican church (Tories). The Tories were in the ascendancy under Queen Anne but after the accession of George I in 1714 the Whigs became the natural party of power and government for the rest of the century. The main link between the Crown and the two houses of parliament now became the cabinet, which gradually superseded the large and unwieldy Privy Council as the primary instrument of executive power.

These changes were important because in comparison to Charles II's court, that of Queen Anne was often on the periphery of real power and patronage, and access to the person of the monarch was not the prize it had once been. Ambitious, clever and power-hungry individuals now looked towards parliament, the government bureaucracy, the armed forces and trade rather than just to the court. At first glance, it is difficult to perceive this shift. The round of receptions, dining, progresses, hunting, meetings, repair, redecoration, refurnishing, christenings, coronations and funerals continued without apparent change. Yet the power was vanishing from what were increasingly ceremonial rather than executive events.[1]

The loss of Whitehall as the architectural and geographical nexus between monarch, court and ministers must have been felt by Anne, who had seen first-hand how Charles II had bound the sinews of state together in the chambers and galleries of the great palace. But there was no way that she could afford to rebuild Whitehall. Although the queen had been granted £700,000 a year by parliament at her accession, it was dependent on unsecured revenue, and by 1710 this had fallen short by a total of £868,335. On her death in 1714 she owed her household servants over £150,000. The situation at the Office of Works was little better. In 1702 Wren was seventy and still, after nearly fifty years, surveyor of the Royal Works. His department had been starved of cash and debts left over from King William's time alone totalled some £57,000. Wren was starting to lose his grip on the office and there was a view that he was too old to be in charge.[2]

Anne used Hampton Court and Windsor as her country retreats. She had owned a private residence in Windsor town since the late 1690s and was drawn back each summer to hunt and enjoy herself. For her, as for Charles II, Hampton Court was a convenient place for the Privy Council to meet, equidistant between St James's and Windsor. In London Anne preferred the newer and more private metropolitan palace at

Kensington to the official seat of power at St James's. In short, St James's and Hampton Court were for business, Kensington and Windsor for pleasure.[3]

Now at the centre of national government and ceremonial it was realised that St James's urgently needed remodelling to take on some of the former functions of Whitehall. The most important of these were the meeting of the Privy Council, the queen's public attendance at chapel and her ability to host large social gatherings.

Crucial to the workings of the state was the council. Anne was highly conscientious, attending long meetings twice a week, and received a constant stream of ambassadors and petitioners, and papers to sign. Although parliament had a decisive power in affairs of state, the formulation of foreign policy, the appointment of ministers, and the distribution of patronage were still central concerns of the monarch. All these she managed from St James's.[4]

In March 1703 work started on a £7,000 extension to the royal lodgings. There were to be two very large new rooms: a council chamber and a drawing room. The council chamber had a private backstair that gave access to a waiting room and a room for the clerks. The two new rooms completely changed the scale of St James's, at 48 feet long the council chamber was the size of the then unfinished queen's presence chamber at Hampton Court, itself a room larger than any room at St James's.

Running down the middle was a long table covered in a carpet with thirty chairs and, at its head, a chair of state under a canopy for the queen. The walls were hung in tapestry on which hung silver sconces, there were heavy curtains and over the fireplace was a painting of St Catherine by Correggio; over the doors to the waiting room and stairs were portraits of doges of Venice.

The Privy Council had an official membership of fifty-five in 1708 and, although it was rare for everyone to attend, there were occasions when the whole council assembled. Indeed, when it met at Hampton Court, it gathered in the enormous cartoon gallery. The new room at St James's came to be known as the 'great council chamber', but most

Figure 138: The entry of George I and the Prince of Wales into London, 1714, from a Dutch newsletter. The wing on the left of St James's Palace is the one containing Queen Anne's council and audience chambers.

council meetings were smaller, and when the queen met with her smaller, cabinet committee they met in a room known as the 'little council chamber' near the chapel.[5]

Next to the council chamber was the new drawing room-cum-audience chamber. This was a new concept in royal accommodation and the first room in an English royal palace that was formally called an audience chamber. Since the time of Henrietta Maria, the queen's drawing room was one of the most important rooms at court. In here the queen held weekly circles or drawing rooms in which the king, free from the formal restrictions of etiquette in his own rooms, could mix more relaxedly with courtiers. Anne was the first queen regnant since the establishment of the drawing room as the premier event at court. Her drawing rooms were held in the monarch's apartment under rules of etiquette pertaining to the sovereign and were therefore much more rigid affairs.

Anne's drawing rooms were more like formal audiences than the convivial gatherings of Catherine of Braganza's time. Like her forebears Anne was a stickler for proper ceremony and form. But unlike her uncle, Charles II, who had used court ceremonial to brilliant effect to enhance his majesty and to entertain his court, Anne, although articulate and fun-loving in her prime, never had the gift of showing people a good time. At a typical drawing room, the queen sat immobile on her chair of state beneath a canopy surrounded by ladies in waiting; she didn't circulate and people who wanted to speak to her had to be introduced.[6]

After Whitehall burnt down a temporary chapel royal was set up in the Banqueting House, but as St James's was being set up as a permanent headquarters for the monarchy it was necessary to bring the queen's public worship together with the council chamber and withdrawing room. When in London, Anne, like her predecessors attended chapel in public and in state. In 1702 a German visitor saw the procession to chapel proceeding down the main stairs and into its west end, the sword of state and four great maces carried before the queen. The St James's chapel was not rebuilt, but the gallery to it was widened to take the queen's procession to her closet.[7]

There is a danger of painting Queen Anne as a boring and lacklustre monarch. This would be wrong for she was a great outdoor sportsman and a lover of parties and dancing. In February 1703 she had her first birthday ball as queen at St James's. It was said that 'there had not been such a magnificent appearance at court for 20 years past'. In 1711 her birthday was celebrated 'in richer habits than has been known since 1660'. On her birthday in February 1714 she was at Windsor where there was 'a great Appearance of Foreign Ministers, Nobility and Gentry, sumptuously Dressed who, about Two a Clock in the Afternoon, paid their compliments to her majesty; And at Night there was a ball and splendid entertainment in the castle'.[8]

At St James's she ordered the construction of a large portico to make the entrance to the state rooms seem more imposing and ambassadors who were received there seem to have been impressed. Yet, despite attempts of historians to rehabilitate the court of Queen Anne, the fact was that the energy and drive that came from sovereign power had vanished from English royal palaces. St James's was a poor stub of a place in which the queen did not even want to live.

The history of royal building in Britain did not end with Queen Anne. The first three Georges modified and modernised some of the royal palaces, and the fourth George was the greatest royal builder since Henry VIII. But never again was architecture and power bonded in brick and stone as it had been in the seventeenth century and never again was the drama of constitutional change played out on a royal stage. British monarchs now reigned and not ruled, and parliament had become the theatre of state, rather than the homes of the sovereign. What were once houses of power were now merely hollow citadels of ceremony.

Notes

ABBREVIATIONS

BL   British Library

Cal. SP. Dom.   *Calendar of State Papers Domestic*, 1547–1603, R. Lemon
                and M. A. E. Green (eds), 8 vols (London, 1856–72)

Cal. SP. Scot.   *Calendar of State Papers Scotland*, W. K. Boyd and
                H. W. Meikle (eds), 11 vols (Edinburgh, 1936)

Cal. SP. Ven.   *Calendar of State Papers Venetian*, R. Brown et al. (eds),
                38 vols (London, 1864–1940)

CHR   *The History of the Rebellion and Civil Wars in England
                begun in the year 1641*, E. Hyde, Earl of Clarendon,
                W. Dunn Macray (ed.), 6 vols (Oxford, 1888)

CKJ   J. Brewer (ed.), G. Goodman, *The Court of King James
                the First*, 2 vols (Oxford, 1839)

CL   *The Letters of John Chamberlain*, J. Chamberlain,
                N. E. McClure (ed.), 2 vols (American Philosophical
                Society, Philadelphia, 1939)

DSP   R. Latham and W. Matthews, *The diary of Samuel Pepys: a new and complete transcription,* 11 vols (London, |1970–83)

FP   Sir John Finet, *Finetti Philoxenis. Som Choice Observations of Sir John Finet Knight and Master of Ceremonies to two kings* (London, 1656)

HCP   S. Thurley, *Hampton Court Palace: A Social and Architectural History* (New Haven and London, 2004)

HKW   *The History of the King's Works,* H. M. Colvin (ed.), 6 vols (London, 1963–73)

HMC   Historical Manuscripts Commission

HoP   *History of Parliament.* Online edition

HP   S. Thurley, *Houses of Power: The Places That Shaped the Tudor World* (London, 2017)

KJP   *The progresses, processions, and magnificent festivities, of King James the First, his royal consort, family, and court,* J. Nichols, 4 vols (London, 1828)

ODNB   *Oxford Dictionary of National Biography*

SH   S. Thurley, *Somerset House, The Palace of England's Queens 1551–1692* (London Topographical Society, 2009)

SLD   *The Earl of Strafforde's Letters and Dispatches,* T. Wentworth, 1st Earl of Strafford, W. Knowler (ed.), 2 vols (London, 1739)

TNA   The National Archives

WP   S. Thurley, *Whitehall Palace and Architectural History of the Royal Apartments 1240–1698* (Yale, 1999)

PROLOGUE

1 C. Smith and M. Gnudi (trans and ed.), *The pirotechnia of Vannoccio Biringuccio: the classic 16th-century treatise on metals and metallurgy by Biringucci, Vannoccio* (New York, 1990), pp. 291–2; H. White and T. Kearns, *Legge's Mount, The Tower of London, Scientific Analysis of the Crucibles* (Historic England Research Department Report Series 76-2010); Z. Hazell, *Legge's Mount, The Tower of London, Analysis of wood charcoal from deposits associated with the Tudor Royal Mint* (Historic England Research Report Series 6-2012); A. Keay, *The Elizabethan Tower of London. The Haiward and Gascoyne plan of 1597* (London Topographical Society, 2001), pp. 32–3; C. Challis (ed.), *A New History of the Royal Mint* (Cambridge, 1992), pp. 286–96; V. Pearl, *London and the Outbreak of the Puritan Revolution* (Oxford, 1964), pp. 328–31; A. Keay, *The Crown Jewels* (London, 2011), pp. 32–43; A. Barclay, 'The 1661 St Edward's Crown – Refurbished, Recycled or Replaced?', *The Court Historian*, xiii (2008), pp. 149–70; *KJP*, i, p. 320.

CHAPTER 1: SCOTLAND

1 M. Glendinning, R. MacInnes and A. MacKechnie, *A History of Scottish Architecture from the Renaissance to the Present Day* (Edinburgh, 2002), pp. 6–9.

2 R. Fawcett, *Stirling Castle* (London, 1995), pp. 55–64; J. G. Dunbar, *Scottish Royal Palaces* (East Linton, 1999), pp. 49–55. My plan of Stirling is based on a survey of 1708, National Library of Scotland NLS MS.1646 Z.02/17 and figure 7.2 in G. Ewart and D. Gallagher, *With thy Towers High. The Archaeology of Stirling Castle and Palace* (Historic Scotland Archaeology Report 9, 2015).

3 C. McKean, 'The Palace at Edinburgh Castle', *Book of the Old Edinburgh Club*, n.s. iv (1997), pp. 89–102; J. G. Dunbar, *Scottish Royal Palaces* (East Linton, 1999), pp. 75–83.

4 'The history of Scotland, from the death of King James I . . ., by John Lesley, Bishop of Ross', *Bannatyne Club*, xxxviii (Edinburgh, 1830), p. 154.

5 J. G. Dunbar, 'The Palace of Holyroodhouse during the first half of the 16th century', *Archaeological Journal*, cxx (1964), pp. 242–54; J. G. Dunbar, 'Some aspects of the planning of Scottish royal palaces in the 16th Century', *Architectural History*, xxvii (1984), pp. 15–19; R. Fawcett, *Scottish Architecture from the Accession of the Stewarts to the Reformation 1371–1560* (Edinburgh,

1994), pp. 320–2. My plan of Holyrood is based on John Mylne's survey of 1663, Bodleian Library Gough Maps 39.iv and fig. 1 in John Dunbar's 1964 article.

6 A. L. Juhala, 'The Household and Court of King James VI of Scotland, 1567–1603' (unpublished PhD thesis, University of Edinburgh, 2000), pp. 124–8.

7 HMC, *Marquis of Salisbury*, iii, p. 54; A. L. Juhala, 'The Household and Court of King James VI of Scotland, 1567–1603' (unpublished PhD thesis, University of Edinburgh, 2000), pp. 46–7; A. Juhala, '"For the king favours them very strangely": the rise of James VI's chamber 1580–1603', M. Kerr-Peterson and S. Reid (eds), *James VI and Noble Power in Scotland 1578–1603* (London, 2017), pp. 155–66; S. Doran, 'Loving and Affectionate Cousins? The Relationship between Elizabeth I and James VI of Scotland 1586–1603', S. Doran and G. Richardson (eds), *Tudor England and its Neighbours* (Basingstoke, 2005), pp. 207–9, 227–8; J. Goodare, 'James VI's English Subsidy', J. Goodare and M. Lynch (eds), *The Reign of James VI* (East Linton, 2000), pp. 110–25.

8 *Cal. SP. Scot., 1589–93*, p. 12.

9 D. Stevenson, *Scotland's Last Royal Wedding. The Marriage of James VI and Anne of Denmark* (Edinburgh, 1997); *Papers Relative to the Marriage of King James VI of Scotland, with the Princess Anna of Denmark, and the form and manner of Her Majesty's Coronation at Holyroodhouse AD 1590* (Edinburgh, 1828).

10 B. Mikkelsen, *Kronborg* (Elsinore, 1997); J. Skovgaard, *A King's Architecture, Christian IV and his Buildings* (London, 1973), pp. 17–21; *Christian IV and Europe* (19th Art Exhibition of the Council of Europe, Denmark, 1988), pp. 464–6.

11 *Cal SP. Scot., 1589–93*, p. 175.

12 *ibid.*, pp. 295–6; R. Fawcett, *Dunfermline Abbey and Palace* (Historic Scotland, 2004); A. MacKechnie, 'The Royal Palace of Dunfermline', R. Fawcett (ed.), *Royal Dunfermline* (Society of Antiquaries of Scotland, 2005), pp. 101–38; J. G. Dunbar, *Scottish Royal Palaces* (East Linton, 1999), pp. 87–94; D. Howard, *Scottish Architecture. Reformation to Restoration 1560–1660* (Edinburgh, 1995), pp. 26–30.

13 *Cal. SP. Scot., 1584–5*, p. 274.

14 My plan is based on D. MacGibbon and T. Ross, *The castellated and domestic architecture of Scotland*, I (Edinburgh, 1887), p. 488.

15 J. G. Dunbar, 'Some aspects of the planning of Scottish royal palaces in the 16th Century', *Architectural History*, xxvii (1984), pp. 21–3.

16 *Cal. SP. Scot.*, x, nos. 408, 365, 409, p. 306; *Register of the Privy Council of Scotland, 1599–1604*, pp. 207–8.

17 A. L. Juhala, 'The Household and Court of King James VI of Scotland, 1567–1603' (unpublished PhD thesis, University of Edinburgh, 2000), p. 305.

18 H. M. Paton, *Accounts of the Masters of Works for Building and Repairing Royal Palaces and Castles 1529–1615* (Edinburgh, 1957), p. 311.

19 *Cal. SP. Scot.*, xiii, no. 496; A. L. Juhala, 'The Household and Court of King James VI of Scotland, 1567–1603' (unpublished PhD thesis, University of Edinburgh, 2000), p. 126.

20 H. Meikle (ed.), *The Works of William Fowler*, ii (Scottish Text Society, 3rd ser. 7, 1936), p. 171; J. Nichols, *The Progresses and Public Processions of Queen Elizabeth*, iii (London, 1823), pp. 353–5; R. Fawcett, *Stirling Castle* (London, 1995), pp. 72–6; D. Howard, *Scottish Architecture. Reformation to Restoration 1560–1660* (Edinburgh, 1995), pp. 30–5.

21 I. Campbell and A. MacKechnie, 'The Great Temple of Solomon at Stirling Castle', *Architectural History*, liv (2011), pp. 91–118; M. Lynch, 'Court Ceremony and Ritual during the Personal Reign of James VI', J. Goodare and M. Lynch (eds), *The Reign of James VI* (East Linton, 2000), pp. 74–5.

22 *Register of the Privy Council of Scotland 1599–1604*, p. 576.

23 The account of the king's progress south follows *KJP*, i, pp. 52, 63–113.

24 G. Akrigg, *The Letters of James VI & I* (Berkeley, CA, 1984), pp. 212–13.

25 C. Norton, 'The Buildings of St Mary's Abbey, York and their Destruction', *Antiquaries Journal*, lxxiv (1994), pp. 267-80; *Royal Commission on Historical Monuments of England, York*, iv, pp. 31–4; *HKW*, iv, pp. 355–61; TNA SP14/50 no. 71. *HKW* and *RCHME* both confuse the two royal houses at York. My plan is based on Jacob Richards' survey of 1685, Staffordshire County Record Office Dartmouth MSS D(W) 1778/8/02 and the phase plan in the *RCHME* volume.

26 *CKJ*, i, p. 30.

CHAPTER 2: FIRST STEPS

1 J. Nichols, *The Progresses and Public Processions of Queen Elizabeth*, i (London, 1823), p. 146.

2 A. L. Juhala, '"For the king favours them very strangely". The rise of James VI's chamber 1580–1603', M. Kerr-Peterson and S. J. Reid (eds), *James VI and Noble Power in Scotland 1578–1603* (London, 2017), pp. 155–66.

3 *Cal. SP. Ven., 1603–7*, p. 33.

4 L. Pearsall Smith (ed.), *The Life and Letters of Sir Henry Wotton*, i (Oxford, 1966), pp. 314–15.

5 R. Holinshed, *Chronicle* (London, 1588), p. 195; G. Groos (ed.), *The Diary of Baron Waldstein* (London, 1981), p. 71.

6 P. Temple, *The Charterhouse* (Survey London 18th Monograph, 2010), pp. 54–8.

7 I have not been able to consult the original of the letter from Roger Aston to the Privy Council in 1603 cited by D. H. Willison, *King James VI and I*, (London, 1956), p. 171.

8 F. Wilson, *The Plague in Shakespeare's London* (Oxford, 1927), pp. 85–92.

9 *HP*, p. 129.

10 *Cal. SP. Ven., 1603–7*, p. 39.

11 M. de Béthune, C. Lennox (trans.), *The memoirs of the Duke of Sully*, iii (London, 1817), pp. 105–20.

12 *ODNB*; *HoP* sub Sir Lewis Lewknor.

13 Sir Thomas Edmonds to the Earl of Shrewsbury 15 June 1603, in E. Lodge, *Illustrations of British history, biography, and manners,: in the reigns of Henry VIII, Edward VI, Mary, Elizabeth, and James I, exhibited in a series of original papers*, iii (London, 1791), pp. 163–5; T. Wilson, 'Thomas Wilson to Sir Thomas Parry 22nd June 1603', in Sir Henry Ellis, *Original letters illustrative of English history: including numerous royal letters; from autographs in the British Museum, the State Paper office, and one or two other collections* (2nd series), iii (London, 1846), p. 201.

14 M. Lee Jr., *Dudley Carleton to Jon Chamberlain 1603–1624 Jacobean Letters* (New Jersey, 1972), pp. 34–5.

CHAPTER 3: ROYAL PLEASURES

1 F. Wilson, *The Plague in Shakespeare's London* (Oxford, 1927), pp. 92–100.

2 S. Harrison, *The arch's of triumph erected in honor of the high and mighty prince. Iames. the first of that name. King, of England. and the sixt of Scotland at his Maiesties entrance and passage through his honorable citty & chamber of London. vpon the 15th. day of march 1603.*

3 G. Parry, *The Golden Age Restored. The Culture of the Stuart Court 1603–42* (Manchester, 1981), pp. 1–21; M. Hutchings and B. Cano-Echevarría, 'The Spanish Ambassador's account of James I's entry into London, 1604', *The Seventeenth Century Journal*, xxxiii (2017), pp. 255–77.

4 D. Bergeron, 'Gilbert Dugdale and the Royal Entry of James', *The Journal of Medieval and Renaissance Studies*, xiii (1983), pp. 111–25.

5 T. Thompson (ed.), D. Calderwood, *The History of the Kirk of Scotland*, iii (Wodrow Society, Edinburgh, 1842–9), pp. 457–9.

6 F. Bamford, *A Royalist Notebook: The Commonplace book of Sir John Oglander* (London, 1936), p. 197.

7 R. Dutton (ed.), *Jacobean Civic Pageants* (Keele, 1995); James I, *Basilicon Doron* (1599) (Scholar Press, 1969); 'Advertisments of a Loyall Subiect to His Gratious Soveraigne Drawn from the Observations of the Peoples Speache', B. L. Cotton MS. Faustina C II ii.

8 D. Carleton, *Letters from and to Sir Dudley Carleton . . . during his embassy in Holland, from January 1615/16, to December 1620* (London, 1775), p. 35; H. Scott (ed.), 'The Journal of Sir Roger Wilbraham', *Camden Miscellany*, x (1902), pp. 58–60.

9 G. Akrigg, *The Letters of King James VI & I* (Berkeley, CA, 1984), pp. 246–7; HMC, *Cecil*, xvii, p. 349; *HKW*, iv, pp. 45–6.

10 C. Rogers, *Estimate of the Scottish Nobility during the Minority of James VI* (Grampian Club, 1873), p. 48; *Cal. SP. Ven., 1603–7*, p. 513; *Cal. SP. Ven., 1603–7*, p. 441.

11 *Cal SP. Dom., James I, 1628–9*, p. 31; *Cal. SP. Dom., 1623–5*, pp. 105, 107; *Cal. SP. Dom., 1611–18*, p. 488.

12 *KJP*, i, pp. 464–5.

13 TNA E351/3240, E351/3241.

14 TNA E351/3243.

15 *Cal. SP. Dom., 1603–10*, p. 624; TNA E351/3244; A. Kingston, *A History of Royston* (London, 1906), pp. 109–10.

16 TNA E351/3249.

17 P. Ranson, *Royston's Heritage Buildings* (Royston and District Local History Society, 2017); TNA E317/Cambs no. 4 and 5 in J. Beldam, 'Royston Court House and its Appurtenances', *Archaeologia*, xl (1866), pp. 120–37. The reconstruction in this article is not to be trusted.

18 S. Thurley, 'Turning a Town into a Palace', *Country Life* (14 August 2019), pp. 48–53.

19 W. Rye, *England as Seen by Foreigners* (London, 1865), pp. 62–3.

20 *Cal. SP. Dom., 1603–10*, pp. 403, 449; TNA E351/3243; TNA E351/3244; P. May, *The Changing Face of Newmarket. A History from 1600 to 1760* (Newmarket, 1984), p. 3.

21 *CL*, i, p. 434.

22 TNA E351/3249, the king's rooms identified in TNA E351/3254.

23 The parliamentary survey describes the layout in some detail: TNA Cambs. E317 no. 3. I'm grateful to John Sutton for his help in plotting out the king's house on the modern town plan.

24 TNA E351/3254, E351/3255, E351/3256, E351/3257.

25 R. Blome, *The Gentleman's Recreation*, ii (London, 1686), pp. 91–5; G. Turbervile, *Turbervile's Booke of Hunting 1576* (Oxford, 1907), pp. 160–78, 246; H. Stokes, 'Cambridgeshire Forests', *Proceedings of the Cambridge Antiquarian Society*, xvii (1922), pp. 70–5; *CL*, ii, p. 539; J. P. Hore, *The History of Newmarket and the Annals of the Turf* (London, 1886), pp. 218, 157, 249, 252–4.

26 TNA E351/3250; J. Hacket (ed.), *Scrinia reserata: a memorial offer'd to the great deservings of John Williams, D.D., who some time held the places of Ld Keeper of the Great Seal of England, Ld Bishop of Lincoln, and Ld Archbishop of York. Containing a series of the most remarkable occurrences and transactions of his life, in relation both to Church and State* (London, 1693), p. 227; *Cal. SP. Dom., 1611–18*, p. 167; C. Rogers, *Estimate of the Scottish Nobility during the Minority of James VI* (Grampian Club, 1873), p. 48; *CL*, i, pp. 330–1.

27 *FP*, pp. 42–4, 120, 124–5. Also see p. 136; J. P. Hore, *The History of Newmarket and the Annals of the Turf* (London, 1886), pp. 161, 179, 208; *CL*, ii, pp. 192, 483.

28 *CL*, i, p. 566, ii, pp. 243, 325, 535; *Cal. SP. Ven., 1617–19*, p. 420.

29 *HKW*, iv, pp. 84–6; TNA E351/3239.

30 *HCP*, pp. 107–10.

31 S. Thurley, 'Elizabeth I and the Early Stuarts', S. Brindle (ed.), *Windsor Castle. A Thousand Years of a Royal Palace* (Royal Collection Trust, 2018), pp. 190–1.

32 HMC, *Rutland*, i, p. 150.

33 E. Cole, 'Theobalds, Herefordshire: The Plan and Interiors of an Elizabethan Country House', *Architectural History*, lx (2017), p. 105.

34 G. Groos (ed.), *The Diary of Baron Waldstein* (London, 1981), p. 85; TNA C89/10/55.

35 *The Workes of Benjamin Jonson* (London, 1616), pp. 887–90.

36 *Cal. SP. Dom., Addenda, 1580–1625*, p. 498; TNA E351/3244.

37 TNA E317/Herts/26; J. Summerson, 'The Building of Theobalds 1564–1585', *Archaeologia*, xcvii (1959), pp. 107–26; E. Cole, 'Theobalds, Herefordshire: The Plan and Interiors of an Elizabethan Country House', *Architectural History*, lx (2017), pp. 71–109. My plan is based on the royal building accounts

and Sir John Soane's Museum T245-6 and T243 illustrated in J. Summerson, 'The Book of Architecture of John Thorpe in Sir John Soane's Museum', *Walpole Society*, xl (1966), pp. 8 and 105.

38 *CL*, i, p. 316, ii, pp. 426, 496.

CHAPTER 4: THE ROYAL FAMILY

1 *WP*, pp. 75–6.

2 *Cal. SP. Dom., James I, 1603–10*, pp. 35, 45, 51.

3 HMC, *Salisbury*, xv, p. 348, in E. Lodge *Illustrations of British History . . .* (London, 1791), pp. 206–7, 210–12; for a full list of the jointure. Grants: TNA SP 14/65 no. 89; TNA SP14/141 p. 102; *Victoria County History: Surrey*, iii, p. 401.

4 W. B. Rye (ed.), *England as seen by Foreigners, in the days of Elizabeth and James the First* (London, 1865), p. 117; HMC, *Salisbury*, xvi, p. 212, xvii, pp. 441, 520; *Cal. SP. Ven.*, no. 10, p. 143.

5 T. Riis, 'Theatre and Architecture: Anne, Dunfermline and Christian IV', R. Fawcett (ed.), *Royal Dunfermline* (Society of Antiquaries of Scotland, 2005), pp. 187–9.

6 *Cal. SP. Scot., 1593–5*, no. 290.

7 E. Henderson, *The annals of Dunfermline and vicinity, from the earliest authentic period to the present time, A.D. 1069–1878* (Glasgow, 1879), p. 254.

8 The key information from which my plan has been drawn is: P. Chalmers, *Historical and Statistical Account of Dunfermline*, ii (Edinburgh, 1859), plan facing p. 1; *View of the Abbey and palace from the west* by John Clerk of Eldin (National Galleries of Scotland); SRO GD 28/1705 (glazing estimate, 1654).

9 T. Riis, *Should Auld Acquaintance Be Forgot . . . Scottish Danish Relations c.1450–1707* (Odense, 1988), p. 275; R. Chambers, *Domestic Annals of Scotland from the Reformation to the Revolution*, ii (Edinburgh, 1858), p. 358; *Cal. SP. Scot., 1597–1603*, ii, no. 705.

10 C. McKean, *The Scottish Chateau. The Country House of Renaissance Scotland* (Stroud, 2001), pp. 190–2; D. Stevenson, *The Origins of Freemasonry. Scotland's century 1590–1710* (Cambridge, 1988), pp. 26–31.

11 H. M. Paton (ed.), *Accounts of the Masters of Works*, i (Edinburgh, 1957), p. xxix; *HKW*, i, pp. 105–20; A. MacKechnie, 'Sir David Cunningham of Robertland: Murderer and "Magna Britannia's" first Architect', *Architectural History*, lii (2009), pp. 79–106.

12 *Cal. SP. Ven., 1603–07*, p. 248; *FP*, p. 40.

13 For the above see *SH*, pp. 38–43; M. T. W. Payne, 'An Inventory of Queen Anne of Denmark's "Ornaments, furniture, householde stuffe, and other parcells" at Denmark House, 1619', *Journal of the History of Collections*, xiii (i) (2001), pp. 37–8.

14 R. Poulton with major contributions by A. Cook and S. Thurley, *Excavations at Oatlands Palace 1968–73 and 1983–4* (Guildford, 2009), p. 161.

15 HMC, *Salisbury*, xxi, pp. 130–1.

16 M. M. Meikle, 'Holde her at the Oeconomike rule of the House: Anne of Denmark and Scottish Court Finances, 1589–1603' in E. Ewan and M. M. Meikle (eds), *Women in Scotland c.1100–c.1750* (East Linton, 1999), p. 107; *CKJ*, p. 37.

17 M. R. Wade, *Triumphus Nuptialis Danicus. German Court culture and Denmark. The "Great Wedding" of 1634* (Wiesbaden, 1996), pp. 47–56.

18 *ibid.*, pp. 47–56, 75–6; S. Orgel and R. Strong, *Inigo Jones and the Theatre of the Stuart Court*, i (California, 1973), pp. 1–14.

19 *ibid.*, pp. 89–93.

20 L. Stone, 'Inigo Jones and the New Exchange', *Archaeological Journal*, cxiv (1957), pp. 106–21; G. Worsley, *Inigo Jones and the European Classicist Tradition* (Yale, 2007), pp. 10–11; J. Harris and A. A. Tait, *Catalogue of the Drawings by Inigo Jones, John Webb and Isaac de Caus at Worcester College Oxford* (Oxford, 1979), pp. 13–14; J. Harris and G. Higgott, *Inigo Jones, Complete Architectural Drawings* (London, 1989), pp. 36–7.

21 J. Pitcher (ed.), *Samuel Daniel, Hymen's Triumph* (Oxford, Malone Society reprints, 1994); E. K. Chambers, *The Elizabethan Stage*, iii, p. 277.

22 See J. Knowles 'To Enlight the darksome Night, Pale Cinthia Doth Arise: Anne of Denmark, Elizabeth I and the Images of Royalty', in C. McManus (ed.), *Women and Culture at the Courts of the Stuart Queens* (Basingstoke, 2003), pp. 30–3.

23 TNA SP14/90, Chamberlain to Carleton 8 March 1616/17 'The King dined that day [4 March] with the queen at Somerset house, which was then new christened and must hence forward be called Denmark house'; *Cal. SP. Dom., 1611–18*, pp. 422, 514. Also see E. K. Chamberlain, *The Elizabethan Stage*, i, p. 12.

24 L. Barroll, 'The court of the first Stuart queen', L. Levy Peck (ed.), *The Mental World of the Jacobean Court*, (Cambridge, 1991), p. 199.

25 I. Jeayes and F. Bickley (eds.), *Letters of Philip Gawdy of West Harling, Norfolk, and of London to various members of his family, 1579–1616* (Roxburghe Club, 1906), p. 162; TNA SP14\67 p. 79.

26 R. Poulton with major contributions by A. Cook and S. Thurley, *Excavations at Oatlands Palace 1968–73 and 1983–4* (Guildford, 2009), pp. 10–11, 160–2.

27 *Cal. SP. Dom., 1611–18*, pp. 212, 224; *Cal. SP. Ven., 1613–15*, p. 92; *Cal. SP. Ven., 1615–17*, pp. 334, 495; *Cal. SP. Dom., 1611–18*, pp. 361, 460, 464, 473, 537. My plan is based on sources listed in S. Thurley *English Royal Palaces 1450–1550* unpublished PhD Thesis London 1992, II, Greenwich Palace, note 33. And amended through recent results of geophysics.

28 *Cal. SP. Ven., 1610–13*, p. 160; *CL*, ii, p. 263.

29 'The Journey to England: The Royal visit of King Christian IV in the Summer of 1606', p. 27.

30 *CL*, ii, p. 83; *HKW*, ii, pp. 114–15; *HP*, pp. 102, 259–61.

31 G. Higgott, 'Inigo Jones's Designs for the Queen's House in 1616', M. Airs and G. Tyack (eds), *The Renaissance Villa in Britain 1500–1700* (Reading, 2007), pp. 140–66; G. Higgott, 'The Design and Setting of the Queen's House 1616–40', *The Court Historian*, xi (2006), pp. 135–48.

32 TNA E351/3384; TNA E351/3257.

33 O. Millar, *The Tudor, Stuart and Early Georgian Pictures in the Collection of Her Majesty the Queen* (London, 1963), no. 106.

34 *Cal. SP. Dom., James I, 1603–10*, p. 132.

35 TNA E351/3239; BL Add. MS 12,498 f. 3v; BL Add. MS 12,498 ff. 3, 3v, 4.

36 TNA E351/3239, E351/3241; R. Strong, *Henry Prince of Wales and England's Lost Renaissance* (London, 1986), pp. 42–4; *CKJ*, ii, pp. 16–18.

37 T. Birch, *The Life of Henry, Prince of Wales: Eldest Son of King James I* (London, 1760), pp. 128–9; J. Sears and F. R. Johnson (eds), *The Lumley Library, the Catalogue of 1609* (London, 1956), pp. 14–17.

38 A. White, 'A Biographical Dictionary of London Tomb Sculptors c.1560–1660', *Walpole Society*, lxi (1999), pp. 29–31.

39 TNA E351/3244; TNA SP14/63 no. 55; C. Gapper, J. Newman and A. Ricketts, 'Hatfield: A House for a Lord Treasurer', P. Croft (ed.), *Patronage, Culture and Power. The Early Cecils* (Yale, 2002), pp. 77–8.

40 TNA E351/3242; G. Worsley, *The British Stable* (Yale, 2004), pp. 52–68.

41 RIBA Smythson 1/14; M. Girouard, 'The Smythson Collection of the Royal Institute of British Architects', *Architectural History*, v (1962), pp. 33, 76.

42 TNA LR1/56 f. 226; TNA E317/Middx/42; Sir Charles Cornwallis, *A Discourse of the Most Illustrious Prince, Henry, Prince of Wales* (London, 1641), pp. 16–17; *Cal. SP. Dom., James I, 1611–18*, p. 86; *Cal. SP. Dom., Charles I, 1625–6*, p. 577; *Cal. SP. Dom., Charles I, 1636–7*, p. 463; Sieur de la Serre, *Histoire de l'Entrée de la Royne Mere . . . dans la Grande Bretagne* (London, 1639), here the translation used is in 'The Entry of Mary de Medicis to

England in 1638 by the Sieur de la Terre', F. Grose, *The Antiquarian Repertory*, i (London, 1775), p. 264; TNA AO1/2425/57 f. 9r; E351/3257.

43 T. Birch, *The Life of Henry, Prince of Wales: Eldest Son of King James I* (London, 1760), p. 97; 'Particulars of the Expense of the Royal Household in the Reigns of Henry VII, Henry VIII, Elizabeth etc', *Archaeologia*, xii (1796), pp. 85–6; W. Bray, 'An Account of the Revenue, the Expenses, the Jewels etc. of Prince Henry', *Archaeologia*, xv (1806), pp. 22–6.

44 *Cal. SP. Dom., James I, 1603–10*, pp. 75, 629.

45 P. Croft, 'The Parliamentary installation of Henry, Prince of Wales', *Historical Research*, lxv (1992), pp. 177–93.

46 S. Thurley (ed.), *St James's Palace from Leper Hospital to Royal Palace* (London, forthcoming) the evidence for my reconstruction of the first floor plan is presented in this book; T. Birch, *The Life of Henry, Prince of Wales: Eldest Son of King James I* (London, 1760), pp. 184–6; *CL*, i, p. 293; HMC, *Downshire*, iii, p. 216.

47 *KJP*, ii, pp. 324–35; E. Foster, 'Staging a Parliament in early Stuart England', P. Clark, N. Smith and N. Tyacke (eds), *The English Commonwealth 1547–1640* (Leicester, 1979), pp. 131–5.

48 P. Croft, 'The Parliamentary installation of Henry, Prince of Wales', *Historical Research*, lxv (1992), pp. 177–93; TNA E351/3244.

49 Hatfield House CP 134/163; BL, Harley Manuscripts, 252/3 printed in *A Collection of Household Ordinances* (Society of Antiquaries of London, 1790), pp. 324–34.

50 *Cal. SP. Ven., 1612–13*, xii, no. 159; G. Haslam, 'Jacobean Phoenix: The Duchy of Cornwall in the Principates of Henry Frederick and Charles', R. Hoyle (ed.), *The Estates of the English Crown, 1558–1640* (Cambridge, 1992), pp. 263–74; *HP supra* Richard Connock.

51 R. Strong, *Henry Prince of Wales and England's Lost Renaissance* (London, 1986), pp. 88–96; S. Eiche, 'Prince Henry's Richmond. The Project by Costantino de' Servi', *Apollo*, cxlviii (November 1998), pp. 10–14.

52 G. Haslam, 'Jacobean Phoenix: The Duchy of Cornwall in the Principates of Henry Frederick and Charles', R. Hoyle, (ed.), *The Estates of the English Crown, 1558–1640* (Cambridge, 1992), pp. 269–71; T. Wilks, ' "Forbear the Heat and Haste of Building": Rivalries among the designers at Prince Henry's Court 1610–12', *The Court Historian*, vi (2010), p. 63; T. Wilks, 'The Court Culture of Prince Henry and his Circle, 1603–1613' (unpublished PhD dissertation, University of Oxford, 1988), p. 283. I am grateful to Dr Wilks for supplying me with a copy of the relevant parts of his dissertation.

53 *Cal. SP. Ven., 1603–7,* no. 739, p. 513.

54 A. Keay, 'The best proportioned old building in England: Kenilworth Castle 1588–1722', *English Heritage Historical Review,* v (2010), pp. 83–7; *HP,* pp. 355–8.

55 *HKW,* iii, pp. 105–15.

56 G. Akrigg, *The Letters of King James VI & I* (Berkeley, CA, 1984), pp. 227, 270, 291–2.

57 *CKJ,* ii, pp. 199–200; F. Dietz, *English Public Finance 1558–1641* (London, 1964), pp. 103–13.

58 I was unable to consult the original of this document which is TNA 30/24/7.

59 J. Orrell, *The theatres of Inigo Jones and John Webb* (Cambridge, 1985), pp. 15–16.

60 J. Webb, *A Vindication of Stone-Heng Restored* (London, 1665), p. 119; R. Wittkower, 'Inigo Jones – "Puritanissimo Fiero"', *Burlington Magazine,* xc (1948), pp. 50–1.

CHAPTER 5: JACOBUS REX MAGNAE BRITANNIAE

1 S. T. Bindoff, 'The Stuarts and Their Style', *The English Historical Review,* vol. lx, no. ccxxxvii (May, 1945), pp. 192–216.

2 N. Brett-James, *The Growth of Stuart London* (London, 1935), pp. 67–126; *HKW* III, pp. 139–147.

3 P. Temple, *The Charterhouse* (Survey London 18th Monograph, 2010), p. 59; L. Stone, 'Inigo Jones and the New Exchange', *Archaeological Journal,* cxiv (1957), pp. 106–21; *Survey of London,* xlvi, South and East Clerkenwell (London, 2008), pp. 204–10.

4 *Survey of London,* 3, St Giles-in-The-Fields, Pt I: Lincoln's Inn Fields, pp. 3–22.

5 For the following paragraphs see *WP,* pp. 69–73, 78–82.

6 TNA E351/3239; TNA E351/3240.

7 TNA E351/3243; S. Orgel and R. Strong, *Inigo Jones and the Theatre of the Stuart Court,* i (California, 1973), p. 95.

8 BL, Harley Manuscripts, 1653, pp. 13–49.

9 S. Orgel and R. Strong, *Inigo Jones and the Theatre of the Stuart Court,* i (California, 1973), p. 282.

10 *CKJ,* ii, p. 174; T. Birch, *The Court and Times of James the First,* ii (London, 1848), p. 127; *CL,* ii, p. 204; *KJP,* iii, p. 523 ff.

11 P. Palme, *Triumph of Peace. A Study of the Whitehall Banqueting House* (London 1957), pp. 52–5.

12 TNA SP14/108 no. 55; *WP*, pp. 82–90.

13 *CL*, ii, p. 367.

14 TNA SP124/131; D. Howarth, *Images of Rule* (London, 1997), pp. 34, 298; *Cal. SP. Dom., 1619–23*, p. 331.

15 James I, *The peace-maker: or, Great Brittaines blessing* (London, 1619); *Cal. SP. Dom., 1619*, p. 8; A. Bullen, *The Works of Thomas Middleton*, vii (London, 1886), pp. 344–6.

16 The definitive account of this is G. Martin, *Rubens. The Ceiling Decoration of the Banqueting Hall*, i (London, 2005), pp. 19–52.

17 *CL*, ii, p. 323; TNA SP14/124/130; O. Millar, *The Tudor, Stuart and Early Georgian Pictures in the Collection of Her Majesty the Queen* (London, 1963), no. 104.

18 S. Orgel and R. Strong, *Inigo Jones and the Theatre of the Stuart Court*, i (California, 1973), pp. 348–60.

19 BL, Lansdowne Manuscripts, 225 f. 305; E351/3256.

20 C. Kyle, 'Parliament and the Palace of Westminster: An Exploration of Public Space in the Early 17th Century', C. Jones and S. Kelsey, *Housing Parliament, Dublin, Edinburgh and Westminster* (Edinburgh, 2002), pp. 84–92; C. Kyle and J. Peacey, '"Under cover of so much coming and going": Public Access to Parliament and the Political Process in Early Modern England', C. Kyle and J. Peacey (eds), *Parliament at Work: Parliamentary Committees, Political Power, and Public Access in Early Modern England* (Woodbridge, 2002); M. Collins, 'The Medieval and Early Tudor Topography of Westminster', T. Tatton-Brown and R. Rodwell (eds), *Westminster: the art, architecture and archaeology of the Royal Abbey and Palace*, part i (British Archaeological Association, Conference Transactions, 39:1, Leeds, 2015), pp. 214–21.

21 C. Kyle and J. Peacey, '"Under cover of so much coming and going" . . .', C. Kyle and J. Peacey (eds), *Parliament at Work . . .* (Woodbridge, 2002), pp. 3–17.

22 E. Foster, 'Staging a Parliament in Early Stuart England', P. Clark, A. Smith and N. Tyacke (eds), *The English Commonwealth 1547–1640* (Leicester, 1979), pp. 129–46. My plan is based on the plans published in *Architectural History*, d, (1966) figs 57 and 85 and All Souls College plan III.13. My base survey is from *HKW* plan portfolio.

23 S. Gardiner, *What Gunpowder Plot Was* (London, 1897), pp. 1–138; M. Nicholls, *Investigating Gunpowder Plot* (Manchester, 1991), pp. 3–18.

24 TNA E351/3246; TNA E351/3249; H. J. M. Green and S. Thurley, 'Excavations

on the West Side of Whitehall 1960–2 Part I: From the Building of the Tudor Palace to the Construction of the Modern Offices of State', *The London and Middlesex Archaeological Society Transactions* (1990), pp. 107–10.

25 *CL*, i, pp. 366, 566, 590, 623, ii, pp. 243, 245–7, 432, 535; The remarks below on James's movements are based on the comprehensive referenced itinerary compiled by Emily Cole which has transformed our ability to study James and his court: E. V. Cole, 'The State Apartment in the Jacobean Country House 1603–1625' (DPhil thesis, University of Sussex, 2010), pp. 365–416.

26 E. Croft-Murray, *Decorative Painting in England 1537–1837*, i (London, 1962), pp. 198–200, 206; J. Orrell, 'The London Court Stage in the Savoy Correspondence 1613–1675', *Theatre Research*, iii (1979), pp. 157–76.

27 S. Thurley (ed.), *St James's Palace from Leper Hospital to Royal Palace* (London, forthcoming).

28 For instance TNA E351/3255; *FP*, pp. 34, 95, and pp. 33–4, 52–3, 63–4, 76.

29 A. Young, *Tudor and Jacobean Tournaments* (London, 1987), pp. 33–42.

30 E. Law, *Shakespeare as a Groom of the Chamber* (London, 1910), pp. 39–40.

31 A. Kernan, *Shakespeare, the King's Playwright 1603–1613* (Yale, 1995), p. 16; *FP*, p. 8.

32 *HP*, pp. 374–8; E. K. Chambers, *The Elizabethan Stage*, i (Oxford, 1923), pp. 100–5.

33 *HP*, pp. 374–94.

34 N. Cuddy, 'The Revival of the Entourage: the Bedchamber of James I, 1603–1625', D. Starkey et al., *The English Court: from the Wars of the Roses to the Civil War* (London, 1987), pp. 173–225.

35 F. Dietz, *English Public Finance 1558–1641* (London, 1964), p. 411; S. Pegge, *Curialia or an Historical Account of some Branches of the Royal Household*, i (London, 1791), pp. 33–5.

36 *Cal. SP. Ven., 1603–7*, no. 72. Also see L. Pearsall Smith, *The Life and Letters of Sir Henry Wotton*, i (Oxford, 1907), pp. 314–15.

37 *CL*, i, p. 409; I was unable to check the original of this letter in the British Library Trumbull MSS 18/138; P. Croft, 'Robert Cecil and the Early Jacobean Court', L. Levy Peck (ed.), *The Mental World of the Jacobean Court* (Cambridge, 1991), pp. 134–47.

38 HMC, *Portland*, ix, p. 113.

39 *KJP*, ii, p. 38; R. Ashton, *James I by his Contemporaries* (London, 1969), p. 14; A. Loomie, *Ceremonies of Charles I. The Note Books of John Finet 1628–1641* (Fordham, 1987), pp. 9–10; *ODNB supra* Herbert, Philip, first earl of Montgomery and fourth earl of Pembroke.

40 *WP*, p. 76; *FP*, pp. 64, 74, 104, 156; TNA E351/3254.

CHAPTER 6: THE CONNOISSEUR KING

1 J. W. Stoye, *English Travellers Abroad 1604–1667* (London, 1952), pp. 328–36.

2 J. Pérez Gil, *El Palacio Real de Valladolid, sede de la Corte de Felipe III 1601–1606* (Universidad de Valladolid, 2012), p. 227 ff.; *A relation of such things as were observed to happen in the journey of the right Honourable Charles Earle of Nottingham, L. High Admirall of England, his highnesse ambassadour to the King of Spaine London 1605*; BL Trumbull MSS 20/20 f. 6v.

3 D. Howard and H. McBurney (eds), *The Image of Venice. Fialetti's view and Sir Henry Wotton* (London, 2014), pp. 100–13.

4 C. Hope, *Titian* (London, 2003); L. Pearsall Smith, *Life and Letters of Sir Henry Wotton*, ii (Oxford, 1907), p. 419. This was the same advice given to Mary I when she received a Titian from Philip II; C. Hope, 'Titian, Philip II and Mary Tudor', E. Chaney and P. Mack (eds), *England and the Continental Renaissance* (Woodbridge, 1994), pp. 53–65.

5 T. P. Campbell, 'Collectors and Connoisseurs: The Status and Perception of Tapestry, 1600–1660', T. P. Campbell (ed.), *Tapestry in the Baroque. Threads of Splendor* (Metropolitan Museum of Art, New York, 2008), pp. 325–38.

6 A. Ribeiro, *Fashion and Fiction. Dress in Art and Literature in Stuart England* (Yale, 2005), p. 96.

7 *Acts of the Privy Council 1618–19*, p. 264; L. Martin, 'Sir Francis Crane: Director of the Mortlake Tapestry manufactory and Chancellor of the Order of the Garter', *Apollo*, cxiii (1981), pp. 90–6; W. Hefford, 'The Mortlake Manufactory, 1618–49', T. P. Campbell (ed.), *Tapestry in the Baroque. Threads of Splendor* (Metropolitan Museum of Art, New York, 2008), pp. 171–82; W. G. Thomson, *Tapestry Weaving in England from the Earliest Times to the end of the 18th Century* (London, 1914), pp. 66–71.

8 D. Howarth, 'William Trumbull and art collecting in Jacobean England', *The British Library Journal*, xx (1994), pp. 149–59; TNA E407/78/1; J. Shearman, *Raphael's Cartoons in the Collection of Her Majesty the Queen and the Tapestries in the Sistine Chapel* (London, 1972), pp. 146–7.

9 TNA E404/153 (1pl.1), ff. 9, 10; E403/1746 (unpaginated); P. Austin Nuttall, *The History of the Worthies of England by Thomas Fuller*, iii (London, 1840), pp. 201–2.

10 *CKJ*, ii, pp. 369–70.

11 The best account of the Spanish adventure is G. Redworth, *The Prince and the Infanta. The Cultural Politics of the Spanish Match* (Yale, 2003).

12 *CKJ*, ii, p. 254; C. Petrie, *The Letters, Speeches and Proclamations of King Charles I* (London, 1935), pp. 7–8. The principal primary sources I have used

for the king's time in Spain are: T. Hearne, *Historia vitæ et regni Ricardi II* . . . *et D. Ricardi Wynni, baronetti. Narratio historica de Caroli, Walliæ prinicpis, famulorum in Hispaniam itinere* (Oxford, 1729), pp. 299–341; J. Digby, Earl of Bristol, *A true relation and Journall, of the manner of the arrivall, and magnificent entertainment, given to the high and mighty Prince Charles, Prince of Great Britaine, by the King of Spaine in his court at Madrid* (London, 1623); J. Digby, Earl of Bristol, *A continuation of a former relation concerning the entertainment given to Prince His Highnesse by the King of Spaine in his court at Madrid* (London, 1623); 'A Relation of the Departure of the most Illustrious Prince of Wales from Madrid the 9th September 1623', W. Scott (ed.), *A collection of scarce and valuable tracts . . . Selected from an infinite number in print and manuscript, in the Royal, Cotton, Sion, and other public, as well as private libraries; particularly that of the late Lord Somers*, 2nd ed., 1809–15, ii, pp. 540–50.

13   T. Hearne, *Historia vitæ et regni Ricardi II . . . et D. Ricardi Wynni, baronetti. Narratio historica de Caroli, Walliæ prinicpis, famulorum in Hispaniam itinere* (Oxford, 1729), pp. 327–8.

14   C. Petrie, *The Letters, Speeches and Proclamations of King Charles I* (London, 1935), pp. 10–11.

15   *CKJ*, ii, pp. 259–60.

16   T. Hearne, *Historia vitæ et regni Ricardi II . . . et D. Ricardi Wynni, baronetti. Narratio historica de Caroli, Walliæ prinicpis, famulorum in Hispaniam itinere* (Oxford, 1729), p. 328; BL, Trumbull MSS, 20/20 f. 6.

17   S. Orso, *Philip IV and the Decoration of the Alcazar of Madrid* (Princeton, 1986), pp. 17–23. My plan is based on Juan Gómez de Mora's plan in the Vatican Biblioteca Apostolica.

18   J. H. Elliott, 'The Court of the Spanish Hapsburgs: A Peculiar Institution?', J. H. Elliott, *Spain and its World 1500–1700* (Yale, 1989), pp. 142–61.

19   T. Hearne, *Historia vitæ et regni Ricardi II . . .* (Oxford, 1729), pp. 330–1.

20   *A True relation and journal of the manner of arrival and magnificent entertainment given to the high and mighty Prince Charles Prince of Great Britain by the King of Spaine in his court in Madrid* (London, 1623), pp. 30–2.

21   D. Sánchez Cano, 'Entertainments in Madrid for the Prince of Wales: Political Functions of Festivals', A. Samson (ed.), *The Spanish Match. Prince Charles's Journey to Madrid 1623* (Aldershot, 2006), pp. 51–73.

22   J. Digby, Earl of Bristol, *A continuation of a former relation concerning the entertainment given to Prince His Highnesse by the King of Spaine in his court at Madrid* (London, 1623), p. 2; For the following paragraphs see J. Brown,

'Artistic Relations between Spain and England 1604–1655', J. Brown and J. Elliott (eds), *The Sale of the Century. Artistic Relations between Spain and Great Britain 1604–1655* (Yale, 2002), pp. 41–50, 158–91; J. Brotton, 'Buying the Renaissance: Prince Charles's Art Purchases in Madrid 1623', A. Samson (ed.), *The Spanish Match. Prince Charles's Journey to Madrid 1623* (Aldershot, 2006), pp. 9–26.

23 F. Calvo Serraller (ed.), *V. Carducho, Diálogos e la pintura* (Madrid, 1970), p. 435.

24 BL, Trumbull MSS 20/20 f. 6v; T. Hearne, *Historia vitæ et regni Ricardi II . . . et D. Ricardi Wynni, baronetti. Narratio historica de Caroli, Walliæ prinicpis, famulorum in Hispaniam itinere* (Oxford, 1729), pp. 334–5.

25 J. Brown and J. Elliott, *A Palace for a King. The Buien Retiro and the Court of Philip IV* (Yale, 1980), pp. 44–5; P. Shakeshaft, 'Elsheimer and G. B. Crescenzi', *Burlington Magazine*, cxxiii (1981), pp. 550–1.

26 'A Relation of the Departure of the most Illustrious Prince of Wales from Madrid the 9th September 1623', W. Scott (ed.), *A collection of scarce and valuable tracts . . . Selected from an infinite number in print and manuscript, in the Royal, Cotton, Sion, and other public, as well as private libraries; particularly that of the late Lord Somers.* 2nd ed., ii (1809–15), pp. 540–50.

27 TNA SP14/139 no. 63; TNA SP14/140 no. 21; *Cal. SP. Dom., James I, 1611–18*, pp. 516, 536, 563.

28 *CL*, p. 494; S. R. Gardiner (trans. and ed.), 'El hecho de los tratados del matrimonio pretendido por el Principe de Gales con la serenissima Infante de Espana Maria, tomado desde sus principios para maior demostracion de la verdad, y ajustado con los papeles originales desde consta', *Camden Society*, ci (1869), pp. 120, 299–300; *Cal. SP. Ven., 1621–3*, xvii, no. 771.

29 T. Birch, *The Court and Times of James the First*, ii (London, 1848), p. 400; TNA SP14/144 no. 42; HMC, Appendix to 7th Report, p. 258; *CL*, ii, p. 494; *Cal. SP. Ven., 1623–5*, nos. 55, 65; The houses were ordered to be vacated: *Acts of the Privy Council, James I, VI* (1621–23), p. 493.

30 G. Beltramini (ed.), *Andrea Palladio the Complete Illustrated Works* (New York, 2001), pp. 96–9; O. Bertotti Scamozzi, *Le Fabbriche e i Disegni di Andrea Palladio*, 4 vols. i (Vicenza, 1776–83), plates 37–9.

31 J. Harris and G. Higgott, *Inigo Jones, Complete Architectural Drawings* (London, 1990), pp. 103–5.

32 TNA E351/3260; A. Palladio, *I Quattro Libri dell'architecttura* (Venice, 1570), Book iv, plate xxiii.

33 R. Cust, *Charles I, A Political Life* (Harlow, 2005), pp. 36–44; R. Lockyer,

Buckingham. *The Life and Political Career of George Villiers, First Duke of Buckingham 1592–1628* (Harlow, 1981), pp. 180–98.

34 TNA E351/3257, E351/3258; A. Hawkyard, 'Inigo Jones, the Surveyors of the Works and the Parliament House', *Parliamentary History*, xxxii (2013), pp. 31–7.

CHAPTER 7: DIGNITY AND ORDER

1 J. F. Larkin, *Stuart Royal Proclamations*, ii (Oxford, 1983), no. 14, p. 37; *Cal. SP. Ven., 1625–6*, p. 21; HMC, 11th Report appendix part i p. 6; HMC, *Cooper*, i, p. 382; *CL*, ii, p. 609; P. Warwick, *Memoirs of the Reign of King Charles* I (London, 1701), p. 113; C. H. Firth, *Memoirs of the Life of Colonel Hutchinsoln Governor of Nottingham by his widow Lucy* (London, 1906), p. 69.

2 *SLD*, ii, pp. 140–1, and for the above see K. Sharpe, *The Personal Rule of Charles I* (Yale, 1992), pp. 209–22; K. Sharpe, 'The Image of Virtue: the Court and Household of Charles I, 1625–1642', D. Starkey et al., *The English Court: from the Wars of the Roses to the Civil War* (London, 1987), pp. 226–60.

3 *FP*, pp. 145–6.

4 *CL*, i, pp. 127, 251; C. White, *The Dutch Pictures in the Collection of Her Majesty the Queen* (Cambridge, 1982), no. 87; A. Wheelock, 'Gerard Houckgeest and Emanuel de Witte: Architectural Painting in Delft around 1650', *Simiolus*, viii (1975–6), pp. 167–85; Charles I regulations for dining are in TNA LC5/180 ff. 9r–10 and BL Stowe 561 ff. 4v–5.

5 *CL*, i, p. 25.

6 *Cal. SP. Ven., 1625–6*, ixx, no. 4, p. 3; *Cal. SP. Ven.*, no. 17, p. 11; T. Birch, *The Court and Times of Charles the First*, i (London, 1848), pp. 3–4; *Acts of the Privy Council, Charles I* (1625–6), p. 3.

7 In a letter from Rubens in 1619 he describes the Banqueting House as in a 'new palace', but this is likely to be a misunderstanding as it is not mentioned anywhere else and the architectural evidence does not support it being anything other than a stand-alone commission, see R. Strong, 'Britannia Triumphans. Inigo Jones, Rubens and the Whitehall Banqueting House', R. Strong, *The Tudor and Stuart Monarchy: Pageantry, Painting, Iconography iii Jacobean and Caroline* (Woodbridge, 1998). Examples of blending in are in TNA E325/3241, E351/3244, E351/3248.

8 Berkshire Record Office Microfilm 10113 frame 0402; TNA C115/N4/8606;, *Wren Society*, vii, p. 234; J. Harris and A. Tait (eds), *Catalogue of the Drawings*

by Inigo Jones, John Webb and Isaac de Caus at Worcester College Oxford (Oxford, 1979), fig. 107.

9   TNA LC5/132 f. 188; *Cal. SP. Ven., 1623-6*, no. 195, p. 146, no. 202; *Cal. SP. Ven., 1636–9*, no. 156, p. 143.

10 TNA SP16/168 no. 64; Bodleian Library MS Eng. Hist. E 28 f. 8v; Eyewitness accounts are in A. J. Loomie, *Ceremonies of Charles I. The Note Books of John Finet 1628–1641* (Fordham, 1987), pp. 88–90; BL Egerton MS 2553, f. 34r; BL Egerton MS 1818 ff. 78r–v; BL. Harl. MS 791 f. 40r; See also *Cal. SP. Dom., Charles I, 1629–31*, pp. 269, 282; TNA LC5/132 p. 196, 201; AO1/2426/60 f. 8v.

11 TNA E351/3258, E351/3262, E351/3263.

12 TNA E351/3265; TNA E351/3271.

13 TNA LC5/134 pp. 50, 185, 242; TNA E351/3269.

14 TNA AO1/2429/73; *Cal. SP. Dom., Charles I, 1629–31*, p. 313; A. J. Loomie, *Ceremonies of Charles I. The Note Books of John Finet 1628–1641* (Fordham, 1987), pp. 195, 244, 246; A. MacGregor, *The Late King's Goods. Collections, Possessions and Patronage of Charles I in the light of the Commonwealth Sale Inventories* (London, 1989), pp. 360–1; A. Keay, *The Magnificent Monarch. Charles II and the Ceremonies of Power* (London, 2008), pp. 21–7.

15 *Cal. SP. Dom., Charles I, 1629–31*, p. 165; M. A. Everett Green, *Letters of Henrietta Maria* (London, 1857), pp. 19–20; *Les Voyages de Sieur Albert de Mandelslo* (Leiden, 1719), p. 749; S. Thurley (ed.), *St James's Palace from Leper Hospital to Royal Palace* (London, forthcoming).

16 C. McGee, '"Strangest consequence from remotest cause": the second performance of The Triumph of Peace', *Medieval and Renaissance Drama in England*, v (1991), p. 331; J. Orrell, 'The Agent of Savoy at The Somerset Masque', *The Review of English Studies*, NS xxviii (1977), pp. 301–4; *SLD*, ii, p. 148; S. Orgel and R. Strong, *Inigo Jones the Theatre of the Stuart Court*, ii (London, 1973), pp. 662, 631–59; B. Gerbier, *A Brief Discourse Concerning the Three Chief Principles of Magnificent Building* (London, 1662), p. 40; TNA E351/3255; A. J. Loomie, *Ceremonies of Charles I. The Note Books of John Finet 1628–1641* (Fordham, 1987), pp. 120, 152–3, 174.

17 J. Orrell, *The Theatres of Inigo Jones and John Webb* (Cambridge, 1985), pp. 128–48.

18 PRO LC5/134 f. 195; TNA E351/3271; *SLD*, ii, pp. 130, 140; HMC, *De L'Isle and Dudley*, vi, p. 127.

19 A. J. Loomie, *Ceremonies of Charles I. The Note Books of John Finet 1628–1641* (Fordham, 1987), p. 272; A. Pelzer (ed.), *Joachim von Sandarts Academie der*

Bau-, Buil- und Mahlerey-Künste von 1675 (Munich, 1925), p. 173; C. White, *The Dutch Pictures in the Collection of Her Majesty the Queen* (Cambridge, 1982), cat. 53.

20 D. Cressy, *Charles I and the People of England* (Oxford, 2015), p. 159; *SLD*, ii, p. 140; J. Murray, *Memoirs of the Embassy of the Marshal de Bassompierre to the Court of England* (London, 1819), pp. 95–6.

21 H. J. M. Green and S. Thurley, 'Excavations on the West Side of Whitehall 1960–2 Part I: From the Building of the Tudor Palace to the Construction of the Modern Offices of State', *The London and Middlesex Archaeological Society Transactions* (1990), pp. 107–10; J. Orrell, *The Theatres of Inigo Jones and John Webb* (Cambridge, 1985), pp. 90–103; G. E. Bentley, *The Jacobean and Caroline Stage*, i, (Oxford, 1941), p. 23; J. Harris and A. A. Tait, *Catalogue of Drawings by Inigo Jones, John Webb and Isaac de Caus at Worcester College Oxford* (Oxford, 1979), pp. 11–12; *SLD*, p. 177.

22 T. Wilks, 'Art Collecting at the English Court from the death of Henry Prince of Wales to the death of Anne of Denmark', *Journal of the History of Collections*, ix (1997), pp. 34–5; R. M. Smuts, 'Art and the Material Culture of Majesty in Early Stuart England', R. M. Smuts (ed.), *The Stuart Court and Europe* (Cambridge, 1996), p. 102.

23 *FP*, pp. 156, 200. My plan of Whitehall first floor is drawn from material published in WP and on inventories published in *Walpole Society* xxxvii and building and repair accounts in the National Archives.

24 *Cal. SP. Dom., 1625–6*, p. 402; *Cal. SP. Dom., 1637–8*, p. 148; *FP*, pp. 137–8; O. Millar (ed.), 'Abraham van der Doort's Catalogue of the Collections of Charles I', *Walpole Society*, xxxvii (1958–60), pp. 76–156.

25 *ODNB*; O. Millar (ed.), 'Abraham van der Doort's Catalogue of the Collections of Charles I', *Walpole Society*, xxxvii (1958–60), pp. xiii–xvi.

26 TNA AO1/2429/73; AO1/2428/69.

27 O. Millar, *The Tudor, Stuart and Early Georgian Pictures in the Collection of Her Majesty the Queen* (London, 1963), no. 143, pp. 93–5; S. J. Barnes, N. de Poorter, O. Millar and H. Vey, *Van Dyck. A Complete Catalogue of the Paintings* (Yale, 2004), nos. iv.66 & iv.47, pp. 460–4.

28 *HCP*, pp. 112–15.

29 J. Fielding (ed.), 'Diary of Robert Woodford 1637–1641', *Camden Society*, 5th ser., xlii (2012), p. 246.

30 W. Kelly, *Royal Progresses and Visits to Leicester* (Leicester, 1884), pp. 382–93.

31 Huntingdon Library CA. HA Misc. Box 1 (15); TNA E351/3408; M. Kishlansky, 'Charles I: A Case of Mistaken Identity', *Past & Present*, clxxxix

(2005), pp. 63–9; D. Cressy, *Charles I and the People of England* (Oxford, 2015), pp. 161–76.

CHAPTER 8: QUEEN CONSORT

1 Hastily done, the work was accounted for in the following accounting period. TNA E351/3258; TNA E351/3259, in G. Higgott, 'A Royal Lodging: the Great Tower from *c.*1480 to *c.*1700', P. Pattison, S. Brindle and D Robinson (eds), *The Great Tower of Dover Castle History, Architecture and Context* (Liverpool, forthcoming). I'm grateful to Paul Pattison for sight of this ahead of publication; *Cal. SP. Ven., 1625–6*, p. 87.

2 *Cal. SP. Ven., 1625–6*, no. 125; The most often quoted description of the queen's arrival at Dover is by a disaffected opponent of her marriage: M. C. Hippeau, *Mémoires Inédits du comte Leveneur de Tillières* (Paris, 1862), pp. 89, 91. Another more balanced view is in the 'Mémories du Comte de Brienne' in J. Michaud and J. Poujoulat, *Nouvelle Collection Des Memoires Relatifs a L'histoire De France Despuis Le XIII Siecle Jusqua' La Fin Du XVIII Siecle*, xxvii (Paris, 1854), p. 38; L. Wickham Legg, 'A relation of a short survey of the western counties, made by a lieutenant of the Military Company in Norwich in 1635', *Camden Miscellany*, xvi (1936), p. 25.

3 *A true discourse of all the royal passages, tryumphs and ceremonies, obserued at the contract and mariage of the high and mighty Charles, King of Great Britaine, and the most excellentest of ladies, the Lady Henrietta Maria of Burbon, sister to the most Christian King of France* (London, 1625); *FP*, pp. 151–3; M. Toynbee, 'The Wedding Journey of King Charles I', *Archaeologia Cantiana*, lxix (1955), pp. 82–3.

4 E. Griffey, *On Display. Henrietta Maria and the Materials of Magnificence at the Stuart Court* (Yale, 2015), is a mine of information on this subject.

5 C. Hibbard, 'By our Direction and For Our Use: The Queen's patronage of Artists and Artisans seen through her household accounts', E. Griffey (ed.), *Henrietta Maria, Piety, Politics and Patronage* (Aldershot, 2008), pp. 118–20; T. Rymer, *Foedera*, viii (i), (1743), pp. 211–12: *Cal. SP. Dom., 1625–6*, p. 561; T. Rymer, *Foedera*, xviii, p. 685; *Cal. SP. Dom., 1627–8*, pp. 84, 89; *Cal. SP. Dom., 1628–9*, pp. 214, 215; *Cal. SP. Dom., 1629–31*, p. 37.

6 This is based on an itinerary that I have compiled from printed primary sources.

7 TNA LR5/65.

8 *Cal. SP. Ven., 1625–6*, nos. 34, 52; T. Birch, *The Court and Times of Charles the First*, i (London, 1848), p. 33.

9 S. Thurley (ed.), *St James's Palace from Leper Hospital to Royal Palace* (London, forthcoming).

10 T. Birch, *The Court and Times of Charles the First*, i (London, 1848), p. 52.

11 For the following see *SH*.

12 C. Avery, 'The Collector Earl and his Modern Marbles. Thomas Howard and François Dieussart', *Apollo*, clxiii (June 2006), pp. 46–53; E. Veevers, *Images of Love and Religion. Henrietta Maria and Court Entertainments* (Cambridge, 1989), pp. 165–71. *Cal. SP. Ven.*, *1636–9*, pp. 120–1; T. Birch (ed.), *The Court and Times of Charles I*, ii, pp. 311–14, 343.

13 E. Lodge, *Illustrations of British History* (London, 1791), pp. 227–8; BL Stowe MS 561 ff. 12r–17v.

14 BL King's MSS 136 f. 441.

15 E. Griffey, *On Display. Henrietta Maria and the Materials of Magnificence at the Stuart Court* (Yale, 2015), pp. 75–6; G. Beard, *Upholsterers and Interior Furnishing in England 1530–1840* (Yale, 1997), pp. 60–2.

16 C. Carlton, *Charles I. The Personal Monarch*, 2nd ed. (London, 1995), p. 186; W. L. Spiers, 'The Note Book and Account Book of Nicholas Stone', *Walpole Society*, vii (1918–19), pp. 86, 88; E351/3266 f. 9v; LR5/65 (Grynder's bill Jan, Feb, Mar 1632); *HCP*, p. 119.

17 *Cal. SP. Ven.*, *1636–9*, p. 356; HMC, *Viscount De L'Isle*, vi (Sydney papers, 1626–98), pp. 122–3; A. Keay, 'The Ceremonies of Charles II Court' (unpublished PhD thesis, London, 2004), pp. 116–26; S. Thurley, 'The King in the queen's lodgings: The rise of the drawing room at the English court', M. Chatenet and K. De Jonghe (eds), *Le Prince, la Princesse et leurs Logis* (Paris, 2014), pp. 67–74.

18 A. Loomie, *Ceremonies of Charles I. The Note Books of John Finet 1628–1641* (New York, 1987), pp. 32–3, 85–6, 168; *FP*, pp. 222–3; C. Hibbard, 'The Role of a Queen Consort. The Household and Court of Henrietta Maria 1625–1642', R. Asch and A. Birke (eds), *Princes, Patronage, and the Nobility. The Court at the Beginning of the Modern Age c.1450–1650* (Oxford, 1991), pp. 393–414.

19 I. Atherton and J. Sanders, *The 1630s. Interdisciplinary essays on culture and politics in the Caroline era* (Manchester, 2006), especially the introduction and Caroline Hibbard's essay on Henrietta Maria pp. 92–106; *CHR*, i, p. 84.

20 O. Miller, *Pictures . . .* cat. 197; see payment to Belcamp in the queen's personal accounts National Library of Wales Wynnstay 174.

21 G. Higgott, 'Inigo Jones's Designs for the Queen's House in 1616', M. Airs and G. Tyack (eds), *The Renaissance Villa in Britain* (Reading, 2007),

pp. 140–263; J. Harris and G. Higgott, *Inigo Jones: Complete Architectural Drawings* (London, 1989), pp. 226–7.

22 G. H. Chettle, *The Queen's House Greenwich* (Survey of London 14th Monograph, 1937), which also prints many key documents; J. Bold, *Greenwich. An Architectural History of the Royal Hospital for Seamen and the Queen's House* (Yale, 2000), pp. 52–76; *Cal. SP. Ven., 1632–6*, pp. 386–7; *Cal. SP. Ven., 1636–9*, p. 120; For the pleasaunce *HP,* pp. 73–4.

23 G. Finaldi (ed.), *Orazio Gentileschi at the Court of Charles I* (London, 1999), pp. 9–32.

24 J. Bold, *Greenwich. An Architectural History of the Royal Hospital for Seamen and the Queen's House* (Yale, 2000), pp. 63–76.

25 C. Knight, 'The Cecils at Wimbledon', P. Croft (ed.), *Patronage, Culture and Power. The Early Cecils* (Yale, 2002), pp. 47–63; R. Strong, *The Renaissance Garden in England* (London, 1998), pp. 57–63.

26 My plan is based on John Thorpe's Plan: J. Summerson, 'The Book of Architecture of John Thorpe in Sir John Soane's Museum' (*Walpole Society*, xl, 1966), pp. 77–8, pl. 54; Robert Smythson's Plan: M. Girouard, 'The Smythson Collection of the Royal Institute of British Architects', *Architectural History*, v (1962), p. 37; Nicholas Hawksmoor's Plan: A. Geraghty, *The Architectural Drawings of Sir Christopher Wren at All Souls College, Oxford* (Aldershot, 2007), p. 217; Two views by Henry Winstanley: British Museum 1881,0611.353; Financial accounts in National Library of Wales Wynnstay MSS 167, 170, 172, 173, 176, 185; Survey of 1649 printed in W. Hart, 'Parliamentary Surveys of Richmond Wimbledon and Nonsuch in Surrey AD 1649', *Surrey Archaeological Collections*, v (1871), pp. 105–12.

27 *Cal. SP. Dom., 1639–40*, pp. 157, 342.

28 R. Strong, *The Renaissance Garden in England* (London, 1998), pp. 191–7.

29 'Parliamentary Surveys of Richmond Wimbledon and Nonsuch in Surrey AD 1649', *Surrey Archaeological Collections*, v (1871), p. 109; O. Millar (ed.), 'The Inventories and Valuations of the King's Goods 1649–1651', *Walpole Society*, xliii (1970–2), p. 57.

30 M. Girouard, *Life in the French Country House* (London, 2000), pp. 120–3.

CHAPTER 9: CAPITAL IMPROVEMENTS

1 A. Thrush and J. P. Ferris (eds), *The History of Parliament: the House of Commons 1604–1629* (Cambridge, 2010).

2 J. Escobar, *The Plaza Mayor and the Shaping of Baroque Madrid* (Cambridge,

2004); D. Duggan, '"London the Ring, Covent Garden the Jewell of that Ring", New Light on Covent Garden', *Architectural History*, xliii (2000), pp. 141–9.

3 E. S. de Beer (ed.), *The Diary of John Evelyn*, ii (Oxford, 1955), p. 184.

4 S. Thurley (ed.), *St James's Palace from Leper Hospital to Royal Palace* (London, forthcoming); F. H. W. Sheppard (ed.), *Survey of London: Volume 34, St Anne Soho* (London, 1966), pp. 416–18, 441–2.

5 D. Howarth, 'The Politics of Inigo Jones', D. Howarth, *Art and Patronage in the Caroline Courts* (Cambridge, 1993), pp. 68–81.

6 G. Higgott, 'The Fabric to 1670', D. Keene, A. Burns and A. Saint (eds), *St Paul's. The Cathedral Church of London 604–2004* (Yale, 2004), pp. 173–82; C. Anderson, *Inigo Jones and the Classical Tradition* (Cambridge, 2007), p. 185; W. Dugdale, *History of St Paul's Cathedral in London: From its Foundation to these Times* (London, 1658), p. 60.

7 S. Orgel and R. Strong, *Inigo Jones and the Theatre of the Stuart Court*, ii (California, 1973), pp. 452–75.

8 TNA PC2/46 p. 111 (27 April 1636); LMA City of London Repertories, 50, f. 199 (printed in T. C. Noble, *Memorials of Temple Bar* (London, 1869), p. 25); J. Peacock and C. Anderson, 'Inigo Jones, John Webb and Temple Bar', *Architectural History*, xliv (2001), pp. 29–37; J. Harris and G. Higgott, *Inigo Jones, Complete Architectural Drawings* (London, 1989), pp. 251–3.

9 K. Sharpe, *The Personal Rule of Charles I* (Yale, 1992), pp. 769–97; K. Sharpe, *Image Wars. Promoting Kings and Commonwealths in England 1603–1660* (Yale, 2010), pp. 231–9.

10 *SH*, pp. 55–6; J. Harris and A. A. Tait, *Catalogue of Drawings by Inigo Jones, John Webb and Isaac de Caus at Worcester College Oxford* (Oxford, 1979), pp. 18–19; J. Harris, *Catalogue of the R.I.B.A. Drawings Collection: Jones & Webb* (London, 1972), p. 16, cat. 50; G. Worsley, *Inigo Jones* (Yale, 1997), pp. 84–6, 113–14.

11 The key texts for the Whitehall schemes are: J. A. Gotch, *Architectural Review*, June 1912, pp. 1–32, and M. Whinney, 'John Webb's Drawings for Whitehall Palace', *Walpole Society*, xxxi (1942–3), pp. 45–107. Like every scholar since 1943 I accept Whinney's grouping of the drawings. Also see J. Bold, *John Webb, Architectural Theory and Practice in the Seventeenth Century* (Oxford, 1989), pp. 107–25 and J. Summerson, *Inigo Jones* (Yale, 2000), pp. 123–31.

12 The scheme can be dated to 1638–9 by the testimony of William Emmet, (C. Campbell, *Vitruvius Britannicus*, ii (1717), p. 1, pls 1–5) and of Richard Daye (HMC, *Cowper*, ii, p. 186). The scope of the scheme is described in

W. Sanderson, *Compleat History of the Life and Raigne of King Charles* (London, 1658), p. 311.

13 R. Strong, 'Britannia Triumphans. Inigo Jones, Rubens and the Whitehall Banqueting House', R. Strong, *The Tudor and Stuart Monarchy III, Jacobean and Caroline* (Woodbridge, 1998), pp. 150–4; V. Hart, *Art and Magic in the Court of the Stuarts* (London, 1994), pp. 105–16; H. Kamen, *The Escorial. Art and Power in the Renaissance* (Yale, 2010), pp. 94–8.

14 The drawings are Chatsworth House 71 (Whinney P1), 72 (Whinney P12), 73 (Whinney P4).

15 TNA WO49/60 f. 16v; WO47/70 f. 7r; TNA SP16/323 pp. 33–4; E351/3271, 3272; *Cal. SP. Dom. 1639*, p. 380. I owe these references to Anna Keay.

16 N. A. M. Roger, *The Safeguard of the Sea. A Naval History of Britain: I 1660–1649* (London, 1997), pp. 379–91; G. Callender, *The Portrait of Peter Pett and the Sovereign of the Seas* (Newport, Isle of Wight, 1930).

17 T. Heywood, A *true discription of his Majesties royall and most stately ship called the Soveraign of the Seas, built at Wolwitch in Kent 1637* (London, 1638); G. Callender, *The Portrait of Peter Pett and the Sovereign of the Seas* (Newport, 1930); A. Griffiths, *The Stuart Print in Britain 1603–1689* (British Museum, 1998), pp. 102–3.

18 The reference is TNA SP84/ 142.196 80–81 & 34 but I have not been able to check this.

19 E. Walker, *Historical discourses, upon several occasions* . . . (London, 1705), p. 282.

20 G. Worsley, 'Chiswick House: Palladian Paradigm or Symbol of Sovereignty?', *English Heritage Historical Review*, vi (2011), pp. 115–33; G. Worsley, *Inigo Jones and the European Classical Tradition* (Yale, 2007), pp. 123–74.

CHAPTER 10: GOD AND MY RIGHT

1 J. J. Jusserand, *A French Ambassador at the Court of Charles II* (London, 1892), pp. 115–16.

2 S. Thurley, '"The example of princes": The practice and performance of religion at the Tudor court', K. De Jonghe (ed.), forthcoming.

3 J. P. Sommerville (ed.), *James VI and I: Political Writings* (London, 1994), p. 161.

4 C. Rogers, *History of the Chapel Royal of Scotland* (Edinburgh, 1882), pp. lxxv–vi, lxxxi, xcv–civ; H. Paton, *Accounts of the Masters of Works*, i (Edinburgh, 1957), p. 312; A. L. Juhala, 'The Household and Court of King

James VI of Scotland, 1567–1603' (unpublished PhD thesis, University of Edinburgh, 2000), pp. 317, 327.

5 TNA E351/3239; HMC 11th Report appx pt. 7, p. 148; R. Ashton, *James I by his Contemporaries* (London, 1969), p. 10; *Cal. SP. Ven., 1603–7*, no. 739.

6 *CL*, ii, p. 489; *SLD*, i, p. 226.

7 J. P. Hore, *The History of Newmarket and the Annals of the Turf* (London, 1886), pp. 165, 209, 226, 251; *CL*, i, p. 195; TNA E351/3256.

8 *CL*, ii, pp. 42, 63, 82; *KJP*, iii, pp. 307–16, 336; J. Imrie and J. Dunbar, *Accounts of the Masters of Works*, ii (Edinburgh, 1982), pp. lxxxvi–vii, 441–3; W. L. Spiers, 'The Note Book and Account Book of Nicholas Stone', *Walpole Society*, vii (1918–19), pp. 43–4, 137; D. Calderwood, *The True History of the Church of Scotland* (Edinburgh, 1678), pp. 673–5.

9 C. Rogers, *History of the Chapel Royal of Scotland* (Edinburgh, 1882), pp. cxx–cxxv; *KJP*, iii, p. 340.

10 A. Milton, '"That Sacred Oratory": Religion and the Chapel Royal during the Personal Rule of Charles I', A. Ashbee (ed.), *William Lawes 1602–1645: Essays on his Life, Time and Works* (Ashgate, 1998), pp. 69–96; K. Sharpe, *The Personal Rule of Charles I* (Yale, 1992), pp. 284–92; A. Foster, 'Church Policies of the 1630s', *Conflict in Early Stuart England. Studies in Religion and Politics 1603–1642* (London, 1989), pp. 193–223.

11 J. Bickersteth, *Clerks of the Closet in the Royal Household* (Stroud, 1991), pp. 19–21.

12 TNA E351/3255; E351/3268; E351/3270; TNA E351/3240, E351/3257, E351/3258; BL Add. MS 34,324 ff. 215r–216r; *CL*, ii, p. 470.

13 A. J. Loomie, *Spain and the Jacobean Catholics*, ii (Catholic Record Society, 1978), pp. 185–6; D. Sánchez Cano, 'Entertainments in Madrid for the Prince of Wales: Political Functions of Festivals', A. Samson (ed.), *The Spanish Match. Prince Charles's Journey to Madrid, 1623* (Aldershot, 2006), pp. 65–73; G. Redworth, *The Prince and the Infanta* (Yale, 2003), pp. 88–95; J. Davies, *The Caroline Captivity of the Church: Charles I and the Remoulding of Anglicanism 1625–1641* (Oxford, 1992), p. 20.

14 Sharpe, *Charles I*, pp. 280–4; C. Wren, *Parwentalia or Memoirs of the Family of the Wrens* (London, 1750), pp. 46–7; M. Fuller, *The Life of Bishop Davenant 1572–1641* (London, 1897), p. 305; J. Bliss and W. Scott (eds), *The Works of William Laud*, iii (Oxford, 1847–60), p. 197; *Cal. SP. Ven., 1636–7*, p. 125.

15 W. Prynne, *Canterburies Doome* (London, 1646); G. Parry, *Glory Laud and Honour. The Arts of the Anglican Counter-Reformation* (Woodbridge, 2006), pp. 43–6.

16 C. Wren, *Parentalia or Memoirs of the Family of the Wrens* (London, 1750), pp. 15–16.

17 C. Rogers, *History of the Chapel Royal of Scotland* (Edinburgh, 1882), pp. clviii, clxiv–vi.

18 *Register of the Privy Council*, iv, pp. 488–9 and v, pp. 136–7; J. Row, *The History of the Kirk of Scotland, from the Year 1558 to August 1637* (Edinburgh, 1842), pp. 355–6; W. Maitland, *The History of Edinburgh from its Foundation to the Present Time* (Edinburgh, 1753), p. 281; W. Stirling, *Register of Royal Letters Relative to the affairs of Scotland & Nova Scotia from 1615 to 1635* (Edinburgh, 1885), p. 611.

19 A. Spicer, 'Laudianism in Scotland? St Giles' Cathedral, Edinburgh 1633–39 – A Reappraisal', *Architectural History*, xlvi (2003), pp. 95–106.

20 A. MacKechnie, 'The Crisis of Kingship: 1603–1707', M. Glendinning (ed.), *The Architecture of Scottish Government. From Kingship to Parliamentary Democracy* (Dundee, 2004), pp. 82–133; R. Hannay and G. Watson, 'The Building of the Parliament House', *The Book of the Old Edinburgh Club*, xiii (1924), pp. 17–78. My plan is based on those in MacKechnie's chapter, 'The Crisis of Kingship'.

21 D. Shaw, 'St Giles' Church and Charles I's Coronation visit to Scotland', *Historical Research*, 77.198 (2004), pp. 481–502; D. Laing, 'On the state of the Abbey Church of Holyrood subsequently to the devastations committed by the English Forces in the years 1544 and 1547', *Proceedings of the Society of Antiquaries of Scotland*, i (1851–4), pp. 111–15; J. Imrie and J. Dunbar (eds), *Accounts of the Masters of Works*, ii (Edinburgh, 1982), pp. lxxxix, 308–37.

22 J. Spalding, *The History of the Troubles and Memorable Transactions in Scotland from the year 1624 to 1645* (Aberdeen, 1792), p. 23; 'The Coronation of King Charles the first King of Scotland at Holyrood House 18 June 1633', *College of Arms*, MS. I, 7 fo. 78.

23 D. Shaw, 'St Giles' Church and Charles I's Coronation visit to Scotland', *Historical Research*, 77.198 (2004), pp. 497–9; A. Spicer, 'Laudianism in Scotland? St Giles' Cathedral, Edinburgh 1633–39 – A Reappraisal', *Architectural History*, xlvi (2003), pp. 95–106.

24 G. Ewart and D. Gallagher, *With Thy High Towers. The Archaeology of Stirling Castle and Palace* (Historic Scotland, Archaeology Report no. 9, 2015), pp. 150–3; Imrie and Dunbar, *Accounts*, pp. xcii–xciii, 255–7. There is no documentary evidence for this screen. If it was a reredos the paintings of Solomon's temple may have been a later addition to decontaminate its popish

overtones. For Counter-Reformation reredoses see for instance J. Barbe, *Livre d'architecture d'autels, et de cheminées* . . . (Paris, 1633).

25 S. Thurley, 'The Politics of Court Space in Early Stuart London', G. Gorse and M. Smuts (eds), *The Politics of Court Space in Europe and the Mediterranean, ca. 1500–1750* (Rome, 2009), pp. 293–316.

26 J. Vicars, *Magnalia Dei Anglicana, or, Englands Parliamentary – Chronicle. Containing a full and faithfull Series, and Exact Narration of all the most memorable Parliamentary-Mercies, and mighty (if not miraculous) Deliverances* . . ., (London, 1646); H. Van der Pill, *Magna Britannia Divisa or Great Britain Divided 1642* (Amsterdam, 31 December 1642). BM Prints and Drawings 1868-8-8-3355 (4 parts); *Catalogue of the Prints and Drawings in the British Museum*. Division I, Satirical and Personal Subjects (1-1235) (British Museum, 1870), pp. 96–102.

27 K. Lindley, *Popular Politics and Religion in Civil War London* (Aldershot, 1997), pp. 78–9.

28 W. R. Trimble, 'The Embassy Chapel Question 1625-1660', *Journal of Modern History*, xviii (1946), pp. 100–1; B. Manning, *The English People and the English Revolution 1640–1649* (London, 1976), pp. 1–22; K. Lindley, 'London and Popular Freedom', R. C. Richardson and G. M. Ridden (eds.), *Freedom and the English Revolution: Essays in History and Literature* (Manchester, 1988), pp. 118–21; K. Lindley, *Popular Politics and Religion in Civil War London* (Aldershot, 1997), pp. 74–9.

29 I. W. Archer, 'Popular politics in the 16th and early 17th centuries', P. Griffiths and M. S. R. Jenner (eds), *Londonopolis. Essays in the Cultural and Social History of Early Modern London* (Manchester, 2000), pp. 29–30, 37; Lindley, *Popular Politics*, pp. 74–9.

30 BL. Add. MS 31,116 pp. 64, 76; *The Kingdomes Weekly Intelligencer* (4 April 1643).

31 T. Birch (ed.), *The Court and Times of Charles I,* ii, pp. 352, 429; J. Vicars, *JEHOVAH-JIREH. GOD IN THE MOVNT, or, Englands Parliamentarie-Chronicle*, p. 294; A. Loomie, 'The Destruction of Rubens's "Crucifixion" in the Queen's Chapel, Somerset House', *Burlington Magazine*, cxl (October 1998), pp. 680–2.

32 *Journals of the House of Commons 1642-4*, iii (London, 1802), pp. 57, 63; C. H. Firth and R. R. Rait (eds), *Acts and Ordinances of the Interregnum 1642–60* (London, 1911), pp. 265–6; Lindley, *Popular Politics*, pp. 256–60.

33 *Journals of the House of Lords 1642–3*, v (London, 1767–1830), p. 215a [13 September 1643]; B. Manning, 'The English People and the English

Revolution', p. 58 ff.; *Journals of the House of Commons 1642–4*, iii (London, 1802), p. 260; *HKW*, iii, pp. 161–3.

34 *Journals of the House of Commons 1642–4*, iii (London, 1802), pp. 422, 425.

35 *ibid.*, pp. 410–63; HMC, *Portland*, iii (1894), p. 132; *Journals of the House of Commons 1646–8*, v (London, 1808), p. 77.

36 HMC, *Portland*, iii (1894), p. 133.

37 S. Thurley, 'The Stuart Kings, Oliver Cromwell and the Chapel Royal 1618–1685', *Architectural History*, xlv (2002), pp. 248–50.

CHAPTER 11: CIVIL WAR

1 *Cal. SP. Dom.*, *1641–3*, pp. 252, 254, 262, 281.

2 *The Kings Majesties Speech, As It was delivered the second of November before the university and City of Oxford. Together With a gratulatory Replication expressed by that learned Man Doctor William Strode, Orator for the famous university of Oxford* (1642), p. 6.

3 *Statutes of the Colleges of Oxford : with royal Patents of Foundation, Injunctions of Visitors, and Catalogues of Documents relating to The University, preserved in the Public Record Office*, ii (London, 1853), p. 104.

4 A. J. Taylor, 'The Royal Visit to Oxford in 1636', *Oxonensia*, i (1936), pp. 151–8; H. Colvin, *The Canterbury Quadrangle, St John's College, Oxford* (Oxford, 1988).

5 M. Batey and C. Cole, 'The Great Staircase Tower at Christ Church', J. Blair (ed.), *St Frideswide's Monastery at Oxford* (Gloucester, 1990), pp. 212–20.

6 J. F. Larkin, *Stuart Royal Proclamations*, ii (Oxford, 1983), pp. 849–51, 949, 953; J. de Groot, 'Space Patronage, Procedure: The Court at Oxford 1642–46', *English Historical Review*, cxvii (2002), pp. 1208–10; F. Madden, *Oxford Books*, ii (Oxford, 1912), no. 1192, 1514.

7 Larkin, *Proclamations*, p. 902; *The Memoirs of Anne, Lady Fanshawe* (London, 1907), pp. 24–5.

8 My plan is based on a modern measured survey and my own observations. I am very grateful to The Very Reverend Professor Martyn Percy for access to his lodgings. Dean Goodwin's will of 1621 lists the rooms: Oxford University Archives Hyp/B/13 ff. 35–6, I am most grateful to Judith Curthoys for providing me with a copy of this document; J. Curthoys, *The Stones of Christ Church. The Story of the Buildings of Christ Church, Oxford* (London, 2017), pp. 36, 234, no. 82. The 1733 plan which helps fill in details is illustrated on p. 146. The king took the Spanish ambassador aside to a window

in the presence chamber; J. de Groot, 'Space Patronage, Procedure: The Court at Oxford 1642–46', *English Historical Review*, cxvii (2002), p. 1220.

9 The orders were agreed at the Council of War (Add. MS 125750 ff. 16–17) and promulgated and published the same day (Harleian MS 6851 ff. 117 r–v); *Mercurius Aulicus* (26 January 1642).

10 J. Curthoys, *The Stones of Christ Church. The Story of the Buildings of Christ Church, Oxford* (London, 2017), p. 12; I. Roy and D. Reinhardt, 'Oxford and the Civil Wars', N. Tyacke (ed.), *The History of the University of Oxford*, iv (1997), p. 703; A. Clark (ed.), 'The Life and Times of Anthony Wood, Antiquary, of Oxford, 1632-1695', *Oxford Historical Society* (1891–1900), p. 98; W. Hamper (ed.), *The Life, Diary, and Correspondence of Sir William Dugdale* (London, 1827), p. 53; HMC, 5th Report, pp. 61, 76, 77.

11 J. Bliss and W. Scott (eds), *The Works of Archbishop Laud*, v (Oxford, 1853), p. 145; J. Gutch (ed.), *The History and Antiquities of the University of Oxford by Anthony à Wood*, ii (Oxford, 1792–6), pp. 367, 407–13; H. Martin and J. Highfield, *A History of Merton College Oxford* (Oxford, 1997), pp. 204–5; A. Clark (ed.), 'The Life and Times of Anthony Wood, Antiquary, of Oxford, 1632–1695', *Oxford Historical Society* (1891–1900), p. 91; Corpus Christi Archives C/1/1/10 f. 21r–v; *CL*, i, p. 376; T. C. Edwards and J. Reid, *Corpus Christi College, Oxford* (Oxford, 2017), pp. 178–9.

12 J. Catto (ed.), *Oriel College, A History* (Oxford, 2013), p. 129: Clark (ed.), *Anthony Wood*, p. 96.

13 J. Frank, *The Beginnings of the English Newspaper 1620-1660* (Cambridge, MA, 1961), pp. 33–5.

14 J. Barratt, *Cavalier Capital. Oxford in the English Civil War 1642-1646* (Solihull, 2016), pp. 74–9; A. Saunders, *Fortress Builder. Bernard de Gomme, Charles II's Military Engineer* (Exeter, 2004), pp. 70–3, 79; I. Roy, 'The City of Oxford 1640–1660', R.C. Richardson (ed.), *Town and Countryside in the English Revolution* (Manchester, 1992), pp. 144–53; I Roy, 'Royalist Ordnance Papers', *Oxfordshire Record Society*, xliii (1964), pp. 25–8.

15 M. Toynbee, *Strangers in Oxford. A Side Light on the First Civil War 1642–1646* (Chichester, 1973), pp. 6–43; I. Roy and D. Reinhardt, 'Oxford and the Civil Wars', N. Tyacke (ed.), *The History of the University of Oxford*, iv (1997), pp. 703–5.

16 J. Curthoys, *The Cardinal's College. Christ Church, Chapter and Verse* (London, 2012), p. 106.

17 W. Hamper (ed.), *The Life, Diary, and Correspondence of Sir William Dugdale* (London, 1827), p. 59.

18 J. Gutch (ed.), *The History and Antiquities of the University of Oxford by Anthony à Wood*, i (Oxford, 1792–6), p. 103; *Mercurius Aulicus*, 14 & 23 July 1643; I. G. Philip, 'Journal of Sir Samuel Luke: Scoutmaster General to the Earl of Essex, 1643–4', *Oxfordshire Record Society* (1950–53), p. 260.

19 *The Diary of Sir Henry Slingsby* (London, 1836), p. 140; *CHR*, iii, pp. 195–6; F. Madden, *Oxford Books*, ii (Oxford, 1912), p. 318.

20 *ibid.*, no. 1372; *Mercurius Aulicus*, 8 April 1643; J. Aubrey, *Brief Lives* (Harmondsworth, 1972), p. 23; HMC, *Ormond*, ii, pp. 406–10; *Mercurius Aulicus*, 9 August 1644; W. Hamper (ed.), *The Life, Diary, and Correspondence of Sir William Dugdale* (London, 1827), p. 77.

21 I. G. Philip, 'Journal of Sir Samuel Luke: Scoutmaster General to the Earl of Essex, 1643–4', *Oxfordshire Record Society* (1950–53), pp. 173–4; F. J. Varley, *The Siege of Oxford* (Oxford, 1932), pp. 61–2; W. Hamper (ed.), *The Life, Diary, and Correspondence of Sir William Dugdale* (London, 1827), pp. 59, 60–1, 67.

22 R. Spalding (ed.), *The Diary of Bulstrode Whitelocke 1605–1675* (London, 1990), pp. 141–4, 158–9; *CHR*, iii, p. 293; Varley, *Siege*, pp. 47–51; Madden, *Oxford*, p. 311.

23 J. Curthoys, *The King's Cathedral. The Ancient Heart of Christ Church, Oxford* (London, 2019), pp. 105–7.

24 D. Pinto, 'The True Christmas: Carols at the Court of Charles I', A. Ashbee (ed.), *William Lawes (1603–1645), Essays on his Life, Times and Work* (Aldershot, 1998), pp. 97–115; Madden, *Oxford*, no. 1552.

25 A. Bachrach and R. Collmer (trans and eds), *Lodewijck Huygens the English Journal 1651–2* (Leiden, 1982), p. 81; *Journals of the House of Lords 1642–3*, v (London 1767–1830), pp. 559, 641, vi, p. 235; *Journals of the House of Commons 1662*, iii (London, 1802).

26 Madden, *Oxford*, p. 274; *Cal. SP. Dom., 1641–3*, p. 422; *Mercurius Aulicus*, 3 June 1644; I. G. Philip, 'Journal of Sir Samuel Luke : Scoutmaster General to the Earl of Essex, 1643–4', *Oxfordshire Record Society* (1950–53), p. 222; HMC, 5th Report, appendix pp. 2, 3, 113.

27 J. P. Wainwright, 'Images of Virtue and War: Music in Civil War Oxford', A. Ashbee (ed.), *William Lawes (1603–1645), Essays on his Life, Times and Work* (Aldershot, 1998), pp. 121–42; L. Hotson, *The Commonwealth and Restoration Stage* (New York, 1962), pp. 8–10, 19, 22.

28 J. F. Larkin, *Stuart Royal Proclamations*, ii (Oxford, 1983), pp. 992–3; *CHR*, iii, pp. 524–5; E. Besly, *Coins and Medals of the English Civil War* (London, 1990), p. 42.

29 J. S. Clarke, *The Life of James the Second*, i (London, 1816), p. 29.

30 *Journals of the House of Lords 1645-6*, vii (London, 1767–1830), p. 426; *Journals of the House of Commons 1644–6*, iv (London, 1802), p. 597.

31 *HCP*, pp. 121–3.

32 *HKW*, iv, pp. 531–2; W. H. Long (ed.), *The Oglander Memoirs: Extracts from the MSS of Sir John Oglander* (London, 1888), p. 122; P. Stone, *The architectural antiquities of the Isle of Wight from the XIth to the XVIIth centuries* (London, 1891), plate cxvi. My plan is based on TNA MPF1/140, a survey of the lodgings by Richard Popinjay, E351/3566 the building accounts and the plan in Stone's *Antiquities* (plate cxvi).

33 J. D. Jones, *The Royal Prisoner. Charles I at Carisbrooke* (London, 1965), pp. 45–6; W. H. Long (ed.), *The Oglander Memoirs: Extracts from the MSS of Sir John Oglander* (London, 1888), p. 68.

34 BL, Harl. MS 4898, pp. 590–6.

35 *Journals of the House of Commons 1644–6*, v (London, 1802), p. 452.

36 D. Underdown, *Pride's Purge. Politics in the Puritan Revolution* (London, 1985), pp. 106–42; R. Cust, *Charles I, A Political Life* (London, 2005), pp. 441–8.

37 M. Whinney, 'John Webb's Drawings for Whitehall Palace', *Walpole Society*, xxxi (1942–3), pp. 45–107; J. Bold, *John Webb* (Oxford, 1989), pp. 118–21.

38 S. Thurley, *The Royal Palaces of Tudor England* (Yale, 1993), pp. 125–7.

39 E. Walker, *Historical Collections of Several Important Transactions Relating to the Late Rebellion and Civil Wars of England: . . . Written by the Special Command of K. Charles I. Part Whereof was Corrected by His Majesty's Own Hand* (London, 1705); F. Peck (ed.), *Desiderata Curiosa*, ii (London, 1779), pp. 387–410; King Charles I and E. Gauden, *Eikon Basilike. The Portraiture of his Sacred Majesty in his solitudes and sufferings* (London, 1648), p. 247; S. Kelsey, 'The kings' book : Eikon Basilike and the English Revolution of 1649', N. Tyacke (ed.), *The English Revolution c.1590–1720: politics, religion and communities* (Manchester, 2007), p. 152; P. Warwick, *Memoirs of the Reign of King Charles the First by Sir Philip Warwick* (London, 1702), p. 363: *Journals of the House of Commons 1644–6*, v (London, 1802), p. 436; BL, Add. MS 6988 f. 216.

CHAPTER 12: REPUBLICAN RESIDENCES

1 R. Lockyer (ed.), *The Trial of Charles I* (London, 1974), pp. 31–65; C. H. Firth (ed.), 'The Clarke Papers', *Camden Society*, ii (1894), pp. 140–7; R. Tighe and J. Davis, *Annals of Windsor*, ii (London, 1858), pp. 209–31;

S. Brindle (ed.), *Windsor Castle. A Thousand years of a Royal Palace* (London, 2018), pp. 204–10.

2 G. Stevenson, *Charles I in Captivity* (London, 1927), pp. 171–85.

3 J. Nalson, *A True copy of the journal of the High Court of Justice for the tryal of K. Charles I as it was read in the House of Commons and attested under the hand of Phelps, clerk to that infamous court* (London, 1684), pp. 11, 14–15, 18–20; J. Muddiman, *The Trial of King Charles the First* (London, 1928), pp. 75–6.

4 T. Herbert, *Memoirs of the Last Years of the Reign of King Charles I* (London, 1813), pp. 173–95; *CHR*, iv, p. 483; B. Whitelocke, *Memorial of English Affairs from the Beginning of the Reign of Charles the First to the Happy Restoration of King Charles II*, ii (Oxford, 1853), pp. 511–16, 522.

5 *Journals of the House of Lords 1643*, vi (London, 1767–1830), pp. 181, 415; Bod. Lib., *Clarendon MSS* 30 f. 273v; *Mercurius Pragmaticus*, 5–12 December 1648; *Journals of the House of Commons 1644*, iii (London, 1802), [16 Sept 1643], [28 Feb 1644]; *Journals of the House of Lords 1643*, vi (London, 1767–1830), [7 Feb 1644].

6 S. Kelsey, *Inventing a Republic. The Political Culture of the English Commonwealth* (Manchester, 1997), pp. 29–30.

7 PRO SP18/15, no. 15; *Cal. SP. Dom., 1649-50*, pp. 57, 155, 281; *Cal. SP. Dom., 1651-2*, pp. 92, 304; *Cal. SP. Dom., 1656-7*, p. 86; Also see L. Huygens, A. G. H. Bachrach and R. G. Collmer (trans and eds), *The English Journal 1651-2* (Leiden, 1982), pp. 42–3.

8 G. Aylmer, *The State's Servant. The Civil Service of the English Republic 1649–60* (London, 1973), pp. 17–22; *Journals of the House of Commons 1646-8*, v (London, 1802), p. 440; PRO AO1/2431/79; *Cal. SP. Dom.*, iii, p. 401.

9 *ibid.*, pp. 373, 412, 414, 447; *Cal. SP. Dom., 1651–1652*, p. 9; PRO SP25/63 331.

10 Huygens, *English Journal*, pp. 42–3; *Cal. SP. Dom., Commonwealth 1651*, xv, p. 280; S. R. Gardiner, *History of the Commonwealth and Protectorate*, ii (Moreton-in-Marsh, 1987), p. 95.

11 *Cal. SP. Dom., Interregnum 1649–50*, p. 285; *Cal. SP. Dom., Interregnum 1650*, p. 418.

12 O. Fleming, 'The Humble Narrative of Oliver Fleming, Knight shewing the manner how I came to execute the Office of Master of the Ceremonies, with my Comportment and Sufferings therein for the space of near 18 Years', W. Scott, *A collection of scarce and valuable tracts, on the most interesting and entertaining subjects . . .*, vii (London, 1812), pp. 501–2; S. Kelsey, *Inventing a Republic. The Political Culture of the English Commonwealth* (Manchester,

1997), pp. 58–64; D. Crankshaw, 'Community, City and Nation', D. Keene, A. Burns and A. Saint (eds), *St Paul's. The Cathedral Church of London 604–2004* (Yale, 2004), pp. 62–4.

13 J. Merritt, *Westminster 1640–1660. A Royal City in a Time of Revolution* (Manchester, 2013), pp. 99–106.

14 *Cal. SP. Dom., 1649–50*, p. 155; *Journals of the House of Commons*, vi (London, 1802), p. 246; S. J. Madge, *The Domesday of Crown Lands, A Study of the Legislation, Surveys, and Sales of the Royal Estates under the Commonwealth* (London, 1938) pp. 102–3.

15 *Cal. SP. Ven., 1655–6*, p. 308; Merritt, *Westminster*, p. 74; Huygens, *English Journal*, pp. 42–3.

16 M. Jansson, 'Remembering Marston Moor: The Politics of Culture', S. Amussen and M. Kishlansky (eds), *Political culture and cultural politics in early modern England: essays presented to David Underdown* (Manchester, 1995), pp. 255–70; W. Thompson, *Tapestry Weaving in England* (London, 1914), pp. 92–6; K. Thomas, 'English Protestantism and Classical Art', L. Gent (ed.), *Albion's Classicism: The Visual Arts in Britain 1550–1660* (Yale, 1995), pp. 221–33; L. Knoppers, *Constructing Cromwell. Ceremony, Portrait and Print 1645–61* (Cambridge, 2000), pp. 88–92.

17 *Cal. SP. Ven., 1657–59*, pp. 8–9.

18 *The Weekly Intelligencer of the Commonwealth*, no. 223, p. 179; *Several Proceedings of State Affairs*, ccxxxviii [13–20 April 1654]; E. Ludlow, E. Firth (ed.), *The memoirs of Edmund Ludlow*, i (Oxford, 1894), p. 379; *Cal. SP. Dom., 1655*, p. 160; *Cal. SP. Dom., 1654*, p. 394; *The Court and Kitchen of Elizabeth, Commonly Called Joan Cromwell the wife of the late usurper* (London, 1664), p. 25; Ludlow, *Memoirs*, i, p. 379.

19 M. Stace, *Cromwelliana: A chronological detail of events in which Oliver Cromwell was engaged; from the year 1642 to his death 1658* (London, 1910), p. 137; E. S. de Beer (ed.), *The Diary of John Evelyn*, iii (Oxford, 1955), p. 166.

20 P. Hunneyball, 'Cromwellian Style: The Architectural Trappings of the Protectoral Regime', P. Little (ed.), *The Cromwellian Protectorate* (Woodbridge, 2007), pp. 66–7; Stace, *Cromwelliana*, pp. 132, 136; *Several Proceedings of State Affairs*, ccxxxix [20–27 April 1654].

21 *The faithful narrative of the Late Testimony and Demand made to Oliver Cromwell and his Powers* . . . (London, 1655); R. Coke, *A Detection of the Court and State of England During the Last Four Reigns*, iii (London, 1694), p. 58.

22 *Several Proceedings of State Affairs,* p. 3676; *Cal SP. Ven., 1557–9,* p. 106; M. Roberts (trans. and ed.), *Swedish Diplomats at Cromwell's Court* (London, 1988), p. 125; *The Court and Kitchen of Joan Cromwell,* pp. 44–5; *Cal. SP. Ven., 1657–9,* pp. 20–1; *Mercurius Politicus,* cccl, p. 7615.

23 P. Little, 'Music at the Court of King Oliver', *The Court Historian,* xii (2007), pp. 177–80; HMC, 5th Report p. 166. A. Keay, *Interregnum, People's Republic of Britain* (2022, forthcoming).

24 *Cal. SP. Ven., 1653–4,* xxix, no. 109; *Cal. SP. Ven., 1655–6,* xxx, no. 144; *Mercurius Politicus,* cccxlviii, p. 7588 [5–12 February 1657].

25 *Cal. SP. Dom., 1654,* p. 46; *The Protector, so called. In Part Unvailed: By whom the Mystery of Iniquity is now Working* (London, 1655), p. 10; *Cromwelliana,* pp. 132, 141–2.

26 *Cal. SP. Ven., 1655–6,* xxx, p. 109; J. C. Davis, 'Cromwell's Religion', J. Morrill (ed.), *Oliver Cromwell and the English Revolution* (London, 1990), pp. 181–208.

27 *Cromwelliana,* p. 133; *Cal. SP. Dom., 1660,* p. 392; *The Weekly Intelligencer of the Commonwealth,* ccxxxiii, [14–21 March 1654].

28 *HKW,* iii, pp. 165–8.

29 Huygens, *English Journal,* p. 134; *HCP,* pp. 124–5; P. Hunneyball, 'Cromwellian Style: The Architectural Trappings of the Protectoral Regime', P. Little (ed.), *The Cromwellian Protectorate* (Woodbridge, 2007), pp. 53–74.

30 PRO SP18/203, no. 41. My first floor reconstructed plan is based on material publisher in HCP.

31 M. Roberts, 'Swedish Diplomats at Cromwell's Court, 1655-1656, the Missions of Peter Julius Coyet and Christer Bonde', *Camden Society,* 4th ser., xxxvi, (1988), pp. 119–29, and see also 320–1.

32 Ludlow, *Memoirs,* ii, p. 69; *Cal. SP. Dom., Commonwealth 1660,* p. 577; *Cal. SP. Ven., 1659–61,* pp. 121, 148; *Cal. SP. Dom., 1659–60,* p. 595; R. Hutton, G. Monck, *First Duke of Albemarle, ODNB.*

CHAPTER 13: THE COURT IN EXILE

1 *HKW,* iv, pp. 452–3; J. Stevens, *Old Jersey Houses* (Jersey, 1965), p. 143; A. Keay, *The Magnificent Monarch, Charles II and the Ceremonies of Power* (London, 2008), pp. 42–3; J. Messervy (ed.), *Journal de Jean Chevalier,* i (St Helier, 1906), pp. 299–30, 305, 317; N. V. L. Rybot, *The Islet of St. Helier and Elizabeth Castle* (Société Jersiaise, 1986), pp. 58–69. I am extremely grateful to Dr Warwick Rodwell for sharing with me his unpublished report on the governor's house. My plan is based on his survey.

2 R. Hutton, *Charles the Second King of England, Scotland, and Ireland* (Oxford, 1989), pp. 15–19, 42–5; J. Messervy (ed.), *Journal de Jean Chevalier* (St Helier, 1906), pp. 708–13, 717–18, 722, 742, 745, 760.

3 H. Ballon, *The Paris of Henri IV. Architecture and Urbanism* (Cambridge, MA, 1991).

4 *Journal d'Olivier Lefèvre d'Ormesson, et extraits des Mémoires d'André Lefèvre d'Ormesson*, i (Paris, 1860), pp. 225–7.

5 HMC, *Beaufort*, pp. 16–17; E. Griffey, *On Display. Henrietta Maria and the Materials of Magnificence at the Stuart Court* (Yale, 2015), p. 168; *Journal d'Olivier Lefèvre*, i, pp. 224–7; N. Sainctot, 'Mémoires de Sainctot' in A. Duffo (ed.), *Henriette-Marie de France, Reine d'Angleterre* (Paris, 1935), pp. 20–2. Also see N. Reynolds, 'The Stuart Court and Courtiers in Exile 1644–1654' (unpublished PhD dissertation, Cambridge, 1996), pp. 26–8. My plan is based on Jacques Androuet du Cerceau, *Les Plus Excellents Bâtiments de France*, 1576, and a plan of *c.*1603 by an unknown hand in the Biblioteque National de France (Est. rés. Ve 53i, sometimes known as Destailleur 148).

6 G. Hart Seely (trans.), *Memoirs of La Grande Mademoiselle Duchesse de Montpensier* (London, 1928), pp. 52–3; More generally see: K. Britland, 'Exile or Homecoming? Henrietta Maria in France, 1644–1669', P. Mansel and T. Riotte (eds), *Monarchy and Exile: The Politics of Legitimacy from Marie de Médicis to Wilhelm II* (London, 2011), pp. 120–43.

7 *Cal. SP. Ven., 1643–7*, pp. 266, 270, 272, 275; *Memoirs of Mademoiselle de Montpensier, grand-daughter of Henri Quatre, and niece of Queen Henrietta-Maria. Written by herself*, i (London, 1848), p. 93; *CHR*, iv, pp. 206–7.

8 *Cal. SP. Ven., 1643–7*, no. 397.

9 L. Hotson, *The Commonwealth and Restoration Stage* (New York, 1962), pp. 22–3; K. Britland, '"Tyred in her banished dress": Henrietta Maria in exile', *Early Modern Literary Studies*, Special Issue xv (August 2007), pp. 1–39; G. Hart Seely (trans.), *Memoirs of La Grande Mademoiselle Duchesse de Montpensier* (London, 1928), p. 58; *Memoirs of Mademoiselle de Montpensier written by herself*, i (London, 1848), p. 101; M. Sainte-Beuve (ed.), *Mémoires de Madame de Motteville sur Anne D'Autriche et sa Cour*, i (Paris, 1855), pp. 314, 389; K. Wormeley (trans.), *Memoirs of Madame de Motteville on Anne of Austria and her Court. With an introduction by C. A. Sainte-Beuve* (London, 1902), pp. 174–5, 211–12; K. Britland, *Drama at the Courts of Queen Henrietta Maria* (Cambridge, 2006), pp. 208–9.

10 H. Ballon, *The Paris of Henri IV. Architecture and Urbanism* (Cambridge, MA, 1991), pp. 15–56.

11 G. Groen van Prinsterer, *Archives ou correspondance inédite de la maison d'Orange-Nassau*, 2nd series, iv (Utrecht, 1857–61) pp. 265–9.

12 K. van Strien (ed.), *Touring the Low Countries: Accounts of British Travellers, 1660–1720* (Leiden, 1993), p. 191; K. Ottenheym, 'Possessed by Such a Passion for Building, Fredrick Hendrick and Architecture', M. Keblusek and J. Zijlmans, *Princely Display. The Court of Frederick of Orange and Amalia van Solms* (The Hague, 1997), pp. 109–11; R. J. Van Pelt and M. E Tiethoff-Spliethoff, *Het Binnenhof* (Dieren, 1984) passim; W. Kuyper, *Dutch Classicist Architecture: A Survey of Dutch Architecture, Gardens and Anglo-Dutch Architectural Relations from 1625 to 1700* (Delft, 1980), pp. 66–8; T. Birch (ed.), *A Collection of the State Papers of John Thurloe*, i (London, 1742), p. 397; R. Hutton, *Charles II King of England, Scotland, and Ireland* (Oxford, 1990), pp. 27–33.

13 *Cal. SP. Ven., 1647–52*, no. 237; *CHR*, iv, pp. 372, v, pp. 49–50; *Cal. SP. Ven., 1647–52*, no. 305.

14 *Memoirs of Mademoiselle de Montpensier, grand-daughter of Henri Quatre, and niece of Queen Henrietta-Maria. Written by herself*, 3 vols (London, 1848), i, pp. 169–71.

15 TNA SP 78/113 ff. 16–18r; *CHR*, v, pp. 231–2, 243; *Memoirs of Mademoiselle de Montpensier written by herself*, ii, pp. 82, 84.

16 Bod. Lib., MSS *Clarendon*, iii, pp. 107–8; H. Ballon, 'The Architecture of Cardinal Richelieu', H. T. Goldfarb, *Richelieu, Art and Power* (Montreal, 2003), pp. 246–9; A. Gady, 'Le Palais-Royal sous la Régence d'Anne d'Autriche', I. de Conihout, *Mazarin, Les Lettres et Les Arts* (Bibilioteque Mazarine, 2006), pp. 113–20. My plan is based on J. Blondel, *Architecture Françoise*, 1754 III (Paris, 1904), p. 44.

17 T. Sauvel, 'L'Appartement de La Reine Au Palais Royal', *Bulletin de la Société de l'histoire de l'art Français 1951* (1952), pp. 65–79; 'Le Palais-Royal de la mort de Richelieu à l'incendie de 1763', *Bulletin Monumental*, cxx (1962), pp. 173–90.

18 S. Laveissière, 'Counsel and Courage: The Galerie des Hommes Illustres in the Palais Cardinal', H. T. Goldfarb, *Richelieu, Art and Power* (Montreal, 2003), pp. 64–71.

19 *Le Palais Royal* (Musée Carnavalet, 1988), pp. 17–19; D. Langeois, 'Évolution du décor intérieur entre 1600 et 1660', D. Acouffe et al., *Un Temps d'Exubérance. Les Arts Décoratifs sous Louis XIII et Anne d'Autriche* (Grand Palais, Paris, 2002), pp. 119–26.

20 T. Killigrew, *Comedies and Tragedies* (London, 1664), p. 343; P. de Villers

(ed.), *Journal d'un voyage à Paris en 1657–1658* (Paris, 1862), pp. 73, 116; E. Scott, *The King in Exile. The wanderings of Charles II from June 1646 to July 1654* (London, 1905), pp. 434–7; Bod. Lib., MSS *Clarendon*, ii, pp. 114, 220; *Clarendon*, 45 f. 503r; *Clarendon* 37 f. 193r.

21 M. Sainte-Beuve (ed.), *Mémoires de Madame de Motteville sur Anne D'Autriche et sa Cour*, i (Paris, 1855), p. 454; W. Bray (ed.), *The Diary of John Evelyn to which are added a selection from his familiar letters*, iv (London, 1906), p. 269; *Cal. SP. Ven., 1652–3*, p. 23; A. Keay, *The Magnificent Monarch, Charles II and the Ceremonies of Power* (London, 2008), pp. 76–7; *Clarendon*, ii, pp. 218, 220–1, iii, p. 202; K. Britland, *Drama at the Courts of Queen Henrietta Maria* (Cambridge, 2006), p. 209.

22 N. Reynolds, 'The Stuart Court and Courtiers in Exile 1644–1654' (unpublished PhD dissertation, Cambridge, 1996), pp. 97–8, 112–14; *Cal. SP. Ven., 1652–3*, p. 53; G. Warner (ed.), 'The Nicholas Papers', *Camden Society*, ii (1886–7), p. 14; Bod. Lib., MSS *Clarendon*, ii, p. 215.

23 *CHR*, v, p. 355; *Clarendon*, ii, p. 406.

24 Nicholas Papers, iii, p. 61; *Cal. SP. Ven., 1655–6*, p. 123; Dorset Record Office D/SF1 Fox Strangeways Archive box 268, household accounts 1654–5, pp. 49, 52, 62; box 268, kitchen accounts 1656–9, pp. 16, 45.

25 BL *Egerton* MS 2536. fol. 83; *CHR*, vi, p. 15; Nicholas Papers, iii, p. 278.

26 A. de Behault de Doron, *Bruges séjour d'exil d'Edouard IV et de Charles II rois d'Angleterre* (Bruxelles, 1931), pp. 155–215; Dorset Record Office D/FSI box 268, kitchen accounts 1656–9, pp. 80, 97, general accounts 1658–9, unpaginated; A. Keay, *The Magnificent Monarch, Charles II and the Ceremonies of Power* (London, 2008), pp. 51–3.

27 R. Hutton, *Charles the Second King of England, Scotland, and Ireland* (Oxford, 1989), pp. 100–13.

CHAPTER 14: RESTORATION

1 G. Aylmer, *The Crown's Servants. Government and the Civil Service of Charles II* (Oxford, 2002), pp. 69–75.

2 Denham's own account is in the 'letter to the King' at the front of *Poems and Translations,* (London, 1668); Also see B. O'Hehir, *Harmony from Discords. A Life of Sir John Denham* (Berkeley, CA, 1968) esp. pp. 154–6.

3 *Cal. SP. Dom., 1659–60*, p. 600.

4 The pass to travel to France is registered in TNA SP25/114 p. 10 dated 8 July 1656, John Webb's name then appears in Charles II Household list of October

1656 in Bruges; City Archives of Bruges Oud Archief nr. 101 politieke oorkonden, 1st reeks no. 621 f. 5. Of course, it is possible that this was another John Webb. *Cal. SP. Dom., 1660–1*, p. 379; HMC, 7th Report pt i 88a and 92.

5 T. Blount, *Boscobel, or, The history of His Sacred Majesties most miraculous preservation after the battle of Worcester, 3 Sept. 1651* (London, 1660), pp. 24, 31–2; , *Wren Society*, xviii, pp. 155–6; *Journals of the House of Lords*, xi (London, 1767–1830), p. 31; *HKW*, iii, pp. 167–8; J. Bold, *John Webb* (Oxford, 2019), pp. 181–2.

6 *WP*, p. 106; A. Keay, *The Magnificent Monarch, Charles II and the Ceremonies of Power* (London, 2008), pp. 96–101; L. Hautcoeur, *L'Historie des Chateaux du Louvre et des Tuileries*, (Paris, 1927), pp. 50–3.

7 J. Denham, *Poems and Translations,* (London, 1668); B. O'Hehir, *Harmony from Discords. A Life of Sir John Denham* (Berkeley, CA, 1968), pp. 94–5, 162–3.

8 J. Orrell, *The Theatres of Inigo Jones and John Webb* (Cambridge, 1985), pp. 90–112, 168–85; H. J. M. Green and S. Thurley, 'Excavations on the West Side of Whitehall 1960–2 Part I: From the Building of the Tudor Palace to the Construction of the Modern Offices of State', *The London and Middlesex Archaeological Society Transactions* (1990), pp. 107–10; S. Thurley, *Whitehall Palace and Architectural History of the Royal Apartments 1240–1698* (Yale, 1999), pp. 117–18; L. Hotson, *The Commonwealth and Restoration Stage* (New York, 1962), pp. 197–210; E. Boswell, *The Restoration Court Stage* (London, 1966), pp. 9–174.

9 B. O'Hehir, *Expans'd Hieroglyphicks, A Critical Edition of Sir John Denham's Coopers Hill* (Berkeley, CA, 1969).

10 For the following see S. Thurley (ed.), *St James's Palace from Leper Hospital to Royal Palace,* (forthcoming).

11 For the following see S. Thurley, *Whitehall Palace. An Architectural History of the Royal Apartments, 1240–1698* (Yale, 1999), p. 99; M. Whinney, 'John Webb's Drawings for Whitehall Palace', *Walpole Society*, xxxi (1942–3), pp. 88–95; J. Bold, *John Webb, Architectural Theory and Practice in the Seventeenth Century* (Oxford, 1989), pp. 107, 121–5. My plan is based on Whinney plate xx.

12 S. Thurley, 'The Whitehall Palace Plan of 1670', *London Topographical Society*, cliii (1988), pp. 16–55; S. Thurley, 'Lauderdale at Court', C. Rowell (ed.), *Ham House 400 years of collecting and patronage* (Yale, 2013), pp. 136–43.

13 A. Barclay, 'Charles II's Failed Restoration: Administrative Reform below Stairs, 1660–4', E. Cruickshanks, *The Stuart Courts* (Gloucester, 2000), pp. 158–67.

14 *Journals of House of Commons 1660–7*, viii, p. 73; E. Griffey, *On Display,*

Henrietta Maria and the Materials of Display at the Stuart Court (Yale, 2015), pp. 185–6, 202; *VCH, Surrey*, iii, p. 478; J. Dent, *The Quest for Nonsuch* (London, 1962), pp. 199–201; J. Milward, *Wimbledon in the Time of Civil War* (Epsom, 1976), p. 148.

15 *SH*, p. 63. When I proposed May as architect for the Somerset House works in 2009 I did not know of another set of draft accounts in the Duchy of Cornwall Office which conclusively proves he was Surveyor responsible: Duchy of Cornwall Office Royal Household Accounts: Henrietta Maria, Declared accounts in rolls 746, 749 and 750.

16 E. S. de Beer (ed.), *The Diary of John Evelyn*, iii (Oxford, 1955), pp. 300–1, 313; For the following see: *HKW*, v, p. 140; J. Bold, *John Webb*, p. 126; S. Thurley, 'A Country Seat Fit for a King: Charles II, Greenwich and Winchester', E. Cruickshanks, *The Stuart Courts* (Stroud, 2000), pp. 214–15.

17 E. S. de Beer (ed.), *The Diary of John Evelyn*, iii (Oxford, 1955), pp. 322–5.

18 A. Strickland, *Lives of the Queens of England*, viii (London, 1845), pp. 326–9; *DSP*, iii (London, 1970), pp. 174–5.

19 For the following see *SH*, pp. 60–9.

20 H. Louw, 'The Origin of the Sash-Window', *Architectural History*, xxvi (1983), pp. 60–1; Latham, *DSP*, vi, p. 18.

21 *DSP*, iii, pp. 190–1, v, pp. 300–1; E. S. de Beer (ed.), *The Diary of John Evelyn*, iii (Oxford, 1955), p. 334; *The Memoirs of Ann Lady Fanshawe* (London, 1907), pp. 121–2.

22 Duchy of Cornwall Office Roll 744 (under July and December 1663).

23 J Pérouse de Montclos, *Vaux le Vicomte* (London, 1997), pp. 38, 101; Payment of £300 from Henrietta Maria to le Nôtre in 1662 in Duchy of Cornwall Office Roll 744; E. Rockley, *A History of Gardening in England* (London, 1910), p. 186; Thurley, 'A Country Seat', pp. 219–22; *DSP*, iii, p. 63.

24 *HP*, pp. 73–6; S. Thurley, 'Architecture and Diplomacy: Greenwich Palace under the Stuarts', *The Court Historian*, xi (2006), pp. 125–33.

25 For the following see S. Thurley, 'A Country House fit for a King: Charles II, Winchester and Greenwich', E. Cruickshanks (ed.), *The Stuart Court* (2000), pp. 220–25; J. Bold, *John Webb*, pp. 126–46; *HKW*, v, pp. 140–6.

26 Thurley, 'Country House', pp. 220–5; J. Bold, 'The Grott and Ascent by Mr Webb', *Burlington Magazine*, cxxiv (1982), pp. 149–50.

27 J. Bold, *John Webb*, p. 140; G. Worsley, *Classical Architecture in Britain: The Heroic Age*, (Yale, 1995), p. 71.

28 A. Keay, *The Magnificent Monarch, Charles II and the Ceremonies of Power* (London, 2008), pp. 136–43.

CHAPTER 15: THE FIRST DECADE

1 M. Walker, *Architects and Intellectual Culture in Post-Restoration England* (Oxford, 2017), pp. 40–1.

2 P. Fréart, *Parallèle de l'architecture antique avec la moderne*, J. Evelyn, *Tyrannus or the Mode* (London, 1661); E. Harris, *British Architectural Books and Writers 1556–1785* (Cambridge, 1990), pp. 196–201; M. Walker, *Architects and Intellectual Culture in Post-Restoration England* (Oxford, 2017), passim.

3 C. S. L. Davis, 'The Youth and Education of Christopher Wren', *English Historical Review*, cxxiii (2008), pp. 300–27; J. A. Bennett, *The Mathematical Science of Christopher Wren* (Cambridge, 1982), pp. 40, 73.

4 Bennett, *Mathematical Science*, pp. 87–92; A. Geraghty, *The Sheldonian Theatre. Architecture and Learning in Seventeenth-century Oxford* (Yale, 2013), pp. 38–41.

5 K. Downes, *The Architecture of Wren* (Redhedge, 1988), pp. 6–7; A. Geraghty, *The Sheldonian Theatre. Architecture and Learning in Seventeenth-century Oxford* (Yale, 2013), pp. 51–2; G. Higgott, 'The Fabric to 1670', D. Keene, A. Burns and A. Saint (eds), *St Paul's. The Cathedral Church of London 604–2004* (Yale, 2004), pp. 183–4.

6 *ODNB*

7 L. Jardine, *On a Grander Scale, The Outstanding Career of Sir Christopher Wren* (London, 2002), pp. 239–47; H. Robinson and W. Adams, *The Diary of Robert* Hooke (London, 1935), p. 129; A. Geraghty, 'Robert Hooke's Collection of Architectural Books and Prints', *Architectural History*, xlvii (2004), pp. 113–21.

8 A. Bryant, *The Letters, Speeches and Declarations of King Charles II* (London, 1935), pp. 111–12.

9 D. Lunn, *The English Benedictines 1540–1688* (London, 1980), pp. 135–8; A. S. Barnes, 'Catholic chapels royal under the Stuart kings', *Downside Review*, xx (1901), pp. 232–49.

10 S. Thurley (ed.), *St James's Palace from Leper Hospital to Royal Palace* (forthcoming); Thurley, 'The Stuart Kings, Oliver Cromwell and the Chapel Royal 1618–1685', *Architectural History*, xlv (2002), pp. 238–74.

11 S. Thurley (ed.), *St James's Palace from Leper Hospital to Royal Palace* (forthcoming) my plan of the friary is based on material published in this book.; A. S. Barnes, 'Catholic chapels royal under the Stuart kings', *Downside Review*, xx (1901), pp. 232–49; G. Anstruther, 'Cardinal Howard and the English court, 1658–94', *Archivum Fratrum Praedicatorum*, xxviii (1958), pp.

315–61; W. Maziere Brady, *The Episcopal Succession in England, Scotland and Ireland*, iii (Greg Reprints, 1971), pp. 113–14, 125.

12 J. P. Babelon and C. Mignot (eds), *François Mansart, le Génie de L'Architecture* (Blois, 1998), pp. 183–7; J. M. Pérouse de Montclos, *la Guide du Patrimoine, Paris* (Paris, 1994), pp. 370–2, 475–8; Joan Evans, *Monastic Architecture in France from the Renaissance to the Revolution* (Cambridge, 1964), pp. 24–6.

13 *DSP,* viii, pp. 25–7, 116, 154, 588; G. Anstruther, 'Cardinal Howard and the English Court, 1658–94', *Archivum Fratrum Praedicatorum*, xxviii (1958), pp. 320–1; L. Magalotti, *Travels of Cosmo the Third Duke of Tuscany* (London, 1821), pp. 345–6; Maziere Brady, *Episcopal Succession*, iii, p. 112.

14 *SH*, pp. 257–60; S. Thurley, 'The Stuart Kings, Oliver Cromwell and the Chapel Royal 1618–1685', *Architectural History*, xlv (2002), pp. 238–74.

15 S. Porter, *The Great Plague* (Stroud, 1999), pp. 33–78; *DSP*, vi, pp. 141–2, 165–7, 171. On 26 July the king and duke visited Greenwich where Pepys saw them, *ibid.*, p. 169; J. J. Jusserand, *A French Ambassador at the Court of Charles II, Le Comte de Cominges, from his Unpublished Correspondence* (London, 1892), pp. 167–9, 246; *The Newes* (1665) nos. 53, 56, 58.

16 *DSP*, vii, pp. 25–6, 32; Clarendon's account of the fire is printed in F. Grose and T. Astle (eds), *The Antiquarian Repertory*, ii (1775–84), p. 154.

17 *Oxford Gazette* (1666), no. 34; P. Drury, 'No other palace in the Kingdom will compare with it: The evolution of Audley End 1605–1745', *Architectural History*, xxiii (1980), pp. 4–5; *HKW*, v, pp. 131–2.

18 G. Baker, *The History and Antiquities of the County of Northampton*, i (London, 1822–30), pp. 224–6; *The Oceana of James Harrington and his other works, som wherof are now first publish'd from his own manuscripts : the whole collected, methodiz'd, and review'd, with an exact account of his life prefix'd by John Toland* (London, 1700), p. xvi; T. Sprat, *The history of the Royal-Society of London for the improving of natural knowledge* (London, 1667), p. 432; *Journals of the House of Lords 1648–9*, x (London, 1767–1830), pp. 279–81 [24 May 1648].

19 P. Foster and E. Pyatt, *Bushy House* (National Physical Laboratory Museum and Archives publication, Teddington, 1976), pp. 2–7.

20 *HKW*, pp. 208, 214; H. M. Colvin, *A Biographical Dictionary of British Architects*, 4th edition (Yale, 2008), pp. 895–6.

21 T. Reddaway, *The Rebuilding of London after the Great Fire* (London, 1951).

22 *Cal. SP. Dom., 1668–9*, p. 9; TNA WO48/9; WO51/10, 30/11/67; R. Scott Mylne, *The Master Masons to the Crown of Scotland and their Works*

(Edinburgh, 1893), pp. 168–75; M. Lister, *A Journey to Paris in the Year 1698* (London, 1699), pp. 27–8; A. Keay, *The Last Royal Rebel, The Life and Death of James, Duke of Monmouth* (London, 2016), p. 157.

23 W. Bell, *The Great Fire of London in 1666* (London, 1951), pp. 263–5; *HKW*, pp. 345–7; T. Reddaway, 'The London Custom House 1666–1740', *London Topographical Record*, xxi (1958), pp. 1–14.

24 H. Collins, *Edward Jerman* (Cambridge, 2004), p. 132; A. Saunders, 'The Second Exchange', A. Saunders (ed.), *The Royal Exchange* (London Topographical Society publication, 1997), pp. 130–2, 154.

25 For the following: J. Lang, *Rebuilding St Paul's after the Great Fire of London* (Oxford, 1956); K. Downes, *Sir Christopher Wren: The Design of St Paul's Cathedral* (London, 1988).

26 S. Thurley, *Whitehall Palace. An Architectural History of the Royal Apartments 1240–1698* (Yale, 1999), pp. 108–11; N. Roger, *The Command of the Ocean* (London, 2004), p. 99.

27 B. O'Hehir, *Harmony from Discords*, pp. 187–200, 253–4; *Cal SP. Dom., 1668–9*, pp. 224, 227; *HKW*, v, pp. 15–16.

28 H. Jacobson, 'Luxury Consumption, Cultural Politics, and the Career of the Earl of Arlington, 1660–1685', *The Historical Journal*, lii (2009), pp. 295–317; E. S. de Beer, *The Diary of John Evelyn*, iv (Oxford, 1955), p. 44.

29 M. Beryl Curran (ed.), 'The despatches of William Perwich : English agent in Paris, 1669–1677', *Camden Society* (1903), p. 17; A. Geraghty, *The Architectural Drawings of Sir Christopher Wren at All Souls College, Oxford* (Aldershot, 2007), pp. 175–7.

30 S. Thurley, *The Whitehall Palace Plan of 1670* (London Topographical Society, 1988), pp. 16–24.

CHAPTER 16: GRAND FINALE

1 A. Keay, *The Magnificent Monarch. Charles II and the Ceremonies of Power* (London, 2008), pp. 145–69.

2 HMC, *The manuscripts of S. H. Le Fleming, Esq., of Rydal Hall* (London, 1890), p. 112, no. 1543.

3 *Cal. Treasury Books*, v, *1676–1679*, pp. 1152–3.

4 C. D. Chandaman, *English Public Revenue 1660–1688* (Oxford, 1975), pp. 64–5, 235.

5 Jacobson, 'Luxury Consumption', pp. 306–10; C. Brett, 'Antonio Verrio

(*c.*1636–1707). His Career and Surviving Work', *British Art Journal*, x (2009-10), pp. 4–14; E. S. de Beer (ed.), *The Diary of John Evelyn*, iii (Oxford, 1955), p. 573.

6 For the details of this work see *HKW*, v, pp. 321–2.

7 A. Keay, *The Magnificent Monarch. Charles II and the Ceremonies of Power* (London, 2008), pp. 146–59; *WP* pp. 116–17

8 TNA LC5/141 pp. 136, 138, 311; J. Kenyon, *The Popish Plot* (London, 1972), pp. 125–7.

9 *DSP*, v, p. 57; I. MacIvor and B. Petersen, 'Lauderdale at Holyroodhouse 1669–70', D. Breeze (ed.), *Studies in Scottish Antiquity Presented to Stewart Cruden* (Edinburgh, 1984), pp. 249–68; M. Swain, 'The furnishing of Holyroodhouse in 1668', *The Connoisseur*, cxciv (1977), pp. 122–30.

10 A. MacKechnie, 'Sir William Bruce: 'the chief introducer of Architecture in this Country', *Proceedings of the Society of Antiquaries of Scotland*, cxxxii (2002), pp. 499–519; K. Ottenheym, 'Dutch influences in William Bruce's architecture', *Architectural Heritage: The Journal of the Architectural Heritage Society of Scotland*, xviii (2007), pp. 135–49; C. Wemyss, 'Merchant and Citizen of Rotterdam, Tax Collector "The Bitterest factionalist partie man of his quality in all Scotland". The early Career of William Bruce', *Architectural Heritage*, xvi (2005), pp. 14–31; G. Worsley, *Classical Architecture in Britain: The Heroic Age* (Yale, 1995), pp. 153–7.

11 G. Mackenzie, *Memoirs of the Affairs of Scotland from the Restoration of King Charles II* (Edinburgh, 1821), pp. 193–210; C. Terry, *The Cromwellian Union: Papers Relating to the Negotiations for an Incorporating Union Between England and Scotland, 1651–1652, with an Appendix of Papers Relating to the Negotiations in 1670* (Edinburgh, 1902), pp. 188–218.

12 R. Scott Mylne, *The Master Masons to the Crown of Scotland and their Works* (Edinburgh, 1893), pp. 168–75. My plan is based on the plans published by Mylne.

13 M. Swain, 'Flowerpotts and Pilasters: Royal Tapestries at Holyroodhouse', *The Burlington Magazine*, cxxii (1980), pp. 417–18.

14 H. Arthur, 'Some familiar Letters of Charles II. and James Duke of York addressed to their daughter and niece, the Countess of Litchfield', *Archaeologia*, lviii (1902), pp. 153–88.

15 *Memoirs of Thomas, Earl of Ailesbury*, i (Roxburghe Club, 1890), pp. 22, 57; HMC, *Ormonde*, vi, pp. 143–4; A. Keay, *The Last Royal Rebel, The Life and Death of James, Duke of Monmouth*, (London, 2016), pp. 259–64.

16 J. Clarke, *The Life of King James the Second King of England &c Collected*

out of the Memoirs Writ of his Own Hand . . . 2 vols (London, 1816), I, pp. 659–60.

17 A. Keay, *The Magnificent Monarch, Charles II and the Ceremonies of Power* (London, 2008), pp. 188–90.

18 HMC, *Ormonde*, v, p. 310; *True Domestic Intelligence 1680*, no. 87, p. 466; A. Browning (ed.), with preface and notes by M. K. Geiter and W. A. Speck, *The Memoirs of Sir John Reresby*, 2nd edition (London, 1991), p. 194.

19 *WP*, pp. 82–7.

20 TNA AO1/2478/270 ff. 21v–22r; Anon., *Windsor Castle*, a poem.

21 S. Thurley, 'The Stuart Kings, Oliver Cromwell and the Chapel Royal 1618–1685', *Architectural History*, xlv (2002), pp. 265–9; Thurley, 'The Later Stuarts', S. Brindle (ed.), *Windsor Castle: A Thousand Years of a Royal Palace* (London, 2018), pp. 234–9.

22 Keay, *Magnificent Monarch*, pp. 191–4; TNA LC5/66, p. 26; LC5/66, pp. 44–5.

23 HMC, 12th Report, vii, *Fleming*, p. 185; J. Y. Akerman, 'Moneys Received and paid for Secret Services of Charles II and James II', *Camden Society*, lii (1851), p. 50; N. Luttrell, *A Brief Historical Relation of State Affairs From September 1678 to April 1714*, i (Oxford, 1857), p. 172; *London Gazette* no. 1706 [27 March 1682]; TNA Work 5/37 f. 143.

24 S. Thurley, *Lost Buildings of Britain* (London, 2004), pp. 84–8; TNA Work 5/145 p. 145; TNA E101/674/31.

25 S. Thurley (ed.), *St James's Palace from Leper Hospital to Royal Palace* (forthcoming).

26 T. Harris, *London Crowds in the Reign of Charles II: Propaganda and Politics from the Restoration until the Exclusion Crisis* (Cambridge, 1987), pp. 82–9, 108, 157, 174, 186; G. de Krey, *London and the Restoration* (Cambridge, 2006), pp. 335–86; *London Gazette* no. 2292 [5 November 1687].

27 *HCP*, pp. 140–1; S. Thurley, 'A Country Seat Fit for a King: Charles II, Greenwich and Winchester', E. Cruickshanks, *The Stuart Courts* (Stroud, 2000), p. 227.

28 A. Jessop (ed.), *Lives of the Norths*, ii (London, 1890), p. 207; *Cal. Treasury Books*, vii, pp. 705, 707.

29 E. S. de Beer (ed.), *The Diary of John Evelyn*, iv (Oxford, 1955), p. 74.

30 *WP*, pp. 111–13.

CHAPTER 17: NASTY, BRUTISH AND SHORT

1 E. S. de Beer (ed.), *The Diary of John Evelyn*, iv (Oxford, 1955), p. 416; J. Clarke, *Life of James II, King of England etc* (London, 1816), pp. 5–6; C. Fox, *A History of the Early Part of the Reign of James II* (Philadelphia, 1808), p. xlii.

2 A. Barclay, 'The Impact of King James II on the Departments of the Royal Household' (unpublished PhD dissertation, Cambridge, 1993), pp. 92–3.

3 *WP*, pp. 133–7.

4 *Cal. Treasury Books, 1685–9*, viii, pp. 275, 695; TNA 5/39 f. 140, ff. 302–96; J. Y. Akerman, 'Moneys Received and paid for Secret Services of Charles II and James II', *Camden Society*, lii (1851), p. 111. TNA Work 34/121; P. Bagni, *Benedetto Gennari e la Bottega del Guercino* (Bologna, 1986), p. 97, no. 60, p.150, no. 28 and p. 155, nos. 81–2; D. Bennet Weldon (ed.), *Chronological notes, containing the rise, growth and present state of the English congregation of the Order of St Benedict, etc* (London, 1881), p. xxvi; D. Gilbert Dolan, 'James II and the Benedictines in London', *The Downside Review*, xviii (1899), pp. 94–9.

5 C. Fox, *A History of the Early Part of the Reign of James II* (Philadelphia, 1808), pp. lxxxv–lxxxvii; A. Barclay, 'The Impact of King James II on the Departments of the Royal Household', (unpublished PhD dissertation, Cambridge, 1993), pp. 104–15.

6 E. S. de Beer (ed.), *The Diary of John Evelyn*, iv (Oxford, 1955), pp. 418, 433. A. Clark (ed.), 'Memoirs of Nathaniel Lord Crewe', *Camden Society*, liii (1893), pp. 20–1; TNA LC5/201 f. 189.

7 Braybrooke (ed.), 'The Autobiography of Sir John Bramston K. B.', *Camden Society*, xxxii (1845), p. 253; E. S. de Beer (ed.), *The Diary of John Evelyn*, iv (Oxford, 1955), p. 535.

8 Barclay, 'Impact of King James II', p. 112; P. Leech, 'Music and Musicians in the Catholic Chapel of James II at Whitehall 1686–8', *Early Music*, xxxix (2011), pp. 379–400.

9 *WP*, pp. 134–5; PRO LC/5 147 p. 324; HMC, *Downshire*, i, p. 238.

10 Braybrooke (ed.), 'The Autobiography', pp. 231, 280; Akerman (ed.), 'Moneys Received', pp. 143–4, 175, 180, 198; TNA AO1/2479/276 5v, AO1/2479/277 6r.

11 W. Scott (ed.), *Chronological notes of Scottish affairs, from 1680 till 1701; being chiefly taken from the diary of Lord Fountainhall.* (Edinburgh, 1822), p. 241; W. Maitland, *History of Edinburgh* (Edinburgh, 1753), p. 153; J. Harris, *The Palladians* (London, 1981), p. 58; *Register of the Privy Council of Scotland 1686*, pp. 434–5.

12 R. Mylne, *The Master Masons to the Crown of Scotland* (Edinburgh, 1893), pp. 229–30; A. MacKechnie, 'The Earl of Perth's Chapel of 1688 at Drummond Castle and the Roman Catholic Architecture of James VII', *Architectural Heritage*, xxv (2014), pp. 107–31; C. González-Longo, 'James Smith and Rome', *Architectural Heritage*, xxiii (2012), pp. 75–96; H. M. Colvin, *A Biographical Dictionary of British Architects*, 4th edition (Yale, 2008), p. 952.

13 *Wren Society*, xix, pp. 73–5.

14 C. Rogers, *History of the Chapel Royal of Scotland* (Edinburgh, The Grampian Club, 1882), ccxviii–ccxxviii; *Register of the Privy Council of Scotland*, xii, pp. 434–5.

15 *A full Answer to the Depositions and to all other the Pretences and Arguments whatsoever Concerning the Birth of the Prince of Wales the Intrigue therof detected, the whole Design being set forth, with the Way and Manner of Doing it* (London, 1689), p. 8; B. L. Crace XIII 28.

16 *The State Letters of Henry Earl of Clarendon Lord Lieutenant of Ireland during the reign of King James II and his Lordship's Diary for the Years 1687, 1688, 1689 and 1690* (Oxford, 1765), pp. 202–3; TNA Work 5/42 ff. 118, 131, 123, 126; *London Gazette* no. 2391 [15 October 1688]; *The State Letters of Henry Earl of Clarendon Lord Lieutenant of Ireland during the reign of King James II and his Lordship's Diary for the Years 1687, 1688, 1689 and 1690* (Oxford, 1765), p. 229.

17 *The London Courant* no. 2 [12–15 December 1688]; R. Beddard, *A Kingdom Without a King. The Journal of the Provisional Government in the Revolution of 1688* (Oxford, 1988), pp. 79–80; T. Harris, 'London Crowds and the Revolution of 1688', E. Cruikshanks (ed.), *By Force or Default? The Revolution of 1688–9* (Edinburgh, 1989), pp. 44–64.

CHAPTER 18: DOMESTICITY AND SPLENDOUR

1 D. F. Slothouwer, *De Paleizen van Frederik Hendrik* (Leiden, 1945), pp. 39–88; K. Ottenheym, 'Possessed by Such a Passion for Building, Fredrick Hendrick and Architecture', M. Keblusek and J. Zijlmans, *Princely Display. The Court of Frederick of Orange and Amalia van Solms* (The Hague, 1997), pp. 111–16; V. Sellers, *Courtly Gardens in Holland 1600–1650* (Amsterdam, 2001), pp. 15–59.

2 K. van Strien (ed.), *Touring the Low Countries: Accounts of British Travellers, 1660–1720* (Leiden, 1993), pp. 81, 195; Ottenheym, 'Possessed by Such a Passion for Building', pp. 117–19; V. Bezemer Sellers, *Courtly Gardens in Holland 1600–1650* (Amsterdam, 2001), pp. 61–77.

3 Ottenheym, 'Possessed by Such a Passion for Building', pp. 121–3; M. Loonstra, *Het Huis Ten Bosch* (Amsderdam, 1985), pp. 51–9.

4 D. Clifford, *The Diaries of Lady Anne Clifford* (Stroud, 1990), pp. 206–7; E. Thompson (ed.), 'Correspondence of the Family of Hatton', *Camden Society*, i (1878,) p. 59; TNA Work 5/15 ff. 371–6; A. Browning, *Memoirs of Sir John Reresby* (London, 1991), p. 82.

5 H. Margoliouth, *The Poems and Letters of Andrew Marvell*, ii (Oxford, 1971), p. 327.

6 H. Tromp, *Het Koninklijk Paleis Soesdijk Historisch Gezien* (Amsterdam, 1987), pp. 21–49.

7 D. Jacques and A. van der Horst (eds), *The Gardens of William and Mary* (London, 1988), pp. 37–9; J. D. Hunt, 'The Anglo Dutch Garden in the Age of William and Mary', J. D. Hunt and E. de Jong (eds), *Journal of Garden History*, viii (1988), pp. 142–4.

8 TNA LC5/142 pp. 121, 125; TNA LC5/65 pp. 52, 57; LC5/210 p. 374; HMC, *Ormonde*, iv, pp. 53, 370; HMC, *Fleming*, pp. 140–1; G. Elliott (ed.), 'The Diary of Dr Edward Lake', *Camden Society* (1847), pp. 5–10.

9 B. Bathurst, *Letters of Two Queens* (London, 1924), p. 66.

10 *The Life of that incomparable princess, Mary, our late sovereign lady, of ever blessed memory who departed this life, at her royal palace at Kensington, the 28th of December, 1694* (London, 1695), pp. 27–9; Ottenheym, 'Possessed by Such a Passion for Building', pp. 109–11.

11 R. J. Van Pelt and M. E. Tiethoff-Spliethoff, *Het Binnenhof* (Dieren, 1984) passim; K. Freemantle, 'A Visit to the United Provinces and Cleves in the time of William III, described in Edward Southwell's Journal', *Nederlands Kunsthistorisch Jaarboek*, i (1970), p. 49; N. Robb, *William of Orange*, ii (London, 1963), p. 123.

12 A. Prowse, 'Some memorandums concerning Bishop Hooper', Lambeth Palace Library, MS 3016, in A. Trevor, *The Life and Times of William the Third, King of England and Stadtholder of Holland* (London, 1835), pp. 465–8.

13 O. Mörke, 'William III's Stadtholderly Court in the Dutch Republic', E. Mijers and D. Onnekink, *Redefining William III. The Impact of the King-Stadholder in International Context* (Abingdon, 2007), pp. 227–40; V. Sellers, *Courtly Gardens in Holland 1600–50* (Amsterdam, 2001), p. 79.

14 S. van Raaij and P. Spies, *The Royal Progress of William and Mary* (Amsterdam, 1988), pp. 119–22; D. Jacques and A. van der Horst (eds.), *The Gardens of William and Mary* (London, 1988), pp. 40–2.

15 *The Royal Diary containing . . . The Character of his Royal Consort Queen Mary II* (London, 1702), p. 10; R. Doebner, *Memoirs of Mary, Queen of England, 1689–1693, together with her letters and those of King James II. and William III. to the Electress Sophia of Hanover* (London, 1886), p. 23; K. Freemantle, 'A Visit to the United Provinces and Cleves in the time of William III, described in Edward Southwell's Journal', *Nederlands Kunsthistorisch Jaarboek,* i (1970), p. 54; A. Prowse, 'Some memorandums concerning Bishop Hooper', Lambeth Palace Library, MS 3016, in A. Trevor, *The Life and Times of William the Third, King of England and Stadtholder of Holland* (London, 1835), pp. 465–8.

16 Royal Library RCIN 1142245; Doebner, *Memoirs of Mary, Queen of England,* p. 4.

17 *The Life of that incomparable princess, Mary, our late sovereign lady, of ever blessed memory who departed this life, at her royal palace at Kensington, the 28th of December, 1694* (London, 1695), pp. 40–2; *Mémoires de Mr de B***, secrétaire de Mr L.C.D.R,* p. 87.

18 S. van Raaij and Spies, *Royal Progress,* pp. 21–2.

19 K. A. Ottenheym, W. Terlouw and R. van Zoest (eds), *Daniel Marot: Vormgever van een deftig Bestaan* (Zutphen, 1988), pp. 9–13.

20 Jacques and van der Horst (eds), *The Gardens of William and Mary,* p. 45.

21 M. Loonstra, *Het Koninklijk Paleis Huis ten Bosch Historisch Gezien* (Amsterdam, 1985), pp. 51–61; van Strien (ed.), *Touring the Low Countries,* p. 195; M. Ozinga, *Daniel Marot, De Schepper van den Hollandschen Lodewijk XIV-Stijl* (Amsterdam, 1938), pp. 39–41.

22 W. Kuyper, *Dutch Classicist Architecture, A Survey of Dutch Architecture, Gardens and Anglo-Dutch Architectural Relations from 1625 to 1700* (Delft, 1980), pp. 181–3; A. Vliegenthart and A. Erkelens, *Rijksmuseum Paleis Het Loo* (Paleis Het Loo, Apeldoorn, 1988), pp. 3–5; Jacques and van der Horst (eds), *The Gardens of William and Mary,* pp. 45–7.

23 L. van Everdingen, *Het Loo, de Oranjes en de Jacht* (Haarlem, 1984), pp. 60–70; G. Upmark, 'Ein Besuch in Holland 1687 aus den Reisechilderungen des Schwedischen Architekten Nicodemus Tessin', *Oud-Holland 1900* (Amsterdam, 1900), pp. 117–28, 144–52, 199–210; C. Droste, *Overblyfsels van Geheugchinis, der bisonderste voorvallen in het leven van den Heere Coenreat Droste* ('S-Gravenhage, 1728), pp. 178–80.

24 van Strien (ed.), *Touring the Low Countries,* pp. 87, 92; K. Freemantle, 'A Visit to the United Provinces and Cleves in the time of William III, described in Edward Southwell's Journal', *Nederlands Kunsthistorisch Jaarboek,* i (1970), p. 67.

25 R. Beddard, *A Kingdom Without a King. The Journal of the Provisional Government in the Revolution of 1688* (Oxford, 1988), pp. 40, 56–88. H. Ellis, *Letters Illustrative of English History*, 2nd ser., iv (London, 1846), p. 183; S. Weller Singer (ed.), *The correspondence of Henry Hyde, Earl of Clarendon, and of his brother Laurence Hyde, Earl of Rochester : with the diary of Lord Clarendon from 1687 to 1690, containing minute particulars of the events attending the revolution: and the diary of Lord Rochester during his Embassy to Poland in 1676*, ii (London, 1828), pp. 228–30.

26 J. Siccama (ed.), C. Huygens, *Journaal van Constantijn Huygens, 1673–1696*, 4 vols (Utrecht, 1876–88) i, pp. 51, 86.

27 Doebner, *Memoirs of Mary, Queen of England*, pp. 11, 16.

28 A. Barclay, 'William's Court as King', E. Mijers and D. Onnekink, *Redefining William IIII. The Impact of the King-Stadholder in International Context* (London, 2007), pp. 243–6; D. Onnekink, 'Dutch Counsels: the Foreign Entourage of William III', *Dutch Crossing*, xxix (2005), p. 10.

29 Doebner, *Memoirs of Mary, Queen of England*, p. 15; *Lettres et Memoires de Marie Reine d'Angleterre, epouse de Guillaume III. Collection des documents authentiques inedits* (The Hague, 1880), p. 116; G. Burnet, *History of His Own Time*, iv, 2nd edition, enlarged (Oxford, 1833), p. 152; HMC, 14th Report, appendix ii (1894), p. 431.

30 Doebner, *Memoirs of Mary, Queen of England*, p. 17.

31 *London Gazette* nos. 2421, 2458, 2473, 2850; *Lutterell*, iv, p. 49; *The Post Boy*, 299, 428, 595, 625, 632, 890; *Cal. SP. Dom., 1697*, pp. 494, 498 [30 November 1697]; S. Baxter, *The Development of the Treasury 1660–1702* (London, 1957), pp. 19–20, 49.

32 *Bishop Burnet's History of the Reign of King James the Second* (London, 1852), pp. 465–7; E. S. de Beer (ed.), *The Diary of John Evelyn*, iv (Oxford, 1955), pp. 623–5; S. Jennings Churchill, Duchess of Marlborough, *An Account of the Conduct of the Dowager Duchess of Marlborough: From Her first coming to court to the year 1710 in a letter from herself to my Lord —* (London, 1742), pp. 25–6; Doebner, *Memoirs of Mary, Queen of England*, pp. 11, 43–4; WP, pp. 137–42.

33 *Cal. SP. Dom., 1693*, p. 294; Doebner, *Memoirs of Mary, Queen of England*, pp. 36, 37, 39, 47; *London Gazette* nos. 2631, 2640, 2647; W. Speck, 'William – and Mary?', L. Schwoerer, *The Revolution of 1688–89. Changing Perspectives* (Cambridge, 1992), pp. 131–46; *Wren Society*, vii, p. 136.

34 Doebner, *Memoirs of Mary, Queen of England*, p. 47; WP, pp. 137–4; TNA LC9/280.

35 *London Gazette* [31 December 1688]; *Cal. Treasury Books*, xiv, p. 365; TNA work 5/45 ff. 137–8; TNA Work 5/45 f. 145; S. Thurley (ed.), *St James's Palace from Leper Hospital to Royal Court* (London, forthcoming).

36 T. Claydon, *William III and the Godly Revolution* (Cambridge, 1996), passim.

37 A. Ashbee and J. Harley, *The Cheque Books of the Chapel Royal*, ii (Aldershot, 2000), p. 287; PRO Work 5/42 ff. 198r, 199r; Doebner, *Memoirs of Mary, Queen of England*, pp. 12, 19; PRO LC5/149 p. 119; LC5/150 p. 272.

38 Doebner, *Memoirs of Mary, Queen of England* pp. 11–2, 16; Work 5/43 f. 67v, 69; Work 5/44 ff. 123, 134–5; Work 5/45 ff. 37, 47, 80v; Work 5/46 ff. 305, 311.

39 E. Impey, *Kensington* Palace (London, 2003), pp. 14–38; S. Thurley, 'Kensington Palace: An Incident in Anglo-Dutch Architectural Collaboration?', *Georgian Group Journal*, xvii (2009), pp. 1–18.

40 A. Barclay, 'The Impact of King James II on the Departments of the Royal Household' (unpublished PhD thesis, Cambridge, 1993), pp. 205–15; R. O. Bucholz, *The Augustan Court; Queen Anne and the Decline of Court Culture* (Stanford, CA, 1993), pp. 31–3; *HKW*, v, pp. 19–20; C. Rose, *England in the 1690s; Revolution, Religion and War* (Oxford, 1999), pp. 203–5; J. Lang, *Rebuilding St Paul's after the Great Fire of London* (Oxford, 1956), pp. 147–51.

41 M. D. Ozinga, *Daniel Marot, de Schepper van den Hollandschen Lodewijk XIV-stijl* (Amsterdam, 1938), p. 92; A. M. L. E. Erkelens, *Queen Mary's Delft Porcelain* (Het Loo, 1996), pp. 9–34; BL, Add. MS 56078, transcribed in M. Hinton and O. Impey, *Kensington Palace and the Porcelain of Queen Mary II* (Christie's, 1998), pp. 85–99; T. H. Lunsingh Scheurleer, 'Documents on the Furnishing of Kensington House', *Walpole Society*, xxxviii (1960–62), pp. 15–58; *HCP*, pp. 173–6; A. Bowett, 'The Engravings of Daniel Marot', *Furniture History*, xliii (2007), pp. 92–3.

42 My plan of the first floor of Kensington is based on All Souls I.12 that shows the first floor of Nottingham House, All Souls III.4.a that shows the two eastern pavilions at first-floor level and All Souls III.8 that shows the queen's apartment.

43 *Cal. SP. Dom., 1693*, p. 433; *Cal. SP. Dom., 1698*, pp. 30, 118, 156, 168; HMC, *Bath*, pp. 222, 237; HMC, *Buccleuch*, p. 634; S. Strong, *Catalogue of Letters . . . at Welbeck* (London, 1903), p. 263; BM Add. MS 40773 f. 321; Add. MS 9086 ff. 66, 202, 217, 123; *Cal. SP. Dom., 1698*, p. 168; *Cal SP. Dom., 1699–1700*, p. 145; H. Horwitz, *Parliament Policy and Politics in the Reign of William III* (Manchester, 1977), pp. 204–5.

44 W. Kuyper, *Dutch Classicist Architecture, A Survey of Dutch Architecture, Gardens and Anglo-Dutch Architectural Relations from 1625 to 1700* (Delft, 1980), pp. 123–4; J. Siccama (ed.), C. Huygens, *Journaal van Constantijn*

Huygens, 1673–1696, 4 vols (Utrecht, 1876–88), ii, pp. 50, 134; *Wren Society*, vii, p. 182; J. Harris, *William Talman* (London, 1982), pl. 7; *HCP*, p. 167.

45 K. Haley, 'William III as Builder of Het Loo', J. Dixon Hunt (ed.), *The Dutch Garden in the Seventeenth Century* (Dumbarton Oaks Colloquium on the History of Landscape Architecture, xii, 1990), pp. 3–11; H. and B. van der Zee, *William and Mary* (London, 1973), p. 412.

46 P. Rem, 'Restoration of the State Bed Acquired by Het Loo Palace and intended for the Bedchamber of Stadtholder William III', *Textile History*, xxxi (2000), pp. 154–6; C. van Strien, *British Travellers in Holland during the Stuart Period* (Leiden, 1993), p. 153.

47 R. de Hooghe, *A Short Description of the King's Loo* (Amsterdam n.d.) ('The Anglo Dutch Garden in the Age of William and Mary', *Journal of Garden History*, viii (1988), pp. 146-7); D. Jacques and A. van der Horst (eds), *The Gardens of William and Mary* (London, 1988), pp. 55–9; van Strien, *British Travellers*, p. 153; J. Siccama (ed.), C. Huygens, *Journaal van Constantijn Huygens, 1673–1696*, 4 vols (Utrecht, 1897–8), ii, p. 39.

48 *HCP*, pp. 151–84.

49 *HCP*, pp. 193–205.

50 *The London Gazette*, nos. 2768, 2812, 2920, 3028, 3123, 3542, 3648, 3867; *The Post Boy*, nos. 357, 389, 396, 397, 647, 708, 817, 955, 956, 1011; *The Post Man*, no. 222.

51 Garter: *The London Gazette*, nos. 1692, 2181, 2441, 2442, 2453, 2623, 2737, 3265, 3397, 3601, 3608, 3715; *The Post Man*, no. 189; *The Post Boy*, nos. 294, 295; Lord Mayor: *London Gazette*, nos. 2501, 2710, 2814, 3023; Birthday: *London Gazette*, nos. 2503, 2607, 2816, 2920, 3546, 3651; *The Post Boy*, no. 870; *The Post Man*, no. 233; N. Luttrell, *A Brief Account of State Affairs* (Oxford, 1857), ii, p. 608, iii, p. 220; TNA Work 5/51 f. 454: Balls, concerts and theatre: *The Post Boy*, nos. 273, 279, 403, 434, 438, 599, 605, 622, 812; TNA LC5/152, p. 83; LC5/11; LC5/149, p. 321; LC5/150, p. 73; LC5/152, p. 200; TNA Work 5/43 f. 67v; Work 5/46 f. 91; Work 5/49 f. 382; Doebner, *Memoirs of Mary, Queen of England*, p. 36; Luttrell, *State Affairs*, iv, pp. 133, 180; *HCP*, pp. 207–8; E. Boswell, *The Restoration Court Stage 1660–1702* (London, 1960), pp. 98, 292–3; J. Sainty and R. Bucholz, *Officials of the Royal Household, 1660–1837, Part 1 Lord Chamberlain* (London, 1997), pp. lxi–lxiii.

CHAPTER 19: THE MAGNIFICENCE OF SOVEREIGNTY

1 T. Claydon, *William III and the Godly Revolution* (Cambridge, 1996,), pp. 98–9; P. Fritz, 'From Public to Private: the Royal Funerals in England 1500–1830', J. Whaley (ed.), *Mirrors of mortality: studies in the social history of death* (London, 1981), pp. 65–8; R. Hyde, 'Romeyn de Hooghe and the Funeral of the People's Queen', *Print Quarterly*, xv (1998), pp. 150–72.

2 R. O. Bucholz, *The Augustan Court, Queen Anne and the Decline of Court Culture* (Stanford, CA, 1993), pp. 26–31.

3 My plans are drawn from an estimate in TNA Work 6/2 ff. 65–6 and an enrolled account in TNA E351/3467 printed from an Audit Office duplicate in *Wren Society*, vii, pp. 179–83; Historic plans All Souls 237 and 240 which is part ground, part first floor (A. Geraghty, *The Architectural Drawings . . .* pp. 154, 158, 159). 1699 inventory printed in T. Scheurleer, 'Documents of the furnishing of Kensington House', *Walpole Society*, xxxviii (1960–2) pp. 50–3. Later accounts: TNA Work 5/47 ff. 348v, 353, 358v.

4 *The Post Boy*, no. 725; A. Boyer, *Letters of Wit, Politicks and Morality* (London, 1701), pp. 210–14; T. Scheurleer, 'Documents of the furnishing of Kensington House', *Walpole Society*, xxxviii (1960–2), p. 21; In 1701–2 the king's apartment was rearranged and the position of the little bedchamber, closet and backstairs relocated. TNA Work 5/52 ff. 489, 506; Work 5/53 ff. 296, 331v, 338.

5 D. Jacques, *Gardens of Court and Country. English Design 1630–1730* (Yale, 2017), pp. 170–3.

6 *The Royal Progress; or, A diary of the King's journey from His Majesty's setting out from Kensington, till His return. By a person of quality* (London, 1695); *The Lexington papers or Some Account of the Courts of London and Vienna* (London, 1851), pp. 138–44; HMC, *Downshire*, i, ii, pp. 569–80; J. Siccama (ed.), C. Huygens *Journaal van Constantijn Huygens, 1673–1696*, 4 vols (Utrecht, 1876–88), ii, pp. 551–3, 568.

7 *The Post Man*, no. 92 [Tuesday 10 December], no. 92/3 [Thursday 12 December]; *The Post Boy*, no. 95 [Tuesday 17 December]; N. Luttrell, *A Brief Relation of State Affairs*, iii (Oxford, 1857), pp. 426, 531–2, 551; *Cal. Treasury Papers, 1697–1701*, p. 556; *Cal. SP. Dom., 1697*, p. 293; W. Hilton, 'A Dance for Kings: The 17th-Century French "Courante", its Character, Step-Patterns, Metric and Proportional Foundations', *Early Music*, v (1977), pp. 160–72; M. Goff, '"The Art of Dancing, Demonstrated by Characters and Figures": French and English sources for Court and Theatre Dance,

1700–1750', *The British Library Journal*, xxi (1995), pp. 202–31; *DSP*, iii, pp. 300–1, vii, pp. 371–3; HMC, *Portland*, iii, p. 294.

8 TNA work 5/53 f. 130. For the queen's birthday ball: *Camden Miscellany*, i (1847), 'The Diary of Edward Lake', p. 9; *DSP*, vii, pp. 371–3; HMC, *Rutland*, ii, p. 32.

9 *The Post Boy*, nos. 273, 279, 430, 434, 438, 599, 605, 737. Also see J. Anderson Winn, *Queen Anne Patroness of Arts* (Oxford, 2014), pp. 224–6.

10 'Hatton Correspondence', ii, *Camden Society* (1878), pp. 231–2; W. H. Lewis (ed.), *Memoirs of the Duc de Saint-Simon* (New York, 1964), p. 23; P. Grimbolt (ed.), *Letters of William III and Louis XIV and of their Ministers . . .*, i (London, 1848), p. 144; Luttrell, *State Affairs*, iv, p. 329.

11 TNA Work 5/49 f. 381v; *The Post Man*, no. 99; *The Post Boy*, nos. 610, 614, 625, 632, 643 747, 760, 774, 783, 909, 916, 921; *The Post Boy*, nos. 428, 595, 890; Luttrell, *State Affairs*, iv, p. 351.

12 A. Geraghty, *The Architectural Drawings of Sir Christopher Wren at All Souls College Oxford: A complete Catalogue* (Aldershot, 2007), pp. 180–90.

13 Claydon, *William III*, pp. 14–15; S. Groenveld, 'William III as Stadtholder: Prince or Minister?', E. Mijers and D. Onnekink, *Redefining William III. The Impact of the King-Stadholder in International Context* (Abingdon, 2007), pp. 17–37.

14 *London Gazette*, nos. 3388, 3393; *Cal. SP. Dom, William III, 1698*, pp. 200, 205, 207, 214, 261; *The Post Boy*, nos. 639, 650; J. P. Hoare, *The History of the Royal Buckhounds* (Newmarket, 1895), p. 200; Geraghty, *Wren Architectural Drawings*, pp. 196–9; J. Roberts, *Royal Landscape. The Gardens and Parks of Windsor* (Yale, 1997), pp. 175–9.

15 *Cal. Treasury Books*, xvi, p. 81, xvii, p. 118.

16 J. Harris, *William Talman* (London, 1982), p. 31; Luttrell, *State Affairs*, iv, p. 553; BM Add. MS 20,101 f. 69 (printed in *Wren Society*, iv, pp. 59–60).

17 Luttrell, *State Affairs*, iv, p. 565.

18 M. Grew, *William Bentinck and William III. The Life of Bentinck Earl of Portland from the Welbeck Correspondence* (London, 1924), pp. 316, 320, 322, 334, 339, 342; M. Kroll (ed.), *Letters from Liselotte* (London, 1970), p. 171; G. F. Wingfield Digby, 'Damasks and Velvets at Hampton Court', *Connoisseur*, ciii (May 1939), pp. 248–53.

19 J. Siccama (ed.), C. Huygens, *Journaal van Constantijn Huygens, 1673–1696*, 4 vols (Utrecht, 1876–88), i, pp. 118, 174–5, 187, 193, 216, 221, 226, 517, ii, p. 550; S. Jenkins, 'A Sense of History. The Artistic Taste of William III', *Apollo*, cxl, no. 390 (August 1994), pp. 4–9. This edition of the journal is

devoted to the king's apartments at Hampton Court and covers the internal decoration; E. Croft Murray, *Decorative Painting in England 1537–1837* (London, 1962), pp. 57–9.

20 J. Siccama (ed.), C. Huygens, *Journaal van Constantijn Huygens, 1673–1696*, 4 vols (Utrecht, 1876–88), i, pp. 35–6; B. Brenninkmeyer de Rooij, 'William III and the Royal Collections', R. van Leeuwen (ed.), *William III and the Royal Collections* (The Hague, 1988), pp. 17–34; N. Robb, *William of Orange*, 2 vols (London, 1963), p.447.

21 W. Camden, *Britannia* (Edmund Gibson, London, 1695), p. 368; H. M. Colvin, 'Roger North and Sir Christopher Wren', *The Architectural Review*, x (1962), p. 259. See also his comments in his treatise on building, in H. Colvin and J. Newman (eds), *Of Building. Roger North's Writings on Architecture* (Oxford, 1981), p. 57: 'It is new built, but the old had a better view, for that had gate towers, and some risings, but this is all of an height: balustred, flatt, which looks like combs stuck at the topp, and a series of round windoes, like the ports of a ship.'

EPILOGUE

1 R. O. Bucholz, *The Augustan Court. Queen Anne and the Decline of Court Culture* (Stanford, CA, 1993).

2 Bucholz, *Augustan Court*, pp. 57, 63; *HKW*, v, pp. 47–51.

3 R. Tighe and J. Davis, *Annals of Windsor, being a History of the Castle and Town*, ii (London, 1858), pp. 485–6, 494–5.

4 Bucholz, *Augustan Court*, pp. 235–6; *The Journeys of Celia Fiennes*, pp. 355–6; G. Bickham, *Deliciae Britannicae* (London, 1742), pp. 103–10.

5 E. Gregg, *Queen Anne* (London, 1980), pp. 140–1; *London Gazette*, no. 4240 [27 June 1706], no. 4242 [23 July 1706], *Daily Courant*, no. 1378 [13 September 1706]; *London Gazette*, no. 4840 [23 April 1711].

6 H. Williams (ed.), J. Swift, *Journal to Stella* (Oxford, 1948), pp. 322–3, 328, 363, 421, 490, 522, 595–6, 603, 629, 645, 659.

7 W. H. Quarrell and M. Mare (trans and eds), *London in 1700 from the Travels of Zacharias Conrad von Uffenbach* (London, 1934), pp. 115–16.

8 A. Boyer, *Quadriennium Annae Postremum; or the Political State of Great Britain*, vii (London, 1918–19), p. 184.

Bibliography

Akerman, J. Y., 'Moneys Received and paid for Secret Services of Charles II and James II', *Camden Society*, lii (1851)

Akrigg, G., *The Letters of King James VI & I* (Berkeley, CA, 1984)

Anderson, C., *Inigo Jones and the Classical Tradition* (Cambridge, 2007)

Anstruther, G., 'Cardinal Howard and the English court, 1658–94', *Archivum Fratrum Praedicatorum*, xxviii (1958), pp. 315–61

Archer, I. W., 'Popular politics in the 16th and early 17th centuries', P. Griffiths and M. S. R. Jenner (eds), *Londonopolis. Essays in the Cultural and Social History of Early Modern London* (Manchester, 2000), pp. 26–46

Arthur, H., 'Some familiar Letters of Charles II. and James Duke of York addressed to their daughter and niece, the Countess of Litchfield', *Archaeologia*, lviii (1902)

Ashbee, A., and J. Harley, *The Cheque Books of the Chapel Royal*, 2 vols (Aldershot, 2000)

Ashton, R., *James I by his Contemporaries* (London, 1969)

Atherton, I., and J. Sanders, *The 1630s. Interdisciplinary essays on culture and politics in the Caroline era* (Manchester, 2006)

Aubrey, J., *Brief Lives* (Harmondsworth, 1972)

Austin Nuttall, P., *The History of the Worthies of England by Thomas Fuller*, 3 vols (London, 1840)

Avery, C., 'The Collector Earl and his Modern Marbles. Thomas Howard and François Dieussart', *Apollo*, clxiii (June 2006), pp. 46–53

Aylmer, G., *The State's Servant. The Civil Service of the English Republic 1649–60* (London, 1973)

Aylmer, G., *The Crown's Servants. Government and the Civil Service of Charles II* (Oxford, 2002)

Babelon, J. P., and C. Mignot (eds), *François Mansart, le Génie de L'Architecture* (Blois, 1998)

Bachrach, A., and R. Collmer (trans and eds), *Lodewijck Huygens the English Journal 1651–2* (Leiden, 1982)

Bagni, P., *Benedetto Gennari e la Bottega del Guercino* (Bologna, 1986)

Baker, G., *The History and Antiquities of the County of Northampton*, 2 vols (London, 1822–30)

Ballon, H., *The Paris of Henri IV. Architecture and Urbanism* (Cambridge, MA, 1991)

Ballon, H., 'The Architecture of Cardinal Richelieu', H. T. Goldfarb, *Richelieu, Art and Power* (Montreal, 2003)

Bamford, F., *A Royalist Notebook: The Commonplace book of Sir John Oglander* (London, 1936)

Barbe, J., *Livre d'architecture d'autels, et de cheminées . . .* (Paris, 1633)

Barclay, A., 'The Impact of King James II on the Departments of the Royal Household' (unpublished PhD dissertation, Cambridge, 1993)

Barclay, A., 'Charles II's Failed Restoration: Administrative Reform below Stairs, 1660–4', E. Cruickshanks, *The Stuart Courts* (Gloucester, 2000), pp. 158–70

Barclay, A., 'William's Court as King', E. Mijers and D. Onnekink, *Redefining William IIII. The Impact of the King-Stadholder in International Context* (London, 2007), pp. 241–61

Barclay, A., 'The 1661 St Edward's Crown – Refurbished, Recycled or Replaced?', *The Court Historian*, xiii (2008), pp. 149–70

Barnes, A. S., 'Catholic chapels royal under the Stuart kings', *Downside Review*, xx (1901), pp. 232–49

Barnes, S. J., N. de Poorter, O. Millar and H. Vey, *Van Dyck. A Complete Catalogue of the Paintings* (Yale, 2004)

Barratt, J., *Cavalier Capital. Oxford in the English Civil War 1642–1646* (Solihull, 2016)

L. Barroll, 'The court of the first Stuart queen', L. Levy Peck (ed.), *The Mental World of the Jacobean Court* (Cambridge, 1991), pp. 191–208

Batey, M., and C. Cole, 'The Great Staircase Tower at Christ Church', J. Blair (ed.), *St Frideswide's Monastery at Oxford* (Gloucester, 1990), pp. 212–20

Bathurst, B., *Letters of Two Queens* (London, 1924)

Baxter, S., *The Development of the Treasury 1660–1702* (London, 1957)

Beard, G., *Upholsterers and Interior Furnishing in England 1530–1840* (Yale, 1997)

Beddard, R., *A Kingdom Without a King. The Journal of the Provisional Government in the Revolution of 1688* (Oxford, 1988)

Bell, W., *The Great Fire of London in 1666* (London, 1951)

Beltramini, G. (ed.), *Andrea Palladio the Complete Illustrated Works* (New York, 2001)

Bennet Weldon, D. (ed.), *Chronological notes, containing the rise, growth and present state of the English congregation of the Order of St Benedict, etc* (London, 1881)

Bennett, J. A., *The Mathematical Science of Christopher Wren* (Cambridge, 1982)

Bentley, G. E., *The Jacobean and Caroline Stage*, 2 vols (Oxford, 1941)

Bergeron, D., 'Gilbert Dugdale and the Royal Entry of James', *The Journal of Medieval and Renaissance Studies*, xiii (1983), pp. 101–25

Bertotti Scamozzi, O., *Le Fabbriche e i Disegni di Andrea Palladio*, i (Vicenza, 1776–83)

Beryl Curran. M. (ed.), 'The despatches of William Perwich : English agent in Paris, 1669–1677', *Camden Society* (1903)

Besly, E., *Coins and Medals of the English Civil War* (London, 1990)

Bezemer Sellers, V., *Courtly Gardens in Holland 1600–1650* (Amsterdam, 2001)

Bickersteth, J., *Clerks of the Closet in the Royal Household* (Stroud, 1991)

Bickham, G., *Deliciae Britannicae* (London, 1742)

Bindoff, S. T., 'The Stuarts and Their Style', *The English Historical Review*, vol. lx, no. ccxxxvii (May 1945), pp. 192–216

Birch, T. (ed.), *A Collection of the State Papers of John Thurloe*, 7 vols (London, 1742)

Birch, T., *The Life of Henry, Prince of Wales: Eldest Son of King James I* (London, 1760)

Birch, T., *The Court and Times of Charles the First*, 2 vols (London, 1848)

Bliss, J., and W. Scott (eds), *The Works of Archbishop William Laud*, 7 vols (Oxford, 1847–60)

Blome, R., *The Gentleman's Recreation* (London, 1686)

Blount, T., *Boscobel, or, The history of His Sacred Majesties most miraculous preservation after the battle of Worcester, 3 Sept. 1651* (London, 1660)

Bold, J., 'The Grott and Ascent by Mr Webb', *Burlington Magazine*, cxxiv (1982), pp. 149–50

Bold, J., *John Webb, Architectural Theory and Practice in the Seventeenth Century* (Oxford, 1989)

Bold, J., *Greenwich. An Architectural History of the Royal Hospital for Seamen and the Queen's House* (Yale, 2000)

Boswell, E., *The Restoration Court Stage 1660–1702* (London, 1960)

Bowett, A., 'The Engravings of Daniel Marot', *Furniture History*, xliii (2007), pp. 85–100

Boyer, A., *Letters of Wit, Politicks and Morality* (London, 1701)

Boyer, A., *Quadriennium Annae Postremum; or the Political State of Great Britain*, 8 vols (London, 1718–19)

Bray, W., 'An Account of the Revenue, the Expenses, the Jewels etc. of Prince Henry', *Archaeologia*, xv (1806), pp. 22–6

Bray, W. (ed.), *The Diary of John Evelyn to which are added a selection from his familiar letters*, 4 vols (London, 1906)

Braybrooke (ed.), 'The Autobiography of Sir John Bramston K. B.', *Camden Society*, xxxii (1845), p. 253

Brenninkmeyer de Rooij, B., 'William III and the Royal Collections', R. van Leeuwen (ed.), *William III and the Royal Collections* (The Hague, 1988), pp. 17–34

Brett, C., 'Antonio Verrio (*c*.1636–1707). His Career and Surviving Work', *British Art Journal*, x (2009–10), pp. 4–14

Brett-James, C., *The Growth of Stuart London* (London, 1935)

Brewer, J. (ed.), G. Goodman, *The Court of King James the First*, 2 vols (Oxford, 1839)

Brindle, S. (ed.), *Windsor Castle. A Thousand Years of a Royal Palace* (London, 2018)

Britland, K., *Drama at the Courts of Queen Henrietta Maria* (Cambridge, 2006)

Britland, K., '"Tyred in her banished dress": Henrietta Maria in exile', *Early Modern Literary Studies*, Special Issue xv (August 2007), pp. 1–39

Brotton, J., 'Buying the Renaissance: Prince Charles's Art Purchases in Madrid 1623', A. Samson (ed.), *The Spanish Match. Prince Charles's Journey to Madrid 1623* (Aldershot, 2006), pp. 9–26

Brown, J., and J. Elliott, *A Palace for a King. The Buien Retiro and the Court of Philip IV* (Yale, 1980)

Brown, J., 'Artistic Relations between Spain and England 1604–1655', J. Brown and J. Elliott (eds), *The Sale of the Century. Artistic Relations between Spain and Great Britain 1604–1655* (Yale, 2002)

Browning, A. (ed.), with preface and notes by M. K. Geiter and W. A. Speck, *The Memoirs of Sir John Reresby*, 2nd edition (London, 1991)

Bryant, A., *The Letters, Speeches and Declarations of King Charles II* (London, 1935)

Bucholz, R. O., *The Augustan Court, Queen Anne and the Decline of Court Culture* (Stanford, CA, 1993)

Bullen, A., *The Works of Thomas Middleton*, 8 vols (London, 1886)

Burnet, G., *History of His Own Time*, iv, 2nd edition, enlarged (Oxford, 1833)

Calderwood, D., *The True History of the Church of Scotland* (Edinburgh, 1678)

Callender, G., *The Portrait of Peter Pett and the Sovereign of the Seas* (Newport, 1930)

Calvo Serraller, F. (ed.), *V. Carducho, Diálogos e la pintura* (Madrid, 1970)

Camden, W., *Britannia* (Edmund Gibson, London, 1695)

Campbell, I., and A. MacKechnie, 'The Great Temple of Solomon at Stirling Castle', *Architectural History,* liv (2011), pp. 91–118

Campbell, T. P., 'Collectors and Connoisseurs: The Status and Perception of Tapestry, 1600–1660', T. P. Campbell (ed.), *Tapestry in the Baroque. Threads of Splendor* (Metropolitan Museum of Art, New York, 2008), pp. 325–38

Carleton, D., *Letters from and to Sir Dudley Carleton . . . during his embassy in Holland, from January 1615/16, to December 1620* (London, 1775)

Carlton, C., *Charles I. The Personal Monarch*, 2nd ed. (London, 1995)

Catto, J. (ed.), *Oriel College, A History* (Oxford, 2013)

Challis, C. (ed.), *A New History of the Royal Mint* (Cambridge, 1992)

Chalmers, P., *Historical and Statistical Account of Dunfermline*, 2 vols (Edinburgh, 1859)

Chambers, E. K., *The Elizabethan Stage*, 4 vols (Oxford, 1923)

Chambers, R., *Domestic Annals of Scotland from the Reformation to the Revolution*, 2 vols (Edinburgh, 1858)

Chandaman, C. D., *English Public Revenue 1660–1688* (Oxford, 1975)

Charles I, and E. Gauden, *Eikon Basilike. The Portraiture of his Sacred Majesty in his solitudes and sufferings* (London, 1648)

Chettle, G. H., *The Queen's House Greenwich* (Survey of London 14th Monograph, 1937)

Clark, A. (ed.), 'The Life and Times of Anthony Wood, Antiquary, of Oxford, 1632–1695', *Oxford Historical Society* (1891–1900)

Clark, A. (ed)., 'Memoirs of Nathaniel Lord Crewe', *Camden Society,* liii (1893)

Clarke, J. S., *The Life of James II, King of England,* 2 vols (London, 1816)

Claydon, T., *William III and the Godly Revolution* (Cambridge, 1996)

Clifford, D., *The Diaries of Lady Anne Clifford* (Stroud, 1990)

Coke, R., *A Detection of the Court and State of England During the Last Four Reigns*, 3 vols (London, 1694)

Cole, E., 'Theobalds, Herefordshire: The Plan and Interiors of an Elizabethan Country House', *Architectural History*, lx (2017), pp. 71–109

Collins, H., *Edward Jerman* (Cambridge, 2004)

Collins, M., 'The Medieval and Early Tudor Topography of Westminster', T. Tatton-Brown and R. Rodwell (eds), *Westminster: the art, architecture and archaeology of the Royal Abbey and Palace*, part ii (British Archaeological Association, Conference Transactions, 39:1, Leeds, 2015), pp. 206–56

Colvin, H. M., 'Roger North and Sir Christopher Wren', *The Architectural Review*, x (1962), p. 259

Colvin, H. M., et al. (eds), *The History of the King's Works*, 6 vols (London, 1963–73)

Colvin, H. M., and J. Newman (eds), *Of Building. Roger North's Writings on Architecture* (Oxford, 1981)

Colvin, H. M., *The Canterbury Quadrangle, St John's College, Oxford* (Oxford, 1988)

Colvin, H. M., *A Biographical Dictionary of British Architects*, 4th edition (Yale, 2008)

Cornwallis, Sir Charles, *A Discourse of the Most Illustrious Prince, Henry, Prince of Wales* (London, 1641)

Crankshaw, D., 'Community, City and Nation', D. Keene, A. Burns and A. Saint (eds), *St Paul's. The Cathedral Church of London 604–2004* (Yale, 2004), pp. 45–70

Cressy, D., *Charles I and the People of England* (Oxford, 2015)

Croft Murray, E., *Decorative Painting in England 1537–1837*, 2 vols (London, 1962)

Croft, P., 'Robert Cecil and the Early Jacobean Court', L. Levy Peck (ed.), *The Mental World of the Jacobean Court* (Cambridge, 1991), pp. 134–47

Croft, P., 'The Parliamentary installation of Henry, Prince of Wales', *Historical Research*, lxv (1992), pp. 177–93

Cuddy, N., 'The Revival of the Entourage: the Bedchamber of James I, 1603–1625', D. Starkey et al., *The English Court: from the Wars of the Roses to the Civil War* (London, 1987), pp. 173–225

Curthoys, J., *The Cardinal's College. Christ Church, Chapter and Verse* (London, 2012)

Curthoys, J., *The Stones of Christ Church. The Story of the Buildings of Christ Church, Oxford* (London, 2017)

Curthoys, J., *The King's Cathedral. The Ancient Heart of Christ Church, Oxford* (London, 2019)

Cust, R., *Charles I, A Political Life* (London, 2005)

Davies, J., *The Caroline Captivity of the Church: Charles I and the Remoulding of Anglicanism 1625–1641* (Oxford, 1992)

Davis, C. S. L., 'The Youth and Education of Christopher Wren', *English Historical Review*, cxxiii (2008), pp. 300–27

Davis, J. C., 'Cromwell's Religion', J. Morrill (ed.), *Oliver Cromwell and the English Revolution* (London, 1990), pp. 181–208

De Beer, E. S. (ed.), *The Diary of John Evelyn*, 6 vols (Oxford, 1955)

De Behault de Doron, A., *Bruges séjour d'exil d'Edouard IV et de Charles II rois d'Angleterre* (Bruxelles, 1931)

De Béthune, M., C. Lennox (trans.), *The memoirs of the Duke of Sully*, 5 vols (London, 1817)

De Groot, J., 'Space Patronage, Procedure: The Court at Oxford 1642–46', *English Historical Review*, cxvii (2002), pp. 1208–10

De Hooghe, R., *A Short Description of the King's Loo* (Amsterdam n.d.) 'The Anglo Dutch Garden in the Age of William and Mary', *Journal of Garden History*, viii (1988), pp. 146–7

De Krey, G., *London and the Restoration* (Cambridge, 2006)

De Villers, P. (ed.), *Journal d'un voyage à Paris en 1657–1658* (Paris, 1862)

Denham, J., *Poems and Translations* (London, 1668)

Dent, J., *The Quest for Nonsuch* (London, 1962)

Dietz, F., *English Public Finance 1558–1641* (London, 1964)

Digby, J., Earl of Bristol, *A continuation of a former relation concerning the entertainment given to Prince His Highnesse by the King of Spaine in his court at Madrid* (London, 1623)

Doebner, R., *Memoirs of Mary, Queen of England, 1689–1693, together with her letters and those of King James II. and William III. to the Electress Sophia of Hanover* (London, 1886)

Doran, S., 'Loving and Affectionate Cousins? The Relationship between Elizabeth I and James VI of Scotland 1586–1603', S. Doran and G. Richardson (eds), *Tudor England and its Neighbours* (Basingstoke, 2005), pp. 203–34

Downes, K., *Sir Christopher Wren: The Design of St Paul's Cathedral* (London, 1988)

Downes, K., *The Architecture of Wren* (Redhedge, 1988)

Droste, C., *Overblyfsels van Geheugchinis, der bisonderste voorvallen in het leven van den Heere Coenreat Droste* ('S-Gravenhage, 1728)

Drury, P., 'No other palace in the Kingdom will compare with it: The evolution of Audley End 1605–1745', *Architectural History,* xxiii (1980), pp. 1–39

Duffo, A. (ed.), *Henriette-Marie de France, Reine d'Angleterre* (Paris, 1935)

Dugdale, W., *History of St Paul's Cathedral in London: From its Foundation to these Times* (London, 1658)

Duggan, D., '"London the Ring, Covent Garden the Jewell of that Ring", New Light on Covent Garden', *Architectural History,* xliii (2000), pp. 140–61

Dunbar, J. G., 'The Palace of Holyroodhouse during the first half of the 16th century', *Archaeological Journal,* cxx (1964), pp. 242–54

Dunbar, J. G., 'Some aspects of the planning of Scottish royal palaces in the 16th Century', *Architectural History,* xxvii (1984), pp. 15–24

Dunbar, J. G., *Scottish Royal Palaces* (East Linton, 1999)

Dutton, R. (ed.), *Jacobean Civic Pageants* (Keele, 1995)

Edwards, T. C., and J. Reid, *Corpus Christi College, Oxford* (Oxford, 2017)

Eiche, S., 'Prince Henry's Richmond. The Project by Costantino de' Servi', *Apollo,* cxlviii (November 1998), pp. 10–14

Elliott, G. (ed.), 'The Diary of Dr Edward Lake', *Camden Society* (1847)

Elliott, J. H., 'The Court of the Spanish Hapsburgs: A Peculiar Institution?', J. H. Elliott, *Spain and its World 1500–1700* (Yale, 1989), pp. 142–61

Ellis, H., *Letters Illustrative of English History*, 2nd ser., 4 vols (London, 1846)

Erkelens, A. M. L. E., *Queen Mary's Delft Porcelain* (Het Loo, 1996)

Escobar, J., *The Plaza Mayor and the Shaping of Baroque Madrid* (Cambridge, 2004)

Evans, J., *Monastic Architecture in France from the Renaissance to the Revolution* (Cambridge, 1964)

Everett Green, M. A., *Letters of Henrietta Maria* (London, 1857)

Ewart, G., and D. Gallagher, *With Thy High Towers. The Archaeology of Stirling Castle and Palace* (Historic Scotland, Archaeology Report no. 9, 2015)

Fawcett, R., *Scottish Architecture from the Accession of the Stewarts to the Reformation 1371–1560* (Edinburgh, 1994)

Fawcett, R., *Stirling Castle* (London, 1995)

Fawcett, R., *Dunfermline Abbey and Palace* (Historic Scotland, 2004)

Fielding, J. (ed.), 'Diary of Robert Woodford 1637–1641', *Camden Society*, 5th ser., xlii (2012)

Finaldi, G. (ed.), *Orazio Gentileschi at the Court of Charles I* (London, 1999)

Finet, Sir John, *Finetti Philoxenis. Som Choice Observations of Sir John Finet Knight and Master of Ceremonies to two kings* (London, 1656)

Firth, C. H. (ed.), 'The Clarke Papers', *Camden Society*, ii (1894), pp. 140–7

Firth, C. H., *Memoirs of the Life of Colonel Hutchinson Governor of Nottingham by his widow Lucy* (London, 1906)

Firth, C. H., and R. R. Rait (eds), *Acts and Ordinances of the Interregnum 1642–60* (London, 1911), pp. 265–6

Fleming, O., 'The Humble Narrative of Oliver Fleming, Knight shewing the manner how I came to execute the Office of Master of the Ceremonies, with my Comportment and Sufferings therein for the space of near 18 Years', W. Scott, *A collection of scarce and valuable tracts, on the most interesting and entertaining subjects . . .*, 12 vols (London, 1812), vii, pp. 501–2

Foster, A., 'Church Policies of the 1630s', *Conflict in Early Stuart England. Studies in Religion and Politics 1603–1642* (London, 1989), pp. 193–223

Foster, E., 'Staging a Parliament in early Stuart England', P. Clark, N. Smith and N. Tyacke (eds), *The English Commonwealth 1547–1640* (Leicester, 1979), pp. 129–46

Foster, P., and E. Pyatt, *Bushy House* (National Physical Laboratory Museum and Archives publication, Teddington, 1976)

Fox, C., *A History of the Early Part of the Reign of James II* (Philadelphia, 1808)

Frank, J., *The Beginnings of the English Newspaper 1620–1660* (Cambridge, MA, 1961)

Fréart, P., *Parallèle de l'architecture antique avec la moderne*, J. Evelyn, *Tyrannus or the Mode* (London, 1661)

Freemantle, K., 'A Visit to the United Provinces and Cleves in the time of William III, described in Edward Southwell's Journal', *Nederlands Kunsthistorisch Jaarboek*, i (1970), pp. 39–68

Fritz, P., 'From Public to Private: the Royal Funerals in England 1500–1830', J. Whaley (ed.), *Mirrors of mortality: studies in the social history of death* (London, 1981), pp. 65–8

Fuller, M., *The Life of Bishop Davenant 1572–1641* (London, 1897)

Gady, A., 'Le Palais-Royal sous la Régence d'Anne d'Autriche', I. de Conihout, *Mazarin, Les Lettres et Les Arts* (Bibilioteque Mazarine, 2006), pp. 113–20

Gapper, C., J. Newman and A. Ricketts, 'Hatfield: A House for a Lord Treasurer', P. Croft (ed.), *Patronage, Culture and Power. The Early Cecils* (Yale, 2002), pp. 67–98

Gardiner, S. R. (trans. and ed.), 'El hecho de los tratados del matrimonio pretendido por el Principe de Gales con la serenissima Infante de Espana Maria, tomado desde sus principios para maior demostracion de la verdad, y ajustado con los papeles originales desde consta', *Camden Society*, ci (1869), pp. 120, 229–300

Gardiner, S. R., *What Gunpowder Plot Was* (London, 1897)

Gardiner, S. R., *History of the Commonwealth and Protectorate*, 4 vols (Moreton-in-Marsh, 1987)

Geraghty, A., 'Robert Hooke's Collection of Architectural Books and Prints', *Architectural History*, xlvii (2004), pp. 113–21

Geraghty, A., *The Architectural Drawings of Sir Christopher Wren at All Souls College, Oxford* (Aldershot, 2007)

Geraghty, A., *The Sheldonian Theatre. Architecture and Learning in Seventeenth-century Oxford* (Yale, 2013)

Gerbier, B., *A Brief Discourse Concerning the Three Chief Principles of Magnificent Building* (London, 1662)

Gilbert Dolan, D., 'James II and the Benedictines in London', *The Downside Review*, xviii (1899), pp. 94–9

Girouard, M., 'The Smythson Collection of the Royal Institute of British Architects', *Architectural History*, v (1962), pp. 33, 37, 76

Girouard, M., *Life in the French Country House*, (London, 2000)

Glendinning, M., R. MacInnes and A. MacKechnie, *A History of Scottish Architecture from the Renaissance to the Present Day* (Edinburgh, 2002)

Goff, M., '"The Art of Dancing, Demonstrated by Characters and Figures": French and English sources for Court and Theatre Dance, 1700–1750', *The British Library Journal*, xxi (1995), pp. 202–31

González-Longo, C., 'James Smith and Rome', *Architectural Heritage*, xxiii (2012), pp. 75–96

Goodare, J., 'James VI's English Subsidy', J. Goodare and M. Lynch (eds), *The Reign of James VI* (East Linton, 2000), pp. 110–25

Green, H. J. M., and S. Thurley, 'Excavations on the West Side of Whitehall 1960–2 Part I: From the Building of the Tudor Palace to the Construction of the Modern Offices of State', *The London and Middlesex Archaeological Society Transactions* (1990), pp. 59–130

Gregg, E., *Queen Anne* (London, 1980)

Grew, M., *William Bentinck and William III. The Life of Bentinck Earl of Portland from the Welbeck Correspondence* (London, 1924)

Griffey, E., *On Display, Henrietta Maria and the Materials of Display at the Stuart Court* (Yale, 2015)

Griffiths, A., *The Stuart Print in Britain 1603–89* (British Museum, 1998)

Grimbolt, P. (ed.), *Letters of William III and Louis XIV and of their Ministers . . .*, 6 vols (London, 1848)

Groen van Prinsterer, G., *Archives ou correspondance inédite de la maison d'Orange-Nassau*, 2nd series, 5 vols (Utrecht, 1857–61)

Groenveld, S., 'William III as Stadtholder: Prince or Minister?', E. Mijers and D. Onnekink, *Redefining William III. The Impact of the King-Stadholder in International Context* (Abingdon, 2007), pp. 17–37

Groos, G. (ed.), *The Diary of Baron Waldstein* (London, 1981)

Grose, F., and T. Astle (eds), *The Antiquarian Repertory* (1775–84)

Gutch, J. (ed.), *The History and Antiquities of the University of Oxford by Anthony à Wood*, 3 vols (Oxford, 1792–6)

Hacket, J. (ed.), *Scrinia reserata: a memorial offer'd to the great deservings of John Williams, D.D., who some time held the places of Ld Keeper of the Great Seal of England, Ld Bishop of Lincoln, and Ld Archbishop of York. Containing a series of the most remarkable occurrences and transactions of his life, in relation both to Church and State* (London, 1693)

Haley, K. H. D., 'William III as Builder of Het Loo', J. Dixon Hunt (ed.), *The Dutch Garden in the Seventeenth Century* (Dumbarton Oaks Colloquium on the History of Landscape Architecture, xii, 1990), pp. 3–11

Hamper, W. (ed.), *The Life, Diary, and Correspondence of Sir William Dugdale* (London, 1827)

Hannay, R., and G. Watson, 'The Building of the Parliament House', *The Book of the Old Edinburgh Club*, xiii (1924), pp. 17–78

Harris, E., *British Architectural Books and Writers 1556–1785* (Cambridge, 1990)

Harris, J., *Catalogue of the R.I.B.A. Drawings Collection: Jones & Webb* (London, 1972)

Harris, J., and A. Tait (eds), *Catalogue of the Drawings by Inigo Jones, John Webb and Isaac de Caus at Worcester College Oxford* (Oxford, 1979)

Harris, J., *The Palladians* (London, 1981)

Harris, J., *William Talman* (London, 1982)

Harris, J., and G. Higgott, *Inigo Jones, Complete Architectural Drawings* (London, 1989)

Harris, T., *London Crowds in the Reign of Charles II: Propaganda and Politics from the Restoration until the Exclusion Crisis* (Cambridge, 1987)

Harris, T., 'London Crowds and the Revolution of 1688', E. Cruikshanks (ed.), *By Force or Default? The Revolution of 1688–9* (Edinburgh, 1989), pp. 44–64

Harrison, S., *The arch's of triumph erected in honor of the high and mighty prince. Iames. the first of that name. King, of England. and the sixt of Scotland at his Maiesties entrance and passage through his honorable citty & chamber of London. vpon the 15th. day of March 1603.*

Hart Seely, G. (trans.), *Memoirs of La Grande Mademoiselle Duchesse de Montpensier* (London, 1928)

Hart, V., *Art and Magic in the Court of the Stuarts* (London, 1994)

Haslam, G., 'Jacobean Phoenix: The Duchy of Cornwall in the Principates of Henry Frederick and Charles', R. Hoyle (ed.), *The Estates of the English Crown, 1558–1640* (Cambridge, 1992), pp. 263–96

Hawkyard, A., 'Inigo Jones, the Surveyors of the Works and the Parliament House', *Parliamentary History*, xxxii (2013), pp. 16–59

Hazell, Z., *Legge's Mount, The Tower of London, Analysis of wood charcoal from deposits associated with the Tudor Royal Mint* (Historic England Research Report Series 6-2012)

Hearne, T., *Historia vitæ et regni Ricardi II . . . et D. Ricardi Wynni, baronetti. Narratio historica de Caroli, Walliæ prinicpis, famulorum in Hispaniam itinere* (Oxford, 1729)

Hefford, W., 'The Mortlake Manufactory, 1618–49', T. P. Campbell (ed.), *Tapestry in the Baroque. Threads of Splendor* (Metropolitan Museum of Art, New York, 2008) pp. 171–84

Henderson, E., *The annals of Dunfermline and vicinity, from the earliest authentic period to the present time, A.D. 1069–1878* (Glasgow, 1879)

Herbert, T., *Memoirs of the Last Years of the Reign of King Charles I* (London, 1813)

Heywood, T., A *true discription of his Majesties royall and most stately* ship called the Soveraign of the Seas, built at Wolwitch in Kent 1637 (London, 1638)

Hibbard, C., 'The Role of a Queen Consort. The Household and Court of Henrietta Maria 1625–1642', R. Asch and A. Birke (eds), *Princes, Patronage, and the Nobility. The Court at the Beginning of the Modern Age c.1450–1650* (Oxford, 1991), pp. 393–414

Hibbard, C., 'By our Direction and For Our Use: The Queen's patronage of Artists and Artisans seen through her household accounts', E. Griffey (ed.), *Henrietta Maria, Piety, Politics and Patronage* (Aldershot, 2008), pp. 115–38

Higgott, G., 'The Fabric to 1670', D. Keene, A. Burns and A. Saint (eds), *St Paul's. The Cathedral Church of London 604–2004* (Yale, 2004), pp. 171–90

Higgott, G., 'The Design and Setting of the Queen's House 1616–40', *The Court Historian*, xi (2006), pp. 135–48

Higgott, G., 'Inigo Jones's Designs for the Queen's House in 1616', M. Airs and G. Tyack (eds), *The Renaissance Villa in Britain 1500–1700* (Reading, 2007), pp. 140–66

Higgott, G., 'A Royal Lodging: the Great Tower from c.1480 to c.1700', P. Pattison, S. Brindle and D Robinson (eds), *The Great Tower of Dover Castle History, Architecture and Context* (Liverpool, forthcoming)

Hilton, W., 'A Dance for Kings: The 17th-Century French "Courante", its Character, Step-Patterns, Metric and Proportional Foundations', *Early Music*, v (1977), pp. 160–72

Hoare, J. P., *The History of the Royal Buckhounds* (Newmarket, 1895)

Holinshed, R., *Chronicle* (London, 1588)

Hope, C., 'Titian, Philip II and Mary Tudor', E. Chaney and P. Mack (eds), *England and the Continental Renaissance* (Woodbridge, 1994), pp. 53–65

Hore, J. P., *The History of Newmarket and the Annals of the Turf* (London, 1886)

Horwitz, H., *Parliament Policy and Politics in the Reign of William III* (Manchester, 1977)

Hotson, L., *The Commonwealth and Restoration Stage* (New York, 1962)

Howard, D., *Scottish Architecture. Reformation to Restoration 1560–1660* (Edinburgh, 1995)

Howard, D., and H. McBurney (eds), *The Image of Venice. Fialetti's view and Sir Henry Wotton* (London, 2014)

Howarth, D., 'The Politics of Inigo Jones', D. Howarth, *Art and Patronage in the Caroline Courts* (Cambridge, 1993), pp. 68–81

Howarth, D., 'William Trumbull and art collecting in Jacobean England', *The British Library Journal*, xx (1994), pp. 149–59

Howarth, D., *Images of Rule* (London, 1997)

Hunneyball, P., 'Cromwellian Style: The Architectural Trappings of the Protectoral Regime', P. Little (ed.), *The Cromwellian Protectorate* (Woodbridge, 2007), pp. 53–74

Hunt, J. D., 'The Anglo Dutch Garden in the Age of William and Mary', J. D. Hunt and E. de Jong (eds), *Journal of Garden History*, viii (1988)

Hutchings, M., and B. Cano-Echevarría, 'The Spanish Ambassador's account of James I's entry into London, 1604', *The Seventeenth Century Journal*, xxxiii (2017), pp. 255–77

Hutton, R., *Charles II King of England, Scotland, and Ireland* (Oxford, 1990)

Huygens, L., A. G. H. Bachrach and R. G. Collmer (trans and eds), *The English Journal 1651–2* (Leiden, 1982)

Hyde, E., Earl of Clarendon, W. Dunn Macray (ed.), *The History of the Rebellion and Civil Wars in England begun in the year 1641*, 6 vols (Oxford, 1888)

Hyde, R., 'Romeyn de Hooghe and the Funeral of the People's Queen', *Print Quarterly*, xv (1998), pp. 150–72

Impey, E., *Kensington Palace* (London, 2003)

Imrie, J., and J. Dunbar (eds), *Accounts of the Masters of Works*, 2 vols (Edinburgh, 1957, 1982)

Jacobson, H., 'Luxury Consumption, Cultural Politics, and the Career of the Earl of Arlington, 1660–1685', *The Historical Journal*, lii (2009), pp. 295–317

Jacques, D., and A. van der Horst (eds), *The Gardens of William and Mary* (London, 1988)

Jacques, D., *Gardens of Court and Country. English Design 1630–1730* (Yale, 2017)

James I, *Basilicon Doron* (1599)

James I, *The peace-maker: or, Great Brittaines blessing* (London, 1619)

Jansson, M., 'Remembering Marston Moor: The Politics of Culture', S. Amussen and M. Kishlansky (eds), *Political culture and cultural politics in early modern England: essays presented to David Underdown* (Manchester, 1995), pp. 255–70

Jardine, L., *On a Grander Scale, The Outstanding Career of Sir Christopher Wren* (London, 2002)

Jeayes, I., and F. Bickley (eds), *Letters of Philip Gawdy of West Harling, Norfolk, and of London to various members of his family, 1579–1616* (Roxburghe Club, 1906)

Jenkins, S., 'A Sense of History. The Artistic Taste of William III', *Apollo*, cxl, no. 390 (August 1994), pp. 4–9

Jennings Churchill, S., Duchess of Marlborough, *An Account of the Conduct of the Dowager Duchess of Marlborough: From Her first coming to court to the year 1710 in a letter from herself to my Lord —* (London, 1742)

Jessop, A. (ed.), *Lives of the Norths*, 3 vols (London, 1890)

Jones, J. D., *The Royal Prisoner. Charles I at Carisbrooke* (London, 1965)

Juhala, A. L., 'The Household and Court of King James VI of Scotland, 1567–1603' (unpublished PhD thesis, University of Edinburgh, 2000)

Juhala, A. L., '"For the king favours them very strangely". The rise of James VI's chamber 1580–1603', M. Kerr-Peterson and S. J. Reid (eds), *James VI and Noble Power in Scotland 1578–1603* (London, 2017), pp. 155–66

Jusserand, J. J., *A French Ambassador at the Court of Charles II, Le Comte de Cominges, from his Unpublished Correspondence* (London, 1892)

Kamen, H., *The Escorial. Art and Power in the Renaissance* (Yale, 2010)

Keay, A., *The Elizabethan Tower of London. The Haiward and Gascoyne plan of 1597* (London Topographical Society, 2001)

Keay, A., 'The Ceremonies of Charles II Court' (unpublished PhD thesis, London, 2004)

Keay, A., *The Magnificent Monarch, Charles II and the Ceremonies of Power* (London, 2008)

Keay, A., 'The best proportioned old building in England: Kenilworth Castle 1588–1722', *English Heritage Historical Review*, v (2010), pp. 82–93

Keay, A., *The Crown Jewels* (London, 2011)

Keay, A., *The Last Royal Rebel, The Life and Death of James, Duke of Monmouth* (London, 2016)

A. Keay, *Interregnum, People's Republic of Britain* (London, 2022, forthcoming)

Kelly, W., *Royal Progresses and Visits to Leicester* (Leicester, 1884)

Kelsey, S., *Inventing a Republic. The Political Culture of the English Commonwealth* (Manchester, 1997)

Kelsey, S., 'The kings' book : Eikon Basilike and the English Revolution of 1649', N. Tyacke (ed.), *The English Revolution c.1590–1720: politics, religion and communities* (Manchester, 2007), pp. 150–68

Kenyon, J., *The Popish Plot* (London, 1972)

Kernan, A., *Shakespeare, the King's Playwright 1603–1613* (Yale, 1995)

Killigrew, T., *Comedies and Tragedies* (London, 1664)

Kingston, A., *A History of Royston* (London, 1906)

Kishlansky, M., 'Charles I: A Case of Mistaken Identity', *Past & Present*, clxxxix (2005), pp. 41–80

Knight, C., 'The Cecils at Wimbledon', P. Croft (ed.), *Patronage, Culture and Power. The Early Cecils* (Yale, 2002), pp. 47–63

Knoppers, L., *Constructing Cromwell. Ceremony, Portrait and Print 1645–61* (Cambridge, 2000)

Kroll, M. (ed.), *Letters from Liselotte* (London, 1970)

Kuyper, W., *Dutch Classicist Architecture, A Survey of Dutch Architecture, Gardens and Anglo-Dutch Architectural Relations from 1625 to 1700* (Delft, 1980)

Kyle, C., and J. Peacey, '"Under cover of so much coming and going": Public Access to Parliament and the Political Process in Early Modern

England', C. Kyle and J. Peacey (eds), *Parliament at Work: Parliamentary Committees, Political Power, and Public Access in Early Modern England* (Woodbridge, 2002), pp. 1–23

Kyle, C., 'Parliament and the Palace of Westminster: An Exploration of Public Space in the Early 17th Century', C. Jones and S. Kelsey, *Housing Parliament, Dublin, Edinburgh and Westminster* (Edinburgh, 2002), pp. 85–98

Laing, D., 'On the state of the Abbey Church of Holyrood subsequently to the devastations committed by the English Forces in the years 1544 and 1547', *Proceedings of the Society of Antiquaries of Scotland* (1851–4), pp. 101–15

Lang, J., *Rebuilding St Paul's after the Great Fire of London* (Oxford, 1956)

Langeois, D., 'Évolution du décor intérieur entre 1600 et 1660', D. Alcouffe et al., *Un Temps d'Exubérance. Les Arts Décoratifs sous Louis XIII et Anne d'Autriche* (Grand Palais, Paris, 2002), pp. 119–26

Larkin, J. F., *Stuart Royal Proclamations*, ii (Oxford, 1983)

Latham, R. and W. Matthews, *The diary of Samuel Pepys: a new and complete transcription*, 11 vols (London, 1970–83)

Laveissière, S., 'Counsel and Courage: The Galerie des Hommes Illustres in the Palais Cardinal', H. T. Goldfarb, *Richelieu, Art and Power* (Montreal, 2003), pp. 64–71

Law, E., *Shakespeare as a Groom of the Chamber* (London, 1910)

Lee Jr., M., *Dudley Carleton to Jon Chamberlain 1603–1624 Jacobean Letters* (New Jersey, 1972)

Leech, P., 'Music and Musicians in the Catholic Chapel of James II at Whitehall 1686-8', *Early Music*, xxxix (2011), pp. 379–400

Lewis, W. H. (ed.), *Memoirs of the Duc de Saint-Simon* (New York, 1964)

Lindley, K., 'London and Popular Freedom in the 1640s' in R. C. Richardson, G. M. Ridden, *Freedom and the English Revolution: Essays in History and Literature* (Manchester, 1988), pp. 111–50

Lindley, K., *Popular Politics and Religion in Civil War London* (Aldershot, 1997)

Lister, M., *A Journey to Paris in the Year 1698* (London, 1699)

Little, P., 'Music at the Court of King Oliver', *The Court Historian*, xii (2007), pp. 177–80

Lockyer, R. (ed.), *The Trial of Charles I* (London, 1974)

Lockyer, R., *Buckingham. The Life and Political Career of George Villiers, First Duke of Buckingham 1592–1628* (Harlow, 1981)

Lodge, E., *Illustrations of British history, biography, and manners,: in the reigns of Henry VIII, Edward VI, Mary, Elizabeth, and James I, exhibited in a series of original papers*, iii (London, 1791)

Long, W. H. (ed.), *The Oglander Memoirs: Extracts from the MSS of Sir John Oglander* (London, 1888)

Loomie, A. J., *Spain and the Jacobean Catholics*, 2 vols (Catholic Record Society, 1978)

Loomie, A. J., *Ceremonies of Charles I. The Note Books of John Finet 1628–1641* (Fordham, 1987)

Loomie, A. J., 'The Destruction of Rubens's "Crucifixion" in the Queen's Chapel, Somerset House', *Burlington Magazine*, cxl (October 1998), pp. 680–2

Loonstra, M., *Het Huis Ten Bosch* (Amsderdam, 1985)

Loonstra, M., *Het Koninklijk Paleis Huis ten Bosch Historisch Gezien* (Amsterdam, 1985)

Louw, H., 'The Origin of the Sash-Window', *Architectural History*, xxvi (1983), pp. 49–72

Ludlow, E., E. Firth (ed.), *The memoirs of Edmund Ludlow*, 2 vols (Oxford, 1894)

Lunn, D., *The English Benedictines 1540–1688* (London, 1980)

Lunsingh Scheurleer, T. H., 'Documents on the Furnishing of Kensington House', *Walpole Society*, xxxviii (1960–62), pp. 15–58

Luttrell, N., *A Brief Historical Relation of State Affairs From September 1678 to April 1714*, 6 vols (Oxford, 1857)

Lynch, M., 'Court Ceremony and Ritual during the Personal Reign of James VI', J. Goodare and M. Lynch (eds), *The Reign of James VI* (East Linton, 2000), pp. 71–92

MacGregor, A., *The Late King's Goods. Collections, Possessions and Patronage of Charles I in the light of the Commonwealth Sale Inventories* (London, 1989)

MacIvor, I., and B. Petersen, 'Lauderdale at Holyroodhouse 1669–70', D. Breeze (ed.), *Studies in Scottish Antiquity Presented to Stewart Cruden* (Edinburgh, 1984), pp. 249–68

MacKechnie, A., 'Sir William Bruce: 'the chief introducer of Architecture in this Country', *Proceedings of the Society of Antiquaries of Scotland*, cxxxii (2002), pp. 499–519

MacKechnie, A., 'The Crisis of Kingship: 1603–1707', M. Glendinning (ed.), *The Architecture of Scottish Government. From Kingship to Parliamentary Democracy* (Dundee, 2004), pp. 82–133

MacKechnie, A., 'The Royal Palace of Dunfermline', R. Fawcett (ed.), *Royal Dunfermline* (Society of Antiquaries of Scotland, 2005)

MacKechnie, A., 'Sir David Cunningham of Robertland: Murderer and "Magna Britannia's" first Architect', *Architectural History*, lii (2009), pp. 79–106

MacKechnie, A., 'The Earl of Perth's Chapel of 1688 at Drummond Castle and the Roman Catholic Architecture of James VII', *Architectural Heritage*, xxv (2014), pp. 107–31

Mackenzie, G., *Memoirs of the Affairs of Scotland from the Restoration of King Charles II* (Edinburgh, 1821)

Madden, F., *Oxford Books* (Oxford, 1912)

Madge, S. J., *The Domesday of Crown Lands, A Study of the Legislation, Surveys, and Sales of the Royal Estates under the Commonwealth* (London, 1938)

Magalotti, L., *Travels of Cosmo the Third Duke of Tuscany* (London, 1821)

Maitland, W., *The History of Edinburgh from its Foundation to the Present Time* (Edinburgh, 1753)

Manning, B., *The English People and the English Revolution 1640–1649* (London, 1976)

Margoliouth, H., *The Poems and Letters of Andrew Marvell*, 2 vols (Oxford, 1971)

Martin, H., and J. Highfield, *A History of Merton College Oxford* (Oxford, 1997)

Martin, L., 'Sir Francis Crane: Director of the Mortlake Tapestry manufactory and Chancellor of the Order of the Garter', *Apollo*, cxiii (1981), pp. 90–6

May, P., *The Changing Face of Newmarket. A History from 1600 to 1760* (Newmarket, 1984)

Maziere Brady, W., *The Episcopal Succession in England, Scotland and Ireland*, iii (Greg Reprints, 1971)

McClure, N. E. (ed.), 'The Letters of John Chamberlain', *Memoirs of the American Philosophical Society*, 2 vols (Philadelphia, 1939)

McGee, C., '"Strangest consequence from remotest cause": the second performance of The Triumph of Peace', *Medieval and Renaissance Drama in England*, v (1991), pp. 309–54

McKean, C., 'The Palace at Edinburgh Castle', *Book of the Old Edinburgh Club*, n.s. iv (1997), pp. 89–102

McKean, C., *The Scottish Chateau. The Country House of Renaissance Scotland* (Stroud, 2001)

Meikle, H. (ed.), *The Works of William Fowler*, 2 vols (Scottish Text Society, 3rd ser. 7, 1936)

Meikle, M. M., 'Holde her at the Oeconomike rule of the House: Anne of Denmark and Scottish Court Finances, 1589–1603' in E. Ewan and M. M. Meikle (eds), *Women in Scotland c.1100–c.1750* (East Linton, 1999), pp. 105–111

Merritt, J., *Westminster 1640–1660. A Royal City in a Time of Revolution* (Manchester, 2013)

Messervy, J. (ed.), *Journal de Jean Chevalier* (St Helier, 1906)

Mikkelsen, B., *Kronborg* (Elsinore, 1997)

Millar, O. (ed.), 'Abraham van der Doort's Catalogue of the Collections of Charles I', *Walpole Society*, xxxvii (1958–60)

Millar, O., *The Tudor, Stuart and Early Georgian Pictures in the Collection of Her Majesty the Queen* (London, 1963)

Millar, O. (ed.), 'The Inventories and Valuations of the King's Goods 1649–1651', *Walpole Society*, xliii (1970–2)

Milton, A., '"That Sacred Oratory": Religion and the Chapel Royal during the Personal Rule of Charles I', A. Ashbee (ed.), *William Lawes 1602–1645: Essays on his Life, Time and Works* (Ashgate, 1998), pp. 69–96

Milward, J., *Wimbledon in the Time of Civil War* (Epsom, 1976)

Mörke, O., 'William III's Stadtholderly Court in the Dutch Republic', E. Mijers and D. Onnekink, *Redefining William III. The Impact of the King-Stadholder in International Context* (Abingdon, 2007), pp. 227–40

Muddiman, J., *The Trial of King Charles the First* (London, 1928)

Murray, J., *Memoirs of the Embassy of the Marshal de Bassompierre to the Court of England* (London, 1819)

Mylne, R., *The Master Masons to the Crown of Scotland* (Edinburgh, 1893)

Nalson, J., *A True copy of the journal of the High Court of Justice for the tryal of K. Charles I as it was read in the House of Commons and attested under the hand of Phelps, clerk to that infamous court* (London, 1684)

Needham, R., and A. Webster, *Somerset House, Past and Present* (London, 1905)

Nicholls, M., *Investigating Gunpowder Plot* (Manchester, 1991)

Nichols, J., *The Progresses and Public Processions of Queen Elizabeth*, 3 vols (London, 1823)

Nichols, J., *The progresses, processions, and magnificent festivities, of King James the First, his royal consort, family, and court*, 4 vols (London, 1828)

Norton, C., 'The Buildings of St Mary's Abbey, York and their Destruction', *Antiquaries Journal*, lxxiv (1994), pp. 267–80

O'Hehir, B., *Harmony from Discords. A Life of Sir John Denham* (Berkeley, CA, 1968)

O'Hehir, B., *Expans'd Hieroglyphicks, A Critical Edition of Sir John Denham's Coopers Hill* (Berkeley, CA, 1969)

Onnekink, D., 'Dutch Counsels: the Foreign Entourage of William III', *Dutch Crossing*, xxix (2005), pp. 5–20

Orgel, S., and R. Strong, *Inigo Jones and the Theatre of the Stuart Court*, 2 vols (California, 1973)

Orrell, J., 'The Agent of Savoy at The Somerset Masque', *The Review of English Studies*, NS xxviii (1977), pp. 301–4

Orrell, J., 'The London Court Stage in the Savoy Correspondence 1613–1675', *Theatre Research*, iii (1979), pp. 157–76

Orrell, J., *The theatres of Inigo Jones and John Webb* (Cambridge, 1985)

Orso, S., *Philip IV and the Decoration of the Alcazar of Madrid* (Princeton, 1986)

Ottenheym, K., W. Terlouw and R. van Zoest (eds), *Daniel Marot: Vormgever van een deftig Bestaan* (Zutphen, 1988)

Ottenheym, K., 'Possessed by such a Passion for Building, Fredrick Hendrick and Architecture', M. Keblusek and J. Zijlmans, *Princely Display. The Court of Frederick of Orange and Amalia van Solms* (The Hague, 1997), pp. 109–23

Ottenheym, K., 'Dutch influences in William Bruce's architecture', *Architectural Heritage: The Journal of the Architectural Heritage Society of Scotland*, xviii (2007), pp. 135–49

Ozinga, M. D., *Daniel Marot, de Schepper van den Hollandschen Lodewijk XIV-stijl* (Amsterdam, 1938)

Palladio, A., *I Quattro Libri dell'architecttura* (Venice, 1570)

Palme, P. *Triumph of Peace. A Study of the Whitehall Banqueting House* (London, 1957)

Parry, G., *The Golden Age Restored. The Culture of the Stuart Court 1603–42* (Manchester, 1981)

Parry, G., *Glory Laud and Honour. The Arts of the Anglican Counter-Reformation* (Woodbridge, 2006)

Payne, M. T. W., 'An Inventory of Queen Anne of Denmark's "Ornaments, furniture, householde stuffe, and other parcells" at Denmark House, 1619', *Journal of the History of Collections*, xiii (i) (2001), pp. 23–44

Peacock, J., and C. Anderson, 'Inigo Jones, John Webb and Temple Bar', *Architectural History*, xliv (2001), pp. 29–37

Pearl, V., *London and the Outbreak of the Puritan Revolution* (Oxford, 1964)

Pearsall Smith, L. (ed.), *The Life and Letters of Sir Henry Wotton*, 2 vols (Oxford, 1966)

Peck, F. (ed.), *Desiderata Curiosa*, 2 vols (London, 1779)

Pegge, S., *Curialia or an Historical Account of some Branches of the Royal Household* (London, 1791)

Pelzer, A. (ed.), *Joachim von Sandarts Academie der Bau-, Buil- und Mahlerey-Künste von 1675* (Munich, 1925)

Pérez Gil, J., *El Palacio Real de Valladolid, sede de la Corte de Felipe III 1601–1606* (Universidad de Valladolid, 2012)

Pérouse de Montclos, J. M., *La Guide du Patrimoine, Paris* (Paris, 1994)

Pérouse de Montclos, J. M., *Vaux le Vicomte* (London, 1997)

Petrie, C., *The Letters, Speeches and Proclamations of King Charles I* (London, 1935)

Philip, I. G., 'Journal of Sir Samuel Luke: Scoutmaster General to the Earl of Essex, 1643–4', *Oxfordshire Record Society* (1950–53)

Pinto, D., 'The True Christmas: Carols at the Court of Charles I', A. Ashbee (ed.), *William Lawes (1603–1645), Essays on his Life, Times and Work* (Aldershot, 1998), pp. 97–115

Pitcher, J. (ed.), *Samuel Daniel, Hymen's Triumph* (Oxford, Malone Society reprints, 1994)

Porter, S., *The Great Plague* (Stroud, 1999)

Poulton, R., with major contributions by A. Cook and S. Thurley, *Excavations at Oatlands Palace 1968–73 and 1983–4* (Guildford, 2009)

Prynne, W., *Canterburies Doome* (London, 1646)

Quarrell, W. H., and M. Mare (trans and eds), *London in 1700 from the Travels of Zacharias Conrad von Uffenbach* (London, 1934)

Ranson, P., *Royston's Heritage Buildings* (Royston and District Local History Society, 2017)

Reddaway, T., *The Rebuilding of London after the Great Fire* (London, 1951)

Reddaway, T., 'The London Custom House 1666–1740', *London Topographical Record* , xxi (1958), pp. 1–14

Redworth, G., *The Prince and the Infanta* (Yale, 2003)

Rem, P., 'Restoration of the State Bed Acquired by Het Loo Palace and intended for the Bedchamber of Stadtholder William III', *Textile History*, xxxi (2000), pp. 154–6

Reynolds, N., 'The Stuart Court and Courtiers in Exile 1644–1654', (unpublished PhD dissertation, Cambridge, 1996)

Ribeiro, A., *Fashion and Fiction. Dress in Art and Literature in Stuart England* (Yale, 2005)

Riis, T., *Should Auld Acquaintance Be Forgot . . . Scottish Danish Relations c.1450–1707* (Odense, 1988)

Riis, T., 'Theatre and Architecture: Anne, Dunfermline and Christian IV', R. Fawcett (ed.), *Royal Dunfermline* (Society of Antiquaries of Scotland, 2005), pp. 187–98

Robb, N., *William of Orange*, 2 vols (London, 1963)

Roberts, J., *Royal Landscape. The Gardens and Parks of Windsor* (Yale, 1997)

Roberts, M. (trans. and ed.), *Swedish Diplomats at Cromwell's Court* (London, 1988)

Roberts, M., 'Swedish Diplomats at Cromwell's Court, 1655–1656, the Missions of Peter Julius Coyet and Christer Bonde', *Camden Society*, 4th ser., xxxvi, (1988)

Robinson, H., and W. Adams, *The Diary of Robert Hooke* (London, 1935)

Rockley, E., *A History of Gardening in England* (London, 1910)

Rodger, N. A. M., *The Safeguard of the Sea. A Naval History of Britain: I 1660–1649* (London, 1997)

Rodger, N. A. M., *The Command of the Ocean* (London, 2004)

Rogers, C., *Estimate of the Scottish Nobility during the Minority of James VI* (Grampian Club, 1873)

Rogers, C., *History of the Chapel Royal of Scotland* (Edinburgh, 1882)

Rose, C., *England in the 1690s* (New Jersey, 1999)

Row, J., *The History of the Kirk of Scotland, from the Year 1558 to August 1637* (Edinburgh, 1842)

Roy, I., 'Royalist Ordnance Papers', *Oxfordshire Record Society,* xliii (1964), pp. 25–8

Roy, I., 'The City of Oxford 1640–1660', R. C. Richardson (ed.), *Town and Countryside in the English Revolution* (Manchester, 1992), pp. 130–68

Roy, I., and D. Reinhardt, 'Oxford and the Civil Wars', N. Tyacke (ed.), *The History of the University of Oxford,* iv (1997), pp. 688–731

Rybot, N. V. L., *The Islet of St Helier and Elizabeth Castle* (Société Jersiaise, 1986)

Rye, W. B. (ed.), *England as seen by Foreigners, in the days of Elizabeth and James the First* (London, 1865)

Rymer, T., *Foedera,* 16 vols (1743)

Sainte-Beuve, M. (ed.), *Mémoires de Madame de Motteville sur Anne D'Autriche et sa Cour,* 3 vols (Paris, 1855)

Sainty, J., and R. Bucholz, *Officials of the Royal Household, 1660–1837, Part 1 Lord Chamberlain* (London, 1997)

Sánchez Cano, D., 'Entertainments in Madrid for the Prince of Wales: Political Functions of Festivals', A. Samson (ed.), *The Spanish Match. Prince Charles's Journey to Madrid 1623* (Aldershot, 2006), pp. 51–74

Saunders, A., 'The Second Exchange', A. Saunders (ed.), *The Royal Exchange* (London Topographical Society publication, 1997), pp. 121–35

Saunders, A., *Fortress Builder. Bernard de Gomme, Charles II's Military Engineer* (Exeter, 2004)

Sauvel, T., 'L'Appartement de La Reine Au Palais Royal', *Bulletin de la Société de l'histoire de l'art Français 1951* (1952), pp. 65–79

Scott Mylne, R., *The Master Masons to the Crown of Scotland and their Works* (Edinburgh, 1893)

Scott, E., *The King in Exile. The wanderings of Charles II from June 1646 to July 1654* (London, 1905)

Scott, H. (ed.), 'The Journal of Sir Roger Wilbraham', *Camden Miscellany,* x (1902)

Scott, W. (ed.), *Chronological notes of Scottish affairs, from 1680 till 1701;*

being chiefly taken from the diary of Lord Fountainhall. (Edinburgh, 1822)

Sears, J., and F. R. Johnson (eds), *The Lumley Library, the Catalogue of 1609* (London, 1956)

Shakeshaft, P., 'Elsheimer and G.B. Crescenzi', *Burlington Magazine*, cxxiii (1981), pp. 550–1

Sharpe, K., 'The Image of Virtue: the Court and Household of Charles I, 1625–1642', D. Starkey et al., *The English Court: from the Wars of the Roses to the Civil War* (London, 1987), pp. 226–60

Sharpe, K., *The Personal Rule of Charles I* (Yale, 1992)

Sharpe, K., *Image Wars. Promoting Kings and Commonwealths in England 1603–1660* (Yale, 2010)

Shaw, D., 'St Giles' Church and Charles I's Coronation visit to Scotland', *Historical Research*, 77.198 (2004), pp. 481–502

Shearman, J., *Raphael's Cartoons in the Collection of Her Majesty the Queen and the Tapestries in the Sistine Chapel* (London, 1972)

Sheppard, F. H. W. (ed.), *Survey of London: Volume 34, St Anne Soho* (London, 1966)

Siccama, J. (ed.), C. Huygens, *Journaal van Constantijn Huygens, 1673–1696*, 4 vols (Utrecht, 1876–88)

Sieur de la Serre, *Histoire de l'Entréé de la Royne Mere . . . dans la Grande Bretagne* (London, 1639), here the translation used is in 'The Entry of Mary de Medicis to England in 1638 by the Sieur de la Terre', F. Grose, *The Antiquarian Repertory*, i (London, 1775)

Skovgaard, J., *A King's Architecture, Christian IV and his Buildings* (London, 1973)

Slothouwer, D. F., *De Paleizen van Frederik Hendrik* (Leiden, 1945)

Smith, C., and M. Gnudi (trans and eds), *The pirotechnia of Vannoccio Biringuccio: the classic 16th-century treatise on metals and metallurgy by Biringucci, Vannoccio* (New York, 1990)

Smuts, R. M., 'Art and the Material Culture of Majesty in Early Stuart England', R. M. Smuts (ed.), *The Stuart Court and Europe* (Cambridge, 1996), pp. 86–112

Sommerville, J. P. (ed.), *James VI and I: Political Writings* (London, 1994)

Spalding, J., *The History of the Troubles and Memorable Transactions in Scotland from the year 1624 to 1645* (Aberdeen, 1792)

Spalding, R. (ed.), *The Diary of Bulstrode Whitelocke 1605–1675* (London, 1990)

Speck, W., 'William – and Mary?', L. Schwoerer, *The Revolution of 1688–89. Changing Perspectives* (Cambridge, 1992), pp. 131–48

Spicer, A., 'Laudianism in Scotland? St Giles' Cathedral, Edinburgh 1633–39 – A Reappraisal', *Architectural History*, xlvi (2003), pp. 95–106

Spiers, W. L., 'The Note Book and Account Book of Nicholas Stone', *Walpole Society*, vii (1918–19)

Sprat, T., *The history of the Royal-Society of London for the improving of natural knowledge* (London, 1667)

Stace, M., *Cromwelliana: A chronological detail of events in which Oliver Cromwell was engaged* (London, 1810)

Stevens, J., *Old Jersey Houses* (Jersey, 1965)

Stevenson, D., *The Origins of Freemasonry. Scotland's century 1590–1710* (Cambridge, 1988)

Stevenson, D., *Scotland's Last Royal Wedding. The Marriage of James VI and Anne of Denmark* (Edinburgh, 1997)

Stevenson, G., *Charles I in Captivity* (London, 1927)

Stirling, W., *Register of Royal Letters Relative to the affairs of Scotland & Nova Scotia from 1615 to 1635* (Edinburgh, 1885)

Stokes, H., 'Cambridgeshire Forests', *Proceedings of the Cambridge Antiquarian Society*, xvii (1922), pp. 70–5

Stone, L., 'Inigo Jones and the New Exchange', *Archaeological Journal*, cxiv (1957), pp. 106–21

Stone. P., *The architectural antiquities of the Isle of Wight from the XIth to the XVIIth centuries* (London, 1891)

Stoye, J. W., *English Travellers Abroad 1604–1667* (London, 1952)

Strickland, A., *Lives of the Queens of England*, 12 vols (London, 1845)

Strong, R., *Henry Prince of Wales and England's Lost Renaissance* (London, 1986)

Strong, R., *The Tudor and Stuart Monarchy III, Jacobean and Caroline* (Woodbridge, 1998)

Strong, R., *The Renaissance Garden in England* (London, 1998)

Strong, S., *Catalogue of Letters . . . at Welbeck* (London, 1903)

Summerson, J., 'The Building of Theobalds 1564–1585', *Archaeologia*, xcvii (1959), pp. 107–26

Summerson, J., 'The Book of Architecture of John Thorpe in Sir John Soane's Museum', *Walpole Society*, xl (1966)

Swain, M., 'The furnishing of Holyroodhouse in 1668', *The Connoisseur*, cxciv (1977), pp. 122–30

Swain, M., '"Flowerpotts and Pilasters": Royal Tapestries at Holyroodhouse', *The Burlington Magazine*, cxxii (1980), pp. 417–18

Taylor, A. J., 'The Royal Visit to Oxford in 1636', *Oxonensia*, i (1936), pp. 151–8

Temple, P., *The Charterhouse* (Survey London 18th Monograph, 2010)

Terry, C., *The Cromwellian Union: Papers Relating to the Negotiations for an Incorporating Union Between England and Scotland, 1651–1652, with an Appendix of Papers Relating to the Negotiations in 1670* (Edinburgh, 1902)

Thomas, K., 'English Protestantism and Classical Art', L. Gent (ed.), *Albion's Classicism: The Visual Arts in Britain 1550–1660* (Yale, 1995), pp. 221–38

Thompson, E. (ed.), 'Correspondence of the Family of Hatton', *Camden Society*, i (1878)

Thompson, T. (ed.), D. Calderwood, *The History of the Kirk of Scotland*, 8 vols (Wodrow Society, Edinburgh, 1842–9)

Thomson, W. G., *Tapestry Weaving in England from the Earliest Times to the end of the 18th Century* (London, 1914)

Thrush, A., and J. P. Ferris (eds), *The History of Parliament: the House of Commons 1604–1629* (Cambridge, 2010)

Thurley, S., 'The Whitehall Palace Plan of 1670', *London Topographical Society*, cliii (1988)

Thurley, S., *The Royal Palaces of Tudor England* (Yale, 1993)

Thurley, S., *Whitehall Palace and Architectural History of the Royal Apartments 1240–1698* (Yale, 1999)

Thurley, S., 'A Country Seat Fit for a King: Charles II, Greenwich and Winchester', E. Cruickshanks, *The Stuart Courts* (Stroud, 2000), pp. 214–39

Thurley, S., 'The Stuart Kings, Oliver Cromwell and the Chapel Royal 1618–1685', *Architectural History*, xlv (2002), pp. 238–74

Thurley, S., *Hampton Court Palace: A Social and Architectural History* (New Haven and London, 2004)

Thurley, S., *Lost Buildings of Britain* (London, 2004)

Thurley, S., 'Architecture and Diplomacy: Greenwich Palace under the Stuarts', *The Court Historian,* xi (2006), pp. 125–33

Thurley, S., 'Kensington Palace: An Incident in Anglo-Dutch Architectural Collaboration?', *Georgian Group Journal,* xvii (2009), pp. 1–18

Thurley, S., *Somerset House, The Palace of England's Queens 1551–1692* (London Topographical Society, 2009)

Thurley, S., 'The Politics of Court Space in Early Stuart London', G. Gorst and M. Smuts (eds), *The Politics of Court Space in Europe and the Mediterranean, ca. 1500–1750* (Rome, 2009), pp. 293–316

Thurley, S., 'Lauderdale at Court', C. Rowell (ed.), *Ham House 400 years of collecting and patronage* (Yale, 2013), pp. 136–43

Thurley, S., 'The King in the queen's lodgings: The rise of the drawing room at the English court', M. Chatenet and K. De Jonghe (eds), *Le Prince, la Princesse et leurs Logis* (Paris, 2014), pp. 67–74

Thurley, S., *Houses of Power: The Places That Shaped the Tudor World* (London, 2017)

Thurley, S., 'Elizabeth I and the Early Stuarts', S. Brindle (ed.), *Windsor Castle: A Thousand Years of a Royal Palace* (Royal Collection Trust, 2018), pp. 180–93

Thurley, S., 'The Later Stuarts', S. Brindle (ed.), *Windsor Castle: A Thousand Years of a Royal Palace* (London, 2018), pp. 240–9

Thurley, S., 'Turning a Town into a Palace', *Country Life* (14 August 2019), pp. 48–53

Thurley, S. (ed.), *St James's Palace from Leper Hospital to Royal Palace* (London, forthcoming)

Thurley, S., '"The example of princes": The practice and performance of Religion at the Tudor Court', K. De Jonghe (ed.), forthcoming

Tighe, R., and J. Davis, *Annals of Windsor, being a History of the Castle and Town*, 2 vols (London, 1858)

Toynbee, M., 'The Wedding Journey of King Charles I', *Archaeologia Cantiana*, lxix (1955), pp. 75–89

Toynbee, M., *Strangers in Oxford. A Side Light on the First Civil War 1642–1646* (Chichester, 1973)

Trevor, A., *The Life and Times of William the Third, King of England and Stadtholder of Holland* (London, 1835)

Trimble, W. R., 'The Embassy Chapel Question 1625–1660', *Journal of Modern History*, xviii (1946), pp. 97–107

Tromp, H., *Het Koninklijk Paleis Soesdijk Historisch Gezien* (Amsterdam, 1987)

Turbervile, G., *Turbervile's Booke of Hunting 1576* (Oxford, 1907)

Underdown, D., *Pride's Purge. Politics in the Puritan Revolution* (London, 1985)

Upmark, G., 'Ein Besuch in Holland 1687 aus den Reisechilderungen des Schwedischen Architekten Nicodemus Tessin', *Oud-Holland 1900* (Amsterdam, 1900)

Van der Zee, H., and B., *William and Mary* (London, 1973)

Van Everdingen, L., *Het Loo, de Oranjes en de Jacht* (Haarlem, 1984)

Van Pelt, R. J., and M. E. Tiethoff-Spliethoff, *Het Binnenhof* (Dieren, 1984)

Van Raaij, S., and P. Spies, *The Royal Progress of William and Mary* (Amsterdam, 1988)

Van Strien, C. D., *British Travellers in Holland during the Stuart Period* (Leiden, 1993)

Van Strien, K. (ed.), *Touring the Low Countries: Accounts of British Travellers, 1660–1720* (Leiden, 1993)

Varley, F. J., *The Siege of Oxford* (Oxford, 1932)

Veevers, E., *Images of Love and Religion. Henrietta Maria and Court Entertainments* (Cambridge, 1989)

Vicars, J., *JEHOVAH-JIREH. GOD IN THE MOVNT, or, Englands Parliamentarie-Chronicle* (London, 1644)

Vicars, J., *Magnalia Dei Anglicana, or, Englands Parliamentary – Chronicle. Containing a full and faithfull* Series, *and Exact* Narration *of all the most memorable Parliamentary-Mercies, and mighty (if not miraculous) Deliverances . . .,* (London, 1646)

Vliegenthart, A., and A. Erkelens, *Rijksmuseum Paleis Het Loo* (Paleis Het Loo, Apeldoorn, 1988)

Wade, M. R., *Triumphus Nuptialis Danicus. German Court culture and Denmark. The 'Great Wedding' of 1634* (Wiesbaden, 1996)

Wainwright, J. P., 'Images of Virtue and War: Music in Civil War Oxford', A. Ashbee (ed.), *William Lawes (1603–1645), Essays on his Life, Times and Work* (Aldershot, 1998), pp. 121–42

Walker, E., *Historical Collections of Several Important Transactions Relating to the Late Rebellion and Civil Wars of England: . . . Written by the Special Command of K. Charles I. Part Whereof was Corrected by His Majesty's Own Hand* (London, 1705)

Walker, M., *Architects and Intellectual Culture in Post-Restoration England* (Oxford, 2017)

Warner, G. (ed.), 'The Nicholas Papers', 4 vols, *Camden Society*, ii (1886–7)

Warwick, P., *Memoirs of the Reign of King Charles I* (London, 1701)

Webb, J., *A Vindication of Stone-Heng Restored* (London, 1665)

Weller Singer, S. (ed.), *The correspondence of Henry Hyde, Earl of Clarendon, and of his brother Laurence Hyde, Earl of Rochester: with the diary of Lord Clarendon from 1687 to 1690, containing minute particulars of the events attending the revolution: and the diary of Lord Rochester during his Embassy to Poland in 1676,* 2 vols (London, 1828)

Wemyss, C., 'Merchant and Citizen of Rotterdam, Tax Collector "The Bitterest factionalist partie man of his quality in all Scotland". The early Career of William Bruce', *Architectural Heritage*, xvi (2005), pp. 14–31

Wentworth, T., 1st Earl of Strafford, W. Knowler (ed.), *The Earl of Strafforde's Letters and Dispatches,* 2 vols (London, 1739)

Wheelock, A., 'Gerard Houckgeest and Emanuel de Witte: Architectural Painting in Delft around 1650', *Simiolus*, viii (1975–6), pp. 167–85

Whinney, M., 'John Webb's Drawings for Whitehall Palace', *Walpole Society*, xxxi (1942–3), pp. 45–107, 118–21

White, A., 'A Biographical Dictionary of London Tomb Sculptors c.1560–1660', *Walpole Society*, lxi (1999), pp. 29–31

White, C., *The Dutch Pictures in the Collection of Her Majesty the Queen* (Cambridge, 1982)

White, H., and T. Kearns, *Legge's Mount, The Tower of London, Scientific Analysis of the Crucibles* (Historic England Research Department Report Series 76-2010)

Whitelocke, B., *Memorial of English Affairs from the Beginning of the Reign of Charles the First to the Happy Restoration of King Charles II*, ii (Oxford, 1853)

Wickham Legg, L., 'A relation of a short survey of the western counties, made by a lieutenant of the Military Company in Norwich in 1635', *Camden Miscellany*, xvi (1936)

Wilks, T., 'The Court Culture of Prince Henry and his Circle, 1603–1613' (unpublished PhD dissertation, University of Oxford, 1988)

Wilks, T., 'Art Collecting at the English Court from the death of Henry Prince of Wales to the death of Anne of Denmark', *Journal of the History of Collections*, ix, (1997), pp. 31–48

Wilks, T., '"Forbear the Heat and Haste of Building": Rivalries among the designers at Prince Henry's Court 1610–12', *The Court Historian*, vi (2010), pp. 49–65

Williams, H. (ed.), J. Swift, *Journal to Stella* (Oxford, 1948)

Wilson, F., *The Plague in Shakespeare's London* (Oxford, 1927)

Wingfield Digby, G. F., 'Damasks and Velvets at Hampton Court', *Connoisseur*, ciii (May 1939), pp. 248–53

Wittkower, R., 'Inigo Jones – 'Puritanissimo Fiero', *Burlington Magazine*, xc (1948), pp. 50–1

Wormeley, K. (trans.), *Memoirs of Madame de Motteville on Anne of Austria and her Court. With an introduction by C. A. Sainte-Beuve* (London, 1902)

Worsley, G., *Classical Architecture in Britain: The Heroic Age* (Yale, 1995)

Worsley, G., *Inigo Jones* (Yale, 1997)

Worsley, G., *The British Stable* (Yale, 2004)

Worsley, G., *Inigo Jones and the European Classical Tradition* (Yale, 2007)

Worsley, G., 'Chiswick House: Palladian Paradigm or Symbol of Sovereignty?', *English Heritage Historical Review*, vi (2011), pp. 115–33

Wren, C., *Parentalia or Memoirs of the Family of the Wrens* (London, 1750)

Young, A., *Tudor and Jacobean Tournaments* (London, 1987)

Image Credits

All images not credited here are courtesy of the author.

Colour plate section 1

Plate 1   Stephen Conlin

Plate 2   Royal Collection Trust / © Her Majesty Queen Elizabeth II 2020

Plate 3   Royal Collection Trust / © Her Majesty Queen Elizabeth II 2020

Plate 4   Musei Reali, Turin

Plate 5   Public domain, sourced from Wikimedia Commons

Plate 6   Public domain, sourced from Wikimedia Commons

Plate 7   Royal Collection Trust / © Her Majesty Queen Elizabeth II 2020

Plate 8   Royal Collection Trust / © Her Majesty Queen Elizabeth II 2021 photograph: Historic Royal Palaces

Plate 9   Public domain, sourced from Wikimedia Commons

Plate 10   Royal Collection Trust / © Her Majesty Queen Elizabeth II 2020

Plate 11   Royal Collection Trust / © Her Majesty Queen Elizabeth II 2020

Colour plate section 2

Plate 12	Royal Collection Trust / © Her Majesty Queen Elizabeth II 2020
Plate 13	National Maritime Museum, Greenwich. London
Plate 14	Public domain, sourced from Wikimedia Commons
Plate 15	Bridgeman Images
Plate 16	© Crown Copyright
Plate 17	© The Warden and Fellows of All Souls College, Oxford
Plate 18	Historic England
Plate 19	xtof.photo
Plate 20	Bridgeman Images
Plate 21	Royal Collection Trust / © Her Majesty Queen Elizabeth II 2020
Plate 22	Royal Collection Trust / © Her Majesty Queen Elizabeth II 2020
Plate 23	Royal Collection Trust / © Her Majesty Queen Elizabeth II 2020
Plate 24	Stephen Conlin
Plate 25	Stephen Conlin

Integrated images

Figure 1	Reproduced with the permission of the National Library of Scotland
Figure 2	© Simon Thurley
Figure 3	Public domain, sourced from Wikimedia Commons
Figure 3b	© Simon Thurley
Figure 5	Thomas Rahbek
Figure 6a	© RCAHMS
Figure 6b	© Simon Thurley
Figure 7	© Simon Thurley
Figure 8	© The Trustees of the British Museum
Figure 11a	RIBA Collections
Figure 11b	The Provost and Fellows of Worcester College, Oxford
Figure 12	© Simon Thurley

Figure 14	Royal Collection Trust / © Her Majesty Queen Elizabeth II 2020
Figure 16	© Simon Thurley
Figure 17	© Sir John Soane's Museum, London
Figure 18	© Simon Thurley
Figure 19	Public domain, sourced from Smithsonian Libraries
Figure 20	© Simon Thurley
Figure 22	RIBA Collections
Figure 23a	© Simon Thurley
Figure 24	Public domain, sourced from the Metropolitan Museum of Art
Figure 25	Public domain, sourced from Ministero dei Beni e delle Attività Culturali e del Turismo
Figure 26	© Chatsworth House Trust
Figure 27	Royal Collection Trust / © Her Majesty Queen Elizabeth II 2020
Figure 28	Public domain, sourced from the Rijksmuseum
Figure 30	Public domain, sourced from the Morgan Library & Museum
Figure 31	© Simon Thurley
Figure 32	Public domain, sourced from Wikimedia Commons
Figure 33	Public domain, sourced from the Rijksmuseum
Figure 35a	Royal Collection Trust / © Her Majesty Queen Elizabeth II 2020
Figure 35b	Royal Collection Trust / © Her Majesty Queen Elizabeth II 2020
Figure 36	RIBA Collections
Figure 37b	Steve Cadman
Figure 38	Public domain, sourced from Wikimedia Commons
Figure 39	Public domain, sourced from the Metropolitan Museum of Art
Figure 40	By permission of The Pepys Library, Magdalene College, Cambridge.
Figure 42	The Provost and Fellows of Worcester College, Oxford

Figure 85   © The Trustees of the British Museum

Figure 86   Royal Collection Trust / © Her Majesty Queen Elizabeth II 2020

Figure 87   Library of Congress, Geography and Maps Division

Figure 88   © Simon Thurley

Figure 89   © Simon Thurley

Figure 90   Public domain, sourced from the Rijksmuseum

Figure 91a   Public domain, sourced from the National Archives

Figure 91b   © Simon Thurley

Figure 93b   © Simon Thurley

Figure 94a   Old Royal Naval College

Figure 94b   © Simon Thurley

Figure 96   © Simon Thurley

Figure 97   Album / Alamy Stock Photo

Figure 98   Royal Collection Trust / © Her Majesty Queen Elizabeth II 2020

Figure 99   Stephen Conlin

Figure 100   Royal Collection Trust / © Her Majesty Queen Elizabeth II 2020

Figure 101   Public domain

Figure 102   Library of Congress, Geography and Map Division

Figure 103   Public domain, sourced from the National Archives

Figure 104   © Simon Thurley

Figure 105   © The Trustees of the British Museum

Figure 106   National Galleries of Scotland

Figure 107   © Simon Thurley

Figure 109   Public domain, sourced from Wikimedia Commons

Figure 110   © The Trustees of the British Museum

Figure 115   Public domain, sourced from the Rijksmuseum

Figure 116   Art World / Alamy Stock Photo

Figure 117a   © Simon Thurley

Figure 117b   Public domain, sourced from Wikimedia Commons

Figure 118   © Simon Thurley

Figure 120a   Public domain, sourced from Wikimedia Commons

Figure 120b © Simon Thurley

Figure 121 © Simon Thurley

Figure 122 Public domain, sourced from the Rijksmuseum

Figure 123b © Simon Thurley

Figure 124b Public domain, sourced from Wikimedia Commons

Figure 125 © Edward Impey

Figure 126 © The Warden and Fellows of All Souls College, Oxford

Figure 127 Public domain, sourced from Wikimedia Commons

Figure 128 © Chatsworth House Trust

Figure 129 © Simon Thurley

Figure 130a Public domain, sourced from the Rijksmuseum

Figure 130b © Simon Thurley

Figure 131 © The Warden and Fellows of All Souls College, Oxford

Figure 132 The Royal Borough of Kensington and Chelsea Libraries (RBKC Libraries)

Figure 133 © The Warden and Fellows of All Souls College, Oxford

Figure 134 © The Warden and Fellows of All Souls College, Oxford

Figure 135 National Galleries of Scotland

Figure 136 © Simon Thurley

Figure 1138 © Royal Collection Trust / © Her Majesty Queen Elizabeth II 2021.

Index

Page references in *italics* indicate images.

Index 531

Cecil, Thomas see Burghley, Thomas Cecil,
Lord
Cecil, William 24, 48, 51
Chaloner, Sir Thomas 70–1
Chamberlain, John 32, 96, 136
Charing Cross 28, 141, 191, 192, 193, 250,
261, 286, 290, 291, 321
Charing, Tudor house at 37
Charles I, King of England, Scotland and
Ireland 2; accession (1625) 3, 135, 139;
aesthete 3, 197, 200; army coup and
245–6; Banqueting House and 143–7,
143, 199, 247, 249, *249*, 250; birth 15;
Buckingham and see Buckingham,
George Villiers, Duke of; Civil War
and 118, 215, 221–44, *227*, *229*, *234*, *238*,
240, *242*, 265; court atmosphere during
reign of 135–9; court regulations,
reintroduction of 135–9; Covent
Garden and 85, 184–6, *185*; Denmark
House and 191–2, *192*; execution of 3,
247, 249–50, *249*, 268, 274; Gonzaga
purchase 157; grand projects 190–7, *192*,
194, *195*, *196*; Hampton Court and 47;
'Heads of Proposals' and 236; Henrietta
Maria and see Henrietta Maria, Queen;
imprisonment by republican forces and
escape 236–8; Infanta Maria Ana and
120–1, 128–9; London, building
projects in 183–200, *185*, *187*, *188*, *189*,
192, *194*, *195*; marriage 98, 120–34, 136,
140, 161–3; Newmarket and 42, 43, 46;
Newport Treaty and 239–40, 245;
Office of Works and 85; Oxford, retreat
to during Civil War 221–35, *224*, *227*,
229, *234*; Parliamentary Rump and 245;
Prince of Wales (childhood) 42, 43, 46,
53, *53*, 73, 104, 106, 107, 120–8;
progress 159–60; religion of 207–9, *209*;
royal chapels attacked 216–19, *217*;
Scotland and 190–1, 210–15, *211*, *213*,
274; *Sovereign of the Seas* and 197–8,
198; Spanish court, lives at 121–32, *123*,
124; St James's and 141–3; St Paul's
Cathedral and 85, 186–7, 188, *188*, 199;
tapestry and 117–19; Temple Bar 188–9,
189; theatre/masques and 147–52, *149*,
152, 186, 187, *187*; Theobalds and 46, 51,

51; Tower of London and 196–7; trial
246–7, 248, *248*; uniformity of religious
practice across dominions, orders 190;
Whitehall and 104, 139–41, 143–7, *143*,
152–9, *155*, 192–7, *194*, *195*, 199, 200,
250–2, 262, 291, 305, 414; Windsor
Castle, imprisoned in 245–6
Charles II, King of England, Scotland and
Ireland 3, 118, 137, 156; birth 15, 140–1,
143; Blackheath, reviews army at 286;
Bruges, exile in 281–2; childhood 141–2,
142, 153, 156, *175*; Civil War and 235,
257, 265, 274–5, 286, 313; Cologne,
exile in 280–1; country houses 317–23,
318, *320*, *321*, *322*; Customs House and
325, 326, *326*; death 354–5, 379;
Declaration of Indulgence 333–4; exile
in Europe 265–82; Fire of London and
323, 324–5, 326, *326*, 327, 328; France,
exiled in 268–73, *271*, *272*, *273*, 275–80,
277, *278*, *279*; Frankfurt, exile in 281;
Fronde and 275; Greenwich Palace and
294–5, 296, *296*, 300–6, *302*, *303*, *304*,
305; Hampton Court and 285–6, 404,
422, 426; Holyrood and 339–44, *343*,
364; Jersey, flees to 265–7, *266*;
marriage 207, 294–7, *297*, *298*; Office
of Works and 284; Palais Royal and
275–80, *277*, *278*, *279*; Parliament,
dissolves 345; religion of court 313–17,
314, *316*, 357; Restoration 3, 152, 255,
264, 283–306, 307–11, 317, 320, 324,
333, 338, 414; Royal Exchange and 327;
Scotland and 274, 275, 339–44, *343*,
364; Somerset House and 297–8, *299*,
299, 300; St James's Park and 289–90,
290; St Paul's Cathedral and 310–11,
327–8; Third Dutch War and 333;
Treaty of Dover (1670) and 333, 335;
United Provinces, exile in 273–4;
Westminster, royal estate recast by
(1661–5) 289–92, *290*; Whitehall Palace
and 286–93, *290*, *292*, 311–12, 328–32,
329, 354–5, 416; William III and 369,
370, 373, 374–5, 390; Windsor Castle
and 334–9, *336*, *337*, *338*, 345–7;
Worcester, defeated by Cromwell at
(1651) 257, 274–5, 286, 313